C·A·N·O·N·S

C·A·N·O·N·S

Edited by Robert von Hallberg

The University of Chicago Press
Chicago and London

Some of the essays in this volume were originally published in various issues of
Critical Inquiry.

The University of Chicago Press, Chicago 60637
The University of Chicago Press, Ltd., London

Library of Congress Cataloging in Publication Data
Main entry under title:

Canons.

  Most of the articles were taken from the Sept. 1983,
Dec. 1983, and Mar. 1984 issues of Critical inquiry.
  Bibliography: p.
  Includes index.
  1. Criticism—Addresses, essays, lectures. 2. Canon
(Literature)—Addresses, essays, lectures. I. Von Hall-
berg, Robert, 1946–   . II. Critical inquiry.
PN85.C34 1984   801'.95   84-2411
ISBN 0-226-86493-6
ISBN 0-226-86494-4 (pbk.)

Contents

Introduction

In the last few years any number of papers and panels on canon-formation have been listed in programs for the Modern Language Association and various conferences on interpretation; the signs of attention to this topic are abundant. Canon-formation is not discussed systematically or comprehensively here; rather, these essays reflect some of the range of current thinking about canon-formation in different areas of interpretation. After the essays by Barbara Herrnstein Smith and Charles Altieri, which argue directly from propositions rather than from texts, the essays are arranged chronologically according to their immediate object of study.

Why this should now seem a timely subject is worth asking, because the answer may alert us to pressures that bear on our thinking about canon-formation. Interest in canons is surely part of a larger inquiry into the institutions of literary study and artistic production. "Politics," "economy," "social," "authority," "power"—these are some of the terms that recur throughout these essays; we are most curious now about those points where art seems less private than social. More particularly, the formation of canons is a measure of the strength of institutions devoted to the study of art. Academic interpreters may be especially curious about strong institutions of interpretation because we are currently in a paradoxical position: there are far more of us than ever before; yet the economic resources directed to our proliferating institutions have not kept pace with our expanding population. Though the subject of canon-formation is addressed now only with irony, it might be thought of as the traditional dream of ambitious critics. A canon is commonly seen as what other people, once powerful, have made and what should now be opened up, demystified, or eliminated altogether. Rarely does one hear a critic, especially a professor, confess to dreams of potency, perhaps because now that canons are recognized as the expression of social and political power, intellectuals are, by virtue of a consensus as to their adversarial role, almost required to view these aspirations skeptically.

Yet the aspirations articulated in the following essays are indeed great, as well as timely. Canons are discussed from three perspectives here: how artists determine canons by selecting certain styles and masters

1

to emulate; how poet-critics and academic critics, through the institutions of literary study, construct canons; and how institutionalized canons effectively govern literary study and instruction. Most of these essays are principally concerned with the second and third perspectives. These authors (Lawrence Lipking, Christine Froula, Jerome J. McGann, John Guillory, and Richard Ohmann) urge that the social, political, and economic forces at work in canon-formation be faced squarely and subjected to critical discussion. One of the issues at stake here—contested most explicitly by Altieri—is whether canons are adequately comprehended as the expression of the interests of one social group or class against those of another. Several authors suggest that critical scrutiny will inevitably discount the authority of established canons, exactly because canons are only the instruments of entrenched interests. However, whether new canons, expressing as yet unestablished interests, ought now to be formed is an open question even for those who put their faith in the interest model. Guillory concludes that principles upon which a canon might be based are perhaps permanently inaccessible to a literary culture as socially and politically diverse as our own has now become. How the teaching of literature, painting, and music might be altered by the imagined absence of artistic canons is a question barely touched upon in this collection— and perhaps for good reasons.

The prospect of teaching art without canons—quite different from that of teaching a critical approach to canons, as Froula advocates—is not altogether encouraging. Perhaps more importantly, we should recognize that, on this score, there is a danger of academic critics overestimating their own importance and autonomy in the process of canon-formation and wrongly thinking that they can choose to dispense with canons. The first perspective on canon-formation that I mentioned—the one attuned to the ways in which artists, in choosing their models, set the terms for disputes among academic canonizers—is important as a corrective in this regard. For example, the essays by James E. G. Zetzel, Winthrop Wetherbee, and Michael Fried indicate that poets and painters, by emulation, sometimes produce art that (critical polemics aside) institutes the authority of certain earlier art. This perspective on questions of canon-formation may be the one most deserving attention just now, since it may permit us to test not only the limits of institutionalized literary and artistic study—that is, our own limits as students and professors—but those of the interest model of canon-formation as well. For, however certainly the sociopolitical interests of Cleanth Brooks and T. S. Eliot are analyzed by Guillory, or those of the present Professional-Managerial class are by Ohmann, it is less certain that the emulation of Callimachus by Virgil and Horace can be fully explicated by social analysis or that Manet's allusions to Velázquez were politically motivated. The question raised by the tension between these different perspectives on canon-formation is not whether canons serve political functions but rather how fully their political functions account for their origins and limit their utility. Poets, painters, sculptors, and composers are sometimes unwilling to concede that their use of the methods and materials of their masters is either politically motivated or even importantly freighted with ideological significance. They may often be wrong about this, but, as these essays show, even the commentary that has established and challenged canons has for a long time been the work of artists; the professors are newcomers, who may not yet see fully the constraints within which they operate.

Without being directly addressed, two other limits on the process of canon-formation can be glimpsed, if only faintly, behind some of the questions that are raised in these pages. One has to do with timing. Whether a particular canon should be challenged or confirmed is an issue often taken up by both poet-critics and professors, with little sense that certain generic political circumstances may make the alteration of canons more or less feasible at one moment than at another. Zetzel, Gerald Bruns, James Chandler, and Joseph Kerman all see a direct relationship between nationalism and canon-formation. Certain historical moments, those of consolidation, such as after a war, say, when a nation is given to patriotism and appeals to shared traditions, seem especially propitious to canon-formation. No definitive statement on the timing of canon-formation will be found in these pages, but several authors (Fried and Arnold Krupat, as well as the others mentioned) write with a sense that some historical circumstances may in themselves enable successful canon-formation. Even the present discussion of canon-formation may in fact be occasioned not only by the mixed feelings of power and help-lessness among scholars of the humanities, or even by the competition of rival interest-groups within academic institutions, but also by a greater political stability, a sense of pending consolidation, that in itself raises the question of new canon-formation.

The second of these implied limits on changes in canons seems to be generated by the history of technique, and artists feel this constraint more than critics. Whatever leverage poets, painters, and composers may exercise over critics in the making of canons, their efficacy may be reduced by impersonal (perhaps even unideological) forces of tradition. As Krupat shows, although poets like Yvor Winters, N. Scott Momaday, and James Welch have tried to accommodate Native American poems to the canon of American literature, certain differences of style and technique may, despite their individual intentions, have made a successful meeting of poetic traditions impossible. Neither poets nor professors, it seems, are entirely free to devise programs for the future.

The present collection of essays will not contribute much to the casting of new pantheons, though that is what the great canonizers have accomplished (only McGann's essay on Christina Rossetti is aimed in this direction). But these essays may well give some direction to the effort already underway to sort out terms and principles governing evaluation.

All of the authors here agree, I think, that despite our many conflicting interests we now owe each other clear and explicit statements about how we value art.

I am grateful for help I have received from my coeditors, especially W. J. T. Mitchell and Joel Snyder, and from my colleagues Elizabeth Abel, Robert Ferguson, and Robert Kaster. Carolyn Cimon Williams, Mary B. Caraway, and Toby Rachel Gordon all worked unusually hard over a long period of time to see this book into the world, and I am happy now to be able to thank them.

Robert von Hallberg

Contingencies of Value

Barbara Herrnstein Smith

1. The Exile of Evaluation

It is a curious feature of literary studies in America that one of the most venerable, central, theoretically significant, and pragmatically inescapable set of problems relating to literature has not been a subject of serious inquiry for the past fifty years. I refer here to the fact not merely that the study of literary evaluation has been, as we might say, "neglected," but that the entire problematic of value and evaluation has been evaded and explicitly exiled by the literary academy. It is clear, for example, that there has been no broad and sustained investigation of literary evaluation that could compare to the constant and recently intensified attention devoted to every aspect of literary *interpretation*. The past decades have witnessed an extraordinary proliferation of theories, approaches, movements, and entire disciplines focused on interpretive criticism, among them (to recite a familiar litany) New Criticism, structuralism, psychoanalytic criticism, reader-response criticism, reception aesthetics, speech-act theory, deconstructionism, communications theory, semiotics, and hermeneutics. At the same time, however, aside from a number of scattered and secondary essays by theorists and critics who are usually otherwise occupied,[1] no one in particular has been concerned with questions of literary value and evaluation, and such questions regularly go begging—and, of course, begged—even among those whose inquiries into other matters are most rigorous, substantial, and sophisticated.

Reasons for the specific disparity of attention are not hard to locate. One is the obvious attachment of problems of interpretation and meaning to the more general preoccupation with language that has dominated the entire century and probably, as well, the fact that disciplines such as linguistics and the philosophy of language are more accessible to literary scholars than the corresponding disciplines, especially economics and sociology, that are more broadly concerned with the nature of value and evaluative behavior. The reasons for the general neglect and exile, however, are more complex, reflecting, among other things, the fact that literary studies in America, from the time of its inception as an institutionalized academic discipline, has been shaped by two conflicting and mutually compromising intellectual traditions and ideologies, namely—or roughly namely—positivistic philological scholarship and humanistic pedagogy. That is, while professors of literature have sought to claim for their activities the rigor, objectivity, cognitive substantiality, and progress associated with science and the empirical disciplines, they have also attempted to remain faithful to the essentially conservative and didactic mission of humanistic studies: to honor and preserve the culture's traditionally esteemed objects—in this case, its canonized texts—and to illuminate and transmit the traditional cultural values presumably embodied in them. One consequence or manifestation of this conflict has been the continuous absorption of "literary theory" in America with institutional debates over the proper methods and objectives of the academic *study* of literature and, with respect to the topic at hand, the drastic confinement of its concern with literary evaluation to debates over the cognitive status of evaluative criticism and its proper place, if any, in the discipline.

A bit of history will be helpful here. In accord with the traditional empiricist doctrine of a fundamental split or discontinuity between fact and value (or description and evaluation, or knowledge and judgment), it was possible to regard the emerging distinction within literary studies between "scholarship" and "criticism" as a reasonable division of labor. Thus, the scholar who devoted himself to locating and assembling the historical and philological facts necessary to edit and annotate the works of, say, Bartholomew Griffin might remark that, although Griffin was no doubt a less fashionable poet than such contemporaries as Spenser and Shakespeare, the serious and responsible scholar must go about his work in a serious and responsible manner, leaving questions of literary merit "to the critics." The gesture that accompanied the remark, however,

---

Barbara Herrnstein Smith is University Professor of English and communications and director of the Center for the Study of Art and Symbolic Behavior at the University of Pennsylvania. She is the author of, among other works, *Poetic Closure* and *On the Margins of Discourse*. The present essay is part of a full-length study of literary and aesthetic value and evaluation.

was likely to signal not professional deference but intellectual conde-
scension; for the presumably evenhanded distribution of the intellectual
responsibilities of literary study—the determination of facts to the scholar
and value to the critic—depended on an always questionable and increasingly questioned set of assumptions: namely, that literary value was
a determinate property of texts and that the critic, by virtue of certain
innate and acquired capacities (taste, sensibility, etc., which could be seen
as counterparts to the scholar's industry and erudition), was someone
specifically equipped to discriminate it.

The magisterial mode of literary evaluation that issued from this set
of assumptions (and which, in Anglo-American criticism, characteristically
reproduced itself after the image—and in the voice—of Dr. Johnson
and also of such latter-day "master-critics" as Matthew Arnold and T. S.
Eliot) was practiced most notably by F. R. Leavis in England and, in
America, perhaps most egregiously, by Yvor Winters. Its reaches and a
taste of its once familiar flavor can be recalled in this passage from Leavis'
Revaluation:

> There are, of course, discriminations to be made: Tennyson, for
> instance, is a much better poet than any of the pre-Raphaelites.
> And Christina Rossetti deserves to be set apart from them and
> credited with her own thin and limited but very notable distinction. . . .
> There is, too, Emily Brontë, who has hardly yet had full justice as
> a poet. I will record, without offering it as a checked and deliberated
> judgment, the remembered impression that her *Cold in the earth* is
> the finest poem in the nineteenth-century part of *The Oxford Book
> of English Verse.*[2]

Such unabashed "debaucheries of judiciousness" (as Northrop Frye would
later characterize them) were, however, increasingly seen as embarrass-
ments to the discipline, and the practice of evaluative criticism became
more defensive, at least partly in response to the renewed and updated
authority given to axiological skepticism.

In the thirties and forties, a number of prominent philosophers,
among them A. J. Ayer and Rudolph Carnap, began to argue that value
judgments are not merely distinct from empirically verifiable statements
of fact but vacuous pseudostatements, at best suasive and commendatory,
at worst simply the emotive expressions of personal sentiment, and in
any case neither reflecting nor producing genuine knowledge.[3] For the
positivistic literary scholar, such arguments reinforced his impression
that the work of his critical colleague was the intellectually insubstantial
activity of a dilettante, while the true discipline of literary studies was
exhibited in his own labors, in which he had always sought to achieve a
rigor and objectivity as free as possible from the contamination of value
ascription. In the institutional struggles that ensued, various maneuvers
were developed to secure for "criticism" not only a central place in the

discipline but also an intellectual status equal in respectability to that of empirical science and what was commonly referred to as "serious scholarship."

One obvious tactic, still favored in many quarters of the literary academy, was to invoke the humanistic mission of literary studies and turn the fact-value split against the scholars' claim of centrality. Thus Winters would maintain that while science was value-neutral—or, as he put it, "amoral"—literary studies had moral responsibilities. The function of historical scholarship and philology was, accordingly, ancillary: specifically, it was "to lay the groundwork for criticism," while the important job was, precisely, to evaluate literature.[4] For Winters, this meant to declare, forthrightly and unequivocally, what was good and bad literature (which was to say, "moral" or "decadent" literature), and he did not hesitate, himself, to rank-order not only poets and poems but also literary genres, verse forms, and entire centuries.

Winters had a genius for unequivocality that was imitated but never matched by his numerous followers. In any case, a more common tactic, exemplified by a number of the New Critics, was to devise some formulation of critical activity that bridged the fact-value split or at least unobtrusively edged the two sides together. Thus, in 1951, W. K. Wimsatt, Jr., in an important essay titled "Explication as Criticism," observed that it was necessary to find "an escape between the two extremes of sheer affectivism and sheer scientific neutralism" and attempted to demonstrate how evaluation could be assimilated into the typical New Critical production of increasingly exquisite explications and fine-grained analyses: "But then, finally, it is possible to conceive and produce instances where explication in the neutral sense is so integrated with special and local value intimations that it rises from neutrality gradually and convincingly to the point of total judgment."[5]

It may be recalled here that Wimsatt's attempt to expose "the affective fallacy" was directed largely at the "psychological theory of value" developed by I. A. Richards in the twenties, which Wimsatt charged with amounting to subjectivism and leading to impressionism and relativism. Richards' theory was, however, in effect an updated rehearsal of the eighteenth-century empiricist-normative account and, like the latter, designed to *rebut* axiological skepticism.[6] An adequate theory of criticism, Richards wrote, must be able to answer such questions as "What gives the experience of reading a certain poem its value?" and "Why is one opinion about works of art not as good as another?";[7] and while the first of these questions no doubt seemed to Wimsatt altogether different from what, for him, would have been the more proper question of what gives *the poem itself* its value, the second of them makes Richards' normative objectives quite clear. Indeed, he consistently put his psycho-neurological account of value in the service of canonical judgments and repeatedly translated it into versions of evaluative absolutism and objectivism. Thus, the remarkable chapter on "Badness in Poetry" in *Principles of Literary Criticism* concludes its excruciating examination of the failure of a sonnet by Ella Wheeler Wilcox to produce a "high level of organization" of "adequate [neural] impulses" with Richards' observation that, although "those who enjoy [the sonnet] certainly seem to enjoy it to a high degree," nevertheless, with good and bad poetry, as with brandy and beer, the "actual universal preference of those who have tried both fairly is the same as superiority in value of one over the other. Keats, by universal qualified opinion, is a more efficient poet than Wilcox, and that is the same as saying his works are more valuable."[8] The invocation of an "actual" universality coupled with such question-begging hedges as "fairly" and "qualified" is, as we shall see, characteristic of traditional empiricist-normative accounts. It was not, one suspects, its alleged relativism that made Richards' theory so unabsorbable by the literary academy but rather the raw jargon and unedifying physiology that attended it.

The boldest move in the mid-century effort to give disciplinary respectability and cognitive substance to criticism was, or course, Frye's call upon it to redefine itself as a project that banished evaluation altogether. In his "Polemical Introduction" to the *Anatomy of Criticism*, Frye insisted that, if criticism was ever to become a "field of genuine learning" (significantly exemplified by "chemistry or philology"), it would have to "snip . . . off and throw . . . away" that part that had "no organic connection with [it],"—namely, evaluation.[9] For Frye, the shifting assessments and rank-orderings made by critics were not only a noncumulative accumulation of subjective judgments but also irrelevant to "real criticism," since he believed, echoing and endorsing Eliot, that "the existing monuments of literature form an ideal order among themselves." "This," Frye commented, "is criticism, and very fundamental criticism. Much of this book attempts to annotate it" (*AC*, p. 18).

In what proved to be a memorable passage, he derided "all the literary chit-chat which makes the reputations of poets boom and crash in an imaginary stock-exchange," and observed:

> This sort of thing cannot be part of any systematic study, for a systematic study can only progress: whatever dithers or vacillates or reacts is merely leisure-class gossip. The history of taste is no more a part of the *structure* of criticism than the Huxley-Wilberforce debate is a part of the structure of biological science. [*AC*, p. 18]

In view of Frye's Platonic conception of literature and positivistic conception of science, it is not surprising that he failed to recognize that his analogy here cuts both ways. For not only could the Huxley-Wilberforce debate be seen as very much a part of the "structure" of biological science (which, like that of any other science, including any science of literature, is by no means independent of its own intellectual, social, and institutional history), but, since the "order" of "the existing monuments of literature" is the distinctly sublunary product of, among other things, evaluative practices, any truly systematic study of literature would sooner or later have to include a study of *those practices*. In other words, the structure of criticism cannot be so readily disengaged from the history of taste because they are mutually implicating and incorporating.

Joining as it did both an appeal to scientific objectivity and a humanistic conception of literature, while at the same time extending the promise of a high calling and bright future to a project pursued in the name of "criticism," Frye's effort to banish evaluation from literary study was remarkably effective—at least to the extent of haunting a generation of literary scholars, critics, and teachers, many of whom are still inclined to apologize for making overt value judgments, as if for some temporary intellectual or moral lapse.[10] It was hardly the last word on the subject, however, and as late as 1968 we find E. D. Hirsch, Jr., attempting to rehabilitate the cognitive status of evaluative criticism in an essay significantly titled "Evaluation as Knowledge." In the essay, Hirsch argues that the value judgment of a literary work, when properly directed to the work itself and not to a "distorted version of it," closely coordinated with a correct interpretation of its objective meaning and rationally justified with reference to specific criteria, *does* constitute a genuine proposition and, therefore, like a "pure description," does "qualify as objective knowledge."[11] Since just about every concept engaged by Hirsch's argument is at issue in contemporary epistemology and critical theory, it is not surprising that it did not settle the question of the intellectual status of evaluative criticism—for Hirsch or anyone else.[12]

The debate over the proper place of evaluation in literary studies remains unresolved and is, I believe, unresolvable in the terms in which it has been formulated. Meanwhile, although evaluative criticism remains intellectually suspect, it certainly continues to be practiced as a magisterial privilege in the classrooms of the literary academy and granted admission to its journals as long as it comes under cover of other presumably more objective types of literary study, such as historical description, textual analysis, or explication. At the same time, however, the fact that literary evaluation is not merely an aspect of formal academic criticism but a complex set of social and cultural activities central to the very nature of literature has been obscured, and an entire domain that is properly the object of theoretical, historical, and empirical exploration has been lost to serious inquiry.

Although I confine my comments here primarily to the American literary academy and to Anglo-American critical theory, the situation—and its intellectual and institutional history—has not been altogether different in continental Europe. The dominance of language- and interpretation-centered theories, movements, and approaches, for example, is clearly international, and versions of the positivist/humanist conflict have shaped the development of literary studies in Europe as well. Certain exceptions are, however, instructive. When, in the twenties and thirties, East European theorists also sought to transform literary studies into a progressive, systematic science, the problematic of value and evaluation was not excluded from the project. For example, the historically variable functions of texts and the interrelations among canonical and noncanonical works and other cultural products and activities were recognized and documented by, among others, Jurij Tynjanov and Mikhail Bakhtin; and Jan Mukařovský's explorations of the general question of aesthetic value were both original and substantial.[13] Also, studies in the sociology of literature, especially in France and Germany, and the project of reception aesthetics have concerned themselves with aspects of literary evaluation.[14] It should also be noted, however, that the study of value and evaluation remained relatively undeveloped in the later work of formalists and structuralists,[15] while Marxist literary theory has only recently begun to move from minimal revisions of orthodox aesthetic axiology toward a radical reformulation.[16] It may be added that, although the theoretical perspective, conceptual structures, and analytic techniques developed by Jacques Derrida are potentially of great interest here (especially in conjunction with the renewed attention to Nietzsche), their radical axiological implications remain largely unexplored,[17] and, insofar as it has been appropriated by American critical theory, deconstruction has been put almost entirely in the service of antihermeneutics, which is to say that it has been absorbed by our preemptive occupation with interpretive criticism. Recent moves toward opening the question of value and evaluation in the American literary academy have come primarily from those who have sought to subject its canon to dramatic revaluation, notably feminist critics. Although their efforts have been significant to that end, they have not, however, amounted as yet to the articulation of a well-developed noncanonical theory of value and evaluation.

One of the major effects of prohibiting or inhibiting explicit evaluation is to forestall the exhibition and obviate the possible acknowledgment of divergent systems of value and thus to ratify, by default, established evaluative authority. It is worth noting that in none of the debates of the forties and fifties was the traditional academic canon itself questioned, and that where evaluative authority was not ringingly affirmed, asserted, or self-justified, it was simply assumed. Thus Frye himself could speak almost in one breath of the need to "get rid of . . . all casual, sentimental, and prejudiced value-judgments" as "the first step in developing a genuine poetics" and of "the masterpieces of literature" which are "the materials of literary criticism" (*AC*, pp. 18, 15). The identity of those masterpieces, it seemed, could be taken for granted or followed more or less automatically from the "direct value-judgement of informed good taste" or "certain literary values . . . fully established by critical experience" (*AC*, pp. 27, 20).

In a passage of particular interest, Frye wrote:

> Comparative estimates of value are really inferences, most valid when silent ones, from critical practice. . . . The critic will find soon, and constantly, that Milton is a more rewarding and suggestive poet to work with than Blackmore. But the more obvious this becomes, the less time he will want to waste belaboring the point. [*AC*, p. 25]

In addition to the noteworthy correlation of validity with silence (comparable, to some extent, to Wimsatt's discreet "intimations"of value), two other aspects of Frye's remarks here repay some attention. First, in claiming that it is altogether obvious that Milton, rather than Blackmore, is "a more rewarding and suggestive poet [for the critic] to work with," Frye begged the question of *what kind of work* the critic would be doing. For surely if one were concerned with a question such as the relation of canonical and noncanonical texts in the system of literary value in eighteenth-century England, one would find Blackmore just as rewarding and suggestive *to work with* as Milton. Both here and in his repeated insistence that the "material" of criticism must be "the masterpieces of literature" (he refers also to "a feeling we have all had: that the study of mediocre works of art remains a random and peripheral form of critical experience" [*AC*, p. 17]), Frye exhibits a severely limited conception of the potential domain of literary study and of the sort of problems and phenomena with which it could or should deal. In this conceptual and methodological confinement, however (which betrays the conservative force of the ideology of traditional humanism even in the laboratories of the new progressive poetics), he has been joined by just about every other member of the Anglo-American literary academy during the past fifty years.

The second point of interest in Frye's remarks is his significant conjoining of Milton with Blackmore as an illustration of the sort of comparative estimate that is so obvious as not to need belaboring. Blackmore, we recall, was the author of an ambitious epic poem, *The Creation*, notable in literary history primarily as the occasion of some faint praise from Dr. Johnson and otherwise as a topos of literary disvalue; its function—indeed, one might say, its *value*—has been to stand as an instance of bad poetry. This handy conjunction, however (and similar ones, such as Shakespeare and Edgar Guest, John Keats and Joyce Kilmer, T. S. Eliot and Ella Wheeler Wilcox, that occur repeatedly in the debates outlined above), evades the more difficult and consequential questions of judgment posed by genuine evaluative diversity and conflict: questions that are posed, for example, by specific claims of value made for noncanonical works (such as modern texts, especially highly innovative ones, and such culturally exotic works as oral or tribal literature, popular literature, and "ethnic" literature) and also by judgments of literary value made by or on behalf of what might be called noncanonical or culturally exotic audiences (such as all those readers who are not now students, critics, or professors of literature and perhaps never were and never will be within the academy or on its outskirts).

The evasion is dramatized when conflicts of judgment arising from fundamental and perhaps irreconcilable diversity of interest are exhibited in currently charged political contexts. A specific example will illustrate my point here. In 1977 a study of Langston Hughes' poetry was published by Onwuchekwa Jemie, a Nigerian-born, American-educated poet and critic, at that time associate professor of English and Afro-American literature at the University of Minnesota. In one section of his study, Jemie discusses Hughes' poetic cycle, "Madame," in relation to Eliot's "The Love Song of J. Alfred Prufrock" and Ezra Pound's "Hugh Selwyn Mauberly," comparing various formal and thematic aspects of the three works. He observes, for example, that each of them is "consistent in language, tone and attitude with the socio-psychological milieu which it explores: the ghetto dialect and sassy humor [in Hughes' work], the cynical polished talk of literary London [in Pound's], and the bookish ruminations of Prufrock's active mind in inactive body"; he then concludes pointedly: "In short, to fault one poem for not being more like the other, for not dealing with the matter and in the manner of the other, is to err in judgment."[18] Soon after its publication, a reviewer of Jemie's book in the London *Times Literary Supplement* took it very much to task for, among other things, its "painfully irrelevant comparisons," citing the passage quoted above.[19] And, a few weeks later, there appeared in *TLS* an extraordinary letter to the editor from Chinweizu, himself a Nigerian-born, American-educated writer and critic. Responding to the review and particularly to the phrase, "painfully irrelevant comparisons," he shot back:

> Painful to whom? Irrelevant to whom? To idolators of white genius? Who says that Shakespeare, Aristophanes, Dante, Milton, Dostoevsky, Joyce, Pound, Sartre, Eliot, etc. are the last word in literary achievement, unequalled anywhere? . . . The point of these comparisons is not to thrust a black face among these local idols of Europe which, to our grave injury, have been bloated into "universality"; rather it is to help heave them out of our way, clear them from our skies by making clear . . . that we have, among our own, the equals and betters of these chaps. . . . In this day and age, British preferences do not count in the Black World. As Langston Hughes himself put it half a century ago: "If white people are pleased, we are glad. If they are not, it doesn't matter."[20]

This brief case history in the problem of literary evaluation illustrates, among other things, what genuine evaluative conflict sounds like. (It also illustrates that, contrary to Frye's assertion, the history of taste is not "a history where there are no facts" [*AC,* p. 18], though we have barely begun to recognize either how to chronicle its episodes and shape its narrative or its significance not only for "the structure of criticism" but also for the structure of "literature.") I would suggest that it is, also among other things, the very possibility of that sound that is being evaded in Anglo-American literary studies and, furthermore, that when the sound reaches the intensity that we hear in Chinweizu's letter, the literary academy has no way to acknowledge it except, perhaps, in the language of counteroutrage.[21]

It is clear that, with respect to the central pragmatic issues as well as theoretical problems of literary value and evaluation, American critical theory has simply painted itself out of the picture. Beguiled by the humanist's fantasy of transcendence, endurance, and universality, it has been unable to acknowledge the most fundamental character of literary value, which is its mutability and diversity. And, at the same time, magnetized by the goals and ideology of a naive scientism, distracted by the arid concerns of philosophic axiology, obsessed by a misplaced quest for "objectivity," and confined in its very conception of literary studies by the narrow intellectual traditions and professional allegiances of the literary academy, it has foreclosed from its own domain the possibility of investigating the dynamics of that mutability and understanding the nature of that diversity.

The type of investigation I have in mind here would seek neither to establish normative "criteria," devise presumptively objective evaluative procedures, nor discover grounds for the "justification" of critical judgments or practices. It would not, in short, be a literary axiology or, in effect, the counterpart for evaluative criticism of what a literary hermeneutics offers to be for interpretive criticism. It would seek, rather, to clarify the nature of literary—and, more broadly, aesthetic—value in conjunction with a more general rethinking of the concept of value; to explore the multiple forms and functions of literary evaluation, institutional as well as individual, in relation to the circumstantial constraints and conditions to which they are responsive; to chronicle "the history of taste" in relation to a general model of historical evaluative dynamics and specific local conditions; and to describe and account for the various phenomena and activities that appear to be involved in literary and aesthetic evaluation in relation to our more general understanding—as it is and as it develops— of human culture and behavior.

The sort of inquiry suggested here (which obviously could not be pursued within the confines of literary study or critical theory as they are presently conceived and demarcated) might be expected to make its accounts internally consistent, externally connectable, and amenable to continuous extension and refinement; for it is thus that the theoretical power and productivity of those accounts would be served and secured. This is not, however, to imagine a monolithic intellectual project that would offer to yield an ultimately comprehensive, unified, and objective account of its subject; for to imagine it thus would, of course, be to repeat, only on a grander scale, elements of the raw positivism and naive scientism that were, in part, responsible for both the exile of evaluation and the confinements of modern critical theory. What is desirable, rather, is an inquiry pursued with the recognition that, like any other intellectual enterprise, it would consist, at any given time, of a set of heterogeneous projects; that the conceptual structures and methodological practices adopted in those projects would themselves be historically and otherwise contingent (reflecting, among other things, prevailing or currently interesting conceptual structures and methods in related areas of inquiry); that whatever other value the descriptions and accounts produced by any of those projects might and undoubtedly would have (as indices of twentieth-century thought, for example, to future historians), their specific value as descriptions and accounts would be a function of how well they made intelligible the phenomena within their domain to whoever, at whatever time and from whatever perspective, had an interest in them; and that its pursuit would be shaped by—that is, energized and transformed in response to—those interests, and its descriptions and accounts continuously and variously interpreted and employed in accord with them.[22]

The discussion that follows is designed to suggest a theoretical framework for such an inquiry.[23]

2. *The Economics of Literary and Aesthetic Value*

All value is radically contingent, being neither an inherent property of objects nor an arbitrary projection of subjects but, rather, the product of the dynamics of an economic system. It is readily granted, of course, that it is in relation to a system of that sort that commodities such as gold, bread, and paperback editions of *Moby-Dick* acquire the value indicated by their market prices. It is traditional, however, both in economic and aesthetic theory as well as in informal discourse, to distinguish sharply between the value of an entity in that sense (that is, its "exchange-value") and some other type of value that may be referred to as its utility (or "use-value") or, especially with respect to so-called "nonutilitarian" objects such as artworks or works of literature, as its "intrinsic value." Thus, it might be said that whereas the fluctuating price of a particular paperback edition of *Moby-Dick* is a function of such variables as supply and demand, production and distribution costs, and the publisher's calculation of corporate profits, these factors do not affect the value of *Moby-Dick* as experienced by an individual reader or its intrinsic value as a work of literature. These distinctions, however, are not as clear-cut as may appear.

Like its price in the marketplace, the value of an entity to an individual subject is *also* the product of the dynamics of an economic system, specifically the personal economy constituted by the subject's needs, interests, and resources—biological, psychological, material, and experiential. Like any other economy, moreover, this too is a continuously fluctuating or shifting system, for our individual needs, interests, and resources are themselves functions of our continuously changing states in relation to an environment that may be relatively stable but is never absolutely fixed. The two systems are, it may be noted, not only analogous but also interactive and interdependent; for part of our environment *is* the market economy, and, conversely, the market economy is comprised, in part, of the diverse personal economies of individual producers, distributors, consumers, and so forth.

The traditional discourse of value—including a number of terms I have used here, such as "subject," "object," "needs," "interests," and, indeed, "value" itself—reflects an arbitrary arresting, segmentation, and hypostasization of the continuous process of our interactions with our environments—or what could also be described as the continuous interplay among multiple configurable systems. It is difficult to devise (and would be, perhaps, impossible to sustain) a truly Heraclitean discourse that did not reflect such conceptual operations, but we may recognize that, insofar as such terms project images of discrete acts, agents, and entities, fixed attributes, unidirectional forces, and simple causal and temporal relationships, they obscure the dynamics of value and reinforce dubious concepts of noncontingency—that is, concepts such as "intrinsic," "objective," "absolute," "universal," and "transcendent." It is necessary, therefore, to emphasize a number of other interactive relationships and forms of interdependence that are fragmented by our language and commonly ignored in critical theory and aesthetic axiology.

First, as I have already suggested, a subject's experience of an entity is always a function of his or her personal economy: that is, the specific "existence" of an object or event its integrity, coherence, and boundaries, the category of entities to wl ...n it "belongs" and its specific "features," "qualities," or "properties" are all the variable products of the subject's engagement with his or her environment under a particular set of conditions. Not only is an entity always experienced under more or less different conditions, but the various experiences do not yield a simple cumulative (corrected, improved, deeper, more thorough, or complete) knowledge of the entity because they are not additive. Rather, each experience of an entity frames it in a different role and constitutes it as a different configuration, with different "properties" foregrounded and repressed. Moreover, the subject's experiences of an entity are not discrete or, strictly speaking, successive, because recollection and anticipation always overlay perception and the units of what we call "experience" themselves vary and overlap.

Second, what we speak of as a subject's "needs," "interests," and "purposes" are not only always changing (and it may be noted here that a subject's "self"—or that on behalf of which s/he may be said to act with "self-interest"—is also variable, being multiply reconstituted in terms of different roles and relationships), but they are also not altogether independent of or prior to the entities that satisfy or implement them; that is, entities also produce the needs and interests they satisfy and evoke the purposes they implement. Moreover, because our purposes are continuously transformed and redirected by the objects we produce in the very process of implementing them, and because of the complex interrelations among human needs, technological production, and cultural practices, there is a continuous process of mutual modification between our desires and our universe.[24]

Of particular significance for the value of "works of art" and "literature" is the interactive relation between the *classification* of an entity and the functions it is expected or desired to perform. In perceiving an object or artifact in terms of some category—*as*, for example, "a clock," "a dictionary," "a doorstop," "a curio"—we implicitly isolate and foreground certain of its possible functions and typically refer its value to the extent to which it performs those functions more or less effectively. But the relation between function and classification also operates in reverse: thus, under conditions that produce the "need" for a door-stopping object or an "interest" in Victorian artifacts, certain properties and possible functions of various objects in the neighborhood will be foregrounded, and both the classification and value of those objects will follow accordingly. As we commonly put it, one will "realize" the value of the dictionary *as* a doorstop or "appreciate" the value of the clock *as* a curio.[25] (The mutually defining relations among classification, function, and value are nicely exhibited in the *OED*'s definition of "curio" as "an object of art, piece of bric-à-brac, etc., valued as a curiosity," which is, of course, something like—and no less accurate than—defining "clock" as "an object valued as a clock.") It may be noted here that human beings have evolved as distinctly opportunistic creatures and that our survival, both as individuals and as a species, continues to be enhanced by our ability and inclination to reclassify objects and to "realize" and "appreciate" novel and alternate functions for them—which is also to "misuse" them and to fail to respect their presumed purposes and conventional generic classifications.

The various forms of interdependence emphasized here have considerable bearing on what may be recognized as the economics of literary and aesthetic value. The traditional—idealist, humanist, genteel—tendency to isolate or protect certain aspects of life and culture, among them works of art and literature, from consideration in economic terms has had the effect of mystifying the nature—or, more accurately, the dynamics—of their value. In view of the arbitrariness of the exclusion, it is not surprising that the languages of aesthetics and economics nevertheless tend to drift toward each other and that their segregation must be constantly patrolled.[26] (Thus, an aesthetician deplores a pun on "appreciation" appearing in an article on art investment and warns of the dangers of confusing "the uniqueness of a painting that gives it scarcity value . . . with its unique value as a work of art.")[27] To those for whom terms such as "utility," "effectiveness," and "function" suggest gross pragmatic instrumentality, crass material desires, and the satisfaction of animal needs, a concept such as use-value will be seen as irrelevant to or clearly to be distinguished from aesthetic value. There is, however, no good reason to confine the domain of the utilitarian to objects that serve only immediate, specific, and unexalted ends or, for that matter, to assume that the value of artworks has altogether nothing to do with pragmatic instrumentality or animal needs.[28] The recurrent impulse or effort to define aesthetic value by contradistinction to all forms of utility or as the negation of all other nameable sources of interest or forms of value—hedonic, practical, sentimental, ornamental, historical, ideological, and so forth—is, in effect, to define it out of existence; for when all such particular utilities, interests, and sources of value have been subtracted, nothing remains. Or, to put this in other terms: the "essential value" of an artwork consists of everything from which it is usually distinguished.

To be sure, various candidates have been proposed for a pure, non-utilitarian, interest-free, and, in effect, value-free source of aesthetic value, such as the eliciting of "intrinsically rewarding" intellectual, sensory, or perceptual activities, or Kant's "free play of the cognitive faculties." A strict accounting of any of these seemingly gratuitous activities, however, would bring us sooner or later to their biological utility and/or survival value (and indeed to something very much like "animal needs"). For although we may be individually motivated to engage in them "for their own sake" (which is to say, for the sake of the gratifications they provide), our doing so apparently yields a long-term profit in enhanced cognitive development, behavioral flexibility, and thus biological fitness, and our general tendency to do so is in all likelihood the product of evolutionary mechanisms.[29] Moreover, as I have pointed out elsewhere, the occasioning of such activities (or "experiences") is not confined to "works of art" and therefore cannot, without circularity, be said to constitute the defining "aesthetic function" of the objects so labeled.[30] More generally, it may be observed that since there are no functions performed by artworks that may be specified as unique to them and also no way to distinguish the "rewards" provided by the art-related experiences or behavior from those provided by innumerable other kinds of experience and behavior, any distinctions drawn between "aesthetic" and "non- (or "extra-) aesthetic" value are fundamentally problematic.[31]

Suggestions of the radically contingent nature of aesthetic value are commonly countered by evidence of apparent noncontingent value: for example, the endurance of certain classic canonical works (the invocation of Homer being a topos of the critical tradition) and, if not quite Pope's "gen'ral chorus of mankind," then at least the convergent sentiments of people of education and discrimination. Certainly any theory of aesthetic value must be able to account for continuity, stability, and apparent consensus as well as for drift, shift, and diversity. The tendency throughout formal aesthetic axiology has been to explain the constancies and convergences by the inherent qualities of the objects and/or some set of presumed human universals and to explain the variabilities and divergences by the errors, defects, and biases of individual subjects. The classic development of this account is found in Hume's essay, *Of the Standard of Taste*, where the "catholic and universal beauty" is seen to be the result of

> [t]he relation which nature has placed between the form and the sentiment. . . . We shall be able to ascertain its influence . . . from the durable admiration which attends those works that have survived all the caprices of mode and fashion, all the mistakes of ignorance and envy.
>
> The same Homer who pleased at Athens two thousand years ago, is still admired at Paris and London. All the changes of climate, government, religion and language have not been able to obscure his glory. . . .
>
> It appears then, that amidst all the variety and caprice of taste, there are certain general principles of approbation and blame, whose influence a careful eye may trace in all the operations of the mind. Some particular forms or qualities, from the original structure of the internal fabric are calculated to please, and others to displease; and if they fail of their effect in any particular instance, it is from some apparent defect or imperfection in the organ.
>
> Many and frequent are the defects . . . which prevent or weaken the influence of those general principles.[32]

The essay continues by enumerating and elaborating these defects, introducing the familiar catalog (already given vivid expression in, among other places, Pope's *Essay on Criticism*: "Of all the causes which conspire to blind / Man's erring judgment and misguide the mind") with an analogy, also a commonplace of the tradition, between "the perfect beauty," as agreed upon by men "in a sound state of the organ," and "the true and real colors" of objects as they appear "in daylight to the eye of a man in health."[33]

The following is a more recent statement of the traditional view:

> False judgments and intuitions of an object can only be corrected if there is a correct and permanently valid intuition of an object. . . .
> The relativity of value judgments merely proves that subjective judgments are conjoined with the person, that mistaken judgments—

of which there is no dearth in the history of literature—are always the fault of the person.

... Just as the universal validity of a mathematical proposition does not necessarily imply that everyone can understand it, "but merely that everyone who understands it must agree with it," so the universal validity of aesthetic value does not necessarily mean that evidence of it is felt by everyone. Aesthetic values demand an adequate attitude, a trained or reliably functioning organ. Moreover, the fact that the history of literature contains, albeit tacitly, a firm gradation of valuable works of art is an indication that values transcend historicity.

... The value-feeling organ must not be encumbered with pre-judgments, pre-feelings, or arbitrarily formed opinions if it wishes to address itself adequately to the object, a process that is by no means always easy, ... for the human being is in part—an external but not uninfluential part—a historical creature, embedded in a whole cluster of behavior compulsions that stem from his environment.[34]

This conflation of, among others, Hume, Kant, Nicolai Hartmann, and Roman Ingarden is remarkable only in making particularly flagrant the logical incoherence of the standard account, whether in its empiricist, idealist, or phenomenological guise.

Given a more sophisticated formulation, Hume's belief that the individual experience of "beauty" can be related to "forms" and "qualities" that gratify human beings "naturally" by virtue of certain physiological structures and psychological mechanisms is probably not altogether without foundation.[35] Taken as a ground for the justification of normative claims, however, and transformed accordingly into a model of standards-and-deviations, it obliged him (as it did and does many others) to interpret as so many instances of individual pathology what are, rather, the variable products of the interaction between, on the one hand, certain *relatively* uniform innate structures, mechanisms, and tendencies and, on the other, innumerable cultural and contextual variables as well as other individual variables—the latter including particulars of personal history, temperament, age, and so forth. What produces evaluative consensus, such as it is, is not the healthy functioning of universal organs but the playing out of the *same* dynamics and variable contingencies that produce evaluative divergences.

Although value is always subject-relative, not all value is equally subject-variable. Within a particular community, the tastes and preferences of subjects—that is, their tendency to find more satisfaction of a particular kind in one rather than another of some array of comparable items and to select among them accordingly—will be conspicuously *divergent* (or indeed idiosyncratic) to the extent that the satisfactions in question are themselves functions of types of needs, interests, and resources that (*a*) vary individually along a wide spectrum, (*b*) are especially resistant, if not altogether intractable, to cultural channeling, and/or (*c*) are especially responsive to circumstantial context. Conversely, their tastes and preferences will tend to be similar to the extent that the satisfactions in question are functions of types of needs, interests, and resources that (*a*) vary individually within a narrow spectrum, (*b*) are especially tractable to cultural channeling, and (*c*) remain fairly stable under a variety of conditions.

Insofar as satisfactions ("aesthetic" or any other: erotic, for example) with regard to some array of objects are functions of needs, interests, and resources of the first kind, preferences for those objects will appear "subjective," "eccentric," "stubborn," and "capricious." Insofar as they are functions of the second, preferences will seem so obvious, "natural," and "rational" as not to appear to be matters of taste at all. Indeed, it is precisely under the latter conditions that the value of particular objects will appear to be inherent, that distinctions or gradations of value among them will appear to reduce to differences in the properties or qualities of the objects themselves, and that explicit judgments of their value will appear to be objective. In short, here as elsewhere, a co-incidence of contingencies among individual subjects will be interpreted by those subjects as noncontingency.

Because we are dealing here not with two opposed sets of discrete determinants but with the possibility of widely differing specifications for a large number of complexly interacting variables, we may expect to find a continuous exhibition of every degree of divergence and convergence among the subjects in a particular community over the course of its history, depending in each instance on the extent of the disparity and uniformity of each of the relevant contingencies *and* on the strength of various social practices and cultural institutions that control the exhibition of extreme "deviance."[36] It may be noted that the latter—that is, the normative mechanisms within a community that suppress divergence and tend to obscure as well as deny the contingency of value—will always have, as their counterpart, a *counter*mechanism that permits a recognition of that contingency and a more or less genial acknowledgement of the inevitability of divergence: hence the ineradicability, in spite of the efforts of establishment axiology, of what might be called folk-relativism: "Chacun à son goût"; "De gustibus . . ."; "One man's meat is another's poison"; and so forth.

The prevailing structure of tastes and preferences (and the consequent illusion of a consensus based on objective value) will always be implicitly threatened or directly challenged by the divergent tastes and preferences of some subjects within the community (for example, those not yet adequately acculturated, such as the young, and others with "uncultivated" tastes, such as provincials and social upstarts) as well as by most subjects outside it or, more significantly, on its *periphery* and who thus have occasion to interact with its members (for example, exotic visitors, immigrants, colonials, and members of various minority or marginalized groups). Consequently, institutions of evaluative authority will be called upon repeatedly to devise arguments and procedures that validate the community's established tastes and preferences, thereby warding off barbarism and the constant apparition of an imminent collapse of standards and also justifying the exercise of their own normative authority. In Hume's words, "It is natural to seek a Standard of Taste; a rule by which the various sentiments of men may be reconciled; at least a decision afforded confirming one sentiment and denying another"—the usefulness of such a rule to the latter end being illustrated in the essay by that memorable vignette of the barbarian in the drawing room who "would assert an equality of genius and elegance between Ogilby and Milton or Bunyan and Addison" and what ensues: "Though there may be found *persons* who give preference to the former authors, *no one* pays attention to such taste; and *we* pronounce without scruple the sentiment of these pretended critics to be absurd and ridiculous."[37] The sequence emphasized here is no less telling than the embarrassment of the argument by the examples.

Both informally, as in the drawing rooms of men of cultivation and discrimination or the classrooms of the literary academy, and formally, as in Hume's essay and throughout the central tradition of Western critical theory, the validation commonly takes the form of privileging absolutely—that is, "standard"-izing—the particular contingencies that govern the preferences of the members of the group and discounting or, as suggested above, pathologizing all other contingencies.[38] Thus it will be assumed or maintained: (*a*) that the particular *functions* they expect and desire the class of objects in question (for example, "works of art" or "literature") to perform are their intrinsic or proper functions, all other expected, desired, or emergent functions being inappropriate, irrelevant, extrinsic, abuses of the true nature of those objects or violations of their authorially intended or generically intrinsic purposes; (*b*) that the particular *conditions* (circumstantial, technological, institutional, and so forth) under which the members of the group typically interact with those objects are suitable, standard, or necessary for their proper appreciation, all other conditions being irregular, unsuitable, substandard, or outlandish; and, perhaps most significantly, (*c*) that the particular *subjects* who compose the members of the group are of sound mind and body, duly trained and informed, and generally competent, all other subjects being defective, deficient, or deprived—suffering from crudenesses of sensibility, diseases and distortions of perception, weaknesses of character, impoverishment of background-and-education, cultural or historical biases, ideological or personal prejudices, and/or undeveloped, corrupted, or jaded tastes.

With regard to this last point (*c*), we may recall here the familiar specifications of the "ideal critic" as one who, in addition to possessing various exemplary natural endowments and cultural competencies, has, through exacting feats of self-liberation, freed himself of all forms of particularity and individuality, all special interests (or, as in Kant, all interests whatsoever), and thus of all bias—which is to say, one who is "free" of everything in relation to which any experience or judgment of value occurs. (In these respects, the ideal critic of aesthetic axiology is the exact counterpart of the "ideal reader" of literary hermeneutics.)

We may also note, with regard to the first point (*a*), that the privileging of a particular set of functions for artworks or works of literature may be (and often is) itself justified on the grounds that the performance of such functions serves some higher individual, social, or transcendent good, such as the psychic health of the reader, the brotherhood of mankind, the glorification of God, the project of human emancipation, or the survival of Western civilization. Any selection from among these alternate and to some extent mutually exclusive higher goods, however, would itself require justification in terms of some yet *higher* good, and there is no absolute stopping point for this theoretically infinite regress of judgments and justifications. This is not to say that certain functions of artworks do not serve higher—or at least more general, comprehensive, or longer-range—goods better than others. It is to say, however, that our selection among higher goods, like our selection among any array of goods, will always be contingent.

3. The Multiple Forms, Functions, and Contexts of Evaluative Behavior

It follows from the conception of value outlined here that evaluations are not discrete acts or episodes punctuating experience but indistinguishable from the very processes of acting and experiencing themselves. In other words, for a responsive creature, to exist is to evaluate. We are always calculating how things "figure" for us—always pricing them, so to speak, in relation to the total economy of our personal universe. Throughout our lives, we perform a continuous succession of rapid-fire cost-benefit analyses, estimating the probable "worthwhileness" of alternate courses of action in relation to our always limited resources of time and energy, assessing, re-assessing, and classifying entities with respect to their probable capacity to satisfy our current needs and desires and to serve our emergent interests and long-range plans and purposes. We tend to become most conscious of our own evaluative behavior when the need to select among an array of alternate "goods" and/or to resolve an internal "contest of sentiments" moves us to specifically verbal or other symbolic forms of cost accounting: thus we draw up our lists of pros and cons, lose sleep, and bore our friends by overtly rehearsing our options, estimating the risks and probable outcomes of various actions, and so forth. Most of these calculations, however, are performed intuitively and inarticulately, and many of them are so recurrent that the habitual arithmetic becomes part of our personality and comprises the very style of our being and behavior, forming what we may call our principles or tastes—and what others may call our biases and prejudices.

I have been speaking up to this point of the evaluations we make for ourselves. As social creatures, however, we also evaluate for one another through various kinds of individual acts and also through various institutional practices. The long-standing preoccupation of aesthetic axiology with the logical form and cognitive substance of verbal "value judgments" and, in particular, with debates over their "validity," "truth-value," and "verifiability," has obscured the operation and significance of institutional and other less overt forms of evaluation. It has also deflected attention from the social contexts, functions, and consequences of all forms of aesthetic and literary evaluation, including their complex productive relation to literary and aesthetic value. Although I am more concerned here with the latter questions and shall return to them below, some comments on *explicit* aesthetic judgments (and on certain familiar axiological perplexities regarding them) are in order.

Evaluations are among the most fundamental forms of social communication and probably among the most primitive benefits of social interaction. (Animals—insects and birds as well as mammals—evaluate *for* one another, that is, signal to other members of their group the "quality" of a food supply or territory by some form of specialized overt behavior.)[39] We not only produce but also solicit and seek out both "expressions of personal sentiment" and "objective judgments of value" because, although neither will (for nothing can) give us "knowledge" of *the* value of an object, both may let us know other things we could find useful. For example, other people's reports of how well certain objects have gratified them, though "mere expressions of subjective likes and dislikes," may nevertheless be useful to us if we ourselves have produced those objects or if—as lovers, say, or parents or potential associates—we have an independently motivated interest in the current states, specific responses, or general structure of tastes and preferences of those people. Also, an assertion that some object (for example, some artwork) is good, great, bad, or middling can, no matter how magisterially delivered or with what attendant claims or convictions of absoluteness, usually be unpacked as a judgment of its *contingent* value: specifically, as the evaluator's observation and/or estimate of how well that object, relative to others of the same implied category, has performed and/or is likely to perform certain particular (though taken-for-granted) functions for some particular (though only implicitly defined) set of subjects under some particular (unspecified but assumed) set or range of conditions. Any evaluation, therefore, is "cognitively substantial" in the sense of being potentially informative about *something*. The actual interest of that information, however, and hence the value of that evaluation to *us* (and "we" are always heterogeneous) will vary, depending on, among other things, the extent to which we have any interest in the object evaluated, believe that we take for granted the same taken-for-granted functions and assume the same assumed conditions, and also think that we (or others whose interests are of interest to us) are among that implicitly defined set of subjects—or, of course, the extent to which we have an interest in the evaluator's sentiments by reason of our independently motivated interest in him or her.

In view of the centrality of the question in post-Kantian aesthetic axiology, it may be noted that if the set of relevant subjects implied by an evaluation is not contextually defined or otherwise indicated, it will usually be appropriately taken to consist of the evaluator himself and all others whom s/he believes are *like* himself or herself in the pertinent respects. Of course, some evaluators believe that *all* other people are—or should be—like themselves in the pertinent respects: hence, apparently, the curious and distracting notion that every aesthetic judgment "claims universal subjective validity."[40] The familiar subjectivist/objectivist controversy is commonly seen to turn on whether, in making an aesthetic judgment, I speak "for myself *alone*" or "for *everyone*." A consideration of the social functions of such judgments, however, suggests that, if such a formulation is wanted at all, it should be that, in making aesthetic judgments, I tend to speak "for myself *and some others*."

We may also consider here what is thought to be the suspect propositional status of value judgments as distinguished from and compared to that of so-called factual statements and the consequent demotion of the former to the status of "pseudostatements." There is, of course, no way for us to be certain that someone's reports of his or her personal likes or dislikes are sincere, or that the estimates and observations offered are the estimates and observations actually made. Like all other utterances, value judgments are context-dependent and shaped by the relation of the speaker to his or her audience and by the structure of interests that sustains the verbal transaction between them. (In effect, there is no such thing as an honest opinion.) For this reason, we will always interpret (supplement and discount) evaluations in the light of other knowledge we have of the evaluator (or think we have: there is no absolute end to this regress, though in practice we do the best we can), including our sense—on whatever grounds—of the possibility of flattery or other kinds of deception: the evaluator may be the author's personal friend or professional rival, s/he may not want to hurt the cook's feelings, s/he may want to recommend himself or herself by creating the impression that s/he shares our tastes, and so forth. In all these respects, however, value judgments are no different from any other kind of utterance, and neither their reliability nor their "validity" as "propositions" is any more (or any less) compromised by these possibilities than that of any other type of verbal behavior, from someone's saying (or otherwise implying) that s/he has a headache to his or her solemn report of the measurement of a scientific instrument.

There is a tenacious conviction among those who argue these questions that unless one judgment can be said or shown to be more "valid" than another, then all judgments must be "equal" or "equally valid." Indeed, it is the horror or apparent absurdity of such egalitarianism that commonly gives force to the charge that "relativism" produces social chaos or is a logically untenable position. While the radical contingency of all value certainly does imply that no value judgment can be more valid than another in the sense of being a more accurate statement of *the* value of an object (for the latter concept then becomes vacuous), it does not follow that all value judgments are equal or equally valid. On the contrary, what does follow is that the concept of "validity" is *inappropriate* with regard to evaluations and that there is no nontrivial parameter with respect to which they *could* be "equal." This is not to say that no evaluations can be better or worse than others. What must be emphasized, however, is that the value—the "goodness" or "badness"—of an evaluation, like that of anything else (including any other type of utterance), is *itself* contingent, and thus a matter not of its abstract "truth-value" but of how well it performs various desired/able functions for the various people who may at any time be concretely involved with it. In the case of an aesthetic evaluation, these people will always include the evaluator, who will have his or her own particular interest in the various effects of the judgments s/he produces, and may also include anyone from the artist to a potential publisher or patron, various current or future audiences of the work, and perhaps someone who just likes to know what's going on and what other people think is going on. Each of them will have his or her own interest in the evaluation, and it will be better or worse for each of them in relation to a different set of desired/able functions. What all this suggests is that the obsessive debates over the cognitive substance, logical status, and "truth-value" of aesthetic judgments are not only unresolvable in the terms given but, strictly speaking, pointless.

As was indicated above, the value of an explicit verbal evaluation— that is, its utility to those who produce and receive it—will, like that of any other type of utterance, always be a function of specific features of the various transactions of which it may be a part, including the relevant interests of the speaker and any of those who, at any time, become members of his or her de facto audience. It follows that the value of a value judgment may also be quite minimal or negative. For example, depending on specific (and readily imaginable) contextual features, an aesthetic judgment may be excruciatingly *un*interesting to the listener or elicited from the speaker at considerable expense to himself or herself. Also, aesthetic judgments, like any other use of language, may be intimidating, coercive, and otherwise socially and politically oppressive. If they are so, however, it is not because of any characteristic frailty of their propositional status (and "justifying" them—that is, giving a show of justice to their claims of objectivity or universal validity—will not eliminate the oppression) but, once again, because of the nature of the transactions of which they are a part, particularly the social or political relationship between the evaluator and his or her audience (professor and student, for example, or censor and citizen) and the structure of power that governs that relationship.[41] We may return now from the discussion of individual overt value judgments to the more general consideration of evaluative behavior, normative institutions, and the social mechanisms by which literary and aesthetic value are produced.

4. The Cultural Re-Production of Value

We do not move about in a raw universe. Not only are the objects we encounter always to some extent pre-interpreted and preclassified for us by our particular cultures and languages, but also pre-evaluated, bearing the marks and signs of their prior valuings and evaluations by our fellow creatures. Indeed, preclassification is itself a form of pre-evaluation, for the labels or category names under which we encounter objects not only, as was suggested earlier, foreground certain of their possible functions but also operate as signs—in effect, as culturally certified endorsements—of their more or less effective performance of those functions.

Like all other objects, works of art and literature bear the marks of their own evaluational history, signs of value that acquire their force by virtue of various social and cultural practices and, in this case, certain highly specialized and elaborated institutions. The labels "art" and "literature" are, of course, commonly signs of membership in distinctly honorific categories. The particular functions that may be endorsed by these labels, however, are, unlike those of "doorstops" and "clocks," neither narrowly confined nor readily specifiable but, on the contrary, exceptionally heterogeneous, mutable, and elusive. To the extent—always limited—that the relation between these labels and a particular set of expected and desired functions is stabilized within a community, it is largely through the normative activities of various institutions: most significantly, the literary and aesthetic academy which, among other things, develops pedagogic and other acculturative mechanisms directed at maintaining at least (and, commonly, at most) a *sub*population of the community whose members "appreciate the value" of works of art and literature "as such." That is, by providing them with "necessary backgrounds," teaching them "appropriate skills," "cultivating their interests," and, generally, "developing their tastes," the academy produces generation after generation of subjects for whom the objects and texts thus labeled do indeed perform the functions thus privileged, thereby insuring the continuity of mutually defining canonical works, canonical functions, and canonical audiences.[42]

It will be instructive at this point to consider the very beginning of a work's valuational history, namely, its initial evaluation by the artist (here, the author); for it is not only a prefiguration of all the subsequent acts of evaluation of which the work will become the subject but also a model or paradigm of all evaluative activity generally. I refer here not merely to that ultimate gesture of authorial judgment that must exhibit itself negatively—that is, in the author's either letting the work stand or ripping it up—but to the thousand individual acts of approval and rejection, preference and assessment, trial and revision that constitute the entire process of literary composition. The work we receive is not so much the achieved consummation of that process as its enforced abandonment: "abandonment" not because the author's techniques are inadequate to his or her goals but because the goals themselves are inevitably multiple, mixed, mutually competing, and thus mutually constraining, and also because they are inevitably unstable, changing their nature and relative potency and priority during the very course of composition. The completed work is thus always, in a sense, a temporary truce among contending forces, achieved at the point of exhaustion, that is, the literal depletion of the author's current resources or, given the most fundamental principle of the economics of existence, at the point when the author simply has something else—more worthwhile—to do: when, in other words, the time and energy s/he would have to give to further tinkering, testing, and adjustment are no longer compensated for by an adequately rewarding sense of continuing interest in the process or increased satisfaction in the product.

It is for comparable reasons that we, as readers of the work, will later let our own experience of it stand: not because we have fully "appreciated" the work, not because we have exhausted all its possible sources of interest and hence of value, but because we, too, ultimately have something else—more worthwhile—to do. The reader's experience of the work is pre-figured—that is, both calculated and pre-enacted—by the author in other ways as well: for, in selecting this word, adjusting that turn of phrase, preferring this rhyme to that, the author is all the while testing the local and global effectiveness of each decision by impersonating in advance his or her various presumptive audiences, who thereby themselves participate in shaping the work they will later read. Every literary work—and, more generally, artwork—is thus the product of a complex evaluative feedback loop that embraces not only the ever-shifting economy of the artist's own interests and resources as they evolve during and in reaction to the process of composition, but also all the shifting economies of his or her assumed and imagined audiences, including those who do not yet exist but whose emergent interests, variable conditions of encounter, and rival sources of gratification the artist will attempt to predict—or will intuitively surmise—and to which, among other things, his or her own sense of the fittingness of each decision will be responsive.[43]

But this also describes all the other diverse forms of evaluation by which the work will be subsequently marked and its value reproduced and transmitted: that is, the innumerable implicit acts of evaluation performed by those who, as may happen, publish the work, purchase, preserve, display, quote, cite, translate, perform, allude to, and imitate it; the more explicit but casual judgments made, debated, and negotiated in informal contexts by readers and by all those others in whose personal economies the work, in some way, "figures"; and the highly specialized institutionalized forms of evaluation exhibited in the more or less professional activities of scholars, teachers, and academic or journalistic critics—not only their full-dress reviews and explicit rank-orderings, evaluations, and revaluations, but also such activities as the awarding of literary prizes, the commissioning and publishing of articles about certain works, the compiling of anthologies, the writing of introductions, the construction of department curricula, and the drawing up of class reading lists. All these forms of evaluation, whether overt or covert, verbal or inarticulate, and whether performed by the common reader, professional reviewer, big-time bookseller, or small-town librarian, have functions and effects that are significant in the production and maintenance or destruction of literary value, both reflecting and contributing to the various economies in relation to which a work acquires value. And each of the evaluative acts mentioned, like those of the author, represents a set of individual economic decisions, an ajudication among competing claims for limited resources of time, space, energy, attention—or, of course, money—and also, insofar as the evaluation in a socially responsive act or part of a social transaction, a set of surmises, assumptions, or predictions regarding the personal economies of other people.

Although, as I have emphasized, the evaluation of texts is not confined to the formal critical judgments issued within the rooms of the literary academy or upon the pages of its associated publications, the activities of the academy certainly figure significantly in the production of literary value. For example, the repeated inclusion of a particular work in literary anthologies not only promotes the value of that work but goes some distance toward creating its value, as does also its repeated appearance on reading lists or its frequent citation or quotation by professors, scholars, and academic critics. For all these acts, at the least, have the effect of drawing the work into the orbit of attention of a population of potential readers; and, by making it more accessible to the interests of those readers (while, as indicated above, at the same time shaping and supplying the very interests in relation to which they will experience the work), they make it more likely both that the work will be experienced at all and also that it will be experienced as valuable.

The converse side to this process is well known. Those who are in positions to edit anthologies and prepare reading lists are obviously those who occupy positions of some cultural power; and their acts of evaluation—

represented in what they exclude as well as in what they include—constitute not merely recommendations of value but, for the reasons just mentioned, also determinants of value. Moreover, since they will usually exclude not only what they take to be inferior literature but also what they take to be nonliterary, subliterary, or paraliterary, their selections not only imply certain "criteria" of literary value, which may in fact be made explicit, but, more significantly, they produce and maintain certain definitions of "literature" and, thereby, certain assumptions about the desired and ex- pected functions of the texts so classified and about the interests of their appropriate audiences, all of which are usually not explicit and, for that reason, less likely to be questioned, challenged, or even noticed. Thus the privileging power of evaluative authority may be very great, even when it is manifested inarticulately.[44] The academic activities described here, however, are only a small part of the complex process of literary canonization.

When we consider the cultural re-production of value on a larger time scale, the model of evaluative dynamics outlined above suggests that the "survival" or "endurance" of a text—and, it may be, its achievement of high canonical status not only as a "work of literature" but as a "classic"— is the product neither of the objectively (in the Marxist sense) conspiratorial force of establishment institutions nor of the continuous appreciation of the timeless virtues of a fixed object by succeeding generations of isolated readers, but, rather, of a series of continuous interactions among a variably constituted object, emergent conditions, and mechanisms of cultural se- lection and transmission. These interactions are, in certain respects, anal- ogous to those by virtue of which biological species evolve and survive and also analogous to those through which artistic choices evolve and are found fit or fitting by the individual artist. The operation of these cultural-historical dynamics may be briefly indicated here in quite general terms.

At a given time and under the contemporary conditions of available materials, technology, and techniques, a particular object—let us say a verbal artifact or text—may perform certain desired/able functions quite well for some set of subjects. It will do so by virtue of certain of its "properties" as they have been specifically constituted—framed, fore- grounded, and configured—by those subjects under those conditions and in accord with their particular needs, interests, and resources—and also perhaps largely as pre-figured by the artist who, as described earlier, in the very process of producing the work and continuously evaluating its fitness and adjusting it accordingly, will have multiply and variably con- stituted it. Two points implied by this description need emphasis here. One is that the value of a work—that is, its effectiveness in performing desired/able functions for some set of subjects—is not independent of authorial design, labor, and skill. The second, however, is that what may be spoken of as the "properties" of the work—its "structure," "features," "qualities," and, of course, its "meanings"—are not fixed, given, or inherent in the work "itself" but are at every point the variable products of some subject's interaction with it. (It is thus never "the *same* Homer.") To the extent that any aspect of a work is recurrently constituted in similar ways by various subjects at various times, it will be because the subjects who do the constituting, *including the author,* are themselves similar, not only in being human creatures and in occupying a particular universe that may be, for them, in many respects recurrent or relatively continuous and stable, but also in inheriting from one another, through mechanisms of cultural transmission, certain ways of interacting with that universe, including certain ways of interacting with texts and "works of literature."

An object or artifact that performs certain desired/able functions particularly well at a given time for some community of subjects, being perhaps not only "fit" but exemplary—that is, "the best of its kind"—under those conditions, will have an immediate survival advantage; for, relative to (or in competition with) other comparable objects or artifacts available at that time, it will not only be better protected from physical deterioration but will also be more frequently used or widely exhibited and, if it is a text or verbal artifact, more frequently read or recited, copied or reprinted, translated, imitated, cited, and commented upon—in short, culturally re-produced—and thus will be more readily available to perform those or other functions for other subjects at a subsequent time.

Two possible trajectories ensue:

1. If, on the one hand, under the changing and emergent conditions of that subsequent time, the functions for which the text was earlier valued are no longer desired/able or if, in competition with comparable works (including, now, those newly produced with newly available materials and techniques), it no longer performs those original functions particularly well, it will, accordingly, be less well maintained and less frequently cited and recited so that its visibility as well as interest will fade, and it will survive, if at all, simply as a physical relic. It may, of course, be subsequently valued specifically *as* a relic (for its archeological or "historical" interest), in which case it *will* be performing desired/able functions and pursue the trajectory described below. It may also be subsequently "rediscovered" as an "unjustly neglected masterpiece," either when the functions it had originally performed are again desired/able or, what is more likely, when different of its properties and possible functions become foregrounded by a new set of subjects with emergent interests and purposes.

2. If, on the other hand, under changing conditions and in competition with newly produced and other re-produced works, it continues to perform *some* desired/able functions particularly well, even if not the same ones for which it was initially valued (and, accordingly, by virtue of *other* newly

foregrounded or differently framed or configured properties—including, once again, emergent "meanings"), it will continue to be cited and recited, continue to be visible and available to succeeding generations of subjects, and thus continue to be culturally re-produced. A work that has in this way survived for some time can always move into a trajectory of extinction through the sudden emergence or gradual conjunction of unfavorable conditions of the kind described above under (1). There are, however, a number of reasons why, once it has achieved canonical status, it will be more secured from that risk.

First, when the value of a work is seen as unquestionable, those of its features that would, in a noncanonical work, be found alienating— for example, technically crude, philosophically naive, or narrowly topical— will be glozed over or backgrounded. In particular, features that conflict intolerably with the interests and ideologies of subsequent subjects (and, in the West, with those generally benign "humanistic" values for which canonical works are commonly celebrated)—for example, incidents or sentiments of brutality, bigotry, and racial, sexual, or national chauvinism— will be repressed or rationalized, and there will be a tendency among humanistic scholars and academic critics to "save the text" by transferring the locus of its interest to more formal or structural features and/or allegorizing its potentially alienating ideology to some more general ("universal") level where it becomes more tolerable and also more readily interpretable in terms of contemporary ideologies. Thus we make texts timeless by suppressing their temporality. (It may be added that to those scholars and critics for whom those features are not only palatable but for whom the value of the canonical works consists precisely in their "embodying" and "preserving" such "traditional values," the transfer of the locus of value to formal properties will be seen as a descent into formalism and "aestheticism," and the tendency to allegorize it too generally or to interpret it too readily in terms of "modern values" will be seen not as saving the text but as betraying it.)

Second, in addition to whatever various and perhaps continuously differing functions a work performs for succeeding generations of in-dividual subjects, it will also begin to perform certain characteristic cultural functions by virtue of the very fact that it *has* endured—that is, the functions of a canonical work as such—and will be valued and preserved accordingly: as a witness to lost innocence, former glory, and/or apparently persistent communal interests and "values" and thus a banner of communal identity; as a reservoir of images, archtypes, and topoi—characters and episodes, passages and verbal tags—repeatedly invoked and recurrently applied to new situations and circumstances; and as a stylistic and generic exemplar that will energize the production of subsequent works and texts (upon which the latter will be modeled and by which, as a normative "touchstone," they will be measured). In these ways, the canonical work begins increasingly not merely to survive within but to shape and create the culture in which its value is produced and transmitted and, for that very reason, to perpetuate the conditions of its own flourishing. Nothing endures like endurance.

To the extent that we develop within and are formed by a culture that is itself constituted in part *by* canonical texts, it is not surprising that those texts seem, as Hans-Georg Gadamer puts it, to "speak" to us "directly" and even "specially":

> The classical is what is preserved precisely because it signifies and interprets itself; [that is,] that which speaks in such a way that it is not a statement about what is past, as mere testimony to something that needs to be interpreted, but says something to the present as if it were said specially to us. . . . This is just what the word "classical" means, that the duration of the power of a work to speak directly is fundamentally unlimited.[45]

It is hardly, however, as Gadamer implies here, because such texts are uniquely self-mediated or unmediated and hence not needful of interpretation but, rather, because they have already been so thoroughly mediated—evaluated as well as interpreted—for us by the very culture and cultural institutions through which they have been preserved and by which we ourselves have been formed.

What is commonly referred to as "the test of time" (Gadamer, for example, characterizes "the classical" as "a notable mode of 'being historical,' that historical process of preservation that through the constant proving of itself sets before us something that is true")[46] is not, as the figure implies,.an impersonal and impartial mechanism; for the cultural institutions through which it operates (schools, libraries, theaters, museums, publishing and printing houses, editorial boards, prize-awarding commissions, state censors, etc.) are, of course, all managed by persons (who, by definition, are those with cultural power and commonly other forms of power as well), and, since the texts that are selected and preserved by "time" will always tend to be those which "fit" (and, indeed, have often been *designed* to fit) their characteristic needs, interests, resources, and purposes, that testing mechanism has its own built-in partialities accumulated in and thus *intensified by* time. For example, the characteristic resources of the culturally dominant members of a community include access to specific training and the opportunity and occasion to develop not only competence in a large number of cultural codes but also a large number of diverse (or "cosmopolitan") interests. The works that are differentially re-produced, therefore, will often be those that gratify the exercise of such competencies and engage interests of that kind: specifically, works that are structurally complex and, in the technical sense, information-rich—and which, by virtue of those very qualities, are especially amenable to multiple reconfiguration, more likely to enter into relation with the emergent interests of various subjects, and thus more readily adaptable to emergent conditions.[47] Also, as is often remarked, since those with cultural power tend to be members of socially, economically, and politically established classes (or to serve them and identify their own interests with theirs), the texts that survive will tend to be those that appear to reflect and reinforce establishment ideologies. However much canonical works may be seen to "question" secular vanities such as wealth, social position, and political power, "remind" their readers of more elevated values and virtues, and oblige them to "confront" such hard truths and harsh realities as their own mortality and the hidden griefs of obscure people, they would not be found to please long and well if they were seen to undercut establishment interests *radically* or to subvert the ideologies that support them *effectively.* (Construing them to the latter ends, of course, is one of the characteristic ways in which those with antiestablishment interests participate in the cultural re-production of canonical texts and thus in their endurance as well.)

It is clear that the needs, interests, and purposes of culturally and otherwise dominant members of a community do not exclusively or totally determine which works survive. The antiquity and longevity of domestic proverbs, popular tales, children's verbal games, and the entire phenomenon of what we call "folklore," which occurs through the same or corresponding mechanisms of cultural selection and re-production as those described above specifically for "texts," demonstrate that the "endurance" of a verbal artifact (if not its achievement of *academic* canonical status as a "work of literature"—many folkloric works do, however, perform all the functions described above as characteristic of canonical works *as such*) may be more or less independent of institutions controlled by those with political power. Moreover, the interests and purposes of the latter must always operate in interaction with non- or antiestablishment interests and purposes as well as with various other contingencies and "accidents of time" over which they have limited, if any, control, from the burning of libraries to political and social revolutions, religious iconoclasms, and shifts of dominance among entire languages and cultures.

As the preceding discussion suggests, the value of a literary work is continuously produced and re-produced by the very acts of implicit and explicit evaluation that are frequently invoked as "reflecting" its value and therefore as being evidence of it. In other words, what are commonly taken to be the *signs* of literary value are, in effect, also its *springs*. The endurance of a classic canonical author such as Homer, then, owes not to the alleged transcultural or universal value of his works but, on the contrary, to the continuity of their circulation in a particular culture. Repeatedly cited and recited, translated, taught and imitated, and thoroughly enmeshed in the network of intertextuality that continuously *constitutes* the high culture of the orthodoxly educated population of the West (and the Western-educated population of the rest of the world), that highly variable entity we refer to as "Homer" recurrently enters our experience in relation to a large number and variety of our interests and thus can perform a large number of various functions for us and obviously has performed them for many of us over a good bit of the history of our culture. It is well to recall, however, that there are many people in the world who are not—or are not yet, or choose not to be—among the orthodoxly educated population of the West: people who do not encounter Western classics at all or who encounter them under cultural and institutional conditions very different from those of American and European college professors and their students. The fact that Homer, Dante, and Shakespeare do not figure significantly in the personal economies of these people, do not perform individual or social functions that gratify their interests, *do not have value for them*, might properly be taken as qualifying the claims of transcendent universal value made for such works. As we know, however, it is routinely taken instead as evidence or confirmation of the cultural deficiency—or, more piously, "deprivation"— of such people. The fact that other verbal artifacts (not necessarily "works of literature" or even "texts") and other objects and events (not necessarily "works of art" or even artifacts) have performed and do perform for them the various functions that Homer, Dante, and Shakespeare perform for us and, moreover, that the possibility of performing the totality of such functions is always distributed over the totality of texts, artifacts, objects, and events—a possibility continuously realized and thus a value continuously "appreciated"—commonly cannot be grasped or acknowledged by the custodians of the Western canon.

1. The most recent of these include E. D. Hirsch, Jr., *The Aims of Interpretation* (Chicago, 1976), esp. the essays "Evaluation as Knowledge" (1968) and "Privileged Criteria in Evaluation" (1969); Murray Krieger, "Literary Analysis and Evaluation—and the Ambidextrous Critic," in *Criticism: Speculative and Analytic Essays*, ed. L. S. Dembo (Madison, Wis., 1968); a number of brief essays by Anglo-American as well as continental European theorists in *Problems of Literary Evaluation*, ed. Joseph Strelka (University Park, Pa. and London, 1969); and the chapters on value and evaluation in John Ellis, *The Theory of Literary Criticism* (Berkeley and Los Angeles, 1974), John Reichert, *Making Sense of Literature* (Chicago, 1977), and Jeffrey Sammons, *Literary Sociology and Practical Criticism* (Bloomington, Ind. and London, 1977). All of them either participate directly in the self-justifying academic debates outlined below or are haunted by them into equivocation.

2. F. R. Leavis, *Revaluation: Tradition and Development in English Poetry* (London, 1936; New York, 1963), pp. 5–6.

3. See esp. A. J. Ayer, *Language, Truth, and Logic* (London, 1936).

4. Yvor Winters, *The Function of Criticism* (Denver, 1957), p. 17.

5. W. K. Wimsatt, Jr., *The Verbal Icon* (Louisville, Ky., 1954), p. 250.

6. See the discussion of David Hume below, pp. 15–18.

7. I. A. Richards, *Principles of Literary Criticism* (1924; London, 1960), pp. 5–6. "The two pillars upon which a theory of criticism must rest," Richards declared, "are an account

of value and an account of communication" (p. 25). It was, of course, the latter that subsequently became the overriding concern of critical theory.

8. Ibid., p. 206.

9. Northrop Frye, *Anatomy of Criticism: Four Essays* (Princeton, N.J., 1957), pp. 18, 19; all further references to this work, abbreviated *AC*, will be included in the text.

10. It should be recalled that, like many others (e.g., Hirsch [see n. 12 below]), Frye continued to maintain that *interpretive* criticism could lay claim to objectivity. See his remarks in a paper delivered in 1967: "The fundamental critical act . . . is the act of recognition, seeing what is there, as distinguished from merely seeing in a Narcissus mirror of our own experience and social and moral prejudice. . . . When a critic interprets, he is talking about his poet; when he evaluates, he is talking about himself" ("Value Judgements," in *Criticism: Speculative and Analytic Essays*, p. 39).

11. Hirsch, *The Aims of Interpretation*, p. 108. See also n. 40 below, for Hirsch's neo-Kantian formulation.

12. In a recent unpublished essay, "Literary Value: The Short History of a Modern Confusion" (1980), Hirsch argues that, although literary *meaning* is determinate, literary value is not. With respect to the latter, however, he concludes that "there are some stable principles"—namely, ethical ones—"that escape the chaos of purely personal relativity" (p. 22). As will be seen in the analysis below, "personal relativity" neither produces chaos nor is in itself chaotic. The escape route of ethical principles and other appeals to higher goods are discussed below (p. 19).

13. See Jurij Tynjanov, "On Literary Evolution" (Moscow, 1927), trans. Ladislav Matejka and Krystyna Pomorska, in *Readings in Russian Poetics*, ed. Matejka and Pomorska (Cambridge, Mass., 1971); Mikhail Bakhtin, *Rabelais and His World* (Moscow, 1965), trans. Helene Iswolsky (Cambridge, Mass., 1968); and Jan Mukařovský, *Aesthetic Norm, Function, and Value as Social Facts* (Prague, 1934), trans. Mark E. Suino (Ann Arbor, Mich., 1970).

14. For surveys and discussions, see Sammons, *Literary Sociology and Practical Criticism*, and Rien T. Segers, *The Evaluation of Literary Texts: An Experimental Investigation into the Rationalization of Value Judgments with Reference to Semiotics and Esthetics of Reception* (Lisse, 1978). For a recent study of considerable interest, see Jacques Leenhardt and Pierre Józsa, *Lire la lecture: Essai du sociologie de la lecture* (Paris, 1982).

15. It is not mentioned as such, e.g., in Jonathan Culler's *Structuralist Poetics: Structuralism, Linguistics, and the Study of Literature* (Ithaca, N.Y., 1975).

16. See, e.g., the thoroughly equivocal discussions of "objective value" in Stefan Morawski, *Inquiries into Fundamentals of Aesthetics* (Cambridge, Mass. and London, 1974), and the revalorization of the standard Eng. Lit. canon in Althusserian terms in Terry Eagleton, *Criticism and Ideology: A Study in Marxist Literary Theory* (London, 1976), pp. 162–87. For other discussions of this point, see Hans Robert Jauss, "The Idealist Embarrassment: Observations on Marxist Aesthetics," *New Literary History* 7 (Autumn 1975): 191–208; Raymond Williams, *Marxism and Literature* (Oxford, 1977), esp. pp. 45–54 and 151–57; Tony Bennett, *Formalism and Marxism* (London, 1979), esp. pp. 172–75; and Peter Widdowson, " 'Literary Value' and the Reconstruction of Criticism," *Literature and History* 6 (1980): 138–50. See also n. 33 below.

17. See, however, Arkady Plotnitsky, "Constraints of the Unbound: Transformation, Value, and Literary Interpretation" (Ph.D. diss., University of Pennsylvania, 1982), for an extensive and sophisticated effort along such lines.

18. Onwuchekwa Jemie, *Langston Hughes: An Introduction to the Poetry* (New York, 1976), p. 184.

19. C. W. B. Bigsby, "Hand in Hand with the Blues," *Times Literary Supplement*, 17 June 1977, p. 734.

20. Chinweizu, letter to the editor, *Times Literary Supplement*, 15 July 1977, p. 871.

21. Thus Sammons, in his embattled book, writes of "the elements . . . in the canon of great literature" to which we should be attentive so that, faced with charges of elitism, "we will not have to stand mute before claims that inarticulateness, ignorance, occult

mumbling, and loutishness are just as good as fine literature" (*Literary Sociology and Practical Criticism*, p. 134).

22. See Gonzalo Munévar, *Radical Knowledge: A Philosophical Inquiry into the Nature and Limits of Science* (Indianapolis, 1981), for an elaboration of a "performance model" of scientific activity along the lines implied here.

23. For a companion piece to the present essay, see my "Fixed Marks and Variable Constancies: A Parable of Literary Value," *Poetics Today* 1 (Autumn 1979): 7–31.

24. Some aspects of this process are discussed by Pierre Bourdieu in "La Métamorphose des goûts," *Questions de sociologie* (Paris, 1980), pp. 161–72. The more general interrelations among human "needs and wants," cultural practices, and economic production have been examined by Marshall Sahlins in *Culture and Practical Reason* (Chicago, 1976), Mary Douglas in *The World of Goods* (New York, 1979), and Jean Baudrillard in *For a Critique of the Political Economy of the Sign* (Paris, 1972), trans. Charles Levin (St. Louis, 1981). Although Baudrillard's critical analysis of the concept of "use-value"—and, with it, of "sign value"—is of considerable interest for a semiotics of the marketplace, his effort to develop, "as a basis for the practical overthrow of political economy" (p. 122), a theory of a value "beyond value" (created out of what he calls "symbolic exchange") is less successful, partly because of its utopian anthropology and partly because the value in question does not escape economic accounting.

25. For an excellent analysis of the relation between classification and value, see Michael Thompson, *Rubbish Theory: The Creation and Destruction of Value* (Oxford, 1979), esp. pp. 13–56.

26. The magnetism or recurrent mutually metaphoric relation between economic and aesthetic—especially literary—discourse is documented and discussed by Marc Shell in *The Economy of Literature* (Baltimore, 1978) and Kurt Heinzelman in *The Economics of the Imagination* (Amherst, Mass., 1980).

27. Andrew Harrison, *Making and Thinking* (Indianapolis, 1978), p. 100.

28. See George J. Stigler and Gary S. Becker, "De gustibus non est disputandum," *American Economics Review* 67 (March 1977): 76–90, for an ingenious and influential attempt (at the opposite extreme, perhaps, of Baudrillard's [see n. 24 above]) to demonstrate that differences and changes of behavior (including aesthetic behavior) that appear to be matters of "taste" and, as such, beyond explanation in economic terms can be accounted for (*a*) as functions of subtle forms of "price" and "income" and (*b*) on the usual (utilitarian) assumption that we always behave, all things considered, so as to maximize utility. As Stigler and Becker acknowledge, recent experimental studies of "choice behavior" in human (and other) subjects suggest that this latter assumption itself requires modification.

29. See Robert Fagen, *Animal Play Behavior* (Oxford, 1981), pp. 248–358, for an extensive analysis of "intrinsically rewarding" physical activities and an account of the evolutionary mechanisms that apparently produce and sustain them.

30. See the related discussion of "cognitive play" in my *On the Margins of Discourse: The Relation of Literature to Language* (Chicago, 1978), pp. 116–24.

31. Monroe Beardsley's "instrumentalist" (that is, utilitarian) theory of aesthetic value (*Aesthetics: Problems in the Philosophy of Criticism* [New York, 1958], pp. 524–76) and Mukařovský's otherwise quite subtle exploration of these questions (see n. 13, above) do not altogether escape the confinements and circularities of formalist conceptions of, respectively, "aesthetic experience" and "aesthetic function."

32. David Hume, "*Of the Standard of Taste" and Other Essays*, ed. John W. Lenz (Indianapolis, 1965), pp. 8–10.

33. Ibid., p. 10. At the conclusion of the essay, Hume almost—but not quite—reinstalls the very *de gustibus* argument that the standard of taste was presumably designed to answer: "But where there is such a diversity in the internal frame or external situation as is entirely blameless on both sides, . . . a certain degree of diversity of judgment is unavoidable and we seek in vain a standard by which we can reconcile the contrary sentiments" (pp. 19–20). Of course, the qualification ("as is entirely blameless on both sides") that keeps this from being a total turnabout also introduces a new normative consideration (how to determine

whether or not—or to what extent—something "in the internal frame or external situation" is *blamable*) and thus moves again toward the type of potentially infinite regress into which all axiologies typically tumble.

34. Walter Hinderer, "Literary Value Judgments and Value Cognition," trans. Leila Vannewitz, in *Problems of Literary Evaluation*, pp. 58–59.

35. The discipline of "empirical aesthetics" has been developed out of precisely such a belief. For a recent survey and discussion of its findings, see Hans and Shulamith Kreitler, *Psychology of the Arts* (Durham, N.C., 1972). See also n. 47 below.

36. See Morse Peckham, *Explanation and Power: The Control of Human Behavior* (New York, 1979), for an account of deviance (or what he calls "the delta effect") as the product of the relation between cultural practices and the randomness of behavior and, more generally, for a highly original discussion of the processes and institutions of cultural channeling.

37. Hume, *"Of the Standard of Taste,"* pp. 5, 7.

38. Communities are of all sizes and so are drawing rooms: the provincials, colonials, and marginalized groups mentioned above (including the young), insofar as they constitute social communities, may also be expected to have prevailing structures of tastes and preferences and to control them in the same ways as do more obviously "establishment" groups. Folk-relativism is neither confined to the folk nor always exhibited by them.

39. To the extent that such forms of behavior are under the control of innate mechanisms that respond directly to—or, in effect, "register"—the conditions in question, they are not, strictly speaking, verbal or symbolic. For this reason, such evaluations may be "objective" in a way that, for better or worse, no human value judgment can be.

40. Kant's tortured attempt, which occupies most of *The Critique of Judgment*, to ground such a claim on the possibility of a cognition of pure aesthetic value (that is, "beauty") produced by nothing but the free operation of universal cognitive faculties has been recently revived and supplemented by Hirsch's attempt to ground it on the possibility of "correct interpretation," specifically the "re-cognition" of that "universally valid cognition of a work . . . constituted by the kind of subjective stance adopted in its creation" (*The Aims of Interpretation*, pp. 105–6). For a recent and very thorough examination of *The Critique of Judgment*, see Paul Guyer, *Kant and the Claims of Taste* (Cambridge, Mass. and London, 1979); for a thoroughly irreverent examination of it, see Jacques Derrida, "Economimesis," trans. Richard Klein, *Diacritics* 2 (Summer 1981): 3–25.

41. I discuss these and related aspects of verbal transactions in *On the Margins of Discourse*, pp. 15–24 and 82–106, and in "Narrative Versions, Narrative Theories," *Critical Inquiry* 7 (Autumn 1980): 225–26 and 231–36.

42. Pierre Macherey and Etienne Balibar analyze some aspects of this process in "Literature as an Ideological Form: Some Marxist Propositions," trans. James Kavanagh, *Praxis* 5 (1981): 43–58.

43. See Howard Becker, *Art Worlds* (Berkeley, Los Angeles, and London, 1982), pp. 198–209, for a description of some of the specific constraints that shape both the process and its termination and, more generally, for a useful account of the ways in which artworks are produced by "social networks."

44. For a well-documented illustration of the point, see Nina Baym, "Melodramas of Beset Manhood: How Theories of American Fiction Exclude Women Authors," *American Quarterly* 33 (Summer 1981): 125–39. In addition to anthologies, Baym mentions historical studies, psychological and sociological theories of literary production, and particular methods of literary interpretation.

45. Hans-Georg Gadamer, *Truth and Method*, trans. Sheed and Ward, Ltd. (New York, 1982), pp. 257–58.

46. Ibid., p. 255.

47. Structural complexity and information-richness are, of course, subject-relative as "qualities" and also experientially subject-variable: that is, we apparently differ individually in our tolerance for complexity in various sensory/perceptual modes and in our competence

in processing information in different codes, so that what is interestingly complex and engagingly information-rich to one subject may be intolerably chaotic to another. See Gerda Smets, *Aesthetic Judgment and Arousal* (Louvain, 1973), and Sven Sandström, *A Common Taste in Art: An Experimental Attempt* (Lund, 1977), for two recent studies relevant to the point. Its relation to the general problem of aesthetic and literary value, itself a very complex matter, cannot be pursued here but is discussed briefly in *On the Margins of Discourse*, pp. 116–24.

An Idea and Ideal of a Literary Canon

Charles Altieri

> These people think they follow the doctrine of interest, but they
> have only a crude idea of what it is, and, to watch the better over
> what they call their business, they neglect the principal part of it
> which is to remain their own masters.
> —ALEXIS DE TOCQUEVILLE, *Democracy in America*

1

Samuel Johnson is the canonical figure most useful for thinking about
canons. If we are less in need of discovering new truths than of remembering old ones, there are obvious social roles canons can play as selective
memories of traditions or ideals. But how do we decide that the selection
is a good one, that any given canon should have authority? Johnson's
observation on memory suggests an answer to this question. The answer,
however, will lead us into some intricate and tedious arguments. Because
we are not likely to locate truths univocally establishing values a canon
can reflect, we must learn to negotiate the endless circles that constitute
cultural traditions. We must find criteria for canons by provisionally
accepting at least some received cultural values and by exploring hypotheses
about human nature, themselves dependent on experiences mediated
by these traditions. Indeed, we will find the theoretical terms needed to
speak about a canon severely tarnished by the history that authorizes
them. Ideals often cloak the most practical of special interests. Yet I shall
argue that it is a mistake to read cultural history only as a tawdry melodrama
of interests pursued and ideologies produced.

Given our need for memory and the manifest power of various canonical works to transcend any single structure of social interest, I think it is possible to recover some of the force in classical ideals of a canon. Through that effort, we recover modes of thought about value and human agency sorely lacking in the dominant critical attitudes fostered by the hermeneutics of suspicion. That this hermeneutics can produce only demystifying accounts of canons strikes me as a sign of fundamental flaws in its grammar of motives—for texts and for our abilities to use them.

Such charges require particulars. Let me therefore construct a composite antagonist for this essay by attempting to define shared assumptions underlying a variety of "suspicious" critical stances. Jerome McGann's designation of a new principle—critical historicism—will give this antagonist a name and some fundamental beliefs. In contrast to the older hermeneutic ideal that led critics to identify fully with a given imaginative work, critical historicism insists that even the greatest masterpieces are dated: "Scrutinized through the lens of a critical rather than a hermeneutic method . . . [the work] will cease to be an object of faith . . . and become, instead, a human—a social and historical—resource." Scrupulously locating every aspect of the work in its historical setting "inaugurate[s] . . . disbelief" and thus establishes for the reader "ideological differentials that help to define the limits and special functions of . . . current ideological practises. Great works continue to have something to say because what they have to say is so peculiarly and specifically their own that we, who are different, can learn from them."[1] But, McGann asserts, what we learn must acknowledge that difference, must serve our freedom to explain rather than to imitate the values of the text.

Once we emphasize disbelief, we cannot maintain traditional notions of the canon. On the simplest level, what had been treated as transcending history now becomes merely evidence of its positivities. As Frank Kermode puts it in his influential "Institutional Control of Interpretation," canons are essentially strategic constructs by which societies maintain their own interests, since the canon allows control over the texts a culture takes seriously and the methods of interpretation that establish the meaning of "serious."[2] This sense of history has as its correlate Nietzsche's distrust

---

Charles Altieri is professor of English and comparative literature at the University of Washington. He is the author of *Act and Quality: A Theory of Literary Meaning and Humanistic Understanding* (1981) and *Self and Sensibility in Contemporary American Poetry* (forthcoming) and is presently working on value in ethics and aesthetics.

of universals: all efforts to escape history are themselves historically determined. Thus, to accept any claims about transhistorical values is to blind oneself to potential sources of strength within the material differences shaping an agent's life in the present. The ideal of a canon, in this view, makes us a victim of that most dangerous of others—the fantasy of a best self to be excavated from our historical being. In pursuing such a chimera, we purportedly give authority to an other and condemn ourselves to inescapable self-alienation and self-disgust.

Finally, these "suspicious" assumptions about history and the self call for new perspectives on how to value the activities of criticism and the cultural heritage that criticism works upon. Projections of values—by works and by critics—are seen as overdetermined symptoms of needs and underdetermined assertions of hegemony that thus prepare their own undoing. Although McGann never clarifies what specific resources are found in texts liberated by this line of disbelief, there seems to be only one possible answer: historicist disbelief requires the other half of the relativist coin. Instead of idealizing the past (as under the older hermeneutic ideal), we are to impose on texts the forms of scrutiny that we apply to social life. In addition, we are to govern our practices not by the authority attributed to cultural canons but by the most clear-sighted grasp of our own present interests.

If the analytic attitude of critical historicism makes us suspect that canons have always served specifiable social interests, its accompanying political lesson is clear: any desire to put literature to work as a social force would require us self-consciously to build canons that serve our concrete, "political" commitments. Since the valuing dimension of criticism is inescapably ideological, we could either hope to impose a single canon that we see as favoring our own concerns, or we could take a more complex stance emphasizing the liberal play of interests in society.[3] If there are no longer any central stories that unify society but only stories defining the desires of distinctive segments within society, then our view of the canon should supposedly correspond to social reality, should perhaps parlay this fragmentation into articulate differences. Canons are simply ideological banners for social groups: social groups propose them as forms of self-definition, and they engage other proponents to test limitations while exposing the contradictions and incapacities of competing groups.

2

The past as essentially a record of ideological struggle, the present as a domain we liberate from that past by inaugurating disbelief and analyzing ideological overdeterminations, and the future as a conflict among the competing self-interests that determine critical stances—these are the stuff the dreams of contemporary theory are increasingly made on. In opposition, I want to argue that the past that canons preserve is best understood as a permanent theater helping us shape and judge personal and social values, that our self-interest in the present consists primarily in establishing ways of employing that theater to gain distance from our ideological commitments, and that the most plausible hope for the influence of literary study in the future lies in our ability to transmit the past as a set of challenges and models. As ethical agents and as writers, we need examples of the powers that accrue when we turn critically on immediate interests and enter the dialectical process of differing from ourselves, in order to achieve new possibilities for representing and directing our actions.

My arguments involve three basic concerns. I shall analyze the concept of interests to show that one way we can best serve our personal interests is by elaborating transpersonal principles of value that link desires in the present to forms of imaginative discourse preserved from the past. Then I take up the question of how the traditional ideal of the high canon provides certain functions, or resources, of thinking that enable us to satisfy our interests. Finally, from my account of interests and functions, I derive three general criteria I consider deeply entrenched in our judgments of claims to canonical status, and I employ these criteria to advocate a model of reading I believe preferable to those inspired by critical historicism.

All my arguments, however, depend on our understanding why questions of criteria are so problematic for this enterprise. Arguments about canons depend on a certain kind of "foreunderstanding." Clearly, canons are not natural facts and do not warrant the kinds of evidence we use in discussing matters of fact. We are not likely to find general laws governing our acts as canon-formers, nor is extended empirical inquiry likely to resolve any of the essential theoretical issues. Canons are based on both descriptive and normative claims; we cannot escape the problem of judging others' value statements by our own values. What possible criteria could control such a complex evaluative discourse? It seems, in fact, that the critical historicist is on very firm ground, because what I claim to be canonical (or to be a criterion for determining canons) does depend on norms that I establish or, at least, on institutional norms that I certify. The entire process is profoundly circular. So the historicist would insist that no argument is possible: one can only hope to stand outside the claims, exposing the play of interests that create and sustain the circle.

Our attempts to find a way to approach the problem place us at the center of the current reformation created by the overthrow of foundational metaphors for thought. When canons are at stake it is purposes that determine what count as facts, not facts that determine the relevant values. This easy linking, however, makes it crucial to scrutinize the assumptions involved. If antifoundationalist claims like Richard Rorty's are right, and yet if for centuries there has been at least the appearance of cogent discussion about values, we may be doing ourselves a disservice when we simply congratulate ourselves for discovering the circular nature of arguments about canons. Are there not features of circularity itself which enable us to make judgments about values? Even if all our facts are constituted by our practices and purposes, it does not follow that we cannot criticize some practices and purposes on the basis of larger, more comprehensive ones. Circles admit of levels of generality and complex encompassings. Those whose specific beliefs place them in many respects within competing circles may still share wider principles—for example, general rules of evidence or ethical standards of justice—for adjudicating specific differences. In comparison, values prove quite sectarian, usually by not surviving historical changes—the complex of critical assumptions fostered by the New Criticism is a good case in point. But even this example reveals deep affiliations with other, more enduring cultural values, like the ideal of aesthetic unity or the desire to imagine literature as different from history, on the one hand, and philosophy, on the other. We can hope to criticize New Criticism in a way convincing even to New Critics because we can rely on such larger features of circularity. Nonetheless, this general possibility makes it no easier to locate specific circular features we can rely on for my discussion here. That will be a difficult, often elaborate task. But it is very important that we begin with the general awareness of the kind of inquiry we must pursue. I do not propose to offer clinching arguments. Instead, I shall try to elicit a fairly wide circle of shared values deriving from some dimensions of our common literary heritage, so that we can assess claims about roles the canon has played and can continue to play in literary culture.

Indeed, it makes no sense to theorize about canons unless the possibility of finding common principles of judgment within circular conditions is granted. Our practical ideas about the nature and workings of a canon rarely derive from explicit theoretical principles or empirical encounters with a range of texts. We have ideas about canons because we learn to think about literature within cultural frameworks that are in part constituted by notions of the canonical. This becomes apparent when we try to imagine how we could respond to someone demanding noncircular reasons for preferring the texts that are commonly asserted to comprise the core of the Western canon. I do not think we could produce independent reasons; instead, we would have to describe an array of basic works in different genres (like the *Divine Comedy* and *Hamlet*) in order to indicate the concerns they raise and the kind of experience they offer. Ultimately we would have to show the questioner the discourses such works breed and the ways other writers engage them. We would have to teach a literary history charged with struggles to evaluate and use the past. And when we were done, we would have no way to prove that the questioner was wrong if he denied the relevance of those considerations. He could create a canon solely on the basis of what he enjoyed in our survey. We could, however, point out the price he would pay in doing that. For it would be very hard, then, not to take all his comments as circular in the most vicious of ways, because he would not care about contrary evidence. He would be making a canon unconnected to the very examples and arguments that create significant problems of definition in the first place.

Too much contemporary criticism takes the route of willful circularity as its response to the dependence of rationales for valuation on previous decisions about values. Ironically, this refusal to work out ways of locating common grounds for assessing these valuations forces such critics to repeat two of the most serious errors in the foundationalist heritage they reject—an emotivism about values and a narrow sense of literary works as primarily nondiscursive forms for rendering accurate representations of experience. These mistaken repetitions, in turn, compound error in debates about the canon because they deny the principles of idealization that the very idea of a canon requires us to take seriously. Works we canonize tend to project ideals, and the roles we can imagine for the canon require us to consider seriously the place of idealization in social life. By "idealization" I do not mean the projection of propaganda but rather writers' efforts to make the authorial act of mind or certain qualities in their fictional characters seem valuable attitudes with which an audience is moved to identify. In this sense, even the most ironic of writers use their authorial act to idealize their chosen stance. Canons, then, are an institutional form for exposing people to a range of idealized attitudes, a range I shall call a grammar. If a critic refuses to take such idealizations at face value or to locate grounds on which they can be discussed *as* idealizations before systematic suspicion is applied, he in effect binds himself within his own narrow circle. His instruments dictate the result of his inquiry. As an example of such sorry circumscription, consider Kermode's essay. In his concluding remarks, Kermode asserts that the canon is a valuable feature of our institutionalized literary education. But all his considerable interpretive energies have been devoted to de-mystifying the canon so that it appears to be only a means for reinforcing a given set of social values. He has, then, no terms by which to explain his evaluation of the canon's importance except a banal insistence on the variety of interpretations it guarantees. Thousands of years of culture have come to this—a stimulus to subjectivity.

3

It is unfortunately a lot easier to raise an arch eyebrow than it is to describe critical terms that might account for the values in idealization while preserving a pluralistic sense of possible canons and their uses. Instead of facing the challenge directly, I shall rely on what I call a contrastive strategy. Were I simply to assert a traditional psychology with its attendant values, I would expose myself to a host of suspicious charges about my pieties and delusions. So I shall begin by concentrating on the limitations I take to be inherent in the empiricism of the critical historicists' position. If, by deflating idealization, their arguments prove reductive, they should provoke us to ask what it is they reduce. We will find ourselves forced back within the circle of literary and existential expectations I suspect most of us still share. But now we might appreciate the force and possible uses of that training when we measure it against all we cannot do if we accept an alternative stance. That we can measure at all, of course, may emerge as the most significant consequence of this experiment in using contrastive strategies.

The subject of self-interest provides us with a clear test among these competing positions, and it establishes some of the psychological concepts we will need if we are to describe the cultural functions canons can serve. Critical historicism concentrates on two basic aspects of self-interest— the desire for power over others and the pursuit of self-representations that satisfy narcissistic demands. Out of these aspects, ideologies are generated and sustained. But this is hardly an exhaustive account of needs, motives, and powers. I propose that at least two other claims seem plausible, each with important consequences for our understanding of the canon—that some people can understand their empirical interests to a degree sufficient to allow them considerable control over their actions and that a basic motive for such control is to subsume one's actions under a meaning the self can take responsibility for.[4]

There are many general considerations I could invoke to support my two other claims. Theories that we conceal our real interests from ourselves seem self-defeating to assert, since our real interest must belie the assertion. Even less extreme claims about the egoistic basis of all valuations run into obvious problems because they equate with self-interest all the interest the self has and thus equivocate on the term. They produce by definition an equivalence not evident in our varied accounts of our own motives. Finally, there is at least some intuitive evidence for thinking that we do in fact often describe our behavior accurately and take responsibility for it. Indeed, one fairly constant cultural value is respect for persons who stand by their word.

The issues involved in fully testing any of these assertions, however, would lead us too far astray. Instead, let us take up some specifically literary features of experience that a theory of interest should account for. Insistence on the sectarian commitments inherent in self-interest is hard to reconcile with some basic phenomenological features of reading and with expectations about the authority literary texts might wield. Many readers see their interest in reading precisely as an opportunity to *escape* the empirical self, to undergo in imagination protean changes of identity and sympathy. Thus, the pleasure in the text is a pleasure in forms of consciousness or eloquent reponses to experience we can only hope to have and to discover in imaginary worlds not congruent with our sectarian commitments. How else could we attribute the values we do to literary education? And how else can we explain the hopes of writers? Even if the writer wants only to assert power, she must imagine an audience vulnerable to the effort. It is no accident that those reader-response theorists who insist on the primacy of subjective interactions with a text do so not on the basis of literary history but by relying on the authority of contemporary psychological models of the self.[5] Nor is it an accident that claims about ideology rely on a similarly conservative view of the self.

Modern philosophy has for seventy years shared T. S. Eliot's desire to "attack . . . the metaphysical theory of the substantial unity of the soul."[6] But while critical historicists agree that one cannot self-reflexively gather the fragments of self into a coherent "I," they go on to describe or explain the self in action by resorting to the simplest hypothesis about the determining effects of cultural or biographical contexts. Nothing changes in the old "substantial unity" except the agent's ability to recognize and take responsibility for what seems patent to critical historicists. It is clear why they want the unity—they then have in the author's "self" a solid historical phenomenon they can attempt to explain. Were they to acknowledge the full play of interests, as well as the complex mental acts I think necessary to order these interests, their task would be much more difficult. But without an account of ordering powers, critical historicists' own claims to knowledge are subject to the same model of blindness and insight. Their critical behavior must be at least as symptomatic of history as the deeds of the geniuses they manage to disbelieve.

I wish I could consider the internal incoherence resulting from this model of suspicion to be a clinching objection. But there remains a possible defense, which requires me to shift the argument to more prag-matic concerns about the self. Many critical historicists claim no respon-sibility to the traditional imperative that explanation be subject to im-personal, disinterested criteria. Since they see "truth" as only a mask for power, their own work can get directly to the struggle for power without the "detour" of first having to satisfy truth conditions. By reducing truth conditions to features of rhetoric, such thinkers preserve their right to explain—by changing the nature of explanation. Although this shifting of grounds cannot be refuted, it might prove difficult to live by, and the difficulties may make us wonder whether our explanatory ideal is, in fact, reductive about our powers to know and to organize interests in relation to public criteria. If we can ask, as I am asking, whether we ought to enter the practice their claims create, it seems fitting to demand them to explain, in pragmatic terms, why their specific model of inquiry should be pursued at the expense of our older notions. Why should we reject the possibility that we can interpret ourselves and project purposes which integrate various levels of our interests? Why should we reject the idea that the truth requires us to deny some ideas and interests? Finally, why should we reject the possibility of self-consciously articulating what Jürgen Habermas calls our "emancipatory interests"? I doubt that we can base emancipatory interests on Habermas' definitions of rationality or make them the only end of a political system: any public realm will also produce competing, nonemancipatory interests in how we establish authority or develop practical means for preserving order. Yet his model is extremely important for the aims of private subjects and the possible roles idealization can play in public life. Emancipation depends on correlating the negative critical work of demystification with the positive models and powers we can locate in culturally preserved forms of idealization. Once this dialectic between demystifying and idealizing emerges as a possibility, I suspect that our private interests will prove too greedy to condone endlessly repeating the self. We have, or develop, strong interests in expanding, not reducing, our interests. It may even be that linking private interests to models preserved by society will produce an interest in the public good.

4

I seem now to have gotten myself in a bind. I want to deny the substantial self but affirm the powers of consciousness for integrating levels of behavior, judging among interests, and establishing identities that complexly link us to the past. It will be through this bind, however, that we construct a psychological framework allowing us to connect the functions canons can perform to the picture of interests I have been developing.

To begin with, there is no need to equate powers of self-conscious integration with any foundational sense of the unified self. Recursive powers are common in formal systems. The distinctive unity we attribute to human projects need not require a genetic feature deeply private to the self, because that unity can stem simply from the act of establishing reasons or models for an action. As Eliot saw, destabilizing the private self is not debilitating so long as culture preserves a strong conservative element that establishes a repertory of public roles. And if the repertory offers a good deal of variety, the identities constructed need not be themselves wholly conventional. We work within and with conventions, bringing about new syntheses in the process. The public self begins as a simple shifter, an attribution to one physical being of properties available to any person. But because we tend to invest the "I" with imaginary forces, which Jacques Lacan describes, we have an interest in forming for the "I" a distinctive way of relating to the roles we learn to play. So in life, as in literature, convention and distinctive identity are not contradictories but dialectically interconnected principles. We construct selves by weaving relations among conventions and acting in accord with reasons.

Eliot's remarks on the canon reveal the implications of this power to transform convention because he is forced to temper his conservatism with a Romantic codicil. He states that, at one pole, the canon defines genres that minor poets rely on in the same way in which public selves work minor variations on established social roles. But, at the other pole, major writers make something new of their heritage and create demands on others to explore the possibilities it offers for becoming strong identities. Thus, we must read the complete work of major writers, because their identity resides in the pressures they put on their inheritance and in the powers by which they transform empirical personality into an articulate public synthesis.[7]

Charles Taylor's essay "Responsibility for Self" goes a long way toward giving solid philosophical grounding to Eliot's vision of selves formed in a cultural theater.[8] Like Kant, but without any dependence on universals, Taylor makes a sharp distinction between empirical and self-defining choices, or what he calls preferences and strong evaluations. Preferences are judgments that something is good simply by virtue of the direct satisfactions it produces. All preferences are in a sense equal since they conform to no criteria beyond the specific desire of the chooser and no constraints except for practical considerations of possibilities and consequences. Strong evaluations, on the other hand, are second-order choices: something chosen not because of what it is but because it allows a person to represent herself as being an agent of a certain kind, as deserving certain predicates. Strong evaluations place a choice within a network of reasons, where the reasons in effect entitle a person to the self-representation if they fit the situation. The clear sign of second-order status is the nature of the constraints encountered in such choices. If I want to consider myself courageous, there are some cowardly things I cannot do—not because it is impossible or because I will be overtly punished but because the deeds are incompatible with a set of defining terms I have chosen for my actions. Second-order choices are contrastive because they are choices of meanings, not objects. Thus, they are constrained by the network of public associations that establishes meaning. Selves have public identity when they consistently maintain the contrastive schemes projected in their reasons for their actions.

Taylor's model is not without serious problems. There is much room for casuistry here but no more so than in utilitarian models and no less so than we need if we are to honor those who resist the temptation of casuistry. Moreover, in order to maintain a necessary flexibility and set of levels among choices, we must ensure that no single contrast is definitive. The opposition of courage and cowardice can be interpreted in many ways because the interlocking contrastive frameworks are not fixed categories but malleable structures. A person constitutes herself by establishing the specific meaning of the contrast and acting in accord with the implications of that meaning. (Socratic dialogues might be considered complex strong evaluations.) In contradistinction, when we cannot see a connection between words and deeds or cannot place deeds in a contrastive context, then we simply cannot speak of moral identity at all. A person who calls himself courageous but acts in what would normally be called cowardly terms without offering (explicitly or implicitly) any alternative interpretation of those terms has no public identity, except, perhaps, as expressing symptoms. This person, I must add, could still have quite strong and determinate interests. What would be lacking is any process of self-subsumption, any sense that the person determined his interests with a stake in being a certain kind of person. Self-subsumption is a process of projecting images of the self and then adapting one's behavior to them. Within Western cultures these projections sustain claims to freedom and dignity to the degree that the agent can provisionally bracket his specific social setting in order to establish personal meaning for the public values available to him.

5

    The process of strong evaluation dramatizes within practical life the two basic functions that canons serve within the cultural order. One set of functions is curatorial: literary canons preserve rich, complex contrastive frameworks, which create what I call a cultural grammar for interpreting experience. Given the nature of canonical materials, however, there is no way to treat the curatorial function as simply semantic. Canons involve values—both in what they preserve and in the principles of preserving. Thus, the other basic function that canons serve is necessarily normative. Because these functions are interrelated, canons need not present simple dogmas. Instead, canons serve as dialectical resources, at once articulating the differences we need for a rich contrastive language and constituting models of what we can make of ourselves as we employ that language. This interrelation, in turn, applies to two basic kinds of models, each addressing a different dimension of literary works. Canons call attention to examples of what can be done within the literary medium. The canon is a repertory of inventions and a challenge to our capacity to make further developments in a genre or style. But in most cases, craft is both an end in itself and a means for sharpening the texts' capacity to offer a significant stance that gives us access to some aspect of nontextual experience. So in addition to preserving examples of craft, canons also establish models of wisdom, often while training us to search for ways the two connect. This means that when we reflect on general functions that canons serve, we must take as our representative cases not only those works that directly exhibit exemplary features of craft or wisdom but also the works that fundamentally illuminate the contrastive language we must use to describe those exemplary achievements. It matters that we read the *Aeneid* because there are strong reasons to continue valuing the tragic sense of duty the work exemplifies; it matters that we read Thomas Kyd because of the influence he exercised on Shakespeare and Eliot; it matters much less that we read George Gascoigne or Stephen Duck, the Water Poet, because they neither provided significant types exemplifying wisdom or craft nor influenced those whom we think did.

The curatorial and normative practices that we develop for such bodies of texts bring about three possible cultural consequences. The first, and most fundamental, is the most difficult to discuss. Canons play the role of institutionalizing idealization: they provide examples of what ideals can be, of how people have used them as stimuli and contexts for their own self-creation, and of when acts in the present can address more than the present. Harold Bloom offers a compelling account of the struggle a canon elicits, but his reliance on personal strength leads him to pay scant attention to other, equally significant effects of this heritage. It is the very idea of a canon and the example it offers that establish the standards writers try to meet. Indeed, canons are largely responsible for the frame of questions that allows Bloom's "agon," and, equally important, they establish the complex practices of argument by which critical evaluations can be articulated. Canons make us *want* to struggle, and they give us the common questions and interests we need to ennoble that project.

We share enough literary experience to obviate any need to elaborate these pieties. So I will proceed immediately to a second, corollary cultural consequence of canons. If ideals are to play a significant role for a culture, there must be a model of authority that empiricism cannot provide. When we offer an idealization from or about the canon, we must face the question of who will judge those features of the past worthy to become normative models—or, who will judge the kind of reasons we offer in our idealizations of those idealizations. We return to the dilemma of circularity. But by now I hope that our reflections on the canon will manifest some of the immanent capacities of the circle. The judges for the canon must be projections from within the canon as it develops over time. For here we can construct a normative circle, analogous to the principle of competent judgment John Stuart Mill proposes as his way of testing among competing models of happiness. Our judges for ideals must be those whom we admire as ideal figures or those whom these ideal figures admired. Only such an audience of judges can save us from the trap of an even smaller circle. For unless we can project audiences for our evaluations who are beyond the specific interpretive community that shares our reading habits, there is little point in giving reasons for our idealizations at all. All our reasons would do is identify our own community; they would say nothing significant about values in general or would not give us the distance from ourselves requisite for both self-criticism and self-direction. Similarly, unless our audience were as capacious as the ideals we concern ourselves with, we would contaminate them (or ourselves) in the very process of attempting to make our strong evaluations articulate.

Even stating this ideal in a plausible form demands the witness of a canonical figure. I call upon Longinus:

> Accordingly it is well that we ourselves also, when elaborating anything which requires lofty expression and elevated conception, should shape some idea in our minds as to how perchance Homer would have said this very thing, or how it would have been raised to the sublime by Plato or Demosthenes or by the historian Thucydides. For those personages, presenting themselves to us and inflaming our ardor and as it were illuminating our path, will carry our minds in a mysterious way to the high standards of sublimity which are imaged within us. 2. Still more effectual will it be to suggest this question to our thoughts: What sort of hearing would Homer, had he been present, or Demosthenes have given to this or that when said by me, or how would they have been affected by the other? For the ordeal is indeed a severe one, if we presuppose such a tribunal and theater for our own utterances, and imagine that we are undergoing a scrutiny of our writings before these great heroes, acting as judges and witnesses. 3. A greater incentive still will be supplied if you add the question, in what spirit will each succeeding age listen to me who have written thus? But if one shrinks from the very thought of uttering aught that may transcend the term of his own life and time, the conceptions of his mind must necessarily be incomplete, blind, and as it were untimely born, since they are by no means brought to the perfection needed to ensure a futurity of fame.[9]

Of course, gods and heroes do not speak. These imaginative projections offer the typical openings to duplicity; but we know enough about such judges to project reactions we might agree on. Our projections would identify us with the appropriate realm of ideals and would replace the narcissistic circle with a common reference point for presenting and judging reasons. Finally, there is a powerful incentive built into the model because the richer our knowledge of canonical figures like Plato, Demosthenes, and their future incarnations, the sharper and less sectarian our judgments are likely to be. If we know our Plato, we will in all probability not let our reasons imitate the ones Phaedrus might give, especially if we are addressing an actual audience who shares that knowledge. An idealized audience will not sanction easy self-justifications. This model preserves as its arbiter not abstract laws but public images of personal judges capable of fully sympathetic and multifaceted comprehension.

We can now move toward questions of social authority by going back to the issue of a cultural grammar. Canons, I argued, sustain complex contrastive languages by showing in concrete terms what competing choices are likely to involve. That curatorial, or semantic, function takes on considerable normative force when we recognize that the qualities of this idealized audience can also become features of the cultural grammar. We acquire a grammar for describing actions that also conveys a good deal of information about the consequences—the kind of community or kind of approval—we might expect from our choices. This extension of grammar need be no more dogmatic or conservative than the straight semantic functions. Cultural grammars constrain discourse only to the extent necessary to allow us to frame alternatives or pose ways of questioning our choices as we imagine possible judges for them.

Now if this much of my case is acceptable, it seems plausible to make the further claim that the set of values and judgments sustained by the canon helps constitute something like Northrop Frye's alternative society within the existing social order.[10] This is the ultimate consequence of insisting that our acts of forming and using canons are not reducible to interests—needs and desires—fully explainable simply in terms of a specific historical and ideological context. For in what resists such critical appropriations, we find grounds for criticizing any given social practice. If we imagine thinkers and artists over a long period of time criticizing the existing social order, producing alternative models, and seeking judgment from within these alternatives, we see clearly how the very concept of imaginative ideals requires a dialogue between empirical conditions and underlying principles. This dialectic is easily acceptable in relation to private life. We use alternatives the past provides in order to shape possible selves in the present. But once that is accepted, it is imperative that we produce a view of history complex enough to handle the ways agents base their actions on a range of contexts, each creating possible ideals and imaginary judges. In turn, that density within history affords grounds for basing arguments about the public good upon the models writers create as they reflect on the conflicts between the actual present and what the past suggests is possible or desirable. Canons give agents within history the double consciousness basic to the Socratic ideal of lovers of wisdom forming marginal elites to preserve principles that can transform society.

The ground of authority that I propose will always be difficult to gain, because it requires us to convince large segments of those who wield social power that they should submit themselves to the judgments fostered by an ideal community. This difficulty is one of the many reasons canons are not sufficient instruments for social change. But no intellectual critique is. Intellectual constructs move only those whose strong evaluation involves the appropriate contrastive language. For these people, the appeal of an authority based on imaginative projections from the past can be enormously influential. At the very least, appeals to personal example or to ideals apparently shared by most great writers can have stronger claims on us than appeals based on vague assertions about carnival spirits or a political unconsciousness. The ideals are explicit and their authority implicit in our literary activity. In asserting this, I do not mean that canonical ideals can or should directly dictate our actions. In that way lies conservative madness. I claim only that canons afford directions or considerations about ends, which we can reflect upon in relation to practical exigencies. Even with these qualifications, however, our need for such a model of authority is a pressing one, as is all too evident in the problems that arise when critical historicism is extended directly to political issues.

Edward Said provides a telling example. Said now seeks considerable distance from the Foucauldian critical historicism central to most of his previous arguments. To Said, Foucault's unrelenting insistence on power and the traps of being situated within a discursive practice denies the possibility of free criticism and moral witness. Speaking against Foucault's treating the idea of justice as either "an instrument of a certain political and economic power or as a weapon against that power," Said insists:

> If power oppresses and controls and manipulates, then everything that resists it is not morally equal to power, is not neutrally and simply "a weapon against that power!" . . . Even if the distinction is hard to draw, there is a distinction to be made—as, for example, Chomsky does, when he says that he would give his support to an oppressed proletariat if as a class it made an ideal of justice the goal of its struggle.[11]

Said now claims it is the task of intellectuals to produce versions of justice applicable to a given social order. But that claim immediately elicits the counterarguments of Paul Bové, another descendant of Foucault:

> Who measures the *Truth* of this idea? Who determines that the justice pursued is an "ideal" and not "false consciousness"? Who understands how it has been made an "ideal"? In whose interest and why? By what criteria? How is it established that these criteria are not themselves part of the "regime of truth" whose function in our society leads . . . to regulative authority for intellectuals?[12]

Said cannot appeal against this to rationality per se because rationality characteristically produces means rather than ends. This is especially relevant if one is sensitive to the ethnocentric uses to which a foundationalist sense of rationality has been put in past discussions about values. Nor can Said appeal to common sense or ordinary morality since these are precisely what the critic of power must often oppose. Common sense is often the blindest of ideological forces. I see no way Said can find the authority he desires for his resistance, unless he grounds his claims against power, on ideals he derives from what our culture tells us we can be, or must be, if we want to measure up to a certain kind of judgment. Only those models from the past that have survived such judgments can serve as basic moral arbiters of our future. Intellectuals do have a special political role to play—but only if they are faithful to levels of experience where the products of intellect have had substantial effects.

Implicit in this discussion of authority is the third cultural consequence of the curatorial and normative functions of canons, well worth elaborating in its own right. As Longinus saw, custodial concerns for past ideals have projective dimensions especially important for contemporary writing. The weight of the past puts pressure on writers to handle certain tasks or roles, and it establishes a level of questioning necessary if a critic is to propose a work as capable of shaping values in the future. Under this dispensation, critics impose on new texts the same kind of expectations they bring to classical works. Such impositions are not often greeted with gracious submission by writers. The typical role of contemporary writers is to create stances that oppose the overt claims their culture derives from the canon. But for the opposition to matter over time, it will probably need to address specific canonical works and engage the same degree of emotional and intellectual energy that canonical works provide. Critical pressure makes these needs explicit and helps focus the writer's response.

One measure of our age is the difficulty we are likely to have in coming up with a good example of a poet who satisfies the standards of a high, transhistorical canon. With enough time I think I could argue that Bloom's misguided efforts to canonize John Ashbery as a visionary poet have, in fact, led us to concentrate on qualities of Ashbery's work that align him with great meditative poets like Wordsworth and Wallace Stevens. But negative examples from the contemporary scene can be briefer and more telling. Most criticism of contemporary poets seems to be content with questions that establish much weaker demands than those we characteristically impose on classical works. We often treat our writers as if they were descendants of Johnson's lady preacher, figures whom we praise not for doing a job well but for showing that it can be done at all. Both critics and poets have renounced, for the most part, the revolutionary spiritual ambitions of the sixties but not its distrust of the past. As a result they have nowhere to turn but to the ideals of earnest sincerity, careful attention to moments of delicate vision, and, above all, intricate manipulation of subtle features of the medium. Without a deeper and broader frame of reference and sense of cultural demands, we find only an impoverished vocabulary of motives masking as a careful, self-conscious commitment to lyricism. The ultimate irony is that such weakness allows poetry's role to be usurped by a theoretical criticism whose pro-grammatic suspiciousness ensures a different but equally narrow human theater.

6

Once we know the roles a cultural structure plays, or could play, in our lives, we know how to assess any particular claims to be good instances of that structure. Functions establish criteria. Considerable difficulties remain in spelling out the appropriate criteria because, ideally, we would derive them from the canonical models of canon-formation we inherit and from analytic attempts (such as this one) to disclose the intrinsic principles within the circle of values we inhabit. Criteria for canons, in short, share the mix of historical and idealized features we have found wherever we looked. By now it should be clear that I take this circular feature as a strength in my argument, one more arc for the geodesic dome we build as we study our past. Here I want simply to offer the hypothesis that we can find within most disputes over a general high canon, three basic criteria that rightfully shape the process of discussion.[13] If the high canon transmits contrastive frameworks, exemplifies forms of imagination considered valuable in a culture, and provides figures of judgment for our actions, then our actual practice of judging literary works for the canon ought to capture these concerns. Conversely, spelling out the relation between our expectations and our evaluations should sharpen our sense of what we can or do share despite our differences.

These three criteria are difficult to state precisely, because they usually appear combined within specific discussions. The first is the most amorphous, requiring loose analogies to strong evaluation. I call it a criterion of forceful self-subsumption. For a work to play canonical roles, it must exhibit qualities which define it as a significant distinctive entity. Preeminent among these qualities is a capacity to interpret its own features by establishing a contrastive language for the situation it projects. *Paradise Lost*, in Addison's and Johnson's terms, presents a single action which integrates our most important concerns and establishes compelling moral categories for them. Flaubert's *Sentimental Education* integrates many of those same concerns by reversing Milton's moral categories and suggesting through its plays on language why this reversal is necessary and how it is possible. These cases are different enough from one another to indicate why I have little to say here beyond pointing out their conditions. All they have in common is that each establishes a model of what it means to have the self-defining strength to be a model on one's own terms. Conversely, all that good criticism of either work need have in common is a willingness to preserve demanding comparative standards that lead us to elicit the work's basic force.

If we ask what uses such force can have, we find ourselves in the central paradox of literary studies: the force of individual works qua self-subsuming individuals is important primarily because of the way it allows a work to become representative. Thus we arrive at a second criterion, best expressed in Johnson's motto, "Nothing can please many and please long, but just representations of general nature." But this neoclassic formulation will not apply widely enough without a redefinition of what "representations of general nature" can mean. Canonical works are expected to provide knowledge of the world represented, to exemplify powers for making representations that express possible attitudes or produce artistic models, and to articulate shared values in a past culture that influence the present or to clarify means of reading other works we have reason to care about. But "representation" accounts only for the descriptive force of a work. The other, constitutive features of a work, which create a grammar of examples, require the broader concept of representativeness.[14]

With this concept we can organize discussions of cognition in terms of two opposed but overlapping directions of thought. In one direction, representativeness is a measure of semantic scope. A work is representative when it provides and responds to a sense of the typical or the general in any of the areas of expectation I just listed. The other direction involves measures of intensiveness. Representativeness is not usually determined by reference to specific states of affairs. Rather, the test of a work's force in this respect is its capacity to enable a reader to identify with the work so as to find in it the power to experience fully the central existential or literary situation it presents. These two features of representativeness— the sense of type and the sense of assuming a power of imaginative action—create a good deal of room for interpretive conflicts, often within the same cultural circle. For example, standards for how works provide the forms of knowledge worthy of a canon vacillate between demands for symbolic generality and demands for approaching the universal through a precise grasp of particulars. Similarly, one can emphasize or dismiss the emotional properties of a work, depending on one's sense of how emotions fit into claims about knowledge. So long as we insist that canons help us to know, we will have to argue about how we know and what best facilitates powers of action.

We need a third criterion because not all works of comparable scope and intensity have the same canonical status. We must, then, acknowledge the critical obligation to describe what we take to be the value of technical innovations or the wisdom and ethical significance of a work's overall content. We must evaluate by examining the powers of action a work clarifies or cultivates. Such questions soon lead to embarrassing impasses, because they pressure us to accept sectarian answers, either as dogma or as the liberal model of each sect's own ethical canons. And, indeed, the more we demand actual models of behavior rather than elements of a contrastive language, the more we will equate the ethical power of a work with an authoritarian program. But if we concentrate on the display of qualities in literary works and the creation of very general ideals, we have grounds for treating the ethical forms of a canon less on the model of a military academy than of a theater. The ethical force of canonical models becomes a way of sustaining simultaneous levels of performance in a wide variety of roles. In fact, some canonical works—*Ulysses*, for instance—dramatize precisely this theatrical pluralism created by the synchronic presence of the canon. Here I cannot claim that competing critics share the same ethical concerns. Nonetheless, I can suggest that we can, to a large extent, get beyond our differences if we adapt an attitude similar to Joyce's. Then our basic ethical criterion becomes not what behavior a text will prescribe but what qualities of being it would make available for a variety of practical stances. On this model, works do not address social life directly but elicit fundamental forms of desire and admiration that can motivate efforts to produce social change. This is why and how Eliot can insist on testing works in terms of their power to make available a unified sensibility. And it is why Wordsworth dismisses works that do not align the intensities of subjective life with the "inherent and indestructible qualities of the human mind, and likewise of certain powers in the great and permanent objects that act upon it, which are equally inherent and indestructible."[15] Finally, this is why Johnson's classicism seeks harmony not with external nature but with the emotions and judgments that align agents of diverse cultures and interests in a shared identification with the text. Canons themselves may form the very society they lead us to dream of and, as we dream, to see ourselves in our limits and our possibilities.

7

I can imagine three basic critiques of my general argument: that I am more ideological than the ideological analysts I fault for being narrow, that my efforts to restore "transideological" grounds of intelligibility and value only repeat the bourgeois fantasy of universalizing a limited set of interests, and that all this talk of idealization is empty piety that has no practical effect except to delude us into believing in the health and possible authority of literary studies. In response, I want to call upon an unwilling ally, W. J. T. Mitchell:

> The more one reflects on the notion of "institutions of criticism," the more difficult it becomes to think of any kind of critical activity that is autonomous and independent of institutional involvement. And yet the idea that criticism has, or should aspire to, this sort of autonomy is a persistent illusion that has prevented criticism from taking a clear look at itself. . . . The question is not whether criticism will be involved in institutions but rather what kind of institutions we will devise to structure our activities and whether criticism is capable of turning its gaze upon its own institutional base.[16]

As soon as we deny foundationalism, we are likely to end up embracing a version of Mitchell's stance. But we must also worry about taking too myopic a gaze at institutional bases. What, we may ask, sustains specific institutions or allows criticism of them? And how do we know differences are irreducible? If there is to be anything like the critical dialogue Mitchell dreams of, must there not be levels of institutional encompassing through which criteria are imposed on the participants and their gazes focused? How shall we invest our attention to avoid becoming a mirror image of what we reject (as, for example, by proposing claims about the primacy of self-interest as our critique of bourgeois ideology)? If we are not to deny the possibility of authority from within literature, we must direct our gaze at the complex relationship between institutions and what can possibly justify or extend their practices. Or, to put the same point another way, we must recognize the general role of institutions as constitutions, as structures with many strata capable of directing and organizing power to enable certain forms of activity. Criticism cannot be autonomous, but its primary role may be to use institutional materials as means for capacitating autonomous individuals—that is, individuals with the capacity to make strong evaluations on the basis of contrastive language constructed from a variety of institutional contexts.

Criticism's dependence on institutions does not entail its devoting itself to analyzing those dependencies. At the very least, there may be very different kinds of critical activities—one for analyzing institutional dependencies and another for actualizing what the institution makes available. The ultimate danger in the critical historicism Mitchell represents is that it undermines precisely what the traditional bases for literary study offer as values. Specific dependencies on social institutions are best defined by purely analytic or purely historical disciplines. But if we want to know what any given institution offers as valuable, we need ways of responding to the constitutive forces within a tradition. What positive terms critical historicism affords for these enterprises will not derive from literary material nor apply to the forms of life individuals can construct for themselves. As I see it, critical historicism relies on a grammar of motives capable of praising only the powers of criticism the institution makes available and the general political forces it marshalls against prevailing values. If we confine literary criticism to this model of inquiry, we must employ the same predicates about actions as the social sciences do—thus depriving us of one of the very few disciplines with the potential power to establish goals that individuals might pursue and to construct audiences that make the pursuit plausible and desirable. In surrendering this power, we risk producing a world where only humanistic psychology would claim authority to clarify the ends of individual self-definition. I cannot imagine that being OK for me or for you.

These arguments all come to bear on one pressing practical issue: How do we teach reading and, through that, create hierarchies for the uses of criticism? Positions like Mitchell's follow inescapably from the ideal of reading as a process of inaugurating disbelief, or, in Geoffrey

Hartman's term, of reading *against* a text. But then how does one defend the texts one reads *with?* How can criticism hope to mediate texts as anything more than cautionary examples? We may, in fact, have already developed a richer grammar for the symptoms in our texts than we have for the varieties of intended meanings. It would be foolish to deny the power, interest, or even utility of such cautionary efforts. This, however, is not the route to reconstructing a Longinian audience or readers capable of using the contrastive language that audience authorizes for their own lives. I think we do better—that is, we better fit the ideals about reading developed by those writers whom we take the time to read—if we imagine ourselves as reading *through* the work. By submitting ourselves to its provisional authority as an integrated work, we can hope to construct the best possible case for the text as a window on possible values in experience. This saves us from a rather vulnerable smugness; it forces us to extend our imaginations; and it keeps authority within the imaginative processes of a dialogue with great minds, rather than placing it in some contemporary interpretive practice.

This is not the place to work out all the implications of reading through texts. It should suffice here simply to indicate how such a model of reading enables us to preserve for a culture the functions of the canon I have tried to describe. The crucial enabling step is to insist on reading authors as I think most of them intended to be read—that is, as agents constructing a version of experience with a claim to influence the ways generations of readers would view themselves and their world. This does entail partially reading against historical specificity, so as to highlight those qualities of the work that transcend the genetic situation. Highlighting transcendent qualities does not mean ignoring the history nor does it require our denying the historical commitments of a given writer. We need the specificity of a work, need it to maintain an otherness with something different to say to us. Models of dialogue like Hans-Georg Gadamer's tend to deny this difference. In my view, we do not want dialogue with texts; we want to encounter the full force of what the author imagined, in the terms the author chose to present it. However, we have a specific use in mind for that force. We want to see how strongly it asserts claims on us—both as a model of behavior and as a possible audience figure in an ideal community. Texts can enter this canonical theater in a variety of ways—for example, by their power to interpret their own historicity, by their deep grasp of perennial features of human experience, or by their construction of compelling ideals for human work. In order to participate as readers in any of these achievements, we must try to state the author's probable intended action within history in the most abstract context of problems and responses. Then the author's achievement can step out of history. Dante's intense imaginative reconstruction of his world becomes a potentially timeless grappling with problems of exile, with concrete challenges for the reader to satisfactorily respond to a range of perennial character traits and action types, with questions of how an individual comes to understand the nature of justice and love, and, finally, with dialectical paths through which one can give order to experiences that, taken singly, overwhelm one's ordinary understanding. Similarly, we can read Augustine for the drama of inventing autobiography and a psychology appropriate for resisting mainstream culture and its canons. All these themes obviously lead back to particular dramatic and stylistic observations but under the crucial pressure that we judge our own reading as commensurate with the strong evaluations others' readings have given of the author. We may not agree with those readings, but if we are to appreciate the power of identification and identities a canon gives, we should be able to offer competing reasons for our interpretive acts that are intended for the same level of audience. By seeing how canons can be normative, by understanding the judgments of judgments that form them, we are likely to make demands on ourselves to be strong readers who are also faithful readers. Anything more private is not in our interest, at least if we believe it possible to find in history, texts or agents who do not simply repeat an endless, self-justifying, self-deluding farce.

I cannot provide that my model of reading should dominate. I cannot even wish that it exclude others. But I hope I can persuade some readers to reexamine our current critical preferences in relation to more traditional notions of canons, to help us at least work through the cultural circle of values we inherit as we define our allegiances. We have possible selves; we need possible worlds—much more than we need to base self-congratulations on the narrow analytic power of critical historicism. We must refuse to let it undermine perhaps the only hope we have of preventing our suspicious attitudes from becoming sufficient accounts of literary works. Instead, we owe it to ourselves to explore the stance that Ashbery's self-irony allows him to recoup from history:

> So I cradle this average violin that knows
> Only forgotten showtunes, but argues
> The possibility of free declamation anchored
> To a dull refrain, . . .
> . . . .
> Our question of a place of origin hangs
> Like smoke: how we picnicked in pine forests,
> In coves with the water always seeping up, and left
> Our trash, sperm and excrement everywhere, smeared
> On the landscape, to make of us what we could.[17]

1. Jerome J. McGann, "The Meaning of The Ancient Mariner," *Critical Inquiry* 8 (Autumn 1981): 67, 65, 55. The term "critical historicism" applies to all schools of criticism— Marxist, feminist, or modified deconstructionist—which insist, with Terry Eagleton, that "criticism is not a passage from text to reader: its task is not to redouble the text's self-

understanding, to collude with its object in a conspiracy of eloquence. Its task is to show the text as it cannot know itself, to manifest those conditions of its making . . . about which it is necessarily silent" (*Criticism and Ideology: A Study in Marxist Literary Theory* [London, 1978], p. 43). The differences among critical historicists occur over how criticism can situate itself "outside the space of the text." Eagleton claims "scientific" knowledge; McGann is studiedly vague on this point; Jacques Derrida's deconstruction uses the issue of situating to reverse priorities so that historicism itself must be criticized as an evasion of what perpetually cannot be known however it influences our discourse.

2. See Frank Kermode, "Institutional Control of Interpretation," *Salmagundi* 43 (Winter 1979): 72–86. Kermode is not one of the full-fledged critical historicists. Like Jonathan Culler and Stanley Fish, he shares their relativism but not their passion about demystification, presumably because that too is only a reliance on one among many possible contexts.

3. Claims about self-interest exploit a basic equivocation. At times it is said that we are *determined* to pursue our self-interests, at times, that we *ought* to pursue our self-interests by developing the critical means necessary for freedom.

4. I use the term "empirical interests" in what I take to be a Kantian sense. "Empirical" refers to interests one simply accepts as preferences, without any need for justification. These interests invite ideological analysis, since, for Kant, they come essentially from outside as heteronomous rather than autonomous features of a subject's life. The opposite of "empirical," in this sense, is interests one tries to rationalize on principles that, at some level, have criteria not selected by the agent and also applicable to some other agents. For a historical account of the concept of interests, see Albert O. Hirschman, *The Passions and the Interests: Political Arguments for Capitalism before Its Triumph* (Princeton, N.J., 1977). For a clear conceptual analysis of problems in attributing all motives to self-interest, see Paul W. Taylor, *Principles of Ethics: An Introduction* (Belmont, Calif., 1978), chap. 3.

5. For a fuller analysis of reader-response theory, as well as defenses of the concepts of exemplification, strong evaluation, grammar, intention, and classic that I employ here, see my *Act and Quality: A Theory of Literary Meaning and Humanistic Understanding* (Amherst, Mass., 1981).

6. T. S. Eliot, "Tradition and the Individual Talent," *Selected Essays* (New York, 1950), p. 9. For a contemporary indexical account of the self that provides plausible alternatives to models of "substantial unity," see John Perry, "Perception, Action, and the Structure of Believing," forthcoming in a festschrift for Paul Grice. We find strange confirmation of my case about the "I" in relation to interests if we reflect on a problem of defining canon that I have so far ignored. My discussion has in effect stipulated the relevant idea of canon to be those texts a culture takes as absolutely basic to its literary education. I suspect that all my readers entered this circle sufficiently to understand that without this note. Yet the act of understanding requires considerable abstraction. There are many different kinds of canons, several of which an individual agent might subscribe to. There are personal canons and official canons, canons for what one needs to know and canons for undermining all one is told one needs to know—and each of these classes has several subdivisions. There are probably even canons for bathroom reading. Canons, then, reveal the same diversity and flexibility we find in the self's affairs. Does any one set of them comprise the self? Yet despite this diversity, we produce hierarchies of interests or stipulative constructs of selves appropriate for given situations and practices.

7. "It is the function of the superior members and superior families to preserve the group culture, as it is the function of the producers to alter it" (Eliot, "Notes towards the Definition of Culture," *Christianity and Culture* [New York, 1949], p. 115). Both the preservation of order and the production of change will require complex models of sameness and difference manifest in levels within the canon: "The Faith can, and must, find room for many degrees of intellectual, imaginative, and emotional receptivity to the same doctrines, just as it can embrace many variations of order and ritual" (ibid., p. 101; see also pp. 105–6). My comments on Eliot depend on his "What Is Minor Poetry?" and "What Is a Classic?," *On Poetry and Poets* (London, 1957), pp. 39–52 and 53–71.

8. See Charles Taylor, "Responsibility for Self," in *The Identities of Persons,* ed. Amélie Oksenberg Rorty (Berkeley and Los Angeles, 1976), pp. 281–300. On the actual workings of a self not dependent on substantial unity yet basic to the use of idealizations within public life, see Michael Oakeshott, *On Human Conduct* (Oxford, 1975).

9. Longinus, *On the Sublime,* trans. W. R. Roberts, in *Critical Theory since Plato,* ed. Hazard Adams (New York, 1971), p. 86.

10. See Northrop Frye's essay on myths in *Anatomy of Criticism: Four Essays* (Princeton, N.J., 1957), and his discussions of authority in *The Stubborn Structure: Essays on Criticism and Society* (London, 1970), pp. 22–56 and 241–56.

11. Edward W. Said, "Travelling Theory," *Raritan* 1 (Winter 1982): 65–66.

12. Paul A. Bové, "Intellectuals at War: Michel Foucault and the Analytics of Power," p. 27.

13. The evaluations I speak about involve the status of a work's content as a historical act. It is also possible to suggest questions we ask of candidates for a canon in terms of aesthetic properties of the work, as Monroe Beardsley does in establishing criteria of unity, complexity, and intensity. I suspect, however, that criteria like Beardsley's will not explain the power of a work to affect our sense of existential values, unless he defines "intensity" along lines similar to the themes I argue. Ironically, criteria of content may also prove more resistant to the historical change which now makes notions like unity very problematic.

14. I elaborate the concept of representativeness both in my "Representation, Representativeness, and Non-Representational Art," *Journal of Comparative Aesthetics* (forthcoming), and "Going On and Going Nowhere: Wittgenstein and Questions of Criteria in Literary Criticism," in *Literature and Philosophy,* ed. William Cain (forthcoming). That elaboration, of course, derives from Kenneth Burke.

15. William Wordsworth, "Preface to the Second Edition of *Lyrical Ballads* (1800)," *William Wordsworth: Selected Poems and Prefaces,* ed. Jack Stillinger, 2d ed. (Boston, 1965), p. 449.

16. W. J. T. Mitchell, "*Critical Inquiry* and the Ideology of Pluralism," *Critical Inquiry* 8 (Summer 1982): 610–11.

17. John Ashbery, from "Street Musicians," *Houseboat Days: Poems* (New York, 1977), p. 1.

Canon and Power in the Hebrew Scriptures

Gerald L. Bruns

It is not so with the man who applies himself,
And studies the Law of the Most High.
He searches out the wisdom of the ancients,
And busies himself with prophecies;
He observes the discourse of famous men,
And penetrates the intricacies of figures.
He searches out the hidden meaning of proverbs,
And acquaints himself with the obscurities of figures.
He will serve among great men,
And appear before rulers.
—BEN SIRA, Ecclesiasticus

The first thing to be said about the Hebrew Scriptures is that we have very little evidence as to how they came into existence. Nineteenth-century textual criticism dispelled once and for all the idea that Moses was the author of the sacred books; indeed, it is now hard to see how a notion of authorship can be applied to these texts in any significant way. The great British scholar, Peter R. Ackroyd, has summarized the current opinion as follows: "It is only rarely that we can point to individuals as authors—the author of Job, the author of Ecclesiastes perhaps, and a few more; more often we can point to compilers, single figures or schools—the Deuteronomists, the Priestly Writers, and the Chronicler whose work has undergone some substantial amplification in the same spirit."[1] The Scriptures are the heterogeneous product of various scribal traditions that flourished at odd times (beginning no later than the eighth century

B.C.E.) and frequently under circumstances of great national disaster (the Babylonian Exile, the Diaspora). To put the matter as plainly as possible, all we know is that the texts we now call the Hebrew Bible are rooted in centuries of scribal activity that originated, borrowed, compiled, revised, amplified, and redacted various sorts of biblical material in ways no longer possible to describe. As Brevard Childs says, in this process "particular editors, religious groups, and even political parties were involved. At times one can describe these groups historically or sociologically, such as the reforming Deuteronomic party of Jerusalem, or the editors associated with Hezekiah's court (Prov. 25.1). But basic to the canonical process is that those responsible for the actual editing of the text did their best to obscure their own identity. [The] actual process by which the text was reworked lies in almost total obscurity."[2]

It is only very late—in the first and second centuries of the common era, as part of the development of rabbinic Judaism, and in the context of conflicting scriptural traditions—that it was thought necessary to cast the Scriptures into something like a canonical form of single, fixed, authoritative versions (as in the Masoretic texts, which give us the modern Hebrew Bible).[3] Prior to this we can refer only generally to Persian or Babylonian, Palestinian, Samaritan, Aramaic, and Greek textual traditions, and there are many others besides, as we know from the scrolls found at Qumran.[4] The Greek tradition gives us (about the third or second century B.C.E.) the Septuagint, which is based on lost Hebrew versions and upon which the Christian Old Testament was based until Jerome's Vulgate in late antiquity; in fact the Septuagint remains authoritative today for many Eastern churches. As for the notion of canonization, this is a patristic idea with applications of its own and is not easy to map onto earlier periods, especially not before the Scriptures had stabilized into what we would recognize as formal texts.[5] Thus some scholars distinguish sharply between Scripture and canon, where the one is authoritative and open (that is, open to supplementation and in constant revision), and the other is closed and fixed.[6] Or, in other words, from the technical standpoint of literary or textual criticism, with its special concern for the final form of documents, canonization frequently refers simply to an official closing and fixing of texts in a form that is declared to be authoritative (for whatever particular tradition) against all prior, competing, eccentric, and subsequent books and versions.

Gerald L. Bruns is professor of English at the University of Iowa. He is the author of *Modern Poetry and the Idea of Language* (1974) and *Inventions: Writing, Textuality, and Understanding in Literary History* (1982). The present essay is from a work in progress, *Hermeneutics, Ancient and Modern*.

However—and here I come round to the point of this paper—the canonization of the Scriptures may be said to have a hermeneutical as well as a textual meaning, for what is important is not only the formation, collection, and fixing of the sacred texts but also their application to particular situations. A text, after all, is canonical, not in virtue of being final and correct and part of an official library, but because it becomes *binding* upon a group of people. The whole point of canonization is to underwrite the authority of a text, not merely with respect to its origin as against competitors in the field—this, technically, would simply be a question of authenticity—but with respect to the present and future in which it will reign or govern as a binding text. The distinction between canonical and noncanonical is thus not just a distinction between authentic and inauthentic texts—that is, it is not reducible to the usual oppositions between the inspired and the mundane, the true and the apocryphal, the sacred and the profane, and so on. On the contrary, it is a distinction between texts that are forceful in a given situation and those which are not. From a hermeneutical standpoint, in which the relation of a text to a situation is always of primary interest, the theme of canonization is *power*.

The Hebrew notion of Torah helps us to see this aspect of canonization with great clarity. The word *tôrāh* is normally used to refer to the Pentateuch, or the first five books of the Scriptures—the "Torah of Moses" or the "Priestly Torah"—but it is frequently extended to include the books of the prophets (the *nᵉbî'îm*) and the Writings (the *kᵉtubîm*) as well. And in various subsequent traditions, the term also embraces the entire sacred literature of the Jews, including principally the Mishna, the Talmuds, and the great midrashic collections that continue down to the tenth century. What the word *tôrāh* embraces as a body of texts, however, is not what matters. More important is the force implicit in the word, which derives from the legal and political thinking of the Deuteronomists in the seventh and sixth centuries.[7] In the third century, *tôrāh* (meaning "directive" or "instruction") was translated into Greek as nomos ("law"), and since that time the characterization of the books of the Torah as Law has become commonplace, if not accurate in every sense, since the Scriptures contain many sorts of writing besides legal material. Nevertheless—and here is the whole point—the books of the Torah have the force, if not everywhere the form, of law. The Hebrew Torah is the first and best example of a binding text; its significance lies not only in what it contains or means but also in its power over those who stand within its jurisdiction. It is precisely within such a textual jurisdiction that the true meaning of canonicity begins to emerge. To inquire into the canonization of the books of the Torah is to ask how they came to possess their power over a nation and a people. What did it mean for these books to become binding? More important, what were the conditions under which such a thing occurred? Or, to put the question in its simplest form:

Torah—as opposed to what? Against what forces were the books of the
Torah put into play—and by whom, and toward what end?

The best way to begin is with the famous canonization story told in
2 Kings, in which, in the eighteenth year of his reign, Josiah, king of
Judah, sends Shaphan the scribe on business to Hilkiah, the High Priest
of the Temple at Jerusalem. The Temple has been undergoing repairs
and the workmen need to be paid. Unexpectedly, and perhaps quite
casually, apropos of nothing at all, Hilkiah mentions that he has discovered
a book:

> And Hilkiah the high priest said unto Shaphan the scribe: "I
> have found the book of the Law [Torah] in the house of the Lord."
> And Hilkiah delivered the book to Shaphan, and he read it. And
> Shaphan the scribe came to the king, and . . . told the king, saying:
> "Hilkiah the priest hath delivered me a book." And it came to pass,
> when the king had heard the words of the book of the Law, that
> he rent his clothes. And the king commanded Hilkiah the priest,
> and Ahikam the son of Shaphan, and Achbor the son of Micaiah,
> and Shaphan the scribe, and Asaiah the king's servant, saying: "Go
> ye, inquire of the Lord for me, and for the people, and for all
> Judah, concerning the words of this book that is found; for great
> is the wrath of the Lord that is kindled against us, because our
> fathers have not hearkened unto the words of this book, to do
> according unto all that which is written concerning us."
>
> So Hilkiah the priest, and Ahikam, and Achbor, and Shaphan,
> and Asaiah, went unto Huldah the prophetess, the wife of Shallum
> the son of Tikvah, the son of Harhas, keeper of the wardrobe—
> now she dwelt in Jerusalem in the second quarter—and they spoke
> with her. And she said unto them: "Thus saith the Lord, the God
> of Israel: Tell ye the man that sent you unto me: Thus saith the
> Lord: Behold, I will bring evil upon this place, and upon the in-
> habitants thereof, even all the words of the book which the king of
> Judah hath read; because they have forsaken Me, and have offered
> unto other gods. . . ."
>
> And the king sent, and they gathered unto him all the elders
> of Judah and of Jerusalem. And the king went up to the house of
> the Lord, and all the men of Judah and all the inhabitants of Jerusalem
> with him, and the priests, and the prophets, and all the people,
> both small and great; and he read in their ears all the words of the
> book of the covenant which was found in the house of the Lord.
> And the king stood on the platform, and made a covenant before
> the Lord, to walk after the Lord, and to keep His commandments,
> and His testimonies, and His statutes, with all his heart, and all his
> soul, to confirm the words of this covenant that were written in this
> book; and all the people stood to the covenant. [2 Kings 22:8–
> 23:3][8]

If you want to know what it means for a text to be canonical, that is,
forceful in a given situation, here you have an answer. Josiah recognizes

a binding text when he sees one—and his recognition is the decisive thing. Naturally we would like to know what it is *in* the text that causes Josiah to respond so decisively—rending his garments, a ritual act of testimony or witness to the truth—but, strictly speaking, it does not matter. The power of the text is not intrinsic to it. On the contrary, the text draws its power from the situation in which it makes its unexpected appearance, because this is a situation which belongs to a definite history and which is structured by this history to receive just this text as it will no other. This is a text which (whatever it says) speaks to the situation at hand.

The history to which the text belongs is the one inaugurated by the covenant that Moses made with Yahweh on Sinai (see Exod.19–40:38). In another situation, containing other people with a different history, this text would be mute or idle in the manner of a foreign law—an object of curiosity, something eventually to be put back where it was found. But its applicability in the present situation cannot be escaped; this is just what Josiah recognizes in the text. What he knows is the history in which this text emerges as *the* book of the Torah, the book of the covenant before which Josiah is accountable, notwithstanding the disregard in which the covenant had been held by his predecessors (Solomon, for example, who set up altars to the gods of his foreign wives). Josiah, recognizing the history and, therefore, the claim of the text, sets in motion a process (call it "canonization") that includes the underwriting of the text by a local oracle and an impressive public reading or promulgation in which the words of the book are confirmed and in which the people are bound by the text as by an oath. The ceremony is a reenactment of the original Mosaic or Sinai covenant. It is a renewal of Israel's Yahwist faith.

The point for us to notice, however, is that canonization here is essentially a legal process in which "binding" means binding with the force of a contract; in fact, it means a good deal more, because binding is a political as well as a legal metaphor. The canonization story occurs at the end of a group of texts which scholars sometimes identify as the Deuteronomic History (Joshua—2 Kings). In the context of this version of Israel's history, the book said to have been discovered by the priest of the Temple would be some early edition of what is now the Book of Deuteronomy (an *Urdeuteronium*), which is a collection of laws, codes, or regulations governing the whole range of life—religious, political, military, social, ethical, domestic, and so on. Deuteronomy is a series of addresses of Moses to his people, including his last words before dying (something like a will or legacy), in which he commands the people to adhere to the covenant, which is here said to be the same thing as following "all the words of this law [Torah]" (Deut. 32:46). Essentially Deuteronomy is a retelling of the Sinai story (in which Sinai is now named Horeb) from the point of view of the monarchy and the priestly cult, institutions which came into existence long after the wilderness experience commemorated in the Exodus narrative. Deuteronomy represents Moses as the founder of these institutions, and thus it invests them with the highest authority. In this same fashion the story of Josiah's canonization of the Torah is a careful allusion to the Deuteronomic valediction of Moses; it is clearly designed to dramatize the authority of Deuteronomy or the Deuteronomic Code as *the* book of the covenant. Deuteronomy was the first of the ancient Scriptures (cf. the so-called JE texts) to achieve something like canonical status.[9] Scholars can even pinpoint the date of canonization: the eighteenth year of Josiah's reign would be 621 B.C.E. Deuteronomy underwent, however, considerable revision and amplification during the period of exile, when it was assimilated along with other codes and narratives into the Pentateuch. It serves as a good example of what is sometimes called an "open canon."[10]

This initial Deuteronomic Torah was the basis of (or served to ratify) a number of wide-ranging reforms carried out by Josiah in the years prior to the catastrophe of the Babylonian conquest. These were religious reforms, to be sure, motivated by the desire to restore Israel's commitment to Yahweh against all strange gods, but their undeniable political goal was to strengthen the monarchy and the priesthood by centralizing the court and the Temple cult in Jerusalem. The first canonization of the Scriptures is a crucial part of this political movement. Hilkiah the high priest did not discover the book of the Torah by accident, or, if he did, it was his good fortune to be the one to bring it forward. Indeed, it is the Torah, more than the Temple and its sacrifices, that is the real source of priestly power in ancient Judaism, because the Torah was not simply a liturgical and pedagogical document.

In an excellent study, *Deuteronomy and the Deuteronomic School,* Moshe Weinfeld points out that the "book of Deuteronomy appears . . . to have the character of an ideal national constitution representing all the official institutions of the state: the monarchy, the judiciary, the priesthood, and prophecy"—where prophecy, Weinfeld explains, means "official cultic prophecy and not classical prophecy."[11] This is a vital distinction, especially from a political standpoint. Huldah the prophetess, who speaks on behalf of the priestly Torah, is a cultic or court prophet and (2 Kings underscores this fact) a resident of Jerusalem, in contrast to Jeremiah, for example, whose relationship to Jerusalem is always that of an outsider and an adversary. Jeremiah is a contemporary of the Deuteronomists and their Torah, but it is no accident that Deuteronomy does not mention him (or any of the classical prophets: Elijah, Isaiah, and so on). From the Deuteronomic standpoint, Huldah is an authoritative prophet. Weinfeld's opinion is that Jeremiah was sympathetic to the Deuteronomic reforms— as we shall see, this is a highly controversial issue—but there is no doubt that he stood completely outside "the official institutions of the state" and would never have done what Huldah did.

For Weinfeld, the crucial figure in the canonization story is Shaphan, who is a good example of what is meant by a Deuteronomist or a Deuteronomic scribe. Together with Hilkiah, and evidently under Hilkiah's guidance and in service to the king, Shaphan is officially responsible for the Scriptures. The Scriptures are traditional material handed down through him, and he reshapes them and adapts them according to current exigencies. It is thus important to know, as Weinfeld says, that the scribes "regarded the institution of monarchy as essential for the proper functioning of society. The premonarchic period, the period of the judges, is depicted by the Deuteronomist as one of religious and political anarchy. . . . This sombre depiction . . . finds expression in the formula 'In those days there was no king in Israel; every man did what was right in his own eyes' that recurs in the literary unit comprising chs. 17–21 of [Deuteronomy]" (p. 169). It is this relativism that the Deuteronomic reforms, and in particular the canonization of the Torah, were meant to overcome. As Weinfeld says, to the mind of the Deuteronomic scribe, " 'the written Torah of Moses' (= the book of Deuteronomy) was designed for kings and *quasi*-regal leaders, who alone were capable of enforcing its sway over the people. It is indeed only when referring to kings and leaders of a regal type (Moses and Joshua, David and Solomon, and other kings) that the Deuteronomist alludes to the 'book of the Torah', whereas in the anarchic period of the judges, when each man did 'as was right in his eyes', no mention is made of it because the 'book of the Torah' could be implemented only in a society governed by a centralized government, that is, a king" (p. 171).

It is against this Deuteronomic background, in which the Scriptures are not just sacred texts but legal and political as well—texts in a real, historical world in which power is grasped and put into play—it is against this background that the book of Jeremiah becomes a rich and puzzling collection of writings. And it *is* a collection of writings, not a work: it is composed of heterogeneous material (sayings, sermons, various sorts of matter about Jeremiah) that we really don't know how to read. The famous crux is the following from Jeremiah:

> How do ye say: "We are wise,
> And the Law [Torah] is with us"?
> Lo, certainly in vain hath wrought
> The vain pen of the scribes.
> The wise men are ashamed,
> They are dismayed and taken;
> Lo, they have rejected the word of the Lord;
> And what wisdom is in them?
>
> [Jer. 8:8–9]

This text is important for the opposition it constructs between a written Torah and the word of Yahweh, where the acceptance of the one amounts to a rejection of the other. How is this opposition to be understood? This is one of those great questions of biblical scholarship that will always remain open, and for this very reason it provides a rich field for speculation. It is worth our reflection because, from a hermeneutical standpoint, we can learn a good deal about the nature of canonization from the topics which this question opens up.

Scholars continue to quarrel over what text Jeremiah could have been thinking of in this passage—was it canonical or was it some forgery? The general opinion is that the reference is nothing less than to Deuteronomy itself. For example, about forty years ago the distinguished Jeremiah scholar, J. Philip Hyatt, argued that "Jeremiah, in 8:8–9, 13, expressed opposition to the claim that the Torah of Yahweh is contained in some written book or books, including the original edition of Deuteronomy, and that he considered it false because it did not agree with the 'word of Yahweh' given to the prophets."[12] Jeremiah, Hyatt added, "opposed the claim of the priests that Torah was their special prerogative, and he opposed the activity of the *sôf^erîm* ["scribes"] and the *tôf^esê hat-tôrāh* ["handlers or holders of Torah"]. He also denied that true Torah was contained in some written book, probably including Deuteronomy." Indeed, what we need to understand, according to Hyatt, is that "the concept of Torah was not a very important one in Jeremiah's thinking" (pp. 394, 395).

This view of the opposition between prophetic word and written Torah can be correlated in fruitful ways with Max Weber's famous distinction between charismatic and institutional authority. On the basis of this distinction, one can see in the biblical period (one can never be sure how truly) a necessary and inevitable conflict between the Hebrew prophets and the priestly class, with its ties to the monarchy, its Temple in Jerusalem, its teaching role, and its command of the scribes and the written Torah that possesses the authority of law. Charismatic authority, Weber says, is highly individualistic and ad hoc; that is, "it is sharply opposed to rational, and particularly bureaucratic, authority, and to traditional authority, whether in its patriarchal, patrimonial, or estate variants, all of which are everyday forms of domination."[13] The relation of the classical prophets to Moses, the first prophet, is on this model a relationship of equivalence rather than of descent—or very nearly so: the figure of Moses is unique in the biblical period because he is represented as a charismatic or prophetic lawgiver or *aisymnete*.[14] His relationship to Yahweh is direct, personal, and thus prophetic, but at the same time it is Moses who establishes the covenant, who promulgates the law, and who founds the institutions by which the law and the covenant are handed down. Thus the Deuteronomic scribes, when they write, do not do so as authors; that is, they do not compose in their own name but only in the name of Moses. Their authority is Mosaic or traditional rather than authorial and is institutional rather than charismatic or prophetic—and the same is true of the priests of the

Temple, especially the priests of the postexilic period or the theocracy of the Second Temple, who are represented as descendents from Aaron, the brother of Moses, and the one who handled religious, legal, and political affairs. If you ask, Who speaks for Yahweh? the Deuteronomic and priestly answer is that the Torah of Moses, the "Priestly Torah," contains the message of Yahweh to his people.

By contrast, the authority of men like Elijah, Isaiah, and Jeremiah is equal to the unmediated authority of Moses. If you ask, Who speaks for Yahweh? the answer here is that Yahweh speaks directly through his prophets, which is to say that the prophets do not themselves speak (they do not speak in their own names or in the name of Moses), but rather the message of Yahweh speaks itself through them. He speaks, moreover, in ways that are entirely unpredictable and which no one can control, neither king nor priest nor, indeed, the prophet himself, who characteristically finds himself (as in Jer. 20:9) speaking the prophetic word against his own will and his own best interests. The most important point, however, is that the prophetic word is always addressed to the situation in which it is uttered, that is, to the moment at hand; it is not a traditional idea, intended as part of a permanent record. It does not bind the future but only addresses the present, which it frequently judges from the standpoint of the future. The prophetic word has something unwritable about it.

The nineteenth-century biblical scholar Julius Wellhausen, who emphasized the opposition of priest and prophet in an uncompromising way, characterized prophecy as follows: "The element in which the prophets live is the storm of the world's history, which sweeps away human institutions; in which the rubbish of past generations with the houses built on it begins to shake, and that foundation alone remains firm, which needs no support but itself. . . . They do not preach on set texts; they speak out of the spirit which judges all things and itself is judged of no man. Where do they ever lean on any other authority than the truth of what they say; where do they rest on any other foundation than their own certainty?"[15] It is this nineteenth-century Romantic and antinomian theory of prophecy which underlies Weber's distinction between charismatic and institutional authority. On this model, the authority of the prophet derives exclusively from Yahweh and is inaugurated in the prophetic call, as when God cleanses the lips of Isaiah with a burning coal (see Isa. 6:6–7). Such authority is completely outside the jurisdiction of monarchy, Temple, and Torah. The prophet is bound by nothing but the necessity of speaking. The question is, What can the canonization of a written Torah mean in the context of biblical prophecy understood in this way? How, for example, are we to read the canonization story in 2 Kings (and other, similar stories in the Scriptures) if we entertain the hypothesis of a fundamental opposition between Hebrew prophets and those who produced and canonized the sacred texts? And, most important, what are we to make of the production and canonization of texts like the Book of Jeremiah? What happens to the prophetic word when it is turned into a scriptural and, eventually, a canonical text? Let me try to work out some answers to these questions.

It is important to emphasize that, in contrast to Wellhausen's time, the inclination of modern biblical scholars, especially those working from a theological base, has been to qualify or underplay (and sometimes to argue strongly against) any conflict between priestly class and prophetic oracle. This is partly due to an assumption, widely held, that, in spite of the heterogeneous and frequently contradictory character of the biblical texts, these texts are to be read from the standpoint of a unified religious outlook. The strongest advocate of this principle of harmony, at least in the context of Jeremiah versus Deuteronomy, has been H. H. Rowley,[16] but the most recent persuasive voice would be Weinfeld's. Weinfeld confronts the crux of Jer. 8:8–9 directly and without blinking: "Jeremiah fully identified himself with the religious ideology of the book of Deuteronomy and also appears to have supported the Josianic reforms (Jer. 11:1–8). . . . The prophet in our verse [Jer. 8:8–9] is not denouncing the book of Deuteronomy but condemning the [scribes] for not observing the teaching that they themselves had committed to writing: the pen of the scribes has made (i.e., composed) to no purpose, the scribes have written in vain" (p. 160).

And it is true that Jeremiah rails principally against the Judah and Jerusalem of Jehoiakim, son of Josiah and a backslider into pre-Deuteronomic idolatry. There is a wonderful story in Jer. 36:1–3, in which God commands Jeremiah, now well into his prophetic career, to " 'Take thee a roll of a book, and write therein all the words that I have spoken unto thee against Israel, and against Judah, and against all the nations, from the day I spoke unto thee, from the days of Josiah, even unto this day.' " Jeremiah summons Baruch, a scribe, and dictates "all the words of the Lord, which He had spoken unto him." Baruch then takes the book to Jerusalem and reads it aloud in the Temple—to the alarm of the princes of Jehoiakim, who urge Baruch and Jeremiah to go into hiding. The princes then read the book to Jehoiakim:

> And Jehudi read it in the ears of the king, and in the ears of all the princes that stood beside the king. Now the king was sitting in the winter-house in the ninth month; and the brazier was burning before him. And it came to pass, when Jehudi had read three or four columns, that he cut it with the penknife, and cast it into the fire that was in the brazier, until all the roll was consumed in the fire that was in the brazier. Yet they were not afraid, nor rent their garments, neither the king, nor any of his servants that heard these words. Moreover Elnathan and Delaiah and Gemariah had entreated the king not to burn the roll; but he would not hear them. And the king commanded Jerahmeel the king's son, and Seraiah the son

of Azriel, and Shelemiah the son of Abdeel, to take Baruch the scribe and Jeremiah the prophet; but the Lord hid them. [Jer. 36:21–26]

This is another canonization story, with its own variation on the theme of power; but what is interesting is that there are no priests mentioned in the story, and the scribes are on the side of Jeremiah (and Yahweh) against the idolatrous Jehoiakim. Jehoiakim does not rend his garments when he hears what is said in the book; he refuses to be bound by the text—even as he refuses to be bound by the Deuteronomic Torah and the reforms of his father. But Yahweh brushes Jehoiakim aside and commands Jeremiah to produce another prophetic text: "Then took Jeremiah another roll, and gave it to Baruch the scribe, the son of Neriah; who wrote therein from the mouth of Jeremiah all the words of the book which Jehoiakim king of Judah had burned in the fire; and there were added besides unto them many like words" (Jer. 36:32)—the second version, in other words, is an amplification of the first!

This story of the production of a Jeremianic Torah needs to be read in conjunction with Jer. 11:1–5, which Weinfeld cites in support of the view of Jeremiah's allegiance to Deuteronomy:

The word that came to Jeremiah from the Lord, saying: "Hear ye the words of this covenant, and speak unto the men of Judah, and to the inhabitants of Jerusalem; and say thou unto them: Thus saith the Lord, the God of Israel: Cursed be the man that heareth not the words of this covenant, which I commanded your fathers in the day that I brought them forth out of the land of Egypt, out of the iron furnace, saying: Hearken to My voice, and do them, according to all which I command you; so shall ye be My people, and I will be your God; that I may establish the oath which I swore unto your fathers, to give them a land flowing with milk and honey, as at this day." Then answered I [Jeremiah], and said: "Amen, O Lord."

This passage expresses the central motif of Deuteronomic covenant theology, together with the allegiance to Torah and nationhood that such a motif presupposes. There is no conflict in this passage between prophetic word and written text; on the contrary, the prophetic word (like the word of Huldah in 2 Kings) clearly underwrites the authority of Deuteronomy and the covenant tradition.

From the standpoint of a Romantic theory of prophecy, however, we are compelled to ask, Who produced this passage? Here we must remind ourselves that little or nothing in the Scriptures is an authored text. What we have in Jer. 11:1–5 appears to be the result of an unseen Deuteronomic hand, writing as if in Jeremiah's name but secretly on behalf of covenant, law, and priesthood. This was, for example, Hyatt's view: "The Book of Jeremiah as we now have it, however, has received expansion and redaction at the hands of 'Deuteronomic' editors, whose purpose in part was to claim for Deuteronomy the sanction of the great prophet."[17] Thoughts naturally fly to Baruch the scribe: Was he a Deuteronomist or a disciple of the prophet—or perhaps someone friendly to both sides?[18]

Deuteronomic recension of Jeremianic material is generally acknowledged by scholars, but it is hard to reach a final opinion as to how this recension is to be understood. Childs explains that the Book of Jeremiah is the product of three sources or traditions: an original poetic tradition made up of sayings or oracles handed down by the prophet's disciples; a secondary prose tradition containing sermons and stories about Jeremiah, including the one about Baruch and the making of a prophetic text; and a Deuteronomic redaction investing this prophetic material with a priestly understanding.

Childs, for his part, stresses the hermeneutical nature of this redaction. "From a historical critical perspective," he says, "the authentic poetic tradition of Jeremiah was transformed by cloaking the prophet's message in the later, prose language of the Deuteronomic tradition. From the perspective of the tradition, a new understanding of Jeremiah emerged from the events of history, which, far from being a distortion, confirmed the prior word of Scripture. The canonical shaping of the Jeremianic tradition accepted the Deuteronomic framework as an authentic interpretation of Jeremiah's ministry which it used to frame the earlier poetic material" (p. 346). From the purely analytical standpoint of literary criticism, with its concern for authorship and authenticity, the Book of Jeremiah is a doctored text. But from a hermeneutical standpoint this doctoring was an attempt of the Deuteronomists to make sense of the prophetic message in order to understand and account for their own situation, particularly after the failure of the Josianic reforms under Jehoiakim and, subsequently, the destruction of Jerusalem and the exile in Babylon. Similarly, Ernest Nicholson has argued that the reshaping of the "Jeremianic prose tradition" by the Deuteronomists was an attempt not only to interpret Jeremiah within the context of national catastrophe but also to apply Jeremiah's message as a way of understanding this catastrophe. The Book of Jeremiah, as we now have it, reflects the understanding of Jeremiah by the exiles in Babylon.[19]

The hermeneutical principle at work here is, in fact, very ancient,[20] but it has recently been given a modern formulation in Hans-Georg Gadamer's conception of the "fusion of horizons" that goes on in any understanding of a text that comes down from the past. Childs calls it the principle of " 'actualization' " (*Vergegenwärtigung*) or the "process by which an ancient historical text . . . derives chiefly from a need to 'update' an original tradition." The whole canonical process by which the Scriptures reached their final form is governed by this principle of actualization. For Childs "it is constitutive of the canon to seek to transmit the tradition in such a way as to prevent its being moored in the past. Actualization derives from a hermeneutical concern which was present during the different stages of the book's canonization. It is built into the structure of the text itself, and reveals an enormous richness of theological interpretation by which to render the text religiously accessible" (p. 79). As a redacted rather than an authored text, the Scriptures are structurally oriented away from an original intention toward the manifold possibilities of future understanding. They possess the openness to future interpretation that is characteristic of, for example, a good law. Thus, according to this argument, what we have in the Book of Jeremiah as a canonical text is not what Jeremiah said in his own historical moment but the way his words were received and understood by those who heard them in circumstances radically different from those in which Jeremiah originally spoke. The Book of Jeremiah as a canonical text is a fusion of prophetic and Deuteronomic horizons.

However, let me now give an equally compelling but considerably less benevolent version of this hermeneutical view of the canonical process. The thesis here is that canonization is the priestly appropriation of prophetic authority by means of the superior forces of writing and textuality; or, in other words, writing was a way of getting rid of prophecy. This had been Wellhausen's thesis in the nineteenth century. He wrote: "With the appearance of the law came to an end the old [prophetic] freedom, not only in the sphere of worship, now restricted to Jerusalem, but in the sphere of the religious spirit as well. There was now in existence an authority as objective as could be [namely, the Priestly Torah]; and this was the death of prophecy."[21]

In a valuable but neglected book, *Prophecy and Canon*, Joseph Blenkinsopp has made a bold attempt to rehabilitate Wellhausen's thesis (relieving it, meanwhile, of some of its Romantic melodrama). Blenkinsopp follows the canonical arguments of Childs, but he does so explicitly within the context of Weber's analysis of the structural incompatibility of prophetic oracle and written Torah. Blenkinsopp's view is that Jeremiah would not necessarily have opposed the *message* of a written Torah; or, more accurately, there is no reason to suppose that Jeremiah would not have supported the Mosaic covenant as this was understood in Deuteronomic theology and in the Josianic reforms—the difficulty is that we really don't have the evidence to answer this question one way or the other. What we can say is that prophecy and priesthood are intrinsic to Israel's Yahwist traditions, but they are political as well as religious phenomena, and on political grounds it is easy to see how it would have been in the interest of a prophet like Jeremiah to oppose the institution of a written Torah as the canonical form of the Yahwist tradition. The crux of Jer. 8:8—

How do ye say: "We are wise,
And the Law [Torah] of the Lord is with us"?

Lo, certainly in vain hath wrought
The vain pen of the scribes.

—does not demand a choice between written law and prophetic word; rather, according to Blenkinsopp, Jeremiah's attack is aimed "at a misplaced confidence arising out of possession of a law written down, edited and authoritatively interpreted. This confidence, he is saying, blinds the official political and religious leadership, including priests, scribes and stipended prophets [like Huldah], to what is actually taking place or, to put it more prophetically, to what God is doing in the world."[22] A written text is an agent of fixity and rule; it sets boundaries and establishes precedents that can only constrict the improvisation that characterizes Hebrew prophecy. Jeremiah's basic insight, in fact, is that writing is a force superior to prophecy in establishing a claim to Yahwistic authority; in Blenkinsopp's words, "writing is the way of making a claim stick," in contrast to the prophetic word, which has to reassert its claim again and again on every occasion of its utterance (p. 38).

Thus it would not be the content or meaning of a written Torah that Jeremiah would attack; rather it would be the Deuteronomic "claim to final and exclusive authority *by means of writing*" (pp. 38–39). Jeremiah's problem is political rather than theological. He knows that writing is more powerful than prophecy and that he will not be able to withstand it—and he knows that the Deuteronomists know no less. As Blenkinsopp says, "Deuteronomy produced a situation in which prophecy could not continue to exist without undergoing profound transformations" (p. 39)— that is, without ceasing to be "free prophecy," or prophecy unbound by any text, *including its own*. "It might be considered misleading or flippant to say that for [Deuteronomy], as for rabbinic orthodoxy, the only good prophet is a dead prophet. But in point of fact the Deuteronomic scribes, despite their evident debt to and respect for the prophets, contributed decisively to the eclipse of the kind of historically oriented prophecy *(Geschichtsprophetie)* represented by Jeremiah and the emergence in due course of quite different forms of scribal prophecy" (pp. 38–39; see also pp. 119–20).

It is at this point that we reach a sort of outer limit of biblical criticism—a threshold that scholars, with their foundations in literary criticism, their analytical attitude toward texts, and their theological concerns, are not inclined to cross. In any case, it is no accident that the political meaning of the conflict of prophecy and canon has received its most serious attention not from a biblical scholar but from a radical historian, Ellis Rivkin. In *The Shaping of Jewish History*, a brilliant and tendentious book, Rivkin proposes to treat the question of canon-formation and the promulgation of canonical texts of the Scriptures, not according to *literary* criteria but according to *power* criteria. For Rivkin, the production of the Hebrew Scriptures "was not primarily the work of scribes, scholars, or editors who sought out neglected traditions about wilderness experience, but of a class struggling to gain power."[23]

Rivkin's "power hypothesis" is squarely in the Wellhausen-Weber tradition: the theological unity of ancient Yahwism that the Scriptures exhibit conceals a politically unstable situation in which there was not one but several versions of Yahwism. "There was the Yahwism of the tribal phase; the Yahwism of the wilderness phase; the Yahwism of the premonarchical agricultural and urban phase; the Yahwism of cult and priesthood; and the Yahwism of the new [that is, the post-Mosaic or classical] prophecy" (pp. 16–17). For Rivkin, the canonization of Deuteronomy in 621 B.C.E. was an attempt by the Jerusalem coalition of Court and Temple to resolve the crisis of authority that the heterogeneous character of Yahwism entailed. In particular, the institution of an authorized version of Yahwism centered in Jerusalem meant that, above everything else, prophetic power has to be brought under control. "So long as prophets had the freedom to speak out in Yahweh's name," Rivkin says, "no institution was safe, and no authority, other than prophecy, sacrosanct" (p. 20). Deuteronomy, in other words, was promulgated as an official countertext to prophecy. It was not only a political and religious constitution enshrining the monarchy and Temple priesthood, with its scribes and oracles; it also proclaimed unambiguously that true charismatic prophecy began and ended with Moses. Deuteronomy concludes dramatically with the statement, inscribed with the force of law, that "there hath not arisen a prophet since in Israel like unto Moses, whom the Lord knew face to face" (Deut. 34:10). As Rivkin says, "Prophetic authority, though recognized [by Deuteronomy], was curbed. It was not permitted to challenge the Mosaic laws, or the legitimacy of the priesthood or the monarchy. The authenticity of a prophet was now to be measured against the Book of Deuteronomy. In case of conflict, the book would prevail" (p. 18).

And prevail it did, but not in its Deuteronomic form. The backsliding of Jehoiakim, Nebuchadnezzar's conquest of Judah, the destruction of Jerusalem and the Temple, and the subsequent exile exploded the Deuteronomic program. "Prophets such as Jeremiah and Ezekiel refused to give up their prophetic freedom," Rivkin says. "They continued to exercise their prophetic prerogative as though Deuteronomy had never been promulgated" (p. 19). Nevertheless, the years of exile were evidently a period of furious scribal activity. We know virtually nothing about this period, but we know that when it came to an end with the return to Jerusalem and the restoration of the Temple (anywhere from the middle of the fifth century to the beginning of the fourth), there, suddenly, stood a monumental Torah: the Pentateuch. For Rivkin, the appearance of the Pentateuch is decisive. The monarchy is no more, nor are there any prophets. "Before the canonization of the Pentateuch, even as late as the time of Nehemiah's visit to Judea about 445 B.C., prophecy is still alive. And then, in the fourth century, there is the Pentateuch and prophecy has evaporated." Never again is there an Elijah, Isaiah, Jeremiah, or Ezekiel. "Exercising authority in [their] stead is a priestly class of Aaronides, unknown to Moses, unmentioned in Deuteronomy, unheard of by Ezekiel, and outside the ken of even so late a prophet as Malachi" (p. 23). The Aaronides are priests of the Second Temple and the founders of the theocracy which resolved the crisis of Yahwism once and for all by centering Yahwism in a book. "The Aaronides succeeded," Rivkin says, "where Deuteronomy had failed. They saw Yahwism threatened unless they wielded absolute authority. They therefore designed the Pentateuch to attain this end, arrogating to themselves not only altar rights but also control over the process of expiation from sin. They broke prophetic authority by having Moses invest Aaron and his sons with the priesthood forever" (p. 31).

The great legendary figure in this political drama is Ezra, priest and ruler, who embodies the characters of prophet and scribe and is sometimes called the Second Moses, since it was he whom God commanded to rewrite the Torah after it had been lost in a fire. The story of the rewriting of the Torah is preserved in a very late text, 2 Esdras, which does not exist in a Hebrew version and so is placed among the apocrypha, where, however, "apocrypha" refers not to bogus texts and discredited stories but (among other things) to writings set aside for private study—learned rather than liturgical texts. In 2 Esdras, Ezra is represented as a prophetic figure, but he is plainly an aisymnetic rather than charismatic figure: a prophet in the manner of Moses or, more accurately perhaps, a scribal prophet of the sort described by Blenkinsopp. Here is part of the account of Ezra's call:

> "Ezra [God says], open your mouth, and drink what I give you to drink."
> And I opened my mouth, and, behold, a full cup was offered me. It was full of what looked like water, but the color of it was like fire. And I took it, and drank, and when I had drunk it my heart gushed forth understanding, and wisdom grew in my breast, for my spirit retained its memory, and my mouth opened and was no longer closed. Moreover, the Most High gave understanding to the five men [Ezra's scribes], and they wrote what was said, one after another, in letters that they did not know. [2 Esd. 14:40–48][24]

Ninety-four books are composed in only forty days of dictation, at which point God instructs Ezra to "publish the twenty-four books that you wrote first, for the worthy and the unworthy to hear, but keep the seventy books that were written last to hand down to the wise men among your people, for in them is the source of understanding, the spring of wisdom, and the stream of knowledge" (2 Esd. 14:45–48). This is important for the way it implies the existence of a double canon, one public and one hidden, one for all the people to hear and one for the wise or for those who can understand what is written.

Who were these people of understanding? In later years they are easily indentified as the sages or *sofᵉrîm* described by Ben Sira in the epigraph to this paper, ancestors of the great rabbinical scholars of the Diaspora, who were able to maintain Judaism as a living tradition in defiance of every conceivable worldly catastrophe. In Ezra's time, however, they are not sages but priests. The last canonization story told by the Hebrew Scriptures is in Nehemiah, in which Ezra promulgates his Second Torah, doing so, we should notice, on the Deuteronomic model of 2 Kings:

> And Ezra the priest brought the Law [Torah] before the congregation, both men and women, and all that could hear with understanding. . . . And he read therein before the broad place that was before the water gate from early morning until midday, in the presence of the men and the women, and of those that could understand; and the ears of all the people were attentive unto the book of the Law. And Ezra the scribe stood upon a pulpit of wood, which they had made for the purpose; and beside him stood Mattithiah, and Shema, and Anaiah, and Uriah, and Hilkiah. [Neh. 8:2–4]

Hilkiah! The name is an allegory of priestly power. He is listed along with those who stood beside Ezra as he read and who walked among the people, "[causing] the people to understand the Law." One senses that the occasion would be incomplete, and the status of the Torah less than certain, without him.

The lesson of Hilkiah is that canon is not a literary category but a category of power; or, in Blenkinsopp's words, "what we call 'canon' is intelligible only in the context of conflicting claims to control the redemptive media and, in particular, to mediate and interpret authoritatively the common tradition" (p. 96). One can see how the canonization of Books of the Prophets would naturally follow the promulgation of the Pentateuch, since the process of turning prophecy into a text would only be complete when fugitive texts become bound to the Torah as an integral part of its canonical domain. Henceforward, when the prophet speaks, it will only be to disclose a written Torah. Let me conclude by quoting my favorite canonization story, which is part of the account of Ezekiel's call to prophetic utterance:

> "And thou, son of man, hear what I say unto thee: be not thou rebellious like that rebellious house; open thy mouth, and eat that which I give thee." And when I looked, behold, a hand was put forth unto me; and, lo, a roll of a book was therein; and He spread it before me, and it was written within and without; and there was written therein lamentations, and moaning, and woe.

And He said unto me: "Son of man, eat that which thou findest; eat this roll, and go, speak unto the house of Israel." So I opened my mouth, and He caused me to eat that roll. And He said unto me: "Son of man, cause thy belly to eat, and fill thy bowels with this roll that I give thee." Then did I eat it; and it was in my mouth as honey for sweetness. [Ezek. 2:8–3:3]

The whole fate of prophecy is contained in this figure of Ezekiel eating the scroll: one could not assert the power and authority of written texts more dramatically than this.

1. P. R. Ackroyd, "The Old Testament in the Making," in *The Cambridge History of the Bible*, 3 vols. (Cambridge, 1963–70), vol. 1, *From the Beginnings to Jerome*, ed. Ackroyd and C. F. Evans (1970), p. 112.

2. Brevard S. Childs, *Introduction to the Old Testament as Scripture* (Philadelphia, 1979), p. 78; all further references to this work will be included in the text.

3. There is an excellent account of early rabbinic textual scholarship by J. Weingreen, *From Bible to Mishna: The Continuity of Tradition* (Manchester, 1976), pp. 1–33. I have discussed the fixing of the biblical texts in *Inventions: Writing, Textuality, and Understanding in Literary History* (New Haven, Conn., 1982), pp. 25–38.

4. See J. R. Roberts, "The Textual Transmission of the Old Testament," in *Tradition and Interpretation: Essays by Members of the Society for Old Testament Study*, ed. G. W. Anderson (Oxford, 1979), pp. 1–30.

5. See M. H. Segal, "The Promulgation of the Authoritative Text of the Hebrew Bible," *Journal of Biblical Literature* 72 (1953): 35–47, rpt. in *The Canon and Masorah of the Hebrew Bible*, ed. Sid Z. Leiman (New York, 1974), pp. 285–97. See esp. p. 289: "We have conclusive evidence, both internal and external, that for a long time in the age of the sopherim the text was in a fluid condition, and that scribes were not tied to a standard model text."

6. E.g., see Albert C. Sundberg, Jr., *The Old Testament of the Early Church*, Harvard Theological Studies, no. 20 (Cambridge, Mass., 1964), and Childs, *Introduction to the Old Testament as Scripture*, pp. 57–62.

7. See Barnabas Lindars, S.S.F., "Torah in Deuteronomy," in *Words and Meanings: Essays Presented to David Winton Thomas*, ed. Ackroyd and Lindars (Cambridge, 1968), pp. 117–36.

8. I have used the Jewish Publication Society of America translation of the Hebrew Bible (Philadelphia, 1917); all further scriptural references, unless otherwise indicated, will be to this edition and included in the text.

9. Nineteenth-century biblical scholars (Christian Friedrich Illgen, Hermann Hupfield, Karl Heinrich Graf, Julius Wellhausen) arrived at the view that the Pentateuch was a composite of various sources: J and E, after the two versions of the Genesis story, one of which identifies God as Yahweh (or Jahweh), the other as Elohim. Deuteronomy (D) is a third source, and the Priestly Code (P) is the fourth. The theory of the J, E, D, and P composite is known as the Graf-Wellhausen thesis. Almost no one agrees with this thesis nowadays, since the evidence for it is so thin and confused, but no one has ever come up with a compelling alternative, whence the thesis, in spite of itself, continues to reign.

10. See Ackroyd, "The Open Canon," *Colloquium: The Australian and New Zealand Theological Review* 3 (Autumn 1970): 279–91.

11. Moshe Weinfeld, *Deuteronomy and the Deuteronomic School* (Oxford, 1972), p. 168 and n. 3; all further references to this work will be included in the text. Weinfeld's discussion of "The Scribes and the 'Book of the Torah' " is the best on the subject.

12. J. Philip Hyatt, "Torah in the Book of Jeremiah," *Journal of Biblical Literature* 60 (1941): 384; all further references to this work will be included in the text.

13. Max Weber, *Economy and Society: An Outline of Interpretive Sociology*, ed. Guenther Roth and Claus Wittich, trans. Ephraim Fischoff et al., 2 vols. (Berkeley and Los Angeles, 1978), 1:244.

14. Weber's sociological analysis of prophecy appears to have little authority among biblical scholars—the major exception of Joseph Blenkinsopp is cited below—but it is indispensable for an understanding of the relationship between prophecy and Scripture from the hermeneutical standpoint of the theme of power. See *Economy and Society*, 1:439–51; see also pp. 457–63 for Weber's discussion of canonization. For example, Weber says: "Most, though not all, canonical sacred collections became officially closed against secular or religiously undesirable additions as a consequence of a struggle between various competing groups and prophecies for the control of the community" (pp. 458–59). It is this idea of canon as a category of power that I am arguing for in this paper.

15. Wellhausen, *Prolegomena to the History of Israel* (1878), trans. J. Sutherland Black and Allan Menzies (Edinburgh, n.d.), p. 398.

16. See particularly H. H. Rowley, "The Prophet Jeremiah and the Book of Deuteronomy," *From Moses to Qumran: Studies in the Old Testament* (New York, 1963), pp. 187–208, and "The Early Prophecies of Jeremiah in their Setting," *Men of God: Studies in Old Testament History and Prophecy* (London, 1963), pp. 133–68.

17. Hyatt, "Jeremiah and Deuteronomy," *Journal of Near Eastern Studies* 1 (1942): 158.

18. See James Muilenburg, "Baruch the Scribe," in *Proclamation and Presence: Old Testament Essays in Honour of Gwynne Henton Davies*, ed. John I. Durham and J. R. Porter (Richmond, Va., 1970), pp. 215–38. See esp. p. 237: "It has been our contention that the so-called 'Deuteronomic additions' by no means represent a separate source, but conform to conventional scribal composition and are therefore to be assigned to Baruch."

19. See E. W. Nicholson, *Preaching to the Exiles: A Study of the Prose Tradition in the Book of Jeremiah* (Oxford, 1970), esp. p. 92, and Robert P. Carroll, *From Chaos to Covenant: Prophecy in the Book of Jeremiah* (New York, 1981), esp. pp. 158–97.

20. See G. Vermes, "Bible and Midrash: Early Old Testament Exegesis," in *From the Beginnings to Jerome*, pp. 199–231, esp. pp. 225–31, in which Vermes discusses "fulfillment-interpretation," where received texts are interpreted as referring to the events in which interpretation occurs. In the Qumran scrolls the term for this sort of interpretation is *pēšĕr*. The Christian interpretation of the Old Testament as a book of prophecies concerning Christ is a species of *pēšĕr* or fulfillment-interpretation. A very valuable book in this context is Carroll, *When Prophecy Failed: Cognitive Dissonance in the Prophetic Traditions of the Old Testament* (New York, 1979), esp. pp. 111–28.

21. Wellhausen, *Prolegomena to the History of Israel*, p. 402.

22. Blenkinsopp, *Prophecy and Canon: A Contribution to the Study of Jewish Origins* (Notre Dame, Ind., 1977), p. 38; all further references to this work will be included in the text.

23. Ellis Rivkin, *The Shaping of Jewish History: A Radical New Interpretation* (New York, 1971), p. 30; all further references to this work will be included in the text.

24. The Complete Bible: An American Translation; the Old Testament, trans. J. M. Powis Smith and scholars; the Apocrypha and the New Testament, trans. Edgar J. Goodspeed (Chicago, 1939).

Aristotle's Sister: A Poetics of Abandonment

Lawrence Lipking

The silence of Shakespeare's sister, described so vividly by Virginia Woolf, has left a vast black hole in the canon of poets. But what words can express the silence of Aristotle's sister? To begin with, we cannot be sure that she ever existed. A few of the ancient accounts do mention a name, Arimneste; and scraps of tradition suggest that she may have helped raise her brother. Yet he never refers to her except as "Nicanor's mother," and the rest of the record is bare.[1] No word of her own survives, of course. No word survives from any classic female literary theorist. Indeed, compared with Arimneste, Judith Shakespeare and her kind seem quite talkative. A few literary women—Gaspara Stampa, Louise Labé, the Countess of Pembroke—did manage to achieve some limited recognition in Shakespeare's sister's time; and anyone seriously concerned with literature ought to know that the first author whose name and works have been preserved was a woman, that a woman wrote the greatest and most influential Japanese classic, and that the Greeks themselves acknowledged a woman as their best lyric poet. Nor can even the most incorrigible misogynist keep Emily Dickinson and Anna Akhmatova out of the anthologies. Yet the standard, large-scale anthology of *Critical Theory since Plato* does not find room for a single woman in its 1,249 double-columned small-printed pages.[2] Unlike Shakespeare's sister, Aristotle's sister has yet to break her silence.

In one respect the exclusion of women from literary theory has been still more extreme than it appears. Most great literature has taken at least occasional notice, after all, of women and their concerns. Shakespeare speaks for his sister by lending her the voices of Rosalind, Cleopatra,

Cordelia, and Lucrece. It would have been better had she spoken for herself; yet even these male-begotten images can still provide women with mirrors (however warped) in which to study their features. But no one speaks for Aristotle's sister. The classic line of literary theory has hardly acknowledged the existence of two sexes, let alone the possibility that women might read and interpret literature in some way of their own. From Aristotle to Northrop Frye, women are assumed to be a subspecies of men. If Arimneste read the *Poetics*, for instance, her one chance for self-recognition would have come in chapter 15, with the description of good and appropriate characters. "Even a woman or a slave may be 'good,' though no doubt a woman is an inferior being and a slave beneath consideration. . . . A character may be brave, but it is not appropriate for a woman to be brave or clever." So much for brotherly love! Yet most poetics are not contemptuous but oblivious of women. The mainstream of theory glides over sexual issues without a ripple. It cannot be an accident that the two most sustained attempts to place women at the center of literature, Samuel Butler's *Authoress of the Odyssey* and Robert Graves' *White Goddess*, are both regarded as irredeemably crackpot.

In another respect the silence of Arimneste might be considered a rare piece of good fortune—at least for her later sisters. No dead hand of tradition grips feminist literary theory. Its time is the present. During the past decade more and better criticism has been written by women than in all previous history. And much of that criticism fairly gleams, from a distance, with promise and daring. The canon itself cannot be immune from this change of air, this revolutionary wind blowing from resisting readers and madwomen unchained and Great Mothers and loaded guns. Like Lady Lazarus, Arimneste rises from her ashes. Surely some new poetics is at hand.[3]

Close up, the situation does not look quite so promising. Despite the brilliant achievements of feminist literary criticism and feminist literary history, few women as yet have cracked the admittedly mandarin but highly prestigious bastions of literary theory. A classic woman's poetics

---

Lawrence Lipking is Chester D. Tripp Professor of Humanities at Northwestern University and director of the program in comparative literature and theory. He is the author of *The Ordering of the Arts in Eighteenth-Century England* and *The Life of the Poet*, which won the Christian Gauss Award of Phi Beta Kappa in 1982. The present essay was originally given as a lecture at the School of Criticism and Theory in the summer of 1982. It is part of a book, *Abandoned Women and Poetic Tradition*, which is to appear in 1984.

has yet to be written. Many reasons have been offered to explain this, and some of them—for instance, male prejudice or the native good sense of women—undoubtedly deserve a hearing.[4] But another reason seems still more plausible to me: the very lack of tradition that provides the opportunity. The best female literary theorists have grown up in the same schools of thought as men, and often they stand in the forefront of the most advanced critical cohorts. There are excellent female neo-Marxists, female semiologists, female Lacanians, female deconstructionists, female readers responding, antithetical females; and already some female post-post-structuralists have been glimpsed on the horizon. Nor do such women leave out of account—as might have been charged against an earlier generation—their own special position as women. Indeed, much of the liveliest current theory explicitly sets out to show how women fit in:[5] to show that, despite Marx's own sexism, the alienated labor of women constitutes the prime example of class struggle in history; that phallus is not a masculine noun; that women respond to different signs than men; that the mischievous free play of deconstruction exactly parallels the skepticism of every woman toward schemes of domination. I sympathize with such efforts. Yet I often hear in them a note of desperation.

They are desperate, I think, because they know no mothers. No school exists of neo-Arimnesteans, of neo-Diotimists. Thus female literary theorists tend to define themselves by giving the lie to daddy, reacting against his power. Certainly they ask very leading questions: What am I to think of this work as a Marxist and a woman? But Marx precedes woman. The boundaries of male-created, male-elaborated theories may be stretched to accommodate the challenges of women, but no amount of stretching will put women at the center. At best the process leaves a space of her own to the daughter-disciple-rebel. And no established literary theory has yet been devised that builds from the ground up on women's own experience of literature, on women's own ways of thinking.[6] Even the most revolutionary feminist thought, it seems to me, has tended to ground its theory of revolution on masculine modes. In the absence of mothers, a father must raise the right issues. Yet historically men have shown no interest at all in a woman's poetics. There must be some better way.

That way exists, I believe. It has been carved out across the centuries by thousands of women, in the innumerable acts of response and commentary on which every poetics depends. For the absence of formal theory does not mean that women have never thought hard about literature. It only means that we must search for the evidence and use some imagination in putting it together. The outline of a woman's poetics is traced in poems and novels and plays, in essays and pamphlets and letters and diaries, and even in records of conversation. The line goes back to Ur (where Enheduanna, history's first poet, left her mark). From this point of view, the problem appears less Arimneste's failure to talk than our failure to listen. The documents where women's ideas about literature are already inscribed have only recently been opened for inspection, and much more digging remains to be done.[7] Yet the fragments do cohere. A patient look at history reveals some consistent patterns in literary criticism by women, as well as some significant differences from the theories of men. As other voices join with Arimneste's, she begins to make herself understood. It is time to sketch her poetics.

I can think of many reasons not to undertake this project. First, I do not know enough. Second, I am a man. Third, the construction of a woman's poetics rests on conjectures and presumptions, not on the hard rock of documentation. Fourth, its distinction between the sexes, not only biologically but ideologically, will inevitably serve to perpetuate sexual stereotypes. Fifth, the notion of *a* woman's poetics suggests an agreement or uniformity among women that cannot stand the test of history.[8] Finally, the attempt to locate such a poetics throughout historical time, not solely in the present, falsely assumes that somehow I can escape my own historical moment and speak for the past.

Like most reasons for not writing something, all these seem plausible to me. Aristotle's sister has not authorized me to speak for her. Doubtless many women would know more and do better. And certainly any man who purports to tell women what they think ought to be aware how offensive he may sound. Other theorists might reach different conclusions from the same evidence; nor would I deny the risk of projecting my own assumptions and stereotypes into the silence of the past. But I do plead innocent to the charge of supposing that a poetics like this one can stand apart from its time. Ten years ago this project would have been inconceivable (at least for me). Indeed, it is precisely the current atmosphere of scholarship and thought, especially by women, that makes it possible to imagine the minds of women in other ages. That past depends on this present; at no earlier moment, in more than two thousand years, has anyone been interested in Aristotle's sister. But I am interested now. A well-grounded woman's poetics remains to be written. It is in the hope of contributing to those who have kindled this interest, and who will write that poetics, that I offer this sketch.

* * *

In the beginning was an aborted word. The first example of a woman's literary criticism in Western tradition, or more accurately the first miscarriage of a woman's criticism, occurs early in the *Odyssey*. High in her room above the hall of suitors, Penelope can hear a famous minstrel sing that most painful of stories, the Greek homecoming from Troy—significantly, the matter of the *Odyssey* itself. That is no song for a woman. She comes down the stairs to protest.

> "Phêmios, other spells you know, high deeds
> of gods and heroes, as the poets tell them;

> let these men hear some other, while they sit
> silent and drink their wine. But sing no more
> this bitter tale that wears my heart away.
> It opens in me again the wound of longing
> for one incomparable, ever in my mind—
> his fame all Hellas knows, and midland Argos."

It seems a reasonable request. But her words meet an immediate brutal rebuff from an unexpected source: her own son Telemachus.

> "Mother, why do you grudge our own dear minstrel
> joy of song, wherever his thought may lead?
> Poets are not to blame, but Zeus who gives
> what fate he pleases to adventurous men.
> Here is no reason for reproof: to sing
> the news of the Danaans! Men like best
> a song that rings like morning on the ear.
> But you must nerve yourself and try to listen.
> Odysseus was not the only one at Troy
> never to know the day of his homecoming.
> Others, how many others, lost their lives!"[9]

Men like to hear the news; women must learn not to take songs so personally! And Penelope gives in. Marveling at the wisdom of her son, she goes back to her room and cries herself to sleep.

Telemachus' words do not seem very much to the point. Penelope had not asked Phêmios to stop singing, after all, or to sing something fit for women; she only asked him to choose some other adventure. And to reproach her for not considering that others besides Odysseus had failed to come home seems irrelevant as well as cruel. The fact that others feel pain is hardly a reason for her not to feel it. Penelope cannot bear even to name her husband, but Telemachus seems to take pleasure in saying "Odysseus." By proclaiming his own indifference to pain, he argues just like a man. And that, of course, is the point. The scene has been contrived exactly to show his new maturity. He proves himself no longer a boy in the time-honored fashion, by rejecting any tenderness of heart and by putting down a woman. Henceforth he will be equal to the suitors.

In the manuscripts of the *Odyssey*, Telemachus' scolding of his mother concludes with four strong lines, suppressed by Aristarchus and omitted from the Fitzgerald translation. These lines are identical, except for a single word, with two other well-known Homeric passages: the speech in which Hector tells Andromache to return to her spindle, since the business of war and the *Iliad* is for men; and the later moment of the *Odyssey* in which Telemachus himself will tell Penelope that archery is man's affair, not woman's.[10] But the single word makes a difference.

"Go back within the house and see to your daily duties,
your loom, your distaff, and the ordering of your servants;
for speech is man's matter, and mine above all others,
for it is I who am master here."[11]

The crucial word is *mythos,* speech or discourse; and what Telemachus chides his mother for is thinking that she has a right to take part in the conversation—especially literary conversation.[12] Like warfare or drawing a bow, *mythos* is barred to women.

This passage has exerted an irresistible attraction for male commentators. A short history of misogyny could be strung together from interpretations like those of the twelfth-century scholiast Eustachius. "Women are not forbidden entirely to speak, for women are talking animals, they have the faculty of talking, and indeed are rational creatures; but they must not give too much liberty to that unruly member, in the company of men. Sophocles advises well, 'O woman, silence is the ornament of thy sex' "; and the Pope-Fenton *Odyssey,* which quotes this wise counsel, cannot resist adding that "Madam *Dacier,* tho' she plunders almost every thing, has spared this observation."[13] The snide reference to Dacier is singularly pointed, since she had made her reputation as the first distinguished female critic in the history of Europe precisely by defending Homer's judgment against all his enemies. When her hero himself betrays her, the male critic hints, she can respond only by maintaining a most uncharacteristic silence. Many later female critics have been scarred by the same brand of masculine logic: a woman proves herself worthy of the faculty of speech through her prudence in never exercising it.

Not all women have been so prudent. Indeed, the first important work of literary criticism to defend the integrity of a woman's point of view begins specifically with the Homeric put-down. Mme de Staël was no Penelope. In *Literature Considered in Its Relation to Social Institutions* (1800), she traces a theory of literature that takes the silence of Greek women as its founding, original fact.

> Shameless prostitutes, slaves degraded by their fate, women secluded in their homes and unknown to the rest of the world, strangers to the concerns of their husbands, reared to have neither ideas nor feelings—this is all the Greeks knew of the ties of love. Even sons hardly respected their mothers. Telemachus orders Penelope to be silent and she leaves imbued with admiration for his wisdom. . . . Sorrow, tender and lasting grief, was not in their nature; it is in the hearts of women that enduring memories dwell. I shall often have the occasion to note the changes wrought in literature since the time women began to share the intellectual and emotional life of men.[14]

De Staël demands her right to *mythos.* Directly contradicting Telemachus' doctrine, she argues that the exclusion of women from poetry fatally impairs the quality of its news. The health of literature depends on keeping the conversation open, making room for those ideas and emotions that women know best. Thus even the *Odyssey* itself defines its hero through his relations with women. If Penelope did not preserve the memory of Odysseus in her heart, he would remain forever a stranger, and the epic would lose its pathos. The woman must have her share— not simply for the sake of justice but for the sake of everything that will be missing from the story when Penelope does not speak.

The argument continues to the present. In the second volume of *A History of Modern Criticism,* the most authoritative modern discussion of de Staël as a critic, René Wellek returns to the same passage and the same emphasis on conversation. "Details in Madame de Staël's literary history are often vague, wrong, or simply absent. Her discussion of Greek literature is almost grotesque. . . . The main offense of the Greeks is the low status granted to women: Telemachus ordering Penelope to be silent must have conjured the vision of some man giving the same order to Madame de Staël."[15] Almost inevitably, it seems, the male critic comes round to Telemachus' manner of argument: women take literature too *personally.* The vision that caps the last sentence is entirely Wellek's invention. It is as if any judgment by a woman needs to be assigned some self-regarding motive to make it intelligible. New Critics consider themselves immune from such motives. They, of course, are objective; and so were the Greeks. Yet on reflection it seems far from clear that de Staël would have been unjustified in associating herself with Penelope, just as Dacier might have seen another Telemachus in Pope, or a current female critic in Wellek himself. Being deprived of *mythos* is not to be taken lightly. The command to be silent prevails over all others, in literary conversation, by shutting off the means of participation or appeal. Silence is not negotiable. And how else can a woman estimate what is missing in literature, after all, than by measuring it against what she herself has not been allowed to say?

A woman's poetics must begin, that is to say, with a fact that few male theorists have ever had to confront: the possibility of never having been empowered to speak. The right to *mythos* is the first law of literary creation; not even God could have created light without a word. And women have not been able to forget that law. Aristotle's sister could hardly have been unaware that he considered her inferior on exactly Eustachius' grounds, as in the *Politics:* "All classes must be deemed to have their special attributes; as the poet says of women, 'Silence is a woman's glory,' but this is not equally the glory of man."[16] If Arimneste knew Sophocles' *Ajax,* she might have replied that the phrase (already an old saw) comes from the mouth of a crazed and violent man resisting his wife's efforts to calm him; to borrow the Homeric formula, vainglory and bloodlust are not the business of women. Yet men do not listen to reason when speech comes into question. Though Dante may have recommended the use of the vernacular in order to permit women as well as men to hear him, he becomes most uneasy when he reads in Genesis that "a woman, that is, the most presumptuous Eve, is found to have spoken before all others." The text needs correction. "But although in Scripture woman is found to have spoken first, it is nevertheless more reasonable for us to believe that man spoke first; for it is against what is fitting to think that such a noble act of the human race did not flow from the lips of man before woman."[17] The moral could not be plainer: man was created to talk, and woman to listen.

A woman who reads and writes, therefore, implicitly challenges silence.[18] The oppositions that inform so much traditional theory, the distinctions between the fictive and the real, literary and nonliterary language, poetry and prose, grammar and rhetoric, or even the signifier and the signified, tend to yield in women's theory to a prior distinction: the spoken and unspoken word. Sappho herself might have been kept from writing; nor did the greatness of her poems protect them from being burned. All works of literature exist against a ground of nonexistence. And women know this truth not through a chain of reasoning or metaphysics but as an urgent pressure on the brain. Before Woolf can address any other question about the great age of English literature, she must face the "perennial puzzle why no woman wrote a word" of it.[19] Most theorists consider such questions beneath them, but that is where her theory starts. More than four thousand years earlier, when another great woman writer complained of her banishment from Ur, the image she used was the blurring of light by a sandstorm, her mouth choked with dust.[20] Historically most women have lived in that storm. Hence female critics, even when aggressive and confident, rarely escape a certain dryness in the back of the mouth. The privilege of writing cannot be taken for granted; a woman who turns the pages of the canon can hardly fail to perceive how much of her is not there.

She also tends to look for what *is* there. The charge made by Telemachus and Wellek and almost every male critic between them, that women react to literature by thinking about themselves, is sustained not only by prejudice but by massive evidence from the writings of women. When Samuel Richardson's female correspondents implored him to spare Clarissa's life, they clearly felt their own lives were at stake. A literary theory based on such evidence cannot pretend to be impersonal. Most criticism that has made a difference to women, in our own time and others', has gained its ground precisely by identifying with the problems of literary women and taking them personally. Thus Kate Millett opens *Sexual Politics* by imagining herself one of those women trapped in the novels of Henry Miller, Norman Mailer, and Jean Genet; Ellen Moers reconceives Frankenstein's filthy creation as a woman delivering a stillborn child; and Sandra Gilbert and Susan Gubar gaze at the mad and outcast heroines of the nineteenth century as if into a mirror.[21] The boundaries between truth and fiction or between reader, author, and character tend to blur in such readings. Women, male critics like to say, consistently fail to maintain "aesthetic distance."

An ingenious example both of the charge and of a proper rebuttal occurs in the famous discussion of fiction in part 3 of *The Tale of Genji*. Visiting his "foster daughter" Tamakazura (whom he is both protecting and trying to seduce), Genji finds her immersed in old romances, where she searches for some parallel to her own situation. " 'What a nuisance this all is,' he said one day. 'Women seem to have been born to be cheerfully deceived. They know perfectly well that in all these old stories there is scarcely a shred of truth, and yet they are captured and made sport of by the whole range of trivialities and go on scribbling them down, quite unaware that in these warm rains their hair is all dank and knotted. . . . I think that these yarns must come from people much practiced in lying.' " But Tamakazura comes back with a smart reply: " 'I can see that that would be the view of someone much given to lying himself. For my part, I am convinced of their truthfulness.' "[22] Her response to Genji's remarks, like her reading of the romances, applies them in the most personal way. The truth of fictions lies in the eye of the beholder: a seducer will naturally think them seductive, but an honest spirit can trust whatever they tell her. Women certainly have less to fear from romances than from men. And Genji, himself the creature both of romance and woman, laughs and good-naturedly concedes the point. Romances *are* true, he admits, both because they record the intimate details of life that slip through chronicles and because they present parables of good and evil, telling the reader how to live. Domestic truth deserves as much attention as the fate of princes.

Beneath the surface of the argument another subtle drama is enacted. When Genji rallies Tamakazura for being so absorbed by her romances, he clearly wants to redirect her interest to himself. A shining hero cannot bear a rival for the woman's mind and heart. Even in a situation where the man seems absolute master, he feels the threat of allowing her an inner life to which he has no access. Hence Genji's apparent curiosity about what Tamakazura is reading covers a brazen ulterior motive: he wants to insinuate himself into her dreams. " 'But tell me: is there in any of your old stories a proper, upright fool like myself?' He came closer. 'I doubt that even among the most unworldly of your heroines there is one who manages to be as distant and unnoticing as you are. Suppose the two of us set down our story and give the world a really interesting one.' " And lest the reader mistake the intent of such "literary criticism," Lady Murasaki prefaces it with a crisp, revealing sentence: "He now seemed bent on establishing the uses of fiction."[23]

If men use fiction for such worldly designs, however, women may use it precisely to claim a part of themselves that does not belong to the world. What Genji and Tamakazura contest is less her virginity than her self-consciousness. He tries to make her aware of her surroundings and appearance, of how she looks while she reads—her dank and knotted hair. She tries to preserve a private realm where he cannot follow, to lose herself in the unworldliness of romances. Where else can she hide? The growth of those long prose fictions intended specifically for women, in medieval Japan as well as modern Europe, seems directly related to the need of women for a private space and time: a sanctuary where the person can be forgotten and the self remembered. The reader as well as the author requires a room of her own.

A literary theory true to women's experience, therefore, is likely to view "aesthetic distance" as a sham, a denial of women's rights to literature. A reader absorbed by a text finds her own identity there, and a man who tells her to stand back probably does so because he is after her place. When women come into question, male critics quickly expose the personal bias of their own judgments. Thus Wellek, like Telemachus and Genji before him, descends to personal remarks in order to accuse a woman of reading too personally—the argument *ad feminam*. From this point of view, it is men themselves who are responsible for the self-absorption of female readers, since men never allow women to forget their sex. Consider the outcome of Penelope's complaint. Curiously enough, she does get her way—not because anyone pays attention to her argument but because of her sex appeal. The sight of her inflames the suitors so much that they fall to quarreling about which one will sleep with her first. Hence they drown out the minstrel and stop the song; Penelope has her wish. But sex has done the work of reason. Many debates between male and female critics seem to have the same structure: a logic that masks the real issues of power and desire. Small wonder, then, that so few women are willing to put their trust in any theory that neglects the importance of persons and sexes.

The exclusion of Penelope herself from the argument, however, may point another moral: works of literature depend on the audience to which they are addressed, and women cannot assume themselves to be part of that audience. If a woman's literary theory cannot take the right to *mythos* for granted and cannot ignore the relation of literature to private life, neither can it leave matters of *community* out of account. Male critics often seem to regard the history of poetry as a sequence of heroic individuals, each of them sustained only by himself. And feminist critics have been tempted by the same mythology, emphasizing the ability of a few extraordinary women to rise above their place and time. But most women have always known better. Great poets go to school. They learn from their teachers, their parents, their peers; they catch the infection of poetry from those around them. Whatever the nature of Sappho's community of women—and scholars continue to disagree about it—her poems themselves record a society that cares about love and poetry and performance, that values intelligent women and saves their art. Not many later female authors have been so well supported. Hence the genius of

Sappho can stir utopian longings, a vision of women in congress together, mutually sustaining and indifferent to any bonds but those of sisterhood. Certainly women require some sort of community. And a woman's poetics, more than a man's, must pay attention to the way that poets and readers have been schooled.[24]

Consider, for instance, the kind of poetics that might have been conceived by Aristotle's sister. We shall assume that Arimneste had her share of *mythos*—that is, that she could read and write and was occasionally permitted to think and argue, at least in private. We shall also assume that, like other women, she had learned to take poetry personally, defining her identity in part by what she found there. These seem like modest assumptions (though not many ancient women, we should remember, actually did read and write). Yet even so, the conditions for a poetics are far from satisfied. For we still do not know how much literature Arimneste was acquainted with or how well she had absorbed what Werner Jaeger calls *paideia:* the unity of culture and education which, according to Greek thought, literature embodied. The *paideia* of Aristotle's *Poetics* is not in question. Much of its power derives from its easy familiarity with epic and tragic tradition, and still more from its sense of shared understandings and ethical verities. The truth of *mimesis* can hardly be doubted by an audience that agrees about the nature of the thing imitated. Indeed, since the epics of Homer and the great tragedies had taught that audience the nature of things in the first place, through Greek education, it is not surprising that Greek men found their masterpieces the image of truth itself.

Greek women may have been different.[25] To begin with, they may not have been able to view those great works of art. Whether women were admitted to tragic festivals or recitals of epics remains a vexed question. In any case, few such works seem to include women among their *implied* audience. Aristotle's lectures certainly do not. Thus de Staël was not far wrong when she accused Greek writers of catering almost entirely to masculine attitudes (with the exception of Euripides).[26] We have already seen that Aristotle himself tends to regard women as a lower species. Hence Arimneste would have had no reason to recognize herself or the truth that she knew in the *Iliad* or the *Oedipus*, even if she were allowed to see them. I do not imply that she must have been a rebel; only that she would have been most unlikely to belong to her brother's consensus. The ideal of the *polis* that still attracts so many scholars to the Greeks, an ideal enforced by the arts and by the public gatherings where men participated in communal rites, holds much less attraction for women. A woman's poetics must find its community elsewhere.

Indeed, for many women literature itself has served in place of a community—not as an occasion to affirm the general voice of the state or the will of the gods but as an interlude in which private feelings are shared. The women of Fez who gather around the well to sing together about what is on their minds—"I see a man who is dull / and boring like no one else"—the women of Lesbos who prepare the bride for her evening's ordeal—"O Hesperus, you bring all things together"—the women of the Papago who sit at the bedside of the dying and teach them the songs of the dead—"In the great night my heart will go out, / Toward me the darkness comes rattling. / In the great night my heart will go out"—all help to instruct each other about what it means to be a woman.[27] There is nothing official about such songs. They have seldom been designed for publication, and often they sound best in intimate circumstances, as a mother croons to her child. Even to eavesdrop upon them may seem to violate a confidence. *Anon* was a woman, as scholars have lately been reminding us, and much of the best literature by women has come to us draped in a veil. Yet Arimneste's poetics, unlike her brother's, would have had to listen carefully to *Anon*. From her she might have learned how much of poetry escapes official forms and public rituals, and so gained access to that secret society united not by myths of culture but by common experience and common suffering. A woman's poetics will be attuned to voices that it cannot name, so close to inner voices that at times they may sound like one's own.

The literary history of women suggests the plausibility of a view that joins writers and readers together in an anonymous community.[28] Until the last few centuries, not many female authors achieved great names. Once again Woolf can be helpful by calling attention to the social conventions (especially the equation of chastity with obscurity) that kept women under a cloud. "Currer Bell, George Eliot, George Sand, all the victims of inner strife as their writings prove, sought ineffectively to veil themselves by using the name of a man. . . . Anonymity runs in their blood. The desire to be veiled still possesses them."[29] From this perspective, the invention of the printing press and the resulting opportunities for pseudonymity and secret reading constitute a crucial stage in the emancipation of literate women. An author can hide in print. Moreover, the thirstiness of presses for readers, and the becoming modesty in which women can read behind closed doors, gradually allowed a vast audience of women to discover the pleasures of literature and to demand the satisfaction of their desires. Such communities never meet in public; and even publication, for writers like Jane Austen, may have to take place under a veil. Yet no one can deny that Austen's readers make up a society—invisible, unknown to each other, but tied with threads of steel.

Despite Woolf's justified resentment of the convention that "publicity in women is detestable," none knew better than she the costs of masculine privilege or the uses of anonymity.[30] Eventually her hatred of the raw ego, its hunger for publicity and greatness, may have cost her her life. But a more positive view of the situation of women might emphasize the advantages of cutting texts free from names. Anonymous writers and anonymous readers can share their secret lives without fear of exposure. Historically, men have tended to use this cloak of namelessness for pornography; women, for expressing their real feelings. More recently, the fashionable critical skepticism about "works" and "authors," the insistence that all of us are swimming in a boundless sea of textuality or polysemous bliss, has suggested that all writing might be returned to its primal anonymous state, to be made use of as we will. But more than one moral can be drawn from such notions. Though many men have viewed the "sea of textuality" as fostering a radical independence, allowing every text a protean or pornographic shape to feed the reader's desire, some women have viewed it instead as promising a free sharing of meanings and interests, a place for meeting the world without defenses.[31] To be at home in that sea would mean putting aside the fear of life without a name. More practically, it would mean reading texts not as performances but as silent conversations or webs of relationship to which each reader might bring her own confidences. The attempt to build a literary theory on principles of "affiliation" rather than "authority" seems to me one of the most promising avenues of recent feminist criticism;[32] and it also reflects the way that women have usually read.

The first major female critic, in fact, consciously built her own program from relations and affiliations that go beyond author and text. Others before de Staël had studied the "rapport" of literature with social institutions, but none had tried so ambitiously to associate the grand sweep of history with the intimate experiences of every reader—history as it affects the individual mind. The project was of course too large to be carried out convincingly. Most literary historians would agree with Wellek about the shallowness of her historicism, the narrowness of her knowledge and taste: "abstract declamation about virtue, glory, liberty, and happiness, fuzzy and pompous and so empty of concrete content that it is difficult to summarize."[33] Yet the project also has an originality that is all the more significant because it has yet to be carried out. What de Staël aimed at was nothing less than an alternative literary canon, adequate to the needs of women as well as men, that would define civilization not in terms of power, refinement, or national pride but as the communion of sensitive and enlightened beings—beings, needless to say, much like herself. This is the great idea that unifies her work. It is a commonplace to contrast her sanguine faith in the virtues of enlightenment with her fervent and morbid sensibility (a reproach that has also been leveled at her heroine Corinne). As Wellek says, her "emotionalist theory is combined, rather incongruously, with a belief in perfectibility, a frantic faith in progress, which clashes oddly with her taste for melancholy and her admiration for Ossian."[34] But de Staël herself saw no such conflict. The perfectibility of the human species, she believed, culminates at its best in a sensitive soul. When men and women are free at last to be themselves, they will still be tied together by love and death.

The central place of literature in this idea of progress is sketched by a brief chapter on the connection of literature with *happiness*. A universal selfishness, de Staël argues, now bars the sort of happiness that a sensitive person might find in an act of good will: "Public opinion itself would condemn it, for it censures those who seek to escape the circle of selfishness everyone wants to preserve as his inviolable asylum." In this desperate situation, only writings filled with sensibility can protect the reader from a cold and uncompassionate loneliness.

> Such writings can draw tears from people in any situation; they elevate the soul to more general contemplation, which diverts the mind from personal pain; they create for us a community, a relationship, with the writers of the past and those still living, with men who share our love for literature. . . . and by feeling similar emotions I enter into some sort of communion with those whose fate I so deeply grieve. [*MS*, p. 151]

What sort of writings does de Staël have in mind? Her earlier "Essay on Fiction" proposes a modern canon: the *Letters of a Portuguese Nun, Eloisa to Abelard, Clarissa, The Sorrows of Werther*, and above all *The New Heloise*. "Such works of fiction are in a class by themselves" (*MS*, p. 265). They link all feeling people together in a human chain; they dissolve the distinctions among eras and social classes, among authors, readers, and fictional characters, and persuade the loneliest outcast that she is not alone. And they also appeal especially to women. As the social order and the sense of interdependence crumble, in modern times, the literature of sensibility takes their place.

Whatever one thinks of de Staël's taste in fiction (as many readers have noticed, the author of *Delphine, Corinne,* and *Sappho* has a weakness for the lugubrious and a blind spot for the comic), her theory retains its interest.[35] A literary critic who took it seriously would begin to evaluate works on different principles, according to their success in creating affiliations or communion. As well as placing literature in the context of its society, such a critic might examine the society within the work, observing not only the ties among characters but the modes of relation between writer and reader. Thus a Staëlian or Arimnestean analysis of the *Oedipus* might focus less on the suspenseful working out of its plot or the tragic flaw of its hero than on the initial predicament: the man who rules the city is a stranger. Oedipus knows that he is not at home in Thebes or the world, and all his relations with other people—his superiority to the Thebans, his "children," his suspicion and resentment of Teiresias and Creon, his curious lack of intimacy with Jocasta—only confirm his loneliness and exile. Unlike the audience at a theater, swept away by the action, the solitary reader communes with that loneliness. Hence the play no longer appears an infernal machine of kinship rules or scapegoating but a sorrow in which we are invited to participate. The true community is not the one that casts the hero out but that which shares his strangeness.

My description has left out of account, however, the point that de Staël herself thought most important: the tragic concern with suffering and death. Indeed, she goes so far as to condemn the Greeks for mitigating the fear of death, as well as underestimating the violent passions of love. "Greek tragedies were, therefore, I believe, very much inferior to our own modern tragedies, because dramatic ability consists not only of the art of poetry but also of a profound knowledge of the emotions; and in this respect tragedy has had to keep up with the progress of the human mind" (*MS*, p. 161). Evidently Sophocles would have profited from familiarity with de Staël's own *Treatise on the Influence of the Passions on the Happiness of Individuals and Nations* (1796). There he would have learned something not to be found in Aristotle: the superior sophistication of women in matters of feeling. Nor can such matters be omitted from a woman's poetics. When analyzing literature, de Staël and other women traditionally look for not only affiliation but passion.[36] The theory that supports them might be called a poetics of abandonment.

Already in her first book, the *Letters on Rousseau*, the future de Staël had stated her theme: literature depends on passion, especially the passion of love, and love is known best through its torments. If women could only express what they feel, "this sublime sorrow, that melancholy grief, those all-powerful sentiments which enable them to live or die, would perhaps produce more deep emotions in the heart of the reader than all the transports to which the exalted imaginations of poets and lovers give birth."[37] The theme may sound like mere adolescent yearning or support for the cliché that men think and women feel; but later writings lend it more substance. The *Treatise on the Passions* sketches the progress of love. Despite its ability to take one temporarily outside oneself, de Staël argues, in the end love always leads to melancholy. There are two main reasons for this. First, the obsession with the loved one completely separates the lover from the rest of the world, leaving her "solitary and concentered." By making women indifferent to society or the ordinary decencies of life, love breaks those rules on which tranquillity and strength depend; a woman in love is "abandoned." Second, she will inevitably be abandoned in deadly earnest. Since the intensity of woman's love surpasses man's, and indeed may even become a source of fear and disgust to him, the plot has a predictable outcome: he leaves, she stays and pines. "Alone in secret, our whole being is changed from life to death." The rest of her life may well be spent mourning or re-creating the scene of her desertion. "How bitterly must a woman regret that she has ever loved."[38] The secret story of the greatest passions—the love almost unknown to men—is always abandonment.

Abandonment may also be the secret of literature. The writings most admired by de Staël, we have seen, invariably present an archetype of solitary abandoned pain, an Eloisa or Portuguese Nun. The sensitive reader recognizes herself in such figures, and so does the sensitive author. Our sympathy for a Werther may become so intense as to tempt us to suicide.[39] And de Staël knows the risks. In one respect the *Treatise on the*

Passions might be considered a continuation of *The Anatomy of Melancholy* or Johnson's *Rambler*, warning readers against the sway of the passions and the dangers of solitude. "The meditations of the *impassioned* man beget monsters" (clearly the Terror is in de Staël's mind).[40] Nor can she ignore the relations between melancholy and writing itself. If an author writes in order to disperse her phantoms and establish "communion" with other minds, the act of composition requires solitude and the imaginative recollection of past ecstasies and pains. The lunatic, the lover, and the poet all fear abandonment.

Hence the most moving literature, on de Staël's analysis, not only gives us images of absence and loneliness but is itself their product. Poetry is a companion that makes the reader feel more alone. Doubling its solitude, she becomes a secret sharer. "Grief can only be assuaged by the power of weeping over our destiny, and of taking that interest in what concerns ourselves, so as to divide us in some sort into two separate beings, the one of whom commiserates the other."[41] Thus the hunger for literary affiliations, the search for an absent friend, finally throws the reader back on herself. The sense of abandonment that poetry consoles, it also confirms. The separation of author, character, and reader, like their communion, is an emblem of that love that women pursue forever, even at the cost of being forever disappointed.

Not every woman will agree with de Staël's formulation. But most women's literary theories, as well as women's preferences in literature, have placed a similar strong emphasis on love and its discontents.[42] Much of this must surely be attributed to the historical oppression of women, forbidden any interests that do not circle around some man and, therefore, doomed to have some man betray them. Yet a considerable amount of evidence suggests that female concern with abandonment has deep psychological roots. While masculine fantasies and myths compulsively reenact the rise and fall of Phaethon, his premature ambition and precipitate plunge (according to Robert May), the dreams of women shape themselves after Demeter—the sundering, the long delay, eventual reunion, "all that pain."[43] Recently psychologists have begun to suggest that women's development is characterized by "separation anxiety," a fear of being parted from others that is the female counterpart to the male fear of intimacy in Freud's Oedipus complex.[44] (A more extreme version of this theory would claim that separation anxiety dominates men as well, as emblemized by the fact that all Oedipus' problems stem from his original abandonment by his parents.) The need to stay close to others, the difficulty of sustaining and perpetuating the frail ties of affection, preoccupy women from infancy. Hence female growth, on this analysis, necessitates the complex bargain of Demeter and Persephone: a balance between the worlds of relationship and separation.

The truth of this theory is certainly open to question. Yet it does help to account for the internal tensions of much of the literature that has meant most to women across the centuries. From Enheduanna to the Three Marias, from Penelope and the *Heroides* through patient Griselda to Jean Rhys, women have tended to see themselves in heroines who suffer loss before they find their way. These models are often repulsive. To modern eyes, the way that masochism becomes Griselda as she colludes in her own victimization may seem to prove the virtue of impatience— or rage, or revenge. Such rage has been put to use in current fiction, which offers more active models of how to resent being hurt. Hence abandonment has gone out of style (though not, of course, in popular forms like soap operas and drugstore romances). Good riddance, we might say: "Well now that's done: and I'm glad it's over." Yet the aversion to images of female suffering should not blot out their role in making women strong. Much of the finest poetry has followed de Staël's prescription: abandonment steels the soul. Thus each of Sappho's two great surviving odes records her separation from a lover, her pain, and perhaps her endurance. Those poems speak for many women. When the lover has gone, survival demands that a woman learn how to endure. "From that arid sadness which we feel when abandoned and forlorn, . . . we are rescued in some measure by those writings."[45] De Staël was not alone in seeking that restoration. Women have sought it from writing throughout the ages; and it ought to appear again in a woman's poetics.

It is time for Arimneste to try definitions. "Tragedy," she reads over her brother's shoulder, "is the imitation of an action. . . ." But something in that phrase does not sound right, and she goes off by herself to think again. Though history has abandoned her, I shall take the liberty of giving her some company: Sappho, Lady Murasaki, Christine de Pisan, Louise Labé, Saint Theresa, Lady Mary Wortley Montagu, Mme de Staël, Margaret Fuller, Marina Tsvetayeva, Virginia Woolf, Simone de Beauvoir—and perhaps the Authoress of the *Odyssey*, the White Goddess, and the Wife of Bath. These women are necessary to Arimneste, for they know something that she has yet to learn—her silence can be broken— and thus can instruct her in the prior tragedy that consists not of acting and mirroring but of doing and saying nothing, or of looking in the mirror and finding no face there. Now she begins her poetics. "Poetry," she writes, "is the expression of a life, personal, incomplete, and proportioned to the self; employing whatever language and conventions one has been allowed to acquire; presented in fragments; and achieving, through sharing the emotions of loneliness and abandonment, a momentary sense of not being alone." She pauses and waits for examples. Eventually the murmur of women's voices—whispers at first, and then a many-languaged chorus—swells and inhabits the room. Her page begins to fill.

What use is this woman's poetics? It cannot compete, of course, with the brother's tradition. Nature and Aristotle are the same, as Pope and Northrop Frye remind us, not because the *Poetics* captured the whole truth about literature but because it established those critical conventions whose adaptations and transformations are identical with the history of theory itself, at least in the West. Nor can the poetics of Aristotle's sister conceivably satisfy all women. Insofar as it accurately represents the strategies of female authors within and against the dominant culture, it stands for a history of subordination and reaction that many women oppose more strenuously than they do the patriarchs themselves. The poetics I have tried to sketch remains within history, if only as a voice of dissent, and those who are trying to awake from that history may be forgiven for remembering Arimneste as one more bad dream. Yet her theory does have its uses. First of all, it reminds us not to confuse the relative silence of women, across the centuries, with a lack of intelligent convictions. Minds can exist without names. Moreover, the thought of a woman's poetics can help to create that sense of community that so many women have looked for and have not found. The history of poetry contains many sisters, in reading as well as in writing. Arimneste has always existed. Imagining her modes of perception, we put women back into time.

A woman's poetics can also repair the balance of theory itself. One use of this way of thinking is that it reveals how much literary theory serves exclusively masculine interests. "Man" and "human" are not synonymous, and a poetics that takes sexual differences seriously will raise some questions that men have preferred to ignore. When Aristotle located "the origin of the art of poetry" in man's "natural" pleasure in imitation and harmony, for instance, to what extent did his analysis presuppose a way of being at home in the world to which most women feel foreign? Abandoned women know that the world can shift too fast to be imitated, that the harmony of art is made to be broken. Hence their poetics obeys another law of nature, the unsatisfied craving of children who cry to be held. That law has its own coherence. A theory based on it will begin not with means and objects and manners of imitation but with the needs that men and women share. Most women who have devoted themselves to literature, at least since de Staël, have stressed needs rather than forms. The project deserves more attention. Women do not have exclusive rights, of course, to a poetics of need, but women do bring one advantage to questions of theory: unlike men, they have never been able to identify the laws of literature with their own forms.

Nor have they been able to count on being heard. Denial of *mythos* has sensitized many women to the privilege that sustains masculine theories even at their most revisionary or ironic: the privilege of being *important*. Literary theories acquire their importance, as everyone knows, by establishing some relation (whether of continuity or confutation) with Plato, Aristotle, Saint Augustine, Descartes, Rousseau, Hegel, Marx, Nietzsche, Freud, or about a dozen other great names—all of them male. And the important fields of theory are metaphysics, epistemology, and the philosophy of language—in none of which any woman has ever become famous. Perhaps it is not surprising, then, that so many women insist on the priority of another set of questions about literature and literary studies: Who is allowed to write and why? Why is it that certain theorists are endlessly quoted, discussed, and imitated, while others of seemingly equivalent merit are hardly ever mentioned? On what principles are critics published by the best presses and journals, assigned to reading lists, reviewed, invited to teach at schools of criticism and theory? These are very annoying questions, but they need to be asked. Indeed, the silence of most theorists about such issues of publicity and career comes close to being the dirty little secret of current theory. A woman's poetics is likely to take them to heart. If Penelope and Arimneste do not claim that their problems are as important as those of Telemachus and Aristotle, they do have the right to inquire about the grounds of importance itself.

The final use of a woman's poetics, however, may bear less on theory than practice: it gives us new ways of reading. Already the surge of interest in women's studies has recovered a hoard of neglected texts from *Anon* to *The Awakening,* and theory adapts to those texts by developing principles that will do them justice. Arimneste rethinks the canon. Rereading literary history through her eyes, we begin to revise the anthologies and to discover that Shakespeare had more sisters than even Woolf knew. Yet the function of a woman's poetics is not limited to the light it sheds on works by women. It also revises our view of the masculine canon. Something peculiar has been happening lately to the classics. Some of them now seem less heroic, and some of them less funny.[46] Those "irrelevant" scenes of cruelty to women, those obsessions with chastity and purity, those all-male debates about the nature and future of the human race, those sacrifices of feeling to duty have changed their character. Some old masters even look silly. Under the gaze of women, strong writers turn pale. Hence the concern often voiced about theory in our time, that all its sophisticated speculations and deconstructions leave the canon firmly in place—"An agony of flame that cannot singe a sleeve"—falls away from a woman's poetics. Its flames can scorch and burn, refining some authors and wasting others forever. Not even our secret places— our language, our habits of reading—can be immune from that fire. Arimneste is learning to speak; it is our turn to listen. Perhaps she has started now. I know that she has not finished.

1. The phrase occurs in Aristotle's will, preserved by Diogenes Laertius. For a summary of facts and hypotheses about Arimneste, see Anton-Hermann Choust, *Aristotle,* 2 vols. (London, 1973), 1:76–79.

2. See *Critical Theory since Plato,* ed. Hazard Adams (New York, 1971). Adams assures me that any future edition of this anthology will contain at least one woman.

3. See Elaine Showalter, "Feminist Criticism in the Wilderness," *Critical Inquiry* 8 (Winter 1981): 179–205, for a useful survey of the recent past and possible future of feminist poetics.

4. See Sniader Lanser and Evelyn Torton Beck, "[Why] Are There No Great Women Critics? And What Difference Does It Make?," in *The Prism of Sex: Essays in the Sociology of Knowledge*, ed. Beck and Julia A. Sherman (Madison, Wis., 1979), pp. 79–91.

5. See, for instance, two recent collections: *New French Feminisms: An Anthology*, ed. Elaine Marks and Isabelle de Courtivron (Amherst, Mass., 1979), and *The Representation of Women in Fiction*, ed. Carolyn G. Heilbrun and Margaret R. Higonnet (Baltimore and London, 1983).

6. The effort to remedy this situation has been the starting point for much of the most influential criticism by women, such as Patricia Ann Meyer Spacks, *The Female Imagination* (New York, 1975).

7. The Modern Language Association has recently sponsored a survey, *Women in Print I: Opportunities for Women's Studies Research in Language and Literature*, ed. Joan E. Hartman and Ellen Messer-Davidow (New York, 1982).

8. The case for a more eclectic view of feminist theory has been made by Annette Kolodny, "Dancing through the Minefield: Some Observations on the Theory, Practice, and Politics of a Feminist Literary Criticism," *Feminist Studies* 6 (Spring 1980): 1–25.

9. Homer, *Odyssey*, trans. Robert Fitzgerald (Garden City, N.Y., 1961), pp. 23–24 (1. 337–55).

10. See *Iliad* 6. 490–93, and *Odyssey* 21. 350–53.

11. Samuel Butler's translation, *The Authoress of the Odyssey* (1897; Chicago, 1967), p. 20.

12. Heilbrun comments on Penelope's position as an "outsider" in *Reinventing Womanhood* (New York, 1979), pp. 40–41.

13. Alexander Pope, *The Odyssey of Homer*, 2 vols. (London and New Haven, Conn., 1967), 1:54 n.

14. Mme de Staël, *Madame de Staël on Politics, Literature, and National Character*, trans. Morroe Berger (Garden City, N.Y., 1964), pp. 157–58; all further references to this work, abbreviated *MS*, will be included in the text.

15. René Wellek, *A History of Modern Criticism: 1750–1950*, 4 vols. (New Haven, Conn., 1955), 2:221, 222.

16. Aristotle *Politics* 1. 13. Susan Groag Bell has gathered Aristotle's remarks on women in *Women: From the Greeks to the French Revolution* (Stanford, Calif., 1980), pp. 17–21.

17. Dante Alighieri, *Literary Criticism of Dante Alighieri*, trans. Robert S. Haller (Lincoln, Nebr., 1973), p. 6.

18. Tillie Olsen's *Silences* (New York, 1978) is a powerful indictment of the forces that keep women from writing.

19. Virginia Woolf, *A Room of One's Own* (New York, 1965), p. 71.

20. See Enheduanna, *The Exaltation of Inanna*, ed. and trans. William W. Hallo and J. J. A. van Dijk (New Haven, Conn. and London, 1968), p. 25.

21. See Kate Millett, *Sexual Politics* (Garden City, N.Y., 1970); Ellen Moers, *Literary Women* (Garden City, N.Y., 1976), pp. 90–99; and Sandra M. Gilbert and Susan Gubar, *The Madwoman in the Attic: The Woman Writer and the Nineteenth-Century Literary Imagination* (New Haven, Conn., and London, 1979).

22. Murasaki Shikibu, *The Tale of Genji*, trans. Edward G. Seidensticker (New York, 1978), p. 437.

23. Ibid., p. 438.

24. Catharine R. Stimpson discusses the special problems that women have faced in developing a sense of community in "Ad/d Feminam: Women, Literature, and Society," in *Literature and Society*, ed. Edward W. Said, Selected Papers from the English Institute, 1978, n.s. 3 (Baltimore, 1980), pp. 174–92.

25. On the situation of women in antiquity, see Sarah B. Pomeroy, *Goddesses, Whores, Wives, and Slaves: Women in Classical Antiquity* (New York, 1975). Translations of sources

are provided by Mary R. Lefkowitz and Maureen B. Fant, *Women's Life in Greece and Rome* (Baltimore, 1982).

26. See Pomeroy, *Goddesses*, pp. 103–12. A more positive view of the role of women in classical literature is taken by some of the contributors to *Reflections of Women in Antiquity*, ed. Helene Foley (London, 1981).

27. *A Book of Woman Poets from Antiquity to Now*, ed. Aliki and Willis Barnstone (New York, 1980), pp. 100, 424.

28. Nina Auerbach stresses the importance of such communities in providing images of female independence in *Communities of Women: An Idea in Fiction* (Cambridge, Mass., 1978).

29. Woolf, *A Room of One's Own*, p. 87.

30. Ibid.

31. See, e.g., Marcia Landy, "The Silent Woman: Towards a Feminist Critique," in *The Authority of Experience: Essays in Feminist Criticism*, ed. Arlyn Diamond and Lee R. Edwards (Amherst, Mass., 1977), pp. 24–25.

32. A criticism founded on object-relations theory is debated by Elizabeth Abel, "(E)Merging Identities: The Dynamics of Female Friendship in Contemporary Fiction by Women," *Signs* 6 (Spring 1981): 413–35 (see also the response by Judith Kegan Gardiner and the reply by Abel in the same issue, pp. 436–44), and Gardiner, "On Female Identity and Writing by Women," *Critical Inquiry* 8 (Winter 1981): 347–61.

33. Wellek, *A History of Modern Criticism*, 2:220.

34. Ibid., p. 221.

35. Madelyn Gutwirth offers a spirited defense of de Staël's genius in *Madame de Staël, Novelist: The Emergence of the Artist as Woman* (Urbana, Ill., 1978).

36. It might be objected that what I have characterized as a *woman's* poetics is merely a branch of *Romantic* poetics. There is obviously some truth in this; nor could there fail to be, since only in the Romantic period did women begin to construct a poetics. But one should also note that Romanticism itself emerged only at the point when women began to play an important role in literature as writers and readers.

37. De Staël, *Letters on the Works and Character of J. J. Rousseau* (London, 1789), p. 18.

38. De Staël, *A Treatise on the Influence of the Passions* (London, 1798), pp. 142, 154.

39. Jean Starobinski emphasizes the logic by which love leads to suicide in "Suicide et mélancolie chez Mme de Staël," *Preuves* 16 (Dec. 1966): 41–48.

40. De Staël, *Treatise on the Passions*, p. 297.

41. De Staël, *The Influence of Literature Upon Society*, 2 vols. (London, 1812), 1:68.

42. In *Fictions of Feminine Desire: Disclosures of Heloise* (Lincoln, Nebr. and London, 1982), Peggy Kamuf uses a canon very similar to de Staël's in order to trace structures "working to appropriate and disguise the force of a woman's passion" (p. xvi).

43. See Robert May, *Sex and Fantasy: Patterns of Male and Female Development* (New York, 1980).

44. A very brief introduction to this large and growing field might include Hans Loewald, "Internalization, Separation, Mourning, and the Superego," *Psychoanalytic Quarterly* 31 (1962): 483–504; John Bowlby, *Attachment and Loss*, 3 vols. (New York, 1969–80), *Separation*, vol. 2 (New York, 1973), which contains an appendix on "Separation Anxiety: Review of Literature," pp. 375–98; and Nancy Chodorow, "Gender, Relation, and Difference in Psychoanalytic Perspective," in *The Future of Difference*, ed. Hester Eisenstein and Alice Jardine (Boston, 1980), pp. 3–19.

45. De Staël, *The Influence of Literature Upon Society*, 1:67.

46. Wayne C. Booth discusses his own turn away from Rabelais' humor in "Freedom of Interpretation: Bakhtin and the Challenge of Feminist Criticism," *Critical Inquiry* 9 (Sept. 1982): 45–76.

Re-creating the Canon: Augustan Poetry and the Alexandrian Past

James E. G. Zetzel

> A genre revived is different from its first avatar, and different also from what it would be if works of its type "just were not written" for a while.
> —ALASTAIR FOWLER, "The Life and Death of Literary Forms"

1

Of the surviving corpus of Latin literature, there is only one work that has always been considered canonical, in any sense of the word, and that is Virgil's *Aeneid*. It is canonical in that it has been, since the poet's death in 19 B.C., a school text and thus a part of the literary vocabulary of all educated people; it is canonical in T. S. Eliot's refined and delicate definition of the "classic" in exhibiting an extraordinary range of sympathies and sensibilities in a pure and elegant diction; and it is canonical in what might be called the ancient sense (although the word "canon" was not applied to literature until the eighteenth century) as an epic poem of broad scale and heroic subject, the highest and most important of all literary genres.[1]

In its historical context, the *Aeneid* is part of a much larger literary development, what seems (at least in retrospect) to have been a deliberate attempt to create a Roman national literature to rival the artistic monuments of classical and archaic Greece. Even before it was completed, Virgil's poem was greeted as a Roman equivalent of the Homeric epics.[2] Horace, too, explicitly saw himself as a new classic. In introducing his first three books of *Odes*, he expressed the hope that his work might rival that of the great lyric poets of archaic Greece, particularly Sappho and Alcaeus, and, in book 4 (published much later), he saw himself as a Roman Pindar. The elegist Propertius, who began his poetic career as a writer of love poetry, scornful of the public and official society of Rome, came at the end of his life to describe himself as the poet of early Roman cult and custom and, in the last poem of his last book, composed an obituary for Cornelia, an aristocratic connection of the emperor himself. These three poets, Virgil, Horace, and Propertius, take very different approaches to their subjects, and opinions of their attitudes to Augustus and Augustan Rome differ considerably. But their shared concern with serious themes is evident, as is their shared desire to write something large and significant. And at least two of them were consciously re-creating for Rome the classical literature of early Greece.

The impetus for their grand undertaking is not hard to find. In 31 B.C., in the battle of Actium, Octavian (not yet Augustus) defeated Antony, Cleopatra, and the forces of Eastern barbarism; in August of 29 B.C., he returned to Rome in triumph, closed the gates of war, brought an end to a century of social upheaval and civil war, and set about his radical restoration of Roman society. Whatever the poets thought about the Augustan regime, the end of civil war was obviously a major event and worthy of poetic recognition; and it was during the decade following Actium that the *Aeneid* and the *Odes* were composed. Indeed, the literary and social developments of that decade share certain paradoxical qualities. While establishing a monarchy and totally reorganizing the structure of Roman government and society, Augustus loudly proclaimed his restoration of republican government and his desire for a return to the manners and morals of early Rome. Similarly, Virgil and Horace made their adherence to the poetic forms of archaic Greece immediately apparent, but they, too, totally altered the nature of the forms they professed to emulate.

Endowed with the wisdom of two thousand years of hindsight, we find it easy to think of the development of Augustan poetry as natural and somehow inexorable: all three poets progressed, as they matured, from slighter forms to more ambitious ones, from private to public themes. No contemporary of theirs, however, would have seen that progression as natural. According to the literary theory of the third-century B.C. Alexandrian poet-scholar Callimachus of Cyrene, dominant in Rome from the time of Catullus and his friends (the so-called new poets or

James E. G. Zetzel is associate professor of classics at Princeton University and editor of the *Transactions of the American Philological Association*. He is the author of *Latin Textual Criticism in Antiquity* (1981) and, with Anthony T. Grafton and Glenn W. Most, has translated Friedrich August Wolf's *Prolegomena ad Homerum* (forthcoming).

neoterics), an unbridgeable gap separated the small, elegant, learned forms of poetry (including both pastoral and didactic) from the large, turgid, and sloppy genre of epic. In the opening of *Eclogue* 6, Virgil adapted one of Callimachus' statements to his own poem: "When I was trying to sing of kings and battles, Cynthian Apollo plucked my ear and said: 'A shepherd, Tityrus, should feed his sheep fat but speak a slender song'" (*Eclogues* 6. 3–5). It is not easy to understand how that poet came to write the *Aeneid*.

The Augustan poets' seemingly conscious emulation of the canonical works of early Greek literature suggests an avenue of explanation not often tried: to see the background to the *Aeneid* and the *Odes* in formal terms, concentrating on questions of poetic genre. For ancient poets the choice of a genre had far-reaching implications. Early in the second century A.D., the younger Pliny described a literary recitation: "I have just heard Vergilius Romanus reading to a small audience a comedy which was so skilfully modelled on the lines of the Old Comedy that one day it may serve as a model itself."[3] According to the theory implicit here and in other passages, the goal of poetry is not to be original but to follow a model so closely that the new work might be taken for the old. The truly successful poet was one who imitated his *exemplar* so faithfully that he became an *exemplar* himself.

Horace also conceived the choice of a model in generic terms: "If I am unable and unwilling to preserve the established manners and styles of works, why should I be called a poet?" (*Ars poetica* 86–87). What is more, in the Augustan period virtually every poetic work announces an explicit model—classical, Hellenistic, or archaic Roman. We cannot escape the idea that this is a highly derivative literature, modeling itself closely on the genres and, occasionally, the specific poetic works of another culture. It is striking, however, that the texts themselves convey no such impression of slavish dependency. This contrast is both curious and significant, and we need to understand its causes to explain the revival of high-style literature in Augustus' reign. I shall first describe some of the formal differences between the Augustan classics and their archaic Greek models and then examine them not only in the context of Augustan and pre-Augustan theories of poetic genre but also in relation to the origins of Augustan poetry in Alexandrian literature of the third century B.C. Finally, to demonstrate the importance and pervasiveness of the extremely formal Alexandrian categories of genre, I shall consider the Alexandrian classification of literature and the origins of the literary canon itself. Only then can we understand the boldness and significance of the Augustan literary revival.[4]

2

It is clear on formal grounds alone that the *Aeneid* is a singularly un-Homeric epic. The Roman epic, unlike the Homeric poems, is a

literary composition, not an oral-formulaic narrative. Its style, to use
Brooks Otis' terms, is subjective rather than objective.[5] Virgil's epic constantly emphasizes the presence of the poet as interpreter, from its initial
cano, "I sing"—replacing the Homeric request to the Muse—to its constant
emphases on relations between the mythic subject and the events of the
poet's own day. In the more technical aspects of genre, moreover, the
Aeneid is also extremely different from the Homeric paradigm. For instance,
book 4 of the poem has often been called a tragedy, and it functions as
one not merely because of its subject matter but because it displays
numerous characteristics of tragic form. It is divided into episodes; it
concentrates, to a much greater degree than the rest of the *Aeneid*, on
direct speech; it even ends with a version of the *deus ex machina*. In its
emphasis on the psychology of Dido, it bears a close resemblance both
to Euripidean tragedy—particularly the *Medea* and the *Hippolytus*—and
to Hellenistic rather than archaic epic. Virgil's Dido is kin to Apollonius
of Rhodes' Medea and Hypsipyle. What is more, by referring to the
theater and to the subjects of Euripidean tragedy, Virgil deliberately
points out to the reader that he is mixing tragedy with epic.[6]

The Dido episode provides another, smaller example of Virgil's
curious mixture of archaic and postclassical elements in the *Aeneid*. At
the very end of book 1, during the banquet which Dido gives for Aeneas,
the minstrel Iopas—Virgil's equivalent to the Odyssean Demodocus—
performs for the guests before Aeneas is asked to recount the adventures
which brought him to Troy. In the equivalent situation in the *Odyssey*,
Demodocus had sung of heroic and mythological topics, but Iopas sings
of cosmogony and cosmology:

> hic canit errantem lunam solisque labores,
> unde hominum genus et pecudes, unde imber et ignes,
> Arcturum pluviasque Hyadas geminosque Triones,
> quid tantum Oceano properent se tinguere soles
> hiberni, vel quae tardis mora noctibus obstet.
>
> [*Aeneid* 1. 742–46]

> [He sings of the wandering moon and the labors of the sun,
> the source of men and cattle, of rain and fire,
> Arcturus and the rainy Hyades and the twin Wains,
> why the winter suns so hurry to quench themselves in the ocean,
> or what the delay that holds up the slow nights.]

The audience of Carthaginian nobles and Trojan sailors are, curiously,
most enthusiastic about this song, one not likely to have appealed to
their Phaeacian equivalents. The topic of the poem is not archaic but
Hellenistic, and it is not only more like Aratus than Hesiod or Homer,
it consists of verses taken from Virgil's own *Georgics* (see *Georgics* 2. 475–
82). The abstruse learning, the scientific subject, and the self-reference

are all un-Homeric and give this passage a very different tone from its model.

The *Aeneid* is also radically different from the *Iliad* and the *Odyssey* on a much broader scale. Both Homeric epics announce a precise subject at the beginning: the anger of Achilles and its effects, the wanderings and homecoming of Odysseus. Virgil starts by alluding to both of these, "arms and the man," but the direction of his poem rapidly changes. After a very brief summary of the history of Aeneas, he identifies the eventual goal of Aeneas' efforts, "to found a city, bring the gods to Latium, whence the Latin race, the Alban fathers, and the walls of lofty Rome" (*Aeneid* 1. 5–7). The direct linking of myth to history is not only unlike Homer, it has a remarkable affinity with a form popular in Hellenistic times, the *ktisis*, or poem about the founding of a city. The *Aeneid*'s emphasis on causes and connections, the incessant linking of the narrative with the history of Rome in more recent times (through the narrator's presence, divine prophecy, the vision in the underworld, and the scenes on the shield), offsets its Homeric epic framework with a decidedly un-Homeric tone and content.

These characteristics of the *Aeneid* can be found in equal or greater profusion in the other major work of the period, the first three books of Horace's *Odes*, published as a unit in about 23 B.C. In the address in the opening poem to his patron Maecenas, Horace announces his desire:

> quod si me lyricis vatibus inseres,
> sublimi feriam sidera vertice.
> > [*Odes* 1. 1. 35–36]

> [If you include me among the lyric bards,
> I shall strike the stars with head on high.]

The "lyric bards" among whom Horace wishes to be included are, of course, the great lyric poets of archaic Greece, notably Sappho and Alcaeus, and the inclusion he requests is to be numbered in the canonical list of those poets compiled in Alexandria in the third century B.C.[7] No more straightforward indication of adherence to a classical model could possibly be imagined; and yet this poem, and these words themselves, contradict that desire. Not only is the meter which Horace uses here Hellenistic rather than classical, but the very phrase "lyricis vatibus" combines a transliterated Greek term with *vates*, a recently resurrected archaic Roman word for "poet." Horace, like Virgil, is combining classical Greek, Hellenistic, and Roman elements in what is in fact a radical transformation of the lyric forms of early Greece.[8]

Horace's alteration of his alleged models is apparent on every level from the individual poem to the entire collection. For example, in one of the poems that seems most closely to follow Alcaeus, the so-called

"Cleopatra Ode" (*Odes* 1. 37), the beginning is like Alcaeus, but the development is very different.[9] Horace starts with a virtual translation of the beginning of Alcaeus' poem celebrating the death of the tyrant Myrsilus:

> Nunc est bibendum, nunc pede libero
> pulsanda tellus . . .
>
> [*Odes* 1. 37. 1–2]
>
> [Now is the time to drink, now to strike
> the earth with a free foot . . .]

We do not know how Alcaeus' poem progresses after its instructions for celebration, though it was almost certainly—to judge from other fragments—not at all like Horace's conclusion but showed an unselfconscious glee at the downfall of an enemy. Horace, on the other hand, moves from a description of Cleopatra as a monster surrounded by decadent and diseased creatures of the East, to a simile in which she is a dove or rabbit in the snow, pursued by a hawklike Caesar. And by the end of the poem, she has been transformed from a monster to a worthy and honorable enemy, whose death is perhaps not to be greeted with unmixed rejoicing.

Besides Horace's continual departures from his classical models, the *Odes* are filled with variations in tone and mood foreign to the manner of Greek lyric. Book 2 opens with a poem that starts by praising Asinius Pollio for his history of the Roman civil wars and warning him of the dangers of his subject. Horace then offers his own poetic meditation on the same martial theme, in a remarkably elevated style. In the last stanza, however, he addresses his Muse and summons her back to lighter themes, thus revealing that this poem is yet another variation (compare *Odes* 1. 6) on the standard neoteric and elegiac refusal to write an epic poem, a topic thoroughly grounded in Alexandrian, not archaic, poetry.[10] In the "Archytas Ode" (*Odes* 1. 28), what begins as an address, apparently by a passing stranger, to the tomb of the Pythagorean mathematician, abruptly turns out to be a speech by an unburied body at the same site. The famous *Integer vitae* (*Odes* 1. 22) starts as a pious sermon on purity of life but suddenly becomes a poem on the safety of the lover, another elegiac conceit. In general, the allusion or the subject proposed in the opening verses of a Horatian ode is a sure indication that the end will be something quite different. The Greek lyric poems that Horace claims to emulate tended to be strictly bound by the generic conventions of the occasion for which they were composed: an athletic victory, a religious festival, a symposium. Horace uses the expectations aroused by conventional openings as a foil to create something new; his is a thoroughly literary, and heavily ironic, adaptation of models.

The difference between Horace and his Greek predecessors is apparent in more than just individual poems. The early lyric poets, to the best of our knowledge, wrote individual poems for particular occasions; their works were not assembled into books until centuries later, by the Alexandrian scholars of the third century B.C., and were then arranged according to formal criteria of occasion, subject, and meter.[11] None of those criteria is observed by Horace. He begins book 1 with a series of nine poems in different meters; book 2 alternates between Sapphic and Alcaic stanzas for the first eleven poems; book 3 opens with a series of six poems (the "Roman Odes") on related subjects and in the same meter. The tone and subject of adjacent poems vary considerably: into the series of introductory poems to major political or literary figures of his day (*Odes* 1. 1–4, 6), Horace inserts the slight and witty "Pyrrha Ode" (*Odes* 1. 5), and he makes a similar amatory poem to Asteria (*Odes* 3. 7) follow the "Roman Odes." The sense of structure, pattern, and organization of the *Odes* as a whole and of its individual books is foreign both to the Greek lyric poets and to the compilations of the Hellenistic librarians. When Horace, in the last ode of the collection (*Odes* 3. 30), refers to himself as a poetic *princeps* who has conquered the Aeolic poets and adapted them to Italic measures, he speaks no less than the truth.

In the scale of their undertakings as in their adoption of the major literary genres of classical and archaic Greece, the *Aeneid* and the *Odes* stand alone in Latin literature of the first century B.C. In certain respects, however, they do share significant features with other Augustan poetry. Of the blending of Greek elements—both classical and Hellenistic—with Roman or Italian themes, little need be said; that is characteristic of much Latin poetry from the earliest times until well after the Augustan age and is only to be expected in a literature whose basic impetus had come from another culture.[12] More noteworthy is that they also share with other poetry of their day a concentration on problems of form and genre foreign to most earlier Roman poetry, emphasizing the organization of the poetic book and expanding the poetic genres to include a much wider spectrum of styles and subjects.

The best and the earliest Latin example of the first of these tendencies, the organization of the book, is Virgil's *Liber bucolicon*, the *Eclogues*, completed in about 35 B.C.[13] Like two other works composed in the same period, Horace's *Liber sermonum* and Propertius' *Monobiblos*, the *Eclogues* displays an artful and complex pattern, balancing each poem against those around it and at the same time balancing the beginning and ending poems to enhance the central ones. The *Eclogues* also provides the best example of the second tendency: it is intensely concerned with the nature and function of poetry in an unsettled and rapidly changing society. As a result, although the overt model of his book is Theocritean pastoral poetry, Virgil deliberately extends the concerns and possibilities of that form. Not only does he include poems modeled on Theocritus' nonpastoral poems, he also addresses himself to the concerns of both epic poetry (in *Eclogue* 4) and the new genre of love-elegy (in *Eclogue* 10). Most significant for poetic theory, however, is *Eclogue* 6. There Virgil begins by adapting the prologue of Callimachus' *Aetia* (see p. 85 above), with its rejection of epic in favor of slighter forms and more elegant poetry. He then proceeds to recount the song of Silenus, which begins from cosmogony and progresses through the romantic myths favored by the Hellenistic poets, to tell of the poetic initiation of Virgil's friend and fellow poet Cornelius Gallus. Gallus is summoned to Mount Helicon, where Apollo and the Muses give him the poetic pipes associated with the poetic heroes of the Hellenistic world—Orpheus, Linus, Hesiod. The goal of *Eclogue* 6, as of the book of the *Eclogues* as a whole, is to demonstrate that within a formal unity—hexameter pastoral poetry—it is possible to create a poetic universe, a poetry which transcends all formal and generic restrictions to encompass all, or at least many, of the varieties of poetic creation.[14]

3

Much of what has been identified in the stylistic manipulations of both the *Aeneid* and the *Odes*, therefore, can be found in a highly developed form in the previous decade and in Virgil's own earlier work. There is, nevertheless, a vast gap between extending the bounds of a slight and nonclassical genre and creating a heroic work on an immense scale. While Virgil and Horace did progress to larger forms, not all poets did. In particular, the elegist Propertius steadfastly chose to remain within the humbler limits of his preferred form. It is not relevant here to discuss in any detail the significance of the formal genre of elegy in Augustan Rome. As in Horace's time, the origin and the primitive connotations of that meter are uncertain (see *Ars poetica* 77–78). It can, however, be safely said that its major period of popularity was in the Hellenistic, not the Classical period, and that its connection with amatory themes was primarily the work of the Roman poets, including Propertius himself.

The *Monobiblos* (Single book), Propertius' earliest work and the first book of his *Elegies*, shows him to be the true heir of Catullus' smaller poems. He is resolutely concerned with his own passion, with his mistress Cynthia, and with his poetry itself. He explicity rejects not only heroic poetry but heroic actions. The elegiac stance, as established in this work for all subsequent elegy, is one of self-absorbed concentration on private affairs and erotic exploits. But by the time Propertius began book 2 of the *Elegies*—written while Virgil and Horace were composing the *Aeneid* and the *Odes*—even the elegist's narrow vision of the nature of his genre had somehow expanded and, by the end of his life, was to expand even further. The opening poem of book 2 is addressed—as are Virgil's *Georgics* and all Horace's early works—to Maecenas, Augustus' chief minister and the day's leading patron of poetry. It is, in proper neoteric and elegiac fashion, a refusal to write an epic about the deeds of the emperor, not on the grounds of political disagreement but of poetic incapacity. Propertius declares that just as Callimachus does not sing of the battles of gods and giants, so his own talent is not suitable for an epic on Caesar: "The sailor tells of winds, the ploughman of bulls; the soldier counts his wounds, the shepherd his flocks; I am concerned with the battles in a narrow bed; each man spends his time on the skill at which he is adept" (*Elegies* 2. 1. 43–46).

Bedroom battles are a stock element in the elegist's vocabulary: they represent the rejection of public affairs in favor of private ones. But before he turned to Maecenas with this disclaimer of poetic incapacity, Propertius had begun the poem in a slightly different vein, one which seems to expand the possibilities of his genre within the limits of his subject. He started the poem, and the book, by imagining his readers' wonder at his apparently limitless poetic variations on the same topic, the overlapping themes of love and love poetry:

> Quaeritis, unde mihi totiens scribantur amores,
>   unde meus veniat mollis in ora liber.
> non haec Calliope, non haec mihi cantat Apollo:
>   ingenium nobis ipsa puella facit.
> sive illam Cois fulgentem incedere †cogis†,
>   hac totum e Coa veste volumen erit;
> seu vidi ad frontem sparsos errare capillos,
>   gaudet laudatis ire superba comis;
> sive lyrae carmen digitis percussit eburnis,
>   miramur, facilis ut premat arte manus;
> seu cum poscentis somnum declinat ocellos,
>   invenio causas mille poeta novas;
> seu nuda erepto mecum luctatur amictu,
>   tum vero longas condimus Iliadas;
> seu quidquid fecit, sive est quodcumque locuta,
>   maxima de nihilo nascitur historia.
>
> [*Elegies* 2. 1. 1–16]

[You ask the source of my writing loves so often, the source of my book that comes softly to the mouth. It is not Calliope nor Apollo that sings these things to me; my mistress herself creates my talent. If [it pleases] her to walk, gleaming in Coan silks, the whole volume will be cut from that cloth; if I have seen her scattered locks wandering on her brow, she rejoices to go proud of the praises of her hair; if she has struck a song from the lyre with ivory fingers, I marvel how skillfully she controls her supple hands; when she lowers her eyes that demand sleep, I find a thousand new causes as a poet; or if she struggles naked with me, her cloak torn off, then in truth we establish new *Iliads*; whatever she has done, whatever she has said, the greatest history arises from nothing.]

After establishing in the first two couplets the traditional elegiac character of his poetry as a slight form that does not receive the divine afflatus of Apollo or Calliope, Propertius proceeds in the following six couplets to extend the boundaries of his humble genre in a new and different way. Saying that the poet and his mistress compose *Iliad*s in bed is significantly different from representing his task as the description of battles in bed; it puts the emphasis less on the events than on the literary form in which they are most commonly found. And in the same way, the final couplet in this quotation suggests that his mistress' slightest word or deed is worthy of recording on a far grander scale, "maxima ... historia." These two couplets seem to imply that, just as the events of a lover's life are preferable to those of a political or military career (as Propertius himself had argued, for instance, in *Elegies* 1. 6), so too the literary record of those events can in some fashion rival, or perhaps replace, the works or genres in which public events are traditionally inscribed—epic and history.

The two couplets just discussed come at the end of six parallel pairs of verses and serve as their climax before Propertius goes on to defend his refusal to write epic or history on more traditional themes. In one way or another, it seems that the poet is using each of these couplets to allude to a different form of verse, now to be subsumed in his own poetry. The reference to Coan silks in lines 5 and 6 is generally taken as a description only of Cynthia's seductive garb—but in other passages such references contain riddling allusions to Philetas of Cos, a poet whose elegies Propertius elsewhere claims as a model.[15] In the following couplet "laudatis ... comis" ("praised hair") seems to be a bilingual pun on the Greek *engkomion*, the poetry of praise, an important genre in both archaic and Hellenistic times.[16] The description of Cynthia's musical talents in lines 9 and 10 is an obvious allusion to the genre of lyric. As for the remaining couplet, it is at least curious that "causas" in line 12 is a translation of the Greek *aetia*—the title of the greatest work of the influential Alexandrian poet Callimachus. The list of Cynthia's endearing and inspiring activities thus becomes an oblique and riddling set of poetic genres, beginning from Propertius' own elegy, through encomiastic poetry, lyric, etiological poetry, epic, and history. Propertius is suggesting that love elegy, even though it is a self-absorbed and private poetic form, can be a vehicle for expressing the concerns of far grander forms.

My interpretation of the opening lines of *Elegies* 2. 1 may seem farfetched and hermetic, and it certainly does not admit of definitive proof. Nonetheless, over the course of his career Propertius very clearly did come to show far more concern with larger subjects and to see his poetry on a much grander scale. In the last poem of book 2, he puts his own poetry in the context of other contemporary writing, not least the as yet unfinished *Aeneid*. At the opening of book 3, under the obvious influence of Horace's *Odes*, Propertius produces five related poems, on his own poetic inspiration and achievements and on his place in Rome, that are clearly intended to match the "Roman Odes" of Horace. And in book 4, he presents an astonishing group of long elegies that leave the topic of his love for Cynthia, in favor of Roman themes, the origins of various Roman customs and cults: a true Roman *Aetia*, based largely on the *Aeneid*.

4

A modern reader endowed with hindsight easily sees the progression in all three Augustan poets, Virgil, Horace, and Propertius, from small forms and subjects to heroic themes and grander genres as natural, the logical maturing of the poetic voice. Certainly, many later writers have appropriated the Virgilian model. In its historical context, however, the progression must have been anything but natural. All three poets, and the poets of the preceding generation, were deeply imbued with the postclassical culture of Alexandria. That city, in the third century B.C., supported a group of poet-scholars—most notably, Callimachus, Theocritus, and Apollonius—whose shared belief was that there was no place at all for the grand heroics of classical Greek poetry, whose goal was elegance and learning, and who despised the familiar forms and subjects as unworthy of a true poet's talents.[17]

A good indication of both their style and poetic theory is given in the conclusion of Callimachus' *Hymn to Apollo*. The poet turns aside from his subject to offer an attack on his poetic detractors:

> Jealousy spoke secretly into Apollo's ears: "I do not love the poet who does not sing even so much as the sea." Apollo kicked Envy and said: "Great is the stream of the river of Assyria, but it carries many scourings of earth and much garbage on its water. Bees do not carry water to Demeter from every source but from the spring which comes up pure and unsullied from a holy source, a small libation, the highest bloom." [*Hymn to Apollo* 105–112]

In other words, they preferred quality to quantity, and epic poetry above all was to be shunned. "I hate the cyclical poem," said Callimachus in his *Epigram* 28, "I do not drink from the common well. I despise everything public."[18] To be a true poet, it was considered necessary to drink from a pure spring, to avoid the wagon track and seek the untrodden path. In the passage of Alexandrian poetry that most influenced Roman poets, the preface to his *Aetia*, Callimachus related from the perspective of old age his first encounter with poetry in the person of its presiding deity, Apollo. "When first I set my tablet on my knees, Lycian Apollo said to me '. . . poet, feed your victim as fat as possible but, my friend, keep your Muse slender'" (*Aetia* fragment 1. 21–24). From that memory, the poet goes on to establish the basic metaphors for the proper attitude of the poet: poetry should be judged by its skill, not by a surveyor's rope; the poet's voice should emulate the sound of the cicada, sweet and small, and not the braying of asses; "it is Zeus' part to thunder, not mine."

Brevity, then, was a desirable characteristic, and not only brevity but the choice of a suitably delicate subject. It was far better to write an exquisite epigram on a trivial or personal theme—and the *Greek Anthology* attests to the popularity of the epigram as a literary form in Alexandria— than to write a turgid and bombastic eulogy of a king. Callimachus eschewed the major literary forms of the classical period and concentrated, as almost all his contemporaries did, on lesser genres—epigram, mime, iamb, elegy—in some cases elevating to literary status forms of expression that had previously existed only in popular culture. Theocritus' pastoral poems and Herodas' mimes are clear examples of this tendency. In fact, the mismatching of singer and song was deliberate: an uncouth shepherd, an urban housewife, or even a Cyclops singing a highly refined poem was intended to amuse the learned audience.

Even when writing of themes that would seem to lend themselves to expansiveness or hyperbole, Callimachus and his friends restrained themselves to a remarkable degree. Instead of an epic, Callimachus wrote an epyllion (now highly fragmentary), the *Hecale*, whose principal subject was Theseus' defeat of the Marathonian bull. In telling, in a fairly short poem, this minor episode of Theseus' life, he managed to devote far less attention to Theseus' heroic exploit than to the thunderstorm which forced the hero to seek refuge in the hut of the old woman Hecale, to a description of her poverty and of the conversation that she and Theseus had that night, and to a very mysterious discussion between two birds in a tree. The conclusion of the poem was not the triumphant return of the hero, but his sadness on returning to Hecale's hut and finding that she had died in the interval, and his establishment of a cult in her honor.

In avoiding heroic exploits, eclipsing narrative, and concentrating on description, humble life, and conversation, the *Hecale* displays the techniques and concerns of Alexandrian poetry. There is a strong tendency, not only in Callimachus, to focus on the childhood or minor exploits of a hero, and that is matched by an interest in the accurate portrayal of unheroic characters—old women, peasants, the petty bourgeoisie of Alexandria, shepherds, farmhands, witches. Jason, the hero of the one extant Alexandrian epic, Apollonius' *Argonautica*, is primarily remarkable for his lack of most of the traditional heroic attributes. As a member of the Museum and hence a functionary of the Ptolemaic court, Callimachus necessarily composed panegyrics on the royal house, but they too tend to be delicate and subtle, not bombastic. The *Victoria*, the recently discovered poem on Berenice's victory (by proxy) at Nemea, features a Pindaric myth on the origins of the Nemean games, founded by Heracles after he killed the Nemean lion; but the poem concentrates on the hero's visit to the hut of a peasant, as does the *Hecale*, and it includes a tale on the invention of the mousetrap, as a delicate counterpoint to the killing of the lion.[19] Similarly, the concluding poem of the *Aetia*, the *Coma Berenices* (Lock of Berenice), dwells not on Ptolemy's expedition to Syria, the occasion for which Berenice dedicates a lock of her hair, but on the lock's grief at being parted from its mistress.

The Alexandrian emphasis on smallness, elegance, and slightness at the expense of grand themes in major poetic genres was not preciosity for its own sake: although the poetry was written by and for scholars, it had much larger sources than the bibliothecal context in which it was composed. Since the time of the classical poets, much had changed. Earlier Greek poetry was an intimate part of the life of the city-state, written for its religious occasions and performed by its citizens. But the conquests of Alexander had altered the structure and the boundaries of the Greek world to an astonishing degree. Alexandria, the center of the poetic culture of the new age, was a city that had not even existed at the time of Euripides; it was in Egypt, not in Greece, and was a huge, polyglot community. As immigrants immersed in a new, impersonal, and bureaucratic society, the poets not unreasonably sought out what was small, intimate, and personal in their verses. The heroes of early Greek poetry are larger than life; those of Alexandrian poetry are life-size. They are human, like us; they have a childhood and an old age; they are afraid or in love or caught in a rainstorm. It was simply one way of reducing the world to more manageable dimensions. At the same time, the new world of Alexandria needed a new poetry. To continue writing epics about a mythology that seemed very far away was senseless; it was impossible to recapture either the style or the immediacy of Homer, lyric poetry, or Attic tragedy. The scholar-poets of Alexandria admired the literature of classical Greece; for them Homer was incomparable and inimitable, to be studied—but not to be copied. Far better, then, to find a new voice on a more manageable scale: instead of oral epic, erudite epyllion; instead of lyric, epigram; instead of tragedy, mime. The poets of an urban and unheroic world might long for but could never re-create the grandeur of the past.

From the very beginnings of Latin literature, the Greece that the Romans encountered was not the Greece of Homer or Pindar but the Alexandria of Callimachus—a literature not of heroism but of erudition and ironic urbanity. The early Roman poets did not by any means follow all the strictures of the Alexandrians, but they never entirely ignored them. The first work of Latin literature of which we have any significant fragments, the translation of the *Odyssey* by Livius Andronicus, made use of Alexandrian learning in order to adapt Homer to the Latin language.[20] Early Roman tragedy shows the influence of Hellenistic character portrayal, emphasizing psychological conflicts and irrational emotions. Ennius, the greatest early Roman poet, opens his *Annales* with an account of his very

Callimachean dream on Mount Helicon; but instead of being forbidden by Apollo to write an epic, he encounters the shade of Homer who tells him to go ahead, on the grounds that Ennius is himself the reincarnation of Homer and thus capable of writing epic.[21]

The full force of Callimachean theory, however, did not reach Rome until sometime in the first century B.C., and its clearest manifestation is in the poetry of Catullus, composed in the decade of the 50s. In a highly polemical epigram, he unfavorably compared the unknown poet Volusius' epic *Annales* to his friend Cinna's epyllion on the myth of Zmyrna. The *Zmyrna* had taken nine years to write, but it would be read forever and throughout the world; the *Annales* was huge and rapidly written, and it would soon be used as fish wrappings in its author's hometown.[22] Catullus also understood the wider implications of Callimachus' poetics; but with him and his contemporaries, the reduction of poetry to a manageable size and scope had less to do with the world's increasing complexity than with its increasing disruption and corruption. The rejection of epic, implicit in Catullus' rejection of Caesar's deeds, was combined with the rejection of not only the standard uses of the vocabulary of political life but also the orotund language of Ciceronian rhetoric.[23]

This is not the place to offer a history of Latin poetry in the late Republic, or even of the different perceptions of Callimachean poetics. It is enough to point out that, before Virgil and Horace undertook their major works, no serious poet contemplated composing in the grand style. Catullus' greatest contemporary, Lucretius, was not a devotee of the neoterics' elegant verse, but neither was he the herald of great deeds and heroic manners. His poem *On Nature* is Alexandrian in its very essence: it is a didactic poem, a form beloved of the Alexandrian poets; it is extraordinary in its poetic treatment of a singularly unpoetic subject, another Alexandrian trait; and in its manifold erudition and allusions to the Alexandrian poets themselves, it is clearly a product of Callimachean poetics.[24]

In the approximately twenty-five years that elapsed between the deaths of Catullus and Lucretius and the time when Virgil began the *Aeneid* and Horace, the *Odes,* literary composition seems to have followed the lines laid down by Callimachus and Catullus. Gallus and others continued to produce epyllia and epigrams; Gallus is also said to have "invented" love elegy in the form we know from the poetry of Propertius, Tibullus, and Ovid. In the triumviral period, the subjects of poetry seem to have moved, to some extent, away from purely personal topics toward more public themes, but the forms remained small: Virgil wrote pastoral poetry; Horace wrote the *Satires* and *Epodes;* Propertius, the *Monobiblos.* And while all these works show awareness of and concern with the larger events of the day, the tone remains slight and personal, the style, relatively low. The genres chosen are those popular in Alexandria, except for Horace's *Satires;* but that is a deliberately humble form, and Horace, with less than perfect seriousness, denies that it is poetry at all.[25] It is only in what is probably the last work of the triumviral period, Virgil's *Georgics*, that there are intimations of something higher, in the prayer to Augustus in the proem of book 1 and in the promise to write something larger in book 3. But even there the language is veiled, the genre, Alexandrian.

5

If the step from the *Georgics* to the *Aeneid* is gradual in terms of content, it is still huge in terms of poetic form and theoretical orientation. An Alexandrian or neoteric poet could legitimately aspire to be a new Hesiod; he could not aspire to be a new Homer. Strangely enough, however, the explanation for the change from lesser to greater forms, from Alexandrian to classical genres, lies in the literary theories of the Alexandrians themselves. It is here, finally, that the two aspects of a canonical text—its creation and its reception into a literary canon—finally meet, and here it is possible to see the ways in which the very structure of the canon has an influence on subsequent writers.

I have already shown that the Alexandrian poets were consciously concerned with the problems of genre and imitation, but there is con-siderably more to be said on the subject. For the members of the Museum, in their role as scholars rather than poets, were responsible for the clas-sification of earlier Greek literature and its codification in a list, an actual canon of "chosen" authors.

Our major source for the Alexandrian canon is the rhetorician Quin-tilian, who compiled in the first chapter of book 10 of his *Institutio oratoria* an annotated list of authors, both Greek and Latin, that the aspiring rhetorician should study in order to develop his vocabulary and style.[26] The list is arranged in parallel sections, one for Greek authors, one for Latin, and it is clear that the Greek section, at least, is much older than Quintilian's time, the first century A.D. It is organized by genre: starting from epic, he proceeds through the various poetic forms from elegy, to iamb, lyric, and, finally, drama and concludes with the three major forms of artistic prose—history, oratory, and philosophy. With slight exceptions resulting from differences between the two literatures, the order in the Latin section is the same.

That the canon of authors is arranged by genre is not unreasonable—although it leads, in the Latin list, to the peculiarity of having Ovid appear in three categories and Cicero and Horace, in two each—but Quintilian's definition of genre is strange, at least to modern eyes. Genres, in poetry, are defined by their metrical form alone, not their content. And the definition is quite rigid: when Quintilian lists Horace's *Epodes*, together with some poems of Catullus and Bibaculus, under the rubric "iamb," he feels the need to explain that they are placed there "although an epodic verse [i.e., one written in a different meter] intervenes" (*Institutio oratoria* 10. 1. 97). Horace's having written the *Epodes* in imitation of the personal, and often invective, poetry of Archilochus and Hipponax only partially makes up for the dactylic verses between the iambs in some poems. The very first subdivision of Quintilian's list, epic, reminds us of how strictly these formal definitions were upheld. Homer, of course, is at the head of the list—but he is followed not only by Hesiod but by the Hellenistic didactic poets Aratus and Nicander and the pastoral poet Theocritus. Although Quintilian describes Theocritus' style as "rustic," there can be no doubt that, by the criteria of the ancient canon, it was rustic epic.[27]

Quintilian also provides evidence about the authorship and the extent of the Alexandrian canon. When he lists Hellenistic poets under the rubric of epic, he remarks that Apollonius "does not come into the order given by the grammarians, because Aristarchus and Aristophanes, the judges of poets, included no one of their own day" (*Institutio oratoria* 10. 1. 55). He later says that this list included only three iambic poets. In other words, it was a selection and not, as has sometimes been thought, a complete list of all early authors—it was explicitly a list of earlier authors, stopping with the fourth century B.C. It was a codification of what was most worthwhile in classical Greek literature: in short, a canon.

We are sadly lacking in evidence about the criteria used by these grammarians in selecting or rejecting authors; some genres seem to have a great many authors, including mediocre ones, while others are extremely sparse. Nor do we know precisely what genres were included or in what order, except that epic is always first and Homer, always first in epic. There is, however, more evidence about the system of classification. Aristophanes and his successor, Aristarchus—better known for their Homeric scholarship—were not the first to make up an ordered list of earlier literature; they were preceded, as is so often the case, by Callimachus.

Callimachus' *Pinakes* (Tables) was not a selection; it was intended to be a complete list, in 120 books, of all earlier literature, arranged by formal genre and including a brief biography of each author and a list of his works.[28] In effect, the *Pinakes* was a catalog of the holdings of the great library of Alexandria, and in such a context the use of purely formal criteria made perfect sense, not only as an objective and immediately verifiable tool for the location of volumes on the shelf but also because most classical and preclassical poets wrote in only one, or primarily one, metrical genre. By cataloging works formally, therefore, Callimachus could indicate author and subject at one time, in the most economical fashion.

The formal principles of classification, moreover, were carried to considerable lengths. In the lyric section, about which we have the most evidence, Callimachus employed two types of subdivision.[29] In Sappho's case, most of her poems were arranged in books according to meter, except for the wedding songs, which were organized into a single book. Different criteria were necessary for lyric poets who employed more complex metrical systems. Pindar's lyrics were classified by the occasion for which they were composed—paeans, dithyrambs, epinicia, and the like—and the epinicia, the major surviving portion of his works, were further subdivided by the particular festival—Olympian, Pythian, Isthmian, and Nemean—at which the victory was gained. For Pindar's contemporary Simonides, however, a slightly different organization was used: there the epinicia were classified by the event—footrace, chariot race, wrestling— in which the athlete had won his victory.

While the system of classification used by the Alexandrians was not entirely satisfactory in coping with Roman literature (as it would not be for most other literatures), it was eminently suitable for describing the literature of pre-Alexandrian Greece. Its presuppositions deserve to be emphasized: it assumes both that an author composed in only one poetic form and that all the major characteristics of a poetic form—style, diction, subject—are implicit in its meter and/or the occasion for which it was written. Any poem written to celebrate an athletic victory, any poem written for a wedding, any poem written in iambs or epic hexameters should have certain well-defined characteristics, and, we may presume, the quality of any given poem was judged by how well it fulfilled its genre's implicit goals. But if Callimachus shared these presuppositions about earlier literature, it is all too obvious that, in his own poetry, he consistently and deliberately violated them.

I have already pointed out that one of the most striking characteristics of Alexandrian poetry was its tendency to avoid the major classical genres and even to elevate to literary status forms probably not recognized previously as literature at all.[30] But the Alexandrian poets, particularly Callimachus, did more than simply repudiate the literary canon; they repudiated the presuppositions behind it as well. The rule that a poet composes in only one genre was not strictly true at any period: in the archaic age, Solon had written elegies and iambs, and so had Archilochus. Homer himself was believed to have written the comic epic *Margites* in mixed meters along with the *Iliad* and *Odyssey*. But Callimachus went considerably further than that. His extant works include the *Hymns*, mostly in hexameters, the *Hecale*, the elegiac *Aetia*, the *Iambs*, a great many epigrams, and a few, highly fragmentary, lyric poems. In the final poem of the book of *Iambs*, moreover, he went so far as to justify his action, defending what the ancient summary of the poem calls *polyeideia* ("writing in many genres") against alleged criticisms of this practice and invoking the somewhat obscure precedent of the fifth-century B.C. poet and tragedian Ion of Chios. In other words, the cataloger deliberately made himself uncatalogable.

Much more important, however, is that Callimachus constantly and consciously removed the connections between the formal characteristics of a genre and its subject and style. Victory odes were traditionally written in lyric meters; Callimachus has one in elegiacs, one in the *Iambs*. Hymns were traditionally written in Ionic dialect and in hexameters; Callimachus wrote two in Doric and one of those in elegiacs. The *Hecale* has considerable overtones of the language of tragedy rather than epic. Similarly, Callimachus' fellow poet Aratus begins his didactic poem, the *Phaenomena,* as a hymn. This stylistic trait has been christened *Kreuzung der Gattungen* ("blending of genres"), and examples of it are to be found in every Alexandrian poet and in almost every poem.[31]

Callimachus' literary ideas led in many directions. The separation of poetry from its formal occasions and metrical bonds allowed immense versatility and originality. The twin ideas that a poet need not be limited to one genre and that a genre need not be limited by classical strictures on the relationship between meter and subject permitted the poet to develop his own ideas in his own way.[32] Most important, it showed that a great subject need not be dealt with in a grand style, and Callimachus' own political poems—the *Hymn to Zeus,* the *Victoria,* and above all the *Coma Berenices*—show that the goals of panegyric could be achieved more subtly but no less seriously in a smaller voice. So, too, the most important Roman poets made use of the same techniques—Catullus, in his epigrams, a few of his polymetrics, and, more obliquely, his epyllion on the wedding of Peleus and Thetis; Virgil and Horace, in all their early works. The small could easily include the large, at least by implication. I hardly need to add that Callimachean theory could, of course, have less salubrious results: an incessant search for novelty for its own sake, a concentration on obscurity and elegance at the expense of content, a scorn for all that was serious or difficult in poetry. In Greek this led to such minor Callimacheans as Euphorion and Parthenius; in Latin it can be found in some aspects of Ovid's poetry and in the (lost) poems parodied in the pseudo-Virgilian *Culex.*[33]

6

We may return, finally, to the major writers of the Augustan age. Thoroughly schooled in Callimachean poetics, each of them followed the master in different ways, and each broke through the now-empty prohibition on canonical forms. The ultimate import of the Alexandrian definition of genre in strictly formal terms was that genre no longer mattered. The true poet could shape his chosen genre or genres in whatever way he chose; as a poet, his sole obligation was to leave his own stamp on what he wrote, to become the master of tradition, not, as had been the case with the oral poets of early Greece, its vehicle. In Callimachus' day, the prohibition on grand themes and classical forms was necessary for the revitalization of poetry, as it was, for different reasons, in Catullus' day. But as Virgil, Horace, and Propertius came to maturity, circumstances had changed, and there was room for a new Homer, a new Pindar—not mere copies of the old ones, of course, but with the subtlety, complexity, and versatility required of an Alexandrian poet.

The three Augustan poets met the challenge of generic freedom in different ways. Horace was in many respects the closest follower of Callimachean *polyeideia*, writing throughout his life in a multitude of forms, hexameter, lyric, and iambic. Propertius chose to emphasize the universality now possible within one genre and allowed his elegy to change and grow from love poetry to the etiological Roman tales of book 4, the closest Roman equivalent to the *Aetia* itself. Virgil, like Propertius, chose to remain constant in his choice of poetic form, the epic hexameter, progressing upward in genre and backward in time from the Alexandrian *Eclogues* to the Hesiodic *Georgics* to the Homeric *Aeneid*. But we are constantly aware that—although from the *Eclogues* one could never expect the *Aeneid*—they are all part of one larger whole, that all three works taken together create a poetic universe united by the mastery of one poetic voice. Each of these poets, in fact, constantly revised himself in such a way that developments unpredictable in advance seem natural by hindsight.[34] And, remarkably, each aimed for canonicity in a new way, through the changes in his works and the blending of genres. Rather than seeking a single niche in a formal list, each poet sought to encompass the range of poetry within a single life, to become a part of the canon by making the canon a part of himself.

Alexandrian formalism and blending of genres had even wider ramifications in terms of style and attitude, in Rome as in Alexandria. Horatian political odes, such as the "Cleopatra Ode," offer a deliberately double perspective: the archaic and bloodthirsty exaltation of an Alcaeus on the one hand, the cosmopolitan Alexandrian sense of shared humanity on the other. Propertius' "Roman Elegies" are never simplemindedly antiquarian or patriotic; they are not the ancient equivalent of Thomas Macaulay's "Lays of Ancient Rome." Instead, a poem like the "Tarpeia Elegy" (*Elegies* 4. 4) makes the primitive Roman traitress as sympathetic as any modern woman smitten with a hapless love. The combination of large and small, old and new, personal and heroic that is found in all good Alexandrian poetry brings with it an essential complexity and doubleness of vision.

Of no poem is a purely formal description less adequate than of the *Aeneid*. The epic does contain, along with its epic scheme, considerable signs of the blending of genres: tragedy in book 4, scientific and philosophical poetry in parts of books 1 and 6, pastoral in 7 and 8, Hellenistic whimsy in the metamorphosis of ships to nymphs in 9, religious hymns in 8, and others elsewhere. But Virgil, to a greater extent than lesser poets, diverts the reader's attention from such purely formal versatility. What is more pervasive than in any other ancient poem, however, is the sense of ambiguity, the doubleness of vision that is the direct result of the Alexandrian deconstruction of poetic genre.

There is no need to rehearse in detail the elements of the *Aeneid* that contribute to its overwhelming sense of doubt and pathos—the frequent tragic and unnecessary deaths, especially of the young; the constant emphasis on the ignorance of Aeneas contrasted with the knowledge of the reader; Aeneas' departure from the underworld through the gate of false dreams; his lack of understanding about the meaning of his shield; and at the poem's end, his yielding to emotion and killing Turnus. At the same time, it would be wrong to underestimate the genuinely heroic, Augustan elements—Jupiter's prophecy of eternal empire, the vision of Roman heroes in book 6 and Italian strength in book 7, and, above all, the battle of Actium at the center of Aeneas' shield, with Augustus leading his troops into battle "with the senate and the people, the Penates and the great gods" (*Aeneid* 8. 679). Given the universality implicit in Alexandrian poetics, the emphasis on the small and humble together with the grand and heroic, it is important to recognize that both sides of the poem are necessary, that neither would be possible without the other.

When Augustus returned to Rome in triumph in 29 B.C., he had a great many plans for reform and renewal: the revival of sound morals and religion, the establishment of orderly government at Rome, the enhancement of the grandeur of Rome as an imperial capital. He also directed his attention to literature. Through Maecenas, he cultivated the support and even the friendship of the most talented writers of the day. Varius' *Thyestes*, written for the celebration of his triumph, he rewarded with an immense sum. He established a new library in the temple of Palatine Apollo, the god who was patron of literature and Augustus' own personal divinity. He is said to have encouraged poets to address works to him—but only works on serious subjects. Clearly, Augustus hoped that the splendor and achievements of his reign would be immortalized in literary works of dignity and grandeur.

Augustus was a man of considerable taste and refinement, and it may be that he never really expected Virgil to compose an epic on the civil wars, filled with deeds of heroic valor and featuring Augustus himself as some new Achilles. If that is what he wanted, he never got it, and that is just as well. The classics of Augustan literature match and in some ways even surpass their canonical models. In creating a new type of canon, one in which each author somehow encompasses all the varieties of poetic mode, they reinvented genres that were at once old and new, archaic and Alexandrian, and, in a word, Augustan.

---

1. My goal in this essay is to suggest an explanation, largely in generic and formal terms, for the high literature of the Augustan age and at the same time to make accessible to students of modern literature some of the less familiar areas of ancient literary history.

Since the subject is large and the secondary literature immense, I have tried to give references only to secondary works that have directly influenced my interpretations (where they are at all unusual), to works which provide fuller discussions of the evidence that I have used, and to the ancient works themselves. Most of my references to ancient works will appear parenthetically in the text. All translations, unless otherwise noted, are my own and aim at literalness rather than elegance. I have discussed a number of the topics considered here with many friends and colleagues over several years; my greatest debt is to my wife, Susanna Stambler, who helped me find an argument in an undigested mass of antiquarian details.

For various definitions of "canon," see Alastair Fowler, "Genre and the Literary Canon," *New Literary History* 11 (Autumn 1979): 97–119, an article to which my approach owes a great deal. For T. S. Eliot, see *What Is a Classic?* (London, 1945)—a lecture addressed to the Virgil Society. In dealing with English literature, Eliot's elevation of minor writers—discussed by John Guillory in this volume—is remarkably similar to the Alexandrian literary theory I discuss in this essay. David Ruhnken, in 1768, was the first to use the word "canon" to describe a selective list of literary works; see Rudolf Pfeiffer, *History of Classical Scholarship,* 2 vols. (Oxford, 1968–76), 1:207. The ancient terms *engkrino* ("select") in Greek and *recipio* ("receive") in Latin imply the existence of such a list, but no word for it exists.

2. So, Propertius *Elegies* 2. 34. 65–66: "Give way, Roman writers; give way, Greeks! Something bigger than the *Iliad* is being born." Whether this was meant to be completely laudatory is open to question.

3. Pliny *The Letters of the Young Pliny* (Penguin Classics, trans. Betty Radice) 6. 21.

4. Let me note here that I shall say nothing in this essay about the history of ancient drama and its place in the Augustan revival—not because it is not important but because we know virtually nothing about Augustan tragedy. For a tentative reconstuction of some of the features of Augustan tragedy that supports some of my observations here about epic and lyric, see R. J. Tarrant, "Senecan Drama and Its Antecedents," *Harvard Studies in Classical Philology* 82 (1978): 213–63, esp. pp. 258–61.

5. See Brooks Otis, *Virgil: A Study in Civilized Poetry* (Oxford, 1964), esp. pp. 41–96, one of the few works that tries to explain the *Aeneid* through its Alexandrian background.

6. Note particularly that Dido in her madness is compared to Pentheus or "Orestes driven from the stage" ("scaenis agitatus Orestes" [*Aeneid* 4. 471]), an anachronism that has troubled many critics but should be seen in the context of *Aeneid* 1. 164, where the woods shading Aeneas' landing site are described as a *scaena,* and *Aeneid* 1. 427–29, where the construction of a new theater is among the first things that Aeneas sees in Carthage. It should also be noted that the erotic language of the opening lines of book 4—wounding, fire, poison—was by the time of the *Aeneid* the shared idiom of Hellenistic epic (Apollonius of Rhodes' *Medea*), early Roman tragedy (Ennius' *Medea*), neoteric epyllion (Catullus' *Ariadne*), and elegy (Propertius' *Monobiblos*). Whatever associations the reader brought to these lines were in any case not Homeric.

7. See Pfeiffer, *History of Classical Scholarship,* 1: 206, and the commentary of R. G. M. Nisbet and Margaret Hubbard (*A Commentary on Horace: Odes* [Oxford, 1970]) on these lines. On the Alexandrian canon, see below, pp. 97–99.

8. On *vates,* see J. K. Newman, *Augustus and the New Poetry* (Brussels, 1967), pp. 99–206. My interpretation here of Horace is scarcely new; I am particularly indebted to David O. Ross, Jr., *Backgrounds to Augustan Poetry: Gallus, Elegy, and Rome* (Cambridge, 1975), pp. 131–52, who gives further references.

9. See the discussion of Horace's odes in the manner of Alcaeus, in Giorgio Pasquali, *Orazio Lirico,* 2d ed. (Florence, 1964), pp. 1–140, and Eduard Fraenkel, *Horace* (Oxford, 1957), pp. 154–78, together with Nisbet and Hubbard's *Commentary.*

10. On this ode, see Fraenkel, *Horace,* pp. 234–39, and Ross, *Backgrounds to Augustan Poetry,* pp. 141–42, with careful comparisons to other similar passages.

11. See A. E. Harvey, "The Classification of Greek Lyric Poetry," *Classical Quarterly,* n.s. 5 (1955): 158–59; Pfeiffer, *History of Classical Scholarship,* 1:130 and 183–84; and below, pp. 98–99.

12. On this topic, see, for instance, Wilhelm Kroll, *Studien zum Verständnis der römischen Literatur*, 2d ed. (Darmstadt, 1973), esp. pp. 1–23, and Gordon Willis Williams, *Tradition and Originality in Roman Poetry* (Oxford, 1968), pp. 250–357.

13. There has been much debate recently about the date of the *Eclogues*, whether it is 38 or 35 B.C. For my point that question is irrelevant, although I favor the later date. On the poetic book in antiquity, see Kroll, *Studien zum Verständnis*, pp. 225–46. The Spring 1980 issue of the periodical *Arethusa* (vol. 13) contains five articles and a copious bibliography on the Augustan poetic book.

14. In this account of *Eclogue* 6, I am indebted to Ross, *Backgrounds to Augustan Poetry*, pp. 18–38; but see also my "Gallus, Elegy, and Ross," *Classical Philology* 72 (July 1977): 249–60.

15. See Propertius *Elegies* 3. 1. 1 and 3. 9. 44, and see also Ross, *Backgrounds to Augustan Poetry*, p. 59 n.2.

16. On the *engkomion*, see Harvey, "Classification of Greek Lyric Poetry," pp. 163–64.

17. The basic study of Hellenistic poetry—altered and supplanted in details but not replaced—is Ulrich von Wilamowitz-Moellendorff, *Hellenistische Dichtung in der Zeit des Kallimachos*, 3d ed. (Zurich, 1973). Two articles useful for the relationship of Roman to Hellenistic poetry are Erich Reitzenstein, "Zur Stiltheorie des Kallimachos," in *Festschrift Richard Reitzenstein* (Leipzig and Berlin, 1931), pp. 23–69, and Wendell Clausen, "Callimachus and Latin Poetry," *Greek, Roman, and Byzantine Studies* 5 (1964): 181–96.

18. I cite Callimachus' works according to the numeration in Pfeiffer's edition, *Callimachus*, 2 vols. (Oxford, 1949–53).

19. The major publication of the new fragments is that of P. J. Parsons, "Callimachus: *Victoria Berenices*," *Zeitschrift für Papyrologie und Epigraphik* 25 (1977): 1–50. The mousetrap (fragment 177) was connected to the new fragment by Enrico Livrea, "Der Liller Kallimachos und die Mausefallen," *Zeitschrift für Papyrologie und Epigraphik* 34 (1979): 37–42, and "Polittico Callimacheo," *Zeitschrift für Papyrologie und Epigraphik* 40 (1980): 21–23.

20. See George A. Sheets, "The Dialect Gloss, Hellenistic Poetics, and Livius Andronicus," *American Journal of Philology* 102 (Winter 1981): 58–78.

21. The soul had also been lodged in the body of a peacock in the interval between its human incarnations. On Ennius' dream, see Otto Skutsch, *Studia Enniana* (London, 1968), pp. 6–9.

22. On this epigram, Catullus 95, see Clausen, "Callimachus and Latin Poetry," pp. 188–91.

23. See Ross, *Backgrounds to Augustan Poetry*, pp. 8–15, for a clear discussion of the question of "political language" in Catullus. For a fuller exposition of the views presented here, see my "Catullus," in *Ancient Writers: Greece and Rome*, ed. T. James Luce, 2 vols. (New York, 1982), 2: 643–67, and "The Poetics of Patronage in the Late First Century B.C.," in *Literary and Artistic Patronage in Ancient Rome*, ed. Barbara K. Gold (Austin, Tex., 1982), pp. 99–101.

24. There is as yet no full study of Lucretius' Alexandrianism, but see E. J. Kenney, "Doctus Lucretius," *Mnemosyne* 23 (1970): 366–92, and Robert D. Brown, "Lucretius and Callimachus," *Illinois Classical Studies* 7, pt. 1 (Spring 1982): 77–97.

25. See Horace *Satires* 1. 4. 39–42.

26. On the canon, see (briefly) Pfeiffer, *History of Classical Scholarship*, 1: 203–8, and (in detail) Ludwig Rademacher in *Real-Encyclopädie der classischen Altertumswissenschaft* (1919), s.v. "Kanon."

27. Fowler, in his "Genre and the Literary Canon," is wrong to list pastoral as a separate genre in Quintilian, although he recognizes the nature of the principles involved (see pp. 103 and 104).

28. On the *Pinakes*, see Pfeiffer, *History of Classical Scholarship*, 1: 127–34, and Otto Regenbogen in *Real-Encyclopädie* (1950), s.v. "Pinax." The evidence for alphabetic order cited by Pfeiffer in his edition of the fragments is very weak. It will be clear that Callimachus' principles of classification—those favored throughout most of antiquity—were opposed to those of Aristotle, who dismissed the use of metrical criteria (see *Poetics* 1447b).

29. On the classification of lyric, see n. 11 above, and L. E. Rossi, "I Generi letterari e le loro leggi scritte e non scritte nelle letterature classiche," *Bulletin of the Institute of Classical Studies* (University of London) 18 (1971): 69–94, esp. pp. 75–77.

30. For the subjects of this and the next paragraph, see Kroll, *Studien zum Verständnis*, pp. 202–44, and Rossi, "I Generi letterari," pp. 83–86, two works to which I owe much elsewhere in this essay.

31. With the one caveat that Fowler's definition of genre is not formal enough to suit Alexandrian theory, the characteristics of most Alexandrian poetry are very much like the secondary forms of genre described in his "The Life and Death of Literary Forms," in *New Directions in Literary History,* ed. Ralph Cohen (Baltimore, 1974), pp. 91–92.

32. This is, essentially, the conclusion drawn by Ross, *Backgrounds to Augustan Poetry,* pp. 36–38, from the poetic genealogy of *Eclogue* 6.

33. For this tendency and the parodies of it, see Ross, "The *Culex* and *Moretum* as Post-Augustan Literary Parodies," *Harvard Studies in Classical Philology* 79 (1975): 235–63.

34. It should be noted that in their constant self-revision, as in other characteristics, the Augustans were the heirs of Callimachus, who was the first poet to arrange (and revise for the purpose) his own collected works.

Poeta che mi guidi: Dante, Lucan, and Virgil

Winthrop Wetherbee

Few writers have been as concerned as Dante to give objective definition to the standards of their art or as conscious of working in a clearly defined tradition. From the earliest stage of his poetic autobiography, when he circulated the opening sonnet of *La Vita nuova* and was answered by his "first friend" Guido Cavalcanti, Dante is acutely and constantly aware of the relation of his own work to that of his contemporaries and predecessors in the vernacular. And as his career progresses, he is increasingly conscious of those great forebears, the classical practitioners of the *suprema constructio*, to whom he grants the name *poeta*.[1]

One purpose of this essay is to determine the value Dante imputed to these designated "poets," and I will be using the term *poeta* in the specific sense he assigns it in the *Commedia*. Though in earlier writings *poeta* often has a general significance encompassing versifiers in the vernacular as well as in Latin and can be extended to Greek writers so unlikely or obscure as Aesop and Simonides, in the *Commedia* it distinguishes the Latin authors who constitute the "bella scola" of the "sovereign poet," Homer: Virgil, Ovid, Horace, Lucan, and Statius (*Inferno* 4. 94).[2] The status of Homer is of course both unique and remote, "above the rest, like an eagle" (*Inferno* 4. 96). Horace is for Dante primarily a satirist and the author of that treatise which he calls *Poetria*. Ovid, at once everywhere and nowhere in the *Commedia,* is present in innumerable echoes and allusions but never confronted directly. The *poetae* whom Dante does confront, who are present to him at significant stages in the evolution of his narrative, are Virgil, Lucan, and Statius.

What I will be concerned with here is *how* these poets are present to Dante and what was at stake for him as he sought to establish a new kind of relationship with them. For there is, I will argue, something significantly new in his engagement with classical poetry—an attempt to experience its influence directly and as nearly as possible on its own terms—which has no precedent in earlier medieval writers' appropriations and imitations of classical material and which Dante criticism has acknowledged only tentatively. I will focus on moments at which we can see Dante reading his *poetae* critically at the literal level and responding to their complexities in ways which are not simply conditioned by his larger religious design. Like Augustine and Milton, Dante knew, and conveys through his own language, how it *feels* to read the *poetae*. We can fully understand his appropriation of them only when we have recognized how he came to terms with what he saw as their authentic poetic qualities by sharing the limitations of their spiritual and historical vision through an act of sympathetic imagination and by undergoing in his own literary persona the experience of their pagan heroes.

To a great extent my project amounts to an attempt to refine certain aspects of Erich Auerbach's method. Auerbach showed long ago that Dante's debt to the classical poets is largely a matter of style and the poetic rendering of concrete reality. For Auerbach, the great achievement of the *Commedia* is its presentation of the earthly, historical world and its people as God views them, "already subjected to God's final judgment," their earthly characters integral to their ultimate fate.[3] In a later development of this approach, Auerbach claimed that the very "classical" concreteness with which Dante represents human values and actions in their earthly context provides the basis for a "figural" reading that incorporates them into the providential scheme much as the events and personae of the Old Testament can be related to those of the New Testament.[4] More recently Giuseppe Mazzotta has argued that Dante's emphasis on the historical is more radical and bears a more complex relation to his spiritual purpose. By giving typological status to a Cato or Aeneas, Dante is not simply isolating the individual character and its *telos* from their secular context. Rather, he is inviting us to view their development *within* that context from a "redeeming" historical perspective, in which the concrete events of pagan history and the moral choices they involve assume an integral relation to the pattern of spiritual history.[5]

Mazzotta's formulation of the notion of a "redeemed secular history" is, like Auerbach's application of the principle of *figura*, a major contribution to Dante criticism (*DPD*, p. 59). And since classical poetry is an important

Winthrop Wetherbee is professor of English at the University of Chicago. He is the author of *Platonism and Poetry in the Twelfth Century* (1972), *The Cosmographia of Bernardus Silvestris* (1973), and *Chaucer and the Poets: An Essay on "Troilus and Criseyde"* (1984).

repository of this redeemed history (see *DPD*, pp. 3–4, 66–68, and 170–80), Mazzotta's approach is important for my immediate purpose, as a step toward the kind of direct engagement with the *poetae* I want to demonstrate. Whereas in Auerbach's readings there is always something arbitrary about the relation between the original figure and its meaning—a gap between concreteness and "figurality" that he does not appear concerned to bridge—Mazzotta seems to posit a situation in which the more we know of the original context from which the figure derives, the richer will be the typological reading this figure can be made to yield. Potentially, at least, he encourages the broadest possible freedom in reading the texts of the *poetae* into Dante's own, a freedom for which I will argue in what follows.

Nevertheless, a certain arbitrariness is probably inseparable from any attempt to establish Dante's mode of figuration. In Mazzotta's readings, too, founded though they are on the concrete details of Dante's sources, there is a good deal of selectivity, a privileging of certain details and a suppression of others. According to Mazzotta, texts of the *poetae* exist in an indeterminate state, suspended between pagan and Christian views of history and allegory. Everything depends on our ability to read properly, to resist the seductive appeal of an alienated desire which the pagan text harbors. In the face of the threat it poses—"the trap of narcissistic literary identification"—we must instead open the text to new meaning by the "violent" act of interpretation. In practice this means accepting the allegories of the neo-Platonist encyclopedists at one moment and rejecting them at another, sometimes affirming and sometimes dismissing the religious intuitions of the pagan author, and in the broadest sense constituting for ourselves the "*sensus proprius*" of the text (*DPD*, pp. 191, 190, and see pp. 188–91).

That some such selective strategy is ultimately necessary to the right reading of the *Commedia*, I do not doubt, but I would argue that Dante's engagement with his pagan authors is often more extensive and less forcefully interpretative than even Mazzotta's careful analyses suggest. I contend that we can understand the problematics of Dante's use of those classical poets who contribute so much of the history in the *Commedia*, and the basis this history provides for allegory, only by fully considering those moments which reveal Dante responding to precisely the seductive and unredeemed qualities of the texts of the *poetae*. My main illustration of the sort of reading I propose will be Dante's encounter with Virgil in the opening cantos of the *Inferno*, an encounter which involves him as well with the *Aeneid*, the great "text . . . of desire" that poses the most formidable challenge for the experience of interpretation to which Dante subjects himself and his reader (*DPD*, p. 150, and see pp. 150–58). First, however, I would like to look at what Auerbach, Mazzotta, and many others have viewed as the example par excellence of Dante's assimilation of a figure from pagan poetry and history. I refer of course to the Roman statesman and general Cato, hero of Lucan's *Pharsalia,* who had committed suicide rather than submit to Caesar but who appears in *Purgatorio* 1 as the guardian of the shores of the island on which the mountain of Purgatory rises.

Auerbach's definition of Cato's status is clear and decisive: Cato is no mere personification but a unique individual whose historical commitment to liberty justifies his transposition from his "tentative earthly state" to "a state of definitive fulfillment, concerned no longer with the earthly works of civic virtue or the law, but with . . . the freedom of the immortal soul in the sight of God."[6] Mazzotta refines Auerbach's view. To account for Dante's choice of Cato in particular, Mazzotta locates in the texts of Lucan and Virgil the concrete details of Cato's experience which seemed to medieval historians and commentators to manifest a Christ-like selflessness. He shows how Cato's life can be conformed to the redemptive pattern of Exodus and concludes that Dante's revisionary treatment of him constitutes "a mimetic representation of the redemption of history" (*DPD,* p. 65, and see pp. 60–65). As further evidence of Cato's personal redemption, which seems to be implied by Virgil's reference to the radiance his body will emanate at "the great day" (*Purgatorio* 1. 75), Mazzotta cites the four stars which illumine Cato's face and which, though ascribable also to contexts in pagan moral philosophy, intimate the restorative "*gratia sanans*" (*DPD,* p. 36, and see pp. 36–37 and 48–51).[7] When Cato professes himself unmoved by Virgil's appeal to him in the name of his earthly wife Marcia, the assertion amounts to a "palinode of earthly love," marking Cato's spiritual regeneration and indicating as well that "no reciprocity is possible between the lost and the elect" (*DPD,* p. 52).

But it is possible to look at Dante's Cato in quite another way, as one who has freed himself from the constraints and enticements of the world yet who exhibits no clear sign of any capacity for participation in the dynamic spiritual life of Purgatory. It is surely strange that in the *Purgatorio,* which begins with rejoicing over the escape from the "aura morta" of the underworld, the first figure we meet should be Cato and that his first act should be to menace Virgil and Dante with the very laws of hell (*Purgatorio* 1. 17, and see 1. 13–18 and 40–48). Though the light which illumines Cato's face may be considered a sign of grace, there is also something faintly hypothetical about it, derived as it is from four stars "never seen before save by the first people" and referable to no authentic cosmology (*Purgatorio* 1. 24). Cato himself vanishes at the rising of the sun (see *Purgatorio* 1. 107–9). And a number of other details conspire to render his status problematic. In a realm where grace is the operative power, Cato is associated emphatically with old and unalterable laws. Where pliant humility is the dominant virtue, Cato maintains the unbending rigor of his earthly self.[8] In a canto whose first lines promise the renewal of the power of "poesì," Cato remains wholly immune to what he views as the mere "lusinghe" of Virgil's eloquence, of that same "parola ornata" which has been capable of mediating to Dante the will of the court of Heaven and arousing the aspiring love which sustains him in his journey (*Purgatorio* 1. 7, 92; *Inferno* 2. 67). Cato can acknowledge at second hand the influence of the celestial "donna" who "moves" Virgil and Dante, but he shows no sign of any comparable motivation. He is precisely unmoved by the memory of Marcia, and indeed the only motion attributed to him is that of his venerable white hair (*Purgatorio* 1. 91, and see 1. 89 and 42). He says nothing to confirm or deny the pagan Virgil's apparent assumption that he will be among the saved, and when he rebukes the "slothful" pilgrims in canto 2, bidding them rid themselves of "the slough which prevents God from being manifested to you," his words may hint that he himself has not been granted religious vision (*Purgatorio* 2. 122–23).[9]

In short, the Cato whose ascetic life and passion for liberty have seemed to promise so much may be interpreted, from a different point of view, as providing a standard that is as much negative as positive—an example of perfect self-mastery utterly uninformed by any trace of the aspiration which love arouses in the pilgrim. Having pursued his own path, what Lucan calls his "inreducem . . . viam" (*Pharsalia* 9. 408), into the desert, Cato has reappeared, removed from any living relation to humanity or history, to preside over a realm of his own ("le mie grotte" [*Purgatorio* 1. 48]) whose spiritual significance, like that of Limbo, is effectively neutral.

To the extent that such complicating undertones are present in Dante's text, they show him closely attentive to his source, Lucan's *Pharsalia*, where the characterization of Cato is at once idealizing and faithful to the evidently unsympathetic personality of the historical man. From his first appearance, Lucan's Cato fairly begs to be understood as a secular Christ, selflessly concerned for Rome and mankind.[10] The first speech that issues, in the form of "sacras . . . voces," from the "shrine" of his heart ("Arcano . . . pectore") includes six distinct expressions of the wish that he might die for Rome and his blood "redeem" her people (*Pharsalia* 2. 285, 312, and see 2. 306–18). But there is something desperate about the violent energy of this commitment and something oddly hollow about Cato's selfless desire to give himself for Roman freedom.[11] From the beginning, he seems to sense—indeed, to insist—that the cause is a lost one, Rome a lifeless body, and liberty herself a name, an "inanem . . . umbram," which he will follow to the grave (*Pharsalia* 2. 303, and see 2. 301–3).[12] The same emptiness appears again in the renewal of his marriage vows with Marcia, the wife whom he had presented to his friend Hortensius after she had borne three children. The seemingly affectionate tone in which Dante's Cato recalls having granted Marcia "whatever favor she wished" (*Purgatorio* 1. 87) is offset somewhat by Lucan's portrayal of their relationship. What Lucan's Marcia had asked was precisely the name, the "nomen inane," of marriage: Cato's "rigidity" had allowed no indulgence in even the "just" love of the marriage bed (*Pharsalia* 2. 342, 378, 379–80). Even when he appears at his most actively heroic, during the desert march of *Pharsalia* 9, Cato's role is expressed largely in negative terms. He can promise his followers no salvation beyond that of dying "indomita cervice" (*Pharsalia* 9. 380). The half-taunting lines in which he bids those whose patriotism is less than extreme to choose an alternative course, a path he himself could never follow, sound like a prefiguration of Dante's own journey:

> At qui sponsore salutis
> Miles eget capiturque animae dulcedine, vadat
> Ad dominum meliore via.
>
> [*Pharsalia* 9. 392–94]

[But should any soldier require a guarantee of safety, or feel the desire to give delight to his spirit, let him take a more favorable path and seek (another) master.]

It would be a mistake, I think, to assume on the basis of the passages I have cited that Lucan's high praise of Cato is wholly ironic. There is good reason to believe that he saw Cato's role as the noblest available to a Roman of his time.[13] But for Dante the image of a self-martyred saint, a man whose very virtues had finally cut him off from any positive role in life or history, might well suggest the fatal impasse of a spirituality suspended in a world without gods. And Cato's role only translates into human terms what Dante seems to have regarded as Lucan's place in literary history. For when he makes Cato reject as mere "lusinghe" the words in which Virgil, invoking both "donna del ciel" and the "occhi casti" of Cato's own Marcia, seeks to win his favor, Dante shows himself to have sensed with remarkable astuteness what modern criticism has only lately been rediscovering—how essential it was to Lucan's purpose to expel Virgilian values from the world of his poem (*Purgatorio* 1. 92, 91, 78).[14] Lucan repudiated what seemed to him false and self-betraying in Virgil's cult of *pietas* and in his devotion to the Roman gods, but the price is a failure at the human level, a total absence of the responsiveness to love which makes Virgil's language a communicative vehicle for that promise of "great good" which elicits Dante's "buono ardire" (*Inferno* 2. 126, 131). The isolation of Lucan and his Cato will become still plainer when, toward the summit of Purgatory, Dante encounters a poet of the next generation, Statius, in whose equally tormented verse he discovered intimations of a new, dynamic spirituality and in whose company he continues his journey.

But the poetic canon that we see here defining itself in both literary and religious terms is grounded in Virgil's *Aeneid,* the text in which seduction and aspiration conflict most powerfully. Although there can be no doubt that Dante saw the *Aeneid* as a "poem of history" in the highest sense, the appeal of its language is ambiguous, wavering, as Mazzotta suggests, "between good and evil" and so expressing "the open-ended ambiguous process of history" (*DPD*, pp. 158, 159). To understand Virgil's canon-forming role in the *Commedia*, we must recognize that the reminiscences of the *Aeneid* in the poem, particularly those in the early cantos of the *Inferno*, tend to evoke Virgil's poetry at its most seductive.

For a medieval poet, confronting the complexities of Virgil directly meant distancing himself not only from traditional allegorizations of the *Aeneid* but also from the practice of the medieval romance tradition.[15] Medieval romance had adapted Virgil to its own purposes by simplifying his treatment of character and muting his emphasis on the pain and irresolution of human experience, keeping death and destructive desire at bay and sustaining a meliorist faith in the power of *courtoisie*. This is the tradition of the Old French *Eneas*, where Dido's last word is the name of a forgiven Aeneas, where Turnus dies unmurmuring (his death separated by a bare twenty lines from the naming of Eneas and Lavine's wedding day), and where the prevailing courtly decorum minimizes the sense of loss and sacrifice.[16] The Virgil of romance tradition has subtle and complex affinities with elements of pathos, nostalgia, and fascination with death which appear in a partly repressed form in the *Aeneid* itself. Dante, acutely aware of the power of Virgilian pathos, was equally aware of how this pathos could be isolated and heightened in the mind of a reader conditioned by romance.

The false reading of Virgil to which such a conditioning can lead is well illustrated by the pilgrim's encounter with Paolo and Francesca in *Inferno* 5. Like their own hapless identification with the lovers of *Lancelot du Lac*, Dante's response to Paolo and Francesca is mediated. This episode occurs, as we are twice reminded, in the circle of hell "ov' è Dido" (*Inferno* 5. 85), and as Mazzotta has shown, it reenacts Augustine's description of the effect on his younger self of Virgil's powerful account of Dido's suicide (see *DPD*, pp. 165–70). As Augustine had dwelt on Dido's suffering to the exclusion of any sense of the larger meaning of the *Aeneid* (Aeneas' voyages are mere "errores," the fall of Troy a "spectaculum vanitatis" [*Confessions* 1. 13], so Dante's *pietà* isolates the victims of destructive passion from history and responsibility, reducing them to "the ladies and the knights of old" betrayed by the power of love (*Inferno* 5. 71).

The important thing about this famous canto for my purposes is the prominence and complexity of the role of the *Aeneid* in the pilgrim's experience. Dante's response to Paolo and Francesca is conditioned not only by the young Augustine's experience of Dido. It is also impressed, like Augustine's and to a much greater extent, by the guilty compassion with which Aeneas responds upon encountering the shade of Dido in

Virgil's underworld as he seeks to reaffirm a bond totally at odds with his own larger mission.[17] As for Aeneas, so for Dante the encounter takes place in an atmosphere suffused by the memory of "sweet love," and both seek in the spirits they meet a reflection of their own tender feelings (*Aeneid* 6. 455). For both, the indulgence of these feelings is of primary importance, and both episodes end with their heroes wholly absorbed in reflection on the sorrows of love. But while Dido's unresponsiveness finally shocks Aeneas into a partial appreciation of her suffering, her "casu . . . iniquo" (*Aeneid* 6. 475), Dante's *pietà* is wholly unreflecting, a connoisseur's response to the sheer pathos of Francesca's tale, and it is in an excess of *pietà* that he succumbs to a deathlike swoon at the end of the canto.

Another indication of the role that a romanticized Virgil is playing in Dante's experience is the image which describes Paolo and Francesca at their first appearance:

> Quali colombe dal disio chiamate
>   con l'ali alzate e ferme al dolce nido
>   vegnon per l'aere, dal voler portate;
> cotali uscir de la schiera ov' è Dido
>
> [*Inferno* 5. 82–85]

[As doves called by desire, with wings raised and steady, come through the air, borne by the will to the sweet nest, so did these issue from the troop where Dido is]

Though Dante's birds are damned souls as well as signs, their response to the pilgrim recalls the apparition of the twin doves who guide Aeneas through the "antiquam siluam" to the entrance of the underworld, where he discovers and claims the golden bough (*Aeneid* 6. 179). As Virgil's doves are sent by Venus in response to Aeneas' half-conscious prayer, Dante's are "summoned by desire," and in both cases their behavior is precisely adapted to the eager responsiveness of the human seeker (*Inferno* 5. 82; and see *Aeneid* 6. 190–92). Venus' doves pace their flight to ensure that Aeneas can keep them in sight (see *Aeneid* 6. 199–200), and Dante's dove-spirits will lead him on by making their message to him mirror his own desire:

> "Di quel che udire e che parlar vi piace,
>   noi udiremo e parleremo a voi"
>
> [*Inferno* 5. 94–95]

["Of that which it pleases you to hear and speak, we will hear and speak with you"][18]

In both cases the birds' hypnotic power draws the hero toward an experience that promises a profound but uncertain knowledge, to be assimilated
only imperfectly and with great difficulty. And in Dante's case, clearly,
his subjective engagement with this experience has, for the moment,
overwhelmed his ability to reflect on its meaning. Whereas Virgil turns
Aeneas away from thoughts of lost love with a brusque reminder of the
"datum . . . iter" (*Aeneid* 6. 477), Dante is borne forward unconscious and
awakens in canto 6 still preoccupied with the "pietà" and "trestizia" of
what he has just undergone (*Purgatorio* 6. 2, 3).

There is evidently something demoralizing about the influence Virgil
exerts in programming the pilgrim's response to his meeting with Paolo
and Francesca, and there are a number of other such moments in the
early cantos. Virgil's explicit declarations to Dante inspire him with a
sense of his great mission, but his presence also triggers a series of
reminiscences of the *Aeneid* which evoke the somber side of Virgil's vision
and charge the descent to the underworld with hints of anxiety and
disorientation. This dual process is initiated by Virgil's first entry into
the poem.

At the moment when Virgil appears to Dante, the pilgrim, menaced
by a wolf and forced, little by little, to turn from his ascent of "the
mountain of delight," has suddenly begun rushing headlong downward
"in basso loco" (*Inferno* 1. 77, 61, and see 1. 49–61). In a region of
unfathomable obscurity, "where the sun does not speak," there appears
before his eyes "one who appeared indistinct through long silence" (*Inferno*
1. 60, 63). These odd, synesthetic images are complementary, and it is
important to see them in their context, for they provide us with an index
to the immense responsibility Dante will be assigning to poetry, poetic
language, and the figure of Virgil as the episode develops.

It is, we are told, dawn on a day in late March, the season of both
the Creation and the Incarnation. When the sun first appears, attended
by stars, it recalls to Dante's mind the time "when Divine Love first set
these beautiful things in motion," and he sets off with good hope. But
the beasts which menace his ascent disrupt this vision, and his headlong
descent to "where the sun is silent" is a way of characterizing a condition
in which the natural universe no longer has meaning, no longer com-
municates a sense of orientation to the hapless human sinner or speaks
to him of his Creator (*Inferno* 1. 39–40, 60).

The "long silence" which renders "indistinct" the figure who eventually
reveals himself to be Virgil has sometimes been taken to refer to the
vast empty space in which Dante encounters him. Its more significant
reference, however, is to the centuries during which the authentic character
of Virgil's poetry has been neglected—that character which Dante will
revive in the *Commedia*.[19] For Dante will claim to have realized in his own
poetry the "bello stilo" of Virgil, and in fact Virgil's noble language, his

"parlare onesto," plays a vital role in the scheme of the poem (*Inferno* 1. 87, 2. 113). As we learn in canto 2, it is in Virgil's language that Beatrice and the ladies of the court of Heaven have invested their hope of drawing Dante back to the path of salvation. The link between divine mercy and Virgil's "parole" and the effect of both on Dante are evinced at the end of canto 2 (*Inferno* 2. 137). There Dante responds to Virgil's account of having been sought in Limbo by Beatrice and charged with the task of ministering to Dante:

> "Oh pietosa colei che mi soccorse!
> e te cortese ch'ubidisti tosto
> a le vere parole che ti porse!
> Tu m'hai con disiderio il cor disposto
> sì al venir con le parole tue,
> ch'i' son tornato nel primo proposto."
> [*Inferno* 2. 133–38]

["Oh how compassionate was she who helped me, and how courteous were you, so quick to obey the true words she spoke to you! By your words you have made me so eager to come with you that I have returned to my first resolve."]

Exalted by his sense of the divine powers at work on his behalf, Dante feels himself and Virgil to be impelled by "a single will." Virgil is "set in motion" by the pilgrim's "ardor," and the two together proceed into canto 3 (*Inferno* 2. 139, 141, 131).[20]

Like the sun from whose eloquent light Dante has been driven, the poetry of Virgil—or, more properly, his poetic language—can, it seems, function as a means of access to divine love and mercy. By mastering Virgil's "bello stilo," Dante can write a poem which will express that "buono ardire" which the love of Beatrice arouses in him. Virgilian poetry will thereby be reborn, its language wrought into a new, spiritual design, as the elements of the visible universe assume deeper meaning when seen as ordered by divine love. Through this design, Dante will reestablish himself in his right relation to that love.

But it is made clear that before all this can happen, Dante must come to terms with the figure of Virgil himself, a poet with a history and vision of his own. Virgil's first reply to the pilgrim's hapless " '*Miserere* di me' " amounts to a reconstitution of himself as he had existed in the world (Mantua, Lombardy, Rome), in history (the pagan era of Julius and Augustus Caesar), and in poetry (as the poet of Aeneas' journeying after the fall of Troy) (*Inferno* 1. 65, and see 1. 67–75). Only after having thus asserted his own identity does he make any response to the pilgrim and his situation, and his abrupt question seems oddly detached and imperceptive, a dismissal of Dante's plight as mere folly:

"Ma tu perché ritorni a tanta noia?
  perché non sali il dilettoso monte
  ch'è principio e cagion di tutta gioia?"
                                    [*Inferno* 1. 76–78]

["But you, why do you return to so much woe? Why do you not climb the delectable mountain, the source and cause of every happiness?"]

Dante seems not to hear this question and instead reacts directly to the information the shade has given about himself. Identifying the shade as Virgil, Dante then, in effect, proceeds to redefine him in his own terms, as a resource of his own poetry:

"Or se' tu quel Virgilio e quella fonte
  che spandi di parlar sì largo fiume?"
rispuos' io con vergognosa fronte.
"O de li altri poeti onore e lume,
  vagliami 'l lungo studio e 'l grande amore
  che m'ha fatto cercar lo tuo volume.
Tu se' lo mio maestro e 'l mio autore,
  tu se' solo colui da cu' io tolsi
  lo bello stilo che m'ha fatto onore."
                                    [*Inferno* 1. 79–87]

["Are you, then, that Virgil, that fount which pours forth so broad a stream of speech?" I answered him, my brow covered with shame. "O glory and light of other poets, may the long study and the great love that have made me search your volume avail me! You are my master and my author. You alone are he from whom I took the fair style that has done me honor."]

Dante's words reinforce the point of the concession with which Virgil had prefaced his first speech: " 'No, [I am] not a living man, though once I was" (*Inferno* 1. 67). The Virgil to whom Dante responds ("*quel* Virgilio" [my emphasis]) is no longer a man who lived and wrote but a poetic source, a fountain of language, and the verb "spandi," which describes the operation of this source, both emphasizes its power and denies it a self-determining character, relegating it to a constant, depersonalized function. The zeal and love which Dante feels for Virgil, his "maestro" and "autore," have been devoted to a book, a "volume" from which, Dante says, he "took" his famous style.[21] The title "autore" is the highest praise and, together with "volume," suggests for Virgil and his text a quasi-biblical status. "Maestro," on the other hand, suggests the more practical function attendant upon Virgil's role as a figure of authority, and the verb "tolsi," which describes Dante's appropriation of the master's language and technique, is often used to denote deprivation, dispossession, even robbery.[22]

But there is, moreover, a third aspect to Virgil's role, in which his poetry is neither a secular Testament, nor simply a resource of Dante's own poetry, but its own preserve of autonomous character and power. And there is much in the scene we are considering to suggest that Dante's engagement with this authentic Virgil is a complex one. The moment at which Virgil appears to Dante, while itself reminiscent of numerous moments of prophetic reassurance in the *Aeneid*, is prepared by a Virgilian echo marking the haplessness of the unguided pilgrim. His rush toward the depths ("i' rovinava in basso loco" [*Inferno* 1. 61]) echoes the desperation of Aeneas, who reenters the burning city of Troy in search of his wife Creusa and whom we see in a near-frenzy "tectis urbis sine fine ruenti" (*Aeneid* 2. 771). A moment later Creusa is before his eyes ("ante oculos" [*Aeneid* 2. 773]), as the shade of Virgil appears "dinanzi a li occhi" of Dante (*Inferno* 1. 62). And Creusa's words clearly establish that Aeneas' journey is overseen by divine powers (see *Aeneid* 2. 777–78), as Virgil recounts the heavenly impetus of his mission to the pilgrim. But the "sine fine" of Virgil's line has an ominous indeterminacy, echoed in Dante's "in basso loco," which reminds us that Virgil, before arriving to serve as Dante's guide, had already opened the depths of hell to Dante's imagination. Both poets are acutely aware of the horrible fascination of certain kinds of despair: Aeneas' rush through the streets, though prompted by the loss of his wife, is also impelled by his need to reexperience the disaster of the fall of Troy (see *Aeneid* 2. 750–51); Dante's Virgil discerns in the pilgrim's downhill flight a confused will to return to the "noia" from which he had been fleeing (*Inferno* 1. 76, and see 1. 76–78).[23]

The *Aeneid* contains still other precedents for Virgil's role in the *Commedia*. The "od omo certo" of Dante's first appeal to the shade of his mentor echoes the "o, dea certe" with which Aeneas expresses his intuition of the divine presence beneath the disguise in which Venus appears to him on the African shore (*Inferno* 1. 66; *Aeneid* 1. 328). The guidance Venus offers her son leads him to the uncertain comforts of Dido's Carthage—this should remind us that Dante's Virgil, too, will lead the pilgrim inevitably to the circle where Dido is: Virgil's paradoxical role requires that he serve Dante's desires in the course of disciplining them. Again, the bluntness and apparent detachment of the question revealing Virgil's puzzlement at Dante's flight from the "delectable mountain" recall the Sibyl of *Aeneid* 6. Like Virgil, the Sibyl is capable of both high prophecy and sympathetic counsel in preparing Aeneas for his descent into hell, but there is a sense in which the "facilis descensus" appears to her as a madness which she is yet bound to indulge (*Aeneid* 6. 126). We are reminded for a moment that both guides are, in their very different ways, mere enablers, agents of higher powers and larger designs by which they themselves are unaffected:

> quod si tantus amor menti, si tanta cupido est
> bis Stygios innare lacus, bis nigra uidere
> Tartara, et insano iuuat indulgere labori
>
> [*Aeneid* 6. 133–35]

[Yet if your mind has such a desire, such a passion to be borne twice across the Stygian lake, twice to see black Tartarus, and if it pleases you to give yourself to this mad undertaking]

The conjunction of "amor" and "cupido" is always a danger sign in the *Aeneid*, and its implications bear even more tellingly on Dante's situation. Both the Sibyl and Dante's Virgil mediate to the heroes they serve the influence of divine powers, but both also expose them to horrors and fascinations that at times threaten to subvert the divine influence they convey. For Aeneas the underworld journey is a test which will confirm the *virtus* acquired through a long schooling in privation and dedication. For Dante, to compare Aeneas' role with his own is to feel his own inadequacy, a "viltade" which it is Virgil's task to overcome (*Inferno* 2. 45, and see 2. 32–33 and 43–45) but which will be all the more apparent as the pilgrim is exposed to experiences which reveal his own confusion, doubt, and often desperate attachment to the very life he is privileged to view in the light of divine judgment.

To put the problem in terms of literary influence, the aspects of Virgil and his poetic voice that Dante revives are as complex in their effect as Virgil's own vision, a vision in which affirmation and despair are strangely combined. Virgil's sense of the destiny of Rome, which meant so much to Dante, coexists with a deep and often overwhelming sense of the price of empire in loss and destruction. Dante is fully aware of the ambivalence of Virgil's vision. It is the pilgrim, rather than Virgil himself, who links Virgil's poetry with the glorious theme "de l'alma Roma e di suo impero" that established the future seat of the Papacy (*Inferno* 2. 20). For Dante's Virgil, the *Aeneid* is the story simply of Anchises' just son "who came from Troy"; when he speaks of Italy, it is of a lost Italy, the resting place of the youthful heroes, Trojan and Italian alike, who died in Aeneas' war of conquest (*Inferno* 1. 74, and see 1. 106–8).

The complexities of Virgil's tone and outlook are nowhere greater than in book 6 of the *Aeneid*, the great precedent for the *Inferno*. Dante must have been acutely conscious, in accepting Virgil's invitation to descend to the world of the "antichi spiriti dolenti," that for Virgil this was very largely a world of tragic unfulfillment, its moral and spiritual order uncertain and circumscribed by darkness (*Inferno* 1. 116).[24] It must indeed have seemed at times that in appropriating Virgil's poetic style, he was drawing on a resource as ominously ambiguous as the golden bough itself.

I could continue by indicating a number of well-known moments later in the *Inferno* which bear out the complex suggestiveness of Virgil's initial appearance in the poem, showing the pilgrim distracted or demoralized by the powerful memory of Virgil's language or by the precedent of Aeneas' experience. But perhaps the most unnerving moment is one which has received little notice, no doubt because the Virgilian reminiscence is so obvious as to have seemed perfunctory. This moment occurs at the end of canto 3, when Dante and Virgil arrive at the shore of Acheron. The entire episode closely recalls the corresponding moment in *Aeneid* 6, and its centerpiece is the simile in which Dante describes the souls of the damned, who hurl themselves from the shore at the command of Charon:

> Come d'autunno si levan le foglie
>   l'una appresso de l'altra, fin che 'l ramo
>   vede a la terra tutte le sue spoglie,
> similemente il mal seme d'Adamo
>   gittansi di quel lito ad una ad una,
>   per cenni come augel per suo richiamo.
> [*Inferno* 3. 112–17]

[As the leaves fall away in autumn, one after another, till the bough sees all its spoils upon the ground, so there the evil seed of Adam one by one cast themselves from the shore at signals, like a bird at its call.]

Earlier, Dante places the catalyst of this activity in the cruel words, the "parole crude," with which Charon "the demon" bids the damned souls abandon hope (*Inferno* 3. 102, and see 3. 100–102 and 109). In the *Aeneid* Virgil had used the Latin adjective "cruda" to describe the strange, supernatural energy enabling Charon in old age to keep ferrying the endless procession of souls to the further shore (*Aeneid* 6. 304, and see 6. 302–4). Dante's use of the Italian cognate has the effect of locating something of this same demonic power in Charon's speech, and the slight displacement emphasizes the important role played by language in the episode. For while the damned souls are responding to the cruel words of Charon, Dante himself is responding both to what he sees and to his memory of the words in which Virgil had described the same scene:

> huc omnis turba ad ripas effusa ruebat,
> . . . .
> quam multa in siluis autumni frigore primo
> lapsa cadunt folia, aut ad terram gurgite ab alto

quam multae glomerantur aues, ubi frigidus annus
trans pontum fugat et terris immittit apricis.
                                              [*Aeneid* 6. 305–12]

[Here the whole throng of souls rushed forward toward the bank
. . . : as many as the leaves which fall in the forest at the first chill
of autumn, or as the birds which flock from the deep water to shore,
when the cold of the year drives them over the sea and bids them
flee to sunny lands.]

The imagery here is closely recalled in Dante's similes, but Dante has
introduced alterations which show him enthralled by the spectacle he
beholds as if seized by the same demonic force that drives the damned
souls. For Dante the falling leaves are less important than the bough,
which "sees" them as they lie on the earth. The leaves themselves, moreover,
fall one by one, "l'una appresso de l'altra." The unnaturalness of the two
details diverts us from the beauty of the image in itself and directs us
toward its significance in the context of the *Inferno:* the "ramo" is the
pilgrim; the leaves which fall in sequence mirror the sequency of his
imaginative and verbal response to the controlling influence of Virgil's
words. The same sense of control appears again as the migrant birds of
the *Aeneid,* fleeing instinctively before the winter wind, are reduced in
the *Inferno* to a single bird trained to respond to its master's signal. The
double simile is a forceful expression of Dante's sense of the challenge,
spiritual and artistic, involved in imitating a great poetic forebear and
gives an added point to the final term of the comparison. For the action
of the "evil seed of Adam" represents not only the self-destructive impulse
of the damned soul but the self-diminishing effect of Dante's identification,
under Virgil's spell, with this impulse. The leaves, his own words, are
the "seed" he spends in an ejaculation of vicarious participation in the
scene he beholds. Like the bird drawn by the master's lure, he has suspended
his own flight and given himself wholly to a repetition of the bleak finality
of the Virgilian moment. The words of the *Aeneid* have themselves become
"parole crude," and when Virgil intrudes on Dante's reverie, reminding
him of the spiritual meaning of what he sees and of his own status as
one of the elect, the shock of the contradiction between his real and his
imagined state is overwhelming (see *Inferno* 3. 122–29). The earth trembles
and "gives forth" wind and flashing light, and Dante falls "like one seized
by sleep" (*Inferno* 3. 133, 136).

Of course, it would be wrong to concentrate exclusively on the immediate psychological impact of this moment. Like everything in the
Commedia, it has its place in the providential economy. Dante's descent
into hell is a miraculous event, and the violent events that herald his
crossing over Acheron represent the suspension of natural laws which
any miracle involves. But it is equally mistaken to stress only this aspect

of the episode. Both the divine event and the psychological event are crucially important, and the point of the scene is largely to emphasize the enormous gap between the levels at which the two events are enacted.

This point is reinforced by Dante's experience in canto 5, where he is again overcome by his imaginative involvement in a situation he wholly fails to understand. The verbal echoes which link the accounts of his fainting in the two episodes (see *Inferno* 3. 136 and 5. 142) acknowledge a similar linkage between the precisely corresponding moments in *Aeneid* 6, which are also the two moments at which we see Aeneas reflecting inwardly on the suffering he confronts. Both the clustering souls on the shores of the Styx and Dido in her silent rage move him to ponder the injustice of their fate, their "casus iniquus" (see *Aeneid* 6. 331–32 and 475–76). Aeneas' feelings at these moments are far from simple, but the contrast between his capacity to reflect and Dante's unreflecting identification with the damned is plain. The pilgrim has assimilated Virgil's power but not his knowledge, and his own spiritual resources are wholly at the mercy of a self-diminishing *pietà*.

In Dante's engagement with Virgil, then, we can see a unique instance of a medieval poet responding to what Harold Bloom (in a more modern context at least) would call a "strong" poetic ancestor: unprotected by the evasions and transformations of courtly romance, Dante is deliberately seeking to experience for himself the tragic aspect of his forebear's poetry.[25] In a fuller survey, I would go on to note the symptoms of a dawning awareness of Virgil's problematic influence in the interval of anxious delay before the citadel of Dis in canto 9 and in the episode of Piero delle Vigne in canto 13. I would also consider moments in later cantos when Dante openly or implicitly challenges comparison with Virgil and other great exemplars and when poetic power is shown as a source of spiritual temptation. At such moments Dante is no longer caught unawares by a too human involvement with what he sees but menaced by the dangers of presumption and inhumanity inherent in his willing participation virtually as an agent in the damnation he describes. Here and throughout the *Inferno,* the *poetae* are present as a constant force, collaborating in the necessary process of drawing the pilgrim through the stages which review his engagement with sin and the tragic errors which lead to damnation.

In the *Purgatorio* the living world will speak to Dante once again. His own poetry will assume new powers, and he will be released, by the exercise of a new freedom to revise literary history, from the encroaching influence of his models' spiritual limitations. The great example of this new freedom is Statius and Dante's invention of a secret conversion to Christianity for him, which Dante attributes to Statius' revisionary reading of Virgil. At this point, it may well seem, literary history has become purely symbolic, rendering the intrinsic character of the works of the *poetae* and any authentic relationship among them irrelevant. Thus many scholars have treated the Statius cantos as if Statius' own poetry were as much of a fiction as his conversion. But it would be possible to show that the Dantean Statius of the *Purgatorio* is derived from a reading of the *Thebaid* and *Achilleid* as direct, as extensive, and as uncontaminated by allegorization as the readings of the *Aeneid* and the *Pharsalia* that produced the Dantean versions of Virgil and Cato. Statius' conversion is a development of intuitions present in Statius' own poetry; Dante's assignment to Statius in *Purgatorio* 25 of a discourse on the development of the soul is a ratification of these intuitions.

The heart of this discourse is a description of the informing of the embryonic soul by divine "virtù" which leads directly to an account of the soul's death and afterlife (*Purgatorio* 25. 59, and see 25. 68–87). The passage is modeled on Statius' account of the ritual suicide of Menoeceus, son of Creon, in *Thebaid* 10, an act inspired by the goddess Virtus and important to Dante because of Statius' emphasis on the immortality it gained for Menoeceus.[26] For Dante, and evidently for the historical Statius, Menoeceus' suicide provided an affirmative answer to questions about the meaning of self-sacrifice and heroic action which Virgil had raised and left unresolved in the *Aeneid* and which receive only a problematic resolution in the life and death of Lucan's Cato.[27] Dante's use of the episode may serve as a final measure of the depth and precision of his reading of the *poetae*, the care with which he inscribed their works within his own, and his discovery, in the process, of a canon grounded in a mutually confirmatory relationship between literary and spiritual history.

1. See Alfredo Schiaffini, "*Poesis* e *poeta* in Dante," in *Studia philologica et litteraria in honorem L. Spitzer,* ed. A. G. Hatcher and K. L. Selig (Bern, 1958), pp. 385–87. See also Dante Alighieri, *The Divine Comedy,* trans. Charles S. Singleton, 3 vols. (Princeton, N.J., 1970–75); all further references to this work will be included in the text, with book titles and canto and line numbers in parentheses. Occasionally I have modified Singleton's renderings; unless otherwise noted, all further translations in this paper are my own. References to classical works will be included parenthetically in the text.

2. The one near-exception to this restricted usage occurs in *Paradiso* 25, where Dante, who has already referred to his *Commedia* as a *poema* and to its medium as *poesì,* imagines returning to his native Florence in triumph and there claiming the title of *poeta,* once and for all, for himself.

3. Erich Auerbach, *Dante: Poet of the Secular World,* trans. Ralph Manheim (1929; Chicago, 1961), p. 86, and see p. 90.

4. See Auerbach, " 'Figura,' " trans. Manheim, *Scenes from the Drama of European Literature: Six Essays,* trans. Manheim and Catherine Garvin (New York, 1959), pp. 60–76.

5. See Giuseppe Mazzotta, *Dante, Poet of the Desert: History and Allegory in the "Divine Comedy"* (Princeton, N.J., 1979), pp. 58–59; all further references to this work, abbreviated *DPD,* will be included parenthetically in the text.

6. Auerbach, " 'Figura,' " p. 67.

7. Mazzotta discusses the same motif with reference to Macrobius and Cicero; see *DPD*, pp. 55–58.

8. The symbol of humility is the pliant rush, to which Cato himself refers (see *Purgatorio* 1. 101–5) and which Dante calls "the humble plant" (*Purgatorio* 1. 135).

9. On this question, see Ettore Paratore, *Antico e nuovo* (Rome, 1965), p. 198.

10. See Lucan *Pharsalia* 2. 240–41, where Cato first appears, sleeplessly thinking on the common weal, "cunctisque timentem / Securumque sui."

11. Its effect on the younger Brutus is to arouse in him a "too great" desire for civil war (see *Pharsalia* 2. 323–25), and so, in effect, to point him toward the tyrannicide which leads Dante to place him in the jaws of Satan in *Inferno* 34.

12. The idea is repeated at *Pharsalia* 9. 204–6.

13. See Frederick M. Ahl, *Lucan: An Introduction* (Ithaca, N.Y., 1976), pp. 240–47.

14. See Ahl, *Lucan,* pp. 64–67 and 274–78.

15. See Ulrich Leo, "The Unfinished *Convivio* and Dante's Rereading of the *Aeneid,*" *Medieval Studies* 13 (1951): 41–64, and Mazzotta, *DPD,* pp. 52–53 and 154–57.

16. See Daniel Poirion, "De l'*Enéide* à l'*Eneas:* Mythologie et moralisation," *Cahiers de civilisation médiévale* 19 (1976): 213–29.

17. The Virgilian phrase with which Augustine recalls Dido, "exstinctam ferroque extrema secutam," is part of Aeneas' first outburst on encountering Dido's shade and expresses a dawning awareness of his responsibility for her death (*Aeneid* 6. 457).

18. On this aspect of Dante's experience in the canto, see Roger Dragonetti, "L'Episode de Francesca dans le cadre de la convention courtoise," *Aux Frontières du langage poétique: Etudes sur Dante, Mallarmé, Valéry,* Romanica Gandensia, vol. 9 (Ghent, 1961), pp. 99–100.

19. See Domenico Consoli, *Significato del Virgilio dantesco* (Florence, 1967), pp. 34–45, and Antonino Pagliaro, " '. . . Chi per lungo silenzio parea fioco' (*Inf.* I. 63)," *Altri saggi di critica semantica* (Messina and Florence, 1961), pp. 271–72.

20. Virgil's response to Dante's "ardor" is clearly indicated by the use of the passive "mosso fue." So Beatrice is "moved," and her speech inspired, by Love. At the end of canto 1, where Dante is still unaware of the hierarchy of forces at work on his behalf, Virgil appears to move himself (*Inferno* 2. 141, 72, and see 1. 136).

21. On Dante's use of "volume" and "autore," see Robert Hollander, "Dante's Use of *Aeneid* I in *Inferno* I and II," *Comparative Literature* 20 (1968): 144–45; on the relation of "maestro" and "autore," see Mazzotta, *DPD,* pp. 154–55.

22. The verb *togliere* is used again to describe Statius' taking from Virgil "forte" or "forte a cantar" (*Purgatorio* 21. 125–26). In the *Inferno* it frequently describes the removal of the damned from earthly life; in addition to Francesca's reference to "la bella persona / che mi fu *tolta*" (*Inferno* 5. 101–2; my emphasis), see *Inferno* 7. 59, 13. 105, 24. 135, and 33. 130.

23. Augustine acknowledges Aeneas' complex impulse when he ends his account of reading Virgil by recalling the "sweetness" of the double spectacle of "Troiae incendium, atque ipsius umbra Creusae" (*Confessions* 1. 13).

24. See Auerbach, *Dante: Poet of the Secular World,* pp. 88–91.

25. See, however, Harold Bloom, *The Anxiety of Influence: A Theory of Poetry* (Oxford, 1973), pp. 122–23, which offers a rather cosy picture of the relations of Dante and Virgil.

26. See Statius *Thebaid* 10. 628–85 and 756–82. Virtus promises Menoeceus immortality at 10. 654–55, and his ascent to heaven occurs at 10. 781–82.

27. With the account of Virtus in *Thebaid* 10. 628–37, cf. *Aeneid* 9. 184–87, and see C. S. Lewis, "Dante's Statius," *Medium Aevum* 25, no. 3 (1956): 138. On the critique of Virgil implicit in Lucan's treatment of Cato's suicide, see Ahl, *Lucan,* pp. 240–42.

When Eve Reads Milton: Undoing the Canonical Economy

Christine Froula

> Let a woman learn in silence with all submissiveness. I permit no
> woman to teach or to have authority over men; she is to keep silent.
> —1 Tim. 2:11–12

In *Jacob's Room*, with her nose pressed against a Cambridge window,
Virginia Woolf's narrator describes the don within holding forth in speech
that is at once coin and communion wafer to an audience of admiring
undergraduates:

> Sopwith went on talking . . . The soul itself slipped through the
> lips in thin silver disks which dissolve in young men's minds like
> silver . . . manliness. He loved it. Indeed to Sopwith a man could
> say anything, until perhaps he'd grown old, or gone under, gone
> deep, when the silver disks would tinkle hollow, and the inscription
> read a little too simple, and the old stamp look too pure, and the
> impress always the same—a Greek boy's head. But he would respect
> still. A woman, divining the priest, would, involuntarily, despise.[1]

In the sixty years since Woolf wrote this passage, women in significant
numbers have broken the barriers which excluded Woolf herself from
"Oxbridge," and now inhabit some of the rooms formerly occupied by
Jacob and his dons. I begin with it, however, not to measure women's

I am indebted to Adrienne Munich, Paul Wallich, Maureen Quilligan, and Robert von
Hallberg for provocative dialogue on the issues of this paper and helpful criticism of the
manuscript.

149

progress from cultural exclusion but because in contrasting the places and stances of "man" and "woman" in the cultural economy, Woolf opens a more complicated question concerning the effects of women's *in*clusion: How are the dynamics of canonists selecting, readers interpreting, teachers teaching, and students learning affected by what is beginning to be a critical mass of women in the academy? Woolf's image is useful to a feminist critique of the literary canon because, rather than focusing on a canonical work, it abstracts what we might call the canonical mode of authority embodied in the don's speech and presents different responses of "man" and "woman" to this authority. The don, as "priest," mediates between his sacred books and his flock. A man, partaking of the "silver disks," respects; a woman, for whom the male-impressed currency is both inaccessible and foreign, involuntarily despises priestly authority. That woman can "divine" for herself challenges such authority, implying independence of the don's exclusive mediation. Further, even if we suppose her to have acceded to the don's role as cultural mediator, both her historical exclusion and her independent view suggest that she must play that part in a different way, reforming the traditional model of cultural authority in fidelity to her own experience.

But how might Woolf's "woman" transform the priestly model that has been instrumental in her own cultural oppression? To ask this question is to conceive cultural authority not merely as a commodity which women seek to possess equally with men but as power which has a political dimension realized in particular stances toward literary texts and literary history, toward language and stories, students and curricula. As the traditional literary canon exists in problematic relation to women, so do the modes of literary authority enshrined in those texts, upon which the social authority that institutes the canon and draws our models of literary history patterns itself. Sixty years after Woolf wrote, it is not only—nor even all—women who are alienated from the modes of authority invoked by cultural canons and priests; for present purposes, therefore, I will borrow Woolf's representation of "man" as one who "respect[s] still" the don's mystified cultural authority and "woman" as one who, "divining the priest," raises questions about the sources, motives, and interests of this authority. This definition identifies "woman" not by sex but by a complex relation to the cultural authority which has traditionally silenced and excluded her. She resists the attitude of blind submission which that authority threatens to imprint upon her; further, her resistance takes form not as envy of the "priest" and desire to possess his authority herself

---

Christine Froula, associate professor of English at Yale University, is the author of *A Guide to Ezra Pound's "Selected Poems"* and of the forthcoming *"To Write Paradise": Style and Error in Pound's Cantos.* She is currently working on a book about literary authority in James Joyce and Virginia Woolf.

but as a debunking of the "priestly" deployment of cultural authority and a refusal to adopt that stance herself. Women, under this local rule, can be "men," as men can be "women."[2]

Following the ground-breaking studies of Simone de Beauvoir, Mary Ellmann, and Kate Millett, many feminists have explored the politics of reading the patriarchal canon, which, as Elaine Showalter points out, holds up to the female no less than to the male reader the ideal of thinking "like a man."[3] Judith Fetterley, for example, has shown how the study of the traditional American literary canon presses the female reader to identify with the male point of view—the position of power—against herself.[4] In the last fifteen years, women professors of literature have begun to redress the male bias, both by including women authors in the curriculum—in established courses which their very presence exposes as having been previously, and invisibly, preoccupied with "men's studies," as well as in courses focused on women writers—and by employing the critical and pedagogical strategies of the "resisting reader" exemplified by de Beauvoir, Millett, Fetterley, and many others.

The effect of this work has been not simply to balance male bias with female (or marginal) bias—the "opening" of the canon—but to disrupt the canonical economy as such, the dynamics of cultural authority.[5] Feminists have moved from advocating representation of voices formerly silenced or "marginalized" by the established curriculum to recognizing that such representation implies and effects a profound transformation of the very terms *authority* and *value*—cultural and aesthetic or literary— that underwrite the traditional idea of the canon.[6] As Fetterley puts it: "To expose and question that complex of ideas and mythologies about women and men which exist in our society and are confirmed in our literature is to make the system of power embodied in the literature open not only to discussion but . . . to change."[7] Since the opening of the literary canon has been in some degree accomplished, we can now begin to analyze the impact of formerly silenced voices on the political economy of the literary canon, on the "system of power" that controls which texts are taught and how they are taught. How are "women" writers and teachers, formerly excluded from positions of cultural authority, affecting the economy of literature? I will take up two aspects of this large question: first, the radical challenge that feminist perspectives pose to the concept of a canon as such—not merely to the history and politics of canon-formation but to the *idea* (and ideal) of "the canon"—and, second, the critique of traditional modes of literary authority that emerges from reading "canonical" and "marginal" texts side by side.

1. The Politics of Orthodoxy: Canonists vs. Gnostics

I begin by extrapolating from Elaine Pagels' book, *The Gnostic Gospels*, to the power dynamics of literary authority, first, as claimed by texts and, second, as "respected" or "despised" by readers, teachers, and students. Pagels' study of the second-century gnostic writings discovered at Nag Hammadi in 1945 illuminates the politics implied in the canonist's stance by showing how the rediscovery of the gnostic texts—successfully suppressed by the church fathers in the struggle to establish a unified Church— dispels the widespread myth that all Christians shared the same doctrine in the apostles' time. She shows that early Christianity appears to have been "far more diverse than nearly anyone expected before the Nag Hammadi discoveries" and that the establishment of the "one, holy, catholic, and apostolic Church" required the suppression not merely of dissenting voices but of an antithetical conception of spiritual authority embodied in certain gnostic writings.[8]

There are, of course, many important differences between the deployment of cultural authority in the social context of second-century Christianity and that of twentieth-century academia. The editors of the *Norton Anthology,* for example, do not actively seek to suppress those voices which they exclude, nor are their principles for inclusion so narrowly defined as were the church fathers'. But the literary academy and its institutions developed from those of the Church and continue to wield a derivative, secular version of its social and cultural authority. Since Matthew Arnold, the institution of literature has been described in terms which liken its authority to that of religion, not only by outsiders— Woolf's woman "divining the priest"—but by insiders who continue to employ the stances and language of religious authority; see, for instance, J. Hillis Miller's credo in a recent issue of the *ADE Bulletin:* "I believe in the established canon of English and American literature and in the validity of the concept of privileged texts. I think it is more important to read Spenser, Shakespeare, or Milton than to read Borges in translation, or even, to say the truth, to read Virginia Woolf."[9] Such rhetoric suggests that the religious resonances in literary texts are not entirely figurative, a point brought out strikingly by revisionary religious figures in feminist texts. In her recent essay " 'The Blank Page' and the Issues of Female Creativity," Susan Gubar cites as some of the "many parables in an ongoing revisionary female theology" Florence Nightingale's tentative prophecy that "the next Christ will perhaps be a female Christ," H. D.'s blessed Lady carrying a "Bible of blank pages," and Gertrude Stein's celebration of *The Mother of Us All.*[10] The *revisionary* female theology promoted in *literary* writing by women implicitly counters the patriarchal theology which is *already* inscribed in literature. The prophesied female Christ, blank Bible, and female Creator revise images familiar in the literary tradition, and, in contrast to earlier appropriations of religious imagery by Metaphysical, Pre-Raphaelite, and other poets, make visible the patriarchal preoccupations of literary "theology." These voices, like the gnostic voices recovered at Nag Hammadi, are only now being heard in chorus; and Pagels' study of "the gnostic feminism" (as the *New York Review of*

Books labeled it) helps to illuminate some aspects of a cultural authority predicated on the suppression or domination of other voices.

Reconsidering patristic writings in light of the contemporary gnostic writings, Pagels argues that claims for exclusive authority made by the self-styled orthodoxy of the early Christian Church depended upon a mystification of history: the church fathers, in order to establish privileged texts, claimed that Jesus himself had invested the spiritual authority of the Church in certain individuals, who in turn passed this power on to their chosen successors. Their claim to a privileged spiritual authority rested upon the interpretation of the Resurrection as a historical event witnessed by the eleven remaining disciples. By this interpretation, all "true" spiritual authority derives from the apostles' witnessing of the literally resurrected Christ—an unrepeatable experience. Remarking the political genius of this doctrine, Pagels outlines its consequences, showing how the restriction of authority to this small band and their chosen successors divided the community into those who had power and those who didn't, privileged authorities and those whom such claims to privilege would dispossess of authority. The interpretation of the Resurrection as a historical event placed its advocates in a position of unchallengeable political dominance: "It legitimized a hierarchy of persons through whose authority all others must approach God" (*GG*, p. 27).

By contrast, the gnostics, interpreting the Resurrection in symbolic terms, resisted the mediating spiritual authority that the "orthodox" sought to institute in the Church. Pagels illustrates this conflict between the orthodox and gnostic positions by analyzing a passage from the gnostic "Gospel of Mary" in which Mary Magdalene comforts the disciples as they mourn after Jesus' death. Mary tells them: " 'Do not weep, and do not grieve, and do not doubt; for his grace will be with you completely, and will protect you.' " Peter then invites Mary, Pagels writes, " 'to tell us the words of the Savior which you remember.' But to Peter's surprise, Mary does not tell anecdotes from the past; instead, she explains that she has just seen the Lord in a vision received through the mind, and she goes on to tell what he revealed to her." Andrew and Peter ridicule Mary's claim that the Lord appeared in her vision, but Levi defends her: " 'Peter, . . . if the Savior made her worthy, who are you to reject her?' . . . Peter, apparently representing the orthodox position, looks to past events, suspicious of those who 'see the Lord' in visions: Mary, representing the gnostic, claims to experience his continuing presence" (*GG*, p. 13).[11]

The gnostic position, then, held that those who had received *gnosis*, that is, self-knowledge as knowledge of divinity,

> had gone beyond the church's teaching and had transcended the authority of its hierarchy. . . . They argued that only one's own experience offers the ultimate criterion of truth, taking precedence over all secondhand testimony and all tradition—even gnostic tra-

dition! They celebrated every form of creative invention as evidence that a person has become spiritually alive. On this theory, the structure of authority can never be fixed into an institutional framework: it must remain spontaneous, charismatic, and open. [*GG*, p. 25]

Pagels' study of "the politics of monotheism" illuminates the fact that the Church's aspirations to "catholicism," or universality, rendered the gnostic and orthodox interpretations of the Resurrection not merely different, nor even antithetical, but mutually exclusive. The coincidence of spiritual and political authority in the Church's self-styled orthodoxy (or "right opinion") made "heretics" of gnostics, defining as politically dangerous those who did not subscribe to the church fathers' mystified historical authority. By contrast, prior to any consideration of the "truth" of their writings, the gnostics neither claimed for themselves nor honored the historically based, absolute authority that the church fathers claimed. It was not, then, a question merely of competing canons, of differing doctrines or guidelines propounded by groups vying for cultural dominance, but of two mutually contradictory stances toward spiritual authority: one defined in such a way as to subsume political power and the other defined in such a way as to preclude the mediation of spiritual authority and, thus, the concept of a transcendentally grounded political authority.

Pagels concludes that the gnostic gospels reopen for our time the central issue of the early Christian controversies—"What is the source of religious authority? . . . What is the relation between the authority of one's own experience and that claimed for the Scriptures, the ritual, and the clergy?" (*GG*, p. 151)—for that issue was formerly settled by fiat, by the violence of political suppression as the cult of orthodoxy, aspiring to *culture*, sought and gained dominance over other cults. In literary culture, the concept of the canon preserves in secularized form some important aspects of the politics of cultural domination which Pagels elucidates in the early Christian Church. As the rediscovery of the repressed gnostic texts casts a new light on the conquests of orthodoxy and the idealization of "one faith" at the cost of many voices, so the entry of marginal texts into the modern literary curriculum not only "opens up" the canon but opens to question the idea of a canon. To explore more fully the workings of canonical authority in a literary context, I will turn now to a passage in *Paradise Lost*—the canonical text par excellence of English literature—which represents the conversion of Eve to orthodoxy. My interest in this passage is not in the dimensions of Milton's views on women as such but in the lines of force already inscribed in the Genesis story that Milton's retelling makes visible.[12]

2. The Invention of Eve and Adam

Eve's story of her first waking in book 4 of *Paradise Lost* is an archetypal scene of canonical instruction. Nowhere are the designs of orthodoxy more vividly displayed than in this passage in which Eve herself utters the words which consign her authority to Adam, and through him to Milton's God, and thence to Milton's poem, and through the poem to the ancient patriarchal tradition.[13] Eve opens her narrative with an apostrophe to Adam—

> O thou for whom
> And from whom I was form'd flesh of thy flesh,
> And without whom am to no end, my Guide
> And Head
>
> [4.440–43]

—which shows that she has already absorbed the wisdom of her teachers, for she echoes Adam's naming of her (see 8.494–97) adapted from Genesis 2:23. She repeats this gesture of self-subordination at the end of her own reminiscences. In the space between, however, Eve remembers an origin innocent of patriarchal indoctrination, one whose resonances the covering trope of narcissism does not entirely suffice to control. Recalling her first waking "Under a shade on flow'rs," Eve remembers that she heard a "murmuring sound / Of Waters issu'd from a Cave," which led her to a "green bank" where she lay down to "look into the clear / Smooth Lake, that to me seem'd another Sky" (4.451–59). But it is not, of course, only "another Sky" that Eve sees reflected in the pool; she also sees what she does not yet understand to be her own image:

> A Shape within the wat'ry gleam appear'd
> Bending to look on me, I started back,
> It started back, but pleas'd I soon return'd,
> Pleas'd it return'd as soon with answering looks
> Of sympathy and love; there I had fixt
> Mine eyes till now, and pin'd with vain desire,
> Had not a voice thus warned me, What thou seest,
> What there thou seest fair Creature is thyself,
> With thee it came and goes; but follow me,
> And I will bring thee where no shadow stays
> Thy coming, and thy soft imbraces, hee
> Whose image thou art, him thou shalt enjoy
> Inseparably thine, to him shalt bear
> Multitudes like thyself, and thence be call'd
> Mother of human Race
>
> [4.461–75]

This scenario imputes to the newborn Eve as her first desire a "vain" narcissism, against which her gently accomplished conversion to the wiser purposes of Adam and God seems a fortunate rise. But the master plot in which the untutored Eve plays the role of doomed narcissist only partially obscures the actual terms of her conversion, which require that she abandon not merely her image in the pool but her very self—a self subtly discounted by the explaining "voice," which *equates* it with the insubstantial image in the pool: "What there thou seest . . . is thyself." The reflection is not *of* Eve: according to the voice, it *is* Eve. As the voice interprets her to herself, Eve is not a self, a subject, at all; she is rather a substanceless image, a mere "shadow" without object until the voice unites her to Adam—"hee / Whose image thou art"—much as Wendy stitches Peter Pan to his shadow.

Having reproduced the voice's call, Eve continues in her own voice with a rhetorical question that gestures toward repressed alternatives:

> what could I do,
> But follow straight, invisibly thus led?
> Till I espi'd thee, fair indeed and tall,
> Under a Platan, yet methought less fair,
> Less winning soft, less amiably mild,
> Than that smooth wat'ry image; back I turn'd,
> Thou following cri'd'st aloud, Return fair *Eve*,
> Whom fli'st thou? whom thou fli'st, of him thou art,
> His flesh, his bone; to give thee being I lent
> Out of my side to thee, nearest my heart
> Substantial Life, to have thee by my side
> Henceforth an individual solace dear;
> Part of my Soul I seek thee, and thee claim
> My other half: with that thy gentle hand
> Seiz'd mine, I yielded, and from that time see
> How beauty is excell'd by manly grace
> And wisdom, which alone is truly fair.
>
> [4.475–91]

As the benefits or "graces" of conversion promised by the voice—sexual pleasure and "Multitudes like thyself"—begin to materialize in Adam, the still autonomous Eve repeals the bargain, for the advertised original does not equal in interest the self she has been called upon to renounce. As she turns away to follow her own desire, Adam himself takes over from the voice the burden of educating Eve to her secondariness, recounting the "history" of her derivation from his rib. This tale informs Eve of an ontological debt she has unwittingly incurred to the generous lender of her "Substantial Life"—not that she might exist to, for, and from herself but rather that he might "have thee by my side / . . . an individual [inseparable] solace dear." Eve is "Part" of Adam's whole, his "other half," to which he lays "claim" by an oxymoronic gentle seizure; her debt to him, as he represents it, is such that she can repay it only by ceding to him her very self.

Eve's relation to Adam as mirror and shadow is the paradigmatic relation which canonical authority institutes between itself and its believers in converting them from the authority of their own experience to a "higher" authority. It also illustrates the way in which patriarchal culture at large imprints itself upon the minds of women and men. Eve's indoctrination into her own "identity" is complete at the point at which her imagination is so successfully colonized by patriarchal authority that she literally becomes its voice. As her narrative shows, she has internalized the voices and values of her mentors: her speech reproduces the words of the "voice" and of Adam and concludes with an assurance that she has indeed been successfully taught to "see" for herself the superiority of Adam's virtues to her own, limited as far as she knows to the "beauty" briefly glimpsed in the pool. In this way she becomes a "Part" not only of Adam but of the cultural economy which inscribes itself in her speech— or, more accurately, which takes over her speech: Eve does not speak patriarchal discourse; it speaks her.[14] The outer limits of her speech are given by the possibilities of this discourse. So long as she does not go beyond those limits her "credit" in the patriarchal system is ensured. It is not simply, then, that Eve accepts Milton's cultural currency at "face value." Rather, as the nativity story in which she traces her transformation from newborn innocent—tabula rasa—to patriarchal woman suggests, she *is* its face value. It is her image that appears on its bills of credit, the image of the idealized and objectified woman whose belief in her role underwrites patriarchal power.

The cultural economy erected upon Eve's credence exists on condition that Eve can "read" the world in only one way, by making herself the mirror of the patriarchal authority of Adam, Milton's God, Milton himself, and Western culture that the voice tells her she is. Indeed, the poem's master plot is designed precisely to discourage any "Eve" from reading this authority in any other way. As Diana Hume George points out, it is not primarily narcissism to which the beautiful talking serpent tempts Eve but *knowledge:* to cease respecting the authority fetish of an invisible power and to see the world for herself.[15] That *Paradise Lost*, the story of the Fall, is a violent parable of *gnosis* punished attests to the threat that Eve's desire for experienced rather than mediated knowledge poses to an authority which defines and proves itself chiefly in the successful prohibition of all other authorities.

To question the "face value" of Milton's cultural currency from within the poem, as Milton's Eve does, is to be blasted by the cultural and poetic authority that controls its plot and representation. But a gnostic "Eve," reading outside the bounds of that authority and not crediting the imagery that Milton would make a universal currency, disrupts that economy by a regard which makes visible what can work only so long as it remains hidden—the power moving Eve's conversion, that is, the power of Milton's God. In Eve's nativity scene, this power is imaged in the disembodied "voice"; and it is precisely the *invisibility* of this voice and of the "history"— originating in Adam's dream (see 8.287–484)—by which Adam attributes to Eve her secondary status that strikingly links this imagery to the church fathers' mystified history of the Resurrection, that invisible past invoked to justify their claims to privileged spiritual authority. The invisible voice that guides Eve away from the visible image of herself in the world to him whose image she is allegorizes what is literally the *secret* not only of spiritual and literary authority in Milton's poem but of cultural authority as such. The mystified authority of Christian doctrine underwrites the voice's injunctions, as it does the church fathers' claims to "right opinion." In both literatures, invisibility is a *definitive* attribute of authority: the power of the voice and of the church fathers, like that of the Wizard of Oz, resides in and depends upon invisibility.[16]

The dynamics of visibility and invisibility in Eve's and Adam's nativities uncover the hidden operations of power in Milton's text, which elaborately exfoliates the cultural text it draws upon. Their autobiographical narratives reveal a powerful subtext, at once literary and cultural, that works to associate Eve with visibility and Adam with invisibility from their first moments. As Maureen Quilligan observes, the relation of Eve's nativity imagery to Adam's replicates the relation between Eve and Adam themselves; for when Adam woke, "Straight toward Heav'n my wond'ring Eyes I turn'd, / And gaz'd a while the ample Sky," requesting it and the "enlighten'd Earth" to "Tell, if ye saw, how came I thus, how here?" (8.257–58, 274, 277). "Where Adam looks up at the true sky and then springs up, immediately to intuit his maker," Quilligan writes, "Eve bends down to look into 'another sky'—a secondary, mediated, reflective sky: a mirror, in more ways than one, of her own being."[17]

Adam's leaping upright to apostrophize a transcendent sky while Eve, supine, gazes into a "sky" that is to Adam's as her knowledge is to his—not the thing itself but a watery reflection—indeed supports the ontological hierarchy so crucial to Milton's purposes in *Paradise Lost*. But these images also intimate—or betray—the deep structure of that hierarchy: a defense against the apparent ascendancy of *Eve's* power. Eve's first act is to move toward the maternally murmuring pool that returns an image of herself in the visible world. Her "father" is out of sight and out of mind, but the reflecting face of the maternal waters gives back an image of her visible self. Adam, by contrast, is a motherless child. He sees with joy the "Hill, Dale, and shady Woods, and sunny Plains, / And liquid Lapse of murmuring Streams," but he does not identify with earthly bodies—not even his own (8.262–63). Adam "perus[es]" himself "Limb by Limb" (8.267), but like Emerson concludes that his body is "Not-Him." The sight of it only inspires him with questions that presuppose not the maternal life source from which bodies come but a father:

> Tell, if ye saw, how came I thus, how here?
> Not of myself; by some great Maker then,
> In goodness and in power preëminent;

Tell me, how may I know him, how adore,
From whom I have that thus I move and live
[8.277–81]

Adam projects a specifically male Creator, subordinating body and earth—
all that Adam can see—to an invisible father.

While it might seem that in these two scenes Milton is simply setting
up intimations of Adam's intrinsic spiritual superiority to Eve, Adam's
nativity offers another reading of his orientation toward transcendence.
Adam's turn to "higher" things can also be read as alienation from his
body and the visible world, an alienation which his God and the establishment of a hierarchical relation to Eve are designed to heal. Apostro-
phizing a sky and earth which give back no self-image, Adam finds none
until he succeeds in turning Eve into his reflection: "Whom fli'st thou?
whom thou fli'st, of him thou art." In this relation, Eve's visible, earth-
identified being is subordinated to Adam's intangible spiritual being.
Thus Eve can tell Adam that it is she who enjoys "So far the happier
Lot, enjoying thee / Preëminent by so much odds, while thou / Like
consort to thyself canst nowhere find" (4.446–48) and that he has taught
her to "see / How beauty is excell'd by manly grace / And wisdom, which
alone is truly fair" (4.489–91). The visible "beauty" of Eve's image bows
to the invisible fairness of "manly grace / And wisdom" in a contest which
appears to originate in Adam's need to make the visible world reflect
himself.

Adam's need to possess Eve is usually understood as complemented
by her need for his guidance, but Milton's text suggests a more subtle
and more compelling source for this need: Adam's sense of inadequacy
in face of what he sees as Eve's perfection. The apparent self-sufficiency
glimpsed in her nativity account ("back I turn'd," interestingly misrep-
resented by Adam in book 8, lines 500–510) is amplified by Adam in
talking with Raphael. When he first saw Eve, Adam recalls, "what seem'd
fair in all the World, seem'd now / Mean, or in her summ'd up, in her
contain'd" (8.472–73), and he cannot reconcile her apparent perfection
with God's assurance of his own superiority. He worries about whether:

> Nature fail'd in mee, and left some part
> Not proof enough such Object to sustain,
> Or from my side subducting, took perhaps
> More than enough; . . .
> . . . .
>   [for] when I approach
> Her loveliness, so absolute she seems
> And in herself complete, so well to know
> Her own, that what she wills to do or say,
> Seems wisest, virtuousest, discreetest, best;
> All higher knowledge in her presence falls

> Degraded, Wisdom in discourse with her
> Loses discount'nanc't, and like folly shows;
> Authority and Reason on her wait,
> As one intended first, not after made
> Occasionally; and to consummate all,
> Greatness of mind and nobleness thir seat
> Build in her loveliest, and create an awe
> About her, as a guard Angel plac't.
>
> [8.534–59]

What is interesting about Adam's representation of his own sense of inadequacy with respect to Eve is that it focuses on the body—specifically, *on the rib* which, he fancies, God took from his body to make Eve. That Adam's anxiety should take this particular form suggests that the "completeness" he fears in Eve and lacks in himself attaches to the function Adam associates with his rib: the power to create a human being. Adam's dream of Eve's creation from his rib fulfills his wish for an organ that performs the life-creating function of Eve's womb. The initial difference between Adam and Eve, then, is not Adam's inner superiority but simply sexual difference; Adam's fantasy of Eve's subordinate creation dramatizes an archetypal womb envy as constitutive of male identity.[18]

Considered in this light, the God that Adam projects in his nativity appears designed to institute a hierarchy to compensate for the disparity he feels between himself and Eve. It is not that Adam is an imperfect image of his God, rather, his God is a *perfected* image of Adam: an all-powerful *male* Creator who soothes Adam's fears of female power by Himself claiming credit for the original creation of the world and, further, by bestowing upon Adam "Dominion" over the fruits of this creation through authorizing him to name the animals *and Eve*. The naming ritual enables Adam to translate his fantasy of power from the realm of desire to history and the world, instituting male dominance over language, nature, and woman. The perfection Adam attributes to the God who authorizes his "Dominion" counters the power he perceives in Eve. As Eve seems to him "absolute . . . / And in herself complete" so must his God possess these qualities in order to compete with her. Milton's curious elaboration of Genesis 2:18 makes a point of God's perfection in contrast to Adam's imperfection without Eve: God baits Adam after he requests a companion, saying in effect, "I'm alone; don't you think I'm happy?" and Adam replies, "Thou in thyself art perfet, and in thee / Is no deficience found; not so is Man" (8.415–16). Adam's "perfet" God enables him to contend with the self-sufficiency he sees and fears in Eve, precisely by authorizing Adam's possession of her. Through the dream of the rib Adam both enacts a parody of birth and gains possession of the womb by claiming credit for woman herself. In this way he himself becomes as "perfet" as he can, appropriating in indirect and symbolic but consequential ways the creative power and self-sufficiency he attributes to Eve and to his God.

The shadow of the repressed mother, then, falls as tangibly over Adam's nativity scene as it does upon Eve's. Necessitated by Adam's awe of Eve's life-giving body and his wish to incorporate her power in himself, this repression mutely signals that patriarchal power is not simply one attribute among others of Adam's God but its primary motive and constituent. As the nativity scene represents Him, Adam's God is a personification of patriarchal power, created in the image of and in competition with the maternal power that Adam perceives in Eve. The overt hierarchy of God over Adam and Adam over Eve which is the text's "argument" is underlain (and undermined) by a more ancient *perceived* hierarchy of Eve over Adam, still apparent in the "ghostlier demarcations" of Adam's transumptive myth. In the power dynamics of Adam's nativity scene, the self-sufficient Eve and the compensatory God that Adam projects out of his fear are the true rivals, as Christ's jealous rebuke to Adam after the Fall confirms:

> Was shee thy God, that her thou didst obey
> Before his voice, or was shee made thy guide,
> Superior, or but equal, that to her
> Thou didst resign thy Manhood, and the Place
> Wherein God set thee above her
>
> [10.145–49]

The nativities of Adam and Eve in Milton's poem bear out the archetypal association of maleness with invisibility and of femaleness with visibility that some theorists argue is given in male and female relations to childbirth and, through childbirth, to the world and the future. In *Moses and Monotheism*, Freud celebrates civilization as the triumph of invisibility over visibility. Freud links what he labels "the progress in spirituality" in Western culture to three tropes of invisibility: the triumph of Moses' unrepresentable God over idols, "which means the compulsion to worship an invisible God"; the evolution of symbolic language, through which abstract thinking assumed priority over "lower psychical activity which concerned itself with the immediate perceptions of the sense organs"; and "the turning from the mother to the father," from matriarchy to patriarchy, which, says Freud, "signifies above all a victory of spirituality over the senses . . . since maternity is proved by the senses whereas paternity is a surmise."[19] Following Dorothy Dinnerstein, Jonathan Culler shifts the priorities of Freud's reading of human history. The establishment of patriarchal power, he suggests, is not merely an instance, along with the preference for an invisible God, of the triumph of spirituality; rather, "when we consider that the invisible, omnipotent God is God the Father, not to say God of the Patriarchs, we may well wonder whether, on the contrary, the promotion of the invisible over the visible . . . is not a consequence or effect of the establishment of paternal authority."[20] Dinnerstein and other feminists go further, interpreting hierarchical dualism not as a "consequence or effect" but as the *means* of establishing paternal authority, a *compensatory* effort on the part of the male to control a natural world to which he is bound in relatively remote and mediated ways.[21] Freud himself runs significantly aground on the question of what motivates the hierarchy of the invisible over the visible: "The world of the senses becomes gradually mastered by spirituality, and . . . man feels proud and uplifted by each such step in progress. One does not know, however, why this should be so" (*MM*, p. 151). In fact, a few pages earlier, he argues that the *invisibility* of Moses' divine patriarch aroused in the minds of believers "a much more grandiose idea of their God" and that this august invisible god endowed believers themselves with grandeur by association: "Whoever believed in this God took part in his greatness, so to speak, might feel uplifted himself" (*MM*, pp. 143). So Adam's first colloquy with his God raises him above the earth to literalized heights, the mount of Paradise:

> *Adam,* rise,
> . . . .
> . . . he took me rais'd,
> . . . .
> . . . led me up
> A woody Mountain; whose high top . . .
> [was so beautifully planted], that what I saw
> Of Earth before scarce pleasant seem'd.
> [8.296–306]

Adam's God enables him to transcend earthly being and in so doing to gain a power he hungers for, as his "sudden appetite / To pluck and eat" the fruits of paradise implies (8.308–9).

Returning now to Eve's nativity narrative, we can see that her story allegorizes Freud's analysis of the "triumph" of invisibility. The God that Adam sees is invisible to her; she, too, progresses from a "lowly" absorption in images of the senses to more grandiose "conceptions"; and she turns away from the maternal waters in which she finds her reflected image to identify with a patriarchy whose power is specifically *not* visible, prevailing even though it is to all *appearances* "less fair, / Less winning soft, less amiably mild, / Than that smooth wat'ry image" of herself in the world. The fable of Eve's conversion from her own visible being in the world to invisible patriarchal authority traces a conversion from being in and for herself to serving a "higher" power—from the authority of her own experience to the hidden authority symbolized in the prohibited Tree of Knowledge.

Yet this power is not transcendent; it must be authorized by Eve's belief—a belief enlisted through the invisible voice's claim that it *already* exists and, further, through its equally strategic representation of Eve as a mere "shadow" or image that has and can have no value except for what patriarchal authority attaches to her. Eve's value is created by the patriarchy whose discourse she becomes. Her narrative proves the "triumph" of her education or colonization; she has received the imprimatur of the realm, has *become* its text, image, and token of value. Assuring her own power within the terms it offers her, she also assures its literal power: her discourse makes its invisible power visible *as herself*. Her passive role in the patriarchal cultural economy—"what could I do, / But follow straight invisibly thus led?"—resembles that of the paper on which monetary value is inscribed.[22] The imprinting of patriarchal authority upon Eve, like the printing of paper money, transforms intrinsically worthless material into pure value. Any object chosen to be the medium of trade must, of course, be worth less than its exchange value; otherwise, it is soon de-idealized, reverting from an image of value to an object of value.[23] Similarly, in order for her to serve as the idealized currency of patriarchal culture, Eve's intrinsic value must be denied; her self, her subjectivity, must be *de*valued to resemble the worthless paper on which the inscription designating money, or credit, is stamped. Eve's subjectivity, her being-for-herself, is the "paper" upon which patriarchal authority imprints its own valuation, thereby "uplifting" her allegedly worthless being ("shadow," reflection, "image") to pure value.

Gubar observes that numerous images of women in texts by male authors suggest that "the female body has been feared for its power to articulate itself."[24] Milton's Eve brings the threat of woman's self-articulation into focus: it is the danger posed by her speaking from her body, from an experience that exists outside patriarchal authority, as did the untutored, self-reflective consciousness Milton represents as narcissistic. Such speech threatens the very basis of the cultural currency. As woman begins to speak a discourse no longer defined and limited by the patriarchal inscription, Eve's voice recovers its intrinsic value. Just as paper would no longer be available to serve as a medium of exchange were its use-value to exceed its exchange-value, so it no longer profits Eve to hand over the "blank pages" of her subjectivity to the patriarchal imprint. At this point, the patriarchal currency fails: to overturn a cliché, it is no longer worth the paper it's printed on.

What the failure of its currency means for the patriarchal economy is not that we no longer read its texts but that we read them in a different way, using interpretive strategies that mark a shift from a sacred to a secular interpretive model, from an economy of invisible transactions to one of *visible* exchange. Concluding *A Room of One's Own*, Woolf refers to *Paradise Lost* as "Milton's bogey."[25] From a gnostic vantage point, *Paradise Lost* loses its power as "bogey" or scarecrow and becomes, instead, a cultural artifact situated in history, its power analyzable as that of an ancient and deeply ingrained pattern in Western thought, reinvented to serve the interests of modern society and realized in language of unsurpassed subtlety and *explicable* sublimity. Read in such a way that the invisible becomes visible; the transcendent, historical; the sacred icon, a cultural image; the "bogey," old clothes upon a stick, Milton's poem becomes as powerful an instrument for the undoing of the cultural economy inscribed in it as it was for its institution—more powerful, indeed, than less "pure" forms of patriarchal currency.

The critique of patriarchal / canonical authority assumes that literary authority is a mode of social authority and that literary value is inseparable from ideology. The "Eves" no longer crediting their image in Milton's poem value his literary achievement no less than do such proponents of canon-making ideologies as Harold Bloom; but the poem no longer shuts out the view. Precisely because of the ways in which our own history is implicated in the poem, we continue to hear the other voices which Milton's literary and cultural history making dominates and which, presenting different models of literary / social authority, disrupt the canonical economy of Milton's text as the gnostic voices disrupted the economy of Christian orthodoxy. To explore some implications of this disruption, I will turn now to compare the representation of poetic authority in *Paradise Lost* with that of Isak Dinesen's short story "The Blank Page," a text Susan Gubar recently brought to wide attention. This story about woman's body and spirit relates itself dialectically to the biblical patriarchal tradition which Milton deepens and extends. Existing both inside and outside that tradition, it exemplifies Eve's speech as it breaks through the limits of patriarchal discourse. By comparing the connections drawn between sexuality and authority in these works, I wish to suggest that Milton's patriarchal epic and Dinesen's very short story about women's speaking silence are, in important ways, complementary forms in our literary culture.[26]

3. Counter-Currencies: Milton and "The Blank Page"

"I can conceive," wrote Woolf of *Paradise Lost*, "that this is the essence, of which almost all other poetry is the dilution."[27] Woolf echoes innumerable readers, but the hypothetical cast of her remark unhinges the judgment just enough to expose its presumption of a particular idea of poetry. Her speculative judgment is also a definition, a tautology: *Paradise Lost* is the essence of poetry / the essence of poetry is *Paradise Lost*. In context, the judgment reflects a rather uncomfortable acquiescence to a certain ideal of poetic greatness. Milton, Woolf says, gives her "no help in judging life; I scarcely feel that Milton lived or knew men and women"; yet beside his sublime depth of style, even Shakespeare seems "a little troubled, personal, hot and imperfect," and this sublime, impersonal perfection she names "poetry."[28]

We may wonder, however, how far the Miltonic sublime derives not from sheer linguistic virtuosity but from thematic resonances that history has proved all but invisible to mortal sight. Milton's nativity scenes, I have argued, reveal that the repression of the mother is the genesis of Genesis. As Milton unveils his Muse in the first of his four invocations, the repression that shapes his epic story is found to mirror a similar repression in the representation of his poetic authority. The Muse of book 1 is a protean figure. Opening *Paradise Lost*, Milton invokes what seems at first a perfectly conventional "Heav'nly Muse"—identified by Merritt Hughes with the Urania of book 7 and the Celestial Patroness of book 9—to tell the story of "man's first disobedience" redeemed by "one greater Man" in order to "justify the ways of God to men" (1.6, 1, 4, 26). At line 7, this figure is particularized as Moses' Muse, the Muse of Genesis through whose inspiration Moses "first taught the chosen Seed, / In the Beginning how the Heav'ns and Earth / Rose out of *Chaos*" (1.8–10). At line 17, the Muse undergoes another, more startling, translation, from *witness* of Creation to *Creator*:

> And chiefly Thou O Spirit, that dost prefer
> Before all Temples th'upright heart and pure,
> Instruct me, for Thou know'st; Thou from the first
> Wast present, and with mighty wings outspread
> Dove-like satst brooding on the vast Abyss
> And mad'st it pregnant
>
> [1.17–22]

It is finally this imagined author of Creation that Milton asks to tell the story of Creation (see 1.27–30).

The invocation of the Creator as Muse is surprising; it is rather as though Homer had invoked not Calliope but Zeus to tell the story of the Trojan War. What is at stake in Milton's construction of his Muse is, of course, his own poetic authority. Milton moves past the sublimated social authority of the Homeric Muse to invoke his God directly, thereby creating an image of a poetic authority that mediates between his conception of the absolute and the "nation" for whom he meant his poem to be "example." Like the orthodox doctrine of the Resurrection as historical event upon which the church fathers based their claims for authority, Milton's Muse underwrites his claims to a specific kind of poetic authority, a power grounded in priority of witness to human history—in *having been there* where his hearers were not. Milton's Muse is at once a model for and a projection of his own ambitious poetic authority, which he seeks to ground in first and highest things. Its authority for the creation of song is based on its authority for the Creation itself. In the role of Milton's Muse this "Spirit" becomes the Logos, the Word that calls all things into being. As such, it is a figure for the cultural authority to which Milton aspires as creator and poet, the absolute authority for history that only one who is both creator and namer can claim. Like Moses' invisible God and like Eve's invisible voice, the God / Muse that Milton projects "uplifts" him from the human to the sublime, from blindness to vision, from the limitations of the visible to invisible power. It meets Milton's prayer:

> What in me is dark
> Illumine, what is low raise and support;
> That to the highth of this great Argument
> I may assert Eternal Providence,
> And justify the ways of God to men.
>
> [1.22–26]

As Milton transforms his Muse into his God, an attendant change occurs: the apparently conventional, presumably female, "Heav'nly Muse" is "transsexualized" even as it is elevated, precisely at the point at which Milton has most at stake in establishing his epic authority. That this is no accident of iconographic tradition is clear from Milton's embellishment of the verse "The earth was without form and void, and darkness was upon the face of the deep; and the Spirit of God was moving over the face of the waters" (Gen. 1:2). Milton's apostrophe, "[Thou who] with mighty wings outspread / Dove-like satst brooding on the vast Abyss / And mad'st it pregnant," transforms his Muse not just into a Creator-figure but into that powerful, self-sufficient *male* Creator so crucial to Adam in his relations with Eve. Milton's image heightens the procreative "hovering" or "brooding" of the Hebrew text but in such a way as to annihilate its female aspect: the maternal—and *mate*rial—life-giving waters of Genesis 1:2 become, in Milton, darkness and silence, an "Abyss," whereas the male impregnator, "Spirit" and divine voice, is addressed as the author of both the Creation and the creation story which Milton tells.

Milton's silencing and voiding of female creativity recall the anxiety about female independence allegorized in the nativities, and his invocation brings all the elements of Freud's "progress in spirituality" into play. The male Logos called upon to articulate the cosmos against an abyss of female silence overcomes the anxieties generated by the tension between visible maternity and invisible paternity by appropriating female power to itself in a parody of parthenogenesis. Milton's image of creation is an archetypally patriarchal image, imagining as it does an absolutely original and self-sufficient paternal act, prior to and unthreatened by all others, from which issues the visible world. His image of epic authority thus depicts in small the "genesis" of the patriarchal authority which is the basis of Milton's cultural power and of his epic theme. Milton's emphatic suppression of the female in his transformation of Genesis is integral to his authority in patriarchal culture, preenacting the silencing of Eve and the Fall which follows upon her violation of the orthodox prohibition of knowledge.[29]

Yet the cost of such authority is the repression of another kind of knowledge, that *human* knowledge the absence of which Woolf remarked. In the famous invocation to book 3, Milton writes of his literal blindness in terms which do not represent the invisible power of the sublime as a simple triumph over the visible, or spiritual power as satisfactory compensation for loss of the visible world:

Thus with the Year
Seasons return, but not to me returns
Day, or the sweet approach of Ev'n or Morn,
. . . .
. . . or human face divine;
. . . .
. . . from the cheerful ways of men
Cut off, and for the Book of knowledge fair
Presented with a Universal blanc
Of Nature's works to me expung'd and ras'd,
And wisdom at one entrance quite shut out.
So much the rather thou Celestial Light
Shine inward, . . .
. . . .
. . . that I may see and tell
Of things invisible to mortal sight.

[3.40–55]

These invocations, which play out in small the sexual dynamics of *Paradise Lost*, suggest that the story of the epic enterprise, the victory of invisibility, and the compensations of "Celestial Light" has not yet been fully told. If the epic tradition has in a very real sense been built upon female silence, then the patriarchal authority Milton establishes in *Paradise Lost* is not mere precondition for his story; it *is* that story.

If *Paradise Lost* issues from an epic authority founded upon women's silence, Dinesen's "Blank Page" is the voice of that silence. Dinesen's storyteller compares the power of speaking silence specifically to the Miltonic tradition of "highest inspiration":

> "Where the story-teller is loyal, eternally and unswervingly loyal to the story, there, in the end, silence will speak. Where the story has been betrayed, silence is but emptiness. But we, the faithful, when we have spoken our last word, will hear the voice of silence . . ."
>
> "Who then," she continues, "tells a finer tale than any of us? Silence does. And where does one read a deeper tale than upon the most perfectly printed page of the most precious book? Upon the blank page. When a royal and gallant pen, in the moment of its highest inspiration, has written down its tale with the rarest ink of all—where, then, may one read a still deeper, sweeter, merrier, and more cruel tale than that? Upon the blank page."[30]

Here is the inverted image of the rivalry between female and male creativity found in Milton's imagery of creative power, and here too the contest is obscurely won. In what sense can the story of the "blank page" be understood to triumph over Milton's high inspiration? It would seem that this triumph must be construed as the feat of showing that silence does speak, that Milton's words cannot possess the *absolute* authority claimed in the image of the Muse as Logos. The speaking silence of the blank page undermines the authority of Milton's scriptures in the same way that Eve's untutored speech does. Its story cannot be told within—yet is the suppressed condition of—patriarchal discourse.

Though less than six pages long, "The Blank Page" begins with a leisurely prologue in which Dinesen's storyteller, like Milton, marks out the terms of her authority. As in *Paradise Lost,* her prologue and her story mirror each other; but whereas Milton's imagery of epic authority privileges the Father and the "Spirit," her authority and her story come through her mothers and belong to the *mater*ial world. The story opens with a frame narrator who sets the scene, a nameless ancient city in which the telling of stories is the sustenance of bodies: "By the ancient city gate sat an old coffee-brown, black-veiled woman who made her living telling stories. . . . Now if she is well paid and in good spirits, she will go on" ("BP," pp. 99, 100). Where Milton's poetic ambition fixes upon invisible highest things, the storyteller's are less grand, concerned first with biological economy. Like Milton, she defines her authority in historical terms, but while he obliterates human forebears—even Moses—"soaring above" to unmediated communion with his "Muse," the storyteller literally *embodies* the teaching of a chain of mother's mothers, all better storytellers than she yet now merged with her as she carries on their "work": "They and I have become one" ("BP," p. 99).

That work is itself bound up with the experience of the female body, for the teller is a Scheherazade whose tales defer death at the hand of patriarchal authority. It is not justification of the ways of God to men but woman's life that is at stake in her craft. Her tale defends not against the literal death that threatens Scheherazade but against a death of the spirit imaged in the tales which the storyteller heard in her youth from young men: "I have told many tales, one more than a thousand, since that time when I first let young men tell me, myself, tales of a red rose, two smooth lily buds, and four silky, supple, deadly, entwining snakes" ("BP," p. 99). The young men's tales allegorize a metaphorical death of woman in patriarchal culture, a "deadly" break between the female body and a speaking subject who disappears into silence upon reaching sexual maturity. The disjunction between the fertile female body and speech is exemplified by her grandmother's two bodies—in youth the dancer's, "often-embraced," and in age the storyteller's, a wrinkled apple ("BP," p. 99). As a child in her grandmother's hard school, the storyteller was unable to understand the "loyal[ty] to the story" through which silence is made to speak: having not yet become a woman, she could not distinguish between speaking silence and empty silence nor feel loyalty to the story at once of female sexuality and female creativity in patriarchal culture ("BP," p. 100). The female body in history is not only the story proper of "The Blank Page" but quite directly its source, inspiration, and authority.

The authority of the female storytellers is not circumscribed by patriarchal tradition; yet it is informed by it. Recounting the history of the convent where flax is cultivated and made into the finest "flower-white" linen of Portugal, the storyteller explains that the first seed for the flax was brought by a Portuguese crusader from the Holy Land. The story of the flax seed is also the story of her own tale: "Diligence . . . is a good thing, and religion is a good thing, but the very first germ of a story will come from some mystical place outside the story itself" ("BP," p. 102). These seed images echo many others in the story: the Annunciation scene, pictured as the Virgin gathering eggs in her mother's poultry yard while Gabriel descends from heaven; the sisters' seeding of the flax fields in the spring; and the imagery of impregnation on the marked "pages" of linen framed and hung in the convent. What is interesting about the superposition of linseed and story-germ is that both picture a remote and indirect fertilization of female production and creation. Though the storyteller cannot read, her grandmother's grandmother learned from an old rabbi and passed her knowledge on, and she cites the Book of Joshua (see Josh. 15:17–19) in describing how the flax seed came from the holy lands of Lecha and Maresha. These lands were made fertile by Achsah's demand that her father Caleb "Give me a blessing!" through which she received "the upper springs and the nether springs" to water her land ("BP," p. 102). The storyteller knows the Bible only as she knows her tales, through oral tradition, in this case "seeded" by the old rabbi. Yet in making her own story continuous with it, she augments biblical authority even as she acknowledges its own in her story and in the sisters' flax and linen.

In tracing the linseed back to Achsah's demand, the storyteller simultaneously allegorizes the history of her own authority and of the story that both takes shape within patriarchal culture and escapes it. Achsah's demand of her father for "the blessing of springs of water," the means of creativity, is the creative speech from which the story of the blank page and the industry of the Convento Velho grow ("BP," p. 102). In this economy of female creativity, women use the father's gift to create their own blessings, outside the fatal authority of patriarchy. They invest their patrimony in a new culture which subverts the ancient, deeply engrained mythology of the war between the sexes: woman as scapegoat; the "fallen" state of the body and labor; and the fetishizing of woman as sexual object, virgin, mother, and property.

The Annunciation image, then, is the paradigm for convent and story, representing the seed which comes to woman from "somewhere outside." The convent society is not entirely independent of patriarchal values: it is in concept a kind of harem of "brides of Christ," and its "first privilege" is to supply the matrimonial sheets ceremoniously displayed in proof of noble brides' virginity, "before the morning gift had yet been handed over" ("BP," p. 102). But within the convent walls exists a world in which the concept of a Fall appears to have no meaning. The nuns are "a blithe and active sisterhood. They take much pleasure in their holy meditations, and will busy themselves joyfully" with their work ("BP," p. 101). Nowhere is their independence of the fallen world of hard toil at the accursed ground more evident than in the joy the sisters take in their labor:

> The long field below the convent is plowed with gentle-eyed, milk-white bullocks, and the seed is skillfully sown out by labor-hardened virginal hands with mold under the nails. At the time when the flax field flowers, the whole valley becomes air-blue, the very color of the apron which the blessed virgin put on to go out and collect eggs. . . . During this month the villagers many miles round raise their eyes to the flax field and ask one another: "Has the convent been lifted into heaven? Or have our good little sisters succeeded in pulling down heaven to them?" ["BP," p. 101]

The sisters create a "heaven" in which the visible world and the work of hands coincide with joy of thought. The story celebrates their female economy as innocent of the dichotomies between visibility and invisibility, body and spirit, the human face and divinity, earth and heaven, which in patriarchal culture attach to gender in such a way as to put enmity between woman's seed and man's, imaged and disowned in the phallic serpent. The "blank page" of linen in the convent's gallery tells the story of escape from the patriarchal sexual economy with its fetish of virgin blood on matrimonial sheets, not only in the specific instance it memorializes but in the many which echo it in the story—Achsah, the Virgin Mary, the sisterhood, the storyteller, and the spinster who makes the "sacred and secretly gay" pilgrimage to the convent to view the blank page, pausing like a gnostic Eve on her way up into the mountains "to see the view widen to all sides" ("BP," pp. 103, 104). The indeterminate text of the blank page gestures beyond a sexual economy which makes woman's body the symbol of patriarchal authority—credit or goods—toward body and spirit no longer divided and no longer inscribed with the designs of an external mastery.

To the Adam-and-Eve-like pair who are her audience, the storyteller says that the old women who tell stories "know the story of the blank page. But we are somewhat averse to telling it, for it might well, among the uninitiated, weaken our own credit. All the same . . . my sweet and pretty lady and gentlemen of the generous hearts[,] I shall tell it to you" ("BP," p. 100). As Milton's orthodox story of the Fall is one in which all are initiated and which many still credit, the gnostic "Blank Page" is a riddle, a "counter-currency" of unfamiliar inscription and authority. But cultural authority, like money, is a social convention underwritten by common belief. Within the gender distinctions instituted by patriarchy, epic authority is "male" and the authority of "The Blank Page," which seeks not to dominate other voices but to let silence speak, is "female." But this "pregnant" juxtaposition points beyond static dichotomies to active rereadings of the texts that have shaped our traditions alongside those that have been repressed and toward questioning and reimagining the structures of authority for a world in which authority need no longer be "male" and coercive nor silence "female" and subversive, in which, in other words, speech and silence are no longer tied to an archetypal— and arbitrary—hierarchy of gender.

The problem of revising the ways in which the literary academy deploys its culture-making power is obviously too large to address here. But the feminist (or antipatriarchal) challenge to the ideal of "the literary canon" points to the need to transform a pedagogy which conceives "Great Books" on the model of sacred texts into one which calls into question the unexamined hierarchies invoked by the Arnoldian ideal, "the acquainting ourselves with the best that has been thought and said in the world." A recent exponent of this ideal, Harry Levin, has written that it must not be laid aside, for "without this, we will lose our most valued patrimony, our collective memory."[31] But there can be no hope for a "community of ideas," or for anything like the consensus a "canon" requires, based on a heritage in which domination and hierarchy are the very ground for literary and social authority—a "patrimony" accumulated at the expense of silencing woman's culture-making power in "matrimony." Yet, if the "collective memory" held in the traditional canon of Western literature is a danger to the future so long as it is propagated by a "Great Books" pedagogy in the traditional curriculum, it also has powerful possibilities, read from a critical perspective, as an instrument for change. Few of us can free ourselves completely from the power ideologies inscribed in the idea of the canon and in many of its texts merely by not reading "canonical" texts, because we have been reading the patriarchal "arche-text" all our lives. But we can, through strategies of rereading that expose the deeper structures of authority and through interplay with texts of a different stamp, pursue a kind of collective psychoanalysis, transforming "bogeys" that hide invisible power into investments both visible and al-terable. In doing so, we approach traditional texts not as the mystifying (and self-limiting) "best" that has been thought and said in the world but as a *visible* past against which we can teach our students to imagine a different future. Because its skeptical regard of the past is informed by responsibility to that future, feminist theory is a powerful tool with which to replace Arnold's outworn dictum. As women begin to come into a share of the "patrimony," we can begin to imagine a redistribution of "credit" that will undo the invisible power of the literary tradition and make for a richer world.

1. Virginia Woolf, *Jacob's Room* (1922; New York, 1978), pp. 40–41.
2. Since the male-female relationship is the archetypal hierarchy in Western culture, "woman" has become a fashionable image for analysts of cultural politics, notably in deconstructive theory and practice. The dangers of this appropriation to the interests of actual women have been discussed by Nancy K. Miller in "The Text's Heroine: A Feminist Critic and Her Fictions," *Diacritics* 12 (Summer 1982): 48–53. She argues for combining a post-humanistic theory which throws center, periphery, and subject into question with a critical practice that does not lose sight of the *literally* marginal and precarious position female authors and teachers now hold in the academy. While it is manifestly not true that the "canonical" and "gnostic" stances toward authority that I explore in this essay belong in any simple way to actual men and women, respectively, history—and literary history— render these alignments no more heuristic than descriptive.
3. Elaine Showalter, "Women and the Literary Curriculum," *College English* 32 (May 1971): 855.
4. See Judith Fetterley, *The Resisting Reader: A Feminist Approach to American Fiction* (Bloomington, Ind., 1978).
5. This "opening" was propounded from Third World, feminist, and Marxist points of view in the collection of essays that appeared in the wake of the sixties' questioning of authority, *The Politics of Literature: Dissenting Essays on the Teaching of Literature*, ed. Louis Kampf and Paul Lauter (New York, 1972), and later in *English Literature: Opening Up the Canon*, ed. Leslie A. Fiedler and Houston A. Baker, Jr., Selected Papers from the English Institute, 1979, n.s. 4 (Baltimore, 1981).
In order to situate the issues of my argument, it is useful to recall here Ernst Robert Curtius' description of the intellectual economy that he considered to have replaced the concept of the canon in the twentieth century. Citing Valery Larbaud, he distinguishes between "la carte politique et la carte intellectuelle du monde." The anachronistic French model of national canons competing for the colonization of intellectual territories has ceded, he says, to literary cosmopolitanism, "a politics of mind which has left behind all pretensions to hegemony, and is concerned only with facilitating and accelerating the exchange of intellectual merchandise" (*European Literature and the Latin Middle Ages*, trans. Willard R. Trask [1948; Princeton, N.J., 1973], pp. 271, 272). In Curtius' account, which posits the transformation of cultural imperialism into a world market in which intellectual "goods" are freely exchanged, not only the concept of a closed canon but the canonizing stance itself becomes obsolescent along with the hegemonic and universal (or "catholic") pretensions of parochial cultures—Judeo-Christian, national, or European. The evangelical projects of ethnocentric beliefs are presumed dead or defunct, and belief in the supremacy of a single cultural authority gives way to diverse and mutually translatable cultural "currencies." These admit of equation and free exchange in a global economy governed not by transcendent and hegemonic conceptions of value but by *translatability*—of sensibility as well as language. Curtius' idealized image of a free-market cultural economy usefully distinguishes the cultural issues of the twentieth century from those of earlier periods, but his wishful depoliticization of this economy can be understood only in the context of nationalist politics in the first half of the century. In fact, the "intellectual free market" has the defects of its economic analogue, and both are, in any case, virtually male monopolies.
6. See, for example, Florence Howe, "Those We Still Don't Read," *College English* 43 (Jan. 1981): 16.
7. Fetterley, *The Resisting Reader*, p. xx.

8. Elaine Pagels, *The Gnostic Gospels* (New York, 1979), p. xxii; all further references to this work, abbreviated *GG*, will be included parenthetically in the text. Critics who object that Pagels gives scant attention to the diversity of voices within Christian orthodoxy err in supposing her discussion to concern unity and diversity as such rather than the politics implicit in orthodox and gnostic stances toward spiritual authority. The gnostic position as she describes it leads logically not to political anarchy but rather to a demystification of the political sphere.

9. J. Hillis Miller, "The Function of Rhetorical Study at the Present Time," *The State of the Discipline, 1970s–1980s, ADE Bulletin* 62 (Sept.-Nov. 1979): 12; cited by Sandra Gilbert, "What Do Feminist Critics Want? or, A Postcard from the Volcano," *ADE Bulletin* 66 (Winter 1980): 20. Miller acknowledges the "strongly preservative or conservative" character of his pronouncement (p. 12).

10. Susan Gubar, " 'The Blank Page' and the Issues of Female Creativity," *Writing and Sexual Difference, Critical Inquiry* 8 (Winter 1981): 261, 262.

11. For the complete text, see "The Gospel of Mary," in *The Nag Hammadi Library in English*, ed. James N. Robinson, trans. Members of the Coptic Gnostic Library Project of the Institute for Antiquity and Christianity (New York, 1977), pp. 471–74.

12. John Milton's sexual politics has become an issue of increasing importance in Milton criticism in the last decade; among many illuminating studies are Marcia Landy, "Kinship and the Role of Women in *Paradise Lost*," *Milton Studies* 4 (1972): 3–18, and " 'A Free and Open Encounter': Milton and the Modern Reader," *Milton Studies* 9 (1976): 3–36; Barbara K. Lewalski, "Milton on Women—Yet Once More," *Milton Studies* 6 (1974): 3–20; Diane McColley, " 'Daughter of God and Man': The Subordination of Milton's Eve," in *Familiar Colloquy: Essays Presented to Arthur Edward Barker*, ed. Patricia Bruckmann (Ottawa, 1978), pp. 196–208; Joan Malory Webber, "The Politics of Poetry: Feminism and *Paradise Lost*," *Milton Studies* 14 (1980): 3–24; Northrop Frye, "The Revelation to Eve," in *"Paradise Lost": A Tercentenary Tribute*, ed. Balachandra Rajan (Toronto, 1969), pp. 18–47; and Marilyn R. Farwell, "Eve, the Separation Scene, and the Renaissance Idea of Androgyny," *Milton Studies* 16 (1982): 3–20.

13. See Milton, *Paradise Lost, Complete Poems and Major Prose*, ed. Merritt Y. Hughes (Indianapolis, 1957), bk. 4; all further references to this work will be included in the text, with book and line numbers in parentheses.

Milton draws his account of the creation of Adam and Eve mainly from that by the J[ahwist] scribe (Gen. 2:4–3:20, ninth–tenth century B.C.), rather than from the P[riestly] scribe's account (Gen. 1:26–27, fifth–sixth century B.C.). In the P scribe's text, female and male are co-orginary. But, for a discussion of the exaggeration of patriarchal values in the J scribe's Hebrew text by the translators of the English texts, see Casey Miller and Kate Swift, *Words and Women: New Language in New Times* (New York, 1978), pp. 15–16, citing Phyllis Trible's "Depatriarchalizing in Biblical Interpretation," *Journal of the American Academy of Religion* 41 (Mar. 1973): 35–42.

14. The limits of Eve's discourse in her nativity story illustrate the interest of the concept of authority as reframed by Michel Foucault: " 'What are the modes of existence of this discourse?' 'Where does it come from; how is it circulated; who controls it?' " ("What Is an Author?," *Language, Counter-Memory, Practice: Selected Essays and Interviews*, ed. Donald F. Bouchard, trans. Bouchard and Sherry Simon [Ithaca, N.Y., 1977], p. 138).

15. See Diana Hume George, "Stumbling on Melons: Sexual Dialectics and Discrimination in English Departments," in *English Literature: Opening Up the Canon*, pp. 120–26.

16. Foucault theorizes that invisibility is inherent in and necessary to the workings of power: "Power is tolerable only on condition that it mask a substantial part of itself. Its success is proportional to its ability to hide its own mechanisms. . . . For it, secrecy is not in the nature of an abuse; it is indispensable to its operation" (*The History of Sexuality: Volume I, an Introduction*, trans. Robert Hurley [New York, 1980], p. 86).

17. Maureen Quilligan, *Milton's Spenser: The Politics of Reading* (Ithaca, N.Y., 1983), pp. 227–28. Quilligan pursues a different line of argument, reevaluating Eve's centrality

in the poem read as integrally concerned with instituting "a new kind of family structure concurrent with the 'rises' of protestantism and of capitalism with its free market ideologies" (p. 177).

18. Milton develops with subtlety and precision the motive of womb envy already strikingly apparent in the J scribe's creation story (Gen. 2:4–3:20). The motive of compensation in Adam's appropriation of the power of naming—language—is illuminated by his naming the woman Eve (*Hawwah*), derived from the Hebrew root *havah* ("to live"). Other details contribute to this interpretation of the rib fantasy, not least Eve's impressive birth announcement in Genesis 4:1: "'I have acquired a man with the help of Yahweh.'" Such a reading suggests that the cultural conditions that conduce to the malaise of penis envy are "erected" on a prior malaise of womb envy; and, indeed, so patriarchal a historian as Amaury de Riencourt writes that our "original" creation story "was taken wholesale" from a *more* original Sumerian mythology centered not on patriarchal namers but on female fertility gods (*Sex and Power in History* [New York, 1974], p. 37; see also pp. 36–38). On this last point, see Wolfgang Lederer, "Envy and Loathing—The Patriarchal Revolt," *The Fear of Women* (New York, 1968), pp. 153–68. See also Virginia R. Mollenkott, n. 29 below.

19. Sigmund Freud, *Moses and Monotheism*, trans. Katherine Jones (New York, 1967), pp. 142, 144, 145–46; all further references to this work, abbreviated *MM*, will be included parenthetically in the text.

20. Jonathan Culler, *On Deconstruction: Theory and Criticism after Structuralism* (Ithaca, N.Y., 1982), p. 59; see also pp. 58–60.

21. The most extensive exploration of this theme, linking the structures of individual psychology in Western society to those of its cultural institutions, is Dorothy Dinnerstein, *The Mermaid and the Minotaur: Sexual Arrangements and Human Malaise* (New York, 1976).

22. Feminist theorists have drawn upon Marxist anthropologists' analyses of women as objects of exchange in kinship systems to analyze women as the "goods" through which patriarchal power passes; see, for example, Gayle Rubin, "The Traffic in Women: Notes on the 'Political Economy' of Sex," *Toward an Anthropology of Women*, ed. Rayna R. Reiter (New York, 1975), pp. 157–210, and Luce Irigaray, "Des Marchandises entre elles" [When the goods get together], *Ce sexe qui n'en est pas un* [This sex which isn't one] (Paris, 1977), pp. 189–93, trans. Claudia Reeder in *New French Feminisms: An Anthology*, ed. Elaine Marks and Isabelle de Courtivron (New York, 1981), pp. 107–10. I am conceiving the issue of cultural authority in terms of credit rather than barter or coins in order to analyze the workings of patriarchal authority, but my argument has some parallels to Irigaray's discussion of the disruption of the patriarchal sexual economy effected by women's removing themselves from this market.

23. Ideally, the medium of trade should be intrinsically worthless; Gresham's law that "bad" money (coins of baser metals) drives out "good" money (gold or silver coins) points to the advantage of the almost "pure" credit embodied in paper money. Gold and silver coins are money conceived as portable stores of value rather than as credit.

24. Gubar, "'The Blank Page' and the Issues of Female Creativity," p. 246.

25. Woolf, *A Room of One's Own* (1928; New York, 1957), p. 118. Woolf says that women will write "if we . . . see human beings . . . and the sky, too, and the trees or whatever it may be in themselves; if we look past Milton's bogey, for no human being should shut out the view" (p. 118). Gilbert takes up the image in "Milton's Bogey: Patriarchal Poetry and Women Readers," Gilbert and Gubar, *The Madwoman in the Attic: The Woman Writer and the Nineteenth-Century Literary Imagination* (New Haven, Conn., 1979), pp. 187–212. Gilbert identifies women writers with Eve and Satan, all "resisting readers," but, I think, does not fully rescue their gnostic readings from the patriarchal framework within which they are damned.

26. See Myra Jehlen, "Archimedes and the Paradox of Feminist Criticism," *Signs* 6 (Summer 1981): 575–601, and Coppélia Kahn, "Excavating 'Those Dim Minoan Regions': Maternal Subtexts in Patriarchal Literature," *Diacritics* 12 (Summer 1982): 32–41. Both address "the gender of genre" with respect to the bourgeois novel and Shakespearean tragedy.

27. Woolf, *A Writer's Diary,* ed. Leonard Woolf (New York, 1954), p. 6.

28. Ibid., pp. 5, 6.

29. For a different reading of the sexual ambiguity of Milton's Muse, see Mollenkott, "Some Implications of Milton's Androgynous Muse," *Bucknell Review* 24 (Spring 1978): 27–36. Mollenkott sees the Muse as androgynous and as "beautifully symboli[zing] the womb envy that is so deeply repressed in the human male" (p. 32); however, she does not acknowledge the *appropriation* of female power by the male in Milton's image of his Muse. See also Farwell, n. 12 above.

30. Isak Dinesen, "The Blank Page," *Last Tales* (New York, 1957), p. 100; all further references to this work, abbreviated "BP," will be included parenthetically in the text. I am indebted to Susan Gubar's insightful and suggestive reading of this story; see n.10 above.

31. Harry Levin, "Core, Canon, Curriculum," *College English* 43 (Apr. 1981): 362.

A Few Canonic Variations

Joseph Kerman

1. Thema

"Canon," to musicians, means something else. "Wir haben ein Gesetz." That may be the one reason we feel awkward, even a little uneasy, about using the term as it is used in the other arts, to mean (roughly) an enduring exemplary collection of books, buildings, and paintings authorized in some way for contemplation, admiration, interpretation, and the determination of value. We speak of the repertory, or repertories, not of the canon. A canon is an idea; a repertory is a program of action.

A deeper reason, I think, has to do with some simple and well-known truths about music's evanescence, that evanescence which makes for special difficulties when we try to talk about music's history. Certainly it is difficult to talk about a canon without also talking about history. Perhaps I can begin a discussion of these difficulties through some simple words once spoken by Mantle Hood, following one of his gracefully polemical seminars. Hood had just urged, in effect, that Western art music be viewed not in terms of a canon but rather as a field of social and cultural activity.

> Music persists as it is only to the extent that interlocking requirements allow it to. . . . When a culture has finished with any [musical] tradition, when it no longer communicates or ceases to fill whatever function it has filled esthetically or otherwise, then it will most certainly disappear, particularly in cultures where there is no form of written record of such things. In our culture I think many traditions have not completely disappeared because we do have some kind of written

record. I suspect that in many ways, however, their real identities
are gone. I think we are looking at skeletons, without being sure
what kind of flesh they ought be be clothed in.[1]

Music is process, action, activity; but once it is written down it yields up
an object (a score) and is itself on the way to becoming objectified. The
concept of a musical work or composition, to say nothing of a canon,
depends on such objectification, at least to some extent—on writing,
which is not a musical but a literary mode. What Hood wants to stress
is that "some kind of written record" is neither necessary nor sufficient
to assure the "real" maintenance of a musical tradition. As long as a
tradition persists, musicians continue to internalize the music by a long
and, to them, rewarding process of attending to it, absorbing it, imitating
it, learning it, and repeating it. There may or may not be written aids
to this, but essentially the tradition is passed on orally from musician to
musician and from musician to listener.

It is not surprising to find this model for music insisted on by ethnomusicologists. Coming to an alien music cold, or more or less cold,
and perhaps finding that some sort of notation has been developed for
it, an ethnomusicologist such as Hood becomes only too sharply aware
of how little the documents tell him about time and tempo, nuance and
sonority, the limits of improvisatory practice—everything that gives the
music of the Javanese puppet theater, say, its particular arcane identity.
Often enough the ethnomusicologist finds nothing at all in writing to
help him with his work, whether this consists of describing music or
learning to perform it—often through lengthy apprenticeships—in order
to achieve some measure of the internalization on which that identity
depends.

None of this may seem like much of a problem to those of us who
stick to our own tradition. We have been internalizing this music ever
since our fathers sang us Beatles songs and our mothers shoved our
playpens in front of the TV. It is only on the basis of this unconscious
internalization that musicians can easily learn to read musical scores
straight off—with the feel of other such music in their fingers and throats
and with its sound in their ears. But music in this sense, as must be clear,
does not extend back very far in history. Music in this sense (which is

---

Joseph Kerman, professor of music at the University of California,
Berkeley, is the author of *Opera as Drama, The Beethoven Quartets, The
Masses and Motets of William Byrd,* and (with Alan Tyson) *The New Grove
Beethoven.* He is also coeditor of *Beethoven Studies* and *Nineteenth-Century
Music* and is presently working on a concise study of modern musical
scholarship.

Hood's sense) does not *have* much history. In the absence of an internalized performance tradition, the interpretation of written records of Western music going back two hundred years is already equivocal, five hundred years highly speculative, and a thousand years in certain serious ways hopeless. The notation symbols of the ninth and tenth centuries—staffless neumes—do not even specify pitch or (so far as scholars agree) rhythm, let alone tempo, tone quality, ornamentation, or dynamics—only certain aspects of melodic contour.

So it is not surprising, once again, that among students of Western music the greatest sympathy for the ethnomusicologists' dilemma, and the greatest interest in their model, has been shown to date by medievalists. Leo Treitler now conceives of the history of medieval music in terms of a by no means simple or unilateral transition from what he calls the "medieval paradigm" to the "modern paradigm" or "paradigm of literacy."[2] Gregorian chant was first sung in monastic communities according to an oral, formulaic system, internalized by cantors of ritual texts whom Treitler has compared to Albert Lord's singers of tales. The complex polyphonic music of later centuries was written down by composers—Perotin, Petrus de Cruce, Machaut, Dufay—to be sung, more or less "by the book," by musicians who could read music as well as words. Treitler's medieval paradigm helps explain many things, including some puzzles about the interpretation of the earliest Gregorian chant notation—a notation invented, it is clear, in order to meet Charlemagne's determination to import and standardize the music that went with the canonical words of the Roman Mass and office services. He ran into trouble which is reflected in the chant manuscripts. While the words could be sent to him, it took some time before he could be satisfied about the music, for it was not clear in Rome how an oral tradition could be, in fact, canonized.

Charlemagne's program was the first instance of canon-formation in Western music, and one thing to keep in mind about it is that it called for texts, for written records. This was a new idea as far as music was concerned. When a fresh redaction of the Gregorian canon was demanded by the Counter-Reformation papacy, things went much more smoothly since people were by then accustomed to using musical texts like verbal texts, musical notation was much more highly developed, and, of course, the distribution of texts was now much more efficient. The next official redaction of the Gregorian canon was carried out by the scholarly Benedictines of Solesmes in the later nineteenth century. This was interesting both because of the sophisticated philological principles on which it rested and also because its authority was extended to cover not only the notes on the page but also the way they were to be sung. The Solesmes phenomenon is an early instance of re-creating a historical performance tradition—putting flesh or clothes on those skeletons. I shall return to it later.

2. Canon perpetuus

With some qualifications Richard L. Crocker, another medievalist, accepts Treitler's medieval paradigm for the early Gregorian period but not his paradigm of literacy for the later Middle Ages and beyond.[3] Impressed by work such as Hood's, he does not consider that a musical tradition changes in any essential way under the impact of writing or literacy. Crocker is even ready to take on the art music of the nineteenth century—though if there ever was a time when a canon was consolidated in music outside of the Church, this should be it. Even in the nineteenth century, musicians operated more or less as they always had, relying primarily on the internal dynamic of tradition rather than on the external authority of composers' ideal texts. The points Crocker makes about this are worth summarizing. As he says, performers were (and still are) taught by word and gesture and example those all-important, unwritten nuances that would completely elude someone from Java schooled simply in note reading, although such nuances are required for even the most elementary level of performing competence. Nineteenth-century instrumental and vocal virtuosos improvised freely and often played fast and loose with the text before them. "Throughout the nineteenth century we know of the important role of the performer as 'interpreter,' under which rubric he or she could do and did an endless variety of individual things to whatever written record there was." Scores were neither sacrosanct nor stable; well-liked music was arranged—that is, recast, rescored, and re-composed—into multiple versions for different performing groups. Famous composers kept revising their famous texts, too; so much so, in Verdi's case, that of his twenty-six operas, seventeen (including *Oberto,* the first, and *Falstaff,* the last) exist or existed in more than one version. "The fact that a work can be established to have one original, authentic, final form may not reflect the composer's final authoritative determination, but only that he was never occasioned by performance opportunities to rethink it."

This is spirited and salutary; though for the purposes of his own polemic, Crocker lights up only one face of a notoriously two-faced century. Verdi also wrote contracts stipulating that his operas were to be performed note for note according to the materials supplied by his publisher. Very few are the compositions by Brahms that he allowed to survive in more than one version. No one called Clara Schumann a *virtuosa* or observed her monkeying with a text. The same nineteenth century that spawned all those innumerable arrangements also nurtured the first musical variorums (Bischoff's edition from the 1880s of Bach's keyboard music, now published by Kalmus, is an example that many will know).

What seems to me more significant about the nineteenth century is the fundamental change that took place during this period in the nature of the Western art-music tradition or, more precisely, in the way this tradition changed. In previous centuries the repertory consisted of music of the present generation and one or two preceding generations; it was continuously turning over. Thus in the fifteenth century the insufferable Johannes Tinctoris could announce that there was no music worth listening to that hadn't been written in the last forty years (about his own age at the time); in seventeenth-century Venice, though the opera houses may remind us of a modern city's movie theaters, there were no rerun houses for Monteverdi as there are for Fellini; and Bach's music dropped out of the Leipzig repertory at his death no less promptly than that of his far less eminent predecessors. Under such conditions of evanescence the idea of a canon is scarcely thinkable.

After around 1800 or 1820, however, when new music entered the repertory, old music did not always drop out. Beethoven and Rossini were added to, not replaced. Increasingly the repertory assumed a historical dimension; music assumed a history. There were even conscious efforts to extend the repertory back into the evanesced past.

For "repertory" I should have written "secular repertories"; as has already been noted, the Catholic church had its enduring canon, periodically revised, and by 1800 the Lutheran and Anglican rites also supported musical traditions extending back (even if only tenuously, as the Leipzig case reminds us) two hundred years or more. In the secular sphere an interesting exception is Jean-Baptiste Lully, whose operas held the stage in France for nearly a hundred years after their composition. This exception is revealing because special social-political and also special literary-academic reasons can be adduced for it with such clarity. On the one hand, there was Lully's extraordinary and, it seems, even posthumous power in controlling the resources of artistic monopoly and patronage under the Sun King. On the other, there was the French academic establishment, which took the composer and his librettist Philippe Quinault if not exactly into its heart at least into its canon, even devising a special literary genre, *tragédie lyrique,* to validate the canonization. Quite exceptionally for operas in the seventeenth century, sumptuous scores were printed of the Lully works.

That the new longevity enjoyed (or suffered) by repertories depended on the new social configuration that was formed for music in the nineteenth century is obvious. It may be less obvious that it also depended on the literary phenomenon of canonization. Why would the new social scene for music—the concert series and the virtuoso, the bourgeois as audience and amateur, the freelance composer and critic—in itself have frozen and extended repertories? The social scene exacted, perhaps, its ideology. In any case, the ideology supporting the notion of a canon in music was one of the first precipitates of the post-Kantian revolution in music criticism and aesthetics. Like the expanding, historical repertory, the canon was one of music's legacies from early Romanticism.

Repertories are determined by performers, canons by critics—who are by preference musicians, but by definition literary men or at least effective writers about music. Literary models lie close at hand for the categories that music critics have to manipulate. When E. T. A. Hoffmann in 1810 proclaimed Haydn, Mozart, and Beethoven as the three great Romantic composers—though Beethoven was clearly *primus inter pares*—an idea that caught so much of the resonance of contemporary aesthetics itself resonated hugely into the future. "Romantic" was a term taken from literature (and Hoffmann the arch-Romantic novelist did his unfortunately rather premature best to compose Romantic operas also). What Hoffmann called "romantic," we call "classic," to be sure: a term conflating a stylistic discrimination between these composers and a later generation, which Hoffmann did not live to see, with the honorific that Hoffmann actually intended, whatever his terminology. For him, Haydn, Mozart, and Beethoven constituted the canon.

Literary, too, was the model for the status Hoffmann meant to bestow on his musical trinity. He wanted to erect pedestals for them like those supporting the three great Greek tragedians, thrones like those still being warmed by at least one of the Weimar classics. Beethoven was compared, inevitably, to Shakespeare. The canonization of the Greek tragedians and Shakespeare depended on written texts; there was no concern about the internalization of theatrical performance traditions, nor as yet about recovering such traditions. Hence scores in the nineteenth century assumed a new importance, over and above that of providing guidance for conductors (less anachronistically: leaders of group performances) or fodder for student composers. Scores were now seen as texts for criticism, like literary texts.

Hoffmann's program as a music critic combined metaphysical speculation, Romantic rhetoric, and legislation about the canon with specific, sometimes bar-by-bar musical descriptions—an early form of musical analysis modeled once again on the modes of literary criticism. Hoffmann must be the first of many authors who have badgered journal editors with demands for more and more music illustrations; it is extremely important, he kept saying, for his readers to be able to see the scores—scores which he himself had to prepare, incidentally, since the music he was discussing was issued not in scores (to be studied) but in separate band parts (to be played from). His famous Beethoven reviews were not of live performances but of published sheet music, texts dead on the page save for Hoffmann's internalized musical imagination and that of his readers.[4]

As in the case of plainchant in the ninth century, canonization in the nineteenth was bound up with the whole matter of musical records. Inexpensive *Taschenpartituren* found their way into the pockets of serious concert goers, while expensive fifty-volume critical editions of great composers' scores in folio were prepared by musicologists, a new brand of scholar marching along dutifully in the footsteps of literary historians and philologists. The Romantics did not think like today's ethnomusicologists, for whom the ultimate reality of music resides in the social activity of musical performance. They were idealists enough to see musical scores as primary texts of which performances, or "readings," were successively imperfect representations.

And if this idea was not always spelled out frankly, one reason was, I think, that it clashed with another idea or ideal that was dear to the Romantics. This was the spontaneity of the artist—the performing artist as well as the composer. The performer was thought to have something inspired of his own to bring to the music; yet the underlying assumption was that he should be representing the composer's inspiration and doing his best to convey this faithfully, "authentically." In a similar way, as M. H. Abrams pointed out many years ago, the idea of the work of art growing organically and inevitably as though from a seed clashed with the ideal of the poet's spontaneity, and indeed put in question his very role in making the poem.[5] These conflicts were unresolvable and grew more explicit as the discipline of musical analysis was refined from its adumbrations in the work of Hoffmann. Analysis shows why this sequence of notes in the score is important and that sequence is not, why the main downbeat is here and not there, and why this phrasing is right and that one wrong. Unless the critic conceives of his work as purely theoretical, these are veiled instructions he is issuing to the performer. The analysts' insights, said Edward T. Cone in a famous article, "reveal how a piece of music should be heard, which in turn implies how it should be played. An analysis is a direction for a performance."[6] The idea of a canonical work of music has to imply the idea of a canonical musical performance.

All this was possible, no doubt, only because an entire high culture intoxicated by music had internalized it to so high a degree. Crocker observes that where Treitler's paradigm of literacy works best is in reference to the seemingly perpetual twentieth-century cultivation of nineteenth-century masterpieces:

> If we turn to classical instrumental music—symphonies, chamber works, and solos—especially in twentieth-century institutionalized performances, then indeed we seem to be dealing with the "paradigm of literacy." . . . The most important point about this instrumental repertory seems to me to be that it involves a very specific, restricted list of symphonies, string quartets, sonatas preserved long after origin in a kind of Meistersinger environment—one in which we could imagine the authority of the standard version to derive . . . from factors of reverence for impressive, beloved compositions.[7]

This sounds like a pretty fair definition of a canon, except that Crocker is really speaking about a repertory; but in this case, at least, the canon is at the core of the repertory. It need not be restricted to instrumental music. Equally canonical are vocal works by the instrumental masters — *Don Giovanni, Dichterliebe, Ein deutsches Requiem*—as well as works by other masters who specialized in opera or lieder.

The idea of a canon had taken hold powerfully during the nineteenth century, as the canon itself grew by the accretion of more and more music—though of course the growth was never entirely linear. While Beethoven always stayed at dead center, Haydn and much of Mozart dropped or at least faded out, to be reinstated later, and a major issue developed over the inclusion of Wagner or Brahms or both. Liszt's claim was never properly adjudicated; indeed, members of non-Teutonic nations grew increasingly restive over the difficulty of gaining places for their heroes. For from Hoffmann's time on, the ideology which nurtured that growth included a strong component of nationalism along with historicism, organicism—a concept applied not only to individual artistic structures but also to the canon itself—and what Carl Dahlhaus has aptly called "the metaphysics of instrumental music." This ideology is something I touched on in an earlier *Critical Inquiry* article, which also includes something about the canon and a good deal more about the academic critics—that is, musical analysts—who validated it.[8]

Formed at the outset of Romanticism, this ideology seems to have reached its fullest articulation as a reaction to the advent of modernism, at the very time when the ideology itself came under question. The first of the influential writings of Heinrich Schenker and Donald Francis Tovey appeared in the early 1900s. Of all early twentieth-century critics, Schenker was the most rigidly committed to the concept of a canon, which for him consisted of J. S. and C. P. E. Bach, Handel, Haydn, Mozart, Beethoven, Schubert, Schumann, Mendelssohn, Chopin, Brahms, and no further. Tovey was a little more flexible, partly because, unlike Schenker, he was a practicing musician all his life and, as such, had to deal with the day-to-day reality of repertories—but not much. Both men, incidentally, spent much time editing authoritative editions of Beethoven and the two Bachs.

It is worth repeating that repertories are determined by performers, canons, by critics. How much effect critics have on actual repertories is a matter of much ill-natured debate. In any case, conservative critics at the turn of the century did not all agree on the exact prospectus of the canon, any more than they agreed on correct methods of musical analysis. That would hardly have been natural, would have left hardly anything to argue about. What they did all agree upon was that Western music should be viewed in terms of a canon and that some form of analysis of the scores was the means of determining what music belonged in.

3. Per motum contrarium

A contrary way of viewing music, perhaps even directly opposite, has made great headway in this century. It fixes arts policy in Marxist societies. In the West this view has been building up somewhere in between, I believe, two other contrarieties, which have become fully articulate only when formulated as attacks. One is an attack in the marketplace, an attack on the nineteenth-century repertory. The other is an attack in the academy, an attack on musical analysis.

A nonpareil marketplace warrior was and is Virgil Thomson, ever since the fine fury of his campaign against "the appreciation-racket" and "the fifty pieces" in *The State of Music,* which burst on the scene in 1939. Many critics have followed him—most recently, and most gently, Edward Rothstein of *The New York Times*—in deploring the anacondalike hold that nineteenth-century music persists in maintaining on today's repertory.[9] It is a quixotic attack, for the beast is more likely to laugh all the way to the bank than to holler out "Virgil!" and roll over belly up. Some of the animus here—certainly for Thomson's generation—stems from the anti-Romantic reaction following World War I. People turned against the high emotional and sententious tone that is the hallmark of Romantic music—in Wagner quintessentially, but also even in Beethoven. Those who remember Aldous Huxley's novel *Point Counter Point* may remember how accurately that always trendy author expressed the anti-Beethoven fashion of the 1920s, this by means of the episode in which Maurice Spandrell, dejected after Mark Rampion has listened with him to the *Heiliger Dankgesang* movement of opus 132 and pontificated about its metaphysical emptiness, walks into his self-prepared suicide trap. As his friends rush to the door to confront his assassins, the needle is heard scratching away at the end of the record. The end for Spandrell, it seems, is also the end for Beethoven.

Many needles have scratched on Beethoven records since that fictional day. However, the standard repertory has regrouped appreciably, and with it, the canon, as indeed had been happening all along. Berlioz, Musorgsky, and Verdi have assumed some of the former luster of Mendelssohn and Brahms, as we know, to say nothing of Rachmaninoff and Sibelius. It is surely no accident that the most conspicuous new addition to the repertory, Mahler, should be almost Nietzschean in the combination of nausea and nostalgia which he expresses for ninteenth-century music.

Another outcome of the anti-Romantic reaction that worked against the nineteenth-century repertory was an interest in older, "pre-Bach" music (which did not, however, develop as a major force until after World War II, at a time when the anti-Romantic reaction was waning). More serious than any of this, I suspect, was the dawning realization after World War I that the repertory was no longer growing by the addition of new or at least modernist music. The reasons are well known. Modernist composers, like other modernist artists, dissociate themselves from any audience other than one made up of other artists; listeners have not been able to internalize modern music; and performers, since so much of it is extremely difficult to execute, often do not persevere with material they find unrewarding in several senses of the word. In this situation modernist music is played on relatively few occasions by a relatively small cadre of contemporary-music specialists. It belongs in *their* repertory but not in *the* repertory. The Berg *Altenberg Lieder* does not figure in the corpus of music that sopranos are taught they must master to achieve professional status; the same is true of the Stravinsky and Schoenberg concertos for violinists, the Boulez sonatas for pianists, and even the Elliott Carter quartets for string quartets. These are works we may ache to see included in the canon, but we cannot say they are included in the repertory.

The musical tradition has changed diametrically, both in the music played and listened to and in the social conditons under which playing and listening take place. At first the repertory was nearly all contemporary. Then it extended from some point in the past up to and including the present. Now it seems to hang suspended like a historical clothesline between two fixed points in the past. This new state of affairs must first have caused apprehension and then something like terror; fears for the very life of music seem to underlie attacks on the nineteenth-century repertory as much as any explicit commitment to modernism. I do not suppose people really begrudged the repertory the right to send down taproots, but some seem to have felt like ripping them up when they saw the trunk was no longer growing new leaves and flowers. The repertory was no longer functioning like an organism.

For that matter, was the individual work of art, the autonomous musical structure itself, still functioning like an organism? Had it ever? There has always been a current of opposition to the dominant strain of academic music criticism, analysis, which stands or falls on this very issue of organicism. But these questions were not forced until fairly recently—until the 1960s, when new music in the so-called non-teleological mode began to be taken seriously, and until the 1970s, when various currents of dissatisfaction with or revaluation of Schenkerian analysis finally began finding their way into print.[10] However, it is not only the Schenkerians and the neo-Schenkerians (Eugene Narmour's term for the more system-minded of Schenker's followers) who think in terms of a canon of great works. So does a polemical anti-Schenkerian like Narmour and so do analytically inclined critics of all shades, schools, and descriptions. That categorization covers, I trust, the great majority of musicians who are trying to practice criticism in the academy today. It has been phrased broadly enough, in any case, to cover critics with a wide range of commitment to analysis and of course an equally wide range of methodological preference.

The most coherent attack on this well-entrenched academic position comes from ethnomusicologists of the anthropological school and some systematic musicologists, Americanists, and students of popular music. Scholars who see the reality of a musical tradition in its social function within a supporting culture can only regard the activity of poring over revered scores "in a kind of Meistersinger environment" as not only elitist and compulsive but myopic (and possibly chauvinistic), a deflection of scrutiny from where it belongs. "I am convinced," writes the ethnomusicologist John Blacking, "that an anthropological approach to the study of *all* musical systems makes more sense of them than analyses of the patterns of sound as things in themselves."[11]

Again there is something quixotic about this attack. It may be that Gregorian chant as we now know it is best studied in terms of Frankish culture and politics and that country music yields most as an expression of everything that Robert Altman put into *Nashville*. But if nineteenth-century music is to be approached on the same basis, that is, in terms of its own culture and ideology, the force exerted by the idea of the canon must be recognized and so must the practice of analysis which was developed to validate it. We shall certainly *not* feel bound to study and appreciate this music exclusively in the terms it evolved for itself, and I have argued elsewhere against the exclusive use of formalistic analytical methodologies in current academic music criticism. On the other hand, it would be flying in the face of history to try to view the nineteenth-century musical tradition as though its performers and listeners, let alone its composers, were innocent of the idea of a canon.

It is another question, of course, whether earlier music or very recent music should be viewed in the same way. That might indeed be thought to go against history. As far as older music is concerned my answer to this is rather simple. There was assuredly no canon in the early days; the musical tradition was essentially contemporary and extended back, so Tinctoris assures us, no more than a few generations. Yet from the beginnings we have the names of celebrated composers, wistfully memorialized even though their music was mute. Why? Notker, Léonin, Pérotin, Machaut, Dunstable, Dufay, and Ockeghem (Tinctoris himself mentions these last three)—even their names were probably read infrequently, for their music was no longer sung and its archaic notation could no longer be deciphered, even if anyone had the mind to do so and could have found the written records. In the lifespan of these composers and for a time thereafter they had great reputations, it seems, like those of contemporary artists and writers. For a time their music was considered outstanding, great, canonical.

We can now read archaic notations better. Old written records have been searched and found, codified and transcribed. For some time we have been experimenting with the performance of old music, which is to say experimenting with the internalization of past musical traditions; I shall return to this matter later at greater length. It is not an ahistorical task to seek to explain and exemplify those evanesced reputations. On the contrary, I would say it is one of the primary goals of historical criticism.

4. Per augmentationem

What Spandrell did he would not have been able to do if *Point Counter Point* had been written just a few years earlier. Feeling it a matter of life and death to hear a certain Beethoven movement, he played it on a record. The record, he carefully explained to Rampion, had just been issued. Even if Huxley had decided to have the Flonzaley or the Léner Quartet doing a concert that afternoon at Wigmore Hall, it would not have helped Spandrell, who needed to hear just the *Heiliger Dankgesang* and needed to hear it again and again. In an earlier age he would have reached in his extremity for the Bible or the *Imitation of Christ*.

Sound recording has increased such options. The new form of musical records that this century has developed has changed musical life in the most comprehensive way. One paradox is that although our new records are not in writing at all but in sound, they have brought music in one important sense close to the condition of literature. Once sound recordings can be used as freely (or almost as freely) as books, music can be absorbed as freely (or almost as freely) as literature. No wonder the audience for music has expanded.

We have all gasped at tales of how recording technology and marketing made the careers of such artists as Elvis Presley and set in motion whole waves of popular music. The effect of records on the nineteenth-century repertory must have been and must continue to be enormous, too, though I do not remember ever seeing this discussed systematically. Clearly, the standard repertory would not have regrouped in the way it has without records. Would it even have frozen to the extent it has without records? What is discussed most frequently is the effect of sound recording— usually judged to be dire—on the canonization of musical performance. A symptomatic figure in this regard was B. H. Haggin, a critic who is still writing but whose main period of influence was from around 1935 to 1955. For Haggin, the canon took on the aura of a Great Composers' Club every bit as exclusive as that of Tovey (whom he admired) and Schenker, though the membership list had been revised with the aid of some anti-Romantic blackballs. Haggin's most important book, *Music on Records,* attempted to set forth not only the full canon of music as he saw it but also the full canon of musical performance as frozen on 78 rpm records. Indeed Haggin also took in jazz, a kind of music he probably never would have known if not for records.

In 1938, when Haggin's book first came out, about ten years after the development of electrical recording, there were still few enough commercial records issued so that his project seemed like a feasible one. It did not survive the next technological breakthrough, the development of the long-playing record. Thirty years and several more breakthroughs later, it seems generally agreed that records have contributed to canonization in a way that the older generation may not have foreseen. It is not just a question of influential critics upholding Toscanini recordings; the prestige of certain recordings has led them to be studied in detail and systematically imitated by other performers. As more and more works are recorded again and again, there is a noticeable tendency toward standardization in every aspect of the performer's craft. The loss of spontaneity (for the performer) and variety (for the listener) is often deplored. But for the ideal listener in the ideal sound archive—with its disc collection extending back to Nikisch, Joachim, and Caruso augmented yearly by new recordings of any work holding a secure place in the repertory, with its piano-rolls and off-the-air tapes, and now with its CDs and videodiscs—there is probably variety and spontaneity enough.

Sound recording has worked otherwise with music that does not hold a secure place in the repertory. Of this the most vulnerable category is twentieth-century modernist music, as has already been remarked. It is seldom played in public. The music is evanescent. If a recording of a new piece is issued, the *actualité* far exceeds that provided by a single performance or a single season of performances or by publication of the score (a less likely windfall, in any case, for a composer today). A second recording may never be issued; unless the first was a disaster, this is an eventuality that can be borne. It may be worrying that on the single recording the music always sounds exactly and unspontaneously the same; but it sounds, it sounds, it continues to sound. As one composer, Roger Reynolds, has put it: "The singular representation—the existence as sound (though inflexible)—has a tendency to *become* the work, even for the composer. The authority of sound prevails over the abstract prescription in score. The goal (let alone the fact) of multiple realizations fades, and the creative person's aims are inevitably re-directed."[12]

It becomes possible after all, then, to conceive of works in the canon of music which do not figure in the repertory. There exist key works of contemporary music that are never performed at all because they were composed on tape by means of electronic generators and computers, works which have consciously renounced (or given up on) the flexibility and spontaneity of "multiple realizations." Could not such works enter the canon? And then how would they differ in status from earlier, performed works fixed on tape after the event?

Perhaps we need a new paradigm for music, one centered on the activity—or, if you prefer, the passivity—of listening to music on tapes and records. This modern paradigm would start with the listener but also implicate the performer and the composer, whose "aims are inevitably re-directed." It would not supplant the older paradigm which starts with the performer. Music as action or praxis, also implicating the composer (if any) and the listener, a form of behavior whose continuity is assured not by records in writing or sound but essentially by means of an internalized oral tradition—this describes non-Western music as well as Western popular music (however much this may be affected by sheet music and records). It would not supplant Treitler's paradigm of literacy, which starts with the composer. As even Crocker grants, this describes the standard nineteenth-century repertory as preserved and presented today. What the new paradigm covers is something that now coexists with the above: modernist music and, with some qualifications, older music resuscitated from the past. Music happens in different ways and means different things under these paradigms. Contrast the Javanese puppet theater, a social event loud with cultural resonance for the improvising musicians, puppeteers, and audience alike; the symphony orchestra rehearsal, a highly professional "reading" of the score and parts—the text—of a canonical masterpiece by the conductor and the players; and the solitary willed experience of music in the hi-fi den.

"That which withers in the age of mechanical reproduction is the aura of the work of art. . . . The technique of reproduction detaches the reproduced object from the domain of tradition."[13] Walter Benjamin, who died in 1940, did not talk about music reproduced on records, but T. W. Adorno, who lived to see the LP explosion, hated it. And mandarins of fine printing cannot look at a photoset, ragless page like this one without regretting its detachment from tradition. The rest of us look where we can for the compensations of art without aura. Asocial, amateur, existential, blanketed in anomie, the passive listener to records nonetheless chooses in a way that the Javanese theatergoer and the orchestra musician do not. He does not always choose new and old music in favor of standard fare, obviously—rather the reverse. But those are the categories of music that need him the most.

5. Quaerendo invenietis

Since the idea of a canon seems so closely bound up with the idea of history, there should be something to be learned from the persistent efforts that have been going on for nearly two hundred years to extend the musical repertory back in time. What is involved here is nothing less than a continuous effort to endow music with a history. From the workings of this process in the nineteenth century, we learn that where the ideology is right the past can indeed yield up a canon of works and even a canon of performance.

Bach, to take the most weighty example, would appear to have entered the canon—Hoffmann's canon—before entering the repertory. The history of the nineteenth-century Bach revival begins as a triumph of ideology over practice. Only after J. N. Forkel, in his famous biography, canonized Bach as the archetypal German master was *The Well-tempered Clavier* published for the first time—and if any one work of music deserves to be called canonic, it would have to be *The Well-tempered Clavier*.[14] (But when did it really enter the repertory? Not really until the formation of a new repertory, the repertory of the modern harpsichord, in our own time.) Gradually other Bach works, works which fitted better into nineteenth-century concert life, did enter various nineteenth-century repertories; Mendelssohn's revival of the St. Matthew Passion is a famous landmark, and various piano transcriptions and orchestral arrangements, not to speak of Gounod's "Ave Maria," followed in due course. Bach was made to sound like a premature Romantic. There was as yet no call for historical "authenticity." But I do not think it was Bach that Hood was thinking of when he complained of musical traditions of the past whose "real identities are gone." The skeleton may not have been bodied out with authentic flesh and blood, but it was made into a handsome waxwork which was quite real enough for the nineteenth century.

The Solesmes monks made Gregorian chant, too, sound Romantic. There is a considerable irony here, since in editing the chant texts they went back to the earliest neumes and subjected them to the full rigor of nineteenth-century historical philology. The Church authorities were duly impressed; but for the Solesmes performance style, which was promulgated as zealously as were the texts themselves, the historical underpinnings were much more speculative—and once again, in this matter there was as yet no call for rigor. After successfully making their case for canonization at the turn of the century, the monks made their first commercial records of plainchant as early as 1930. To this day, thanks at least in part to these canonical recordings, Gregorian chant is always sung in their admirably lifelike wax-museum version, even though this certainly reflects the ideals of the Cecilian or Pre-Raphaelite movements more closely than anything that can conceivably be imagined from the ninth century.[15] And if the Church itself saw in sound recordings an important means for stabilizing its canon, sound recordings were to prove even more important for the revival of past secular music.

This is shown graphically, if negatively, by the story of Arnold Dolmetsch, an intimate of William Morris, Bernard Shaw, and William Poel, who was involved in old music long before the reaction against Romanticism. Equal in crankiness to any of the old-music specialists who followed him, in universality he outdid them all—Dolmetsch not only played the first modern harpsichords, recorders, and viols, he also made each of these instruments and more in his own workshop. And he wrote a landmark study of *The Interpretation of the Music of the Seventeenth and Eighteenth Centuries* as early as 1915. The point is that while the instruments he made in the 1900s were unmatched for historical authenticity, sensitivity, and beauty of sound until the 1950s, the old-music revival that might have taken off from his work, both as maker and player, did little more than mark time until the age of LP records. Then it exploded.

The effect of LP records on the dissemination of older music, especially Baroque music, is clearer and possibly more dramatic than on music of any other kind (popular music excepted). Think of the Pachelbel Canon; but think more seriously of the enormously expert and artistic re-creation of past performance styles that has been recorded by the direct and indirect followers of Dolmetsch. What has happened is not so much an expansion of existing repertories as a sudden addition of new ones (though perhaps each is as marginal as the contemporary-music repertory, using this term broadly for music played by contemporary-music specialists): repertories for the harpsichord, the countertenor, the Baroque orchestra, and so on. These repertories, incidentally, have proved to be *less* susceptible to canonization of performance than has the nineteenth-century repertory in one way and modernist music in another. A single recording of a modern piece can attain canonical status because usually the composer has been involved with it, at least indirectly; while the result may not do full justice to the composer's conception, it will probably come close enough not to offend him. This is exactly what we do not know about with performances of old music. In this area, performance styles change almost as frequently, it sometimes seems, as fashions change in clothes — precisely because what to do with those skeletons is the subject of so much busy debate and experiment. Although some years ago it was generally felt that the cause of "authenticity" was best served by an anodyne and mechanical style of playing, today there is probably more variety and vitality of performance to be heard on old-music records than on those of the standard repertory.

And what about the canon of old music? This is not, in fact, a question that seems to interest most old-music performers. They approach whatever old music attracts them with internalization in mind, not discrimination.[16] It will be historians or, rather, historical critics who will be interested in establishing or clarifying the canon of old music, as I have already suggested. The problem is that historians of music have typically veered away from criticism. To go with Hood's irresistible metaphor once again, their best work has been a sort of musical paleontology devoted to restoring the skeletons; they have not even gone forward very often to assume the role of those ingenious taxidermists who make the animals we see in museums of natural history, nor of those artists who create the delectable swamp and tundra scenes in which they are exhibited. That work has been left, by and large, to musicians and craftsmen like Dolmetsch and his successors, who have mostly tended to pick up just a little from the research of scholars, a little from the lore of cabinetmakers, and a little more from their own continuous exercise of the aural historical imagination.

Still, there have always been some maverick musicologists—I count Treitler and Crocker in that category—and I believe that in the last half-dozen years there has been a real tropism toward criticism in the musicological community.[17] Symptomatic of this is Treitler's discussion of the interrelations of history and criticism in his article "History, Criticism, and Beethoven's Ninth Symphony," the powerful argument of which falters only very occasionally.

> This discussion provokes reflection on the possibility of practicing criticism with respect to the music of the Middle Ages and even the Renaissance, that is, of having historical knowledge of it in Croce's and Collingwood's sense. It sometimes seems that we can hope to do no more than identify the range of choices that performers and composers *could* make, without being able to count on any persuasive hypotheses for the choices they *did* make. That would be a way of saying that their traditions are no longer alive.[18]

This thought is expressed tentatively, by Treitler's standards, and is relegated to a footnote, but in any case the pessimism he appears to be flirting with here seems to me unfounded. Like Hood, he speaks of traditions that "are no longer alive" without acknowledging the accomplishments of today's old-music revivers and their allies in the recording industry. Modern performers of medieval and Renaissance music are making choices with increasing confidence and persuasiveness.

Those accomplishments seem to me as remarkable and as historically significant as those of the Bach and Solesmes revivals in the nineteenth century. Dufay was no longer alive in 1950 just as, I suppose, Theocritus was no longer alive in 1450. But after musicologists like Guillaume de Van and Heinrich Besseler have reconstructed the skeletons, and after Charles Hamm, Craig Wright, and David Fallows have polished them up, and after performers like Thomas Binkley, Fallows, Michael Morrow, and Alejandro Planchart have provided flesh or clothes—it does not matter which—Treitler himself as well as Patricia Carpenter and Don M. Randel have started a criticism for Dufay which can indeed lay the basis for the kind of knowledge Treitler seeks. Oliver Neighbour and I have done the same for William Byrd. Winton Dean has done the same for Handel's oratorios and operas. Crocker has done the same for the ninth-century sequences of Notker of St. Gall.

* * *

There has been more about the history and the ontology of the canon in these remarks than about the philosophy and politics of canon-formation. They are coming to an end at a point where many readers, I rather think, would have liked to see them begin: *How* are canons determined, *why*, and on *what* authority? The situation in music, in my view, is such that we have first to build up serious criticism so that when we ask these questions of critics, we can ask them seriously. My closing point, and I am sorry if it seems a self-serving one, is that the old music which now occupies so large a part of our sound-world needs a sensible criticism. But a sensible criticism for Boulez and Carter is needed only slightly less than for Gregorian chant, Dufay, Byrd, and Monteverdi—and there is certainly no reason to exclude the authors of the St. Matthew Passion and the Ninth Symphony from this list. Everyone now sees that analysis cannot serve as the sole critical methodology, not even for the nineteenth-century canon in aid of which it was developed, let alone for earlier and later music. Those critics who still believe in the canon must work to keep it viable, and work freshly.

1. Mantle Hood, *Perspectives in Musicology*, ed. Barry S. Brook, Edward O. D. Downes, and Sherman van Solkema (New York, 1972), pp. 203–4.

2. Leo Treitler, "Transmission and the Study of History," *International Musicological Society, Twelfth Congress, Berkeley 1977: Report* (Cassel, 1981), p. 202; cf. his "Oral, Written, and Literate Process in the Transmission of Medieval Music," *Speculum* 56 (July 1981): 471–91.

3. See Richard L. Crocker, "Is There Really a 'Written Tradition' in Music?" (Music Colloquium paper, Berkeley, May 12, 1982).

4. E. T. A. Hoffmann's role in the history of criticism has been analyzed with great perspicacity by Carl Dahlhaus; for a summary see his "Metaphysik der Instrumentalmusik," *Die Musik des 19. Jahrhunderts*, vol. 6, *Neues Handbuch der Musikwissenschaft*, ed. Dahlhaus (Wiesbaden, 1980), pp. 73–79.

5. Some of M. H. Abrams' ideas are placed in a music-historical context by Ruth A. Solie, "The Living Work: Organicism and Musical Analysis," *Nineteenth-Century Music* 4 (Fall 1980): 147–56.

6. Edward T. Cone, "Analysis Today," *Musical Quarterly* 46 (Apr. 1960), rpt. in *Problems of Modern Music*, ed. Paul Henry Láng (New York, 1960), p. 36.

7. Crocker, "Is There Really a 'Written Tradition'?"

8. See my "How We Got into Analysis, and How to Get Out," *Critical Inquiry* 7 (Winter 1980): 311–31; see also my "Tovey's Beethoven," *American Scholar* 45 (1975–76): 795–805.

9. See Edward Rothstein, *New York Times*, 15 July 1982, p. 17.

10. See, e.g., my "How We Got into Analysis"; Eugene Narmour, *Beyond Schenkerism: The Need for Alternatives in Music Analysis* (Chicago, 1977); Charles Rosen, "Art Has Its Reasons," *New York Review of Books*, 17 June 1971, pp. 32–38, and *The Classical Style: Haydn, Mozart, Beethoven* (New York, 1971), pp. 33–36; Solie, "The Living Work"; Treitler, "History, Criticism, and Beethoven's Ninth Symphony," *Nineteenth-Century Music* 3 (March 1980): 193–210; the posthumously published lecture by T. W. Adorno, "On the Problem of Musical Analysis," trans. Max Paddison, *Music Analysis* 1 (July 1982): 169–87; and Dahlhaus, *Analysis and Value Judgment* (1970), trans. Siegmund Levarie (New York, 1983), pp. 8–9. The magisterially critical essays on Schenker written by Roger Sessions in the 1930s ("Talmudic subtleties and febrile dogmatism") were reprinted in 1979 in *Roger Sessions on Music: Collected Essays*, ed. Cone (Princeton, N.J., 1979). Perhaps David Epstein's widely noticed *Beyond Orpheus: Studies in Musical Structure* (Cambridge, Mass., 1979) should be added to this list;

see the review by Arnold Whittall and correspondence in *Journal of Music Theory* 25 (Fall 1981): 319–26 and vol. 26 (Spring 1982): 208–12.

11. John Blacking, *How Musical Is Man?* (Seattle, 1973), p. xi.

12. Roger Reynolds, "Thoughts on What a Record Records," in *The Phonograph and Our Musical Life*, ed. H. Wiley Hitchcock (New York, 1980), p. 33.

13. Walter Benjamin, "The Work of Art in the Age of Mechanical Reproduction," trans. Harry Zohn, in *Marxism in Art*, ed. Maynard Solomon (Detroit, 1979), p. 554.

14. This point is made by Crocker, "Is There Really a 'Written Tradition'?"

15. For an excellent summary of the nineteenth- and twentieth-century chant movement, see the *New Grove Dictionary of Music and Musicians*, s.v. "Plainchant" by John A. Emerson. To him I owe the astonishing information that a recording survives of demonstrations of chant performance by the Solesmes pioneers and others at the Gregorian Congress of 1904 (available on Discant DIS 1–2). The effect of recordings on canonization may have been more decisive in this case than anyone realized.

Efforts to perform Gregorian chant in a more "authentic" fashion have been few, but there are some on records: the remarkable performances from the 1930s for the Anthologie Sonore under Guillaume de Van and Curt Sachs (reissued in the 1950s by Haydn Society, AS–1) and recently those by the Schola Antiqua, "Tenth-Century Liturgical Chant" (Nonesuch H–71348). See Lance W. Brunner, "The Performance of Plainsong," *Early Music* 10 (July 1982): 317–28.

16. Just recently, however, some complaints about this situation have begun to surface in "early music" circles; see Philip Brett, "Facing the Music," *Early Music* 10 (July 1982): 347–50, and David Z. Crookes, "A Turinese Letter [. . .]," *Music Review* 42 (Aug.–Nov. 1981): 169–73.

17. See the group of "state-of-the-art" papers read at the American Musicological Society annual meeting in 1981 and published as *Musicology in the 1980s: Methods, Goals, Opportunities*, ed. D. Kern Holoman and Claude V. Palisca (New York, 1982).

18. Treitler, "History, Criticism," p. 208 n.35.

The Pope Controversy: Romantic Poetics and the English Canon

James Chandler

The topic of canon-formation, with its built-in sense of process, invites a historicizing approach—a criticism responsive to Raymond Williams' complaint that the facts of cultural change are too often "projected into an apparent totality," which contains them and makes them seem to stand still. Though Williams' name for the most common of these false totalities is "tradition," rather than "canon," his claim about it is to the point. He says that we tend to see tradition "not as it is, an active and continuous selection and reselection, which even at its latest point in time is always a set of specific choices, but now more conveniently as an object, a projected reality, with which we have to come to terms on its terms, even though those terms are always and must be the valuations, the selections and omissions, of other men."[1] My discussion here follows generally in the spirit of these remarks. In choosing to investigate the dispute over Alexander Pope, I have taken what is arguably the canonical canon controversy in English literary history, the one associated with that nation's major revolution in poetry and taste. I have explained this dispute as a function of what Williams calls the "active and conflictive human histories" that produce canons and traditions, and I have tried to suggest advantages in such an approach to literary history as compared with, say, a history-of-poetics approach. At the same time, however, I have treated the Pope controversy as marking a crucial stage in the development of just that historicizing attitude toward the question of canon which produces a view like Williams' in the first instance.

Research for this essay was supported by a fellowship from the William Andrews Clark Library at the University of California, Los Angeles.

1

In its narrowest sense, "the Pope controversy" refers to the seven years war of words that was touched off in 1819 by some remarks of Thomas Campbell in defense of Pope. Campbell was defending Pope from charges made years before by William Lisle Bowles. Feeling attacked himself, Bowles immediately published a defense of his comments on Pope. Others soon entered the fray, most notably Byron on the side of Campbell and Hazlitt on the side of Bowles. Byron's 1821 *Letter to **** ******* [John Murray] stands as his only published essay in critical prose. (A sequel to it was not published.) Bowles, for his part, contributed eight different publications to the debate, some of which went through multiple editions. In 1822 and again in 1825 he published book-length collections of these documents. Before hostilities subsided in 1826, Grub Street was littered with some two-dozen pamphlets, articles, and reviews pertaining to the question of Pope and his place in the poetic canon.[2]

Like many of our contemporary critical controversies, this one seems in the end to have generated more heat than light. The words tend to become darkest and hottest in this dispute when the point at issue (to use the distinction of the disputants themselves) was Pope's "moral" as distinct from his "poetical" character. For at such moments the disputants inevitably succumbed to the temptation to discuss the moral characters of one another, though each in his own way. There is Byron's cavalier gossipiness, for example:

> Mr. Bowles was not always a clergyman; and when he was a very young man, was he never seduced into as much [as the alleged "licentiousness" for which, following Colley Cibber, he chastises Pope]? If I were in the humour for story-telling, and relating little anecdotes, I could tell a much better story of Mr. B. than Cibber's, upon much better authority, viz. that of Mr. B. himself. [*WB*, 5: 542]

Bowles' own comments frequently lapse into a kind of vitriolic self-righteousness. Introducing a reply to Octavius Gilchrist, he writes: "Having given a *lash,* as I felt compelled to do, to a rabid and slaver'd barker, I should have turned from him in disdain," but "the reptile which first *defiled* the London Magazine, is HERE again! "[3] Both of these remarks occur relatively early (1821) in the discussion of Pope's moral character; the mutual vilification continues to escalate afterward. But even when the disputants turn to the question of Pope's poetical character, the

---

James Chandler, associate professor of English at the University of Chicago, is the author of *Wordsworth's Second Nature: A Study of the Poetry and Politics* (forthcoming this autumn).

polemic often reflects less on their taste or aesthetics than on their bad humor and petty vanities. In view of the bulk of pages he published on the matter, Bowles ends up saying very little of substance. After his initial publication he tends to become obstinately repetitive and narrowly self-protective. Byron, on the other hand, tends to be carelessly overgeneralized, often self-aggrandizing, and sometimes self-contradictory. It is easy to see why the one book on this controversy focuses so much attention on the tone in which it is carried on.[4]

If there were no more to this matter than the low-level forensics of these two-dozen documents, the whole affair were better left in the oblivion to which such petty quarrels are usually consigned. Yet it is hard to think of another literary controversy more costly than this one in sheer expense of spirit. The very energy of these exchanges suggests that we ought to look a little further into the matter. And one does not have to look far to see the first relevant point: that this seven years campaign is part of a larger and longer controversy over Pope.

I mentioned that Campbell's offending comments in 1819 respond to prior remarks by Bowles. These remarks appeared in the moral and poetical "Observations" on Pope that Bowles included in his 1806 edition of Pope's works. Nearly everything of substance that Bowles had to say about Pope and poetry can be found there without the splenetic defensiveness that colors the later pamphlets.[5] Byron had likewise entered the lists against Bowles long before he took part in the later controversy. His Horatian satire of 1809, *English Bards and Scotch Reviewers*, featured this lampoon:

> BOWLES! in thy memory let this precept dwell:
> Stick to thy Sonnets, man! at least they sell.
> But if some new-born whim, or larger bribe
> Prompt thy crude brain, and claim thee for a scribe,
> If 'chance some bard, though once by dunces fear'd,
> Now, prone in dust, can only be rever'd;
> If POPE, whose fame and genius from the first
> Have foiled the best of critics, needs the worst,
> Do thou essay; each fault, each failing scan;
> The first of poets was, alas! but man!
> . . . .
> Oh! had'st thou liv'd in that congenial time,
> To rave with DENNIS, and with RALPH to rhyme,
> Throng'd with the rest around his living head,
> Not rais'd thy hoof against the lion dead,
> A meet reward had crown'd thy glorious gains,
> And link'd thee to the Dunciad for thy pains.[6]

Like Bowles' early comments on Pope, Byron's on Bowles assume a form less alloyed with personal self-interest than we typically find in the exchanges of the 1820s. This lampoon should be understood as dramatizing the commitment it describes in its final lines, Byron's dedication of himself to Pope's memory, perhaps the finest instinct at work in his long campaign against Pope's detractors. If Bowles had attacked Pope when the latter was still alive, Byron argues, he would have met his just punishment from Pope's own pen. Since Bowles kicks a lion already dead, Byron steps up to respond, as Pope would have done for himself, by putting Bowles in this new *Dunciad* of a poem, *English Bards and Scotch Reviewers*.

Even in this Ur-form of the 1820s controversy, however, Byron and Bowles were reenacting a dispute that was already being played out decades earlier, and Bowles' 1806 comments on Pope quite explicitly locate themselves in respect to this prior debate. In 1756, Joseph Warton published his *Essay on the Writings and Genius of Pope*, which praised Pope as a moralist and versifier but raised serious questions about the ultimate value of Pope's achievement. Coming at a period when Pope's reputation still commanded the extraordinary respect he had gained during his own lifetime, Warton's *Essay* marks the effective starting point of the Pope controversy. It was a serious challenge to Pope's merit by a critic who professed to admire many of Pope's characteristic virtues, and it prompted some serious apologies for Pope's oeuvre.[7] Among them, in fact, we must number the work often called the finest single piece of biographical criticism in English, for we have it on James Boswell's authority that Dr. Johnson wrote his *Life of Pope* specifically to silence "all attempts to lessen his poetical fame by demonstrating his excellence."[8]

Yet not even the powerful hand of Johnson could stem the tide. The *Life of Pope* appeared in 1781. In 1782, Warton answered Johnson in volume two of the *Essay on Pope*, whose publication may actually have been delayed for the purpose. In 1791, Warton published his brother Thomas' poems with the proud announcement that "the ingenious Author of the following Poems was of the SCHOOL of SPENSER and MILTON, rather than that of POPE."[9] By the early 1790s, Bowles' *Sonnets* (first published in 1789) began, as Byron put it, to "sell," and the perceived departures of these poems from the practices of Pope evidently generated further conversation about the Pope question among young literati like Coleridge. Indeed, when readers of the *Biographia Literaria* express dismay over what Coleridge says in chapter 1 about Bowles' impact on his career, they often fail to note Coleridge's stress on the literary context in which these sonnets were received. It was, as Coleridge writes, "the *controversies occasioned by* my unfeigned zeal for [Bowles]" that "were of great advantage in the formation and the establishment of my taste and critical opinions."[10] The topics in these controversies and the identity of his opponents are clear both from chapter 1's critique of Popean poetics and from specific reference: "Among those with whom I conversed there were, of course, very many who had formed their taste and their notions of poetry from the writings of Mr Pope and his followers: or to speak more generally, in that school of French poetry condensed and invigorated by English understanding which had predominated from the last century" (p. 9). I shall return to this last comment presently.

In 1797, Warton's edition of Pope appeared, a reminder to the English public of his earlier critique in the *Essay*. Two years later Coleridge suggested in a letter to Robert Southey that the latter's *Annual Anthology* for 1799 should not open with "Christabel," not because he had not yet finished it but because the first poem should be "a poem in couplets, didactic or satirical—such a one as the lovers of genuine poetry would call sensible and entertaining, such as the Ignoramuses & Pope-admirers would deem genuine Poetry."[11] A year later appeared the 1800 Preface to *Lyrical Ballads*, which explained just how the poems in those two volumes aimed to overthrow the views of the "Ignoramuses & Pope-admirers" as to what was and was not genuine poetry. Wordsworth added his obviously anti-Popean appendix on poetic diction in 1802. I have already mentioned Bowles' edition of 1806 and the publication of *English Bards* in 1809. Further, in the years immediately preceding the later controversy, we find a series of critical and literary documents that are all centrally relevant to the questions raised by Warton and Johnson: Wordsworth's *Essay, Supplementary* to the Preface of 1815; in 1817, Keats' "Sleep and Poetry" and Coleridge's *Biographia;* in 1818, Hazlitt's *Lectures on the English Poets;* and in 1819, Byron's *Don Juan* (canto 1).

The pamphlet war of 1819–26 escalated so quickly, in other words, because lines had already been established and artillery already emplaced in this larger struggle. When Shelley observed to Byron in 1821 that Pope was "the pivot of a dispute in taste," it was surely this larger dispute that he had in mind—the "dispute in taste" associated with what we commonly call the Romantic movement in England.[12]

Of course, it will come as news to no one that certain English Romantic poets took issue with the poetic theory and practice of Pope. But as a rule we tend to approach the connection between Romantic poetics and anti-Popism in England from the side of the former—as if Pope were attacked somehow as a consequence of a revision in poetic principles, as if the revision in principles somehow *preceded* the revision of the canon.[13] An occasion like the present one, with its invitation to focus primary attention on the question of canon and the process of canon-formation, encourages us to consider the connection between poetics and canon from the other side. We shall see that reversing perspectives in this way produces a rather different view from the one we are used to taking. If it does not lead us to go so far as to reverse the usual assumption and thus to conclude that poetic principles changed in the Romantic period as a result of the challenge to Pope's place in the canon, it may at least help us to appreciate how these two developments were mutually generative.

2

To see what might be at stake in the question of Pope's place in the poetic canon—in the question as such, before anything is said of critical theory—we must understand that late eighteenth-century England was developing a different sort of canon from the one which Pope and the Augustans had in view. As everyone knows, Pope's classics were, well, classical. His pantheon was populated with poets of another place and time whose stature was globally recognized. One recalls the tribute to these "Bards triumphant" in *An Essay on Criticism* (1711):

> Still green with Bays each *ancient* Altar stands,
> Above the reach of *Sacrilegious* Hands,
> Secure from *Flames*, from *Envy's* fiercer Rage,
> Destructive *War*, and all-involving *Age*.
> See, from *each Clime* the Learn'd their Incense bring;
> Hear, in *all Tongues* consenting *Paeans* ring!
> In Praise so just, let ev'ry Voice be join'd,
> And fill the *Gen'ral Chorus* of *Mankind!*[14]

Pope's song of praise here forms just a part of mankind's "*Gen'ral Chorus.*" These are poets for all climates and languages, and for all nations, even "Nations *unborn*" and "Worlds . . . that must not yet be *found*" (ll. 193– 94). Although I want to place adequate stress on Pope's deep commitment to this universalized canon, it would be misleading to suggest that he was completely uninterested in the poetry of his own nation. He studied it and imitated it. He even sketched a plan for a possible history of poetry in England. It is to the point here, however, that this project remained only a sketch and that England would have no major overview of its national accomplishment until the 1770s and 1780s, when Thomas Warton issued the first three volumes of his pioneering *History of English Poetry,* and Johnson, his *Lives of the English Poets.*

Building on the scholarship of René Wellek, Lawrence Lipking has offered a compelling account of the emergence of these great works at that time, by reference to the "interested and demanding public" that called for them.[15] What that public wanted and got, Lipking explains, "was a history of English poetry, or a survey of English poets, that would provide a basis for criticism by reviewing the entire range of the art. Warton and Johnson responded to a national desire for an evaluation of what English poets had achieved" (p. 328). Such terms are most useful, although "evaluation" connotes a greater degree of neutrality than even Lipking's own subsequent analysis permits. For example, among the public needs served by such work as Johnson's and Warton's, Lipking lists the "patriotic" and the "political" as primary. These needs are obviously related. The patriotic need expresses itself as a hunger for "a glorious national poetic pantheon" (p. 328); that is, for a specifically national rather than a global canon of classics. Such a canon would in turn serve political purposes that Lipking sees motivating "the poets of mid-century, Thomson and Akenside and Collins and Gray and Mason and Smart," who all "wrote variations on the mythopolitical theme of Milton: sweet Liberty, the nymph who had freed English pens to outstrip the cloistered conservative rule-bound verses of less favored nations." Politically, in other words, and this is the crucial point, "English literary history was shaped by the need for a definition of the superiority of the national character" (p. 329).

Once this point has been established, it is but an easy step to Lipking's somewhat stronger claim that, insofar as they were concerned with identifying a national canon to display the native genius, the "English public looked for historians [like Warton] who would find their enchanted ground on the soil of England herself" (p. 330). To acknowledge the force of this desire is to discover the seeds of a serious dilemma in respect to Pope, for the enchanted ground of Pope and the Augustans was plainly elsewhere. Lipking describes one side of this dilemma incisively: "Augustan poets won their title by establishing commerce with the poetry of Greece and Rome and France, not by planting native roots, and a literary history that appealed to them could not afford to be parochial" (p. 330). So long as the literary dominance of the Augustans operates more powerfully than the nationalist drive to find native literary origins, it makes good sense to put the matter this way. But with sufficient strengthening of the nationalist motive, one might want to reverse the terms: a literary history that insists on discovering native roots for English poetry could not afford to appeal to, or perhaps even to accommodate, Pope and the Augustans. This latter hypothesis is the one I wish to investigate further, for there is good evidence that English nationalism intensified dramatically in the decades that lead from the age of the Wartons to the 1820s.

Among those "less favored nations" against which the English traditionally defined their national identity, France clearly stood foremost. Some sense of Anglo-French cultural relations in the age of the Wartons can be gained from the prologue to George Colman's popular *English Merchant* (1767). These lines, which were published separately in *Gentleman's Magazine,* apologize for Colman's use of Voltaire's *L'Ecossaise* by developing an elaborate analogy between literary influence and economic trade.[16] After opening with the observation that "Each year . . . many English visit France, / To learn the Language, or to learn to dance," the prologue goes on to explain that the author has likewise "made a Trip" and "Brought home, among some more Run-Goods, a Play." The stage on which the actor stands is the metaphorical English dock. He is,

> Here, on this Quay, prepar'd t'unload his Cargo,
> If on the Freight you lay not an Embargo.
>   "What! am I branded for a Smuggler?" cries
> Our little *Bayes,* with Anger in his Eyes.

"No. *English* Poets, *English* Merchants made,
To the whole World of Letters fairly trade:
With the rich Stores of ancient *Rome* and *Greece*,
Imported Duty-free, may fill their Piece:
Or, like *Columbus*, cross th'Atlantick Ocean,
And set *Peru* and *Mexico* in Motion;
Turn *Cherokees* and *Catabaws* to Shape;
Or sail for *Wit* and *Humour* to the *Cape*."
   Is there a *Weaver* here from *Spital-fields*?
To his Award our Author fairly yields.
The *Pattern*, he allows, is not quite new,
And he imports the raw *Materials* too.
Come whence they will, from *Lyons, Genoa, Rome,*
'Tis *English* Silk when wrought in *English* Loom.

This is still only 1767, and Colman seems confident that he can persuade his audience to accept his French-influenced play. They were evidently willing, as he hoped, to "pronounce it *English Stuff*, and let it pass." Just as significant, on the other hand, is Colman's concern to justify the French import, his evident fear of cultural embargo.

   These lines were written in the wake of the Seven Years War. Eighteen years later, William Cowper's *The Task* (1785) addressed the nation in the wake of the war in which France's opposition (as Cowper remarks) cost England most of her Western empire. Here, deeper divisions are asserted and the English nationalist sentiment seems less amenable to cultural compromise. "With all thy loss of empire," Cowper apostrophizes his country, "Thee I account still happy, and the chief / Among the nations, seeing thou art free."[17] The explicit comparison is with France, which utterly lacks liberty and thus suffers an evil that is, conversely, far *greater* than any of her material setbacks:

> Then shame to manhood, and opprobrious more
> To France than all her losses and defeats
> Old or of later date, by sea or land,
> Her house of bondage worse than that of old
> Which God aveng'd on Pharoah—the Bastile!
> Ye horrid tow'rs, th'abode of broken hearts;
> Ye dungeons and ye cages of despair,
> That monarchs have supplied from age to age
> With music such as suits their sov'reign ears—
> The sighs and groans of miserable men!
> There's not an English heart that would not leap
> To hear that ye were fall'n at last; to know
> That ev'n our enemies, so oft employ'd
> In forging chains for us, themselves were free.
>
> [Bk. 5, ll. 379–92]

Neither in politics nor in poetic "music," did "politer" France have anything to teach Cowper's countrymen, despite what he concedes to be a certain "roughness in the grain / Of British natures" (bk. 5, ll. 480–81).[18]

It takes nothing away from Cowper's uncanny prediction about the fall of the Bastille to say that he was only half right about the English response to it. Not all English hearts rejoiced at the event, and many of those who did, turned against England, at least for a time, in favor of France's apparently more progressive example. They became *citoyens du monde*. On the other hand, some of these Francophiles later became sufficiently reentrenched in their English nationalism that they could retrospectively describe the enthusiasm for France in the early 1790s as though they had had nothing to do with it. A clear case in point is the onetime enthusiast Wordsworth, who attacked the Whigs of the 1790s in an 1818 speech. The party had failed miserably, according to Wordsworth, "for the fundamental reason, that neither the religion, the laws, the morals, the manners, nor the literature of the country, especially as contrasted with those of France, were prized by the Leaders of the Party as they deserved."[19] What was needed then, as now, was "a restoration of that genuine English character, by which alone the confidence of the sound part of the People can be recovered" (*PW*, 3:163).

The galvanizer of those Englishmen who initially refused to rejoice at the fall of the Bastille, as Wordsworth noted in 1818, was Edmund Burke: "The most sagacious Politician of his age broke out in an opposite strain" (*PW*, 3:158). And one poet immediately responsive to the aggressive nationalism of Burke's *Reflections on the Revolution in France* (1790) was Bowles, whose *Poetical Address to the Right Honourable Edmund Burke* (1791) appeared two years after the first edition of his *Sonnets*. Much of Bowles' poem is an attempt to clarify Burke's position in the *Reflections*. Bowles argues that Burke did not lament the shows of the dying age of chivalry but only the spirit of "Honour" and "liberal Sentiment" associated with that age. Bowles takes pains to show that Burke has been a lifelong enemy of tyranny (in the form of unscrupulous dealings with America and England) but that this did not make Burke a friend to anarchy, which at that moment threatens to raise "her temple, wet with human gore, / . . . on Gallia's bleeding shore." And following Burke's own lead, Bowles suggests that the alleged chaos in France makes the view of England sweeter than ever:

> With joy we turn to Albion's happier plain,
> Where ancient Freedom holds her temperate reign;
> Where Justice sits majestic on her throne;
> Where Mercy turns her ear to every groan!
> O Albion! fairest Isle, whose verdant plain
> Springs beauteous from the blue and billowy main;
> In peaceful pomp whose tower'd cities rise,

> And lift their glitt'ring foreheads to the skies;
> Whose airy hills with wand'ring flocks are crown'd,
> With tabrets whose green villages resound;
> Whose far-fam'd commerce loads the yielding tides,
> And O'er the darken'd Deep triumphant rides.
> O! mid thy cities old, thy cultur'd vales,
> (That with fond transport Contemplation hails:)
> May Honour's train with liberal manners shine,
> And love, and gallant deeds, and liberty be thine![20]

This is by no means fine verse, but it does fairly represent what Raymond Williams would call the "structure of feeling" of those who, in the first years of the Revolution, opposed France in the name of English liberty and tranquillity.[21] Bowles is of course writing before the establishment of the French Republic, the execution of Louis XVI, the Reign of Terror, and the twenty-two-year war with France, all of which intensified English chauvinism still further.[22]

Because Alfred Cobban has amply documented the evident impact of the Revolution, as interpreted by Burke, on the first-generation Romantics (Wordsworth, Coleridge, and Southey), I will not belabor the matter here.[23] Accepting Cobban's account of how nationalist sentiment deepened among the poets of this generation, I would like to turn instead to what evidence we have that the desire for a national canon intensified accordingly. In 1803, for example, when Southey was contemplating a still unspecified program of scholarship, Coleridge made so bold as to draft up a plan for him: "I write now to propose a scheme . . . of your grand work. . . . I would have the work entitled Bibliotheca Britannica, or an History of British Literature, bibliographical, biographical, and critical." One volume of the work would contain "the history of *English* poetry and poets, in which I would include all prose truly poetical." The first half of this volume "should be dedicated to great single names, Chaucer and Spenser, Shakespeare, Milton and Taylor, Dryden and Pope; the poetry of witty logic,—Swift, Fielding, Richardson, Sterne" (2:955). If the inclusion of the Augustans seems peculiar in view of Coleridge's earlier comment to Southey about the "Ignoramuses & Pope-admirers," we must understand what Coleridge has in mind by "great names" and what he takes to be the "great object" in presenting them: "I mean to say all great names as have either formed epochs in our taste, or such, at least, as are representative; and the great object to be in each instance to determine, first, the true merits and demerits of the *books;* secondly, what of these belong to the age—what to the author *quasi peculium*" (2: 955).

Southey never carried through with Coleridge's idea, but eleven years later he and Coleridge were evidently still talking about the importance of establishing a national canon, as we know from Wordsworth's 1814 letter to Robert Anderson, editor of *A Complete Edition of the Poets of Great Britain* (1792–95). Wordsworth compliments Anderson for the relative comprehensiveness of his anthology but also expresses his urgent wish that "this Collection would have included many valuable works of our elder Poets which have no place there."[24] (By "elder," Wordsworth means roughly pre-Augustan.) Since Wordsworth regards Alexander Chalmers' 1810 anthology of English poetry as imitative of Anderson's and "also very incomplete," he feels obliged to point out to Anderson that "the Public therefore is still unprovided with an entire Body of English Poetry" (*LWW*, p. 152). What Wordsworth goes on to say shows just how live and urgent an issue this was among the Lake Poets:

> I have long wished this to be done; and have talked with several of my Friends Messieurs Coleridge and Southey in particular upon the subject who both participate my desire to see your Edition adequately enlarged. . . . A few days ago I had a conversation with Mr Southey on this subject, and we both agreed that it would be a fortunate thing for the interests of Literature. [*LWW*, p. 152]

He might have added "for the interests of England." A further claim of this letter upon our interests here, in any case, is the list that he and Southey drew up to guide Anderson in his revisions, passing labor on to him somewhat as Coleridge had tried to do with Southey eleven years earlier. The list comprised the names of twenty-seven poets, all pre-Augustan, and five translations (including George Chapman's Homer), the latest of which appeared almost a century before Pope's controversial *Iliad* (see *LWW*, pp. 153–54). Unfortunately for the Lakist cause, the next major anthology to appear in England was not Anderson's but Campbell's *Specimens of the English Poets*. It was the preface to this work that ignited the pamphlet wars over Pope.

Quite apart from questions of Romantic poetics, then, the challenge to Pope comes to seem almost inevitable in light of the movement and the motives for forming a native English canon—and all the more inevitable insofar as Englishmen begin to describe Pope's un-English values as deriving not from ancient Greece and Rome but from modern France. Writing during the 1790s in the *Biographia*, as we saw, Coleridge identified Pope's work specifically with the "school of French poetry." This was no isolated occurrence. Such a view had already been expressed in that same decade by one of Coleridge's friends and one of his enemies. In 1814 Southey observed that "images of nature were not in fashion during the prevalence of the French school: from Dryden to Thomson, there is scarcely a rural image drawn from life to be found in any of the English poets."[25] Three years earlier, Francis Jeffrey wrote more pointedly: "The Restoration brought in a French taste upon us, and what was called a classical and a polite taste; and the wings of our English muses were clipped and trimmed."[26] Like so many other commonplaces in this controversy, however, this one can ultimately be traced back to Joseph Warton, who wrote that Pope's "turn of mind" away from imagination and toward "strong sense and judgment . . . led him to admire French models; he studied *Boileau* attentively; formed himself upon *him*, as Milton formed himself upon the Grecian and Italian Sons of *Fancy*. He stuck to describing *modern manners;* but these *manners,* because they are *familiar, uniform, artificial,* and *polished,* are, for these *four* reasons, in their very nature *unfit* for any lofty effort of the Muse."[27]

3

In the years between Wordsworth's proposal to Anderson and Campbell's *Specimens,* two texts appeared that are particularly illuminative of some of the characteristic connections made at this time among poetics, literary history, and the role of the national canon. The first of these was Wordsworth's *Essay, Supplementary* to the Preface of 1815, an apologia for his own writings that was occasioned by the hostile reviews of *The Excursion* (1814). Wordsworth opens the *Essay* by distinguishing what he calls the three classes of readers and by showing how two of these three groups are nowise trustworthy in their judgments about poetry and how the third is only occasionally so. He then reasons as follows: "If the number of judges who can be confidently relied upon be in reality so small, it ought to follow that partial notice only, or neglect, perhaps long continued, or attention wholly inadequate to their merits—must have been the fate of most works in the higher departments of poetry [works such as Wordsworth's own]; and that, on the other hand, numerous productions have blazed into popularity, and have passed away, leaving scarcely a trace behind them" (*PW,* 3:67). Entering the canon is thus a great struggle for a worthy author, but Wordsworth expresses confidence that time insures eventual recognition. This recognition is the fair and lasting esteem of the trans-generational "People" rather than the whimsical and ephemeral approbation of the immediate readership whom he calls "the Public" (*PW,* 3:84). Furthermore, authors, like himself, who deserve entry into the canon are recompensed for their frustration "by perceiving that there are select Spirits for whom it is ordained that their fame shall be in the world an existence like that of Virtue, which owes its being to the struggles it makes, and its vigour to the enemies whom it provokes" (*PW,* 3:67).

To "support these inferences," Wordsworth offers what he calls "a hasty retrospect of the poetical literature of this Country for the greater part of the last two centuries," and what he says about Pope makes him out to be the antithesis of himself, which is of course to say a poet *not* entitled to be enshrined among the nation's "select Spirits":

> The arts by which Pope . . . contrived to procure to himself a
> more general and a higher reputation than perhaps any English
> Poet ever attained during his life-time are known to the judicious.
> And as well known is it to them, that the undue exertion of those
> arts is the cause why Pope has for some time held a rank in literature,
> to which, if he had not been seduced by an over-love of immediate
> popularity, and had confided more in his native genius, he never
> could have descended. He bewitched the nation by his melody, and
> dazzled it by his polished style, and was himself blinded by his own
> success. [*PW*, 3:72]

As is so often the case in Wordsworth, "native genius" is a pun that
connotes not only personal but also national resources. Pope failed to
confide in his *national* genius in two related ways. First, he went to France
to learn his trade—to those pseudo-enlightened "French Critics" who,
as Wordsworth explains earlier in his retrospect, failed to see the merits
of even the "darling of our Nation," Shakespeare (*PW*, 3:68). But Pope
also lacked confidence in the perceptive powers of the most judicious
readers among the English, those readers to whom Wordsworth, for all
his doubts, finally entrusts his own fate. Pope chose to bewitch and
bedazzle the English nation instead of proceeding as Wordsworth said
every true poet must: as a man speaking to men, an Englishman speaking
to Englishmen.

A year after the *Essay* appeared, Keats composed "Sleep and Poetry."
This poem was probably influenced by Wordsworth's *Essay*, but it offers
an even more striking illustration of how much the categories of canon
and national literary history affected thinking about poetry at this time.
The opening of this early reverie poem seems to promise the sort of self-
indulgent, self-generated fantasy that we find elsewhere in Keats' juvenilia.
Coming early in the poem upon an exclamation like "O for ten years,
that I may overwhelm / Myself in poesy," certainly, no reader would
guess what the middle of the poem holds in store.[28] For before this
"strange assay / Begun in gentleness" is allowed to "die so away" (ll. 313–
14), it offers its own hasty retrospect of England's poetic history.

This account is ostensibly prompted by Keats' apprehension, as he
prepares himself for his poetic career, that "the high / Imagination cannot
freely fly / As she was wont of old" (ll. 163–65). "Of old," as we discover,
refers to the pre-Augustan period, the age of Wordsworth's and Coleridge's
"elder poets." This dating becomes clear when, after summarizing the
achievement of the English Renaissance, Keats asks rhetorically:

> Could all this be forgotten? Yes, a schism
> Nurtured by foppery and barbarism,
> Made great Apollo blush for this his land.
> Men were thought wise who could not understand
> His glories: with a puling infant's force

They sway'd about upon a rocking horse,
And thought it Pegasus. Ah dismal soul'd!
The winds of heaven blew, the ocean roll'd
Its gathering waves—ye felt it not. The blue
Bared its eternal bosom, and the dew
Of summer nights collected still to make
The morning precious: beauty was awake!
Why were ye not awake? But ye were dead
To things ye knew not of,—were closely wed
To musty laws lined out with wretched rule
And compass vile: so that ye taught a school
Of dolts to smooth, inlay, and clip, and fit,
Till, like the certain wands of Jacob's wit,
Their verses tallied. Easy was the task:
A thousand handicraftsmen wore the mask
Of Poesy. Ill-fated, impious race!
That blasphemed the bright Lyrist to his face,
And did not know it,—no, they went about,
Holding a poor, decrepid standard out
Mark'd with most flimsy mottos, and in large
The name of one Boileau!

[ll. 181–206]

Although this reverie poem seems an unlikely place to find a highly nationalized literary history, Keats' treatment of this history and of Pope's place in it is perhaps much what one should expect from a poet so dedicated to extending the achievement of Wordsworth and the first-generation Romantics. Imputing to Apollo a special sense of propriety in England ("this his land"), for example, Keats' account dramatically reveals why the question of poetic canon is so particularly important to the rise of English nationalism. A poetic canon can obviously be useful in the self-definition of any national character, but more especially so where a nation regards itself, as England increasingly does in the late eighteenth and early nineteenth centuries, as having a distinctively *poetic* collective identity.

Keats' poetic history is also useful for documenting how thoroughly Pope was identified in this period with modern French rather than ancient classical ideas about poetry. Indeed, Keats is more broadly defining the (poetic) character of the English nation by setting it against the (calculating, antipoetic) character of France. This point becomes explicit at the end of the passage when the name of Boileau is made to stand at once as the culmination of the vices summarized there and as the origin of the Augustans' treacherous schism. The invidious comparison is already adumbrated at the opening of the passage, however, in the early comment about the Augustans' heretical embrace of "foppery and barbarism." The notion that French culture vacillated between these extremes was a commonplace in English writing even before Burke developed it in the *Reflections*.

Certain stylistic features of this passage demand attention in this context, for Keats has evidently taken pains not to let his satire upon the school of Pope become a Popean satire. Keats' verse here follows from an implicit conjunction—Coleridge would make it explicit in his remarks on Pope's style in chapter 1 of the *Biographia*—between Pope's way of writing heroic couplets and his failure to heed the inspiration of nature. Keats both does and does not want to parody this unnatural style. The lines in which Keats specifically describes how Popeans construct their couplets, for example, seem at first to imitate what they describe:

>   ye taught a school
> Of dolts to smooth, inlay, and clip, and fit,
> Till, like the certain wands of Jacob's wit,
> Their verses tallied.
>
>   [ll. 196–99]

Line 197, which describes the regularity of Popean practice, is itself the most metrically regular line in the passage. It comprises a series of very weak alternating with very strong syllables, and its syntactical and metrical boundaries (the phrase and the foot) coincide perfectly. Lines 197–98, moreover, are the first pair of rhyming, comma–end-stopped lines in the paragraph. Yet on closer inspection, we see that this couplet about couplets makes only a gesture toward the style that Coleridge, in the *Biographia*, called "a *conjunction disjunctive* of epigrams" (p. 9). The couplet fails to achieve epigrammatic integrity because it is introduced by an instance of strong enjambment ("school / Of dolts") which represents it as following from the poem's "natural" flow of thought. Earlier lines in this passage have already marked enjambment as an effect inspired by nature: "the ocean roll'd / Its gathering waves"; "The blue / Bared its eternal bosom"; "the dew / Of summer nights collected still to make / The morning precious." These instances of enjambment are there to show that, while Keats accuses the Popeans of being insensitive to the power of nature, he himself is not. That second example ("The blue / Bared"), with its apparent threat to break the line across an adjective-noun phrase, is perhaps the boldest, "freest" stroke in the poem. Similarly, the double trochee that opens line 193—"beauty was awake! / *Why* were *ye* not" (my emphasis)—means to show the spontaneity and sincerity of Keats' very question about Popean artificiality.

"Sleep and Poetry," then, not only reveals a nationalistically canon-conscious view of the Pope question, it also shows how that question bears upon a mode of verse writing that we associate with high English Romanticism. But Keats' debunking of Pope is instructive in yet another way, for it stands as an example of how the nationalist motive, even where we may feel it to operate most powerfully, is not allowed to stand as the rationale for Pope's rejection. Keats' argument, finally, is not that Pope's reputation should be deflated because his poetry is French-influenced; it is that we must reject Pope because his poetry is blind to the influences of nature. It is bad because it is artificial—like most things influenced by French culture. The "Englishness" of the "elder poets," and presumably also of their recent heirs, the Lake Poets, is to be esteemed not primarily on its own account but on account of the "naturalness" that inheres in it.

4

The point about nature and England is important because although, as I have tried to suggest, it makes some sense to explain the movement to exclude Pope from the canon (or demote him within it) in terms of nationalist interests, the question of Pope's Englishness is almost never raised in the actual controversy over his status. This is the case from the inception of the controversy. The dedication to Warton's *Essay on Pope* does, it is true, announce its concern with locating Pope's rank among "our English poets," but he nowhere directly brings nationalist arguments against Pope's reputation.[29] Warton's method, as readers of the *Essay* will recall, was rather to establish certain major-minor distinctions among the English poets and then to determine "in which of these classes Pope deserves to be placed" (1:viii). Yet the confusions that beset Warton's work are telling, and they survived through much of the subsequent writings about Pope. The ambiguity centers chiefly in the major-minor distinctions. On the one hand, Warton seeks to erect a fourfold hierarchy among English writers, placing Pope in the second group with Dryden, Donne, Denham, Cowley, and Congreve: all writers who "possessed the true poetical genius, in a more moderate degree" than others such as Spenser, Shakespeare, Milton, Otway, and Lee, but who nonetheless "had noble talents for moral, ethical, and panegyrical poetry" (1:vii). On the other hand, Warton wants to make a distinction between the "true poets" and other worthy writers, and to insinuate that Pope was no true poet. After complaining, for example, that his contemporaries do not "sufficiently attend to the difference there is betwixt a MAN OF WIT, a MAN OF SENSE, and a TRUE POET," Warton goes on to ask about Donne (grouped with Pope in the fourfold scheme) and Swift, "undoubted men of wit, and men of sense": "what traces have they left of PURE POETRY?" (1:ii). That Pope is implicated here is clear from a later question, in which Pope is named specifically. After asserting that "the sublime and the Pathetic are the two chief nerves of all genuine poetry," Warton asks pointedly: "What is there very sublime or very pathetic in Pope?" (1:vi). It was to this latter sort of invidious distinction that Johnson was responding in a celebrated question of his own: "If Pope be not a poet, where is poetry to be found?"[30] This confusion, as I said, lasted for decades; in his 1818 *Lectures on the English Poets,* Hazlitt could still declare that "the question, whether Pope was a poet, has hardly yet been settled."[31]

Whichever way we understand Warton's distinctions to cut, however, it remains clear that they do not specifically introduce Pope's national loyalty into the controversy, directing attention instead to the relative "purity" of his poetry. How strongly Warton was actually influenced by the desire to find the enchanted ground of English poetry on English soil is a difficult matter to decide. But it is fair to say that many readers have suspected that Warton's stated reasons for demoting Pope do not correspond to his actual motives. Lipking captures this suspicion in his suggestion that "the interest of the *Essay* can only depend on the search for principles according to which Pope is to be excluded from the first rank of his art" (p. 365). The desire to unseat Pope is represented here as having preexisted definitions (of "pure poetry" and the like) employed for the purpose.

We have seen how far Bowles, as early as 1791, was willing to identify himself in print with a Burkean English nationalism and a corresponding distrust of French cultural influence. Yet when he steps up to mediate the quarrel between Warton and Johnson, the issue of nationalism never emerges. In Bowles' 1806 edition of Pope, the headnote to the "Concluding Observations on the Poetic Character of Pope" explains that Bowles' aim is to "state the grounds of this difference [between Warton and Johnson] upon principles which . . . will be easily recognised."[32] These two principles are stated outright in the ensuing discussion: first, "that 'all images drawn from what is beautiful or sublime in the works of NATURE, are more beautiful and sublime than any images drawn from ART;' and that they are therefore, *per se,* more poetical"; and second, that "in like manner, those *Passions* of the human heart, which belong to Nature in general, are, *per se,* more adapted to the *higher species* of Poetry, than those which are derived from *incidental* and *transient* MANNERS."[33] In these two notions, specifically articulated for the purpose, Bowles claimed to have found the means of establishing the rule by which we would estimate the "general poetic character of Pope" and thus of determining once and for all his proper rank as an English poet: that is, right at the top of the class of second-rate poets. When Campbell sought to reestablish Pope among the very greatest of English poets in the preface to his 1819 *Specimens,* Bowles responded by restating these same two propositions and by re-christening them with the Coleridgean phrase, "The Invariable Principles of Poetry."[34] Insofar as the ensuing controversy had critical substance, it took these principles, either by themselves or in their relation to the case of Pope, as constituting the main item on its agenda.

Many participants in the debate, on both sides, saw that Bowles' principles resembled those by which poets like Wordsworth and Coleridge defended their own poetry. We think of such principles ourselves, I believe, as central to the poetics of high English Romanticism. It is of course possible to explain the emergence of such principles—as Samuel Monk, Walter Jackson Bate, M. H. Abrams, and many since have done—in terms of critical or aesthetic history.[35] Such an account would show the debt of these principles to Longinus, John Dennis, the Edmund Burke of *A Philosophical Inquiry into . . . the Sublime and the Beautiful,* the theoreticians of the picturesque, and so on. As I suggested earlier, I do not propose to argue the extreme case that the principles of Romantic poetics can be explained solely as an ad hoc contrivance to justify the ouster of Pope. And I would not want to deny that many participants in the Pope controversy of the 1820s accepted Bowles' representation of his commitment to these principles at face value—that is, as categories independent of any prior, or extrapoetic, attitude toward Pope. There were, however, two pamphleteers who argued otherwise: Isaac D'Israeli, man of letters and father of the later prime minister, and Lord Byron. Their positions are the ones that merit particular attention here.

D'Israeli's critique of Bowles, which appeared in the July 1820 issue of the *Quarterly Review,* elaborates a central claim in Johnson's response to Joseph Warton decades earlier. This claim, as quoted by D'Israeli himself, is that "To circumscribe poetry . . . by a definition will only shew the narrowness of the definer."[36] In D'Israeli's hands, however, the Johnsonian apothegm expands into a full-blown assault on those who place their trust in theoretical principles. The question at issue for D'Israeli comes down to a choice between what we have been calling the poetic canon and what he, following others before him, calls "canons of criticism" (p. 410). He suggests that where the critical canon, in the form of "invariable" or universalized principles, comes into conflict with a duly canonized poet such as Pope, the former must give way. Obviously, the notion of whether a poet is indeed duly canonized is a problem for this account, but it is not one about which D'Israeli has much to say.

D'Israeli's early summary statement indicates what concerns him most in Bowles' response to Campbell: "Mr Bowles has adopted a system which terminates in an exclusion of a great poet from the highest order of poets" (p. 408). Whether or not we take D'Israeli to be insinuating that Bowles deliberately developed a theory that would demote Pope, he makes it very clear that he bothers to address Bowles' "Invariable Principles" only insofar as they affect the fate of Pope in the canon. This latter issue is indeed a momentous one in D'Israeli's eyes: "How this wonderful operation [the exclusion of Pope] has been carried on, it is of some importance to state—it is the history of the past, if Mr. Bowles triumphs; or the history of the future, should good sense and good taste return to Pope" (p. 408). In order to save Pope, and guarantee a future for English poetry, D'Israeli undertakes to show where Bowles goes wrong.

Perhaps the clearest expression of D'Israeli's priorities is the assertion that he offers as axiomatic for his discussion: "It is clear to us that a theory, which frequently admitting every thing the votary of Pope could desire to substantiate the high genius of his master, yet terminates in excluding the poet from 'the highest order of poets,' must involve some fallacy" (p. 410). One immediately wants to say to this what Bowles in effect says himself in later pamphlets, that the votaries of Pope may be mistaken in their poetic criteria. They might simply be praising Pope for trivial or mistaken reasons. D'Israeli anticipates this objection with the skeptical argument that we have no reliable means of establishing the kinds of principles by which an erroneous view might be categorically refuted. He is especially skeptical about Bowles' specific strategy of refutation, the appeal to "Nature":

> What are we not told of 'Nature!' What chimes and changes has not the delighted critic rung on 'Nature,' on 'General Nature,' on 'External Nature,' and on 'Moral Nature'—and so on! 'Nature' is a critical term, which the Bowleses have been explaining for more than two thousand years—and they still throw us into that nervous agitation of spirits which always arises when we sit down to our favourite studies of squaring the circle, or beginning the perpetual motion. [P. 409]

D'Israeli is careful to suggest that the "Bowleses" have increased in both number and influence over recent years and that they included both Wordsworth, "who is often by genius so true a poet" and "by his theory so mistaken a one," and Coleridge, who is implicated in Bowles' reference to Kant's verbal mystification (p. 411).[37] The grounds upon which D'Israeli can call these theories "mistaken" is, again, a question not itself addressed in his discussion.

In his account of the causes or motives that he sees leading to the malignant opinions of Bowles and the Bowleses, D'Israeli nowhere says that their invidious, pseudonatural principles are motivated by nationalism as such, but what he does say is nonetheless quite compatible with such a conclusion. The root of the problem, as he explains it, is a self-blinding self-centeredness: "It has frequently been attempted to raise up such arbitrary standards and such narrowing theories of art; and these 'criterions' and 'invariable principles' have usually been drawn from the habitual practices and individual tastes of the framers; they are a sort of concealed egotism, a strategem of self-love" (p. 410). Burke, in his attack on the allegedly bogus cosmopolitanism of the French, had argued that self-love grows inevitably into the love of nation. But we needn't rely on Burke to make this sort of connection, for it is suggested by the direction in which D'Israeli himself takes the discussion when he goes on to charge Bowles, and by implication the Lake Poets, with intellectual provincialism:

> We have frequently observed that *rural* editors and writers often incur the danger of effecting discoveries which are not novel, and are apt to imagine that they have completed their journey, when they have only proceeded as far as they were able to go. Plutarch long ago declared that an author should live in a great and populous city, which only could supply him with that abundance of books he requires, and with that traditional knowledge which floats in the memories of men of letters. Matters have by no means altered in this respect, for even at this day, there are some works, particularly an edition of Pope, which cannot properly be prepared in a country town. [P. 411]

D'Israeli's notion is that provincialism, like egotism, leads to a kind of solipsism in literary judgments—"Provincial authors . . . are liable to a sort of literary hypochondriasm, where they see nothing but the creation of a morbid fancy, a phantom in a dark room" (p. 411). Nationalism, then, would represent just an extension of this same debility with similar consequences.[38] (We note, in this connection, that D'Israeli cites a *classical* author to make his point.)

D'Israeli's discussion of Bowles and the Bowleses probably owes a great deal to Byron's *Don Juan,* a poem whose genesis simply cannot be fully explained without reference to the Pope controversy.[39] In April 1818, Byron wrote to Murray of "the unjustifiable attempts at depreciation begun by Warton—& carried on to & at this day by the new School of Critics & Scribblers who think themselves poets because they do *not* write like Pope."[40] On this occasion Byron's invective seems to trail off in fatigue: "I have no patience with such cursed humbug—& bad taste—your whole generation are not worth a Canto of the Rape of the Lock—or the Essay on Man—or the Dunciad—or 'anything that is his' but it is three in the matin & I must go to bed" (*LJ,* 6:31). It was probably late one night just weeks after this that Byron began his witty polemic against the Lakers in the dedicatory stanzas to *Don Juan.* We cannot take it for granted that D'Israeli read the 1818 letter, though he is in fact praised in it and was a member of the circle at Murray's among whom Byron's letters from Italy were circulated.[41] It is probably not even reasonable to assume that D'Israeli saw the suppressed dedicatory stanzas, though their existence was widely known by 1820 and he seems to echo them in the article in Murray's *Quarterly Review.* But D'Israeli would unquestionably have known canto 1 proper of *Don Juan,* with its satire on Lakist system-building and its famous canonical imperative: "Thou shalt believe in Milton, Dryden, Pope; / Thou shalt not set up Wordsworth, Coleridge, Southey."[42] Indeed, the general drift and tone of D'Israeli's critique of Lakist provincialism and self-absorption are too Byronically mordant to be explained as coincidence.

If D'Israeli's 1820 discussion thus develops points initially articulated by Byron, Byron's *Letter to Murray* pamphlet of 1821 may in turn be read as extending what D'Israeli had printed the year before. Byron not only read D'Israeli's article, he even uses its mention of a dinner exchange between himself and Bowles as his explicit point of departure in the *Letter.* We also have evidence that Byron had already been an admirer of D'Israeli's work and that he knew it well enough to identify D'Israeli— Bowles, to his embarrassment, failed to do so—as the author of the anonymous piece in the *Quarterly.*[43] Here is Byron to his friend Francis Hodgson soon after its appearance:

> The Scoundrels of Scribblers are trying to run down *Pope,* but I hope in vain. It is my intention to take up the Cudgels in that controversy, and to do my best to keep the Swan of Thames in his true place. This comes of Southey and Turdsworth and such renegado rascals with their systems. I hope you will not be silent; it is the common concern of all men of common sense, imagination, and a musical ear. I have already written somewhat thereto and shall do more, and will not strike soft blows in the battle. You will have seen that the "Quarterly" has had the sense and spirit to support Pope in an article upon Bowles; it is a good beginning. I do not know the author of that article, but I suspect *Israeli,* an indefatigable and an able writer. [*LJ,* 7:253]

A month earlier Byron had written to Murray even more unequivocally: "D'Israeli wrote the article on Spence—I know him by the mark in his mouth—I'm glad that the Quarterly has had so much Classical honesty and honour as to insert it—it is good & true" (*LJ,* 7:223).

One point that Byron seems to have found especially good and true in D'Israeli's remarks is his debunking of universalized "canons of criticism." Characteristically, Byron is both more emphatic and more personal in his enunciation of the position that D'Israeli only partly spelled out:

> I now come to Mr. B's 'invariable principles of poetry.' . . . I do hate that word '*invariable.*' What is there of *human,* be it poetry, philosophy, wit, wisdom, science, power, glory, mind, matter, life, or death, which is '*invariable?*' Of course I put things divine out of the question. Of all arrogant baptisms of a book, this title to a pamphlet appears the most complacently conceited. [*WB,* 5:543]

Putting D'Israeli's skeptical critique of critical principles so explicitly leaves it even more vulnerable to the sorts of objections we noted in the case of D'Israeli. In his review of Byron's *Letter,* Hazlitt coolly exposed its weaknesses and inconsistencies, especially Byron's attempt, after renouncing invariable principles, to substitute a set of such principles of his own.[44] What is especially germane about the *Letter* here, however, is that Byron also extends D'Israeli's suggestion about the nature of Bowlesian provincialism and about the way a parochial attitude defends itself on universalized principles.

In the concluding paragraph of the *Letter to Murray*, Byron develops a hypothetical case to point up the nationalist motives that underlie the work of the scoundrels who praise system and damn Pope:

> If any great national or natural convulsion could or should overwhelm your country in such sort as to sweep Great Britain from the kingdoms of the earth, and leave only that, after all, the most living of human things, a *dead language*, to be studied and read, and imitated by the wise of future and far generations, upon foreign shores; if your literature should become the learning of mankind, divested of party cabals, temporary fashions, and national pride and prejudice;—an Englishman, anxious that the posterity of strangers should know that there had been such a thing as a British Epic and Tragedy, might wish for the preservation of Shakespeare and Milton; but the surviving World would snatch Pope from the wreck, and let the rest sink with the people. He is the moral poet of all civilisation; and as such, let us hope that he will one day be the national poet of mankind. [*WB*, 5:560]

Like Keats' survey of English literature in "Sleep and Poetry," this passage should probably be read as responding to Wordsworth's remarks in the 1815 *Essay, Supplementary*. Byron's apocalyptic vision of an England in ruin invites us to view the canon of English poetry, much as Wordsworth's Preface does, from the perspective of future generations. But unlike Wordsworth, Byron asks that we become a "posterity of *strangers*" (my emphasis) toward English poetry and that we therefore regard it as part of a canon of international classics. From this perspective, he claims, not only the Bowleses of the world (and of course the Wordsworths, the Keatses, and the Southeys), but even Shakespeare and Milton, will be less highly cherished than Pope.

That this alien or cosmopolitan perspective is to be understood as Byron's own is clear from the pronouns: "*your* country," "*your* literature." Whether or not we accept his implied claim to being above "party cabals, temporary fashions, and national pride and prejudice," we must admit that Byron was perhaps uniquely qualified for the difficult role he tries to play. What other English writer living in 1821 could boast a position sufficiently alienated from contemporary English life to recognize the nationalistic premises of its literary arguments? Who else had so little to lose in exposing them to the world?[45]

5

Byron's *Letter to Murray* seems, then, to offer stiff opposition to the movement to establish a specifically native poetic canon; there is certainly no evidence that Byron thought any such canon would argue for the superiority either of England's national character or its poetic genius. What he urges instead looks like a return to Pope's own notion of a classical canon that cuts across national boundaries and rises above national interests. There is an important difference, however, in the way in which Byron's and Pope's respective classics bear on the practice of poetry. Pope and Pulci cannot be for Byron what Homer and Virgil were for Pope, and the reason lies in the skepticism Byron shared with D'Israeli about "invariable principles."

To see this difference plainly, we need only recall the two celebrated imperatives of Pope's *Essay on Criticism*. This is the first:

> First follow NATURE, and your Judgment frame
> By her just Standard, which is still the same:
> *Unerring Nature*, still divinely bright,
> One *clear, unchang'd,* and *Universal* Light,
> Life, Force, and Beauty, must to all impart,
> At once the *Source,* and *End,* and *Test* of *Art.*
>
> [ll. 68–73]

Here is a power that Pope is, in effect, willing to call "invariable." In terming its light "divinely bright," Pope certainly does not mean to suggest that, like Byron's "things divine," it should be "put . . . out of the question." On the contrary, this invariable force is also invariably essential to success in the human work of writing poetry. According to Pope, the great poetic rules that poets ignore only at their aesthetic peril are but nature self-methodized. "*Nature,*" as he says, "restrain'd / By the same Laws which first *herself* ordain'd" (ll. 90–91).

Pope argues further, however, that we discover these rules by perusing the great works of the classical tradition. In the most famous formulation of the second imperative, Homer stands as a synecdoche for this canon:

> Be *Homer's* Works your *Study,* and *Delight,*
> Read them by Day, and meditate by Night,
> Thence form your Judgment, thence your Maxims bring,
> And trace the Muses *upward* to their *Spring*
>
> [ll. 124–27]

Anticipating those who would question the consistency of these imperatives, Pope recommends the example of Homer's greatest student, Virgil, who is portrayed as initially falling prey to the same suspicion. Starting out on his great work, Virgil is supposed to have thought himself "*above* the Critick's Law, / And but from *Nature's Fountains* scorn'd to draw" (ll. 132–33). Pope then quickly explains that Maro's "boundless Mind" was too keen to remain unbound for long: "But when t'examine ev'ry Part he came, / *Nature* and *Homer* were, he found, the *same*" (ll. 134–35). The moral of this parable would be clear enough even if Pope had not spelled it out: "Learn Hence for Ancient *Rules* a just Esteem; / To copy *Nature* is to copy *Them*" (ll. 139–40). Pope's view, then, is that not just Nature and Homer but also Nature and Homer and Virgil—by implication even Nature and Homer and Virgil and Pope—are the same. They are always "still the same." Together they make up one clear, unchanged, and universal light. The canons of criticism and the canon of classics, in this scheme of things, are one in nature.

In the Romantic period, this doctrine no longer carries weight with either side of the quarrel over Pope. Writers are forced, as it were, to take sides on this matter, too. In elevating the national canon over the classical one, Bowles, Keats, and the Lakers insist on the universality of their critical principles. Seeing in this move a glorification of provincialism in the name of nature, Byron and D'Israeli insist upon a universalized canon of classics but surrender the notion that this canon embodies universally applicable principles.

D'Israeli's version of this argument in the *Quarterly Review* essay is that one must maintain the full range of the canonized classics precisely because they are so various. He holds universalized canons of criticism suspect precisely because he sees the great poets responding *variously* to various historical conditions. This position is sketched out in his account of why an "artifical test" (such as Bowles and the Lakists propose) for poetry must be "repugnant to the man of taste who can take enlarged views":

> In the contrast of human tempers and habits, in the changes of circumstances in society, and the consequent mutations of tastes, the objects of poetry may be different in different periods; preeminent genius obtains its purpose by its adaptation to this eternal variety; and on this principle, if we would justly appreciate the creative faculty, we cannot see why Pope should not class, at least in file, with Dante, or Milton. It is probable that Pope could not have produced an 'Inferno,' or a 'Paradise Lost,' for his invention was elsewhere: but it is equally probable that Dante and Milton, with their cast of mind, could not have so exquisitely touched the refined gaiety of 'the Rape of the Lock.' [P. 410]

Genius finds its merit not in its fidelity to a changeless Nature but rather in its adaptability to the mutations of society and the concomitant variations of culture. According to this historicist "principle"-against-principles, Pope's own representation of the classical canon is just one of many such possibilities among which we cannot readily discriminate a hierarchy.

In making an argument similar to this one, Byron is, again, both more emphatic and more personal than D'Israeli. The emotional climax of his *Letter to Murray* is a passage occasioned by his charge that the present enemies of Pope "have raised a mosque by the side of a Grecian temple of the purest architecture; and, more barbarous than the barbarians from whose practice I have borrowed the figure, they are not contented with their own grotesque edifice, unless they destroy the prior, and purely beautiful fabric which preceded, and which shames them and theirs for ever and ever" (*WB*, 5:559).[46] The climactic moment assumes the form of a confession and a subsequent qualification:

I shall be told that amongst those I *have* been (or it may be still *am*) conspicuous—true, and I am ashamed of it. I *have* been amongst the builders of this Babel, attended by a confusion of tongues, but *never* amongst the envious destroyers of the classic temple of our predecessor. I have loved and honoured the fame and name of that illustrious and unrivalled man, far more than my own paltry renown, and the trashy jingle of the crowd of 'Schools' and upstarts, who pretend to rival, or even surpass them. [*WB*, 5:559]

How is it that Pope's fiercest advocate and most loyal defender can end up at work on the same poetic enterprise as Pope's detractors? How is it, to be specific where Byron is not, that the satirist of *English Bards and Scotch Reviewers* could praise Pope's classicism to the sky in 1809 and then spend the next two years writing and living the life of Childe Harold, that most Romantic of Romantics? The reason can only be that Pope's own principles must themselves somehow cease to apply. Pope's poetic temple should outlast the applicability of the principles by which it was constructed. It is to be admired but not imitated. Byron saves Pope not for the history of the future but only for the history of the past.[47]

We touch here, I believe, on the reason why in *Don Juan* Byron can only parody the laws by which Pope swears. We can tell by the tone not to take him seriously when, midway through canto 1, the Byronic narrator comments: "as I have a high sense / Of Aristotle and the Rules, 'tis fit / To beg his pardon when I err a bit" (1.120). The joke becomes more obvious toward the end of the canto when he promises a work in which he will "carry precept to the highest pitch" (1.204) by setting down his poetical commandments. The title he proposes for this work makes it out to be the epitome of poetic anarchy: "Every Poet his own Aristotle" (1.204). The joke is easy to get but hard to interpret, especially in view of Byron's later comments about how the degradation of Pope by the leveling "poetical populace of the present day" is tied to their obsessive jockeying for fame and recognition: Juan has a vision in canto 11 of "the eighty 'greatest living poets,' / As every paltry magazine can show *its*" (11.54). Byron cracks off in a letter to Murray in 1820 about "the fifteen hundred first of living poets" (*LJ*, 7:168). Perhaps it was this suspicion about an unseemly ambition beneath the surface of their populist rhetoric that led Byron, the most radical Whig among the Romantics, to denounce Wordsworth and his colleagues as too democratic in their poetics, as for example in canto 3, where Byron describes the Lakers as "Jack Cades /

Of sense and song" hissing above the graves of the majestic Pope and Dryden (3.100).[48]

Indeed, in a degenerate age such as his own, Byron seems resigned to seeing a despot emerge from the anarchy, just so long as it is not the hypocrite Wordsworth. "Did you read [Hunt's] skimble-skamble about [Wordsworth] being at the head of his *profession* . . . ?" asked Byron of Moore in 1820. "He is the only one of us (but of us he is not) whose coronation I would oppose. Let them take Scott, Campbell, Crabbe, or you, or me, or any of the living, and throne him;—but not this new Jacob Behmen" (*LJ*, 6:47). Of course, Byron would prefer that the despot be himself. He seems to admit as much when, with a characteristic renunciation of hypocrisy and cant, he sums up the poetical commandments of "Every Poet his own Aristotle":

> Thou shalt not write, in short, but what I choose:
> This is true criticism, and you may kiss—
> Exactly as you please, or not, the rod,
> But if you don't, I'll lay it on, by G_d!
>
> [1.206]

The noble lord was perhaps not altogether uneasy in the role of an enlightened despot thrown up by what he saw as a failed revolution— or as he described himself later in this same poem, "The grand Napoleon of the realms of rhyme" (11.55). But what uneasiness we do discern in Byron's posture—elsewhere in canto 11, for example—sometimes takes the form of a melancholy awareness of the contradictions in his position. And when it does, it can make his high-handed pronouncements seem a kind of twisted elegy for the passing of those fixed laws that guided Pope.

---

1. Raymond Williams, *Problems in Materialism and Culture* (London, 1980), p. 16.

2. R. E. Prothero provides some valuable background information about the controversy. See *Works of Lord Byron,* ed. Prothero and E. H. Coleridge, 13 vols. (London, 1898–1904), esp. the appendix to vol. 5, where he prints the texts of Byron's two *Letters to Murray;* Prothero edited the 6 volumes titled *Letters and Journals.* All further references to *Works of Lord Byron,* abbreviated *WB* and with volume and page numbers, will be included in the text. The fullest compendium of information on the subject is J. J. Van Rennes, *Bowles, Byron, and the Pope-Controversy* (1915; rpt. ed., New York, 1966). The most valuable discussion of Pope's reception at this time is Upali Amarasinghe, *Dryden and Pope in the Early Nineteenth Century: A Study of Changing Literary Taste, 1800–1830* (Cambridge, 1962), which includes a more reliable bibliography of the controversy than Van Rennes'. See also Garland Greever, ed., *A Wiltshire Parson and His Friends: The Correspondence of William Lisle Bowles* (Boston, 1926), pp. 115–36.

3. W. L. Bowles, "Observations on the Poetical Character of Pope . . . with a Sequel in Reply to Octavius Gilchrist," *Pamphleteer* 18 (1821): 242.

4. See Van Rennes, *The Pope-Controversy,* pp. 15–33.

5. See Bowles, ed., *The Works of Alexander Pope,* 10 vols. (London, 1806), 10:363–87; see also Bowles' memoirs of Pope in this edition, 1:xv–cxxxiv.

6. Byron, *English Bards and Scotch Reviewers, The Complete Poetical Works*, ed. Jerome J. McGann, 3 vols. to date (Oxford, 1980–), 1:240–41, ll. 361–84.

7. On the reception of Joseph Warton's *Essay*, see William Darnall MacClintock, *Joseph Warton's "Essay on Pope": A History of the Five Editions* (Chapel Hill, N.C., 1933), pp. 19–33, and W. L. Macdonald, *Pope and His Critics: A Study in Eighteenth-Century Personalities* (London, 1951), pp. 233–330.

8. James Boswell, quoted in *Alexander Pope: A Critical Anthology*, ed. F. W. Bateson and N. A. Joukovsky (Harmondsworth, 1971), p. 160.

9. Joseph Warton, from the advertisement to Thomas Warton, *Poems on Several Occasions* (London, 1791).

10. Samuel Taylor Coleridge, *Biographia Literaria; or, Biographical Sketches of My Literary Life and Opinions*, ed. George Watson (London, 1975), p. 11, my emphasis; all further references to this work will be included in the text.

11. Coleridge, *Collected Letters*, ed. Earl Leslie Griggs, 6 vols. (Oxford, 1956–71), 1: 545; all further references to this work, with volume and page numbers, will be included in the text.

12. Percy Bysshe Shelley, *Complete Works*, ed. Roger Ingpen and Walter E. Peck, 10 vols. (London, 1926–30), 10:265.

13. Amarasinghe's formulation typifies the received view of the matter: "During the early nineteenth century the reputation of the Augustan poets, under the impact of the new Romantic tendencies, underwent a serious crisis" (*Dryden and Pope*, p. 3).

14. Alexander Pope, *An Essay on Criticism*, from the Twickenham text of the *Poems*, ed. John Butt (New Haven, Conn., 1963), ll. 181–88; all further references to this work will be cited by line from this edition and will be included in the text.

15. Lawrence Lipking, *The Ordering of the Arts in Eighteenth-Century England* (Princeton, N.J., 1970), p. 327; all further references to this work will be included in the text. René Wellek's work in this area is to be found primarily in *The Rise of English Literary History* (Chapel Hill, N.C., 1941), esp. pp. 47–94.

16. My citations of George Colman's *English Merchant* are from the second edition (London, 1767). The prologue also appeared in *Gentleman's Magazine* 37 (Mar. 1767): 136.

17. William Cowper, *The Task, Poetical Works*, ed. H. S. Milford, 3d ed. (London, 1926), bk. 5, ll. 457, 460–61; all further references to this work will be cited by book and line from this edition and will be included in the text.

18. For further discussion of the cultural nationalism of Cowper and his times, see Esmé Wingfield-Stratford's chauvinistic *History of English Patriotism*, 2 vols. (London, 1913), 1:594–99.

19. William Wordsworth, *Prose Works*, ed. W. J. B. Owen and Jane Worthington Smyser, 3 vols. (Oxford, 1974), 3:162; all further references to this work, abbreviated *PW* and with volume and page numbers, will be included in the text.

20. Bowles, *Poetical Address to the Right Honourable Edmund Burke, Fourteen Sonnets and Other Poems*, ed. Donald H. Reiman (New York, 1978), pp. 8–9.

21. Williams' fullest discussion of "structures of feeling" appears in *Marxism and Literature* (New York, 1977), pp. 128–35.

22. For a brief but penetrating analysis of the sharp rise of European nationalism in the face of the French Revolution and the Napoleonic Wars, see Georg Lukács, *The Historical Novel*, trans. Hannah and Stanley Mitchell (London, 1962), pp. 23–30.

23. See Alfred Cobban, *Edmund Burke and the Revolt against the Eighteenth Century: A Study of the Political and Social Thinking of Burke, Wordsworth, Coleridge, and Southey* (New York, 1978), chaps. 4–6. I have considered the particular case of Wordsworth's changing relation to Burkean nationalism in some detail in "Wordsworth and Burke," *ELH* 47 (Winter 1980): 741–71, and in an essay on the France books of *The Prelude*, "Wordsworth's Reflections on the Revolution in France," forthcoming in a volume of the 1982–83 Clark Lectures, *The Golden and the Brazen World*, ed. John M. Wallace. Important dissertation work on the literary nationalism of Coleridge and Shelley is now being undertaken by Julie Carlson at the University of Chicago.

24. Wordsworth, *The Letters of William and Dorothy Wordsworth: The Middle Years, Part 2, 1812–1820*, ed. Ernest de Selincourt, revised Mary Moorman and Alan G. Hill (Oxford, 1970), p. 152; all further references to this work, abbreviated *L W W*, will be included in the text.

25. Robert Southey, review of *English Poets* by Alexander Chalmers, *Quarterly Review* 23 (Oct. 1814): 84.

26. Francis Jeffrey, review of *Dramatic Works* by John Ford, *Edinburgh Review* 36 (Aug. 1811): 278. Jeffrey goes on to comment wistfully that if Dryden "had known nothing of foreign literature, and been left to form himself on the models of Shakspeare, Spenser and Milton . . . , there is reason to think that he would have built up the pure and original school of English poetry so firmly, as to have made it impossible for fashion, or caprice, or prejudice of any sort, ever to have rendered any other popular among our own inhabitants" (p. 281). For a contemporary *defense* of Dryden on nationalist grounds, see Percival Stockdale, *Lectures on the Truly Eminent English Poets*, 2 vols. (London, 1807). In saving Dryden for *his* English canon, Stockdale argued that Dryden was a "patriotick, and beneficient dictator, in the republic of letters," who "took the reins of government" at a time when the "region of the British muse was rude, and undetermined"; his genius melted "the ruggedness of its mother-tongue" with "the breath of its inspiration" (1:238, 237, 252). For a later defense on the same grounds, see T. S. Eliot, *John Dryden* (New York, 1932).

27. Joseph Warton, ed., *The Works of Alexander Pope*, 9 vols. (London, 1797), 1:1xviii. Amarasinghe offers much valuable discussion of the various accounts of Pope's "Frenchness" in *Dryden and Pope*.

28. Keats, "Sleep and Poetry," *The Poems of John Keats,* ed. Jack Stillinger (Cambridge, Mass., 1978), ll. 96–97; all further references to this work will be cited by line from this edition and will be included in the text.

29. Joseph Warton, *An Essay on the Genius and Writings of Pope*, 2d ed., 2 vols. (London, 1762), 1:vii; all further references to this work, with volume and page numbers, will be included in the text.

30. Samuel Johnson, *Lives of the English Poets*, ed. George Birkbeck Hill, 3 vols. (Oxford, 1905), 3:251.

31. William Hazlitt, *Complete Works*, ed. P. P. Howe, 21 vols. (London, 1930–34), 5: 69.

32. Bowles, ed., *Works of Pope*, 10:362.

33. Ibid., p. 363.

34. See Bowles, *The Invariable Principles of Poetry . . . Particularly Relating to the Poetical Character of Pope* (London, 1819). Bowles begins by simply quoting verbatim his statements of 1806 (see p. 6).

35. The classic critical histories of the rise of Romantic poetics are Samuel H. Monk, *The Sublime: A Study of Critical Theories in Eighteenth-Century England* (New York, 1935); Walter Jackson Bate, *From Classic to Romantic: Premises of Taste in Eighteenth-Century England* (Cambridge, Mass., 1946); and M. H. Abrams, *The Mirror and the Lamp: Romantic Theory and the Critical Tradition* (Oxford, 1953). An example of important recent work in the area is Thomas Weiskel, *The Romantic Sublime: Studies in the Structure and Psychology of Transcendence* (Baltimore, 1976).

36. Isaac D'Israeli, review of *Anecdotes of Books and Men* by Joseph Spence, *Quarterly Review* 66 (July 1820): 408; all further references to this work will be included in the text.

37. See also p. 409 for D'Israeli's disparaging remarks about the "Kantian transcendental philosophy."

38. For a suggestive recent discussion of classicist ideas about canon-formation and provincialism, see Frank Kermode, *The Classic: Literary Images of Permanence and Change* (New York, 1975), pp. 15–45.

39. See McGann's discussion of the poem as Byron's effort at "Counter-Reformation" in *Don Juan in Context* (Chicago, 1976), pp. 51–67.

40. Byron, *Letters and Journals*, ed. Leslie A. Marchand, 12 vols. (Cambridge, Mass., 1973–82), 6:31; all further references to this work, abbreviated *LJ* and with volume and page numbers, will be included in the text.

41. On D'Israeli's friendship with Murray, see Samuel Smiles, *A Publisher and His Friends: Memoir and Correspondence of the Late John Murray*, 2 vols. (London, 1891), 1:41–55; Smiles cites a letter of Washington Irving's which describes a dinner at Murray's, with D'Israeli present, at which one of Byron's letters from Italy was brought out (see 2:127).

42. Byron, *Don Juan*, cited from the variorum edition, ed. Truman Guy Steffan and Willis W. Pratt, 4 vols. (Austin, Tex., 1957), 2:canto 1, st. 205; all further references to this work will be to canto and stanza from this edition and will be included in the text.

43. Bowles ascribed the *Quarterly Review* piece to Gilchrist, whom he then attacked in "A Reply to the Charges Brought by the Reviewer of Spence's *Anecdotes*, in the Quarterly Review," *Pamphleteer* 17 (1820): 73–102. This set off a further exchange between the two men, from which I quoted above.

44. See Hazlitt, *Complete Works*, 19:62–82.

45. Peter Manning rightly warns me against overstating the case for Byron's literary expatriotism. "He was a poet," as Manning puts it, "who declared that his hopes of being remembered 'were twined with my land's language.' "

46. Byron's use of the figure of the second temple is reminiscent of Dryden's conceit, which has been so effectively elaborated by Bate, *The Burden of the Past and the English Poet* (New York, 1970), pp. 3–27. But the Romantic edifice that Byron regards as the second temple is discussed by Bate as the third (see pp. 95–134).

47. And once we understand the logic of D'Israeli's (Byronic) position, it is not clear how, by saving Pope, he can claim to be saving the poetic history of the future, either.

48. "Jack Cade," as Pratt's note explains, "led the rebellion of commoners against the misrule of Henry VI and his council in 1450" (*Don Juan*, vol. 4, p. 101).

Painting Memories: On the Containment of the Past in Baudelaire and Manet

Michael Fried

Near the beginning of Charles Baudelaire's *Salon of 1846*—one of the most brilliant and intellectually ambitious essays in art criticism ever written—the twenty-five-year-old author states that "the critic should arm himself from the start with a sure criterion, a criterion drawn from nature, and should then carry out his duty with a passion; for a critic does not cease to be a man, and passion draws similar temperaments together and exalts the reason to fresh heights."[1] It may be the emphasis on passion, indeed on strong personal feeling of every kind, not only here but everywhere in the *Salon,* that has prevented commentators from taking wholly seriously the possibility that a single criterion is in fact at work throughout it. But what if that criterion operates in the realm of feeling, if it is itself a feeling or complex of feelings, and if, moreover, as Baudelaire as much as says, no conflict between the claims of reason and of passion exists within his conception of the critical enterprise? Not that scholars have failed to recognize either the brilliance or (within limits) the ambitiousness of the *Salon of 1846;* on the contrary, it is widely regarded as the major extrapoetic text of Baudelaire's early career and especially in recent years has received extensive commentary. But by and large, those who have written about it have focused primarily on topics,

A first version of this essay was presented at a symposium on Edouard Manet at the Center for Advanced Studies in the Visual Arts in Washington, D.C. in March 1983. I am grateful to Jonathan Crewe and Walter Benn Michaels for their criticisms of that version, to Neil Hertz for comments at a later stage, and to Charles Dempsey for helpful conversations early and late.

such as Baudelaire's conception of nature, his vision of the creative process, and the relation of his ideas to those of other critics, that seem to me, if not quite pseudoproblems, at any rate concerns that lead us to ignore what the text may be saying about its own manner of proceeding.[2] I acknowledge, too, that certain features of that manner—the mixture of irony and seriousness in the opening dedication to the bourgeois, the many abrupt fluctuations of tone in the body of the essay, the seeming breaks in the argument from section to section, the texture and movement of the prose—could hardly be less systematic in effect. And yet it would not be hard to show that the *Salon* as a whole is the product of a remarkable effort, not merely to ground the judgment of individual works of art in a single experiential principle but also to bind together a number of diverse concerns—pictorial, literary, political, philosophical—in an intellectually coherent structure every part of which is meant to be consonant with every other. No wonder the last sentence of the *Salon* apostrophizes Balzac: the sheer inclusiveness of Baudelaire's undertaking recalls nothing so much as the scope of the *Comédie humaine.*

My aim in this essay is not, however, to demonstrate the intended unity of the *Salon of 1846.*[3] Instead, I want to pursue the single topic of Baudelaire's "criterion drawn from nature" with a view to developing a comparison, and in the end a contrast, between a previously unremarked, and in fact mostly inexplicit, aspect of Baudelaire's pictorial thought and what I shall maintain is a crucial function of Edouard Manet's ambitious canvases of the first half of the 1860s. Nor will I attempt to summarize the terms in which the relations between Baudelaire and Manet have been understood until now, beyond saying that the two men, whose friendship dates from some time in the 1850s until the poet's death in 1867, have been seen as sharing an intense preoccupation with the conditions of modernity as such.[4] A good deal of previous attention has therefore been paid to the last section of the *Salon of 1846,* entitled "Of the Heroism of Modern Life," as well as to Baudelaire's fascinating late text *The Painter of Modern Life* (about which I shall have something to add toward the close of this essay). My own emphasis will be different, though only up to a point: for there is an important sense in which the issues that I shall be treating, while not primarily concerned with the

Michael Fried, professor of humanities and the history of art and director of the Humanities Center at the Johns Hopkins University, is the author of *Morris Louis* and *Absorption and Theatricality: Painting and Beholder in the Age of Diderot.* He is currently at work on a book on Gustave Courbet.

representation of contemporary reality, are also issues of modernity broadly conceived.

My opening claim is this: the criterion to which Baudelaire refers in the passage from the *Salon of 1846* I began by quoting is that of *memory*. I mean by this that throughout the *Salon*, Baudelaire proceeds on the assumption that those works of art that leave the strongest and most lasting impression on the memory are the best, as opposed to all those others, in modern times the vast majority, that are forgotten virtually as soon as they are seen.[5] The first indication of this that we are given occurs in the course of a brief discussion of "melody" in color, which Baudelaire defines as "unity within color, or overall color." He then observes: "Melody calls for a cadence [*une conclusion*]; it is a whole, in which every effect contributes to a general effect. Thus melody leaves a profound memory in the mind." And in a striking passage to which I shall return, he goes on to say:

> The right way to know if a picture is melodious is to look at it from far enough away to make it impossible to understand its subject or to distinguish its lines. If it is melodious, it already has a meaning, and it has already taken its place in your store of memories [*le répertoire des souvenirs*]. [P. 50; p. 108]

Another revealing passage appears in the long section on Eugène Delacroix, in Baudelaire's estimation by far the greatest painter of the nineteenth century:

> For Eugène Delacroix, nature is a vast dictionary whose leaves he turns and consults with a sure and searching eye; and his painting, which issues above all from the memory [*du souvenir*], speaks above all to the memory [*au souvenir*]. The effect produced upon the spectator's soul is analogous to the artist's means. A painting by Delacroix, *Dante and Virgil* [i.e., *The Bark of Dante* (fig. 1)], for example, always leaves a deep impression whose intensity increases with distance. Ceaselessly sacrificing detail to whole, and reluctant to weaken the vitality of his thought by the drudgery of a neater or more calligraphic execution, he fully enjoys an indefinable [or, ungraspable: *insaisissable*] originality, which is the intimate essence of the project. [Pp. 58–59; p. 119]

I take the opening clause to mean that nature for Delacroix is *merely* a dictionary—a figure that invites diverse readings but, in this instance, seems designed to indicate that while Delacroix turns repeatedly to nature for precise information as to the appearance of things, he would be no more moved to copy nature than a writer would be inclined to transcribe a dictionary.

FIG. 1.—Eugène Delacroix, *The Bark of Dante*, 1822. Louvre, Paris. Phot. Réunion des musées nationaux.

Various other allusions to successes and failures of memory occur here and there in the next few sections, but it is only when we reach section 7, "On the Ideal and the Model," that Baudelaire overtly acknowledges the principle under which he has been operating all along. "I have already remarked," he writes, "that memory [*le souvenir*] is the great criterion of art; art is a mnemotechny of the beautiful" (p. 80; p. 147). Actually, until this point he hadn't stated explicitly that memory was the criterion to which he had referred in the opening pages of the *Salon*, but on the strength of the other quotations we have considered, it is easy to see why he might have thought he had. In any case, he argues that too much particularization and too much generalization are equally destructive of memory (that is, of memorability) and goes on to try to formulate a notion of the ideal that would somehow be poised between the two extremes (see pp. 80–81; pp. 148–49). The same central preoccupation turns up in his critique of two abuses of memory: the *chic*, a sort of manual memory that issues in a mere calligraphy of representations, and the *poncif*, an analogous automatism of the imagination that produces hackneyed, merely conventional depictions of facial expression and bodily gesture (see pp. 92–93; pp. 163–64). A few pages later, he accuses the military painter Horace Vernet of having "no passion and a memory like an almanac," a charge he amplifies by saying that Vernet renders "the correct number of buttons on each uniform, or the anatomy of a gaiter or a boot which is the worse for innumerable days' marching, or the exact spot on a soldier's gear where the copper of his small arms deposits its verdigris" (pp. 94, 95; p. 166). So it would seem that painting must not only issue from and speak to the memory but must do so properly, by virtue of an appeal to the right modality of memory, if it is to have the desired effect.

A few points should be noted before proceeding further. First, the criterion of memory as I have presented it may be considered to be "drawn from nature" in that it concerns a faculty with which individuals are naturally, albeit unequally, endowed. Second, there is a close connection throughout the *Salon* between successful effects of memory and notions associated with that of pictorial unity (for example, ensemble, melody, harmony, unity as such). Thus Baudelaire observes of Corot: "Almost all his works have the particular gift of unity, which is one of the requirements of the memory [*la mémoire*]" (p. 106; p. 180); while the work of those artists Baudelaire calls eclectics, combining as it does disparate and ultimately irreconcilable manners and procedures, is said by him not to leave a memory behind it (see pp. 96–97; pp. 168–69). Third, I want to underscore Baudelaire's use of certain complex spatiotemporal metaphors to figure those effects of memory of which he approves, metaphors that carry with them more than a hint of paradox. For example, what are we to make of the statement that a painting just this instant seen for the first time, at a considerable distance or, for that matter, at any distance, is *already* part of our store of memories? Practically speaking, how would we know or determine that this is so? And if the greatest paintings — say, Delacroix's *Bark of Dante*—leave an impression whose intensity increases with the passage of time, when, if ever, are we in a position to assess definitively the strength of such an impression? And how are we to compare that impression with those left on other occasions by other works? Worse still, how are we to reconcile the claim that an impression's intensity increases with time, which would tend to defer assessment indefinitely, with the statement previously considered, which invokes an assessment via a memory-effect occurring at the moment of, if not before, our very first impression of a work? Reflecting on these questions, we may come to feel that Baudelaire's criterion is not so simply drawn from nature after all.

But there is more to his treatment of memory than I have elicited so far. In an extraordinary footnote to his remark that Vernet lacks passion and has a memory like an almanac, Baudelaire provides, by way of a quotation from the German writer E. T. A. Hoffmann, an account of the workings of memory that presumably is meant to illuminate the argument of the *Salon* as a whole. (Although Baudelaire nowhere says that this is how he means the quotation to be taken, it is impossible not to take it in this spirit; however, it is also true, as we shall see, that its precise relevance to the rest of the *Salon* is far from self-evident.)

"True memory, considered from a philosophical point of view, consists, I think, in nothing else but a very lively and easily-roused imagination, which is consequently given to reinforcing each sensation by evoking scenes from the past, and endowing those scenes, as if by magic, with the life and character proper to each of them; at least I have heard this theory upheld by one of my past teachers who had a prodigious memory, although he could not carry a single date or proper name in his head.—The teacher was right, and in this matter there is, no doubt, a difference between sayings or utterances which have penetrated deeply into the soul and whose intimate and mysterious meaning has been grasped, and words which have merely been learned by heart." [P. 94 n.**; p. 166 n.1][6]

Reconsidered in the light of this passage, the notion that a painting might on first view already be part of our memories becomes more intelligible. For if "true memory" consists simply in a natural propensity to reinforce present sensations or perceptions by calling up certain emotionally charged scenes from earlier times, a primary effect of this will be to superimpose or even to merge present and past. What is more, Hoffmann's account of how true memory works raises the possibility that, in a given instance, the evocation of an earlier scene might be so compelling, so charged with the life and character proper to the original experience, as to gain a kind of ascendancy over the present perception in the very act of coming to its support. (Let the extent to which such a process is in fact sanctioned by the *Salon of 1846* remain an open question for the moment.) Similarly, a memory of a work of art might be imagined to grow more intense with the passage of time in that its revival by subsequent perceptions could be expected to augment its vividness or, at any rate, to establish its place in our store of memories on an ever deeper and more secure basis. In addition, we are better able to interpret the conflation of proximity and remoteness in Baudelaire's key figures: on the one hand, the special evocation of the past that Hoffmann calls true memory is available only in and through an experience of the present; on the other hand, the quotation suggests that our present perceptions not only are receptive to but perhaps stand in need of reinforcement from the past. What is nearest to hand is thus our only access to what is now remote, even while it may require the assistance of the latter to be truly present.

But if the quotation from Hoffmann helps rationalize certain seemingly paradoxical aspects of Baudelaire's claims for memory as the great criterion of art, it also problematizes those claims in ways that are at least as fundamental. For if we ask *how* a scene from our past first took its place among our memories and so became available to be called up by subsequent sensations, the answer would seem to be that, as originally perceived, the scene in question was overlain, suffused, or otherwise reinforced by an earlier scene, which in turn can have assumed *its* place among our memories only by virtue of exactly the same process, and so on ad infinitum.

Here one might wish to argue that such a chain of reinforcements must have a point of origin, a first memory (or primal scene) that provides the grounding for all the rest. But on the Hoffmann-Baudelaire account of the nature of memory, it is impossible to explain how a truly originary scene can have assumed the status of a memory at all, much less how it can have established itself as the master memory that any attempt to ground the chain as a whole requires it to be.

At this juncture, two further lines of inquiry all but propose themselves. One line would seek to integrate the thematics of memory in the *Salon of 1846* with the powerful if somewhat elusive reading of Baudelaire's poetry adumbrated almost fifty years ago by Walter Benjamin in a cluster of essays culminating in the late "On Some Motifs in Baudelaire." In particular, Benjamin's speculations on the intimate connection between what he calls the aura of a work of art (or of any perceived scene or object) and what, following Marcel Proust, he terms the *mémoire involontaire* are deeply suggestive, as is his analysis of the decay of aura in the modern experience of shock.[7] Another line of inquiry, not unrelated to the first, would compare the treatment of memory in the *Salon* with an analogous though immeasurably more developed problematic in Freud's writings — a comparison which, wherever else it might lead, would surely direct attention to the conflictedness of both the Baudelairean and the Freudian texts as regards questions of origin.[8] I am interested, however, in pursuing a third, more restrictedly pictorial, though I hope not excessively reductive, line of attack by suggesting that Baudelaire's use of memory as a criterion of aesthetic judgment in the *Salon of 1846* may be understood as reflecting a central yet, despite recent developments, insufficiently appreciated aspect of the enterprise of representational painting in the West since at least the Renaissance. I mean the remarkable degree to which the products of that enterprise were made from painting, from previous painting, often (though by no means always) with an openness, a frankness in the exploitation of the past, that historians have not infrequently found disconcerting and that we are still far from adequately comprehending.

Now it may seem strange, if not absurd, to say that we have not yet learned to appreciate sufficiently so conspicuous a feature of the Western tradition of picture making. As Rudolf Wittkower remarked more than fifteen years ago, one of the staples of the discipline of art history is the tracing of influences and borrowings, and what are they if not concrete evidence that the art in question was made from previous art in one way or another? And yet, as Wittkower also observed, scholars have mostly shied away from recognizing the ubiquitousness of the phenomenon or, at any rate, from reflecting in a sustained way on what that ubiquitousness implies about the actual functioning of the tradition which generated the objects of their study.[9] Recently the situation has begun to change. In the fairly short time since Wittkower wrote, a number of scholars working primarily in comparative literature but also in intellectual history and the history of art have sought to emphasize the importance for writers and painters from the Renaissance through the eighteenth century of a theory and a practice, and specifically of a theory-oriented practice, of selective imitation of canonical works by ancient and modern masters. This is not the place for even a cursory summary of these developments, but all the indications are that we have only just begun to recognize both the dimensions and the complexity of the general problem now before us. And we have perhaps not yet begun to consider the extent to which that new, acutely intertextual awareness may be at odds with the more or less straightforward evolutionary framework of conventional art history.[10]

Nor is the prevalence over several centuries of a theory and a practice of selective imitation the only factor that conduced to the making of art from art. Another is the persistence of iconographical traditions, often going back to antiquity, the precise articulation of which has been the special study of Aby Warburg, Fritz Saxl, Erwin Panofsky, and their school.[11] Still another is indicated by the growing recognition that the broadly realistic bias of much Western painting from the early Renaissance to the late nineteenth century was never simply a matter of constructing accurate simulacra of visual experience but, instead, crucially involved a highly structured play of codes, schemata, and the like, at least some of which may be understood as "internal" to the pictorial enterprise over considerable stretches of time.[12] (Of course, the ability of certain artists to achieve especially compelling effects of the real was actively emulated by their successors—put another way, realism was itself the object of selective imitation.) In addition, there may well be something about the nature of works of so-called visual art in the West, especially paintings— a particular memorableness associated with the perspicuousness both of their formal gestalten and of their technical or medium-specific characteristics—that makes them even more likely to leave their stamp on those who encounter them than is normally the case as regards works of literature. Thus we habitually speak of a given painting "betraying the fact" that the artist who made it had to have seen a previous work by another painter, and indeed, to enable him to have done so, we routinely posit journeys for which no corroborating evidence exists. As Denis Diderot observed in 1761:

> It seems to me that a great painter who has gone before is more discomforting for his successors than a great writer for us. The imagination seems to me more tenacious than the memory [by which Diderot means that the visual memory seems to him more tenacious than the verbal memory]. Raphael's paintings are more present to me than Corneille's verses, than the most beautiful parts of Racine. There are some figures that never leave me. I see them; they follow me, they obsess me. For example, that St. Barnaby who rends his clothing [in Raphael's *Sacrifice at Lystra*], and many other figures, how can I shake off such spectres? And how can painters do it?[13]

The answer would seem to be that painters can't, which is to say that they are compelled to grapple more or less openly with those specters in painting after painting.

The next step in my argument is perhaps already apparent. I suggest that the thematics of memory in the *Salon of 1846,* whatever relation it may bear to the treatment of memory elsewhere in Baudelaire's oeuvre, reflects a fundamental characteristic of paintings in the Western tradition, namely, that in one way or another, or in a variety of mutually reinforcing ways, they are made from previous paintings, which in turn are made from still previous ones, and so on ad infinitum in an ever ramifying network of associations. To rephrase this slightly, a painting in this tradition is nothing more nor less than the latest term in a chain of memories of works of art that for all practical purposes must be thought of as endlessly regressive, as leading back to no ultimate or primal source or prototype. Inasmuch as all successful paintings in the tradition would have been seen by Baudelaire as instantiations of an ideal of unity, this would help explain why unity is for him one of the requirements of memory: only the experience of a "unified" work in the present would sufficiently recall— would lend itself to being supported by memories of—"unified" works from the past. And I suggest also that Baudelaire's use of memory as the great criterion of art may be understood as calling for the establishment of a particular relationship between a new work of art and its antecedents, one that will trigger rather than block the process Hoffmann describes and Baudelaire himself must be presumed to endorse. For it seems clear on the strength of Baudelaire's condemnation of various abuses of memory and especially on the strength of his distaste for the eclectics that not just any relationship to previous art will set the desired process going. We must, then, return to the *Salon* to try to specify the nature of the relationship to past art that is ultimately, if tacitly, at stake in Baudelaire's repeated appeals to the criterion of memory throughout its pages.

We touch here on one of the most delicate and obscure issues in Baudelaire's aesthetic thought, an issue roughly comparable to another he could never fully resolve concerning the distinction between legitimate and illegitimate uses of poetry in painting. In both cases Baudelaire appears to have resorted to a distinction thematized in terms of a radical difference between naiveté and calculation, between doing something involuntarily or unknowingly and doing it in full consciousness of trying to achieve a particular end. His admiration for Delacroix's naiveté as opposed to Victor Hugo's deliberateness is a case in point, as is his remark that Delacroix "is often, without knowing it, a poet in painting" (p. 57; p. 117). Toward the end of the *Salon* he amplifies this:

> Poetry is not [that is, ought not to be] the painter's immediate aim: when poetry happens to be mixed with painting, the resulting work cannot but be more valuable; but poetry is unable to disguise the

shortcomings of a work. To make a deliberate point of looking for poetry during the conception of a picture is the surest means of not finding it. It must come without the artist's knowledge. It is the result of the art of painting itself; for it lies in the spectator's soul, and it is the mark of genius to awaken it there. [P. 98; p. 171]

On the basis of my discussion so far, we can surmise that what lies in the "spectator's soul" are memories of poems and their characteristic effects and that it is the peculiar achievement of the legitimately poetic painter to unknowingly or involuntarily trigger a process of reinforcement that will bring at least some of these memories into play.[14] Clearly, however, there are serious weaknesses in Baudelaire's formulation, notably, the indeterminateness of the concept of "painting itself," the seeming arbitrariness of the claim that painting mixed with poetry is "more valuable" than painting that is not, and the evident absurdity of implying that Delacroix, who repeatedly turned to Dante, Shakespeare, Scott, Byron, and other writers for his subject matter, was in no sense seeking poetry when he did so.[15]

Consider now a passage quoted by Baudelaire from the young Adolphe Thiers, a gifted art critic before he became a master politician, who in his *Salon of 1822* praised Delacroix's *Bark of Dante* in the following terms:

> "Apart from the poetic imagination which is common to both painter and writer, the author of this picture has another, *artistic* imagination, which one might almost call 'the graphic imagination' and which is quite different from the first. He throws his figures on to the canvas, he groups and bends them at will, with the boldness of Michelangelo and the abundance of Rubens. I don't know what recollection [Je ne sais quel souvenir] of the great masters seized hold of me at the sight of this picture; once more I found that power—wild, ardent, but natural—which yields without effort to its own impulse." [P. 53; pp. 111–12; Thiers' emphasis]

As I read this passage, its special appeal for Baudelaire lies in what it almost says, or rather in what it doesn't quite say. For example, it doesn't say that Delacroix attempted consciously to achieve the boldness of Michelangelo or the abundance of Rubens, only that he did achieve both; and while it evokes a certain memory of the great masters (and thereby, if I am right, approaches Baudelaire's unexpressed thought), it simultaneously characterizes that memory as ineffable, unanalyzable, the effect ultimately of a natural power. And, of course, the object of Thiers' panegyric, Delacroix's *Bark of Dante,* is especially telling in this connection, bearing as it does a manifest relation to Théodore Géricault's *Raft of the "Medusa"* and beyond that (as well as *through* it, which is to say, indirectly, perhaps involuntarily, unknowingly) to works by artists such as Antoine-Jean Gros, Jacques-Louis David, Gabriel-François Doyen, Rubens, Michelangelo . . . the list could go on and on, each name ramifying into many more.[16] (We may recall that it is the *Bark of Dante* that Baudelaire cites as an instance of the way in which Delacroix's paintings leave behind them a deep impression whose intensity increases with distance.)

Other rhetorical strategies allow Baudelaire to achieve analogous results. For example, elsewhere in the "Delacroix" section of the *Salon of 1846,* he remarks that Delacroix "is one of those rare beings who remain original after having drunk deep of all the true wells, and whose indomitable individuality has borne and shaken off the yokes of all the great masters in turn [et dont l'individualité indomptable a passé alternativement sous le joug secoué de tous les grands maîtres]," a characterization which, especially in the odd phrasing of the original, at once asserts and denies a relation to the past (p. 57; p. 117). A few pages later, Baudelaire likens a personage in Delacroix's *Pietà* of 1844, a work that amounts virtually to a paraphrase of Rosso Fiorentino's *Pietà* in the Louvre, to "the most pitiful figures in [Delacroix's] *Hamlet,* with which, besides, this work has more than one affinity," thereby acknowledging a sense of the familiar while deflecting attention, his own first and foremost, from the very possibility of a derivation from the old masters (p. 60; p. 121).[17] But perhaps the most revealing statement in Baudelaire's early criticism touching on the question of the proper relation of present to past art occurs in his *Salon of 1845,* near the end of a long discussion of William Haussoullier's *Fountain of Youth.* Scholars have always found it puzzling that Baudelaire thought so highly of that particular picture, but the crucial passage is one in which he draws back somewhat from his admiration to consider a possible flaw in Haussoullier's performance:

> Dare we, after having so frankly displayed our sympathies . . . say that following our pleasant contemplation of this work the names of Giovanni Bellini and some early Venetian painters crossed our memory? Is M. Haussoullier perhaps one of those men who know a little too much about their art? That is a truly dangerous scourge, and one that compromises the naiveté of many excellent impulses.[18]

As I read these remarks, they not only express Baudelaire's final, almost belated reservations about Haussoullier's picture but also go a long way toward accounting for its strong appeal to him in the first place.

Here it is important to observe that a version of the practice of selective imitation of the great masters, to speak only of that, was by no means foreign to the procedures of the leading French painters of the first half of the nineteenth century. Wittkower is undoubtedly correct when he says that the later eighteenth and early nineteenth centuries saw a valorization of ideas of genius, originality, and naiveté at the expense of the traditional doctrine of imitation.[19] But the triumph of the new idea-complex was far from total, and if we call to mind recent scholarship on Delacroix, Jean-Auguste-Dominique Ingres, and Thomas Couture, the last of whom was Manet's teacher, it becomes apparent that an intense and often highly explicit involvement with canonical works and painters continued unabated through the period and indeed gathered fresh momentum, for reasons that merit investigation in their own right.[20]

In the *Salon of 1846,* Baudelaire's expressions of revulsion against eclecticism testify to his sense of the pervasiveness of that general phenomenon in the art of his time. And what has so far emerged about the thematics of memory in the *Salon* leads me to suggest that it, too, should be construed as a response not simply to the larger post-Renaissance tradition to which I have alluded but specifically to the new phase of interest in and exploitation of the styles and monuments of the past that took place throughout French painting in the 1830s and '40s. More precisely, Baudelaire's appeal to memory as the great criterion of art may be understood simultaneously as according with contemporaneous developments, in its unstated but implicit demand that a new work contain within it traces of its antecedents, and as reacting against those developments, in its scarcely more articulated requirement that the antecedents' traces not announce themselves as such. Or, to rephrase this double demand in terms that approach those of his quotation from Hoffmann cited earlier, the perception of a new work must trigger or activate an endlessly regressive sequence of memories of earlier works, but not only must those memories not be allowed to overwhelm or otherwise displace that perception (this is the answer to the question left open on page 515), *they must remain below the threshold of conscious awareness,* investing the present with the aura and significance of memory without for a moment appearing on its stage.[21] It should also be stressed, on logical grounds, that *neither must they quite be forgotten,* for in that event they would no longer be available to come to the support of new perceptions, with disastrous consequences for the future of painting. In fact, Baudelaire explains what he regards as the inherent deficiency of the art of sculpture partly on just this basis, writing in the opening sentence of section 16 ("Why Sculpture Is Tiresome"): *"The origin of sculpture is lost in the night of time,* it is therefore a Carib art" (p. 111; p. 187; emphasis his). I take this to mean that having irrevocably lost contact with its origins, the art of sculpture is unable to mobilize its past at all and so will forever lack a viable present. This implies, in turn, that the state of affairs in painting is fundamentally different, the entirety of its past being in some sense held in reserve.[22]

What cannot fail to surprise us, having reached this point, is that the author of the *Salon of 1846* singles out Delacroix as the one truly great modern painter: for as I have already noted, and as other critics of the period recognized, Delacroix's paintings often bear a quite specific and wholly unconcealed relation to famous prototypes in earlier art. May we therefore say that Baudelaire's admiration for Delacroix, which anchors not just his first two *Salons* but virtually everything he went on to write about painting, involves what can only be described as a refusal to see or know or (at the very least) acknowledge, even to himself, the truth about Delacroix's unembarrassed exploitation of the past? Or is it rather that the inapplicability to Delacroix's achievement of the double demand that I have drawn from the *Salon of 1846* explains why Baudelaire left those demands mostly implicit, indeed why he *could not* have allowed himself to frame them in as many words, since the moment they were given definite form, their dissonance with Delacroix's art and, more generally, the enormous difficulty (verging on outright contradiction) of imagining how they might be satisfied would threaten to become manifest? And is this also why at certain crucial junctures in the *Salon,* Baudelaire deploys quotations from the writings of others, as if in order to absolve himself, not precisely of responsibility for those quotations but, rather, of something like full consciousness of what they say and entail? Does the preservation of his own and Delacroix's naiveté require nothing less?[23] With these unanswerable, not quite rhetorical questions, I reach the limit of my reading, at least for the time being, of a critico-aesthetic "system" that no one, neither its operator nor its interpreters, may be said to command.

What bearing does the "system" of the *Salon of 1846* have on Manet? In view of his training in Couture's atelier, it is not surprising that the young Manet, Manet of the 1850s, remained comfortably within the Western imitative tradition I have sketched, even to the extent of calling on Delacroix to request permission to copy one of his paintings—as it happens, the *Bark of Dante.* But what of a different Manet, the newly mature Manet of the first half of the 1860s, the painter who, in the space of just a few years, produced a body of work that marks a curious caesura in the history of painting: How are we to understand *his* relation both to that tradition and to what I have interpreted as the response to that tradition in Baudelaire's *Salon of 1846?* In order to pursue this subject further, I am forced to broach the most obdurate and, it may be, the most explosive problem in all of Manet studies: the meaning of his use of sources in the art of the museums.

The problem of the meaning of Manet's use of sources first arose in 1864, when the critic Ernest Chesneau spotted the painter's adaptation in his *Déjeuner sur l'herbe* (1862–63) of a figure group from Marcantonio Raimondi's engraving after Raphael's *Judgment of Paris.* That same year, a more distinguished critic, Théophile Thoré, remarked in the course of a largely favorable review that Manet had "pastiched" Velázquez, Goya, and El Greco and called attention to certain striking similarities between Manet's art and the work of other old masters. Thereafter the topic was largely moot, until 1908, when the German art historian Gustav

Pauli rediscovered the Marcantonio connection. But it was not until the 1930s and '40s that the astonishing range of Manet's quotations from, allusions to, and adaptations of earlier works of art became apparent to scholars. Confronted by a phenomenon seemingly without precedent in their experience, they mostly saw in it either a sign of deficiency—thus Manet was criticized for lacking imagination or being unable to compose— or a hallmark of modernity—indicating a laudably formalist indifference to subject matter as such. By the 1950s and '60s, it was often said or implied that Manet intended by his use of sources at once to identify with and to compete with the old masters, though it was never explained why he should have felt a special need to do so nor, indeed, why he should have chosen to identify with and compete with them in this particular way. Nor was it made clear how those alleged intentions were consistent, if in fact they were, with his basic commitment to a realist aesthetic.[24]

In 1969 I published a long essay, "Manet's Sources: Aspects of His Art, 1859–1865," that advanced a new interpretation of Manet's references to earlier art, and shortly thereafter that essay was severely criticized by Theodore Reff.[25] Let me say at once that many of Reff's criticisms now seem justified to me, though I have always felt that the head and trunk of my argument, as distinct from one or two of its limbs, suffered less damage than has been thought. In any case, in the years since our essays appeared, the question of the overall or strategic significance of Manet's use of sources has been allowed to lapse, partly, no doubt, owing to the force of Reff's critique but, more importantly, because the question has seemed to have little place in the revisionist reading of Manet's art that Beatrice Farwell, Anne Coffin Hanson, Reff, and others have been elaborating.[26] Two recent exhibition catalogs by leading scholars typify this state of affairs: in each of them, Manet's use of past art is discussed in connection with specific works bearing an obvious relation to famous prototypes, but the larger question of the meaning of his involvement with the past is ultimately not addressed.[27] More fundamentally, nor does either catalog address any issue touching on Manet's commitment to an exalted conception of the enterprise of painting, understood as distinct from the production of images—of *mere* images, I am inclined to say.[28] For Manet, as I view him, was essentially a painter of major ambition at a time and in a situation in which it was far from clear what that undertaking entailed or how that ambition was to be expressed, much less realized: this is what it means to characterize Manet as a *modernist* painter, a term that revisionist art history tends to shun as irredeemably tainted with formalism. But there is nothing formalist, acontextual, or suprahistorical about the account I am going to summarize of Manet's involvement with the past nor about the attempt I shall go on to make to relate that involvement to the thematics of memory and its rationale in what might be called the memory-structure of Western painting that I have developed through my reading of Baudelaire's *Salon of 1846*.

Briefly, I see Manet in the early 1860s as pursuing a double strategy in and through his use of sources from the art of the museums. In the first place, his demonstrable interest in the work of the Le Nain, Antoine Watteau, and, surfacing around 1864, Jean-Baptiste Chardin suggests that he wished to associate his own art with an interpretation of the authentic French tradition in painting that was currently being advanced by a number of critic-historians, the most eminent and authoritative of whom was Thoré. At the heart of that interpretation, elements of which go back to the 1830s and '40s, was the belief that the French national genius in painting, as expressed historically in the work of the Le Nain, Watteau, and Chardin, among others, was both realist and democratic, an art of the people rather than of either the church or the crown. Such a characterization of Watteau especially may strike us as surprising; but it is no more limited by cultural assumptions than are more recent assessments of his achievement, and it has the virtue of enabling us to understand how Manet could be a realist in his basic orientation and at the same time be as interested in Watteau's art as I believe he was throughout these years. In any event, Manet's *Old Musician* (1862) (fig. 2), with its conjoined allusions to Louis Le Nain's *Halt of the Horseman* (fig. 3) and/ or Antoine Le Nain's *Old Piper* and to Watteau's *Gilles* (fig. 4), may be seen as a singularly clear statement of Thoré's position, at least up to a point.[29]

FIG. 2.—Edouard Manet, *The Old Musician,* 1862. National Gallery, Washington, D.C., Chester Dale Collection. Phot. Museum.

FIG. 3.—Louis Le Nain, *The Halt of the Horseman*, ca. 1640? Victoria and Albert Museum, London. Phot. Museum.

FIG. 4.—Antoine Watteau, *Gilles,* 1717–19? Louvre, Paris. Phot. Réunion des musées nationaux.

But Manet was not content merely to secure the Frenchness of his art in this manner. Equally important, he wished to go beyond the art of France to comprehend and in effect to subsume the painting of the other major national schools and, by doing so, to establish explicitly the internationalism or, better, the *universality* of his own painting: as witness the deliberate reference in the *Old Musician* to Velázquez's *Drinkers* (fig. 5), a well-known masterpiece that Manet evidently wanted to be seen as presiding over his picture as a whole.[30] Moreover, this ambition, too, finds a reflection, in fact an anticipation, in the art writing of this period, most importantly in several essays by Thoré. Thus Thoré argued that throughout Europe an irresistible desire for a less nationalistic, more universal mode of existence was springing up (despite Thoré's bitter personal experience, his socialism gives his thought a perpetually hopeful cast). He maintained that major international exhibitions such as the one held in Paris in 1855 were at once expressions of that desire and instruments of its further realization, in that they promoted the formation, first, of "a sort of European school [of painting] . . . then of a universal school, familiarized with the world, and to which nothing human would be foreign."[31] In the same spirit, Thoré held that the time had come for art history to go beyond the study of national schools toward a universal history of painting, the exact conceptual basis of which he could not specify beyond asserting that such a history would have above all "to grasp the analogies and the harmonies that link [the different national schools] in a great unity."[32] In the light of the first half of the present essay, we may surmise that the "analogies and the harmonies" to which

FIG. 5.—Diego Velázquez, *Drinkers*, 1628. Prado, Madrid. Phot. Museum.

Thoré referred, and which around this time appear to have become *visible* as such to him and others as never before, were the result of selective imitation over the centuries and, more broadly, of the processes by which European painting since the Renaissance fed on its own past accomplishments.

In my essay of 1969, I suggested that Manet found himself constrained to seek access to the art of the other national schools by relying on publicly recognized links or affinities between the French painters he regarded as canonical and various foreign artists—for example, Watteau was often associated with Rubens, and the Le Nain with both the Flemish and Velázquez. Although I still believe Manet was not indifferent to such connections, I would now qualify my views by saying that he did not require textual sanction to use non-French sources. Rather, I see him as acutely aware of the network of visual analogies and harmonies stretching across national boundaries to which Thoré's remarks also bear witness and as needing no further sanction than that awareness to justify his allusions to a multiplicity of works belonging to at least four major European schools: those of Spain, Flanders, Italy, and Holland. (An explicit acknowledgment of his interest in Japanese art takes place only in the later 1860s, following the International Exhibition of 1867.)[33] Another point in my 1969 essay I would now modify is the claim that Manet followed Thoré, to whom the Italian tradition was anathema, to the extent of staying clear of Italian art until he came to paint the *Déjeuner sur l'herbe*. One of Reff's most telling criticisms was that this view is untenable as it stands.[34] In fact, I wouldn't wish to be understood as saying that Manet followed anyone at all—my claim is rather that when his relation to earlier art is understood against the background of contemporaneous thinking about that art, Thoré and a few other writers must also be counted among his sources.

A point I would insist on, though, against Reff and others who have found my basic argument unconvincing, is that it is not invalidated merely by the discovery of alternative or indeed superior sources for a painting or a figure. For example, I suggested that Manet's *Portrait of the Artist's Parents* (1860) owes a great deal to one or more paintings by Louis Le Nain; this not only is not disproved by, it is entirely compatible with Reff's countersuggestion that the head of Manet *père* recalls Rembrandt's etching *A Bearded Man in a Furred Oriental Cap*, then considered to be a portrait of Rembrandt's father.[35] Or to take an instance which perhaps epitomizes this aspect of Manet's method in the early 1860s, I associated the superb *Mlle V. in the Costume of an Espada* (1862) (fig. 6) with Watteau's paintings of figures from the commedia dell'arte as well as, reaching beyond French painting, with an engraving after a picture by Rubens of a figure of *Venus* or *Fortune* that appeared in the *Gazette des beaux-arts* in 1860 (fig. 7), accompanying a review of Thoré's monograph on the Galerie Suermondt at Aix-la-Chapelle.[36] In refutation of this connection,

FIG. 6.—Manet, *Mlle V. in the Costume of an Espada*, 1862. The Metropolitan Museum of Art, New York, bequest of Mrs. H. O. Havemeyer, 1929, the H. O. Havemeyer Collection. Phot. Museum.

Reff proposed an engraving after Titian's *Girl with a Fruit Dish* (fig. 8) that would have been available to Manet as early as 1855.[37] And at roughly the same moment, Farwell advanced Marcantonio's engraving after Raphael's *Temperance* (fig. 9) as a source for the *Mlle V.*, which, in addition to accounting for salient features of Manet's composition, provides an immediate precedent for his use of Marcantonio/Raphael in the *Déjeuner*.[38]

FIG. 7.—After Peter Paul Rubens, *Venus* or *Fortune*, wood engraving. *Gazette des beaux-arts*, 1860.

FIG. 8.—After Titian, *Girl with a Fruit Dish*, wood engraving. Charles Blanc, *Histoire des peintres de toutes les écoles: Ecole vénitienne*, 1855.

FIG. 9.—Marcantonio Raimondi, after Raphael, *Temperance*, engraving. The Metropolitan Museum of Art, New York, Harris Brisbane Dick Fund, 1926. Phot. Museum.

Now it may seem that Farwell's discovery not only supersedes but invalidates both my Rubens and Reff's Titian, and perhaps it does. But it would be wholly consistent with Manet's project as I have interpreted it to imagine that he might have been alert to and, in that sense, might have "intended" the resemblance between the posture of the head and upper body in the *Temperance* and in the *Girl with a Fruit Dish,* or, more loosely, between stance and gesture in the *Temperance* and in the Rubens. Such resemblances raise the further possibility that Titian and Rubens may have had this or a related Raphael image in mind when they designed *their* pictures. Somewhere along here, salutarily, the very concept of a source begins to blur.[39]

In summary, I interpret Manet's multiple and often overlapping references to the art of the past as evidence of an attempt both to represent a certain vision of the authentic French tradition and to surpass that tradition in the direction of a universalizing or a *totalizing* of the enterprise of painting. And this brings me at last to the question that has been pending throughout my discussion of Manet. Assuming for the moment that my account of these matters has been at all persuasive, how are we to understand the relationship of Manet's use of sources in previous art to both the thematics of memory in Baudelaire's *Salon of 1846* and the tradition of art making that I have suggested is reflected in that thematics?

The first point to establish is that Manet, like Baudelaire, may be seen as bearing a double relation, at once positive and negative, to the widespread tendency of his contemporaries (it was still widespread in 1860) to make selective use of stylistic and other features of canonical works by earlier masters. Before saying more about the significance of Manet's art in this regard, however, I want to emphasize the profound difference between Baudelaire's and Manet's respective views as to how the art of the past should be used or acknowledged or, in one way or another, allowed to come into play.

As I read the *Salon of 1846,* it implies that a painting will satisfy Baudelaire's criterion of memory only if that painting bears an ineffable, to all intents and purposes undetectable, relation to those earlier works which, near and far, lie behind it. The contrast between this implicit insistence that the past be kept out of sight and Manet's deliberate, specific, and perspicuous references to the art of the old masters could hardly be more striking. But the crucial difference lies deeper. For there is an important sense in which Baudelaire's stricture against any overt acknowledgment of previous works has for its ultimate rationale the production of a memory-effect by virtue of which the art of the past, far from being kept in quarantine, is, on the contrary, brought into intimate commerce with the art of the present, supporting the latter precisely by not quite giving itself away. Conversely, it is possible to see in Manet's attempts at totalization across national schools evidence of a desire, if not exactly to break with or be quits with the past, at any rate to subsume the past synecdochically and, by so doing, to transform fundamentally the terms of its relation to both present and future. It is in this respect above all that Manet may be viewed as departing sharply from the practice of his contemporaries and immediate predecessors, in whose exploitation of the past no comparable ambition can be discerned.

If we try to cast this in terms of metaphors of memory, we might say either that Manet sought once and for all to do away with memory as a medium of painting and its reception or, alternatively, that implicit in Manet's practice was the belief that *true* memory, not in a Hoffmannesque but in a certain Freudian sense, begins only when mere repetition of the past has been brought to an end.[40] In a similarly ambiguous vein, Thoré in 1860 wrote of the need for the history of art to do justice to the various national schools, a task that he characterized as "a sort of Last Judgment, after which, the past being liquidated, we will enter a new world."[41] Thoré's hopes were never exactly fulfilled, at least not in any shape he was able to acknowledge. And it would be equally misleading to think of Manet's canvases of the early 1860s as having foreclosed for subsequent painting of high ambition the possibility of more traditional modes of association with the art of the past. But none of Manet's successors has found it necessary, as in my account he appears to have done, to assume responsibility for the entire history of painting since the Renaissance or, at least, for a particular configuration of that history. And we have only to consider how unburdened the Impressionists were in this regard to appreciate the accuracy of Matisse's dictum that Manet simplified the art of painting.[42] The rider, of course, is that he did so by means that were anything but simple, which is to say that he both did and didn't simplify it for himself.

We gain further insight into what divides Baudelaire and Manet on these issues when we recognize that Manet's historicist undertaking is part of a still larger enterprise. I think of this as his pursuit of *painting altogether,* a pursuit that involved, in addition to his totalizing manipulation of sources, both a search for a more compelling and comprehensive mode of pictorial unity than was provided by the culture of his day and an attempt to establish a relationship between painting and beholder that would address a need to redefine both terms in that highly unstable equation.[43] Thus his search for a new ideal of unity led him to put a premium on the primordial convention that the entire surface of a painting faces the beholder and so is available to be taken in at a glance, in a single instantaneous *coup d'oeil,* which in turn would have militated against the peculiar temporal regressiveness on which the Baudelairean "system" depends, as well as against the attenuation (if not the elision) of visuality implicit in its key figures. Equally important, Manet's paintings of the first half of the 1860s may be seen as rejecting both the Diderotian project of denying the presence of the beholder through dramatic effects of closure and Gustave Courbet's antithetical but equivalent project of removing the beholder (originally the painter-beholder) from in front of the picture by absorbing him quasi-corporeally into it, in favor of a radical, almost Brechtian acknowledgement of the inescapable theatricality of the painting-beholder relationship.[44] And this, too, would have called for the suppression of all Baudelairean memory activity intense enough to threaten to collapse the classical scene of representation—a scene which, in a sense (that is, with a difference), begins a new life in Manet's art—into a giddy, disorienting, mainly "spiritual" space in which nothing like a *confrontation* between painting and beholder could ever quite take place.[45]

One last general point: by concentrating on Baudelaire's *Salon of 1846,* I have left myself open to the objection that too much time intervenes between the writing of that text and Manet's paintings of the early 1860s for any comparison between the two to be meaningful. I would counter that the issues that come to the fore in Manet's art did not spring into being around 1860 but, rather, are the product of a history that Baudelaire's *Salon* can help us to construe. Furthermore, the thematics of memory that I have traced in that *Salon* remained throughout Baudelaire's life fundamental to his vision of painting, though it is also true, as is often claimed, that his ideas on art underwent important changes during the 1850s and after. A glance at three passages will bring out the relevance of the present discussion to an understanding of his later writings.

First, in a memorial essay of 1863, Baudelaire remarks that Delacroix's oeuvre "sometimes seems to be like a kind of mnemotechny of the native greatness and passion of universal man."[46] I take this simile to rest on an intuition, the content of which Baudelaire can acknowledge only indirectly, through the sort of euphemism he employs here, of numerous points of resemblance between, on the one hand, Delacroix's paintings and, on the other, canonical works by Renaissance and baroque masters, not to mention the antique sculptures that helped inspire the latter and to which Delacroix himself was hardly indifferent.

Second, in a letter to Thoré of 1864, Baudelaire protests against Thoré's description of Manet as having "pastiched" Velázquez, Goya, and El Greco, on the grounds that Manet had never seen works by the last two (in effect he concedes Velázquez), and explains the similarity between Manet's painting and theirs as the result of the same type of "mysterious coincidence" that led him to discover anticipations of his own thoughts and phrases in the writings of Edgar Allan Poe. It has always been hard to know how to take Baudelaire's insistence on this point, but in the present context it makes perfect sense: the depth of his commitment to an aesthetics of invisible and indeed unthinkable derivation—rather than of deliberate allusion or even tangible influence—would not have allowed him to view the matter in any other light.[47]

Finally, it has sometimes seemed rather puzzling that the major essay on painting of Baudelaire's later career, *The Painter of Modern Life,* glorifies the work of a distinctly minor figure, Constantin Guys. Of course, Baudelaire's essay is also, is chiefly, a meditation on modernity, using Guys' representations of assorted subjects—prostitutes, fashionable women, dandies, military men, crowds, ceremonies, horses and carriages—as a springboard for his remarks. But it is worth noting, too, that Guys' images, by virtue of their extreme modesty, bear no significant relation to the art of the museums, and in fact Baudelaire strongly implies that he was drawn to Guys as a catalyst for his observations partly on those grounds.[48] In this connection, it is striking that Baudelaire describes Guys' art as essentially mnemonic, by which he now means that it seeks to project a sort of "memory of the present" which, acting despotically on the spectator's imagination, will recreate the impression produced by the original scene on the imagination of the artist.[49] He thus continues to assert the preeminence of memory while confining its operations to the present or, at most, the immediate past. And this suggests that Baudelaire may have come to suspect—though once again he doubtless could not have framed the suspicion—that *all* ambitious new painting inevitably bore a relation to the high art of the past that his gravest predispositions led him to reject: as though only by evading high pictorial ambition could the sheer intrusiveness of the past be brought under control. Manet, too, may be understood as seeking to contain that intrusiveness, though in a largely opposite spirit and by radically different means.[50]

1. Charles Baudelaire, *Salon of 1846, Art in Paris 1845–1862: Salons and Other Exhibitions,* ed. and trans. Jonathan Mayne (Ithaca, N.Y., 1981), p. 45; for the original French, see Baudelaire, *Salon de 1846,* "Curiosités esthétiques," "L'Art romantique," et autres oeuvres critiques, ed. Henri Lemaître (Paris, 1971), pp. 101–2. All further references to the *Salon of 1846* (the translation and the original, in that order) will be included parenthetically in the text (occasionally I have modified Mayne's renderings in the interest of greater exactness). I have also consulted the recent edition, *Baudelaire: "Salon de 1846,"* ed. David Kelley (Oxford, 1975), which includes a useful introduction and bibliography.

2. See, for example, Margaret Gilman, *Baudelaire, the Critic* (New York, 1943), pp. 3–54; Lucie Horner, *Baudelaire, critique de Delacroix* (Ph.D. diss., University of Chicago, 1955; Geneva, 1956), pp. 12–53 and 77–111; F. W. Leakey, "Les Esthétiques de Baudelaire: Le 'Système' des années 1844–1847," *Revue des sciences humaines,* n.s., fasc. 127 (July–Sept. 1967): 481–96, and *Baudelaire and Nature* (Manchester, 1969), pp. 73–88; and Kelley, "Deux Aspects du *Salon de 1846* de Baudelaire: La Dédicace aux bourgeois et la couleur," *Forum for Modern Language Studies* 5 (Oct. 1969): 331–46, and introduction to *Baudelaire: "Salon de 1846,"* pp. 1–114.

3. Such a demonstration might usefully focus on Baudelaire's notion of "individualism rightly understood (*l'individualisme bien entendu*)" (p. 45; p. 101) and on his attempt to establish the centrality of that notion for diverse regions of experience. I do not claim, however, that he everywhere succeeds in resolving the difficulties inherent in such a project: see, for example, section 7 of the *Salon,* "On the Ideal and the Model," where the strain of distinguishing the correct mode of individualization from both mere particularization,

on the one hand, and mere generalization, on the other, is plainly manifest (see pp. 79–82; pp. 46–51). The problems Baudelaire will be seen to encounter in defining and applying a single criterion of aesthetic judgment may also be understood in this light. Another index of the ambitiousness of his project is the thematizing, starting with the opening sentence of his dedication to the bourgeois, of an opposition between force and justice drawn from Pascal's *Pensées*. And another sign of strain is his strident antirepublicanism, which (at least half seriously) equates republicanism with anarchism and the July Monarchy with a tempered individualism (see pp. 43 and 113–14; pp. 99 and 191–92).

4. See, for example, Nils Gösta Sandblad, *Manet: Three Studies in Artistic Conception*, trans. Walter Nash (Lund, 1954), pp. 17–68; Lois Boe and Francis E. Hyslop, "Baudelaire and Manet: A Re-Appraisal," in *"Baudelaire as a Love Poet" and Other Essays*, ed. Lois Boe Hyslop (University Park, Pa., 1969), pp. 87–130; Anne Coffin Hanson, *Manet and the Modern Tradition* (New Haven, Conn., 1977), esp. pp. 18–22; Beatrice Farwell, *Manet and the Nude: A Study in Iconography in the Second Empire* (Ph.D. diss., University of California, Los Angeles, 1973; New York, 1981), pp. 169–84; and Theodore Reff, catalog of the exhibition *Manet and Modern Paris* at the National Gallery of Art, Washington, D.C., Dec. 1982–Mar. 1983 (pp. 23–28). For another view of thematic connections between Baudelaire and Manet, see George Mauner, *Manet, "Peintre-Philosophe": A Study of the Painter's Themes* (University Park, Pa., 1975).

5. Several scholars have noted the importance of memory in the *Salon of 1846* in a general way, and a few (e.g., Leakey and Kelley) have gone so far as to cite it as one criterion among others, but no one has considered the possibility that memory is the single criterion Baudelaire intends in the passage I quoted earlier. Not surprisingly, therefore, no one has attempted to track its functioning in the *Salon* as a whole.

6. The unannotated quotation is from E. T. A. Hoffmann, "Dernières Aventures du chien Berganza," *Contes fantastiques*, trans. Henri Egmont (Paris, 1836). For a general discussion of Baudelaire's interest in Hoffmann, see Rosemary Lloyd, *Baudelaire et Hoffmann: Affinités et influences* (Cambridge, 1979).

7. See Walter Benjamin, "A Short History of Photography," trans. Stanley Mitchell, *Screen* 13 (Spring 1972): 5–26; "The Work of Art in the Age of Mechanical Reproduction" and "On Some Motifs in Baudelaire," *Illuminations*, ed. Hannah Arendt, trans. Harry Zohn (New York, 1969); and "The Paris of the Second Empire in Baudelaire" and "Paris—Capital of the Nineteenth Century," *Charles Baudelaire: A Lyric Poet in the Era of High Capitalism*, trans. Zohn (London, 1973). See also "The Storyteller: Reflections on the Works of Nicolai Leskov" and "Image of Proust," *Illuminations*. For a brief discussion of the relation of my reading of the thematics of memory in the *Salon of 1846* to Benjamin's ideas, see n. 22 below.

8. The classic instance of this conflictedness within the Freudian corpus is, of course, his "From the History of an Infantile Neurosis" (the Wolf Man case), with its vertiginous unfolding of a memory sequence that leads back via screens and detours to a primal scene that may or may not have taken place. On the problematic of memory, fantasy, and origin in that text, see, for example, Jean Laplanche and J.-B. Pontalis, "Fantasy and the Origins of Sexuality," *International Journal of Psycho-Analysis* 49, pt. 1 (1968): 1–18; David Carroll, "Freud and the Myth of the Origin," *New Literary History* 6 (Spring 1975): 513–28; and Peter Brooks, "Fictions of the Wolfman: Freud and Narrative Understanding," *Diacritics* 9 (Spring 1979): 72–81. See also Laplanche, *Life and Death in Psychoanalysis*, trans. Jeffrey Mehlman (Baltimore, 1976), esp. chap. 2, "Sexuality and the Vital Order in Psychical Conflict"; Leo Bersani, *Baudelaire and Freud* (Berkeley and Los Angeles, 1977); and Jacques Derrida, "Freud and the Scene of Writing," *Writing and Difference*, trans. Alan Bass (Chicago, 1978), pp. 196–231. In n. 22 below, I try briefly to relate my findings to some remarks on memory in another Freudian text.

9. See R. Wittkower, "Imitation, Eclecticism, and Genius," in *Aspects of the Eighteenth Century*, ed. Earl R. Wasserman (Baltimore, 1965), p. 154.

10. Recent studies bearing on these matters include Wittkower, "Imitation, Eclecticism, and Genius"; Nancy S. Struever, *The Language of History in the Renaissance: Rhetoric and Historical Consciousness in Florentine Humanism* (Princeton, N.J., 1970), pp. 46–48, 149–54, 180, and 193–95; Charles Dempsey, *Annibale Carracci and the Beginnings of Baroque Style* (Glückstadt, 1977); Terence Cave, *The Cornucopian Text: Problems of Writing in the French Renaissance* (Oxford, 1979), esp. chap. 2, "Imitation"; G. W. Pigman III, "Versions of Imitation in the Renaissance," *Renaissance Quarterly* 33 (Spring 1980): 1–32; Stephen Orgel, "The Renaissance Artist as Plagiarist," *ELH* 48 (Fall 1981): 476–95; Jeffrey M. Muller, "Rubens's Theory and Practice of the Imitation of Art," *Art Bulletin* 64 (June 1982): 229–47; and Thomas M. Greene, *The Light in Troy: Imitation and Discovery in Renaissance Poetry* (New Haven, Conn., 1982). Greene's chapters 2 and 3, "Historical Solitude" and "Imitation and Anachronism," subtly explore the hermeneutic difficulties raised by an awareness of imitative practice. (My thanks to Joseph Marino and Charles Dempsey for their help in guiding me through this material.) Also pertinent are Harold Bloom's reflections on the struggle of belated "strong" poets to overcome their major predecessors—a kind of tragic version of classical *emulatio*. See, for example, his *The Anxiety of Influence: A Theory of Poetry* (New York, 1973), *A Map of Misreading* (New York, 1975), and *Poetry and Repression: Revisionism from Blake to Stevens* (New Haven, Conn., 1976).

11. See, for example, Aby Warburg, *Gesammelte Schriften*, ed. Gertrud Bing and Fritz Rougemont, 2 vols. (Leipzig and Berlin, 1932); Fritz Saxl, *A Heritage of Images: A Selection of Lectures*, ed. Hugh Honour and John Fleming (Harmondsworth, 1970); and Erwin Panofsky, *Studies in Iconology: Humanist Themes in the Art of the Renaissance* (1939; New York, 1962). In view of the concerns of the present essay, it is striking that Warburg in the late 1920s postulated the existence of a collective memory that kept images of violent feelings in classical art alive across the centuries. For a discussion of Warburg's speculations along these lines, as well as of his project for an illustrated atlas (to be called *Mnemosyne*) that would demonstrate the survival and adaptation to new functions of classical "engrams," see E. H. Gombrich, *Aby Warburg: An Intellectual Biography* (London, 1970), pp. 239–306. Cf. Kurt W. Forster, "Aby Warburg's History of Art: Collective Memory and the Social Mediation of Images," *Daedalus* 105 (Winter 1976): 169–76.

12. For all its confusions and inconsistencies, Gombrich's work has been instrumental in this regard; see, typically, his *Art and Illusion: A Study in the Psychology of Pictorial Representation*, A. W. Mellon Lectures in the Fine Arts, vol. 5 (Princeton, N.J., 1960). Recently some implications for art history of semiotic analyses of literary realism have been drawn by Norman Bryson, *Word and Image: French Painting of the Ancien Regime* (Cambridge, 1981), pp. 1–28. A subsequent book by Bryson, *Vision and Painting: The Logic of the Gaze* (New Haven, Conn., 1983), contains a persuasive critique of Gombrich's perceptualism but otherwise falls short of demonstrating the capability of an "art history of the sign" to account for pictorial realism. In an essay in preparation on Thomas Eakins' *Gross Clinic*, I argue that a close connection holds throughout the Western tradition between a realistic mode of representation and a thematics of absorption that characteristically serves as its matrix.

13. Denis Diderot, *Salon de 1761, Salons*, ed. Jean Seznec and Jean Adhémar, 2d ed., vol. 1 (Oxford, 1975), pp. 133–34; my translation.

14. Baudelaire nearly says as much in his memorial essay on Eugène Delacroix (1863), where he writes: "Delacroix is the most *suggestive* of all painters, he whose works, even secondary and inferior ones, most make us think, and most recall to the memory feelings and poetic thoughts that we already knew but that we believed were buried forever in the night of the past" ("L'Oeuvre et la vie d'Eugène Delacroix," *"Curiosités esthétiques,"* pp. 424–25; my translation). Presumably, it is on this basis that Baudelaire on another occasion admiringly characterizes Delacroix's talent as "essentially literary" ("Exposition Universelle de 1855," *"Curiosités esthétiques,"* p. 239; my translation).

15. Throughout his career as an art critic, Baudelaire returns to this problem. On the one hand, he asserts boldly that, since the advent of Romanticism, "the arts aspire, if

not to take one another's place, at least to lend one another new powers" ("L'Oeuvre et la vie d'Eugène Delacroix," p. 424; my translation); on the other, he continually deplores what he regards as the illegitimate exploitation of the means of poetry by painters such as Ary Scheffer and the "apes of sentiment," though he finds it extremely difficult to distinguish in principle between their procedures and those that underwrite the triumphant literariness of his paragon, Delacroix (see *Salon of 1846*, pp. 98–99; pp. 170–73). As late as 1859, Baudelaire alludes to "a certain fault, horribly difficult to define, which I will call, for want of a better term, the fault of all the *littératisants*." He continues: "I want an artist to be literate, but it distresses me to see him seeking to solicit the imagination by means situated at the extreme limits of his art, if indeed they aren't beyond them" (*Salon de 1859*, "Curiosités esthétiques," p. 355; my translation). Here as elsewhere in Baudelaire's criticism, a discourse on the limits of the arts soon reaches the limit of its own conceptual efficacy.

16. See Lee Johnson, "The Formal Sources of Delacroix's *Barque de Dante*," *Burlington Magazine* 100 (July 1958): 228–32; Frank Anderson Trapp, *The Attainment of Delacroix* (Baltimore, 1970), pp. 18–28; and Lorenz Eitner, *Géricault's "Raft of the 'Medusa'"* (New York, 1972), pp. 44–48.

17. The reference to *Hamlet* is almost certainly to Delacroix's series of lithographs on that subject. On the relationship between the two *Pietàs*, see Trapp, *The Attainment of Delacroix*, pp. 241–42. Trapp also stresses the similarity between Delacroix's *Pietà* and the late works of Titian as regards the treatment of color and surface.

18. Baudelaire, *Salon de 1845*, "Curiosités esthétiques," pp. 18–19; my translation. It is, of course, significant that we have to go outside the *Salon of 1846* for this striking conjunction of motifs of memory, consciousness, and naiveté. But I take it to be at least equally significant that we are invited to do so, by a footnote to the first mention in the later *Salon* of "individualism rightly understood." The footnote reads: "A propos individualism rightly understood, see in my *Salon of 1845* the article on William Haussoullier. In spite of all the reproaches that I have received on this subject, I persist in my opinion; but it is necessary to understand the article" (p. 45 n.∗; p. 101 n.1). Eventually, I shall wish to say that it required all of the *Salon of 1846* to *make* the Haussoullier article understandable, and even then it will remain questionable to what extent Baudelaire himself understood either (see n. 23 below). For an illustration of Haussoullier's picture, see Baudelaire, *Art in Paris*, fig. 2.

19. See Wittkower, "Imitation, Eclecticism, and Genius," pp. 157–61.

20. See, for example, Robert Rosenblum, *Jean-Auguste-Dominique Ingres* (New York, 1967); Trapp, *The Attainment of Delacroix;* and Albert Boime, *Thomas Couture and the Eclectic Vision* (New Haven, Conn., 1980). The first two chapters of Boime's study are an attempt to place the phenomenon in question in a broader cultural context. Boime's remarks on the influence of Victor Cousin and specifically on the role of memory in Cousin's theory of art are particularly relevant to this present essay (see *Thomas Couture*, p. 28). See also the brief discussion of Ingres' relation to the multiplicity of styles available by the early nineteenth century in Bryson, *Word and Image*, pp. 249–53. Also pertinent is Neil Levine, "The Romantic Idea of Architectural Legibility: Henri Labrouste and the Neo-Grec," in *The Architecture of the Ecole des Beaux-Arts*, ed. Arthur Drexler (New York, 1977), pp. 325–416.

21. The insistence on unity as one of the requirements of memory, which I have suggested functions as a principle of equivalence (hence of communication) between new and old paintings, contributes also to the repression of memory, by virtue of its emphasis on the self-sufficiency of individual works. At the same time, the use of musical metaphors of unity—e.g., melody, harmony, counterpoint—represents that self-sufficiency in terms that imply not only temporal repetition but a certain consciousness of repetition. Nothing could be more characteristic of the "system" of the *Salon of 1846* than this double implication.

22. A suggestive parallel to Baudelaire's implicit injunction that memories of previous works remain below the threshold of conscious awareness occurs in Freud, *Beyond the*

Pleasure Principle (*The Standard Edition of the Complete Psychological Works of Sigmund Freud,* ed. and trans. James Strachey, 24 vols. [London, 1953–74], 18:1–64; all further references to Freud's works will be from this edition, abbreviated *Standard Edition,* and will be included in the text). There Freud observes that memory-traces "are often most powerful and most enduring when the process which left them behind was one which never entered consciousness" and goes on to consider the possibility that "becoming conscious and leaving behind a memory-trace are processes incompatible with each other within one and the same system" (p. 25). From this it would follow that memories of previous works of art simultaneously activated and repressed in the perception of a successful new work of art would be rendered all the more memorable on that account, which, on the Hoffmannesque premises examined above, also means that they would be made all the more efficacious *agents* of memorableness with regard to the triggering perception (cf. my earlier gloss on Baudelaire's statement that the greatest paintings leave an impression whose intensity increases with distance). See also Freud, "A Note upon the 'Mystic Writing-Pad'" (*Standard Edition,* 19:225–32), and Derrida's masterly reading of successive thematizations of memory in the Freudian corpus, "Freud and the Scene of Writing."

As for Benjamin's association of what he calls aura with the Proustian *mémoire involontaire,* my reading of the *Salon of 1846* suggests that, at least as regards that particular text, the auratic experience arises when an involuntary memory or chain of memories is simultaneously mobilized by an actual perception and yet not quite allowed to become part of the contents of consciousness. The "inapproachability" that Benjamin associates with the concept of aura would thus be a function of something more than simply the fact that the data of the *mémoire involontaire* cannot be recalled by an act of will, and the inexhaustibleness that he cites Paul Valéry as attributing to the genuine work of art would be accounted for in terms of the endlessness of the memory chain that is brought into play in the perception of a successful new painting (see "On Some Motifs in Baudelaire," pp. 186–88). This in turn yields a more precise basis for the claim that modern techniques of mechanical reproduction, photography in particular, are "decisively implicated in the phenomenon of the 'decline of the aura'" (ibid., p. 187): not, as Benjamin first suggests, because the fact of reproduction somehow divests the original work of art of its authenticity (see "The Work of Art in the Age of Mechanical Reproduction," pp. 220–22), or because mechanical reproduction is inherently on the side of voluntary as opposed to involuntary memory (see "On Some Motifs in Baudelaire," p. 186), but because the proliferation of reproductions of works of art, as well as the advances in art historical knowledge that such a proliferation subtends, make it ever more unlikely that an educated beholder can remain unaware of at least some of the antecedent works that lie behind the work at hand. Perhaps this is the "crisis in perception" to which Benjamin refers in a dense passage in this same essay (ibid., p. 187). Understood in these terms, the phenomenon of aura emerges as a highly specific historical formation (one might say that it emerges contemporaneously with the phenomenon of its decay), not an essential quality of premodern works of art. I might add that Benjamin makes interesting use of the remarks from Freud's *Beyond the Pleasure Principle* quoted earlier in this note (see ibid., pp. 160–62). For a painstaking discussion of varieties of memory in Benjamin, see Irving Wohlfarth, "On the Messianic Structure of Walter Benjamin's Last Reflections," *Glyph* 3 (1978): 148–212. I have also found stimulating two essays that touch indirectly on my concerns: Hans-Jost Frey, "Ueber die Erinnerung bei Baudelaire," *Symposium* 33 (Winter 1979): 312–30, and Paul de Man, introduction to Hans Robert Jauss, *Toward an Aesthetic of Reception,* trans. Timothy Bahti (Minneapolis, 1982), pp. vii–xxv. My thanks to Timothy Bahti for bibliographical suggestions pertaining to Benjamin on aura.

23. For that matter, does this also account for the relegation to a footnote in the *Salon of 1846* of the reference to his discussion of Haussoullier the previous year? Is the job of the footnote quoted in n. 18 above not simply to annex the earlier passage to the later *Salon* but to do so "naively" and, moreover, while keeping what that passage (almost) says out of the body of the text?

Baudelaire's guarded appreciation of Ingres presents similar problems but in a much less extreme form. Thus he characterizes Ingres' method, which he seems to have recognized involved a far more systematic and archaeologically precise exploitation of precedents than was the case with Delacroix, as "frank and, so to speak, involuntary," the latter quality in particular being what set the master apart from his many followers (p. 85; p. 154).

Finally, it should be noted that at three minor junctures in the *Salon of 1846*, Baudelaire does suggest that the positive evocation of memories of earlier paintings, as opposed to their simultaneous activation and repression, might be a virtue. Of Alexandre-Gabriel Decamps he writes: "Sometimes he seemed to stem from the boldest colorists of the old Flemish school, but he had more style than they, and he grouped his figures more harmoniously; sometimes the splendor and the triviality of Rembrandt were his keen preoccupation; at other times one found in his skies a loving memory of the skies of Claude" (p. 74; p. 140). Of Ignazio Manzoni's *Beggar's Duel:* "It has a ferocity and a brutality of manner which suit the subject rather well and recall Goya's violent sketches" (pp. 76–77; p. 143). And of Théodore Rousseau: "Think of certain landscapes by Rubens and Rembrandt; add a few memories of English painting, and assume a deep and serious love of nature dominating and ordering it all—and then perhaps you will be able to form some idea of the magic of his pictures" (p. 109; p. 184). Two of the three passages are importantly concerned with landscapes or landscape elements (Decamps' skies), which suggests that when paintings involve the representation of natural scenes, the demand that a new work not actually recall the previous works lying behind it may be at least partly abrogated. This, in turn, may indicate that for Baudelaire the experience of nature is suffused through and through by memories of the representation of nature in art.

24. A useful brief summary of previous discussions of Manet's use of sources is found in Sandblad, *Manet,* pp. 39–40.

25. See my "Manet's Sources: Aspects of His Art, 1859–1865," *Artforum* 7 (Mar. 1969): 28–82, and Reff, " 'Manet's Sources': A Critical Evaluation," *Artforum* 8 (Sept. 1969): 40–48.

26. See, for example, Farwell, *Manet and the Nude;* Hanson, *Manet and the Modern Tradition;* and Reff, *Manet and Modern Paris.* The object of this revisionist reading would seem to be to involve Manet more fully in his age—for example, by demonstrating his use of ephemeral, popular imagery (Farwell and Hanson), by underscoring the specificity of the locales depicted in his paintings (Reff), and in general by drawing various loose connections between the presumed contents of his pictures and the social-historical reality of France in the 1860s. But the price paid for what at best are somewhat meager gains seems to me exorbitant: an utter indifference to precisely those issues, ambitions, and anxieties that would have engaged Manet *as a painter* and the successful resolution of which would have been his primary concern. An exception to the general tendency I have just described is Mauner's *Manet, "Peintre-Philosophe,"* in which the painter's references to previous works of art are construed as indicating a metaphysical program based on the idea of the doubleness of human nature. As for T. J. Clark's Marxist readings of Manet's art, it would hardly be fair either to their interpretive energy or to their complex relation to the values of modernism to characterize them as "revisionist" in my disparaging use of the term. See Clark, "Preliminaries to a Possible Treatment of *Olympia* in 1865," *Screen* 21 (Spring 1980): 18–41, and "The Bar at the Folies-Bergères," in *The Wolf and the Lamb: Popular Culture in France from the Old Regime to the Twentieth Century,* ed. Jacques Beauroy, Marc Bertrand, and Edward T. Gargan, Stanford French and Italian Studies, vol. 3 (Saratoga, Calif., 1977), pp. 233–52.

27. See Reff, *Manet and Modern Paris,* and Françoise Cachin and Charles S. Moffett, catalog of the exhibition *Manet (1832–1883)* at the Grand Palais, Paris, Apr.–Aug. 1983 and the Metropolitan Museum of Art, New York, Sept.–Nov. 1983. The latter catalog, a monumental production, sums up Manet's relation to his sources in terms that hark back to an earlier, pre-revisionist era. Here, for example, is how Cachin characterizes the unprecedentedness of Manet's procedures: "To paint openly from paintings, almost to the

point of parody, taking painting itself as the object of its own attention; *Olympia*, daughter of Titian, Ingres, and Goya, throws down a challenge to the masters but in contemporary terms" (p. 18). One of the implications of the present essay will be that formulations such as these, while not entirely mistaken, wholly fail to register the historical specificity of Manet's undertaking. See also, in this connection, Cachin's suggestion that Picasso's variations on the *Déjeuner sur l'herbe* "do unto Manet as he had done unto the Italian Renaissance painters" (p. 172).

28. A basic criticism of the traditional methods of art history, including stylistic analysis, would be that they characteristically fail to do justice to the variousness and specificity of the pictorial enterprise as it has been pursued in different contexts and situations. In this connection, one might try to show that the concept of the image has often been tacitly deployed to perform a task of de-historicization—of making disparate phenomena equivalent, of leveling crucial differences not only between works and traditions but also between the viewers they posit and perhaps partly construct—which has been required in order for the approved operations of art history (the production of "art historical" difference) to get under way. Not the least irony in all this is that some revisionist art historians have made a methodological virtue of treating paintings merely as images, as if in its very leveling function the concept of an image provided a means of challenging the disciplinary status quo. Interestingly, the concept of the image is used as a pejorative by a critic of the 1860s who was close to Manet, Zacharie Astruc: for example, Astruc criticizes Rosa Bonheur for allowing the influence of English art to "spoil her work and lead her toward the image" (*L'Etendard*, 27 Feb. 1868; my translation).

29. On Manet's pursuit of Frenchness and the affinity between that aspect of his enterprise and the vision of the French tradition put forward by Théophile Thoré and others, see my "Manet's Sources," esp. pp. 47–49. Starting in the mid-1850s, Thoré wrote under the name William Bürger; for this reason he is often referred to in the secondary literature as Thoré-Bürger. His discussions of Manet's art in his *Salons* of the 1860s are among the most intelligent the painter received. On Thoré's historical thought, see Frances Suzman Jowell, *Thoré-Bürger and the Art of the Past* (Ph.D. diss., Harvard University, 1971; New York, 1977). See also Francis Haskell, *Rediscoveries in Art: Some Aspects of Taste, Fashion, and Collecting in England and France* (Ithaca, N.Y., 1980), pp. 112–17. The composition of the *Old Musician*, particularly as regards the outdoor setting and the relationship between the two boys, is closest to that of the *Halt of the Horseman*, but it cannot be proved that Manet could have seen either of the two versions of that painting that have come down to us. As an alternative source, Reff has proposed the *Old Piper*, which Manet could have known either from an eighteenth-century engraving or from a woodcut in Charles Blanc's *Histoire des peintres de toutes les écoles* (see " 'Manet's Sources': A Critical Evaluation," p. 43). As for Antoine Watteau's *Gilles*, it had recently been shown in a major exhibition of French paintings held in the gallery where Manet himself exhibited his work. Recent discussions of the *Old Musician* include Alain De Leiris, "Manet, Guéroult, and Chrysippos," *Art Bulletin* 46 (Sept. 1964): 401–4; my "Manet's Sources," esp. pp. 29–32; Reff, " 'Manet's Sources': A Critical Evaluation," pp. 42–43, and *Manet and Modern Paris*, pp. 170–91; Hanson, "Popular Imagery and the Work of Edouard Manet," in *French Nineteenth-Century Painting and Literature: With Special Reference to the Relevance of Literary Subject-matter to French Painting*, ed. Ulrich Finke (Manchester and New York, 1972); and Mauner, *Manet, "Peintre-Philosophe,"* pp. 46–78. I might add that I would no longer connect Manet's *Absinthe Drinker* (1859), the source for the standing figure in top hat and cape in the *Old Musician*, with Watteau's *L'Indifferent*, though I continue to see a strongly theatrical element in both "absinthe drinkers' " mode of self-presentation.

30. Reff suggests that Manet may have been familiar with Velázquez's painting through a lithographed copy by Célestin Nanteuil (see *Manet and Modern Paris*, p. 174). Two rather striking details in the *Old Musician*, the foliage at the upper left and the lost profile and unkempt hair of the young girl holding an infant, appear designed chiefly to refer to Velázquez's composition.

31. Théophile Thoré [W. Bürger], "Des Tendances de l'art au dix-neuvième siècle" (intro.) in Maurice Chaumelin, *L'Art contemporain* (Paris, 1873), p. xiv; my translation ("Des Tendances" was originally published in the *Revue universelle des arts* 1 [1855]: 77–85). See also "Nouvelles Tendances de l'art" (datelined "Brussels, 1857"), *Salons de Théophile Thoré* (Paris, 1868), pp. xiv–xv. This is not to say that Manet, too, was a socialist. But political considerations are by no means irrelevant to an understanding of his relation to his sources. For one thing, his own republican sympathies made him all the more receptive to a vision of the French tradition advocated largely by a republican school of critic-historians; for another, as I argue in "Manet's Sources," his dual aspiration to Frenchness and universality has striking affinities with a mode of thought that receives its richest expression in Jules Michelet's writings of the years leading up to 1848 (see pp. 63–67).

32. Thoré [Bürger], *Trésors d'art en Angleterre*, 3d ed. (Paris, 1865), p. viii; my translation. The establishment of a universal art history on different foundations was to be the achievement of Heinrich Wölfflin and his German-language successors starting in the late 1880s. See Michael Podro, *The Critical Historians of Art* (New Haven, Conn., 1982), pp. 98–151, and Joan Hart, "Reinterpreting Wölfflin: Neo-Kantianism and Hermeneutics," *Art Journal* 42 (Winter 1982): 292–300.

33. The key works here are the *Portrait of Emile Zola* (1868) and especially *The Balcony* (1868–69), for which see my "Manet's Sources," pp. 59–60.

34. And yet it is striking how minor a role Italian sources play in Manet's paintings before the *Mlle V. in the Costume of an Espada* (see below), especially compared to the surprisingly large role assigned to Rubens, an artist who hardly seems sympathetic to Manet on stylistic grounds. According to Thoré and other critic-historians of his convictions, a Flemish element in the French painting of the past resisted the influence of Italian art and thus helped preserve the integrity of the beleaguered French school. See my "Manet's Sources," pp. 48–53, and Jowell, *Thoré-Bürger*, pp. 117–43.

35. See my "Manet's Sources," pp. 44–45, and Reff, " 'Manet's Sources': A Critical Evaluation," p. 42. The Le Nain are compared with Rembrandt and his school in an important article by Thoré [Bürger], "Exposition de tableaux de l'école française ancienne tirés de collections d'amateurs," *Gazette des beaux-arts* 7 (1860): 263.

36. See my "Manet's Sources," pp. 52–53.

37. See Reff, " 'Manet's Sources': A Critical Evaluation," p. 41. I have followed Reff in reproducing the woodcut of Titian's picture that appeared in Blanc's *Histoire des peintres*.

38. See Farwell, "Manet's *Espada* and Marcantonio," *Metropolitan Museum Journal* 2 (1969): 197–202. In addition, it has long been recognized that the bullfight scene in the background of the *Mlle V.* is based on prints by Goya. See, for example, the discussion of the *Mlle V.* in Cachin and Moffett, *Manet (1832–1883)*, cat. no. 33, pp. 110–14.

39. Or consider the resemblance between the Roman replica of a Hellenistic statue of the philosopher Chrysippos in the Louvre, which De Leiris was the first to connect, by way of a drawing by Manet, with the figure of the seated violinist in the *Old Musician*, and depictions of seated men in Louis Le Nain's *Halt of the Horseman*, Antoine Le Nain's *Old Piper*, and other works (see "Manet, Guéroult, and Chrysippos"). This, too, is perhaps not coincidental, inasmuch as during the sixteenth and seventeenth centuries, statues roughly of the Chrysippos type became a prototype for representations of seated male figures throughout European painting. In any event, I see no alternative to assuming that Manet was aware of the resemblance and that the squared-off drawing he made of the statue is further proof of a desire to relate his own work to points of maximum resonance in the total repertoire of previous art. Manet's sense of that repertoire and of its internal articulations doubtless owed a great deal not only to contemporary art history but also to the rise of the modern art museum; see, in this connection, the suggestive remarks by Michel Foucault, "Fantasia of the Library," *Language, Counter-Memory, Practice: Selected Essays and Interviews*, ed. Donald F. Bouchard, trans. Bouchard and Sherry Simon (Ithaca, N.Y., 1977), pp. 92–93. Significantly, what was then the relatively haphazard presentation of paintings in the Louvre was strongly criticized by Thoré in articles of 1836 and 1838; see Jowell, *Thoré-*

Bürger, pp. 62–75. On Manet's debt to the most important illustrated art-historical compendium of his time, see Reff, "Manet and Blanc's *Histoire des peintres*," *Burlington Magazine* 112 (July 1970): 456–58.

Still another factor promoting a new awareness of the stereotypical character of European painting was the influx of Japanese prints, products of an altogether different visual culture, in the 1860s. Here, for example, is Astruc on the repetitiveness of contemporary practice: "One can say this in all confidence: originality is absent from our European art. We flow gently in a few accepted molds and that is all. Nothing proceeds from an absolutely independent personal impression. One begins by wanting the approval of the public; and, always anticipating its manner of seeing, its initiative, one is condemned to eternal repetitions [*redites*] which produce neither absolute disgust nor true pleasure—which lead one to say, without further emotion, 'I know that; it's fine' " ("L'Empire du soleil levant," *L'Etendard*, 27 Feb. 1867; my translation).

40. See Freud, "Remembering, Repeating, and Working-Through (Further Recommendations in the Technique of Psycho-analysis II)," *Standard Edition*, 12:145–56. The desire to put an end to the hegemony of the past would therefore be something Manet had in common not only with progressive critics like Thoré and Astruc, for both of whom the previous achievements of Western painting continued to matter profoundly, but also with the hard-line naturalist critic Jules-Antoine Castagnary, who, for example, wrote in 1864: "Our painter will forget the painting prior to him, and the societies that have been, and the interpretations to which they have given rise. A book isn't made with books, a painting isn't made with paintings" (*Salon de 1864*, *Salons [1857–1870]*, 2 vols. [Paris, 1892], 1:288; my translation). Manet's strategic use of the art of the museums implies a conviction of the radical inadequacy of any merely naturalist aesthetic as well as of Castagnary's (unpsychoanalytic) enjoinder simply to forget the painting of earlier ages.

41. Thoré [Bürger], "Exposition de tableaux de l'école française," p. 259; my translation.

42. "[Manet] was the first to *act by reflex* thus simplifying the painter's métier" (Henri Matisse in 1932, emphasis his, quoted in Cachin and Moffett, *Manet [1832–1883]*, p. 18).

43. Still another aspect of this pursuit concerns the role of the traditional genres in his work. In "Manet's Sources," I quote the critic Astruc as arguing that the art of painting must somehow overcome its traditional fragmentation into separate genres, and I go on to suggest that the perspicuous conjunction in the *Déjeuner sur l'herbe* of elements of various distinct genres—*fête champêtre*, landscape, portraiture, still life, and (I would now add) history painting, via the allusion to Raphael, and religious painting, via the parodic significance of the bird hovering in flight in the upper center of the composition—signifies an attempt to bring about a totalization of the pictorial enterprise analogous to the one I see Manet as having tried to effect across national schools (see p. 78, n.228).

44. On the problematic of painting and beholder before Manet, see my *Absorption and Theatricality: Painting and Beholder in the Age of Diderot* (Berkeley and Los Angeles, 1980); "The Beholder in Courbet: His Early Self-Portraits and Their Place in His Art," *Glyph* 4 (1978): 85–129; "Representing Representation: On the Central Group in Courbet's *Studio*," in *Allegory and Representation*, ed. Stephen J. Greenblatt, Selected Papers from the English Institute, 1979–80, n.s. 5 (Baltimore, 1981), pp. 94–127; "Painter into Painting: On Courbet's *After Dinner at Ornans* and *Stonebreakers*," *Critical Inquiry* 8 (Summer 1982): 619–49; and "The Structure of Beholding in Courbet's *Burial at Ornans*," *Critical Inquiry* 9 (June 1983): 635–83.

45. This is much too compressed. By "classical scene of representation," I refer to the basic structure of the relationship between representation and beholder posited by mid–eighteenth-century theorists of painting such as Diderot, Melchior Grimm, and Gotthold Ephraim Lessing, a structure in which the two terms are understood to stand for separate and distinct entities situated at a more or less fixed or at least not wildly fluctuating distance from one another and, in history painting or serious genre painting, taking part in the same imaginary temporal flow, a narrative-dramatic continuum that runs from the inception

of an action through its crisis or crises to its climax and beyond. (It is precisely this ideal spatial separation of representation and beholder that makes possible the Diderotian project of denying the beholder's presence.) What must be emphasized, however, is that from its initial formulation in the 1750s and '60s, the structure in question contained the seeds of its eventual dissolution: as, for example, in Diderot's fictive promenades in his *Salon of 1767* through a series of peopled landscapes by Joseph Vernet, or as in Lessing's insistence that the painter choose the most "suggestive" moment in an action, by which he meant the one that would most effectively evoke the entire trajectory of the action from start to finish. "The more we see, the more we must be able to imagine. And the more we add in our imaginations, the more we must think we see" (Lessing, *Laocoön: An Essay on the Limits of Painting and Poetry*, trans. Edward Allen McCormick [Indianapolis, 1962], pp. 78, 19). From this it is only a step (or a series of steps) to Baudelaire's valorization of suggestiveness at the expense of seeing in the *Salon of 1846*. In Manet's art of the first half of the 1860s, on the other hand, painting and beholder are posited with a vengeance as separate entities, partly owing to a mode of narrative-dramatic *un*intelligibility that effectively blocks or forestalls the supplemental activity Lessing described and, by so doing, establishes a new ideal distance between the one and the other. What might be termed the ideal perceptual instantaneousness of Manet's art may also be viewed as analogous to, though by no means identical with, the "moment" of later eighteenth-century theory and practice.

46. Baudelaire, "L'Oeuvre et la vie d'Eugène Delacroix," p. 425; my translation.

47. For Thoré's remarks on Manet and Baudelaire's letter in defense of the painter, see *Manet raconté par lui-même et par ses amis*, ed. Pierre Courthion and Pierre Cailler, 2 vols. (Geneva, 1953), 1:110–14.

48. See Baudelaire, *Le Peintre de la vie moderne*, "*Curiosités esthétiques*," pp. 468–69 (written in 1859–60 but not published until 1863).

49. See ibid., pp. 468–70. The whole of sections 4 and 5, "Modernity" and "Mnemonic Art," bear directly on the concerns of this essay.

50. This is not to say that there could be no commerce between Guys' modest productions and Manet's ambitious ones. On the contrary, works by Guys have been associated with two of Manet's most "Baudelairean" paintings, the *Concert in the Tuileries* (1862) and the *Olympia* (1863). (On the *Concert*, see Sandblad, *Manet*, pp. 17–68, and Cachin and Moffett, *Manet [1832–1883]*, cat. no. 38, pp. 122–26. On the *Olympia*, see Reff, *Manet: "Olympia"* [London, 1976], pp. 68–69.) We know, too, that at the time of Manet's death, he owned sixty of Guys' drawings (see Cachin and Moffett, *Manet [1832–1883]*, pp. 124–26). Stanley Cavell has read *The Painter of Modern Life* as anticipating the experience of film (see *The World Viewed: Reflections on the Ontology of Film*, enlarged ed. [Cambridge, Mass., 1979], pp. 41–45).

The Religious Poetry of Christina Rossetti

Jerome J. McGann

1

One of the difficulties which an explictly Christian poetry or art presents for criticism is its appearance of thematic uniformity. Readers of such work (even critics of such work) frequently seem to think not merely that religious ideas are in themselves eternal truths which wake to perish never but that these ideas are traditionary, self-consistent, and unchanging—in brief, that the ideas are transcendent rather than historically particular (whatever the scale of their historical particularity may be). Of course, one recognizes that certain doctrinal positions may produce divergent religious emphases in different poets—as, for example, the ideological differences between the Christian poems of Donne, Herbert, Crashaw, and Dryden. But if the specifically controversial poems are set aside (like certain of the Holy Sonnets and *The Hind and the Panther*), the doctrinal variances, we often think, tend to disappear into a basically congruent economy of Christian thought. Christian poetry from the Middle Ages to the present thus comes to us as a body of work which, despite shifting emphases and interests, expresses a uniform world view or ideological focus.[1]

In one sense, of course, this general conception is quite correct: Christian poetry, whether sixteenth or nineteenth century, whether Calvinist or Catholic, Evangelical or Anglican, English or French, rests in a tradition of such length and continuity that all its divergent expressions trade in certain common shares of feeling and thought.[2] Nevertheless, if Christian poetry exhibits many common elements, the individual work of different poets is marked by distinctive qualities. Scholars will try to mark out these distinctive features by restoring the work of the religious poets to their special local habitations. If you map the verse of Donne or Herbert on the grids of a historical or biographical analysis, the peculiar features of their work are forced to yield themselves up. This result is especially ·important in the case of religious poetry read in a culture which maintains and (to a large extent) still propagates the ideological self-representations of such poetry. For in such a culture we are continually tempted to attribute some sort of inherent value to the content of religious verse.

But suppose for a moment you wanted to convince a non-Christian Japanese friend of the power of Christina Rossetti's poetry or—perhaps better—a humanist scholar from the Soviet Union—or simply any non-believer. What line would you take? What would you say?

Rossetti's poetry might be usefully approached in terms of such a problem. For Western scholars and readers like ourselves, who have been brought up within the ideological apparatuses of a Christian culture, such a study of Rossetti's poetry might be useful precisely because her poetry has been largely judged inferior, or at most only of incidental interest, by the chief twentieth-century spokesmen for cultural values. The enormous revival of interest in Christian and even Catholic poetry which began in the modern period and which flourished with the New Criticism did not take any serious account of Rossetti's work. Hopkins yes, Rossetti, no.[3]

Why this choice should have been made by those who celebrated the virtues of so many seventeenth-century religious poets is not a subject to be dealt with in a short essay such as this, for the topic involves the whole de-historicizing program of modernism and the New Criticism. But we must pause to consider the roots of this choice, if only in a brief way. Why is it that not a single critic associated with the New Critical movement ever wrote anything about Rossetti? And what does that disinterest mean?

2

Let me begin with a few commonplaces. The poetry of the English Metaphysicals, particularly their religious poetry, was one of the touchstones

---

Jerome J. McGann is the Doris and Henry Dreyfuss Professor of Humanities at the California Institute of Technology. His two most recent books are *The Romantic Ideology. A Critical Investigation* (1983) and *A Critique of Modern Textual Criticism* (1983).

by which the New Critics would measure a poet's value. This criterion was itself allied to a more general one which prized verse that exhibited a high degree of surface tension, ambiguity, and complexity. Such qualities were associated with the presence of a central conflict or paradox which seemed to define the very nature of the poet and poetry itself: a struggle to reconcile opposite and discordant qualities such as tradition and individual talent, reason and feeling, religion and the secular world. Furthermore, immediately behind the work of the New Critics lay the example of the early modern poets, who seemed to exhibit many of these qualities in their own verse. Most dramatically, the work of the early modern poets sought and found a way to break the spell and authority of Tennyson, Swinburne, and Pre-Raphaelitism, where the poetic surface tended to disguise or sublime all forms of disjunction and irregularity.

The cultural vantage of modernism and New Criticism, then, stood in a hostile relation to much of what the modern poets understood as "the Victorian frame of mind," as manifested in a poetic medium. The model of Donne seemed more useful as a point of departure, for poet and critic alike, than the model of Tennyson. Yet the religious and moral critique of science and the secular modern world, so vigorously maintained (and in certain respects initiated) by the Victorians, was a cultural resource which was far from being abandoned or repudiated. What would greatly benefit the polemic of the New Criticism would be a Victorian religious poet who stood in some clear antithetical relation to his own age—whose verse seemed to stand closer to Donne or Dante than to John Keble's *Christian Year* and the Society for the Propagation of Christian Knowledge.[4]

From various points of view, therefore, Hopkins was just the sort of person whom "the (new) age demanded." He was Victorian, but he didn't sound like Tennyson or Swinburne; his verse displayed an extraordinarily high degree of surface tension (unusual rhythms, obscurity, disjointed syntaxes, startling images and conceits); and—not least of all—he was a religious poet who went virtually unrecognized in his own time. Hopkins was the very epitome of the sort of poet whom Eliot had set up as a model in his 1921 essay "The Metaphysical Poets." The fact that he was a Catholic poet writing in an age dominated by sentimental late-Protestant religious verse only underlined his significance. In Hopkins one discovered an example of resistance to that dissociation of sensibility which had been exerting such an evil effect upon poetry since the seventeenth century. In Hopkins one could discern, as it were, a proof case that the touchstone event of the Metaphysicals might arise at any time and anywhere—might arise as an obscure Jesuit writing agonized verse in what was widely regarded as the most bland and enervated period of English literary history.

If Hopkins had never existed, the New Criticism would have had to invent him (and, to the degree that they elevated him above the master poets of the late Victorian period, this is precisely what they did). It is highly significant that Hopkins only exploded onto the literary scene in

1930, with the publication of the second edition of his *Poems*. The first edition, published in 1918 in a print run of 750 copies, sold slowly over the next twelve years, though the critical notices were favorable and often written by significant critical figures. The first edition was compiled and introduced by Hopkins' friend Robert Bridges, the elegant, learned, and aging poet laureate. Bridges died in 1929, however; so the second edition, when called for, had a new editor—the young Anglo-Catholic Charles Williams. It is with the publication of this second edition that Hopkins' reputation as a major poet begins.[5]

In many ways the early 1930s represent the watershed moment for the next forty years of literary and cultural criticism.[6] John Crowe Ransom's *God Without Thunder. An Unorthodox Defense of Orthodoxy* was published in 1930, Eliot's *Selected Essays* and *After Strange Gods* appeared in 1932 and 1934, and Tate's *Reactionary Essays* came out in 1936. The religious and antihistorical focus which was to dominate the New Criticism is rooted in this period. It is the period of Hopkins' astonishing academic ascendency; it is also the period which marks the virtual disappearance of Rossetti from our cultural consciousness.[7]

Why Rossetti, whom Hopkins admired to a fault, should have thus fallen out of fashion may seem at first rather odd—or at least it may seem odd that the Christian, Anglican, and Anglo-Catholic polemicists should not have maintained her reputation. She was a Dantist, she was Anglican and severely orthodox in her public profession, she was impeccably conservative. Later critics who found a rich mine of ore in the drama of Hopkins' spiritual and psychic life were not interested in these aspects of Rossetti, whose personal life, like her poetry, remained virtually a closed book until the theme of sexual frustration offered itself to certain readers.[8]

But Rossetti's orthodoxy is not sufficiently "unorthodox," at least by New Critical standards. When B. Ifor Evans says of her work that it "is removed from the Elizabethan tradition by infrequency of conceit, and by an increased earnestness," he indicates three of the more apparent (and related) reasons for her lack of favor with the new apologists for poetry.[9] The style of her verse is simple, chaste, and severe, but it is also recognizably in a Victorian stylistic tradition, and in that respect it is "orthodox" precisely where modern poets and New Critics looked for the "unorthodox." Her poetry does not get worked up at the surface.

More crucial, perhaps, is an ideological deviance between Rossetti and certain less explicit aspects of New Critical theory. Consider the conclusion to Ransom's influential *God Without Thunder:*

> With whatever religious institution a modern man may be connected, let him try to turn it back towards orthodoxy.
> Let him insist on a virile and concrete God, and accept no Principle as a substitute.

Let him restore to God the thunder.
Let him resist the usurpation of the Godhead by the soft modern
version of the Christ, and try to keep the Christ for what he
professed to be: the Demigod who came to do honor to the God.[10]

For Rossetti, some of this will do, but some of it will not do; and the final
exhortation about Christ will never do. Worst of all, for a poet such as
she, is the aggressive *maleness* of all this, in that Ransom simply takes his
patriarchalism for granted. Serious issues are at stake for Ransom, and
those issues, therefore, will be conceived in a patriarchal mode such as
this. What Ransom has most in mind is the historical transformations
which Christianity had been undergoing since the early nineteenth century:
the persistent tendency toward Broad Church and liberal doctrinal positions
with their correspondingly innovative interpretations of the Christian
experience. Because religion for Ransom is an original matter, a God
without thunder is seen as a latter-day perversion of Christianity, and a
dangerous apparition. This is the burden of his attack upon the religious
ideologies which spill out from various nineteenth-century forms of Protestant thought.[11]

Related to these issues of poetic style and religious idea is the conviction
that the practice of poetry is a serious intellectual and moral event.
Indeed, it is an event of such moment that it leaves no room for the
sentiment of pathetic or (good) intentional fallacies. Its object is no less
than the Truth, and its function is to seize and define the Truth in times
of crisis (whether personal or cultural). Rossetti's poetry, even among
those critics who profess to admire it, seems to lack the intellectual rigor
which alone can sustain its (evident) moral seriousness. As Lionel Stevenson
has put it: "Christina Rossetti's poetry comes closer to the pure lyric
mode than that of any other Victorian, male or female, for the obvious
reason that it contains a minimum of intellectual substance. Though she
was equipped with a normally keen mind, it was firmly suppressed by
several forces."[12] One might argue with this passage on a number of
counts. Here I want only to call attention to Stevenson's idea that Rossetti's
poetry lacks "intellectual substance." As we shall see shortly, this idea is
profoundly mistaken—*profoundly* not simply because it is not in fact true
but because the error arises out of a lapse in historical awareness.[13]

Indeed, all of the reasons just given might count for little against
Rossetti had the New Criticism not set out, deliberately, to "revolt against
historical scholarship."[14] These words are Tate's own characterization of
the New Critical program, and they go far to explain why and how
Rossetti disappeared so long from our critical consciousness. The restoration
of a historical perspective to the critical task will therefore help us to
understand Rossetti not only in her own terms—from a historicist perspective—but in terms that are important for readers and educators of
this later day.

3

To survey the line of commentary that has preserved the name of Rossetti in twentieth-century literary culture is to discover, first, that the New Criticism ignored her work and, second, that those who praised her did so in terms which were bound to prove largely ineffectual: she is a pure craftswoman, she is the best woman lyricist of the nineteenth century, she is an impassioned mystical poet, she is the poetess of the Tractarian movement; her verse is "spontaneous," "ascetic," "unblemished," and "sweet."[15] There are a few important commentaries on Rossetti in the fifty or sixty years following her death, but they are—in contrast to the critical work on Hopkins—exceptional in every sense.

The consequence of this situation, it seems to me, is that Rossetti has reaped the benefits of what Trotsky once called "the Privilege of Historic Backwardness."[16] Those who gathered the strength of writers like Donne, Herbert, and Hopkins found Rossetti's work variously "morbid," "sterile," "sweet"—in any case, from a Christian perspective, far inferior to the "virile" work of those religious poets of our Great Tradition. This neglect of her verse kept her safe from the critical presuppositions and approaches of modernism and New Criticism. As a consequence, her work is once again being read seriously only in recent years, and her best readers now have nearly all been more or less strongly marked by other critical vantages and presuppositions, not the least of which are those we associate with feminist criticism and its natural ally, historical method.[17]

I want to argue, therefore, that to read Rossetti's religious poetry with understanding (and therefore with profit and appreciation) requires a more or less conscious investment in the *peculiarities* of its Christian orientation, in the social and historical particulars which feed and shape the distinctive features of her work. Because John O. Waller's relatively recent essay on Rossetti, "Christ's Second Coming; Christina Rossetti and the Premillenarianist William Dodsworth," focuses on some of the most important of these particulars, it seems to me one of the most useful pieces of scholarship ever written on the poet. The essay locates the special ground of Rossetti's religious poetry in that peculiar Adventist and premillenarian context which flourished for about fifty years in mid nineteenth-century culture. In point of historical fact—and it is a historical fact which has enormous significance for the aesthetic character of Rossetti's poetry—her religious verse is intimately meshed with a number of particular, even peculiar, religious ideas.[18] From the vantage of her strongest poetry, the most important of these ideas (along with the associated images and symbols they helped to generate) were allied to a once powerful religious movement which later—toward the end of the century—slipped to a marginal position in English culture.

The whole question [of premillenarianism] was overshadowed first and last by the Tractarian Movement, Anglo-Catholicism, and the resulting Protestant reaction. And we can see in retrospect that all through the years [1820–1875] the theological future actually belonged to liberal, or Broad Church, principles. By the middle 1870s, apparently, [the issues raised through the premillenarian movement] were no longer very alive.[19]

In this context we may begin to understand the decline of Rossetti's reputation after the late nineteenth century, when she was still regarded as one of the most powerful and important contemporary English poets. Her reputation was established in the 1860s and 1870s, when Adventism reached the apogee of its brief but influential career. Thereafter, the availability of religious poetry was mediated either through the Broad Church line (which stretches from Coleridge and the Cambridge Apostles and Arnold, to figures like Trilling and Abrams in our own day) or through the High Church and Anglo-Catholic line (which was defined backwards from certain influential twentieth-century figures like Eliot to include the Noetics, Hopkins, and various seventeenth-century religious writers). The premillenarian and evangelist enthusiasm which supported Rossetti's religious poetry had been moved to the periphery of English culture when the canon of such verse began to take shape in the modern period.

To read Rossetti's religious poetry, then, we have to willingly suspend not only our disbelief in her convictions and ideas but also our *belief* in those expectations and presuppositions about religious poetry which we have inherited from those two dominant ideological lines—Broad Church and High Church and Anglo-Catholic. Waller has drawn our attention to the general premillenarian content of her work, and I should like to follow his lead by emphasizing another crucial and even more particular doctrinal feature of her poetry.

4

The well-known lyric "Up-Hill" is a useful place to start. In certain obvious ways, this moving poem follows a traditional model, and its all but explicit forebears are two of Herbert's most familiar pieces, "The Pilgrimage" and the last poem in *The Temple*, "Love (III)." When we set Rossetti's poem beside the two by Herbert we will perhaps be initially struck by the difference in tone: Rossetti's poem is melancholy (one might even say "morbid") whereas Herbert's two lyrics discover and disclose their religious confidence in their respective conclusions:

> My hill was further; so I flung away,
>   Yet heard a crie,
> Just as I went, "None goes that way
> And lives." "If that be all," said I,

> "After so foul a journey death is fair,
> And but a chair."
>
> ["The Pilgrimage"]

> "You must sit down," says Love, "and taste my meat."
> So I did sit and eat.
>
> ["Love (III)"]

If Herbert's pilgrimage has been long and weary, and if his soul—conscious that it is "Guilty of dust and sin"—at first hesitates to accept Love's invitation, in the end all comes to confidence, content, and even joy. For at the end of his life, the Christian (this Christian) comes to the feast of the blessed and a place in the house of God.

In Rossetti it is different, and the difference is signaled in the startling last two lines of her poem "Up-Hill." The speaker questions her divine interlocutor about the pilgrimage, but the answers she gets are strange and mysteriously portentous through the first twelve lines. Finally, however, Rossetti is told, in a disturbingly ambiguous phrase, that her laborious journey will be complete: "Of labour you shall find the sum." The poem then concludes:

> Will there be beds for me and all who seek?
> Yea, beds for all who come.[20]

Surely this seems a peculiar way to end a poem which seems to describe the pilgrimage of the Christian soul to its final reward. No "feast" opens before her final eyes, nor does she seem to believe that the dying Christian should expect to receive anything other than a bed, presumably to sleep in. The image is almost grotesque in its lowliness and not far from a parody of such exalted Christian ideas that at death we go to our eternal rest or to sleep in the bosom of God. Does Rossetti imagine that when we go to heaven we shall sleep away our paradise, or is she simply a weak-minded poet, sentimentally attached to certain traditional phrases and ideas which she has not really thought through?

The conclusion of "Up-Hill" would not have been written as it was if Rossetti had not subscribed to, and thoroughly pondered the artistic possibilities of, the peculiar millenarian and Anabaptist doctrine known popularly as "Soul Sleep."[21] This idea, in a richly dispersed and elaborated variety of poetic forms, pervades the work of her greatest years as a poet, that is, the period from 1848 to 1875. It takes its origin from the time of Luther (whose position on the matter was unsettled), and it means to deal with the problem of the so-called waiting time, that is, the period between a person's death and the Great Advent (or Second Coming). The orthodox view distinguishes between the Particular Judgment, which the soul undergoes at death, and the General Judgment, which takes place at the end of the world. According to traditional doctrine (epitomized in Episcopalian and Roman Catholic theology), the soul at death passes to its final reward (I leave aside here the possibility of a purgatorial period) and suffers no "waiting time." The body corrupts in the grave and is reunited with the emparadised soul on the Last Day. According to Adventist doctrine of Soul Sleep, however, death initiates the period during which the soul is placed in a state of "sleeping" or suspension. Only at the Millennium, on the Last Day, is that sleep broken and the soul confronted with its final reward.

There is no question that Rossetti adhered to the doctrine of Soul Sleep, for it can be found at all levels of tenor and vehicle in her work. From her earliest to her latest poems—from works like "Dream Land" composed in 1849 (and placed third in her first-published volume) to the famous culminant lyric "Sleeping at Last," written in 1893 or early 1894—this premillenarian concept is the single most important enabling principle in Rossetti's religious poetry. By this I mean that no other idea generated such a network of poetic possibilities for her verse, that no other idea contributed so much to the concrete and specific character of her work.

Most obviously, the doctrine provides a ground from which Rossetti can both understand and judge her sense of the insufficiency of a mortal existence. The pervasive theme of *vanitas vanitatum* is generated and maintained through the energy of an emotional weariness, through a sense that living in the world is scarcely worth the effort it requires, since what the world has to offer is, in any case, mere vanity, empty promises, betrayal. Soul Sleep is precisely what would appear to be the first and greatest need of the weary pilgrim under such circumstances; in a word, it answers to the most fundamental emotional demand which Rossetti's poetry sets forth. In addition, however, the doctrine validates Rossetti's peculiarly passive stance toward the world's evil. Rossetti's negative judgments of the world do not take the form of a resistance but of a withdrawal— a strategic withdrawal carried out under the premillenarian consciousness that any commitment to the world is suicidal. It is highly significant that one of the principal sections of her 1893 volume of devotional poems, *Verses*, should have been headed "The World. Self-Destruction."

From the doctrine of Soul Sleep also emerges Rossetti's special employment of the traditional topos of the dream vision. Several of Rossetti's poems set forth paradisal visions, and in each case these proceed from a condition in which the soul, laid asleep, as it were, in the body, is permitted to glimpse the millennial world. In fact, the logic of Rossetti's verse only allows her access to that world through the dream visions that are themselves only enabled by the concept (and the resultant poetic reality) of Soul Sleep. How that logic operates can be readily seen by studying the relations between a group of poems like "Paradise" ("Once in a dream I saw the flowers"), "Mother Country" ("Oh what is that country"), "I Will Lift Up Mine Eyes Unto the Hills," "Advent" ("This Advent moon shines cold and clear"), "Sound Sleep" ("Some are laughing, some are weeping"), "Rest" ("O Earth, lie heavily upon her eyes"), and even the exquisite "Song" ("When I am dead, my dearest"). The sleeping soul is surrounded by a "stillness that is *almost* Paradise" ("Rest," l. 8; my italics), a condition of virtually complete stasis that is also (and paradoxically) premonitory: "Until the morning of Eternity / Her rest shall not begin nor end, but be" ("Rest," ll. 12–13). And in that sleep which is not death what dreams may come? Rossetti says that "Night and morning, noon and even, / Their sound fills her dreams with Heaven" ("Sound Sleep," ll. 17–18). Soul Sleep permits the visions and dream glimpses of paradise which are the objects of those who desire a better country (compare the poem "They Desire a Better Country").

> As I lie dreaming
>   It rises, that land;
> There rises before me,
>   Its green golden strand,
> With the bowing cedars
>   And the shining sand;
> It sparkles and flashes
>   Like a shaken brand.
>   ["Mother Country," ll. 9–16]

The initial rule in Rossetti's ideology is that only the dreams of Soul Sleep give one access to the real details of the Christian paradise (compare her poem "I Will Lift Up Mine Eyes Unto the Hills"). The poetic imagination of what such dreams must be produces, in turn, the actual verse descriptions of paradise which we find in Rossetti's poetry. In all cases, however, the importance of the initial rule is emphasized by a secondary (operating) rule: that Rossetti's poetry will only venture upon a description of paradise through the rite of passage initially defined in the doctrine of Soul Sleep (with its accompanying poetic imagination of the "dreams" and visions which must accompany such a state). So, in the poem "Paradise" Rossetti gives a detailed description of the heaven she saw "Once in a dream," a concrete representation which she draws from various traditionary Christian sources, not the least of which is the New Testament, and in particular the Book of Revelation. The catalog of details which makes up her picture of heaven concludes in an "o altitudo," however, which means to emphasize the secondary nature of the poetic representation. For the poem records, as it were, a dream of the sleeping soul's more final dream, and as such it stands at three removes from paradise. The dream *version* of the sleeping soul's *dream vision* is itself beyond any possibility of an accurate concrete rendering. The closest approximation one can arrive at in this world to the vision that can be expected after death in Soul Sleep is a description not of paradise itself but of the emotional effect which results from the actual desire for such a vision. Thus it is that the poem's description of paradise concludes (indeed, culminates) in the utter defeat of all concrete imaginative detail:

> Oh harps, oh crowns of plenteous stars,
>   Oh green palm branches many-leaved—
> Eye hath not seen, nor ear hath heard,
>   Nor heart conceived.
>   ["Paradise," ll. 37–40]

The premonitory dreams of the sleeping soul take place in a region set far apart from the ordinary, "self-destructive" world; and that world is thereby submitted to the negative judgment implicit in the invocation of such a visionary place.

But that is only one function of the machinery of Soul Sleep as used by Rossetti. Its other principal function is to provide Rossetti with a rationale capable of explaining, and even justifying, her existence in the late Victorian world of getting and spending, which she judged so severely. That is to say, Rossetti consistently used the grammar of the doctrine of Soul Sleep as an analogue for the condition of the contemporary Christian. Rossetti's poems take their model from the visions of Soul Sleep, and the latter state is itself used repeatedly as a model for the state of the Christian soul in the premillennial period of late Victorian England. By thus manipulating the machinery of the doctrine of Soul Sleep, Rossetti was able to produce such famous and beautiful poems as the "Song" ("When I am dead, my dearest"), for in that and so many similar works she elaborated an analogy between the (physical) "resting place" of the body and the (spiritual) place in which the sleeping soul was to be suspended.

This last result has a widespread and profound effect upon the character of Rossetti's poetry. In the first place, it tends to blur any clear distinction between her secular and her religious poetry, since almost all of her best work is generated through a poetic grammar that is fundamentally religious in origin and character. We must, of course, distinguish between her "Devotional" and her nondevotional poetry, partly because *she* made such a distinction and partly because it is an important distinction *in fact.*[22] But if a large part of her work is not specifically *devotional*, it is virtually all "religious" in its orientation.

In the second place, when we begin to see that a specific religious orientation has had a signal impact on all aspects of her verse, we are unexpectedly (and almost paradoxically) provided with a means for gathering the power of her work outside of its own religious self-representations. That is to say, we begin to see how the Christian and Adventist machinery in her work is a historically specific set of images which do not so much describe actual spiritual realities (like paradise and so forth) as they indicate, by poetic obliquity, how difficult it seemed to imagine, least of all actually to live, a fully human life in the real world of her place and time.

This nonreligious, this *human,* view of her poetry is implicit in the following shrewd set of remarks made about Rossetti's work in 1895 by A. C. Benson in the *National Review:*

> Some writers have the power of creating a species of aerial landscape in the minds of their readers, often vague and shadowy, not obtruding itself strongly upon the consciousness, but forming a quiet background, like the scenery of portraits, in which the action of the lyric or the sonnet seems to lie. I am not now speaking of pictorial writing, which definitely aims at producing, with more or less vividness, a house, a park, a valley, but lyrics and poems of pure thought and feeling, which have none the less a haunting sense of locality in which the mood dreams itself out.
>
> Christina Rossetti's *mise-en-scène* is a place of gardens, orchards, wooded dingles, with a churchyard in the distance. The scene shifts a little, but the spirit never wanders far afield; and it is certainly singular that one who lived out almost the whole of her life in a city so majestic, sober, and inspiring as London, should never bring the consciousness of streets and thoroughfares and populous murmur into her writings. She, whose heart was so with birds and fruits, cornfields and farmyard sounds, never even revolts against or despairs of the huge desolation, the laborious monotony of a great town. She does not sing of the caged bird, with exotic memories of freedom stirred by the flashing water, the hanging groundsel of her wired prison, but with a wild voice, with visions only limited by the rustic conventionalities of toil and tillage. The dewy English woodland, the sharp silences of winter, the gloom of low-hung clouds, and the sigh of weeping rains are her backgrounds.[23]

Benson has indeed located the primal scene, as it were, of all of Rossetti's poetry. First, it is a scene which stands in an antithetical relation to the life of Rossetti's immediate experience, to the life and "the way we live now." Second, this scene elaborates a set of images which are, as we have already noted, analogous to those which were generated through Rossetti's use of the doctrine of Soul Sleep. In each case, however, we may come to understand that such "poetical" places and scenes constitute Rossetti's imaginative transpositions—poetic idealizations—of actual places and scenes which she either knew and recoiled from (the Babylon that she saw as the world of London) or that she recollected, dreamed of, and yearned toward. It is beyond question that the charming *mise-en-scène* to which Benson draws our attention is a fantasy delineation of the rural environs of Holmer Green in Buckinghamshire, where Rossetti's grandfather Gaetano Polidori had a cottage and small garden. Rossetti's childhood visits to this place (they ended when she was nine years old) were later to become, by her own acknowledgment, the source of the ideal forms which she associated with the natural world.[24] As such, they allow us to reconceptualize her "religious" idealizations, which are structurally congruent with the "natural" idealizations. In each case we are dealing with symbol structures that express, and re-present, a network of socially and psychologically specific tensions and contradictions. In a word, Rossetti's poetry is not "about" that fantasy scene pointed out by Benson, nor is it about the equally abstract "religious" scenes offered to us at the surface of her poetry. Her poetry is an oblique glimpse into the heaven and the hell of late Victorian England as that world was mediated through the particular experiences of Christina Rossetti.

As I have noted elsewhere, Rossetti's heaven and hell are always conceptualized in terms of personal love relations: true and real love as opposed to the various illusions of happiness, pleasure, and fulfillment.[25] Indeed, hell for Rossetti is merely the culminant experience of any life which has been lived in a "worldly," which is to say in a self-destructive, way. Heaven, conversely, is the achievement of a complete and final escape from such an existence. The importance of the doctrine of Soul Sleep is that it postulates a condition or state which mediates between the finalities of heaven and hell. In that state, according to the doctrinal position adopted by Rossetti's poetry, one achieves an initial release from the wearying confusions of the world as well as one's first visionary glimpses of a paradisal (or nonworldly) existence.

Carried over into her verse, the doctrine of Soul Sleep provides Rossetti with an analogue for poetic vision itself—more specifically, for a poetic vision conceived in certain religious terms which are broadly grounded in the general ideology of Christian ideas. It is as if Rossetti were postulating a doctrinal foundation for Wordsworth's famous Romantic formulation of the state of poetic vision, when one is laid asleep in body to become a living soul, and when one may finally begin to "see into the life of things." This poetic employment of the doctrine of Soul Sleep provides Rossetti, as we have already seen, with the means for generating "paradisal images" which answer to her emotional needs: images which at once sustain her deepest and most frustrate desires, and which also help to reveal the circumstances which are responsible for experiences of misery and betrayal.

The doctrine also helped Rossetti to develop a complex theory of dream vision which can be most graphically seen in poems like "Sleep at Sea" and in particular the great "From House to Home." "Sleep at Sea" narrates the voyage of a ship of fools who are called "the sleepers" and whose ominous fate is specifically connected to the sleep in which they are caught up.[26] In this state they have certain dreams that recall the premonitory dreams of paradise we have already noted in the poems written out of the doctrine of Soul Sleep; but in this case the dreams are represented as perilous illusions, just as the sleep is only a parodic version of a true Soul Sleep:

> Oh soft the streams drop music
>   Between the hills,
> And musical the birds' nests
>   Beside those rills:
> The nests are types of home
>   Love-hidden from ills,
> The nests are types of spirits
>   Love music fills.
>
> So dream the sleepers,
>   Each man in his place;
> The lightning shows the smile
>   Upon each face:
> The ship is driving, driving,
>   It drives apace:
> And sleepers smile, and spirits
>   Bewail their case.
>
> ["Sleep at Sea," ll. 17–32]

The original manuscript title of the poem, "Something Like Truth," indicates the purposefulness with which Rossetti constructed this demonic version of Soul Sleep and dream vision.[27] The doctrinal message of the poem is, of course, quite clear: that the Christian must be watchful on all occasions, that the structures and images of the spiritual life are themselves liable to an evil inversion. Particularly treacherous are the paradisal temptations which are generated out of the desire for rest, comfort, and the eternal life:

> No voice to call the sleepers,
>   No hand to raise:
> They sleep to death in dreaming
>   Of length of days.
> Vanity of vanities,
>   The Preacher says:
> Vanity is the end
>   Of all their ways.
>
> [ll. 81–88]

In "From House to Home" the contrast between illusory dreams and paradisal vision is even more elaborately developed. The first seventy-five lines of the poem construct the dream of "An earthly paradise supremely fair / That lured me from the goal" (ll. 7–8). But the central love-object in that paradise eventually flees, and the speaker is left empty and devastated (see ll. 77–104). The second part of the poem develops an alternative dream sequence in which the goal of a paradisal vision is associated with a nightmare rite of passage. The importance of this association, from a technical (rather than a doctrinal) point of view, is that it forces Rossetti to subject all aspects of her own poetical machinery to a critical examination at all points; and this in its turn frees her to exploit in unusual ways the imagistic, tonal, and symbolic materials which are generated out of that machinery. Specifically, any image, mood, or symbol is laid open to sudden and arbitrary inversions of their apparent poetic value. Indeed, it seems to me that the often-noted melancholia which pervades so much of Rossetti's poetry is a direct function of its openness to such arbitrary inversions—as if she were herself aware of the treacherousness of her own most cherished dreams and ideals, as if she were also aware that all that she might say might just as well have been unsaid, or been said rather differently, or might not even have been said at all. This is the burden that hangs about the touching and plangent lines of a song like "When I am dead, my dearest," where the poetry is haunted by the vanity and inconsequence which it reveals and appears to triumph over, but by which it too is at least partially victimized.

5

Thus, the ultimate marginality of Rossetti's particular Christian stance was to become the source of its final strength, the privilege of its historical backwardness. The ideological triumph of Broad Church Christianity and Anglo-Catholicism in the early twentieth century—in the academy at any rate—drove Rossetti out of the Great Tradition and its attendant anthologies. To us, however, her work seems peculiarly alive, *as poetry,* to her age's cultural contradictions because it is able to reveal how those contradictions are replicated at the heart of her own deepest beliefs and commitments. Moreover, that those commitments should have been located within the tradition of Christianity proves to be the conclusive source of her poetry's importance and power. On the one hand, her poetry contains a forcible and persistent reminder that the themes of Christian poetry— even the greatest of such themes, like those of guilt and redemption, of resurrection, of incarnation—are time and place specific, that they have had a beginning, and a middle, and that they will finally have an end as well. To imagine otherwise is a vanity and an illusion, a peculiar blindness from which only those who recognize their own historical backwardness will be exempt. On the other hand, her poetry also demonstrates, through the self-destruction of its own special worldliness (that is, through the self-destruction of its own religious certainties), the true ground of poetic transcendence. Poetry does not triumph over its times by arriving at a "vision" or idea of the Truth, whether religious or otherwise; it triumphs when it reveals, once again, the local and human origin of all particular and historical events. Hence it is that poetry only maintains its life in later ages and cultures when it preserves its integrity, when it confronts those later ages and cultures with a human world which is important to other human worlds precisely because it is different, local, limited. The survival of that which is specific and therefore obsolete—in particular, the survival of those things which are most conscious of their own limitedness—is the ground of all we can mean by "transcendence." It is the reciprocal, indeed, the dialectical gift which past and present give to each other in order to secure the future.

1. Because the ideological arguments within Christianity were so central during the Renaissance, contemporary writers of various persuasions tended to emphasize the differences between their doctrinal positions. During the Enlightenment a secular challenge began to be raised against Christianity in general, and the consequence of this was the emergence, within the various Christian sects, of a consolidating movement. Broad Church Protestantism gained its ascendancy during the nineteenth and twentieth centuries, a period in which we have also observed, particularly during the last fifty years, several strains of ecumenism. These developments within Christianity follow upon the challenge of humanism and secularism, and they can be seen quite clearly in the world of literary criticism and scholarship as well. M. H. Abrams' *Natural Supernaturalism* is an obvious instance, and the entire corpus of Northrop Frye's work is paradigmatic.

2. The root of the matter probably hinges upon that famous Pauline *sine qua non:* "If Christ be not risen, then is our faith in vain" (1 Cor. 15:13–14). This text contains certain essential features of the Christian economy in all its variant forms: of faith in Jesus as the savior of mankind and of the nature of Christian hope in the individual's own salvation through resurrection. The other key features of Christianity involve the eucharistic feast and its practical/doctrinal concomitant, the ideal of Christian love (cf. especially the Gospel of John 15:12–13 and Matthew 5:43–44; the latter should be compared with what is said in Matthew 22:36–40).

3. See R. W. Crump, *Christina Rossetti: A Reference Guide* (Boston, 1976), where the history of Rossetti's critical reception is schematically presented in a good annotated bibliography. The neglect of Rossetti is especially remarkable when one considers the (often noted) similarity between much of her verse and the work of George Herbert. The latter is, we know, one of the favorite subjects of New Critical and contemporary formalist exegesis.

4. I choose the second example because several of Rossetti's later books were published under the auspices of that society.

5. For a survey of Gerard Manley Hopkins' critical reception, see the first two chapters of Todd K. Bender, *Gerard Manley Hopkins: The Classical Background and Critical Reception of His Work* (Baltimore, 1966).

6. For a survey of some critical views of the New Criticism, see Murray Krieger, *The New Apologists for Poetry* (Minneapolis, 1956); Richard Foster, *The New Romantics; A Reappraisal of the New Criticism* (Bloomington, Ind., 1962); and chaps. 2 and 5 of Gerald Graff, *Literature against Itself* (Chicago, 1979).

7. See Crump, *A Reference Guide.* A number of books about Rossetti appeared in the early 1930s, several quite good, but after that she virtually disappeared from the academic scene for almost three decades; and even then she remained a marginal interest for another ten years or more.

8. This line is epitomized in Lona Mosk Packer, *Christina Rossetti* (Berkeley, 1963).

9. B. Ifor Evans, *English Poetry in the Later Nineteenth Century*, rev. ed. (1933; rpt. New York, 1966), pp. 100–101.

10. John Crowe Ransom, *God Without Thunder. An Unorthodox Defense of Orthodoxy* (New York, 1930), pp. 327–28.

11. See ibid., chap. 1. In literary / critical terms, Ransom sets his face against ideological models which were developed out of Romanticism and Victorianism, including their characteristic tendency to define volatile and problematic issues via historicist and symbolical methods. In England this tendency is epitomized in the work and program initiated by Coleridge. Early twentieth-century reactionary criticism from Irving Babbitt to T. S. Eliot, Allen Tate, and Cleanth Brooks deplored this tendency and its methods. The well-known catchphrase "split religion" accurately describes the double nature of their criticism of Romantic and post-Romantic poetry: that it represented equally a debasement of the proper objects of poetic discourse and the appropriate character of religious experience.

12. Lionel Stevenson, *The Pre-Raphaelite Poets* (Chapel Hill, N.C., 1972), p. 88.

13. I should point out that Stevenson is a distinguished historical scholar. His failure, in this case, to grasp the historical issues at stake in reading Rossetti's poetry is not typical of his work, and least of all is it a function of any New Critical antihistoricism.

14. See "The New Criticism," a discussion involving Tate and several others, *The American Scholar* 20 (Spring 1951): 218–31.

15. These terms and ideas (as well as "morbid" and "sterile," cited below) tend to occur repeatedly in the critical literature on Rossetti.

16. Leon Trotsky, *The Russian Revolution: The Overthrow of Tzarism and the Triumph of the Soviets*, selections from *The History of the Russian Revolution*, ed. F. W. Dupee, trans. Max Eastman (Garden City, N.Y., 1959), p. 3.

17. For recent feminist and feminist-influenced essays on Rossetti, see Barbara Fass, "Christina Rossetti and 'St. Agnes' Eve,'" *Victorian Poetry* 14 (Spring 1976): 33–46, and Nan Miller, "Christina Rossetti and Sarah Woodruff: Two Remedies for a Divided Self," *Journal of Pre-Raphaelite Studies* 3 (1982): 68–77. Significant historical scholarship has been produced in Crump's various works, including *The Complete Poems of Christina Rossetti*, 1 vol. to date (Baton Rouge, La., 1979–) and the *Reference Guide* cited above; in Gwynneth Hatton, "An Edition of the Unpublished Poems of Christina Rossetti with a Critical Introduction and Interpretive Notes to All the Posthumous Poems" (Ph.D. diss., St. Hilda's College, 1955); and in essays like John O. Waller, "Christ's Second Coming; Christina Rossetti and the Premillenarianist William Dodsworth," *Bulletin of the New York Public Library* 73 (1969): 465–82, and Joe K. Law, "William Dyce's *George Herbert at Bemerton:* Its Background and Meaning," *Journal of Pre-Raphaelite Studies* 3 (1982): 45–55.

18. It is a commonplace of Rossetti criticism that her poetry is the best expression we have of the ideas and attitudes of Tractarianism. But this is a most misleading view (though not entirely wrong); one might rather turn to a work such as John Keble's *The Christian Year* for an epitome of Tractarian ideology. Rossetti's evangelical sympathies kept her Protestantism resolute, as one can readily see in her lifelong hostility to the revival of Marianism. Waller's observation is very much to the point: "[Rossetti's] spiritual adviser [i.e., William Dodsworth] during her impressionable adolescence [was an] improbable combination of High Church activist and premillenialist preacher that would mold the peculiar configuration of her religious sensibility" ("Christ's Second Coming," p. 466).

19. Waller, "Christ's Second Coming," p. 477. For a general discussion of millenarianism in the early nineteenth century, see J. E. Harrison, *The Second Coming, Popular Millenarianism, 1780–1850* (London, 1979).

20. "Up-Hill," *The Complete Poems of Christina Rossetti*, ed. Crump, ll. 14–16; all subsequent references to Rossetti's poetry are from this edition and will be included in the text.

21. The technical term for this doctrine is "psychopannychism"; the *OED* defines "psychopannychy" as "the state in which (according to some) the soul sleeps between death and the day of judgment." For further discussion, see O. Cullmann, *Immortality of the Soul; or, Resurrection of the Dead?* (New York, 1958), and two papers by J. Héring, "Entre la mort et la résurrection," *Review of the History of Philosophy and Religion* 40 (1960): 338–48 and "Eschatologie biblique et idéalisme platonicien," in *The Background of the New Testament and Its Eschatology*, ed. W. D. Davies and D. Daube (Cambridge, 1956), pp. 443–63.

22. The distinction is marked in her volumes of poetry, where specifically "devotional" poems are marked off in a separate section at the end. Her 1893 *Verses* is a volume exclusively containing devotional poems. While almost all of her poetry could be called "religious," the "devotional" poems are those which deal with specific liturgical topics and occasions. To a strict Sabbatarian like Rossetti (and many of her readers were Sabbatarians as well), only devotional verse would be suitable for perusal on Sunday. Moreover, the devotional verse is always conceived with an audience in mind which understands and actively practices devotional exercises of various kinds.

23. A. C. Benson, "Christina Rossetti," *National Review* 24 (Feb. 1895): 753, as quoted in Mackenzie Bell, *Christina Rossetti: A Biographical and Critical Study*, 4th ed. (London, 1898), pp. 330–31.

24. See Bell, *Christina Rossetti*, pp. 9–11. See also "Rossetti Family in Bucks," *Notes and Queries* 159 (6 Sept. 1930): 176.

25. See my "Christina Rossetti's Poems: A New Edition and a Revaluation," *Victorian Studies* 23 (Winter 1980): 237–54.

26. I do not know that critics have yet pointed out a signal aspect of this poem: that it is in crucial ways a meditation on, and interpretation of, Coleridge's "Rime of the Ancient Mariner," and especially the (later) parts of the poem which treat the dead mariners and the visiting troupe of animating spirits.

27. See *The Complete Poems of Christina Rossetti*, p. 262.

A History of American Poetry Anthologies

Alan C. Golding

1. Anthologies and the American Poetry Canon: A Historical Overview

In his recent book *Kinds of Literature*, Alastair Fowler distinguishes three main kinds of literary canon: the potential, accessible, and selective canons.[1] He defines the potential canon as consisting of all extant literature, all the literature that, simply because it exists, any reader could potentially read. By the accessible canon, Fowler means that part of the potential canon to which readers have relatively easy access in the form of scholarly reprints, affordable paperbacks, or anthologies. His third category, the selective canon, covers those works in the accessible canon that trained readers have selected as especially worthy of attention. Fowler's categories trace the narrowing-down process by which a selective canon is achieved. They do not fully reveal, however, the complexity of that process. For instance, selection precedes as well as follows the formation of the accessible canon, affecting the form that "accessibility" takes. Some texts are considered worth keeping in print in a readily available form, while others survive only in the darker corners of university libraries. One way this process of selection works, one fundamental means by which the selective canon is formed and transformed, is through the poetry anthology. Examining the often conflicting standards that American anthologists have brought to bear on the problem of selection, then, illuminates more general issues of canon-formation. It helps us understand how an anthology can reflect, expand, or redirect a period's canon; what literary and social principles regulated the poetry canon at different points in American literary history; and how those principles have changed over the years.

Conflicting principles of selection have marked American poetry anthologies from their beginning. When Elihu Hubbard Smith edited the first such anthology, *American Poems, Selected and Original* (1793), he hoped both to preserve poems published in periodicals and newspapers, which might otherwise be lost, and to invite evaluation, "a more certain estimation," of his poets' "comparative merit."² Preservation, logically the first step in canon-formation, gathers an initial accessible canon on which later anthologies can build or from which they can select. At the same time, placing the poems of the accessible canon side by side in one publication invites comparison and evaluation by readers, which eventually narrows the accessible canon. This sequence looks simple and logical: from preservation to evaluation to a more limited preservation. But evaluation actually occurs at two points, performed first by an editor and then by readers, making the sequence more complex than it first appears. Even in the earliest stage of canon-formation, in which one would expect a broad, catholic preservation, evaluation governs the anthologist's work. He inevitably makes evaluative judgments in compiling an anthology. He decides that some poets and poems deserve preservation and others do not. The evaluation by readers that takes place after an accessible canon has been preserved confounds the preservative impulse which led the editor to gather the accessible canon. Preservation, the historian's goal, presumes the value of breadth, of collecting as much poetry as possible; it discourages further comparative evaluations that extract a more selective canon from the whole accessible canon. The preservative impulse assumes the value of a broad, inclusive canon, while evaluation produces a narrowed, exclusive canon. A long-term goal, preservation makes poems available as lasting documents of a literary period. But evaluation determines how long any work, once preserved, receives attention and, consequently, how long it is kept accessible.

Given these conflicts, any editor, either one interested, like Smith, in preserving the beginnings of American poetry or interested, like many later anthologists, in presenting its historical range, has an especially difficult task in weighing historical inclusiveness against evaluation and exclusiveness. The basis on which editors solve such dilemmas will often stay submerged. Thus an anthologist's stated goals may contradict not only each other, as Smith's do, but also the unstated biases on which the selections are founded. Again Smith provides a test case. Personal, regional, and political loyalties all underlie his work. To represent American poetry, he compiled a book dominated by his friends, by Connecticut poets, by

Alan C. Golding, who teaches at the University of California, Los Angeles, has written on Edgar Allan Poe, Jean Toomer, and Charles Olson. He is currently at work on a book about the American poetry canon.

Federalists. Much of the poetry he gathered consists of topical, Federalist satires on the dangers of unbridled populism. Like his stated goal of inviting evaluation, Smith's unstated ideology, which favors occasional poems devoted not to posterity but to the short-term goal of solving immediate political problems, conflicts with his long-term goal of preservation. Smith wanted to gain his poets "a more universal attention" (*AP*, p. iii). But his ideological motive for winning readers was stronger than his altruistic desire to foster awareness of American poetry, and it limited the amount and kind of poetry he made available.

Smith's Federalism underlies what he saw as the use of his anthology: to build America's sense of identity by gathering an independent national literature to match and strengthen the country's newly achieved political independence. The particular political identity which Smith wanted that literature to embody is not what actually evolved, of course. Nevertheless, his and the other early American poetry anthologies, Mathew Carey's *Beauties of Poetry, British and American* (1791) and *The Columbian Muse* (1794), did share this common goal. The term "American literature," rarely used before the 1780s, became commonplace after the 1783 Treaty of Paris. Magazines opened their pages to a flood of American writing, as their editors set out crusading pleas for the creation of a "national" literature. The early anthologies supported this campaign: in *The Beauties of Poetry*, for instance, Carey reprinted large portions of his magazine the *American Museum*.

The literary nationalism fostered in eighteenth-century anthologies became even more programmatic as America moved into the nineteenth century. The country still felt an urgent need to assert that it had an indigenous poetry recognizably different from English poetry. Benjamin Spencer points out that "virtually every major and minor author between 1815 and 1860 felt obliged to expound some version of a national literature."[3] Ralph Waldo Emerson's "American Scholar," in which he asserts that "we have listened too long to the courtly muses of Europe," is only a highlight of an already widespread movement. Some critics and journals, like the *Monthly Anthology and Boston Review*, held out against this inflation of America's literary efforts. But on the whole, American critics until the mid-nineteenth century repeatedly called for a national literature and indiscriminately praised it.[4]

In the 1820s and '30s, as the push to create a national literature gathered a momentum fueled by Washington Irving's success in England and William Cullen Bryant's example at home, the preservative and nation-building impulses behind the early anthologies branched off in two directions. In one direction, anthologists presented the historical range of American poetry, to preserve the poetry that Americans had written so far and thus convince British skeptics that a national literature, an American poetry, was developing. At the same time, "nationality" acquired a moral edge, an alternative to perceived European decadence.

A moral Adamism accompanied the literary Adamism, and as a result the nation-building motive for anthologies led directly to an inspirational one: now that its political institutions were established, America's citizens needed to have them justified and to be told how to live within them. Americans of the time looked to their poets for advice on these matters. Poetry's function, from this view, was to provide a national identity and morality. A poetry that is asked to instruct and inspire needs some degree of ideological conformity to succeed, and American poetry displayed just this conformity. The poetry that stood the best chance of being collected and widely disseminated through anthologies offered comforting and homely truths and affirmed the culture's sense of itself.[5]

These two motives behind nineteenth-century anthologies, the historicizing and the inspirational, were closely related. The logical corollary of the historicizing impulse was to define the distinctively "national" characteristics of the poetry that had been preserved; and anthologists in the first half of the nineteenth century claimed, with some accuracy, that American poetry's defining characteristic was its moral purity. Consequently, since an anthologist like Rufus Griswold could find for *The Poets and Poetry of America* (1842) enough morally orthodox verse to provide both spiritual inspiration and historical breadth, the potential conflict between historical preservation and moral mission (which acts as a force of exclusion) did not arise. Nevertheless, just as evaluation precedes as well as follows preservation, so moral criteria for canonizing poetry not only describe what has been preserved—they also precede and govern the act of historicizing and preserving. Thus the typical anthology of the years 1830–60 included in its historical range only that poetry which fulfilled the book's moral mission. It excluded nonconformist poems by otherwise popular women poets, ignored Puritan poetry, and cowered at the arrival of Walt Whitman.[6]

While America struggled for literary independence, a poem's, or indeed the whole canon's, claim to excellence rested on its embodiment of national characteristics. Once the debate over what constituted American poetry was resolved and the need to extol only poetry that supported America's cultural identity had diminished, however, we might expect claims for transhistorical excellence, excellence judged by universal and international standards, to follow. This is exactly what happened, beginning with Charles A. Dana's *Household Book of Poetry* (1858) and continuing through Emerson's *Parnassus* (1875) and Edmund Clarence Stedman's *American Anthology, 1787–1900* (1900) to the high modernist period. Like the earlier stages of canon-formation, however, this later stage is not easily isolated. Even Smith had avowed universal, not national, standards of taste (although before 1815 and the end of the second war with England, "universal" meant "English," for all practical purposes). Heavily influenced by the critical tenets of the British Lord Kames and Hugh Blair, Smith, according to Spencer, considered "the belles-lettres of all nations as agents of universal taste uniting mankind in 'one vast brother-hood / In equal bonds of knowledge and of right.' "[7]

Just as Smith had used supposedly universal standards in preserving an initial accessible canon, some modernist anthologists claimed to use them in revising the canon. Once an accessible canon develops, preservation becomes a less urgent motive for anthologizing; once a stable literary and political culture is established, literary nationalism and political or-thodoxy also become less urgent. Continued revision is the logical and ongoing final stage, but any revisionist editor who invokes universal standards in his defense walks on shaky ground. That editor will use the principle of transhistorical excellence to propose a new canon: the es-tablished poetry, in this view, does not meet universal standards. A more conservative editor, however, can use the same principle to justify the established canon. In this view, the "best" work rises to the top. A good poem or poet, once recognized, will always be, and will always be considered, good. Both anthologists, then, face a contradiction in this late stage of canon-formation: if transhistorical excellence can be invoked to justify two different kinds of poetry, it offers neither the revisionist nor the more conservative editor a sound basis for his canon.

In the last twenty-five years the American poetry canon has become especially open to revision and expansion. The fragmentation that has always been an unacknowledged part of American literary culture, man-ifesting itself in politically partisan anthologies, women's anthologies, and regional anthologies, has intensified. One feature of this increased frag-mentation has been an unprecedented number of revisionist anthologies. These collections are all intended to shift an academic canon defined mostly by teaching anthologies like *The Norton Anthology of Poetry.* To a large degree, these revisionist anthologies themselves comprise the body of literature from which the academic editor selects. For the editor of the teaching anthology, the old question of what contemporary work to preserve takes a new but still problematic form. Today preservation usually means selecting from abundance, not protecting from oblivion. Due to the lack of general consensus on literary and social values, however, the editor must sift multiple, conflicting claims to poetic worth, making that selection an arduous task.

Because they involve contradictory, often ideologically based defi-nitions of "excellence," these claims undermine the tenability of any single dominant standard for "good" poetry. Evidently excellence *is* historical, *not* transhistorical. Once a putative canon is formed, it exists in a state of constant flux. The guests in the canonical house are continually shuffled from room to room. Broadly, of course, any canon is defined by what it excludes; so changes in the canon look like parts of a larger cycle of inclusion and exclusion. In practice, the cycle's nature is somewhat different. We rarely exclude a poet completely once he has been included for any length of time. A reputation may fluctuate wildly, but it will rarely collapse entirely. Once in, a poet tends to stay in, if only in a small corner of the attic. Getting in is another matter, as we shall see—a matter of meeting the historically specific standards that each literary generation is so easily seduced into thinking "universal," the standards exercised powerfully by each generation's anthologists.

2. Preservation: Elihu Hubbard Smith

When Smith set out to "offer a stronger, and more durable security" to poems otherwise fated to the short life of newspaper clippings, and to win an audience for "many poems, written by the most eminent American Authors . . . known only to a few of their particular acquaintance, and unheard of by the generality of their Countrymen," he was responding to publishing circumstances that made the anthology a genre particularly appropriate to American literature of the period (*AP*, pp. iv, iii). In the late eighteenth and early nineteenth centuries, most poetry appeared only in magazines, and those magazines had short lives. Only two eighteenth-century periodicals, the *New-York Magazine* and the *Massachusetts Magazine*, lasted eight years; the average life of an American magazine in that century was fourteen months. Widely dispersed readership; inadequate supply of affordable, high-quality printing materials; distribution difficulties; lack of advertising support; overdependence on subscriptions that were rarely paid promptly: all these circumstances explain why the early magazines appeared and disappeared at such alarming speed. As the nineteenth century progressed, distribution became easier. Roads and mail service improved, and postal routes were extended. Subscription lists and income from advertising, however, remained small; so magazines continued to blossom and die quickly. Hence, as Fred Lewis Pattee puts it, in "the land of ephemeral periodicals" "there came early the thought of preserving the best of the writings in permanent form."[8]

This attempt to preserve a national literature simultaneously with its creation distinguishes the early American anthologists from their British contemporaries. In America, unlike in England, the survival of the national poetry canon depended largely on the anthologists' success in preserving poetry. Some English anthologies, like Thomas Percy's *Reliques of Ancient English Poetry* (1765), did have preservation as a goal. But Percy wanted to preserve specimens of a particularly ephemeral genre, the ballad; the rest of English poetry was already taken care of. When George Ellis edited *Specimens of the Early English Poets* (1790) and sought to preserve "what is most valuable from the scarcest and least accessible compositions," he had in mind poetry of the tenth century, not of his own.[9] And even Ellis' and Percy's aims were as much historicizing as preservative. Ellis wanted to illustrate "the rise and progress of our language"; Percy wanted to "shew the gradation of our language, exhibit the progress of popular opinions, display the peculiar manners and customs of former ages, or throw light on our earlier classical poets."[10] In America, however, a progressive literary history was something in which to participate in the present, not something to observe about the past. While British editors used their anthologies to review the historical development of an established body of poetry, American editors used theirs to preserve contemporary poems and to record their nation's literary progress as it occurred.

When Smith set out to "preserve" American poetry, however, he faced a conflict of interests. Preservation should have meant including Puritan poetry and a more representative range of Philip Freneau's and Joel Barlow's work. But the Puritans' social ideals conflicted with those of post-Revolutionary America, which saw itself making its own social pattern, not following a God-given pattern. The Declaration of Independence presumed a doctrine of works, not of grace—a conflation, not a separation, of sacred and secular history.[11] Smith had to ask himself this question: Should he choose an eclectic thoroughness, or should he present an ideologically and poetically coherent canon in the service of the Federalist cause? The political situation was volatile enough, and perhaps the pressure (real or imagined) from his friends intense enough, that Smith chose the latter course. Consequently the American poetry canon began to be formalized in a rather surprising way. Instead of preserving a wide and representative accessible canon, which later selections might winnow, Smith began with a narrow, already rigidly selected canon. Preservation was fine, so long as it was the preservation of ideologically acceptable poetry. Whether the later volumes that he planned—cut off by his death in 1796—would have expanded this canon, we cannot know. As it was, America had to wait until Samuel Kettell's *Specimens of American Poetry* (1829) for a historically representative anthology.

Apparently Smith did not have enough confidence in the nation's stability to make a broad selection that embraced conflicting ideologies. His own poetry expressed typical Federalist fears of Jeffersonian democracy; and the other Connecticut Wits, the poets and friends of Smith whom the anthology most fully represents, shared his fears. In one selection Smith made from *The Anarchiad*, a satirical long poem written jointly by Joel Barlow, David Humphreys, John Trumbull, and Lemuel Hopkins to influence the Constitutional Convention in favor of Federalism, the "anonymous" poet warns of

> the certain woe that waits
> The giddy rage of democratic states;
> Whose pop'lar breath, high-blown in restless tide,
> No laws can temper and no reason guide
>
> [*AP*, p. 214]

To control this "giddy rage," the poet offers the Federalist solution of a strong central government: "One potent head, / Must rule your states"

(*AP*, p. 216).[12] Smith reinforced this bias by excluding any politically liberal or Anti-Federalist poetry. Freneau, the most politically inflammatory poet of his age and an Anti-Federalist, is represented by one, apolitical poem, while Barlow is represented by early work written before his alienation from the Connecticut group in the late 1780s.

American Poems also founds the early American poetry canon on regional biases, biases which again suggest a hidden agenda on Smith's part. Although Smith says he intends otherwise, both his collection and Carey's *Beauties of Poetry* amount to regional anthologies. Most of Smith's 250 subscribers came from Connecticut, and both collections heavily favor the Connecticut Wits. Carey gives half his American section to Trumbull, Humphreys, Barlow, and Timothy Dwight, while Smith adds Hopkins and Richard Alsop to this group and similarly gives them half his space.

Smith's and Carey's anthologies were regional or provincial in the sense that all early American poetry was provincial: self-consciously nationalist but lacking indigenous standards, with, in Matthew Arnold's terms, "no centre, no intellectual metropolis." Arnold's essay "The Literary Influence of Academies" is relevant here, because Smith's regional bias can be explained as an attempt to set up Connecticut as an indigenous cultural center with a coherent, authoritative voice. He hoped Connecticut would take over London's role and serve, as Boston did later, an academy's function for the rest of America: "a supposed centre of correct information, correct judgment, correct taste."[13] Thus he used his anthology to try to establish not only a politically narrow canon but also a source of standards by which future poetry might be evaluated. Like any anthology editor, Smith performed silent criticism through what he included and excluded, and, like any editor, he performed that criticism consciously. Even when, like Smith, the editor is mainly preserving an accessible canon, his critical judgment is deliberate and value-laden, not innocent and neutral.

3. Historicizing and Moralizing: Samuel Kettell, Rufus Griswold

During the 1820s America's rampant literary nationalism brought a huge explosion of poetry. In 1822 a British anthology, *Specimens of the American Poets,* featured only 8 poets, with additional fugitive verse, in a book of 283 pages. By the end of the decade, in 1829, Kettell's hugely ambitious *Specimens of American Poetry* comprised three volumes and included the work of 189 poets from Cotton Mather to John Greenleaf Whittier. Kettell faced a monumental task. No complete list of authors was available (Kettell remedies this by recording 429 books of American poetry published since the 1640 Massachusetts Bay Colony edition of the Psalms); texts were not yet collected in public libraries and were therefore hard to get. In gathering this material, he expanded the limited range of the accessible canon more than any anthologist before him and created the first scholarly anthology.

Kettell's goals resemble those of the earlier anthologists: furthering the cause of national literature, gaining an audience for the poetry, preserving texts. He also introduced a new goal to American anthologizing, by claiming historical inclusiveness for his text: "a general and comprehensive view" of what American poets have accomplished. As part of this "general view," Kettell redeems much Puritan poetry. His introduction reviews American poetry from the Bay Psalm Book to the Revolution. In his introduction and his text, he rescues over twenty pre-Revolutionary poets, and grants Benjamin Tompson, born in 1642, "the distinction of being the first native American poet" (*SAP*, 1:v, xxxvii). In discussing Puritan poetry, Kettell permanently broadened the boundaries of what constituted "American" poetry and created a precedent that later anthologists could not ignore, even if they dismissed most of the poetry. Griswold's historical introduction to *The Poets and Poetry of America*, for instance, discusses the same pre-Revolutionary poets as Kettell, in exactly the same order.

Kettell's insertion of Puritan poets into the national canon reflects the changes in political thinking that had occurred since Smith's time. In 1829 most American writers were still obsessed with achieving literary independence from Britain. But as Freneau pointed out, "political and . . . literary independence . . . [are] two very different things—the first was accomplished in about seven years, the latter will not be completely effected, perhaps, in as many centuries."[14] Kettell himself bemoaned America's continued reliance on English models: "The cultivation of literary talent has . . . been retarded by the state of dependence as to literature, in which we have continued, to the writers of Great Britain" (*SAP*, 1:xlvii). But about affairs of state, Americans felt in 1829 what they had felt less confident of in the 1790s—that their republican experiment had succeeded, that political independence was assured. Given this confidence, Kettell did not feel compelled, as Smith had in 1793, to define American poetry by the political principles it adhered to. He could comfortably accord the Puritans, geographically Americans but politically English, a place in American literary history.[15]

To compile not a critical but a historical anthology, covering the whole of American poetry, became a typical approach for the American anthologist, and one that contrasts sharply with the British tendency to select only the best poems.[16] In a historical collection, literary merit is not the overriding criterion for including a poem. Kettell included some pieces because they afford "some insight into the spirit and temper of the times" (*SAP*, 1:iv). Inevitably, dozens of poets appear who have since been consigned to oblivion. But canon-formation is a reductive process, a process of choosing a final few from an initial many, and Kettell's anthology made these initial many more available.

Kettell's ambitions were matched by Griswold, America's first professional anthologist, in *The Poets and Poetry of America* (1842). Griswold, an opportunistic but talented synthesizer, combined all the best features of previous anthologies in his text: a wide range of poets (183 by the time R. H. Stoddard supervised the 1872 edition), lengthy selections, and thorough, if sometimes inaccurate, biographical and critical notices. By 1842 the American public was ready for another major poetry anthology. The collections that had appeared in the thirteen years since Kettell's anthology were limited in either range or depth,[17] and during those years some important new poets had appeared. Henry Wadsworth Longfellow, James Russell Lowell, and Oliver Wendell Holmes had all published their first books of poetry; Edgar Allan Poe, his second; and Whittier, a mixed book of poetry and prose.

Griswold's goals follow Kettell's: to present poetry that is otherwise not easily available and to "exhibit the progress and condition of Poetry in the United States." That condition was one of plenitude, and Griswold exhibited it amply. In doing so, Griswold, like Kettell, faced a conflict between historical range and literary merit. As if to anticipate charges that he lacked discrimination, he says in the preface to the first edition that "the judicious critic will be more likely to censure me for the wide range of my selections than for any omissions."[18] This "wide range" derives from the impulse to include, for the sake of historical representativeness, inferior work along with that of greater merit. Commenting on the first edition, Griswold says, in the preface to the eighth edition, that he "did not consider all the contents of the volume genuine Poetry" and that he "accepted more that was comparatively poor" than good.[19] In basing his text on historical as well as aesthetic considerations, Griswold used a strategy that necessarily admits work of lesser quality. Exhibiting the historical range of American poetry meant exhibiting it at less than its best.

The acceptable limits of this historical breadth were defined by the conviction that American poetry should be represented by specimens of the utmost moral purity, that poetry's function is inspirational. Such moral rectitude became one principle of selection in many nineteenth-century anthologies. Certainly it propels most of Griswold's work.[20] In his *Gems from American Female Poets* (1842), the first anthology of solely American women poets, Griswold asserted that "nearly all American poetry . . . is of the purest moral character" and that it showed "propriety and beauty of thought." A year later, in his school text *Readings in American Poetry,* he reminded his young readers that "a distinguishing characteristic of our poetry is its freedom from all licentiousness."[21] And in *The Poets and Poetry of America,* his most important book, he argued that "the office of the poet" is to create beauty and that "the sense of beauty, next to the miraculous divine suasion, is the means through which the human character is purified and elevated." Hence, although his critical notices counted Freneau the best of the Revolution-era poets, he excluded Freneau's political verses because they lacked "chasteness."[22] (That Griswold meant moral, not stylistic, chasteness, we can infer from the anthology's moralizing tone and from the formally conventional, or stylistically "chaste," nature of Freneau's work.) The principle that American poetry "is of the purest moral character" delayed the acceptance of any poet who appeared to violate it, as Whitman later did, and thus it effectively controlled the moral and intellectual range of subject matter in canonical poetry. No poetry was admitted to the burgeoning canon unless it supported the moral status quo.

Other idiosyncratic biases besides morality propelled Griswold's shaping of the canon. His dislike of the South led him to include only two southern poets and to weight his canon heavily toward New England. This led, appropriately, to charges of sectionalism. The second charge most frequently leveled at Griswold, again appropriately, was that of partiality to personal friends. Griswold's friend Charles Fenno Hoffman, for instance, was for years the most fully represented poet in the anthology. Although he included a substantial amount of Emerson's work, Griswold's distaste for transcendentalism probably turned him away from Henry David Thoreau, whose poetry Emerson had recommended in a letter. And his conviction that "the literature of women . . . is, for the most part, sauzle" caused him to underrepresent women poets; they were in fact weak poets but no more so than most of their male contemporaries.[23] This combination of tastes meant that Griswold proposed an extremely homogeneous canon. His work suggested that American poetry had no tolerance of eccentric philosophies, that it was primarily written by men, and that it was created solely in New York and New England.

Read widely, Griswold's anthology became very influential. It went through seventeen editions in fourteen years, and Stoddard was still refining it in 1872. Frank Luther Mott accounts it one of the best-selling books of the 1840s.[24] The anthology achieved this popularity and influence through its combination of nationalist fervor and moral weight—a combination that captured precisely what its readers looked for in their poetry—and through Griswold's ability to reflect both popular and critical taste. By repeating the poets gathered in earlier anthologies, his anthology perpetuated whatever canon had been established so far. Griswold selected familiar names from among the early poets of the Republic, deriving this part of his canon from the 1790s' anthologies. He began with Freneau and otherwise limited his eighteenth-century selections to works by Dwight, Trumbull, Humphreys, and Barlow, and one poem by Alsop. In his historical introduction, however, he flattered his readers by privileging contemporary American poetry. The representative historical impulse would not allow him to exclude the early poets, but he still asserted that no poetry before Freneau's was worth preserving in bulk. Thus Griswold offered an early version of the now traditional view that each generation of American poets begins anew—a position guaranteed to appeal to readers who held devoutly the doctrines of manifest destiny and of the westward course of empire.

In his selection of early American poetry, Griswold supported these doctrines by preserving the canon of names while radically altering the canon of individual poems. For example, he contrived to make Smith's Federalists look like solid nineteenth-century Democrats. Smith prints thirty poems by the eighteenth-century poets I named above. Griswold, in his 1847 edition, prints thirty-two poems by the same group, but with only one overlap, Dwight's "Columbia." He excludes any poem which suggests a remotely anti-Democratic politics (Dwight's "Address of the Genius of Columbia," Humphreys' "Mount Vernon: An Ode" and "The Genius of America," all of which Smith included) and supplements his selections with work that foregrounds America's independence from England. He selects from Dwight's "Greenfield Hill" a passage that sets England and America at odds, and, to stress the point, he titles the passage "England and America."

In "What Is a Classic?" T. S. Eliot speaks to Griswold's difficulties and those of all anthologists when he observes that a canonical text, a "classic," stands out only in retrospect and that contemporary evaluations usually fail to recognize it: "It is only by hindsight, and in historical perspective, that a classic can be known as such," and the contemporary canon "confounds the contingent with the essential, the ephemeral with the permanent."[25] Any anthologist who seeks historical breadth includes much of the contingent and the ephemeral; Griswold is no exception. A modern reader of Griswold's early editions would disagree with his equal ranking of now forgotten writers alongside the Fireside Poets— Longfellow, Bryant, Lowell, Holmes, Whittier—poets who themselves look minor today. Yet while Griswold rarely expands his selections for the lesser poets, the Fireside Poets all enjoy increased representation through his successive editions, so we can sketch an emerging nineteenth-century canon from his work. And while we should be wary of granting our contemporary sense of the canon too much weight, Griswold deserves credit for raising his estimate of two poets whom recent scholars would rank above the Fireside group: Emerson and Poe.[26] The selection from Emerson, as he produced more poetry and published his first complete volume in 1846, jumped from five poems in 1842 to fifteen in 1855, and Poe's showing jumped from three poems in 1842 to sixteen in 1855— this despite Poe's feud with Griswold and the editor's posthumous character assassination of him.

4. Universal Excellence: Bryant, Emerson, Whittier

After the Civil War, anthologists began to operate more and more on two assumptions: that a stable canon of American poets, complete with greater and lesser lights and reflected in the evolving editions of *The Poets and Poetry of America,* was emerging as a natural product of "time" and "history," and that an undefined community of readers agreed upon that canon. Although anthology editors rarely discussed how this consensus on the canon had been reached, they assumed it to rest on an important new criterion of selection introduced to American poetry anthologies by Charles A. Dana in his well-received *Household Book of Poetry,* first published in 1858 and still being reprinted in 1919. That criterion was the exercise of absolute rather than historically relative critical judgment. Dana attempts "to judge every piece by its poetical merit solely, without regard to the name, nationality, or epoch of its author," a new step for an American editor and a major shift from Griswold's willing inclusion of much "that was comparatively poor."[27] Earlier British anthologists had exercised absolute judgment as their main selective principle; Americans had not. Dana felt, however, that American literature no longer had to have its very existence questioned or be excused in the company of British literature with the argument that its interest was merely historical. Yet even when judged by "poetical merit," his canon of nineteenth-century American poets follows closely the path that the relative reputations of the period were already taking. It consists, in descending order of representation, of Longfellow, Bryant, Emerson, Whittier, and Lowell. Like most anthologists, except Griswold, Dana places Poe well below the New England poets and does not include Whitman in his 1858 or 1868 texts. (Whitman's Civil War poetry was accepted into the 1882 edition, presumably because of its subject matter.) In 1919 the text still did not include Herman Melville or Emily Dickinson.

To justify his canon, Dana appealed to an invisible network of civilized readers, to "the unanimous verdict of the intelligent."[28] The same appeal, stated in similarly vague terms, underlies three anthologies edited within a few years of each other by three of the important New England poets: Bryant's *Library of Poetry and Song* (1870), Emerson's *Parnassus* (1874), and Whittier's *Songs of Three Centuries* (1875). Bryant includes all poets "acknowledged by the intelligent and cultivated to be great." Whittier bases his selections on "the verdicts of Time" and of "critical authorities." Emerson's title assumes an achieved canon, and his preface only mystifies the process by which a poet reaches the Parnassian peak. "The world" selects the "best" poems, "and we select from these our best."[29] Who "we" are remains unidentified. But this mystification does not obscure the fact that, since Griswold first compiled *The Poets and Poetry of America* in 1842, a significant change has occurred in how the poetic canon is selected. By the mid-1870s, editors wanted not merely American poems but the best American poems, poems to stand alongside the best British poems.

What constituted the "best," however, contained no surprises. Because their own status was so great, the judgments about the "best" that Bryant, Emerson, and Whittier made in their anthologies had great influence.

And those anthologies kept the canon stable, self-perpetuating. Bryant, Emerson, and Whittier all agree that the six most important poets in America are themselves, Longfellow, Lowell, and Holmes. They rank Poe below even minor, forgotten figures, and all exclude Whitman and Melville—despite the fact that in 1855 Emerson had been one of the few people to herald the achievement of *Leaves of Grass* and that selections from *Leaves of Grass* and *Battle-Pieces* had appeared in the 1872 edition of *The Poets and Poetry of America.*

The consensus on the American poetry canon that these poet-anthologists and Dana assume did not rest merely on assertion. In part it took the form of literate conversation: critics, poets, publishers, magazine editors all knew each other and formed a tight-knit literary community around Boston and, secondarily, New York. The consensus also had some history to back it up and a sound basis in the critical opinion and popular taste of the time. In the early years of the *Democratic Review,* for instance, different critics on four separate occasions had ranked Bryant as America's leading poet.[30] While some reviewers had carped at Griswold's catholicity, few had argued with his opinion of the period's major names. Jay Martin, in *Harvests of Change,* has documented thoroughly the high popular regard in which the New England poets were held, and as their careers progressed, critical opinion supported further their view of themselves.[31] Assessing American poetry in 1866, the *Nation* considered Emerson, Bryant, Longfellow, and Lowell the four best living American poets, followed by Whittier, with Holmes part of a somewhat lesser but still worthy group. In 1885 a *Critic* plebiscite suggested that the popular canon had shifted to favor Holmes as the leading living poet, followed by Lowell and then Whittier. The relative ranks had changed temporarily but not the names. Predictably, Whitman ranked only twentieth.[32]

That these poets used their anthologies to preserve or enhance their own reputations is hardly surprising. That they showed such a narrow sense of what they would admit into the canon which their anthologies reflected is somewhat more surprising but still explicable: their claims to transhistorical excellence actually rested on historical grounds. To offset the disorienting effects of the Civil War and of rapid economic expansion, the postbellum reading public wanted a stable, ordered art. (In *Parnassus* Emerson talked of "the necessity of printing in every collection many masterpieces which all English-speaking men have agreed in admiring," a necessity perhaps felt most powerfully in a restless time.)[33] Both formally and in their conservation of the European literary tradition (Longfellow translated the *Divine Comedy,* Bryant the *Iliad* and *Odyssey,* Emerson the *Vita Nuova*), the New England poets fit this bill; Whitman's radical experimentation did not. As Martin puts it, these poets "refused to threaten their culture with the new in literature, since Americans were, as they believed, too distracted by the new in life."[34] The New England poets stood for continuity in a disrupted time.

5. *Early Revisionism: Edmund Clarence Stedman*

One stage of canon-formation in American poetry had culminated in the Bryant, Emerson, and Whittier anthologies. At the same time, another stage had already slowly begun, as the claims of Poe and Whitman began to be recognized. In *American Poems: A Collection of Representative Verse* (1872), the English editor William Michael Rossetti proposed a very different balance of reputations from that which had obtained previously, by representing Whitman—whose English reputation far outstripped his American one—as easily the most important American poet of his time.[35] Poe also receives more attention than ever before, while, with the exception of Emerson and Whittier, the New England poets are relegated to minor status. In *Poetry of America* (1878), another English editor, W. J. Linton, grants Whitman as much or more space than all the New England poets; a portrait of Whitman forms his frontispiece. With the appearance of these texts in America, then, the first successful challenges to the nineteenth-century canon came not from the poets who might legitimately claim to have been neglected unfairly, nor from their American apologists, but from two editors who were distant from American literary debate.

The appeal of Poe's aestheticism to the Pre-Raphaelite Rossetti is clear. And when George Santayana coined the term "genteel tradition" in 1911, he explained why an English editor, working outside America's genteel literary circles, might value Whitman so highly. This editor "is looking for what may have arisen in America to express, not the polite and conventional American mind, but the spirit and the inarticulate principles that animate the community."[36] It is not surprising that, at the height of the genteel tradition, English opinion should carry such weight in America. When a history of the genteel tradition characterizes "the genteel endeavor" by its reaction to New England Brahminism and by its Romantic literary program, its desire for a literature "more inclined to self-expression than to self-restraint," one can see why Whitman began to receive a hearing.[37] But the influence of gentility also explains why the limits on that hearing took some years to be lifted. Gentility can tolerate only a certain amount of barbaric yawping about the great "En-Masse," and by most genteel criteria Whitman was just what Santayana described him as: "the one American writer who has left the genteel tradition entirely behind."[38]

This gradual revaluation of Whitman, and to a lesser extent Poe, constitutes the anthologies' main contribution to canon-formation in the last quarter of the nineteenth century. It was forcefully confirmed by Stedman, one of the period's most influential critics, in his voluminous *American Anthology, 1787–1900* (1900). Just as it needs its own literary history, every generation needs its own anthology. Stedman's was the first large anthology by a prestigious American editor since 1875, and the first of solely American poetry since Griswold's 1872 edition. This, combined with Stedman's reputation as a critic, assured the book substantial influence. Despite Longfellow's popularity, Stedman says, it is Emerson, Poe, and Whitman "from whom the old world had most to learn," and he gives them appropriately full coverage. He writes prophetically that "years from now, it will be matter of fact that their influences were as lasting as those of any poets of this century."[39]

Underlying Stedman's judgment is a radical shift from earlier anthologies in the criteria used for canonizing poets. By Stedman's time the tendency to politicize and moralize poetry had largely dropped out of American anthologies. The country's sense of political and literary accomplishment no longer needed the support of anthologies documenting the unique national characteristics and moral purity of American verse. The last collection to use moral virtue as a selective principle was Henry T. Coates' *Fireside Encyclopedia of Poetry* (1878). In that same year, Linton wrote that "hymns and 'religious' poems . . . have been purposely excluded as out of place in such a collection as [*Poetry of America*]."[40] Those whom Stedman saw as the best American poets did not define or confirm their culture's dominant values but revolted against them. Stedman preferred "Poe's renaissance of art for beauty's sake, and Whitman's revolt against social and literary traditions" to Lowell's "homiletic mood." He may, indeed, have derived this suspicion of the didactic from Poe, who he thought "gave a saving grace of melody and illusion . . . to English didactics" (*AA*, pp. xxv, xxiv). Hence, although he still considers Bryant the "progenitor" of American poetry and represents the whole New England group equally and more thoroughly than we might today, Stedman brings Whitman and Poe to the fore of his canon. The earlier rebel Freneau, after suffering from many anthologies that considered poetry before Bryant merely a historical curiosity, also enjoys what has become a lasting resuscitation. And Dickinson gets the space she would not receive again for years. In the absence of easily available editions of Dickinson's work—one factor that delayed her entrance into the canon—Stedman did much to remind later readers of her existence and importance. Except for a predictable overrepresentation of his contemporaries, then, Stedman's choices reflect more closely than any previous anthology our contemporary sense of the American poetry canon through the late nineteenth century.[41]

Stedman's praise for Whitman's "revolt against social and literary traditions" foreshadowed the split between cultivated and popular taste that came to characterize modernism. Since the mid-1870s, fiction had come to dominate the book market at poetry's expense. Stedman saw that this situation showed the "public indifference to the higher forms of poetry" (*AA*, p. xxxi). He and most subsequent anthologists responded by emphatically separating popular and cultivated taste. In 1865 the best poetry was defined largely by popular taste: John W. S. Hows used for his *Golden Leaves from the American Poets* "poems that have, by general acceptance, become identified in the hearts of the People as the choicest and noblest specimens of American National Poetry." In 1912, by contrast, Thomas R. Lounsbury defied in his *Yale Book of American Verse* "the wretchedness of taste displayed by the average man."[42]

Texts such as Lounsbury's *Yale Book, The Chief American Poets* (1905) edited by Curtis Hidden Page of Dartmouth, and *American Poems* (1905) edited by Augustus White Long of Princeton show teachers of literature becoming more responsible for overseeing the canon in the two decades after 1900. The power to direct taste began to shift from individual editors to an institution—the university. These texts suggest that Stedman's revaluations took some time to catch on. Whitman's reputation still fluctuates, and Dickinson does not yet consistently hold a high place. Other important names, however, have become relatively fixed: the New England poets and Poe form the core of the canon. These academic anthologies paradoxically embrace Stedman's values while ignoring his canon. Far from reaffirming popular values and taste, like most earlier anthologists, an editor like Long contrasts the often commercial and popularizing purpose of a nineteenth-century anthology with a book that can "serve as an introduction to the systematic study of American poetry." Yet these anthologists, while demeaning popular taste, generally accepted the canon of poets which that taste had established. They did not significantly change the nineteenth-century canon's makeup; they had simply found a new way to validate the old poetry.

6. Revisionism Continued: Bliss Carman vs. F. O. Matthiessen

This establishment of the pre–twentieth-century canon left modern anthologists free to concentrate on gathering contemporary poetry, often narrowly specified areas of contemporary poetry. They considered Stedman to have taken care of poetry before the twentieth century. Many modernist anthologies were coterie texts that mainly influenced other poets: Ezra Pound's *Des Imagistes* (1914), Amy Lowell's three-volume *Some Imagist Poets* (1915, 1916, 1917), Alfred Kreymborg's *Others* (1916, 1917, 1919). Used in this way, anthologies can become tools of a poetic program, disseminating ideas that are also contained in critical essays, like Pound's imagist manifestos, and thus helping to shift critical thought. Other anthologies of the period— Harriet Monroe and Alice Corbin Henderson's *New Poetry* (1917), Conrad Aiken's *Modern American Poets* (1922), even Louis Untermeyer's quite populist (and certainly popular) *Modern American Poetry: An Introduction* (1919, with seven editions through 1950)—gathered a wider range of poets but shared assumptions similar to the smaller, coterie texts. The central assumption was one that Stedman had introduced to thinking about the canon, an assumption that has become almost a critical article of faith: that the best American poets react against rather than support the poetic and cultural values of their times. Modernist anthologies typically collected poets who wrote against contemporary poetic trends, poets who later became canonized as the major modernists: Pound, Eliot, William Carlos Williams, Marianne Moore, Wallace Stevens.

Stedman's and the modernist anthologies, then, heralded a profound shift in how we evaluate poetry—a shift in the principles by which a canon is selected. Nineteenth-century anthologists praised poetically conservative work; after Stedman, editors began increasingly to value the poetically innovative. Whereas nineteenth-century anthologies tended to reflect and even celebrate popular taste, the modernist anthologies programmatically deviated from it. Kreymborg takes his combative title *Others* from a terse epigraph that opposes new to familiar styles: "The old expressions are with us always, and there are always others." Earlier anthologies stressed how American they were; twentieth-century anthologies stress how up-to-date they are. "New" or "modern" becomes a polemical as much as a temporal category in titles like *The New Poetry* (1917), *Modern American Poetry* (1919), *New Poets of England and America* (1957), *The New American Poetry* (1960), *The New Poetry* (1962), *The New Modern Poetry* (1967)—all a long way from George B. Cheever humbly calling his 1831 collection *The American Common-place Book of Poetry*.

Most modern anthologists were revisionists. Pound, Lowell, Kreymborg, Monroe, Aiken: all used their anthologies to propose a canon written in defiance of inherited poetic norms. (This spirit of defiance partly accounts for the modernist tendency to choose not Freneau or Bryant but Whitman and Dickinson as the progenitors of American poetry.) Since they no longer had to prove the existence of a national literature or set up a national canon from scratch, they could move canon-formation into its final stage, that of reevaluating the received body of texts. They agreed that the literary category "American poetry" was safely established, while they also shared a sense that that established poetry did not speak to modern social or aesthetic concerns. This shared view gave the modern anthologists some common ground and helps explain their revisionist impulse. But their common ground aside, these editors pursued their revision of the poetic canon from a variety of positions. In *American Poetry, 1671–1928* (1929), for example, Aiken dismissed "purely historical considerations" and asserted that "the aesthetic judgment . . . is the only sound basis for [editorial] procedure." While he admits the difficulty of evaluating his contemporaries, Aiken does not admit that aesthetic judgment itself is a "historical consideration."[43] Monroe, on the other hand, viewed American poetry as much from a historical as from an aesthetic angle. While she founds modern poetry on the aesthetic revolution of Whitman's and Dickinson's prosodic experiments—a view of these poets which did not receive wide currency until surprisingly late, in the 1930s—she does not claim to assess what parts of American poetry's subsequent experimentation will have lasting value. It is all temporarily useful, she says, as "an assault against prejudice."[44] Here she aligns herself with the dominant American critical tradition of viewing poetry historically rather than absolutely. Her view recalls the assumption behind Griswold's nationalist anthologies: if the poetry serves the anthologist's purpose at a particular point in cultural history, its transhistorical quality is secondary. But while Griswold risked collecting ephemera because he wanted a representative anthology, Monroe risked doing so as part of an attack on the inherited canon, on the very poetry that Griswold had gathered.

Since a tradition makes an inert antagonist if it has no defenders, revisionist editors thrive on live conservative opposition. No debate on the canon would arise, nor would anthologies compete, if the revisionist editor did not have a more sanguine opposite number. The final stage of canon-formation, which I have called revision, actually involves an ongoing conflict between conserving and revising the canon. This conflict produces difficult choices for the anthologist, who will usually feel compelled to come down on one side or the other. After a selective canon has been formed, every anthologist faces the choice of maintaining or trying to change the canon. In the twentieth century the conflict plays itself out most vividly in two successive editions of *The Oxford Book of American Verse*, the first edited by Carman and the second by Matthiessen.

Carman's *Oxford Book of American Verse* appeared in 1927. Since no inclusive historical anthology had received wide circulation since Stedman's, and no anthologist had attempted to combine the established canon and the new poetry, Carman's was an important publication. Carman does not try to be as encyclopedic as Stedman was, or as thorough as Monroe and Henderson were for the modern period in *The New Poetry*, but he does claim to skim the whole field. The modernist rejection of nineteenth-century verse, however, made it almost impossible for a historical anthologist like Carman to cover both past and present representatively. If he accepted the established nineteenth-century canon, he accepted a poetry that conflicted with contemporary critical taste. If he changed the earlier canon, he failed in his goal of historical inclusiveness. Carman made the former choice. Although he did accept Whitman and Dickinson as central to nineteenth-century American poetry, he refused to rank them any higher than Longfellow or Bryant. He relegated Holmes, Lowell, and Whittier somewhat to suit twentieth-century tastes. But these changes simply juggle with an established body of poetry. They subtly modify rather than change the canon. Generally, Carman does not participate in the modernist shuffling of nineteenth-century reputations. As a predictable corollary, by today's standards he spectacularly underestimates modernist poetry. With critical opinion and other good anthologies to guide him, he nevertheless includes no Eliot, Williams, Moore, Stevens, Hart Crane, or e. e. cummings; only one Pound poem; and no black poets beyond Paul Dunbar. Carman's surprising view of what differentiated the new from the old poetry also contributed to his critical myopia. He saw nineteenth-century American poetry as "imbued with a doleful spirit, or with a desperate resignation at best," while more recent work showed a "valiant and joyous spirit."[45] To consider the spirit of the age as valiant and joyous left little room for *The Waste Land* or *Hugh Selwyn Mauberley*.

Against Carman's more conservative tendencies, Matthiessen set the revisionism of the second *Oxford Book of American Verse* (1950), which brought one of the most radical redefinitions of the canon ever. As an academic editor, Matthiessen was in a position to institutionalize the canonical revisions proposed by the nonacademic modern anthologists like Monroe, Aiken, and Pound. His anthology made the revised canon acceptable for public consumption. He redefined the canon in almost every way imaginable: the canon of individual poems, of genres, of subject matter, and of names. That redefinition, by diminishing many nineteenth-century reputations, helped shape the nineteenth-century canon that we hold today. Matthiessen added 28 poets to Carman's selection and cut a remarkable 147. He demolished the nineteenth century, cutting 91 poets between Lowell and William Vaughn Moody and reducing selections from Bryant, Holmes, Lowell, and Whittier to a mere handful. He increased the representation of those poets on whom he had centered *American Renaissance* (1941): Emerson (8 poems added), Poe (10), Thoreau (4), Whitman (24), Dickinson (27). He also bolstered Edwin Arlington Robinson (18), Edgar Lee Masters (15), Robert Frost (33), Carl Sandburg (14), and Pound (18). The names that Matthiessen added to Carman would make a strong anthology in themselves: Anne Bradstreet, Jones Very, Melville, Eliot, Crane, Moore, Stevens, cummings.

Thus Matthiessen manipulated the canon of names, considering Poe and Whitman the pivotal nineteenth-century figures and confirming the modernist reputations established in Monroe and Henderson's, Untermeyer's, and Aiken's anthologies. His preface corroborates the revisionist impulse implied in all this surgery. Of Longfellow he says "my one aim was to smash the plaster bust of his dead reputation, to eliminate the hackneyed inflated one-time favorites" and to rescue some decent poetry.[46] From Lowell and Holmes he also cut traditional anthology pieces that he considered more popular than good. Like Pound's *Des Imagistes*, but on a more influential scale, Matthiessen's *Oxford Book of American Verse* pushed a critical program, furthering the modernist imperative to wring the neck of rhetoric.

Along with cutting the merely popular, Matthiessen tried to use longer poems, to combat the effect he believed anthologies have of persuading readers that poetry consists solely of lyrics. On this point Matthiessen withstood a strong tradition. Generally, anthologies defined not only what poets but also what *kind* of poem should be canonized, and they defined poetry as lyric. The first critical overview of the American long poem did not appear till the third chapter of Roy Harvey Pearce's *Continuity of American Poetry* in 1961. The British *Specimens of the American Poets* (1822) and Horace E. Scudder's *American Poems* (1879) were early exceptions to the lyric emphasis. But Francis Turner Palgrave's *Golden Treasury,* perhaps the most widely read poetry anthology ever, used only lyrics. In *Songs of Three Centuries* Whittier had suggested that "brief lyrical selections" formed the most appropriate reading for the " 'snatched leisure' " of busy Americans. Many giftbook anthologies presented poetry as something to be dipped into rather than read carefully, while Poe's famous dictum circulated the idea that a genuine poem could not have more than a hundred lines.[47]

Matthiessen, however, adhered to a rule of "not too many sonnets" and thus redeemed a number of subgenres which require length for their effect. He included long narrative poems (Whittier's "Snow-Bound" and Robert Penn Warren's "Ballad of Billie Potts"), philosophical meditations (Stevens' "Comedian as the Letter C"), and spiritual autobiographies (Whitman's "Song of Myself"). Palgrave, by contrast, had excluded narrative, descriptive, and didactic poetry. Matthiessen's commitment to length also reintroduced historical and social subjects to the canon. He excerpted Melville's neglected *Clarel* for its "searching thought upon the dangers threatening American society" and used lengthy extracts from *Hugh Selwyn Mauberley* and *The Bridge* to contrast and supplement the vision of American history contained in "Song of Myself."[48]

7. Teaching and the Contemporary Canon: The Norton Anthology of Poetry

The tug-of-war that Carman and Matthiessen act out between opposing principles for canonizing poetry has become a prominent fact of literary life. In 1960 Robert Lowell commented on the state of American poetry: "Two poetries are now competing, a cooked and a raw. The cooked, marvelously expert, often seems laboriously concocted to be tasted and digested by a graduate seminar. The raw, huge blood-dripping gobbets of unseasoned experience are dished up for midnight listeners. There is a poetry that can only be studied, and a poetry that can only be declaimed, a poetry of pedantry and a poetry of scandal." Lowell added coyly, "I exaggerate, of course."[49] But exaggeration or no, critics of the period accepted Lowell's division of American poetry into "raw" and "cooked," and his distinction was highlighted by what one writer recently called a "cold war" between two competing anthologies: the "cooked" *New Poets of England and America* (1957) edited by Donald Hall, Robert Pack, and Louis Simpson, and the "raw" *New American Poetry* (1960) edited by Donald Allen.[50] The names had changed; the terms of debate had not.

The twenty-odd years since Allen's collection have seen the publication of a vast number of special-interest anthologies and a proliferation of critical methods aimed at opening the accessible canon to historically disenfranchised groups. These trends should warn us against holding rigidly to separable "stages" in canon-formation, fixed in a sequence long since complete. The impulses I have described in this essay—preservation, nationalism and historicizing, the belief in transhistorical excellence, revisionism as a reaction to the established canon—chart accurately how the American poetry canon developed. At the same time, some of these impulses still fuel debate over both the received and the contemporary canon. Many anthologists of black poetry have wanted to preserve black culture's early poetry, trace its generally ignored historical development, and encourage a racial pride that resembles mid–nineteenth-century nationalism. And even in an age of mass reprinting, Allen assumed that texts can be lost in ephemeral little magazines and need to be preserved.[51]

Two main kinds of anthology have emerged both as part of and in response to this pluralism. One is the teaching anthology, to which I will return later. The other continues the tradition of the revisionist anthology designed to increase awareness of particular noncanonical poetry. In its tone this anthology recalls the polemics of Monroe and Henderson's *New Poetry* or Pound's *Des Imagistes*. It is not primarily intended for the classroom, even though it may be used there. The editors avoid the scholarly apparatus of notes and introductions. They are rarely scholars, more often poets— poets aiming not at the aesthetic and social orthodoxy that Bryant, Emerson, and Whittier promoted, however, but at heterodoxy. From their inception, American poetry anthologies have usually pushed a political or literary program, so the contemporary revisionist anthology is not a new *kind* of anthology. Only recently, however, have the revisionist programs that reached a wide public become so many and so vocal, and their number reflects the nonacademic anthologists' increased power to shift the canon.

Many of these polemics from editors outside the academy have succeeded. Anthologists like Allen have gained their favored poets admission into the canon. Allen's "raw" poets are represented almost equally with Hall, Pack, and Simpson's "cooked" poets in the major academic anthologies today.[52] Yet in one sense these poets enter the canon as the victims of a catch-22. Much of the interest and vigor of a book like *The New American Poetry* lay in its extracanonical status. The book's tone and contents assailed the walls of the academically established canon, eventually broke them down, and Charles Olson, Robert Duncan, and such were admitted. But when these poets became tentatively canonized, their combative rhetoric was assimilated by the cultural institution it assailed and lost much of its point. As numerous studies of the avant-garde show, this is the likely fate of any extracanonical group or individual seeking the acknowledgment of canonization.

This canonization is represented and furthered by the teaching anthology, so the modern revisionist collection and the teaching anthology depend on each other. The revisionist editor needs the teaching canon to react against; the teaching editor needs to accommodate extracanonical work if he is to represent the current state of poetry with any accuracy. When a teaching anthology such as *The Norton Anthology of Poetry* canonizes poetic outsiders, however, it renders their work culturally and intellectually harmless. What one might call this detoxification of potent work has two sources: the interpretive community's survival instinct, and the fact that if a pluralist literature is to be taught, it must be systematized. The academy ensures its own survival and that of "literature" by adopting a more pluralist canon. Since the number of possible readings of the "classic" texts must eventually approach a dead end, a revised canon provides new texts for exegesis and keeps alive the whole interpretive enterprise.[53] The teaching anthology is one tool of systematization and of the academy's self-perpetuation.

What problems in selection do the editors of a teaching anthology face in trying to adopt a pluralist canon? More, I suggest, than the polemically minded editor of an extracanonical anthology faces. That editor includes what fits his ideological, poetic, or intellectual program. His program simplifies his choices by narrowing them. This is less true of the editor of the teaching anthology. If he wants to create an inclusive, representative text, a useful teaching tool, that goal complicates his choices. He must respond to heterogeneous audiences of conflicting literary and political interests. He also faces the conflict, which dates back at least to Griswold, between representativeness and quality, in a time when to be representative means to include not just many poems but many different kinds of poem. Simultaneously he faces heavy pressure to expand the canon and heavy pressure to mount a "defence of the classics" against the incursions of what some critics still luridly describe as "feminist *vers libre*" and "obscene black anti-verse."[54] And whereas a nineteenth-century editor like Griswold shared with his age a limited range of aesthetic and ideological criteria for judging poetry, the editor of the contemporary teaching anthology has no such consensus on which to lean.

The *Norton*'s editors have responded to these problems by embracing a heterodoxy that incorporates but also defuses previously extracanonical poetry. In updating the anthology in 1975 from its 1970 edition, they self-consciously announce their text's liberal, pluralist credentials: "Four new black poets amplify the presentation of that tradition" and "there are now twice as many women poets as before."[55] But this surface diversity hides a deeper homogeneity. The *Norton* includes thirty American poets born after Olson in 1910, most of them still alive and working. Richard Ellmann and Robert O'Clair's *Norton Anthology of Modern Poetry* (1973) prints twenty-six of those thirty, and Ellmann's *New Oxford Book of American Verse* (1976) reprints twenty-one. For the *Norton*'s editors, unlike for many readers of contemporary poetry, the canon is not so diverse that it can't be agreed upon. Some of the anthologized poets—Imamu Amiri Baraka, Don L. Lee, Nikki Giovanni, Adrienne Rich—have written poetry sharply critical of American culture. But reading the *Norton,* no one would know it. The book uses poems that stay within acceptable limits of vitriol and thus serves the same function as many nineteenth-century anthologies: maintaining the cultural status quo. A gesture like the inclusion of "four new black poets" partially responds to social pressures to open the canon while fundamentally preserving the canon's hegemonic function.

This function is served further by the quality the *Norton* has of being produced not by people but by a corporation. Because it has not one or two editors but six, it bears the stamp of no individual's personality. This oracular, *ex vacuo* quality, typical of many teaching anthologies with multiple editors, lends the text much of its authority and reduces the likelihood of debate. The anthology alchemically intends "to broaden, and at the same time refine" the selections contained in its earlier editions (*NAP*, p. xlv). The editors never suggest, however, that these simultaneous processes of inclusion and exclusion might be problematic, and they never discuss what governs their choices. Distinctions between "major poets" and "their interesting contemporaries" are assumed to be clear and not open to question (*NAP*, dust jacket). Barbara Herrnstein Smith summarizes the effect of this assumption: "One of the major effects of prohibiting or inhibiting explicit evaluation is to forestall the exhibition and obviate the possible acknowledgment of divergent systems of value and thus to ratify, by default, established evaluative authority."[56]

Nor do the *Norton*'s editors admit as problematic the limited sense that a teaching anthology provides of what kind of poem the canon includes and how to read it. Admitting new work to the canon often requires new ways of reading. You can't read a Charles Olson poem in the same way that you read a Richard Wilbur poem. But the structure and purpose of the teaching anthology limit these new ways of reading, perpetuating old ways of reading the new poetry. By definition the teaching anthology contains poetry that can be readily discussed in university classrooms. That usually means short poems teachable alongside other poems in busy fifty-minute class periods and made more teachable by the scholarly apparatus of footnotes, glossaries, biographical notices, and historical introductions. Conversely the *Norton* editors find it "manifestly impossible" to include something as hard to digest in a class period as "Song of Myself" (*NAP*, p. xlvi). (Recall that Matthiessen did not find this so in 1950, when he inveighed against anthologies of solely lyric poetry.) By this principle of teachability, the *Norton* systematizes a potentially chaotic pluralist canon.

As a compromise the editors include "whole and self-contained seg-ments" of long poems (*NAP*, p. xlvi). But this can mean that even long poems end up being discussed according to criteria more applicable to lyrics. Thus the *Norton* has built into its selections a set of critical assumptions about how poetry should be read. As in many pre–twentieth-century anthologies, the work least likely to appear is that which is least susceptible to accepted methods of reading: for example, the Native American pieces in Jerome Rothenberg's *Technicians of the Sacred* and *Shaking the Pumpkin,* which cannot even be defined as texts in the traditional sense.[57] In times when readers shared narrower definitions of poetry and how to read it, and when form and style carried moral overtones, exclusion on this basis was not surprising; in a pluralist time it is much more surprising. By continuing to exclude this work, the editors of the *Norton* sidestep the problems of selection raised by extreme cultural fragmentation.

On close scrutiny, then, we see that even an apparently inclusive teaching anthology does not adequately represent today's pluralist literary climate. But perhaps, finally, it cannot. Teaching literature requires systematization; pluralism resists it. Since the power of different anthologies to affect the canon is increasing, albeit slowly, it is unlikely that any single anthology will again dominate a period's reading and direct a period's sense of the canon as Griswold's did. The poetry canon remains largely an academic institution, but its boundaries are more flexible than in the past because counter-canons are frequently thrust forward for consideration. The important forces behind canon-formation today make themselves felt less in individual anthologies than in the relationship between the revisionist collection and the canonical teaching text. Each kind of anthology gains its identity in contrast to the other. While texts like the *Norton* define a limited teachable canon, anthologies of noncanonical work will continue to lead toward what Leslie Fiedler and Houston Baker hoped for in their 1981 collection of essays: opening up the canon.[58]

1. See Alastair Fowler, *Kinds of Literature: An Introduction to the Theory of Genres and Modes* (Cambridge, Mass., 1982), pp. 213–16.

2. Elihu Hubbard Smith, ed., *American Poems, Selected and Original,* vol. 1 (Litchfield, Conn., 1793; rpt. [with an intro. by William K. Bottorff], Gainesville, Fla., 1966), p. iv; all further references to this work, abbreviated *AP,* will be included in the text.

3. Benjamin T. Spencer, *The Quest for Nationality: An American Literary Campaign* (Syracuse, N.Y., 1957), p. 77.

4. For brief discussion of some dissenting voices, see Frank Luther Mott, *A History of American Magazines, 1741–1850* (New York, 1930), pp. 176, 185–88. Mott agrees, however, that the period generally was one of critical puffery. For more on the *Monthly Anthology*'s critical position, see Lewis P. Simpson, ed., *The Federalist Literary Mind: Selections from the "Monthly Anthology and Boston Review," 1803–1811, Including Documents Relating to the Boston Athenaeum* (Baton Rouge, La., 1962).

5. See Roy Harvey Pearce, *The Continuity of American Poetry* (Princeton, N.J., 1961), pp. 207–9; R. W. B. Lewis, *The American Adam: Innocence, Tragedy, and Tradition in the Nineteenth Century* (Chicago, 1955), chap. 4; and Claudio Guillén, *Literature as System: Essays toward the Theory of Literary History* (Princeton, N.J., 1971), p. 500.

6. For thorough discussion of the kind of women's poetry that mid–nineteenth-century anthologists ignored, see Emily Stipes Watts, *The Poetry of American Women from 1632 to 1945* (Austin, Tex., 1977), chaps. 3–4.

7. Spencer, *The Quest for Nationality,* p. 37.

8. Fred Lewis Pattee, "Anthologies of American Literature before 1861," *Colophon* 4, pt. 16 (1934), unpaginated. Preservation remained a central goal of poetry anthologies for at least another forty years after Smith's collection. In 1829 Samuel Kettell compiled his

anthology "to rescue from oblivion the efforts of native genius" "by calling into notice and preserving a portion of what is valuable and characteristic in the writings of our native poets" (Specimens of American Poetry, 3 vols. [Boston, 1829], 1:iii; all further references to this work, abbreviated SAP, will be included in the text). In 1840 John Keese, editor of The Poets of America (2 vols. [New York, 1840]), described the usual circumstances of publishing poetry in America: "The main part of our poetical literature . . . has been occasional and fugitive. It has usually come before the public eye in small detached portions, with slight pretension to permanence in the form of its publication" (1:unpaginated). Beginning with Smith's, the earliest American anthologies responded to these circumstances by presenting a coherent body of work in a more lasting format.

For the early history of American magazines, see James Playsted Wood, Magazines in the United States: Their Social and Economic Influence, 2d ed. (New York, 1956).

9. George Ellis, ed., Specimens of the Early English Poets, 5th ed., 3 vols. (London, 1845), 1:v.

10. Ibid., 1:iv; Thomas Percy, ed., Reliques of Ancient English Poetry (London, 1765), p. ix.

11. See Pearce, The Continuity of American Poetry, p. 34.

12. In his intro. to AP, Bottorff discusses the poets' attempt to influence the Constitutional Convention (see p. xvi). On Smith's own Federalism, see Marcia Edgerton Bailey, A Lesser Hartford Wit, Dr. Elihu Hubbard Smith, 1771–1798, University of Maine Studies, 2d ser. 11 (Orono, Maine, 1928), pp. 55–56.

13. Matthew Arnold, "The Literary Influence of Academies," Poetry and Criticism of Matthew Arnold, ed. A. Dwight Culler (Boston, 1961), p. 269.

14. Philip Freneau, "Advice to Authors," The "Poems" (1786) and "Miscellaneous Works" (1788) of Philip Freneau, ed. Lewis Leary (Delmar, N.Y., 1975), pp. 44–45.

15. The debate over whether American literature begins with the Puritans remains unresolved. Those who say it does include Spencer (The Quest for Nationality), Sacvan Bercovitch (The Puritan Origins of the American Self [New Haven, Conn., 1975]), and F. O. Matthiessen (ed., The Oxford Book of American Verse [New York, 1950]). On the other hand, Donald Davie begins American literature in 1776 (see Trying to Explain [Ann Arbor, Mich., 1979], p. 185), while Larzer Ziff begins it with the 1837 appearance of Ralph Waldo Emerson's "The American Scholar" and Nathaniel Hawthorne's Twice-Told Tales (see Literary Democracy: The Declaration of Cultural Independence in America [New York, 1981], pp. xi–xiv). In 1827 two Anne Bradstreet poems appeared in Specimens of British Poetesses, ed. Alexander Dyce (London, 1827), pp. 55–58.

16. For examples of this tendency and of its longevity, see William Hazlitt, ed., Select Poets of Great Britain (London, 1825), who stated that "by leaving out a great deal of uninteresting and common-place poetry, room has been obtained for nearly all that was emphatically excellent" (p. vii); Francis Turner Palgrave, ed., The Golden Treasury (1861; rev. ed., New York, 1929), who used "the best original Lyrical pieces and Songs in our language . . . —and none beside the best" (p. xxv); and Sir Arthur Quiller-Couch, ed., The Oxford Book of English Verse, 1250–1918 (1900; rev. ed., New York, 1941), who set out "to choose the best" and deliberately did not "search out and insert the second-rate" (pp. vii, x).

17. The most widely read of these collections were George B. Cheever, ed., The American Common-place Book of Poetry (Boston, 1831); Sarah Josepha Hale, ed., The Ladies' Wreath: A Selection from the Female Poetic Writers of England and America (Boston, 1837); and William Cullen Bryant, ed., Selections from the American Poets (New York, 1840).

18. Rufus Wilmot Griswold, ed., The Poets and Poetry of America (Philadelphia, 1842), p. vi.

19. Ibid., 8th ed. (Philadelphia, 1847), p. 5.

20. That rectitude was defined partly by the church: Kettell, Griswold, and Cheever were all ministers. On the ministers' role as preservers of culture in mid–nineteenth-century America, see Ann Douglas, The Feminization of American Culture (New York, 1977).

21. Griswold, ed., *Gems from American Female Poets* (Philadelphia, 1842), unpaginated, and *Readings in American Poetry: For the Use of Schools* (New York, 1843), p. 3.

22. Griswold, ed., *Poets and Poetry*, 8th ed., pp. 7, 31.

23. Griswold to James Fields, 7 Mar. 1847, *Passages from the Correspondence and Other Papers of Rufus W. Griswold*, ed. W. M. Griswold (Cambridge, Mass., 1898), p. 224. Despite Griswold's opinion of women's poetry, the lure of the marketplace kept him anthologizing it. After *Gems from American Female Poets*, he also edited *Female Poets of America* (Philadelphia, 1849) to compete with Caroline May's *The American Female Poets* (Philadelphia, 1848) and Thomas Buchanan Read's *The Female Poets of America* (Philadelphia, 1849). On Griswold's commercial intentions, see Joy Bayless, *Rufus Wilmot Griswold, Poe's Literary Executor* (Nashville, Tenn., 1943), p. 144, and Pattee, *The Feminine Fifties* (New York, 1940), p. 99.

   Graham's Lady's and Gentleman's Magazine 20 (June 1842), the *Southern Quarterly Review* 2 (July 1842), and *Magnolia* n.s. 1 (Aug. 1842) all commented on Griswold's regional biases. Edgar Allan Poe gently noted both this bias and Griswold's partiality toward friends in the *Boston Miscellany* (Nov. 1843). Bayless documents Griswold's views both of transcendentalism (see p. 39) and of women writers (see p. 60).

24. See Mott, *Golden Multitudes: The Story of Best Sellers in the United States* (New York, 1947), p. 307.

25. T. S. Eliot, "What Is a Classic?," *Selected Prose of T. S. Eliot*, ed. Frank Kermode (New York, 1975), pp. 116, 129.

26. Also worth noting is Griswold's early support of the long neglected Jones Very. When Yvor Winters championed Very in *Maule's Curse: Seven Studies in the History of American Obscurantism* (Norfolk, Conn., 1938), he thought Very's poetry still so hard to obtain that he ended the book with a selection of that poetry. And as late as 1952, Louis Untermeyer lamented in *Early American Poets* (New York, 1952) that "Very's poetry is little known and practically unread" (p. xv). Griswold had reprinted some of Very's poetry in every edition from the first.

27. Charles A. Dana, ed., *The Household Book of Poetry*, 11th ed. (New York, 1868), p. v.

28. Ibid., p. vi.

29. Publisher's preface to Bryant, ed., *A Library of Poetry and Song*, 20th ed. (New York, 1871), p. iii; John Greenleaf Whittier, ed., *Songs of Three Centuries* (Boston, 1875), p. iv; Emerson, ed., *Parnassus* (Boston, 1874), p. v.

30. See [Park Benjamin], "Recent American Poetry" *United States Magazine and Democratic Review* 5 (June 1839): 523–41; [Parke Godwin], "Bryant's Poems," *United States Magazine and Democratic Review* 6 (Oct. 1839): 273–86; "American Poetry," *United States Magazine and Democratic Review* 8 (Nov.–Dec. 1840): 399–430; and H. T. Tuckerman, "The Poetry of Bryant," *United States Magazine and Democratic Review* 16 (Feb. 1845): 185–91. On the influential critical judgments of the *Democratic Review*, see John Stafford, *The Literary Criticism of "Young America": A Study in the Relationship of Politics and Literature, 1837–1850* (Berkeley, 1952), esp. pp. 95–121, and Perry Miller, *The Raven and the Whale: The War of Wit and Words in the Era of Poe and Melville* (New York, 1956).

31. See Jay Martin, *Harvests of Change: American Literature, 1865–1914* (Englewood Cliffs, N.J., 1967).

32. See Mott, *A History of American Magazines, 1865–1885* (Cambridge, Mass., 1938), pp. 237–38.

33. Emerson, ed., *Parnassus*, p. iii.

34. Martin, *Harvests of Change*, p. 13.

35. William Michael Rossetti had been Walt Whitman's first English editor, editing a selection of his poems in 1868. He concluded an 1870 notice on Henry Wadsworth Longfellow by saying that "the real American poet is a man enormously greater than Longfellow or any other of his poet compatriots—Walt Whitman" (quoted in *The Diary of W. M. Rossetti, 1870–1873*, ed. Odette Bornand [Oxford, 1977], p. 4 n.3).

36. George Santayana, "The Genteel Tradition in American Philosophy" (1911), *The*

Genteel Tradition: Nine Essays by George Santayana, ed. Douglas L. Wilson (Cambridge, Mass., 1967), p. 52.

37. John Tomsich, *A Genteel Endeavor: American Culture and Politics in the Gilded Age* (Stanford, Calif., 1971), p. 27. Tomsich makes the useful point that, in their own time, the "genteel" poets and editors had far more influence than their contemporaries Whitman and Emily Dickinson, who only later came to be considered "great."

38. Santayana, "The Genteel Tradition in American Philosophy," p. 52.

39. Edmund Clarence Stedman, ed., *An American Anthology, 1787–1900* (Boston, 1900), p. xxiv; all further references to this work, abbreviated *AA,* will be included in the text.

40. W. J. Linton, ed., *Poetry of America: Selections from One Hundred American Poets from 1776 to 1876* (London, 1878), p. x.

41. Stedman knew the poetry of his own time was "somewhat timorous," that he lived in an "intermediary lyrical period" which offered at best "a hopeful prelude to whatsoever masterwork the next era [had] in store." But in representing his own period he allowed historical considerations more weight than with earlier periods, collecting that poetry "as an expression and interpretation of the time itself" (*AA,* pp. xxx, xxvi, xxii).

42. John W. S. Hows, ed., *Golden Leaves from the American Poets* (New York, 1865), p. v; Thomas R. Lounsbury, ed., *Yale Book of American Verse* (New Haven, Conn., 1912), p. xliii.

43. Conrad Aiken, ed., *American Poetry, 1671–1928* (New York, 1929), p. v.

44. Harriet Monroe and Alice Corbin Henderson, eds., *The New Poetry: An Anthology* (New York, 1917), p. xii. The canonization of Whitman and Dickinson was furthered by a group of early 1930s anthologies: Alfred Kreymborg, ed., *An Anthology of American Poetry: Lyric America, 1630–1930* (New York, 1930); Untermeyer, ed., *American Poetry from the Beginning to Whitman* (New York, 1931); Frederick C. Prescott and Gerald D. Sanders, eds., *An Introduction to American Poetry* (New York, 1932); and Mark Van Doren, ed., *American Poets, 1630–1930* (Boston, 1932). Yet the changes still moved slowly. Matthiessen complained in *American Renaissance: Art and Expression in the Age of Emerson and Whitman* ([New York, 1941], p. xi) that still no "adequately detailed scrutiny" existed of "When Lilacs Last in the Dooryard Bloom'd," and not until his sixth edition (1944) did the influential Untermeyer begin his *Modern American Poetry* with Whitman.

45. Bliss Carman, ed., *The Oxford Book of American Verse* (New York, 1927), p. v.

46. Matthiessen, ed., *The Oxford Book of American Verse* (1950), p. xviii.

47. Whittier, ed., *Songs of Three Centuries,* p. vi; and see Poe, "The Poetic Principle," *Edgar Allan Poe: Selected Prose and Poetry,* ed. W. H. Auden (New York, 1950), pp. 367–72.

48. Matthiessen, ed., *The Oxford Book of American Verse* (1950), pp. x, xiii.

49. Robert Lowell, National Book Award acceptance speech, quoted in Stanley Kunitz, "The New Books," *Harper's Magazine* 221 (Sept. 1960): 100.

50. See Eric Torgersen, "Cold War in Poetry: Notes of a Conscientious Objector," *American Poetry Review* 11 (July–Aug. 1982): 31–35; see also Donald Hall, Robert Pack, and Louis Simpson, eds., *New Poets of England and America* (New York, 1957), and Donald M. Allen, ed., *The New American Poetry, 1945–1960* (New York, 1960).

51. See Allen, ed., *The New American Poetry,* p. xiv: "Only a fraction of the work [in this anthology] has been published, and that for the most part in fugitive pamphlets and little magazines."

52. To be more specific: nine of Allen's poets and nine of Hall, Pack, and Simpson's poets appear in *The New Oxford Book of American Verse;* eight of Allen's and eleven of Hall, Pack, and Simpson's in *The Norton Anthology of Poetry;* and fourteen of Allen's and seventeen of Hall, Pack, and Simpson's in *The Norton Anthology of Modern Poetry.*

53. On the academy's survival strategies, see Edward W. Said, "Opponents, Audiences, Constituencies, and Community," *Critical Inquiry* 9 (Sept. 1982): 1–26. In *Literature as System,* Guillén shows how literary education creates the need to systematize literature (see p. 380). He goes on to observe how "systems will tend, generally speaking, to absorb change and assimilate innovation" (p. 385).

54. René Wellek, "Respect for Tradition," *TLS*, 10 Dec. 1982, p. 1356; Anthony Burgess, "The Writer among Professors," *TLS*, 10 Dec. 1982, p. 1357; Wellek, "Respect for Tradition," p. 1356.

55. Alexander W. Allison et al., eds., *The Norton Anthology of Poetry*, rev. ed. (New York, 1975), p. xlv; all further references to this work, abbreviated *NAP*, will be included in the text.

56. Barbara Herrnstein Smith, "Contingencies of Value," p. 11, this volume. Smith examines thoroughly the problems in evaluation posed by pluralism.

57. Arnold Krupat discusses the social and critical forces that have kept Native American work outside the poetry canon in "Native American Literature and the Canon" (in this volume), and "An Approach to Native American Texts" (*Critical Inquiry* 9 [Dec. 1982]: 323–38).

58. See Leslie A. Fiedler and Houston A. Baker, Jr., eds., *English Literature: Opening Up the Canon*, Selected Papers from the English Institute, 1979, n.s. 4 (Baltimore, 1981).

Native American Literature and the Canon

Arnold Krupat

1

Although the rich and various literatures of Native American peoples, by virtue of their antiquity and indigenousness, have an important claim to inclusion in the canon of American literature, this claim has not yet fully been acknowledged. From the very first period of invasion and settlement until the close of the "frontier," Americans tended to define their peculiar national distinctiveness in relation to a perceived opposition between the Europeans they no longer were and the Indians they did not wish to become. The development of autobiography as a major genre of American writing is instructive in this regard. Eastern autobiographers like Jonathan Edwards in the colonial period, Benjamin Franklin in the Revolutionary period, and Henry David Thoreau in the period preceding the Civil War, all wrote and thought about Indians, yet chose the European polarity as decisive for self- and literary definition. In contrast, western autobiographers like Daniel Boone, Davy Crockett, Kit Carson, and William F. Cody, all ultimately loyal to white "civilization," nonetheless fashioned themselves and their books on models taken, in varying degrees, from Indian "savagery."[1] But this particular tension never operated in the definition of peculiarly American literature, for the simple reason that Indians, who did not write, were not regarded as possessing a "litterature" available for study and imitation.

I would like to thank Brian Swann and Robert von Hallberg for their help in preparing this essay.

Littera-ture meant the culture of letters, and the man of letters, European or Euramerican, was the man of culture; Native Americans— Indians—were "children of nature" precisely because they were not men of letters. And "oral literature," at that time, could only be a contradiction in terms. American literature, seeking to define itself as a body of national writing (*American* literature) and as a selection of distinctively literary texts (American *literature*), considered only European models because no Native models appeared to be available.

Yet even after Indian literature was "discovered," attempts to open the canon to it and Euramerican work influenced by it based themselves— powerfully but mistakenly—on the "naturalness" of this literature, as though not individuals and cultures but the very rocks and mountains had composed the Native poem or story.[2] Indeed, to the present day the "naturalness" of Indian literatures tends to be assumed by almost everyone other than specialists in its study. The dramatic, performative immediacy of Native literature had, of course, ages of well-established tradition and complex convention behind it. Yet to admire it and urge its inclusion in the canon (even without recognition of its cultural constitution) would have been to question those Eurocentric texts of the canon that seemed especially fixed, distant, and aloof; it would have been to question, as well, the authority of the text in general and thus to propose a revision not only of the literary but of the social order. For the canon, like all cultural production, is never an innocent selection of the best that has been thought and said; rather, it is the institutionalization of those particular verbal artifacts that appear best to convey and sustain the dominant social order.

In our own time, the canon is established primarily by the professoriate, by teacher-critics who variously—passively or actively but for the most part—support the existing order. As Leslie Fiedler has remarked, "Literature is effectively what we teach in departments of English; or, conversely, what we teach in departments of English is literature."[3] Roland Barthes has offered a similar observation. "The 'teaching of literature,' " Barthes said, "is for me almost tautological. Literature is what is taught, that's all."[4] What the pedagogical canon includes from the past and from current production generally and substantially works to ratify the present and to legitimate an established hegemony. As we might expect, the claims of Native American literature have been urged in conjunction with movements toward cultural pluralism and away from monocultural

Arnold Krupat is a member of the literature faculty at Sarah Lawrence College. He is the coeditor of the University of Nebraska Press' Native American Autobiography Series and is currently completing an anthology of Native American autobiographies, *Indian Lives.*

purism, with movements toward racial and sexual equality and away from the Western hierarchies of race and gender. Native American literature and Euramerican writing influenced by it may presently have approached the margins of the canon—as American society has marginally begun to approach the possibility of racial and sexual equality. Whether Native American literature—along with other indigenous, powerful, yet non-canonic cultural production—will enter the anthologies and the university curricula depends upon the development of social forces.

Meanwhile, it must be said that only in the past thirty years or so has philological and, in particular, structural analysis of Indian literatures begun to establish their formal principles on anything like a sound, scientific basis. Not until quite recently could the Native and non-Native student of this rich heritage have an approximately accurate sense of what it actually was and is. In these same thirty years, American society has reached a point where it urgently needs to examine the two central premises of all Native literatures. The first is their ecosystemic—their nonanthropocentric—perspective; the second is their performative—their nontextual—mode of presentation.

Precise relations among the passage of ecology-minded "bottle bills," the gains of antihumanist theorizing in "the highest academies of the empire," and what Father Ong calls the "secondary orality of our electronic age" are not easy to specify.[5] But these relations exist, and, I believe, they may be signs of a social climate in which the canon may at last open itself to Native American literary production. In the following pages, I shall sketch broadly some background of the Euramerican's encounter with the Native American and his literature, paying particular attention to those attempts, to date less than decisive, to open the canon to Native literatures and to writers who have tried to take them as bona fide models for original work.

2

The first invader-settlers of America responded to the verbal pro-ductions of Native orality as a satanic or bestial gibberish that, unmarked in letters nor bound as books, could never be thought to constitute a littera-ture. John Eliot translated the Bible into an Algonquian language in the seventeenth century, but the Puritans did not inscribe the wicked or animal noise of Native song or story. The scientist-revolutionaries of the eighteenth century were more interested in Indian cultural activity than were their Puritan forebears and made efforts to describe, catalog, and subdue its various manifestations—just as they did with other natural phenomena like lightning or steam pressure. Although the child of nature, in this period, was as frequently deemed the noble as the murderous savage—a change prompted less by Rousseau than by the colonists' need to establish trade and military alliances with the powerful interior tribes—it was still difficult to conceive that without writing he could have a littera-ture. Washington, Franklin, and Jefferson "encouraged the collection of Indian wordlists as part of an international project in comparative linguistics," and Jefferson quoted a well-known (perhaps apocryphal) speech of Chief Logan as an example of Native oratorical ability.[6] But this was still far from recognizing an Indian capacity for literary production. Nonetheless, what may be the first translation of an Indian "poem" dates from the pre-Revolutionary period. This appears in the *Memoirs* of Henry Timberlake, a young Virginian, who, after serving under Washington, embarked upon a mission to the Cherokee. Timberlake apparently did not know Cherokee and so had to work from the rendition of an interpreter. In his "Translation of the WAR-SONG. *Caw waw noo dee*, &C.," we encounter Indian poetry in the form of heroic couplets. Here are the first few lines:

> Where'er the earth's enlighten'd by the sun,
> Moon shines by night, grass grows, or waters run,
> Be't known that we are going, like men, afar,
> In hostile fields to wage destructive war;
> Like men we go, to meet our country's foes,
> Who, woman-like, shall fly our dreaded blows[7]

Timberlake made no effort to transcribe the original Cherokee; only scholarly reconstruction might provide an approximation of what this song was like.

In the Romantic nineteenth century, littera-ture came to mean not simply the written culture generally but a selection from it of imaginative and expressive utterance—in writing, to be sure, but also in the speech and song of common men and the "folk" who might themselves be unable to write. "Nature" became the "keyword" of culture, and "oral literature," something other than a contradiction in terms. Once these ideas crossed the ocean to the American East, it was but a short step to hear Native expression as "naturally" poetic and as constituting a literature in need of no more than textualization and formal—"civilized"—supplementation.

English Romanticism had reached the East by the 1830s (Timberlake had reached England earlier: Robert Southey used the *Memoirs* for his 1805 epic, *Madoc*), but in those years the social and cultural dominance of the East was challenged by the Jackson presidency and the "rise of the West." So far as Indians were concerned, the 1830s were the years of President Jackson's Indian Removal policy, which made the forcible relocation of the Eastern tribes to the west of the Mississippi a national priority. During that decade, easterners interested in Indians were primarily concerned to preserve Indian lives and lands before trying to preserve Indian literature. History writing rather than poetry writing appeared the more urgent task. For, as B. B. Thatcher put it in the preface to his *Indian Biography*, published in Boston in 1832, "We owe, and our Fathers owed, too much to the Indians . . . to deny them the poor restitution of historical justice at least."[8]

In the 1840s and 1850s, it was American "civilization" that began to proclaim itself "Nature's nation," in Perry Miller's phrase, proclaiming all the louder as aggressive expansion threatened to destroy the forests, the grasslands, and, as always, their aboriginal inhabitants, nature's children, the Indians.[9] In this period, the work of Henry Rowe Schoolcraft came to wide attention. Schoolcraft, an Indian agent interested in *la pensée sauvage*—"savage mentality," as he called it—had been publishing since 1839, but it was what Roy Harvey Pearce calls his "masterwork," a study undertaken, appropriately, at the instigation of the secretary of war— the *Historical and Statistical Information Respecting the History, Condition, and Prospects of the Indian Tribes of the United States* (1851–57, and reissued under various titles)—that marks the increasingly important contribution of what we would call anthropological scholarship to our understanding of Indian literature.[10] Indeed, according to A. Grove Day, "the beginning of wide interest in native poetry in translation properly dates from the year 1851, when a history of the Indians was published by Henry Rowe Schoolcraft which included samples of Chippewa poetry."[11]

One example from Schoolcraft, quoted by Day, has repeatedly been anthologized; it has also occasioned some trenchant commentary by John Greenway and, particularly, by Dell Hymes. Schoolcraft's procedure— a transcription of the original, a literal translation, and a "literary" translation—continues often to be followed today. His Chippewa "Chant to the Fire-Fly" is literally translated:

> Flitting-white-fire-insect! waving-white-fire-bug! give me light before I go to bed! give me light before I go to sleep. Come, little dancing white-fire-bug! Come, little flitting white-fire-beast! Light me with your bright white-flame-instrument—your little candle.

The first few lines of his "literary" translation read:

> Fire-fly, fire-fly! bright little thing,
> Light me to bed, and my song I will sing.
> Give me your light, as you fly o'er my head,
> That I may merrily go to my bed.[12]

This translation is as typical of its period's deliquescent Romanticism as Timberlake's couplets are of the high Drydenesque. Obviously, the translation of Indian poetry (like poetic translation generally) reveals as much about the translator's culture and literary predilections as it does about the Indian's. Schoolcraft also published, without literary elaboration, some brief Chippewa Midé—medicine society—songs such as the two following:

> All around the circle of the sky I hear the Spirit's voice.

> I walk upon half the sky.[13]

His contemporaries, however, did not seem interested in these—which, today, probably appear both more attractive and more "Indian." In any case, although Schoolcraft's translations spurred interest in Native American poetry, they seem to have had no influence on American poetry in their time. Not Indian poetry but, rather, poetry with an Indian subject did enter the American canon in the 1850s, however.

Composed by a Harvard professor of European literature, the first to teach *Faust* in an American college, Henry Wadsworth Longfellow's *Song of Hiawatha* (1855) sold out its first printing of four thousand copies on the day of its publication and completed its first year in print with sales of thirty-eight thousand. Longfellow derived his Indian materials from Schoolcraft's earlier work, the *Algic Researches* (1839); he derived his attitudes toward Indians from Eastern progressivist thought (Alas, the Noble but Vanishing Savage); and he derived his meter from the Finnish epic, *Kalevala*. Longfellow's Hiawatha comfortably counsels his people to abandon the old ways and adapt themselves to the coming of "civilization," and he does so in a meter that only "civilization" can provide. It is necessary, of course, to mention Longfellow in any consideration of possible Indian influence on the canon of American literature, but *The Song of Hiawatha*, in fact, shows no such influence at all. Longfellow did not make use of Schoolcraft's Chippewa translations (themselves mostly "civilized" in their formal conventions), nor did he have any sense of his own about what Native American literary composition might actually be like or whether it might somehow stand without Finnish support and supplementation. The admission of *Hiawatha* into the American canon had nothing to do with the possibility of naturalizing or expanding the canon; *Hiawatha* merely assimilates the Indian to the persisting Eurocentrism of the East.

Euramericans continued to move westward, appropriating Native American lands by force and by fraud. Once the West had been "won," as the "frontier" approached its "close" in 1890, American thought about Indians situated itself within a broader debate between Americanism and cultural pluralism. The "Indian problem" was related to the "immigrant problem"; the various "solutions" proposed rested upon particular visions of the social order. The "Americanizers" gained the ascendant in 1887 with the passage of the General Allotment Act, known as the Dawes Severalty Act. The Dawes Act was an attack on Indian culture ("for the Indians' own good") by way of an attack on the Indians' collectively held land base—a "mighty pulverizing engine to break up the tribal mass," as Theodore Roosevelt called the act in presciently cyclotronic imagery.[14] The Dawes Act was also—and intended to be—an attack on all "communistic" systems. Opposed (for the most part) to Dawes and the Americanizers were the anthropologists of the newly founded Bureau of Ethnology (1879; after 1894, the Bureau of American Ethnology), whose studies of the rich, Native tribal heritage committed them to its preservation rather than destruction. An important exception, however, was Alice Fletcher. One of the first, in the 1880s, to study the forms of Native American music, Fletcher, nonetheless, was "one of the most vigorous opponents of tribalism and played an influential role in the agitation . . . to force the allotment of land in severalty upon the Indians without tribal consent," as Wilcomb Washburn has commented.[15]

Fletcher was more interested in the music of Indian songs than in their texts; her influence on the study of Native American poetry comes through Frances Densmore and, more particularly, Natalie Curtis [Burlin], whose work she inspired. Densmore, trained in piano, organ, and harmony at the Oberlin Conservatory of Music and at Harvard, began in 1901 a lifetime of work with Indian music by transcribing a Sioux woman's song that she heard near her home in Red Wing, Minnesota. Densmore continued to publish on Indian music until her death in 1957. Of the vast body of material she transcribed and translated, it may be the Midé songs of the Chippewa—these attracted her as they had Schoolcraft—which she published for the Bureau of American Ethnology in 1910, that have most often appeared in the anthologies (although not in the earliest ones).

It was Curtis, the third of these early collectors of Native song, who had the greatest impact on the anthologies. In 1907, Curtis published *The Indians' Book,* a wide-ranging collection which presented not only the music of Native American songs (in special notation) but also poems and short narratives from the tribes. Curtis' particular appreciation of Native artistic production is entirely that of the antiquarian looking back upon what President Theodore Roosevelt called, in a prefatory letter to her book, "the simple beauty and strange charm—the charm of a vanished elder world—of Indian poetry."[16] Like Fletcher, Curtis had no doubt that the "child races" of Indians must give way to the "adult races" of Anglo-Saxon peoples. She recommended the charming and simple songs of the Indians to her white audience for the wisdom they might—somehow, vaguely—teach, and, as well, as an act of—sentimental—justice to this soon-to-be-vanished race. Indeed, Curtis' Indians are so childlike and simple as to be entirely creatures of nature; their art, she says, is "spontaneous," the talent to produce it "inborn" in every member of the race.[17] In these beliefs, Curtis completely ignores the major developments of scientific anthropology in her time, which insisted upon the cultural, not racial, explanation of cultural things. Some of her translations—they are, curiously, the ones chosen by Louis Untermeyer for his 1931 anthology of American poetry, which I note below—are full of exclamation points and archaic diction, but others, like this Winnebago "Holy Song," are somewhat less elaborated and point more nearly forward:

> Let it fly—the arrow,
> Let it fly—the arrow,

> Pierce with a spell the man, oh!
> Let it fly—the arrow.
>
> Let it fly—the arrow,
> Let it fly—the arrow,
> Pierce with a spell the woman!
> Let it fly—the arrow.
>
>   [*IB*, pp. 256–57]

Curtis' work, for all its mistaken inspiration and its partly dubious execution, remains the locus of much that is available nowhere else.

The Dawes Act's policy was a disaster for the Indians; yet it was not officially abandoned until the 1930s. By that time, American anthropology was no longer based in the government bureau, nor in the great urban museum, but, instead, in the university. Franz Boas, who had come to Columbia University just before the turn of the century to train a new generation of anthropologists, was the dominant force in ethnographic science. I will not attempt a full discussion of Boas' contribution to the preservation of Native American culture but, rather, quote Hymes at some length; his description of what happened on the northwest coast of America is largely true for the literatures of most Indian peoples.

> Often non-Indians did not wish to preserve the culture of the Indians. Conviction or guilt persuaded them that it was already gone, or best gone. It is a shameful fact that most of what can be known today about the cultures of the Indians of my state, Oregon, is due to the efforts of men who came across the continent. Franz Boas, a German Jew unable to aspire to scholarly advancement in his native country but versed in the German intellectual tradition that valued individual cultures and their works, recorded Shoalwater and Kathlamet Chinook. His student Sapir recorded Wishram and Takelma; another student, L. J. Frachtenberg, recorded Alsea, Siuslaw, Coos, and Kalapuya. Frachtenberg was followed by a later student with a better ear, Melville Jacobs, who provided superior texts from Coos and Kalapuya, all that has been published so far in Sahaptin, and all that is known, save for one scrap, of Clackamas. To repeat, most of what we can know of the first literature of Oregon is due to representatives of German and Jewish intellectual tradition, who crossed the continent to record it. With regard to that first literature, they are the pioneers. The pioneers of Western song and story and their descendants did little or nothing.[18]

These German and Jewish intellectuals were entirely skeptical of the Americanizers' claims to WASP cultural superiority and asserted their sense of the importance to American culture not only of Continental philosophy and philology but of the aboriginal American culture of the Indians as well. Whereas early attempts at "ethnographic salvage" were

made in the name of history, and the Americanizers' attempts at ethnographic destruction were made, generally, in the name of religion,
what Boas and his students preserved was in the name of science. The
work of Fletcher, Densmore, and Curtis began specifically from an interest
in Indian music and coincided with imagism and a movement in poetry
to privilege the genre of the brief lyric. But Boas and his students sought
knowledge. Although they recorded songs, which would early be anthologized, they also recorded lengthy narratives that were performed
but not sung. Hardly inimical to poetry,[19] their commitment to science
led them to prefer the most literal prose translations—which usually
obscured completely the dynamics of Indian performances and, occasionally, as Dennis Tedlock has remarked, were a "disaster" for anyone
concerned to discover a genuine poetry among Native peoples.[20] The
full value of what Boas and his students recorded would only begin to
be revealed in the 1950s and after, when developments in anthropological
linguistics would permit their translations to be modified for accuracy
and to yield new translations of more apparent poetic value.

3

It was just after World War I that the first concerted effort to bring
Native American poetry into the canon of American literature occurred.
This effort was associated with the American radicals' call for cultural
pluralism, with the imagist challenge to a canon still dominated by Emerson,
Longfellow, and James Russell Lowell, and, in particular, with the work
of Mary Austin. If Schoolcraft's Chippewa translations may be said to
have opened the way to interest in Native American poetry, then it was
George Cronyn's anthology of Indian poetry, *The Path on the Rainbow*
(1918), that began to broaden that way. Cronyn's volume was hardly, as
Austin called it in her introduction, "the first authoritative volume of
aboriginal American verse," for Cronyn was often uncritical and/or mis-
informed.[21] (It might be said that no "authoritative" collection appeared
before Margot Astrov's in 1946; it might also be said that no "authoritative"
collection has yet appeared.) Yet Cronyn had the acumen to take translations
from the superb student of Navajo, Washington Matthews, from John
Swanton, and from Boas himself. Whatever its quality, finally, Cronyn's
volume—which attracted a good deal of attention—at least made it possible
to imagine, as Austin predicted in her introduction, that a relation was
"about to develop between Indian verse and the ultimate literary destiny
of America" (*PR*, pp. xv–xvi).

In Austin's view, to know the Native American heritage was not, as
Curtis believed, for the "adult" American to honor some indigenous
childlike past; rather, it was for the contemporary American poet to "put
himself in touch with the resident genius of his own land" in the living

present (*PR*, p. xxxii). There is an "extraordinary likeness," Austin remarked, "between much of this native product and the recent work of
the Imagists, *vers librists*, and other literary fashionables." Thus, "the first
free movement of poetic originality in America finds us just about where
the last Medicine Man left off" (*PR*, p. xvi).

A year later, in 1919, Austin wrote in the *Dial* that "vers libre and
Imagism are in truth primitive forms, and both of them generically [*sic*]
American forms, forms instinctively selected by people living in America
and freed from outside influence."[22] Austin ascribed these "forms" to
nature, most particularly to what D. H. Lawrence was soon to call "the
spirit of place." In Indian poetry, Austin wrote, "the shape of the lines
is influenced by the contours of the country" (*PRD*, p. 570). So determining
was this geographical influence that "before 1900" she "could listen to
aboriginal verses on the phonograph in unidentified Amerindian languages, and securely refer them by their dominant rhythms to the plains,
the deserts and woodlands," as she explained in 1923, in the introduction
to her own collection of versions of Indian poems, *The American Rhythm*.[23]
Austin wittily admitted that she took the anthropologists of her day more
seriously than they took her; but if she did take them seriously, she
understood them badly, for her sort of simplistic environmental determinism was unacceptable to them as an explanation of cultural variation.

Nonetheless, Austin's often-repeated conviction "that American poetry
must inevitably take, at some period of its history, the mold of Amerind
verse, which is the mold of the American experience shaped by the
American environment" (*AR*, p. 42) took a clear stand on the future of
American poetry. This stand was not only in opposition to the Longfellow-
Emerson-Lowell Eastern past but in opposition, as well, to the futures
envisioned by Austin's contemporaries, T. S. Eliot and Ezra Pound, who
looked not to the West but to the East and Far East, and to a past very
different from that of "the last Medicine Man."[24] Yet Austin shared with
Eliot and Pound what F. H. Matthews has called the "revolt against
Americanism."

"In the 1920's," in Matthews' cogent summary,

> the revulsion from Americanism and the search for a viable cultural
> community intensified into a major quest. Intellectuals in a position
> to assert their identity with some minority now fanned the embers
> of recently-declining traditions, or raised folk arts to self-conscious
> status. . . . Writers who lacked a vital region or ethnic minority with
> which to identify turned instead, like Sherwood Anderson and William
> Carlos William[s], to quarrying the national past in search of lost
> virtue.[25]

This "revulsion from Americanism" serves to link Austin, Williams, Eliot,
and Pound, although the solutions each proposed to the common problem
they shared were incompatible with one another. The modernist inter-

nationalism of the "paleface" and the nativism of the "redskin" were united in the young Yvor Winters.[26] As poet-critic, first, and, subsequently, as scholar-teacher, Winters urged the claims of Indian literatures as part of a broader challenge to the established canon.

In 1922, that *annus mirabilis* of *Ulysses* and *The Waste Land,* Winters published *The Magpie's Shadow;* the "Indians especially were an influence on *The Magpie's Shadow,*" Winters would later write.[27] The linked poems of *The Magpie's Shadow* are introduced by an epigraph from Rimbaud, and Japanese poetry is also an influence, although it is impossible to tell what Winters may have taken from the Native American and what from the Japanese (the two non-Western traditions have often appeared as parallel influences on those poets looking beyond the European tradition— and William Stafford has published a "Sioux Haiku").[28] The brief, titled stanzas of the poem's three sections seem familiar enough from imagist practice. Thus, from part 2, "In Spring":

May

Oh, evening in my hair!

Or, from part 3, "In Summer and Autumn":

The Walker

In dream my feet are still.

Blue Mountain

A deer walks that mountain.[29]

A year earlier, Winters had published in *Poetry* magazine a poem with an Indian subject, "Lament, beside an Acéquia, for the Wife of Awa-Tsireh." He later identified Awa-Tsireh as a painter from the pueblo of San Ildefonso. That was in 1928, in "The Indian in English," a review for *Transition* of two important Native American poetry anthologies, Cronyn's *Path on the Rainbow* and Nellie Barnes' *American Indian Love Lyrics and Other Verse.* Winters quoted from the translators he admired and also offered, "finally," what he called an example of "nonreligious and purely dramatic material" in a "more modern group of Chinook songs" translated by Boas.[30] I should also note Winters' 1926 "Open Letter to the Editors of *This Quarter,*" in which he protested the exploitation of Indian materials. This "notion of interpreting the Indian," Winters wrote, "is too much for me. They are in need of no assistance whatsoever, as anyone is aware who has ever read the really great translations of Frances Densmore, Washington Matthews, Frank Russell, and Jeremiah

Curtin—translations that can take their place with no embar[r]assment beside the best Greek or Chinese versions of H. D. or Ezra Pound and which some day will do so."[31]

Winters' own poetic development would not follow Native American models; yet Winters continued to press the canon to open itself not only to Frederick Tuckerman, Thomas Sturge Moore, and Elizabeth Daryush but to Native American poetry as well. Winters directed A. Grove Day's doctoral dissertation, which became, as I shall note, one of the important anthologies of Indian verse; another of his doctoral students was the Kiowa N. Scott Momaday, whose prose, if not often his poetry, has tried to move beyond Eurocentrism.

In Winters' *Transition* article, he approved of Cronyn's collection as, of the two reviewed, "by all odds the better and larger selection, despite its being saddled with a section of 'interpretations.' "[32] In his approval of Cronyn, he placed himself at odds with Untermeyer, another great canon maker of the time. In 1919, Untermeyer had also reviewed Cronyn's volume, for the *Dial*, rather sniffily concluding that this Indian anthology was "as an ethnic document . . . of indubitable value; as a contribution to creative Americana [?] it may grow to have importance. But as a collection for the mere man of letters it is a rather forbidding pile—a crude and top-heavy monument with a few lovely and even lively decorations."[33] Austin quickly responded in a piece from which I have already quoted. Characterizing Untermeyer as "one whose mind has so evidently never visited west of Broadway," Austin made the telling point that "if Mr. Untermeyer could get his mind off the Indian Anthology as a thing of type and paper, he might have got something more out of it" (*PRD*, p. 569).

By the 1930s, however, Untermeyer had apparently come nearer to Austin's estimate of Native American poetry. His *American Poetry: From the Beginning to Whitman* (1931)—according to H. Bruce Franklin the "most widely used anthology of poetry" in the schools—included a section on American Indian poetry along with sections on Negro spirituals and blues, cowboy songs, and city gutturals.[34] Untermeyer quoted from Austin's introduction to *The Path on the Rainbow* and recommended Curtis' *Indians' Book,* Barnes' *American Indian Love Lyrics,* and Austin's *American Rhythm.* This last, he said, included "a penetrating essay in interpretation."[35] Austin's essay, however, offers no more than the geographical determinism I have already remarked; Untermeyer tended to prefer "adaptations" rather than more literal translations, just the sort of "interpretations" Winters, quite wisely, warned against.

Translation-versions of Native American poetry had earlier appeared in another anthology widely used in the schools. In 1928, Mark Van Doren, also an admirer of Curtis, had published his *Anthology of World Poetry*, consisting of poetic translations from literatures around the world. A section on "American" poetry comes last; this contains twenty poems from translators ranging from Schoolcraft to Austin and Curtis; there is nothing from Boas and his students.

These influential anthologies, for all their confusions about Indians and Indian literature—not to say their thoroughgoing ignorance of what anthropological scholarship of their time had made it possible to understand about Native Americans and their literature—nonetheless were clear gestures toward that pluralism intended to open the canon. In this regard, they were the cultural equivalents of the political change from Herbert Hoover to FDR, from the Dawes Act's policy of cultural destruction and Indian assimilation to the Indian New Deal of Roosevelt's commissioner of Indian affairs, John Collier, who sought to preserve and protect traditional Native cultures.

4

World War II brought Claude Lévi-Strauss to the New School for Social Research in New York, where, as legend has it, he learned structural linguistics from his colleague Roman Jakobson, another displaced European. Lévi-Strauss' essay "The Structural Study of Myth" appeared in the *Journal of American Folklore* in 1955. Whatever its influence on method in America, this text was an important encouragement to the study of Indian "myth," if not—and the two were distinct for Lévi-Strauss—Indian "poetry." It was just after the war, in 1946, that Astrov's anthology of Native prose and poetry, *The Winged Serpent,* was published—still, in 1965, as Hymes judged, one of the "two major contemporary anthologies in English" and, according to William Bevis in 1974, "the best general anthology in paperback."[36] Astrov's introduction and notes pay special attention to the scientific, anthropological contexts of Indian literatures, and the translations she chooses, as well as the commentary she provides, reflect the considerable advances ethnography had made in the Boasian period.

The second of the "two major contemporary anthologies" is Day's *The Sky Clears,* published in 1951. Unlike Astrov, Day pointed, as Austin had, specifically to the possibility of Indian influence on modern American poetry—although only, as Hymes has noted, in relation to existing translations. Day was, as I have said, Winters' doctoral student, and he dedicated the anthology, an outgrowth of his dissertation, to "Yvor Winters, Singer of Power."

Boas had died in 1942; but by that time his students occupied major positions of influence in American anthropology. It was one of Boas' later students, Melville Jacobs, who, in 1958, published the first of an important series of narratives from the Northwest. These appeared as numbers of the *International Journal of American Linguistics,* issued by the Indiana University Research Center in Anthropology, Folklore, and Linguistics. It was also in 1958 at Indiana that Thomas Sebeok convened the interdisciplinary conference on style that provided the occasion for Jakobson's well-known concluding paper, "Linguistics and Poetics." (Sebeok's earlier symposium on myth had provided a forum for Lévi-Strauss' "Structural Study of Myth.") Through the work of Hymes, a participant in that conference, the insights and method of Lévi-Strauss and Jakobson would be brought together to advance the study of Native American literatures as they might be encountered and/or restructured in their original languages.

As early as 1953, while working at Indiana University, Hymes began to conceive the possibility of what he has called "a living relation, through fresh translation and study of the [Native American] originals, to modern poetry."[37] But in the 1950s—to take a single suggestive instance—it was Sputnik and the challenge to further conquest of nature, rather than nature itself, that most engaged Americans. The federal government renewed its efforts to Americanize the Indian under the policy known as "termination"; Washburn has described it as "the forced dissolution of tribal organizations and the break-up of existing tribal assets."[38] This was not a time in which the social order encouraged a cultural opening to Native American influences.

But by 1960, neither presidential candidate supported the termination policy; and by 1970, Richard Nixon, as president, declared government policy toward the Indians to be self-determination without termination. One of Nixon's first official acts was to return the sacred Blue Lake of the Taos Pueblo people. The rights not only of Native peoples but of all those who had traditionally been excluded from full social and literary representation were asserted in the 1970s, arousing a broad increase of interest in traditional Native American culture and literature.

As early as 1951, Gary Snyder, then a senior at Reed College, had written his B.A. thesis on a Haida myth and, in 1960, Snyder's *Myths and Texts,* work done between 1952 and 1956, appeared; I shall return to this shortly. In 1961, Kenneth Rexroth's important essays "The Poet as Translator" and "American Indian Songs" were published, while, a year later, Jerome Rothenberg inaugurated what would be a major and ongoing poetic program with his performance- and event-oriented *From a Shaman's Notebook: Poems from the Floating World.* This was an early attempt, as Rothenberg wrote in 1969, "to get as far away as I could from *writing.*"[39] By that time, Rothenberg had also published *Technicians of the Sacred: A Range of Poetries from Africa, America, Asia, and Oceania* (1968). Rothenberg's presumptuously global reach has been properly and abundantly criticized; yet this volume performed a service for non-Western poetries generally, and for Native American poetry in particular.[40] Rothenberg was not only perspicacious in his selection from the older translators—he included Densmore, Washington Matthews, and Pliny Earle Goddard, while excluding Austin, for example—but also collected newer translations by

William Carlos Williams, W. S. Merwin, and Rochelle Owens.[41] Perhaps most important, Rothenberg went to great lengths to demonstrate the way in which some modern and contemporary poetry follows "primitive" ("'primitive' means complex") directions.[42]

In the section of his "Pre-Face" to *Technicians of the Sacred* called "Primitive and Modern: Intersections and Analogies," Rothenberg tried to show "some of the ways in which primitive poetry and thought are close to an impulse toward unity in our own time, of which the poets are forerunners" (*TS*, p. xxii). Rothenberg lists six "important intersections" in some detail, which I shall abbreviate. These are: (1) "the poem carried by the voice," (2) "a highly developed process of image-thinking," (3) "a 'minimal' art of maximal involvement," (4) "an 'intermedia' situation" in which "the poet's techniques aren't limited to verbal maneuvers but operate also through song, non-verbal sound, visual signs, and the varied activities of the ritual event," (5) "the animal-body-rootedness of 'primitive' poetry," and (6) "the poet as shaman" (*TS*, pp. xxii–xxiii). Some of the "important intersections (analogies)" Rothenberg lists are: jazz and rock poetry, "Blake's multi-images," surrealism, random poetry, concrete poetry, happenings, dada, "lautgedichte (sound poems)," projective verse, "Rimbaud's voyant, Rilke's angel, Lorca's duende," beat poetry and psychedelic "poetry" (*TS*, pp. xxii, xxiii).

Rothenberg then illustrated contemporary intersections with the "primitive" by quoting a number of contemporary poems in his extended commentaries. He drew from his own work, as well as from Owens, Robert Creeley, Denise Levertov, and Diane Wakoski, among others, and included a translation from Pablo Neruda done by Robert Bly. Rothenberg also quoted a poem from Snyder's *Myths and Texts*. This volume of poems, published, as I have noted, in 1960, takes its title, as Snyder later wrote, "from the happy collections Sapir, Boas, Swanton, and others made of American Indian folktales early in this century."[43] It is no surprise, then, to find, as the poet and anthropologist Nathaniel Tarn puts it, "Indians everywhere."[44]

But Snyder does not only write about Indians; some of the time he tries to write like them, to incorporate aspects of their perspective, to approximate their oral modes of presentation. In *Technicians of the Sacred*, Rothenberg quoted Snyder's "First Shaman Song" (see *TS*, p. 429); I will quote here a brief section of "this poem is for bear," number 6 from "Hunting," the second section of *Myths and Texts*. The sources are "Marius Barbeau's Bear-Cult collections, an article by A. O. Hallowell [on the Bear-cult] . . . and Snyder's 'own encounters with Bears' ":[45]

> snare a bear: call him out:
> honey-eater
> forest apple
> light-foot

Old man in the fur coat, Bear! come out!
Die of your own choice
Grandfather black-food!

[*MT*, p. 24]

There is no "intermedia situation" here nor any particular shamanistic
or visionary stance, but the primacy of the voice is assumed; "image-
thinking" and "animal-body-rootedness" are central. These few lines accord
quite well with Rothenberg's account of "primitive" qualities in poetry.
What is also common to a great deal of Native American literature and
this brief quotation from Snyder is mixed tonality—in this instance, joc-
ularity and seriousness. To what extent Native American techniques—
oral and performative and in a "non-Western" language—can directly
or indirectly be incorporated into written verse in English is very difficult
to say. With the exceptions of Snyder and Rothenberg, whose interest
in the complexities of "primitive" technique has persisted, most non-
Native poets interested in Indians, as well as many of the better-known
Native American poets, have been fairly conservative in this regard.

In the 1960s, a considerable number of American poets turned from
European models and sources to acquaint themselves with Native American
models and sources—as they also turned to the cultural productions of
Afro-Americans and women.[46] To turn to Indians was to valorize the
natural (persistently) over the cultural; the communal and collective over
the private and individual; it was to seek the dramatically immediate in
literature and to reject the New Critical conception of the poem as object.
Many poets in the 1960s wrote, in Louis Simpson's phrase, "Indian poems";
so many, that it seemed, in Simpson's 1972 recollection, that

the Indian was being taken up again as a symbol. It was nostalgia,
and something more: in their search for a way of life to identify
with, poets were turning to an idea of the dark, suppressed American. . . . Poems about Indians were a fantasy of sophisticated twentieth-century people who were trying to find ways out of the materialism that was everywhere around them.[47]

In 1975, in response to an interviewer's question, Simpson elaborated:

We were trying to use the Indian as a means of expressing our
feeling about the repressed side of America that should be released.
However, if I or anyone were to continue to try to write Indian
poems, we should know more about Indians than we did, than I
did.[48]

This is surely correct; and it may serve to point up the obvious fact that
poems with Indian subjects do not necessarily have much to do with
Indians or, even less, with Indian models. Poets like Rothenberg and

Snyder have an informed awareness of Native cultures and their literary
productions; others like Stafford and Richard Hugo have a deep feeling
for the places so important to traditional Native cultures. Then there
are poets like James Tate, whose "One Dream of Indians" proclaims:

> When I thought of Indians
> before, I thought of slender
> muscular men with feather
>
> heads wailing hallelujah,
> of blood spears on white flesh, their
> two-toned ponies insane.[49]

But, the speaker tells us, ". . . There was one dream / of Indians I
didn't / dream, however. That was you." Here is that determined reduction
to the merely personal that marked a good deal of writing-school verse
in the 1950s, that carried into the 1960s, and that persists today. The
appearance of Indians in such poems is purely incidental and indicative
of no particular relation whatever to Native Americans and their literature.

5

It was in the 1960s as well that a number of powerful Native American
writers began to appear in print, among them Duane Niatum, Simon J.
Ortiz, Roberta Hill, and James Welch. By the end of the decade, in 1969,
the Pulitzer Prize for literature went to the Kiowa professor of English
literature N. Scott Momaday for his novel *House Made of Dawn*. That
same year, Momaday published his widely noticed, cross-cultural experiment in autobiography, *The Way to Rainy Mountain*. Momaday, as I have
noted, was a student of Winters and for his doctoral dissertation prepared
an edition of the poems of Frederick Tuckerman, Winters' candidate for
major American poet of the nineteenth century. Momaday, like Welch,
writes both poetry and fiction; his verse, however, seems closer to the
formal manner of later Winters than to anything discoverable in traditional
Native literature. Here are the opening stanzas of Momaday's "Angle of
Geese," which appeared in a volume of the same name:

> How shall we adorn
> Recognition with our speech?
> Now the dead firstborn
> Will lag in the wake of words.
>
> Custom intervenes;
> We are civil, something more:
> More than language means,
> The mute presence mulls and marks.[50]

And here is Welch's "Snow Country Weavers":

> A time to tell you things are well.
> Birds flew south a year ago.
> One returned, a blue-wing teal
> wild with news of his mother's love.
>
> Mention me to friends. Say
> wolves are dying at my door,
> the winter drives them from their meat.
> Say this: say in my mind
>
> I saw your spiders weaving threads
> to bandage up the day. And more,
> those webs were filled with words
> that tumbled meaning into wind.[51]

In Welch's poem, regular reference to animals is made, but most all else—the regular stanzas and irregular rhymes (in particular, the final "mind"/"wind" and the brooding-earnest tone—derives from the Eur-american rather than the Native American literary tradition. This is generally true of the work of Hill and Niatum, who, with Welch and Momaday, probably appear most frequently in general anthologies of American poetry. Their technical conservatism seems a recognition of the inevitable presence, in written verse in English, of the European poetic tradition.

I am far from implying, with these observations, a negative judgment upon the work of these writers; obviously, Native American poets are entitled to the same freedom accorded their non-Native counterparts in their choice of subject matter and formal manner. And, in any case, there are decided occasions on which these poets adopt a more open, more voice-oriented style. The relation of other contemporary Indian poets— I think of Ortiz, Ray A. Young Bear, and Joy Harjo—to European poetics is more tentative, more marginal. I will quote in full Ortiz's "This Preparation" as an example:

> these sticks i am holding
> i cut down at the creek.
> i have just come from there.
> i listened to the creek
> speaking to the world,
> i did my praying,
> and then i took my knife
> and cut the sticks.
> there is some sorrow in leaving

fresh wounds in growing things,
but my praying has relieved
some of my sorrow. prayers
make things possible, my uncle said.
before i left i listened again
for words the creek was telling,
and i smelled its smell which
are words also. and then
i tied my sticks into a bundle
and came home, each step a prayer
for this morning and a safe return.
my son is sleeping still
in this quietness, my wife
is stirring at her cooking,
and i am making this preparation.
i wish to make my praying
into these sticks like gods have taught.[52]

The reverential stance toward "ordinary" life, the sense of human responsibility to nature, the commitment to a relationship of "participant maintenance" (in Robert Redfield's phrase) toward the universe: these are all attitudes familiar to the Native tradition. The poem is presented as spoken-performed, with gestures implied, as an aspect of some larger (ritual) event. On the other hand, "This Preparation" is not radically different from poems by certain non-Native poets; it is by and large assimilable to the Euramerican tradition. It will take further work on traditional Native American literatures—new translations and new studies and greater general familiarity—to indicate to what degree its methods as well as its outlook can figure in written verse in English.

In any case, it should be obvious that just as the mere existence of poems with Indian subjects by non-Native poets does not in itself constitute evidence of a genuine opening to Native American influences, so, too, the mere existence of poems in print by Native American poets does not indicate any effective influence of traditional Native American literature on the canon. It does not seem possible or fruitful to attempt strictly to distinguish Native American from European influences in the work of Indian writers and non-Indians interested in Indian traditions, although the nature of the technical mix may well be worth attention. The errors to avoid, I believe, are to urge (as Leslie Marmon Silko has done) that Anglos simply stick to their own traditions, on the one hand, and, on the other, to insist (as Thomas Sanders and Walter Peek have done) that some "remembered Indianness" or "inherited and unconsciously sublimated urge to employ the polysynthetic structure of Native American languages" must somehow come through the English of poetry written by Native Americans.[53]

6

Some other developments of the late 1960s also bear importantly on our subject. For it was in 1968—the year Dover reissued Curtis' *Indians' Book*, while fighting was reported in Vietnam and the streets of Chicago— that rebellion took place among the professoriate at the MLA convention in New York City: a concerted effort to naturalize the canon and to revise its traditional hierarchies of race and gender. Earlier that same year, students in France had rebelled against their professors and the government that employed them, calling for the burning of the libraries and a return to nature: "Sous les paviers, la plage!" (" 'Under the pavement, the beach!' "). Earlier still, in 1966, French structuralism—*hors de Lévi-Strauss*—had arrived in force upon American shores to deliver the fourth blow, as it were, to Western humanistic narcissism (following the first three blows that Freud specified, those delivered by Galileo, Darwin, and Freud himself), with the symposium called "The Languages of Criticism and the Sciences of Man," held at the Johns Hopkins University. Michel Foucault was not present, but Barthes, Jacques Lacan, and the youthful Jacques Derrida were in attendance. At Johns Hopkins, Barthes announced that "to write" might be an intransitive verb; and Lacan dissolved the individual subject as "a fading thing that runs under the chain of signifiers. For the definition of a signifier is that it represents a subject not for another subject but for another signifier."[54] Derrida, already displaying his characteristic total assurance, told his audience that "one can say in total assurance that there is nothing fortuitous about the fact that the critique of ethno-centrism—the very condition of ethnology—should be systematically and historically contemporaneous with the destruction of the history of metaphysics. Both belong to a single and same era."[55] This denial of the privileged place of man—and modern anthropology's contribution to the conditions of possibility for such a denial (an early subject, as well, of Foucault's discourse)—projects exactly the sort of revision of the Western consciousness that would bring it nearer to the world view of Native American peoples and thus contribute to a more ready understanding of traditional Native American literatures and their claims upon the canon.

Throughout the 1970s and to the present moment, the developments I have been tracing have continued. In 1973, an excellent formal textbook, *Literature of the American Indian*, appeared; by 1975 there were at least five available anthologies of American Indian poets, many of whom had originally published in prestigious quarterlies.[56] Just recently, in 1981, Joseph Bruchac, himself part Abnaki and a poet, collected the work of more than thirty Indian poets in *American Indian Writings*, a special issue of the *Greenfield Review*. The 1970s also saw the publication of John Bierhorst's valuable anthologies of Native American materials; Rothenberg's erratic but powerful volume of translation-versions, *Shaking the*

Pumpkin; and Merwin's workings of some of Robert Lowie's *Crow Texts.* Merwin's work appeared in *Alcheringa,* a journal of ethnopoetics, edited by Rothenberg and by the anthropologist Dennis Tedlock. *Alcheringa* not only published non-Western texts but occasionally included recordings with some of its issues. In 1979, Snyder's B.A. thesis was published as *He Who Hunted Birds in His Father's Village: The Dimensions of a Haida Myth,* with a preface by Tarn. *Myths and Texts,* which had been in and out of print since its original appearance in 1960, was finally reissued by Snyder's principal publisher, New Directions, in 1978.

Two important books of poetic translations from the 1970s deserve particular mention—one by Tedlock and one by Howard Norman. On the basis of recent work, I think it's reasonable to require that translations of Native American literature, if they are to be considered approximately authentic, meet two specific conditions. First, they must derive from an actual, taped, or re-creative audition of the Native performance. Second, they must be produced in accord with what Hymes has called "philological recognition of the original, not bilingual control," at least a rough working knowledge of the language in question.[57] To produce his extraordinary translations from the Zuni, *Finding the Center* (1972), Tedlock himself tape-recorded the narratives he would translate. Highly competent in Zuni, Tedlock sought to indicate the structural principles of Zuni narrative performance by attention to its metalinguistic features, its changes of pace and volume, the gestures of the narrator, and the audience responses; these he attempted to present by means of typographical variations. Although a shift from large to small type does not strictly represent a shift in volume from loud to soft, it does insist that something has changed; spaces on the page are not silences—but we are sufficiently accustomed to the analogy to respond to it.

Tedlock's translations are of Zuni *narrative;* yet they are arranged on the page in a manner that corresponds more closely to Euramerican poetry than to the more usual Euramerican medium for narrative, prose. Tedlock has argued long and well, however, that prose has "no existence outside the written page."[58] In one way or another, he has been supported in this conclusion by the practices of Barre Toelken and Hymes, who have both advanced the artful science of what Toelken calls the "poetic retranslation" of Indian narrative that formerly had been transcribed in blocks of "prose."[59]

Similarly, Norman's collection, *The Wishing Bone Cycle: Narrative Poems from the Swampy Cree Indians* (1976), translates Indian stories into what appear, on the page, as poetry. Norman, a non-Native, grew up in proximity to Cree people and learned their language. A poet himself, he gathered these stories and presented them so effectively as to make a strong case for the power of Native American literary production—as well as to point out that traditional examples of that production are still discoverable. (Tedlock's collection performs the same service.)

The Wishing Bone Cycle, according to Norman, is a trickster cycle, but "the inventor and initiator of these particular poems was Jacob Nibenegenesabe, who lived for ninety-four years northeast of Lake Winnipeg, Canada."[60] Nibenegenesabe says, "I go backward, look forward, as the porcupine does," and Norman explains: "The idea is that each time these stories about the past are told they will be learned for the future" (*WBC,* p. 4). These are, again, stories; they are narrated rather than sung or otherwise accompanied by music or dance; and they are both traditional and original, more or less in the same ways that traditional "authors" in Native cultures were always both originators and augmenters—as, indeed, the etymology of our word "author," from the Latin *augere,* indicates. An example:

> One time I wished myself in love.
> I was the little squirrel
> with dark stripes.
> I climbed shaky limbs for fruit for her.
> I even swam with the moon on the water
> to reach her.
> That was a time little troubled me.
> I worked all day to gather food
> and watched her sleep all night.
> It is not the same way now
> but my heart still sings
> when I hear her
> over the leaves.
>
> [*WBC,* p. 8]

Among other interesting texts in Norman's volume are a group of "short poems," which "may be spoken by anyone in a Cree community. Once told, even poems derived from the most personal experiences become community property" (*WBC,* p. 93). Here is one from John Rains:

> I am the poorest one.
> I cook bark.
> I have bad luck in hunting.
> A duck caught my arrow
> and used it
> for her nest.
>
> I am the poorest one.
> I sit in mud and weep.
> I have bad luck in hunting.
> A goose caught my arrow
> and broke it
> in two.

I am old, old.
Don't bring me pity,
but food
yes.

[*WBC,* pp. 93–94]

The two brief examples above show the "highly developed process of image-thinking," the "animal-body-rootedness," of a " 'minimal' art of maximal involvement," a poetry of mixed tonalities, blurring the lines between vision and reality; this is a poetry carried by the voice that is yet richly appealing on the page.

7

Although not exactly continuous, the Native American challenge to the canon, as I have tried to show, has been of comparatively long standing. Nonetheless, inasmuch as Native American literary production and Euramerican writing influenced by it have only barely begun to enter the courses in and the anthologies of general American literature, that challenge cannot be said to have been effective as yet. No doubt it will take more time for poets and teachers to recognize what Native American literatures aboriginally were and, to some extent, still are; to recognize when and if the influence of these literatures is present in work by Native and non-Native writers. It is only since the 1950s and 1960s that philological and structural work has begun to make this recognition possible in any case.

It is only more recently still that an adequately sophisticated criticism for these literatures has begun to develop, with the publication of Abraham Chapman's basic and eclectic collection of essays, *Literature of the American Indians: Views and Interpretations* (1975); Karl Kroeber's uneven but valuable introduction to the subject, *Traditional Literatures of the American Indian: Texts and Interpretations* (1981); and Hymes' *"In Vain I Tried to Tell You": Essays in Native American Ethnopoetics* (1981), a collection of Hymes' seminal and indispensable work. The broadest and most sophisticated collection of essays—gathering work by Hymes, Tedlock, Toelken, Kroeber, and others—has only just appeared: *Smoothing the Ground: Essays on Native American Oral Literature* (1982) is edited by Brian Swann, a poet and translator of Native American songs.[61] These developments are encouraging for Native American literatures. As American society continues to move away from anthropocentrism and textual authority, the Native tradition may for the first time effectively assert its claim upon the canon of American literature.

1. See my "American Autobiography: The Western Tradition," *Georgia Review* 35 (Summer 1981): 307–17.

2. Michael Dorris, a Modoc, makes the point that "there is no such thing as 'Native American literature,' though it may yet, someday, come into being," because there was not and there is not either a single Indian language or a single Indian culture ("Native American Literature in an Ethnohistorical Context," *College English* 41 [Oct. 1979]: 147). This is, of course, true. There is no single Western or European language or culture and, so, no Western or European literature either by this reasoning: nonetheless, as a conceptual entity or heuristic device, the category of "Native American literature" is as tenable, surely, as that of Western or European literature. I shall refer, however warily, to both.

3. Leslie A. Fiedler, "Literature as an Institution: The View from 1980," in *English Literature: Opening Up the Canon*, ed. Fiedler and Houston A. Baker, Jr., Selected Papers from the English Institute, 1979, n.s. 4 (Baltimore, 1981), p. 73.

4. Roland Barthes, "Réflexions sur un manuel," in *L'Enseignement de la littérature*, ed. Serge Doubrovsky and Tzvetan Todorov (Paris, 1971), p. 170; my translation.

5. Walter J. Ong, S.J., *Interfaces of the Word: Studies in the Evolution of Consciousness and Culture* (Ithaca, N.Y., 1977), p. 305.

6. Roy Harvey Pearce, *Savagism and Civilization: A Study of the Indian and the American Mind* (Baltimore, 1965), p. 80.

7. Lieut. Henry Timberlake, *Memoirs: 1756–1765* (Johnson City, Tenn., 1927), p. 81.

8. B. B. Thatcher, *Indian Biography; or, An Historical Account of Those Individuals Who Have Been Distinguished among the North American Natives as Orators, Warriors, Statesmen, and Other Remarkable Characters* (1832; Glorieta, N.Mex., 1973), unpaginated preface.

9. Perry Miller, "Nature and the National Ego," *Errand into the Wilderness* (Cambridge, Mass., 1956), p. 209.

10. Pearce, *Savagism and Civilization*, p. 124.

11. A. Grove Day, *The Sky Clears: Poetry of the American Indians* (New York, 1951), p. 27. Day gives a fairly comprehensive history of American interest in Native American poetry. I have tried to avoid mere duplication in my own account of some of these matters.

12. "Chant to the Fire-Fly," trans. Henry Rowe Schoolcraft, quoted in ibid., p. 28. See also John Greenway, *Literature among the Primitives* (Hatboro, Pa., 1964), pp. 13–14; and Dell Hymes, "Some North Pacific Coast Poems: A Problem in Anthropological Philology," *American Anthropologist* 67 (Apr. 1965): 319–21. Hymes' essay is reprinted with some changes and additions in his *"In Vain I Tried to Tell You": Essays in Native American Ethnopoetics* (Philadelphia, 1981), pp. 35–62. Schoolcraft's translation also appears in John Bierhorst, ed., *Songs of the Chippewa* (New York, 1974).

Hymes' attempts to translate Schoolcraft's text—and others—are particularly instructive because Hymes is committed to the examination of existing Native originals. What Jeffrey Huntsman has called "the translation dilemma" in regard to traditional Native American literatures is considerable (see his "Traditional Native American Literature: The Translation Dilemma," *Shantih* 4 [Summer-Fall 1979]: 5–9; rpt. in *Smoothing the Ground: Essays on Native American Oral Literature*, ed. Brian Swann [Los Angeles, 1982], pp. 87–97). Leslie Marmon Silko has claimed that "white poets use the term 'translation' very loosely when applied to Asian or Native American material; few, if any, of them, are conversant in the Asian or Native American languages they pretend to 'translate.' What they do is sit down and rearrange English transcriptions done by ethnologists, and then call this a 'translation' " ("An Old-Time Indian Attack Conducted in Two Parts," *Shantih* 4 [Summer-Fall 1979]: 3). She is, in general, correct, but the matter is not so simple. "White poets" also "translate" from other white poets whose language—Dutch, Russian, Polish—they may not understand; and all translators, no matter how "conversant" they may be with the language of the original, face choices that cannot be determined strictly on the basis of greater or lesser knowledge. Silko's observation points up the importance of attention to what I have called the mode of production of Native texts (see my "An Approach to Native American Texts," *Critical Inquiry* 9 [Dec. 1982]: 323–38. Hymes' essay cited above is the best single account of translation dilemmas, which I also discuss briefly below, pp. 165–67.

13. "Midé Songs," trans. Schoolcraft, quoted in Day, *The Sky Clears*, p. 146.

14. Theodore Roosevelt, quoted in Wilcomb E. Washburn, *The Indian in America* (New York, 1975), p. 242.

15. Washburn, *The Indian in America*, p. 245.

16. Roosevelt, in *The Indians' Book: An Offering by the American Indians of Indian Lore, Musical and Narrative, to Form a Record of the Songs and Legends of Their Race,* ed. Natalie Curtis [Burlin] (1907; New York, 1968), unpaginated prefatory letter.

17. Curtis, in *The Indians' Book,* pp. xxvii, xxix; all further references to this work, abbreviated *IB,* will be included parenthetically in the text.

18. Hymes, *"In Vain I Tried to Tell You,"* p. 6 (see n. 12 above).

19. Edward Sapir and Ruth Benedict, among Franz Boas' early students, wrote a good deal of verse. Contemporary anthropologist-poets include Dennis Tedlock, Nathaniel Tarn, and Paula Gunn Allen.

20. Tedlock, "On the Translation of Style in Oral Narrative," *Journal of American Folklore* 84 (Jan.-Mar. 1971): 119. This essay is reprinted in *Smoothing the Ground,* pp. 57–77 (see n. 12 above).

21. Mary Austin, introduction to *The Path on the Rainbow: An Anthology of Songs and Chants from the Indians of North America,* ed. George W. Cronyn (New York, 1918), p. xv; all further references to this work, abbreviated *PR,* will be included parenthetically in the text.

22. Austin, "The Path on the Rainbow," *Dial* 31 May 1919, p. 569; all further references to this work, abbreviated *PRD,* will be included parenthetically in the text.

23. Austin, *The American Rhythm: Studies and Reëxpressions of Amerindian Songs* (Boston, 1930), p. 19. This is the "enlarged and expanded edition" of the text published originally in 1923. All further references to this work, abbreviated *AR,* will be included parenthetically in the text.

24. Obviously, T. S. Eliot and Ezra Pound ought not strictly be linked as one. Pound's interest in ideographic language, in varieties of Japanese practice, in charms and spells and incantations makes him available as sympathetic elder to Native American influences in ways that Eliot simply is not. Jerome Rothenberg will offer a "Pre-Face" to a collection of Cree translations (see n. 60 below) with an epigraph from Pound, and Tarn will invoke Pound for a discussion of Gary Snyder's Indian sources (see n. 44 below). For all the concerns Pound shared with Eliot, it is important to acknowledge the concerns the two did not share, as well.

25. F. H. Matthews, "The Revolt against Americanism: Cultural Pluralism and Cultural Relativism as an Ideology of Liberation," *Canadian Review of American Studies* 1 (Spring 1970): 14.

26. The quoted terms are from Philip Rahv; he first offered them in the late 1930s, although, to my knowledge, he was not interested in Indians or in Austin. See Rahv, "Paleface and Redskin," *Literature and the Sixth Sense* (Boston, 1969), pp. 1–6; originally published in *Kenyon Review* 1 (Summer 1939): 251–56.

27. Yvor Winters, *The Collected Poems of Yvor Winters* (Manchester, 1978), p. 13.

28. "I was familiar also with many translations from the poetry of the Japanese" (ibid.).

29. Ibid., pp. 32, 33.

30. Winters, "The Indian in English," rpt. in Winters, *Uncollected Essays and Reviews,* ed. Francis Murphy (Chicago, 1975), p. 39.

31. Winters, "Open Letter to the Editors of *This Quarter,*" rpt. in *Uncollected Essays and Reviews,* p. 33.

32. Winters, "The Indian in English", rpt. in *Uncollected Essays and Reviews,* p. 35.

33. Louis Untermeyer, "The Indian as Poet," *Dial,* 8 Mar. 1919, p. 241.

34. H. Bruce Franklin, "English as an Institution: The Role of Class," in *English Literature: Opening Up the Canon,* p. 100. For an evaluation of the standard school anthologies in relation to the literature of American minorities, see Ernece B. Kelly, ed., *Searching for America,* A Publication of the National Council of Teachers of English Task Force on Racism and Bias in the Teaching of English (Urbana, Ill., 1972).

35. Untermeyer, "Native Ballads and Folk Songs: American Indian Poetry," in *American Poetry: From the Beginning to Whitman*, ed. Untermeyer (New York, 1931), p. 693.

36. Hymes, "Some North Pacific Coast Poems," p. 317; and William Bevis, "American Indian Verse Translations," in *Literature of the American Indians: Views and Interpretations*, ed. Abraham Chapman (New York, 1975), p. 323.

37. Hymes, "Some North Pacific Coast Poems," p. 318.

38. Washburn, *The Indian in America*, p. 268.

39. Rothenberg, "Total Translation: An Experiment in the Presentation of American Indian Poetry," in *Literature of the American Indians*, p. 303.

40. Bevis' "American Indian Verse Translations" contains the most telling critique. More recently, see William M. Clements, "Faking the Pumpkin: On Jerome Rothenberg's Literary Offenses," *Western American Literature* 16 (Nov. 1981): 193–204.

41. These are, for the most part, of just the sort scorned by Silko (see n. 12 above); their value, however, remains to be determined.

42. Rothenberg, "Primitive Means Complex," in *Technicians of the Sacred: A Range of Poetries from Africa, America, Asia, and Oceania*, ed. Rothenberg (New York, 1968), p. xx; all further references to this work, abbreviated *TS*, will be included parenthetically in the text.

43. Snyder, *Myths and Texts* (1960; New York, 1978), p. vii; all further references to this work, abbreviated *MT*, will be included parenthetically in the text.

44. Tarn, preface to Snyder, *He Who Hunted Birds in His Father's Village: The Dimensions of a Haida Myth* (Bolinas, Calif., 1979), p. xv.

45. Lee Bartlett, "Gary Snyder's *Myths and Texts* and the Monomyth," *Western American Literature* 17 (Aug. 1982): 141.

46. Some of the poets who showed interest in Indians in the 1960s were Robert Bly, Robert Creeley, Edward Dorn, Richard Hugo, Galway Kinnell, W. S. Merwin, Rochelle Owens, William Stafford, David Wagoner, and James Wright, among others. Theodore Roethke's 1964 collection, *The Far Field*, contains a "North American Sequence." A section of that sequence called "The Longing" ends (rather awkwardly): "Old men should be explorers? / I'll be an Indian. / Ogalala? / Iroquois." ("The Longing," *Collected Poems of Theodore Roethke* [Garden City, N.Y., 1966], p. 189).

47. Louis Simpson, *North of Jamaica* (New York, 1972), pp. 241–42.

48. Simpson, in Lawrence R. Smith's interview, "A Conversation with Louis Simpson," *Chicago Review* 27 (Summer 1975): 105. Simpson's next sentence reads, "I was writing with sympathy and an historical sense of feeling, but to write about Indians you should in a sense become an Indian." Silko, in *Shantih*, quotes Simpson's remarks in order to observe, "again the unmitigated egotism of the white man, and the belief that he could 'in a sense become an Indian' " ("An Old-Time Indian Attack," p. 3). Unfortunately for Silko's "attack," Simpson had gone on to say, "you have to know how they think and feel. And *that I know I could never do, so I wouldn't even bother trying.* I have enough to do to write about what I do know" (p. 105; my emphasis). This last remark Silko does not quote.

49. James Tate, from "One Dream of Indians," *The Lost Pilot* (1967; New York, 1982), p. 54.

50. N. Scott Momaday, "Angle of Geese," in *Carriers of the Dream Wheel: Contemporary Native American Poetry*, ed. Duane Niatum (New York, 1975), p. 106.

51. James Welch, "Snow Country Weavers," in *Carriers of the Dream Wheel*, p. 249.

52. Simon J. Ortiz, "This Preparation," in *Literature of the American Indian*, ed. Thomas E. Sanders and Walter W. Peek (New York, 1973), p. 467.

53. Sanders and Peek, "Anguished, Angry, Articulate: Current Voices in Poetry, Prose, and Protest," in *Literature of the American Indian*, p. 449. The two Native American editors have put together an extremely fine collection; their commentary, as I find it, varies from excellent to inaccurate.

54. Barthes, "To Write: An Intransitive Verb?" and Jacques Lacan, "Of Structure as an Inmixing of an Otherness Prerequisite to Any Subject Whatever," both in *The Structuralist Controversy: The Languages of Criticism and the Sciences of Man*, ed. Richard Macksey and Eugenio Donato (Baltimore, 1972), pp. 141, 194, respectively.

55. Jacques Derrida, "Structure, Sign, and Play in the Discourse of the Human Sciences," in *The Structuralist Controversy*, pp. 251–52; Derrida goes on to discuss the work of Claude Lévi-Strauss. As interesting a subject, but one excluded, at that time, by Derrida's strict Eurocentrism, would have been the work of Boas.

56. In addition to Niatum's collection, *Carriers of the Dream Wheel*, cited above, see Terry Allen, ed., *The Whispering Wind: Poetry by Young American Indians* (New York, 1972); Robert K. Dodge and Joseph B. McCullough, eds., *Voices from Wah'Kon-Tah: Contemporary Poetry of Native Americans* (New York, 1974); Dick Lourie, ed., *Come to Power: Eleven Contemporary American Indian Poets* (Trumansburg, N.Y., 1974); and Kenneth Rosen, ed., *Voices of the Rainbow: Contemporary Poetry by American Indians* (New York, 1975).

57. Hymes, "Some North Pacific Coast Poems," p. 336. Very little that we have in the anthologies of Indian literature meets the two requirements for approximate authenticity I have posited, but I am far from suggesting that we should ignore all but that little. Rather, we need to pay particularly careful attention to the mode of production of Native American texts, attempting to specify as precisely as we can the division of labor among Native informants, performers, and translators, and non-Native editors, transcribers, and translators. In varying degrees, any knowledge we can have of traditional Native American literatures will always be knowledge, as well, of the role Euramericans have played in its textual production. This is only one price of our history of domestic imperialism.

58. Tedlock, "Toward an Oral Poetics," *New Literary History* 8 (Spring 1977): 513.

59. See Barre Toelken and Tacheeni Scott, "Poetic Retranslation and the 'Pretty Languages' of Yellowman," in *Traditional Literatures of the American Indian: Texts and Interpretations*, ed. and comp. Karl Kroeber (Lincoln, Nebr., 1981), pp. 65–116. In Kroeber's compilation, Hymes offers a poetic retranslation of a Clackamas Chinook tale that had been originally published in prose by Melville Jacobs; see "Reading Clackamas Texts," pp. 117–59. This essay also appears in *"In Vain I Tried to Tell You"* (pp. 342–81), which also contains other retranslations by Hymes. For a detailed consideration of Kroeber's book and the work of Tedlock, Hymes, Toelken, and Jarold Ramsey, see my "Identity and Difference in the Criticism of Native American Literature," *Diacritics* 13 (Summer 1983): 2–28.

60. Howard A. Norman, comp. and trans., *The Wishing Bone Cycle: Narrative Poems from the Swampy Cree Indians* (New York, 1976), p. 3; all further references to this work, abbreviated *WBC*, will be included parenthetically in the text. Several of these poems were first published in the Tedlock-Rothenberg journal, *Alcheringa* (Norman's book has a "Pre-Face" by Rothenberg), where they appeared along with the translator's transcriptions from the Cree. Huntsman has commented on Norman's translations in his "Traditional Native American Literature: The Translation Dilemma" (see n. 12 above).

61. For his translations, see, for example, Swann's *Song of the Sky: Versions of Native American Songs and Poems* (forthcoming). Swann works from texts, not performances, from English language versions, not transcriptions of Native languages; as a result, he has made a point of insisting, "These poems of mine are *not* translations" but instead "versions" of Native American poetry. Although he has given up specific claims to authenticity, Swann has nonetheless shown how much can be done by the non-Native poet and scholar responding to the Native tradition as a powerful source.

The Ideology of Canon-Formation:
T. S. Eliot and Cleanth Brooks

John Guillory

> The canons are falling
> One by one
> Including "*le célèbre*" of Pachelbel
> The final movement of Franck's sonata for
>   piano and violin.
> How about a new kind of hermetic conservatism
> And suffering withdrawal symptoms of same?
> —JOHN ASHBERY, "The Tomb of Stuart Merrill"

1. Ideology

It would be difficult to deny that ideology traverses even the higher regions of textual production, including literature itself; yet the monadic text has offered an impressive resistance to traditional critiques of ideological content. I propose in this essay to shift the attention of such critiques away from the individual text or author and toward that organization of texts known as a "canon."[1] The particular canon to be examined here emerged in T. S. Eliot's earlier criticism, was presented as a canon by Cleanth Brooks in *The Well Wrought Urn*, and has since been institutionalized to a greater or lesser extent in the curricula of university English departments.

The recognition of ideology is usually expressed as an accusation: the ideologue speaks out of his "false consciousness," his state of illusion. Recently it has been possible to conceive of ideology rather as an unconscious "system of representations," a notion probably more appropriate but which also entails a large epistemological problem. It is not at all evident what sort of "truth" is produced by a critique of ideology, except that such truth aspires to overcome the philosophical antitheses between fact and value, the scientific and the emotive, or knowledge and interest.[2] At the least the critique of ideology discloses the complicity of interest in nearly any discourse whatever; and if the process of canon-formation is not excluded from the system of ideological production, it should be possible to move beyond the massively resistant tautology of literary history: that works *ought* to be canonized because they *are* good.

Canon-formation is nevertheless not an obvious production of ideology; the "interests" of Eliot and Brooks—Eliot's Christian authoritarianism or Brooks' association with the neoagrarian movement—are elsewhere expressed quite openly. Though I will glance at some rather more opinionated texts, I want to argue that such texts have not been nearly so effective as those canon-making essays whose serene judgments upon poetic careers or complex close readings seem far removed from the realm of interest, indeed whose very claim upon our admiration is their detachment, their disinterestedness. At the moment, however, I am not concerned with proving that such essays are not disinterested (that proof will take care of itself) but only with pointing out that group whose interest is aroused and expressed by the evaluation of literature; this group is what we know as literary culture, a marginal elite.

The authority of the culture, what maintains it as both marginal and elite, is not to be distinguished from the authority of the canon. For *some* reason *some* literature is worth preserving. We would not expect this or any other conception of authority to have escaped the vicissitudes of social hierarchy, but this is just the claim of the canonical text, which is assumed to be *innately* superior. Indeed we refuse (and this refusal is grounded in much critical theory) to think of the literary work as good or bad for some extrinsic reason; such a possibility can be conceived only as propaganda or censorship, the hot areas of ideological production. When I say, then, that it seems unlikely that the formation of canons is wholly removed from the field of ideological conflict, not much is being asserted. The claim to judge intrinsically, as though the value of a literary work were not mediated by any other concern, has always been suspect. If it *were* possible to form a canon of texts with the easy assurance that only the best literature survives, such a canon would have a structure and genealogy like that of aristocracy in its idealized form: the "rule of the best."

John Guillory, assistant professor of English at Yale University, is the author of *Poetic Authority: Spenser, Milton, and Literary History* (1983). He is currently working on a study of canon-formation.

While the social form of aristocracy has declined, the canon has retained its self-image as an aristocracy of texts. It would be hard to give up this image, as the pure authority of great literature may be the only image of pure authority we have. Yet we can "modernize" canon-formation in just the way that aristocracy was transformed from the sixteenth to the eighteenth century, by all the varieties of persuasion that are supposed to give us a rationalized authority. If we must be persuaded of a work's authority, then it follows that we can be *wrongly* persuaded. The possibility of error is just the precondition of literary culture, which defends the canon and defends itself.

The question I would like to pose about the canon of Eliot can be restated in terms that make unambiguous the ideological burden of canon-formation. For Eliot told us nothing less than that we *had* been wrongly persuaded. The rediscovery of a marginal elite standing in an apocryphal relation to the established canon marks a shifting of authority within the literary culture, as it adjusts to the instabilities of its marginal position. But this hypothesis necessitates an inquiry into the principles of Eliot's canon-making criticism.

2. Orthodoxy

Eliot's canonical motives are of course most visible where his judgments are revisionary. Consider, for example, this very typical evaluation of John Dryden, whose virtues are displayed by contrasting them with Milton's defects:

> The great advantage of Dryden over Milton is that while the former is always in control of his ascent, and can rise or fall at will . . . the latter has elected a perch from which he cannot afford to fall, and from which he is in danger of slipping.[3]

Eliot's image of flight implies an ironic revision òf normative values, because it is not actually the works of the two poets which are being compared but the *choices* which precede composition, the "perches" from which flight is undertaken. The momentary irrelevance of the works themselves discovers a system of value which is already more broadly based than any putative "aesthetic" and which will underlie much more than an attack on Milton.

The effect of the evaluative system can be measured by the deceptive lucidity of Eliot's critical prose: "[Dryden's] powers were, we believe, wider, but no greater, than Milton's; he was confined by boundaries as impassable, though less strait"(*SE*, p. 273). Does this mean Dryden's powers were *as* great *and* wider than Milton's? The neoclassical-sounding rhetoric can be said to do the revolutionary job of displacing the axis of evaluation from the vertical—greatness, height—to the horizontal—width, breadth. The latter figure calls out to its negative image—straitness, narrowness—but with a gesture of reconciliation. Poetic ambition is certainly limited (the sense of Eliot's impassable boundaries), and it would seem to be the ground of Dryden's superiority that he accepts these limitations. His poetry is an art of "mak[ing] the small into the great" (*SE*, p. 269). Eliot's discrimination recapitulates the conventional language by which the canon is divided into major and minor poets and at the same time reverses the polarity of value. He cannot say that Dryden is a greater poet than Milton, but he can suggest that in valuing Milton we have perhaps been valuing the wrong thing. The problem is much larger than the relative status of Milton or Dryden, because it liberates what may be called the canonical engine of Eliot's criticism: the impassable boundary between major and minor.

Impasse is an overdetermined concept in Eliot's career; and I would like to untangle here the several strands of this determination, beginning with a historical example of lifelong interest to Eliot—the decline of poetic drama since the seventeenth century.[4] The existence of the impasse gives Eliot his darker version of literary history, the essay titled "The Possibility of a Poetic Drama," which can be set against the better-known "Tradition and the Individual Talent." I quote first two familiar sentences from the latter essay, with the object of calling attention to the rhetoric of canonization:

> The existing monuments form an ideal order among themselves, which is modified by the introduction of the new (the really new) work of art among them. The existing order is complete before the new work arrives; for order to persist after the supervention of novelty, the *whole* existing order must be, if ever so slightly, altered; and so the relations, proportions, values of each work of art toward the whole are readjusted; and this is conformity between the old and the new.[5]

The idealization of the very order of the monuments means that what the new poet threatens is disorder; he must present himself to his predecessors with a demeanor of conformity if he is to have any chance of altering them or of being admitted to their company. Few writers of our century seem more oppressed than Eliot by the feeling that the canon is by its very nature closed and that it can be reopened only by the most elaborate and even covert of strategies.[6] I read the famous doctrine of impersonality as one such strategy, a sacrifice demanded upon the threshold of the temple. The "continual self-sacrifice," or "extinction of personality," is a preliminary stance on the way to a more subversive posture of *ironic* modesty, a posture which both contains and expresses quite a violent revisionist impulse.

Once Eliot formulates the doctrine of impersonality, he points out a bifurcation of his argument: "There remains to define this process of depersonalization and its relation to [the first subject of the essay] the sense of tradition." Then follows the analogy of the catalyst, which accomplishes just this reconnection. The mind of the poet is merely the shred of platinum in the larger container in which two gases are mixed; but this mind contained is shortly presented as the container itself: "The poet's mind is in fact a receptacle for seizing and storing up numberless feelings, phrases, images, which remain there until all the particles which can unite to form a new compound are present together" (*SW*, p. 55). The reader is intended to understand by this analogy the way in which the deliberate puzzle of tradition and the individual talent is being solved. The impersonal mind is emptied of content (mere emotion, personality), and it thereby becomes only form, the colorless beaker in a laboratory of art. Form has already been monumentalized in "Tradition and the Individual Talent," because it is essentially what the dead poets have become, what Eliot calls "ideal order." What they demand is conformity, which surely has a charged relation to that other word for the poem-as-container. The analogy is geometrically scaled, for the form of any one poem is a small version of literature itself; but in relation to that whole, it is a figure for the mind of the poet—both the container *and* the shred of platinum which has been surreptitiously placed into the otherwise stable mixture, the ideal order of the dead poets. Form and content, container and contained, have just this predictable tendency to exchange places, and Eliot's approach to the sealed canon is wholly dependent upon this useful ambiguity.

If the successful work of art represents a containing of emotion, or conforming to the form which is tradition itself, we are told in "The Possibility of a Poetic Drama" that some forms are inherently more capable of this project than others and that, surprisingly, the drama is most capable of all. It is the drama which stands both as the basic principle of canon-formation and as the arbitrary guarantor of the open-endedness of the canon: "Nevertheless, the drama is perhaps the most permanent, is capable of greater variation and of expressing more varied types of society, than any other. It varied considerably in England alone; but when one day it was discovered lifeless, subsequent forms which had enjoyed a transitory life were dead too" (*SW*, p. 61). It *would* be very interesting to understand the "death" of a form, but the easy mystification of "it was discovered lifeless" points to Eliot's more immediate concern with the effects of this demise. The only hint the essay gives us about causes is contained in a surprising sentence, which sets the drama in *opposition* to tradition: "The Elizabethan Age in England was able to absorb a great quantity of new thoughts and images, almost dispensing with tradition, because it had this great form of its own which imposed itself on everything that came to it" (*SW*, p. 62). This view of tradition is not easily reconciled with that of "Tradition and the Individual Talent," but the rhetoric is fundamentally the same. The Elizabethan freedom from the burden of tradition is the gift mainly of one form, the blank-verse drama, and this fact implies conversely that tradition in the more famous essay is a palliative for the *absence* of form. The "extinction of personality" likewise finds its counterpart in "The Possibility of a Poetic Drama" with Eliot's reflection that the virtues of dramatic form are so great that the personality of the poet is entirely (and happily) submerged. How fortunate to be Shakespeare—not because Shakespeare is great himself but simply because he is the lucky inheritor of a form, the first to see its almost limitless possibilities. "We should see then how little each poet had to do; only so much as would make a play his, only what was really essential to make it different from anyone else's" (*SW*, p. 64).

In the next paragraph Eliot makes an unexpected turn (though in a deeper sense, the digression is determined) to the subject of minor poets:

> Now in a formless age there is very little hope for the minor poet to do anything worth doing; and when I say minor I mean very good poets indeed: such as filled the Greek anthology and the Elizabethan song-books; even a Herrick; but not merely second-rate poets, for Denham and Waller have quite another importance, occupying points in the development of a major form. When every-thing is set out for the minor poet to do, he may quite frequently come upon some *trouvaille*, even in the drama: Peele and Brome are examples. Under the present conditions, the minor poet has too much to do. [*SW*, p. 64]

The reader might well be bewildered by the introduction of this subject, for which no transition is provided. Surely the situation is not different for the major poet? Eliot is saying that "a formless age is one in which minor poetry is all but impossible"—but is this condition unfortunate only for the minor poet? The situation of the minor poet has been taken as normative, or even ideal; in the most desirable of historical circumstances, the individual poet has less to do, and the form more and more. Ideally all poets are minor in a world of major form, and one might argue that this conclusion follows inevitably from Eliot's conception of literary history after Shakespeare and Donne, a history which continues to produce major poets while undergoing a simultaneous atrophy of major form. I do not know how else to interpret a remark such as this from "Tradition and the Individual Talent": "The poet must be very conscious of the main current, which does not flow invariably through the most distin-guished reputations" (*SW*, p. 51). Already in 1919 Eliot is revising the canon.

Most of these revisions are well known, but it is not generally ac-knowledged that Eliot's principle of revision is the high valuation of the minor stance. Eliot's revisions—his preference for the Metaphysicals and Dryden over Spenser and Milton, for the Jacobean dramatists over Shakespeare, and his rejection of virtually all Romantic and Victorian poetry—can be projected from the inner argument of the early essays.[7] The influence of the essays is incalculable, even when their particular theories may be disputed, and despite various recantings by Eliot himself. The scope of his influence is in part attributable to the paradoxical ironizing of the minor stance: the thesis of minority is first conveyed by the haughty and authoritative prose of *The Sacred Wood*. The discordant but revealing stance of the early work is refined into the civilized modesty of later essays, establishing in this transformation the dominant tone of twentieth-century criticism, its ambivalent deference to literature.[8]

At any rate, the grounding of Eliot's canonical principles in a re-estimation of the minor poets is a demonstrable fact. It should be possible to show that his emphasis on craft over inspiration, his conception of wit, of poetry as "objective correlative," and above all the idea of the "dissociation of sensibility" are theories conditioned by his defense of minority, devised in response to the closure of the canon, whose monolithic enclosure is penetrable only by a strategic modesty. In his essay on Andrew Marvell, this covert system of canon-formation is for once made quite explicit, despite the rhetorical effort of denial:

> This virtue of wit is not a peculiar quality of minor poets, or of the minor poets of one age or one school; it is an intellectual quality which perhaps only becomes noticeable by itself, in the work of lesser poets. Furthermore it is absent from the work of Wordsworth, Shelley, and Keats, on whose poetry nineteenth-century criticism has unconsciously been based. [*SE*, p. 262][9]

We do not know, however, which major poets are capable of the wit here praised, and the concept functions more as an exclusive than an inclusive principle. The result is an alternative canon, to which Wordsworth, Shelley, Keats, and many others do not belong. The status of this canon is not competitive (at least not immediately); rather, it rises like a phantom' structure alongside the already finished house of literature. But this image expresses the canon's quality as an inexplicit formulation of Eliot's prose. Its real status is precisely that of Donne's poetry, which circulated among a coterie of admirers, or a marginal elite.

The long-deferred *recognition* of this elite (and "dissociation of sensibility" provides the historical explanation of this deferral) returns us to the problem of impasse, because the marginality of Eliot's canon in English literary history must be what is overcome *in this recognition*. In retrospect, it seems likely that the impasse of verse drama and the related unhappy schism of sensibility are only secondarily theories about the seventeenth century; they are primarily displacements of the recent impasse

of English poetry after the turn of the century. But the proper identification
of that bottleneck does not entirely clear up the constituents of the over-
determination. We are still puzzled by the need for such a theory at all,
after so successful a break in Eliot's own early poetry from an exhausted
tradition. The continued elaboration of a degenerative literary history
suggests that a discontinuity has not been achieved, that the impasse
prevails. I return to Eliot's distinction between Milton and Dryden for
some illumination of this difficulty: "No one, in the whole history of
English literature, has dominated that literature so long, or so completely.
And even in the nineteenth century the language was still the language
of Dryden, as it is to-day."[10] The subject here is really influence, about
which Eliot had usually different and darker things to say:

> Many people will agree that a man may be a great artist, and
> yet have a bad influence. There is more of Milton's influence in
> the badness of the bad verse of the eighteenth century than of
> anybody's else. . . . Milton's bad influence may be traced much farther
> than the eighteenth century, and much farther than upon bad
> poets: if we say that it was an influence against which we still have
> to struggle. [*OPP*, pp. 156–57]

And this would indeed be saying much. That Eliot himself should have
been influenced by Milton seems as inevitable for him as for any English
poet, but surely not to the extent of requiring so great a struggle? One
misses in Eliot's meditations on influence any sense of having to contend
with a *recent* poet, as though the revolution of modern poetry had over-
thrown a ruler long dead.

The charges against Milton are dubious enough to permit me this
violence against Eliot's text: let us suppose that Milton here is the *name*
for the effect of bad influence; that is to say, that Eliot's trope is a kind
of transferred epithet, where the poets *not named* are presumably Eliot's
own bad influences. We should be able to relate this figurative strategy
to the otherwise quite contradictory literary history dominated by Dryden,
whose name signifies benign influence:

> Far below Shakespeare, and even below Milton, as we must put
> him, he yet has, just by reason of his precise degree of inferiority,
> a kind of importance which neither Shakespeare nor Milton has—
> the importance of his *influence*. . . . It was Dryden, more than any
> other individual, who formed a language possible for mediocrity,
> and yet possible for later great writers to do great things with.[11]

Dryden clearly represents literary history as Eliot would have liked it to
be. Further, the dependence of the essay upon the usual valuation of
minority ineluctably points to a conception of healthy influence as em-
anating only from minor poets. In this light, the curious fact that Eliot's

recent major predecessors seem to have no influence comes into view as one *intention* of Eliot's revisionary canon. These later poets cannot be said to have powers of influence, except as they are the devastated remains of the Miltonic legacy. The field is cleared for poets who escaped that influence by not aspiring to the greatness of the progenitor.

It is in this context that we should read the essay "What Is Minor Poetry?," which seems so harmless and reasonable a production of Eliot's critical workshop; it is truly a text that Eliot has been writing all of his life. The essay does largely negative work, demolishing the notion that minor poetry is "failed great poetry," and this evaluative impulse is nothing other than Eliot's stance as a critic of English poetry.[12] We find, for example, that "Milton I" gets under way only by taking up the predictable defense:

> There is a large class of persons, including some who appear in print as critics, who regard any censure upon a "great" poet as a breach of the peace, as an act of wanton iconoclasm, or even hoodlumism. The kind of derogatory criticism that I have to make upon Milton is not intended for such persons, who cannot understand that it is more important, in some vital respects, to be a *good* poet than to be a *great* poet. [*OPP*, p. 157]

The figure of the minor poet cannot be detached from the problematics of influence, and it is this recognition that Eliot achieves in his second essay on Milton:

> There are two kinds of poet who can ordinarily be of use to other poets. There are those who suggest, to one or another of their successors, something which they have not done themselves, or who provoke a different way of doing the same thing: these are likely to be not the greatest, but smaller, imperfect poets with whom later poets discover an affinity. And there are the great poets from whom we can learn negative rules: no poet can teach another to write well, but some great poets can teach others some of the things to avoid. [*OPP*, p. 176]

Eliot has chosen his precursors carefully—Donne, the Jacobeans, the French symbolists—but I suspect that these names are rather after the fact, that they represent a stance that has been adopted toward the major precursors, who need never be named because they are lost in the darkness into which Milton plunged English poetry.

Lost in that darkness are not only the major precursors of Eliot's poetry but the recognition of an ideological force in the making or remaking of the canon. And so I would like to call from the shadows one of the influences upon Eliot's poetry—Tennyson—and permit him to testify about his exclusion from the Eliotic canon. He will speak, of course, in

Eliot's voice, as he would in no other way be able to comment on the meaning of his exclusion. The essay to be considered here is "*In Memoriam*," written in 1936, but I should remind the reader that, in "The Possibility of a Poetic Drama" (1920), Tennyson is said to have been "a master of minor forms," who "took to turning out large patterns on a machine." This early opinion is partially retracted, but the praise of the later essay is reserved for *In Memoriam*, while other works by Tennyson are still found deficient. Both the praise and the condemnation are immediately relevant to Eliot's career as a poet, as it is evident in the course of the essay that "*In Memoriam*" is the occasion of displaced commentary upon the critical reception of *The Waste Land* itself:

> Apparently Tennyson's contemporaries, once they accepted *In Memoriam*, regarded it as a message of hope and reassurance to their rather fading Christian faith. It happens now and then that a poet by some strange accident expresses the mood of his generation, at the same time that he is expressing a mood of his own which is quite remote from his generation. [*SE*, p. 291]

The Waste Land was believed (mistakenly, according to Eliot) to express the "despair" or "disillusion" of a generation, precisely the opposite of what Eliot says Tennyson's poem was *believed* to express.[13] Eliot's attention is then drawn to the question of religious belief, which might have been a spurious criterion in judging the achievement of Tennyson but which becomes crucial for Eliot, again because it is crucial in *his* career. Eliot argues that Tennyson never recovered from the disillusion of his poem; and this is to turn (brilliantly and deviously) the misreading of *The Waste Land* against *In Memoriam*. The real Tennyson is said to be "more interesting and tragic" than his contemporaries knew (*SE*, p. 292). This must mean that Tennyson's career failed after and *because* of *In Memoriam*. The analogy to Eliot's own career is therefore inverse: Eliot did recover from the despair of *The Waste Land*, did recover a religious faith denied in the end to Tennyson, and therefore moved beyond the impasse at which Tennyson was stuck. But this dangerous identification, even for the sake of a necessary difference, has perhaps a more moving effect than Eliot intended, since it gives us the finest of his reflected self-portraits: "Tennyson is not only a minor Virgil, he is also with Virgil as Dante saw him, a Virgil among the Shades, the saddest of all English poets, among the Great in Limbo, the most instinctive rebel against the society in which he was the most perfect conformist" (*SE*, p. 295). We know, of course, that Eliot's poetic scene *is* limbo, the place of those neither saved nor damned. Limbo is both a paradise and a prison, the embodiment of the ambivalence of limits, yet resolves that ambivalence by voiding the pain of the negative image, the circle of the undamned outside of Dante's hell.

The strength of identification is great enough at this point to compel a more vigorous effort by Eliot to distance himself from what might have been his future—which future would be quite evident if we were to substitute "Eliot" for "Tennyson" and *"The Waste Land"* for *"In Memoriam"* in the following passage:

> Tennyson seems to have reached the end of his spiritual development with *In Memoriam:* there followed no reconciliation, no resolution.
>
> > *And now no sacred staff shall break in blossom,*
> > *No choral salutation lure to light*
> > *A spirit sick with perfume and sweet night,*
>
> or rather with twilight, for Tennyson faced neither the darkness nor the light in his later years. The genius, the technical power, persisted to the end, but the spirit had surrendered. [*SE*, p. 295]

The upheaval of elegiac emotion is nothing less than the lament for a poetic career—but not Tennyson's. The poet of twilight, the "violet hour," must say these things about Tennyson and so say them, and not say them, about himself. But the displacement of meaning here is vastly more consequential than even this impasse, the decline of Eliot's poetic career after the composition of *The Waste Land.* The quotation from Swinburne redirects us by its very obliquity to the historical transitions, or failures of transition, over which Eliot is brooding. The elegy encapsulates the mythologies which are the substructures of Eliot's history, as the prelapsarian associated sensibility can be seen as nostalgia for a world in which such a miracle as the blossoming staff is more than an elegiac allusion. The meaning of his canon discloses itself to Eliot as the impasse which marks, like a gravestone, that other passage.

Nostalgia is only the beginning of a recognizably ideological discourse. The way through to the ideological sense of Tennyson's "failure," beneath the phenomenal glow of Eliot's nostalgia, lies in the entanglement of minority in this complex of meanings, the determination that Tennyson is properly placed when seen as a "minor Virgil." The diffusion of a major talent in minor works suggests that what Tennyson *or Eliot* might have been was another Virgil, and for Eliot that means simply a "classic." In "What Is a Classic?," we are told that English literature has no classic poet who would exalt, as Virgil or Dante did, the truths of his age.[14] The absence of a modern classic reflects not an individual failure but rather the absence of a universal truth, which has been hidden in the minor works. Here is the reason both for the ambivalence Eliot expresses about the fact of minority (a valuing of the right things and yet a deferral of greatness) and for the peculiar, and certainly not necessary, association of poetic minority with a marginal elite.[15]

It is the latter point to which I now want to turn. If it has been shown that the canon Eliot legislated in his early career was not merely an arbitrary set of aesthetic preferences, we have not yet fully evinced the ideological sense of Eliot's canonical principle. We have only determined that one way to reconstruct Eliot's canon would be to list those "minor" poets. But the essential quality of their minority, what drives them away from the "mainstream" of English literature, is what Eliot approved as their fidelity to "tradition." Such a concept of tradition must be exclusive as well as revisionary, because it implies that the major poets of English literary history cannot also be "traditional." Eliot finally understood that his canonical principle was the literary reflection of a more fundamental evaluative norm, *extrinsic to literature,* which he identified as "orthodoxy." So he tells us in *After Strange Gods* that he is rewriting "Tradition and the Individual Talent" by substituting "orthodoxy" for "tradition," and this is unquestionably an ideological correction.[16] In the same way, the canon of minor writers is established retrospectively as determined by the rule of orthodoxy. Neither they nor the young Eliot need be orthodox Christians for this rule to have enabled their productions. It is precisely Eliot's meaning that these elite, like the "elect" before them, may come at some point to a conviction of their election, yet they were always the elect. In this sense, Eliot's conversion to Christianity was the recognition that he already belonged to a marginal elite, whose membership had been polemically foreshadowed by the construction of an alternative canon.

Orthodoxy is "true opinion" or, as Eliot calls it, "right tradition," but what is the content of this *doxa?*[17] What does it teach us? It would be a mistake at this point to identify the *doxa* wholly with the truths of Christianity. Eliot does not make this mistake because he senses that orthodoxy is what functions as an effective ideological concept: "A Christian education would primarily train people to be able to think in Christian categories and would not impose the necessity for insincere profession of belief. What the rulers believed would be less important than the beliefs to which they would be obliged to conform."[18] The ideology defines its antithesis as "heresy," a word which is habitually opposed in Eliot's later writings to "tradition," "conformity," and "orthodoxy." I touch here upon *The Idea of a Christian Society,* and Eliot's other atavistic programs, not to deplore them, or to refute them, and certainly not to claim that a preference for Eliot's canon makes one vulnerable to the seduction of Christian belief. I rather take Eliot at his word (perhaps not entirely in his spirit) and say that the beliefs do not matter. What matters is that the dissemination of the alternative canon has an effect which can be described. The "readjustment" of literary history, the ordination of a new canonical principle, makes no difference at all to the marginal community of conservative Anglo-Catholics but quite a lot of difference to the marginal elite to which Eliot belonged as a poet and critic, to literary culture.[19] The complete revision of "Tradition and the Individual Talent" should then read: "Orthodoxy and the Literary Elite."

It is possible to understand by this translation the double consequence of that impasse/passage when orthodoxy was transferred from the major to the minor tradition, and heterodoxy passed from the minor to the major cultural register (this might explain, too, why Eliot revised the theory of dissociation to redeem Dryden, shifting his attack in the 1930s to Milton).[20] It is not the minority of literary culture which is to be lamented, after all; it is rather the decline of that elite which delivers orthodoxy to the rulers *and to the poets.* It is the marginality of the *clergy* which Eliot eventually identifies (with an odd but, I think, quite interesting historical insight) as the origin of that deprivation of "right opinion" in literature, and so of the proliferation of "sects."[21] The literary phenomenon of dissociation was only the consequence of the protracted divorce of church and state; the hypothesis might seem too reductive as an account of history, but it is the motivating force behind the regeneration of Eliot's poetic career and gives him both *Murder in the Cathedral* and the *Four Quartets.* The rift between Thomas and Henry, between the first estate and the second, between Dryden and Milton—these are the determinations of history, factual or mystified, behind the remaking of the canon.

If it is so desirable to seal these divisions, and that depends upon the restoration of authority to a clergy, then we might fairly say that Eliot's canonical reformation embodies only a wish-fulfillment fantasy. I have argued, on the contrary, that his canon, as the central thesis of an ideological discourse, has successfully represented to the agents of literary culture a mutation in the life of that culture. This success can be measured by the influence of one form of Eliot's canonical principle, advanced in his polemic against the Arnoldian substitution of poetry for religion.[22] That literature is historically *related* to religion seems an unavoidable observation. One might think of this relation as constitutive of the "Romanticism," broadly defined, of most literature produced since the sixteenth century. Eliot centers his resistance to a usurping or "vulgar" Romanticism (espoused by Arnold and condemned by Babbitt) in his valuation of the minor stance, which can be understood as a demand for the subordination of poetry to dogma. While this does not mean the deference of poets to clergymen, the structural subordination can be described as *reinstated* within literary culture, a homology we are now able to demonstrate.

What is the function of a clergy? As Eliot sees it, the clergy maintains the continuity of orthodoxy, of right tradition. This it can do only by first maintaining itself, so that it has an instrumental motive to act in accord with a ruling elite. Orthodoxy, as the form of ideology, must conceal its relation to hegemonic elements by incorporating a claim to universality: truth is truth for the whole of society. Since the elite which Eliot has in mind can no longer make this claim openly, it disappears as a social structure and reappears in the mystified form of an *incognito* clergy:

> We need therefore what I have called "the Community of Christians," by which I mean, not local groups, and not the Church in any one of its senses, unless we call it "the Church within the Church." These will be the consciously and thoughtfully practising Christians, especially those of intellectual and spiritual superiority.[23]

Eliot's "Community of Christians," as an invisible power, is surely not even a distant possibility, but neither does the clergy any longer conceive of itself as the transmitter of a surviving *universal* tradition. All that remains of this function has been appropriated by literary culture, which now produces what Edward Said rightly calls "religious criticism."[24] As a spiritual elite, the culture is disinclined to recognize that it has any other interest than the transmission of a valued tradition, one which aspires to define value for the whole of the society. I am arguing, then, that Eliot's description of a "Church within the Church" describes nothing but literary culture, which functions as an *incognito* clergy—not literally but ideologically, in the mode of unconscious representation. The difference between that representation and the world we live in is a world of *difference*, a world in which people differ from one another, physically, culturally, and ideologically. This fact is covertly admitted in the very repression of the clerical function, because no literary orthodoxy can present itself as such—it is just the resistance of literature to right tradition that recalls us to the historical complexity of the relation between the canon of literature and that other sacred and original canon. There must be as many canons as there are clergies, and so, after the long decline of the first estate, as many canonical principles as there are possible ideologies of literary culture.

Nevertheless, literary culture has aspired to canonical consensus, an illusion reinforced by the cognitive silence of the literary work, the silencing of difference. Very simply, canonical authors are made to *agree* with one another; the ambiguity of literary language means nothing less than the *univocity* of the canon. I now want to examine this rule of canonical self-identity as it governs the institutional dissemination of literature. Eliot's fantasy of orthodoxy passes into the university both as an ideology of the marginal elite and as an instruction in the marginal relation of the poem to truth.

3. Paradoxy

I do not imagine that, since the establishment of Eliot's canon, his judgments upon individual poets have been handed down without qualification to our students. I do believe, however, that the rule of the canon has governed our instruction. Eliot is not a teacher, except in the more generous metaphorical sense, but Brooks is in every way a theorist of pedagogy. The latent meaning of canon, as a rule of conduct, can be activated again; indeed, this is the meaning of the canon's dissemination. Let us say, then, that in teaching the canon, we are not only investing a set of texts with authority; we are equally instituting the authority of the teaching profession.

That Brooks takes over almost entirely the canon of Eliot's early essays is obvious to any reader of his *Modern Poetry and the Tradition*. Brooks himself has remarked recently upon Eliot's germinal influence:

> I was particularly stimulated by two paragraphs in one of his essays on the metaphysical poets. In this brief passage, he suggested that the metaphysical poets were not to be regarded as a rather peculiar offshoot of English poetry, but had a deep, hidden connection with its central line of development. This, to me [was a] new way of looking at the tradition of English poetry.[25]

Brooks is perhaps as orthodox a disciple as Eliot created, and given this orthodoxy, it is surprising to discover that he is responsible for one very consequential revision of Eliot's dissociation theory. According to Eliot, the dissociation occurs between "thought" and "sensation" (or sometimes "feeling"). For this event Brooks provides an additional historical cause: the rise of science in the seventeenth century. "We have argued . . . that the critical revolution in the seventeenth century which brought metaphysical poetry to an end was intimately bound up with the beginnings of the New Science."[26] Now this is not Eliot's notion, but it seems to have been authorized by the dichotomy of thought and feeling, and, further, it had the advantage of organizing completely the "split" which widens for both Eliot and Brooks with every following century. The hypothesis about Renaissance science seems to rest on a dubious principle of historical causation (and certainly Thomas Hobbes does not truly have the demonic influence he emanates in *Modern Poetry*). The Brooksian history should be understood in the context of the contemporary conflict between positivism and the humanistic disciplines, a conflict now dated but which had the significant consequence of burdening poetic theory with large, epistemological anxieties. Critics do still debate, along formalist or antiformalist lines, the nature of literature as a mode of proposition.

Of the several ways to argue this issue (along a spectrum, say, from I. A. Richards to Gerald Graff), the stance of Brooks has been most easily assimilated in the American university. I quote here one typical statement of that position in *The Well Wrought Urn:*

> The position developed in earlier pages obviously seeks to take the poem out of competition with scientific, historical, and philosophical

propositions. The poem, it has been argued, does not properly eventuate in a proposition: we can only *abstract* statements from the poem, and in the process of abstraction we necessarily distort the poem itself.[27]

The problem which gives rise to Brooks' statement (and I must enormously simplify its genesis here) seems to involve a lack of distinction between *doxa* and *epistēmē*, with the consequence that *doxa* vanishes from the realm of discourse altogether. All discourse becomes either epistemic or non-sensical. Whether or not we wish to accept a Platonic valuation of *epistēmē* over *doxa*, it is clear that, in the absence of any concept of *doxa*, we might only be able to say, trivially, that a poem does not express "scientific" truth. Brooks can say more than this because his aphasic poetry is given the capacity to point in some other direction. The poem becomes an ostensive act, beyond which lies a conceivably recoverable *doxa*. I believe that "pointing without saying" is what we mean now by New Critical formalism. The pedagogical device of close reading as well as the prohibition of paraphrase relate to the perceived muteness of the literary work, which is imitated by the gestural aphasia of the teacher. He or she can only point to that truth which must not be spoken. I will borrow the Brooksian term "paradox" to name these relations, where the *doxa* standing alongside or beyond the poem is to be identified with the "rule of conduct," the *law*, to which the canon directs us.

The text in which all these problems converge is the first essay of *The Well Wrought Urn*, "The Language of Paradox," which offers a reading of Donne's poem, "The Canonization." Brooks does not pun on the title of this poem, though I intend to make the various puns quite explicit; he is, however, more than willing to acknowledge that his book is a series of canonical readings, a reinterpretation of great works of English literature in the light of Eliot's canonization of Donne.[28] It is even possible for Brooks to waive the question of whether Donne or Yeats (the first and last poets discussed in the book) belongs to "the central stream of the tradition" (*WWU*, p. 192); but this piece of largesse reflects ironically upon those who have not experienced Eliot's revelation of canonical error, who do not know that after Donne, and before the modern poets, the "stream" of tradition had become "hidden." I take it as obvious, then, that "The Language of Paradox" is not just an exemplary close reading, and I think it would be very helpful now to show how heavily determined is Brooks' choice of *this* poem, whether or not the extent of the determination has been evident to Brooks or his readers.

Brooks sets out first to define "paradox," or the nature of poetic language, and this entails the usual contrast of poetry and science:

There is a sense in which paradox is the language appropriate and inevitable to poetry. It is the scientist whose truth requires a language purged of every trace of paradox; apparently the truth which the poet utters can be approached only in terms of paradox. [*WWU,* p. 3]

This tells us not what paradox is, only that it is a sort of language antithetical to the sort science employs; yet we are also told that paradox is "intellectual" and "hard" and that it is not usually thought of as "the language of the soul." In taking over some of the characteristics of scientific language, it is as though paradox had foreclosed any definition that would locate it wholly in the realm of feelings or emotions. This gambit is played against Richards and the positivists, and, successful or not, it determines that the method of analysis (of a metaphor, of a poem) is the method of reconciling contradiction. This is what happens both in a poem and in a critical essay. So the analysis of Wordsworth's lines

> It is a beauteous evening, calm and free,
> The holy time is quiet as a Nun
> Breathless with adoration . . .

fixes upon "Breathless" as the focus of the contradiction between the state of calm and the state of excitement. Brooks concludes: "There is no final contradiction, to be sure: it is *that* kind of calm and *that* kind of excitement, and the two states may well occur together" (*WWU,* p. 9). Not all contradictions can be so resolved: it is possible to be both calm and excited, but it is not possible that it should be both raining and not raining. The rhetoric borrowed from Coleridge, of the "reconciliation of opposites," might lead us to suppose that a *logical* contradiction had been "reconciled," but this can never be the case. Paradox is a kind of semantic confusion, where the two terms in supposed contradiction are not really commensurable. Hence there is no necessity to conclude that if opposing meanings are jammed into one semantic unit, a word or a phrase, those meanings are reconciled.[29]

Nevertheless, there is a great pressure in "The Language of Paradox" to read paradox as the epitome of poetic language, and the reconciliation of opposites as the effect of a poem. Let me ask, then, what needs to be so reconciled for Brooks? I think that all the antinomies concerning Brooks the teacher, or Brooks the ideologist, have been generated from the situation of conflict in the poem by Donne, which is described as follows:

The basic metaphor which underlies the poem (and which is reflected in the title) involves a sort of paradox. For the poet daringly treats profane love as if it were divine love. The canonization is not that of a pair of holy anchorites who have renounced the world and the flesh. The hermitage of each is the other's body; but they do renounce the world, and so their title to sainthood is cunningly argued. The poem then is a parody of Christian sainthood; but it is an intensely serious parody of a sort that modern man, habituated as he is to an easy yes or no, can hardly understand. [*WWU*, p. 11]

The opposition of sacred and secular, or divine and profane, is indeed one premise of "The Canonization," and it is the transference of terms which constitutes in part the wittiness of the argument. But what does it mean to take this transference as paradoxical? The conspicuous rhetorical strategy is of course not paradox but *parody*, as Brooks acknowledges, and the relation between these two devices is by no means a logically necessary one. The difference between the two terms recapitulates the difference between terms that merely *oppose* and terms that *contradict* one another, although it is now clear that something much greater is at stake. There cannot be for Donne, nor for Brooks, any "final contradiction" between the sacred and the secular, but it is not so much the ultimate harmony that Brooks gives us a feeling for as it is the lament that "modern man" cannot understand this harmony. This problem is not Donne's but our own, and the poem thus alerts us prospectively to the possibility of its being misunderstood (religion is not the object of parody).

And yet it is surely not *Donne* who is interested in clarifying this misunderstanding, the notice of which has the effect of foregrounding the distinction between sacred and secular. The parodic motif does not actually come into the poem until the last lines of the penultimate stanza, where it picks up the as yet unremarked title:

> And by these hymnes, all shall approve
> Us *Canoniz'd* for Love.

Until this moment, the speaker has been defending himself against the "chiding" of his friend, who has *not* been complaining about any matter relating to the speaker's religious life. The friend has been worried about the fact that the lover has withdrawn from the world, has let everything go. In emphasizing this point, I do not intend to offer an alternative interpretation of the poem but rather to make opaque Brooks' transparent reading, to read the poem written by his interpretation. In fact, Brooks has not failed to observe that the opening conflict has to do with the lovers' renunciation of the public world: "To use the metaphor on which the poem is built, the friend represents the secular world which the lovers have renounced" (*WWU*, p. 11). This is quite true but at the same time does not achieve its desired transparency by the tactic of reading the poem with its own metaphor. The dramatic situation of Donne's conversation makes a legitimate demand upon us to withhold the dichotomy of sacred and secular until the speaker introduces it. To call the world, at this point, "secular" is already to have made the climactic identification of the lovers with saints, and so undercut the effect of the poem's escalating rhetoric. Whether or not we wish to take the metaphoric transfer of sacred and secular as the subject of the poem (or the parallel distinction Brooks later makes between love and lust), this choice is not predetermined by the title. Might not the choice be the same as that which makes possible the ploy of transforming the love nest into a hermitage, and so *shifting* the evaluative terms from the opposition of public and private to the opposition of profane and sacred?

We might speculate now that Brooks' reading is driven by the same force that drives Donne's hyperbole—*idealization* and a consequent suppression of the conflict behind the need to idealize. What does it mean to think of the "world" in the poem as secular rather than public? The answer to that question is clearly indicated in Brooks' construction of the central paradox, which does in fact turn upon the notion of "world": "The lovers in becoming hermits, find that they have not lost the world, but have gained the world in each other, now a more intense, more meaningful world" (*WWU*, p. 15). But even lovers must go about their mundane business, and the poem is full of the very mundane business it tries to void from its "pretty roomes." If I want to say that the world outside the lovers' room is still there, that is not to be a grudging literalist but only to acknowledge that Donne's paradox disappears when its terms are analyzed. The world of the lovers (the reflection of the world in their eyes) is composed, as Brooks says, of the same " 'Countries, Townes,' and 'Courtes,' which they renounce in the first stanza of the poem." The sentence that follows this one is crucial: "The unworldly lovers thus become the most 'worldly' of all." This is not a "true proposition," of course, any more than the rhetoric it doubles; and Brooks means just this when he puts the second "worldly" in quotation marks. Donne's persona seeks a (partly outrageous) justification of his initial withdrawal, which he discovers in the one precedent within the social context of justified renunciation: the saint's. For many reasons Brooks must understand the analogy as having the force of identity. The idealization of the analogy is evident when he comes to defend the "truth" of the poem on the strange grounds of its supernaturalism, as though the unworldliness of the lovers really were the same thing as saintliness: "What happens to Donne's lovers if we consider them 'scientifically,' without benefit of the supernaturalism which the poet confers on them?" (*WWU*, p. 18). This is a question Brooks can raise only because he is at this point arguing against those Huxleyan positivists who see only (because they can't verify anything else) two animals, "quietly sweating palm to palm" (*WWU*, p. 18).

But surely, we want to respond, the choice between a religious and a secular view of things is not the same as the choice between two readings of the poem, one in which there is love and in the other only animal lust? It is, if the idealizations of the poem are affirmed *against* the world, against business and politics, against the travail of history. The category that goes by the name of the "sacred" grounds the ideal in its most otherworldly mode of appearance and designates as the precondition of all value an act of renunciation. This act achieves an immediate allegorical status in Brooks' reading because it governs the possibility not only of sanctity and love but of poetry, a doctrine which is gleaned from these lines:

> And if no peece of Chronicle wee prove,
> We'll build in sonnets pretty roomes;
> As well a well wrought urne becomes
> The greatest ashes, as halfe-acre tombes,
> And by these hymnes, all shall approve
> Us *Canoniz'd* for Love:

About which Brooks comments:

> The poem is an instance of the doctrine which it asserts; it is both the assertion and the realization of the assertion. The poet has actually before our eyes built within the song the "pretty room" with which he says the lovers can be content. The poem itself is the well-wrought urn which can hold the lovers' ashes and which will not suffer in comparison with the prince's "half-acre tomb." [*WWU*, p. 17]

The "doctrine" here, that the poem is a "well-wrought urn," is not just the proposition that the poem is an artifact—so is the prince's monument—it is rather that the urn belongs to the world of value and not to the world of power. It is a celebration of its own purity, its escape from a mode of "assertion" not only of a scientific *epistēmē* but, in a much more hidden sense, of the assertion of power over other human beings. While renunciation expresses the founding proposition of an ideological discourse, it need not mean anything like a literal withdrawal, such as the lovers have made. Rather, the ideological function of Brooks' reading concerns the demarcation of a spiritual realm between the crudities of power and the crudities of fact. The spiritual realm is *defined* by the audience the essay addresses; the auditors are conceived at a moment of apostolic succession, at just the moment of transition between Eliot and Brooks, as representative figures of literary culture. The *incognito* clergy is relocated within a *visible* social structure: the pedagogical institution. The idealized reading of the lovers' withdrawal must be understood as symptomatic of the professional commitment to the preservation of value: just as the lovers institute love in their act of renunciation, so it is the marginality of value which is both deplored and established by the idealization of literature. There is no other place for this value than the mausoleum of well-wrought urns. That Brooks is speaking now of the institution of criticism is a fact made explicit by the end of his essay, when he openly addresses the teachers (still mainly philologists) who are about to become much more than antiquarians: "The urns are not meant for memorial purposes only, though that often seems to be their chief significance to the professors of literature" (*WWU*, p. 21). "The Canonization" thus figures—as it were, typologically—the displacement of the philologist by the critic.

The urns into which poems have been metamorphosed resolve at the imagistic level the epistemological problem so troubling to the early New Critics, again by manipulating the ambiguity of the container figure. Inside and outside are interchangeable, as the poem's metaphorical room places the world outside, while the poem is at the same time said to be "outside" the world. The interchangeability of the spatial trope is precisely what makes possible the transformation of "profane" love into "divine"— this marks the movement "out" of the world, which is defined retrospectively as "secular." The same moment of transcendence must happen in any canonical poem, and this signifies nothing less than its *canonization*, its elevation to the plane of the ideal. The scene of withdrawal and transcendence can then be generalized as a repeatable canonical principle ("Beg from above / A patterne of your love!"). Let us imagine that Donne's persona speaks here not only to the students of love but to the students of poetry. The pattern *they* will receive can be nothing other than a copy of that transcendentalizing gesture, as the "truth" of every canonical poem retreats before the act of interpretation; our arrival in its pretty room discovers an empty shrine. The poem enjoins upon us the recognition of the externality of dogma and conceals from us the fact that we are already within its truth, that its truth *is* this externality: the poem as paradogmatic text.

The versatility of the urn is not yet exhausted by its function as a container. In fact Brooks goes on to fill the urn/poem with the ashes of the phoenix, fusing two images juxtaposed by Donne. The energy behind this fusion is siphoned from Shakespeare's "The Phoenix and the Turtle," which Brooks quotes at some length in the latter part of his essay. The overt paradoxes of Shakespeare's poem hint at the Coleridgean reconciliation of opposites ("that magic power which Coleridge sought to describe") and prepare the reader for the moment of conflation: "The urn to which we are summoned, the urn which *holds the ashes of the phoenix*, is like the well-wrought urn of Donne's 'Canonization' which holds the phoenix-lovers' ashes: it is the poem itself" (*WWU*, p. 21; italics mine). The phoenix, as a figure for poetic *content*, buttresses the reading of Donne's poem by allowing Brooks to generalize paradox as the mystery of life and death, or rather as the possibility of resurrection: "The phoenix rises from the ashes; or ought to rise"—but what content is resurrected? The rebirth of the phoenix must signify the rebirth of that *doxa* which had so long lain dormant in an ashen state, contained and therefore preserved by the forms of literature. A potential content is restored to the poem. As the urn gestures to the ashes it contains, so the phoenix gestures, by its very allusive density, to the meaning not of any one poem but of poetry: that meaning is to make this allusion, to point to the figure who is historically emblematized as a phoenix, who delivered the *pattern* of resurrection, and who first spoke the paradoxes Brooks cites as exemplary: "He who would save his life, must lose it," and "The Last shall be first" (*WWU*, p. 18). These examples are neither random nor innocent. The allusion to the resurrected Jesus disguises only imperfectly a fantasy of power, which can be figured also as the promise of that day when the mausoleum of urns will revert to what it once was, a temple, and the clergy will resume its "first estate." The last will *again* be first. The power of renunciation here discloses itself as the deferral of power.

The elaboration of the ideology into such allusive structures yields up the New Criticism to the service of the liberal pluralism which is the regnant ideology of the academy and which the pedagogy in no way contradicts. The technique of formalist interpretation subtends the larger ideology, satisfying within a narrower domain of practice the longing for consensus, for a metaphysics of the same—a longing expressed by the posited "unity" of the literary work. But the intensity of the desire for unity is no longer news to us, since its frustration has been marked in recent years by the shattering of hermeneutic serenity and by the rise of a certain dogmatism, perplexingly inconsistent with the public aims of ideological pluralism. It would appear that we mean by consensus what Eliot meant by orthodoxy.

The canon participates centrally in the establishment of consensus as the embodiment of a collective valuation. Hence it is in the interest of canonical reformations to erase the conflictual prehistory of canon-formation or to represent such history as the narrative of error. The canonical authority of *The Well Wrought Urn* is a measure of Brooks' success in this project. So far from merely attaching the names of Donne and Yeats to the beginning and end of canonical history, the curricular shape of English literature is henceforth determined as "From Donne *to* Yeats." The phoenix image emerges from the exemplary text as an emblem of the canonical principle, and this is evidently why the image can be so easily transferred from Donne's poem to Shakespeare's, and so on to the whole of literary history: "A history of poetry from Dryden's time to our own might bear as its subtitle 'The Half-Hearted Phoenix'" (*WWU*, p. 20). Such a narrative is not history at all for Brooks but rather a period during which a certain waiting takes place, when the *doxa* of literature is obscured. The assimilation of "The Phoenix and the Turtle" foreshadows a systematically ideological reading of the canon, a reading capable of absorbing what Eliot's more primitive rule had excluded: the major English poets.

4. Heterodoxy

I have argued that canonical choices are historically overdetermined, that they do not represent necessarily, or only, the arbitrariness of personal preference or the evaluative certainty of consensus. Literary history, however, seldom clearly exhibits the event of a canonical reformation; the canon of Eliot and Brooks has been a hegemonic, though hardly an exclusive, formation. I have not sought to account, therefore, for conflicts between canonizers or all the possible confusions of dissemination. Certainly a work such as F. R. Leavis' *The Great Tradition,* as the most aggressively canonizing text of British criticism, would have demanded a somewhat different analysis.

It should be possible to understand the very divergence of canons and canonizers as a better ground than consensus for a defense of literary culture. The disestablishment of consensus may well have become the project of criticism, the meaning of its new sectarian theories and canons.[30] It can also be said of post-formalist methodologies that they are generally de-idealizing, or programmatically antihumanistic. In another sense, these methodologies have remained well within the Kantian "idealist" tradition, as Richard Rorty has convincingly shown.[31] Nevertheless, the real effect of resisting the idealization of form should not be discounted.

To admit the succession of ideological defenses of the profession is therefore not to deny the necessity of the current de-idealizing move. Ideology does not cease to be functional, whether or not its epistemic falsity can be reduced asymptotically to a zero degree. If the retreat of the New Criticism is now pronounced enough for us to examine in three dimensions its ideological discourse, it is also possible to understand how this discourse produced the very protest against it, the lament for the silence and disenfranchisement of literature. It is really the culture of which we speak, yet it seems as unlikely a program to restore literary culture to a position of power (any power it does not *already* possess) as it is to restore the clergy, for the reason that no contemporary "orthodoxy" can encompass the interests of so many divergent groups, the lateral inequalities (of race, sex, or culture) that have further complicated the material inequalities of social formation. Eliot only proposed his fantasies of orthodoxy on the quite honest premise of an exclusive society such as he hoped to find in England, or the American South, or imagined creating by such extraordinary measures as the exclusion of Jews.[32] If tradition (and all the continuities that literature and religion have been empowered in the past to teach) decays with the decay of orthodoxy, then it is irrecoverable. It is more practical, if not inevitable, that we consider what it means that "difference " has become our central critical category; at the least, this means the permanent difficulty of forming a canon acceptable to a consensus of the literary culture.[33] This condition I would like to describe as the state of heterodoxy, where the *doxa* of literature is not a paralyzed allusion to a hidden god but a teaching that will enact discursively the struggle of difference.

1. Several models of canonical change have recently become current. I mention in particular the generic system of Alastair Fowler, worked out in his *Kinds of Literature: An Introduction to the Theory of Genres and Modes* (Cambridge, Mass., 1982), and the model of the biblical canon, discussed by James Nohrnberg in "On Literature and the Bible," *Centrum* 2 (Fall 1974): 5–43.

2. While it would scarcely be possible here to construct a theory of ideology, antecedent to any use of the term, neither would it be fair to evade altogether the epistemological dilemma. The science/ideology complement, which characterizes Althusserian theories of ideology, seems to me in some sense inescapable. See Louis Althusser, "Ideology and Ideological State Apparatuses," *Lenin and Philosophy*, trans. Ben Brewster (New York, 1971), pp. 127–86. However, the terms of my argument assume only such a conception of "human science" as makes possible the Frankfurt school's practice of *Ideologiekritik*. Perhaps it is also worth invoking Michel Foucault's reservation about the concept of ideology in *Power/ Knowledge: Selected Interviews and Other Writings, 1972–1977*, ed. Colin Gordon, trans. Gordon et al. [New York, 1980], p. 118). On ideology and intellectuals, especially relevant is Antonio Gramsci's distinction between "organic" and "traditional" intellectuals, in *Selections from the Prison Notebooks*, ed. and trans. Quentin Hoare and Geoffrey Nowell Smith (New York, 1971), p. 6.

3. T. S. Eliot, "John Dryden," *Selected Essays* (New York, 1932), p. 270; all further references to this work, abbreviated *SE*, will be included in the text.

4. See Eliot, "Poetry and Drama," *On Poetry and Poets* (New York, 1957): "Reviewing my critical output for the last thirty-odd years, I am surprised to find how constantly I have returned to the drama" (p. 75); all further references to this work, abbreviated *OPP*, will be included in the text.

5. Eliot, "Tradition and the Individual Talent," *The Sacred Wood* (1920; London, 1960), p. 50; all further references to this work, abbreviated *SW*, will be included in the text.

6. A particular passage of Eliot's is worth noting in "What Is a Classic?": "The predecessors should be themselves great and honoured: but their accomplishment must be such as to suggest still undeveloped resources of the language, and not such as to oppress the younger writers with the fear that everything that can be done has been done, in their language" (*OPP*, p. 58). Eliot does not quite say that English literary history either exhibits or escapes this predicament.

7. I emphasize that Eliot's principle of canonical revision does not necessarily mean to decanonize major works but rather to alter principles of valuation. When Eliot attacked *Hamlet* in "Hamlet and His Problems," he knew he could not decanonize such a work, only damage *through it* the principle which had canonized *Hamlet*.

8. Eliot's later essays domesticate this breezy mastery over the canon by projecting it onto his critical precursors, as in this comment on Matthew Arnold: "From time to time, every hundred years or so, it is desirable that some critic shall appear to review the past of our literature, and set the poems in a new order." But this is too much like the persona of *The Sacred Wood*, whose devaluation of literary monuments must be seen rather as a *modest* achievement: "This task is not one of revolution but of readjustment" (*The Use of Poetry and the Use of Criticism* [London, 1933], p. 108).

9. There is an additional motive to be mentioned in this connection—Eliot's unhappy feeling that religious poetry will always be regarded as minor: "For the great majority of people who love poetry, *religious* poetry is a variety of *minor* poetry" ("Religion and Literature," *SE*, p. 345).

10. Eliot, *John Dryden: The Poet, the Dramatist, the Critic* (New York, 1932), p. 24.

11. Ibid., pp. 5, 22.

12. See Eliot, "What Is Minor Poetry?": "What I am concerned to dispel is any derogatory association connected with the term 'minor poetry,' together with the suggestion that minor poetry is easier to read, or less worth while to read, than 'major poetry'" (*OPP*, p. 34).

13. See also Eliot's remark in "Virgil and the Christian World": "A poet may believe that he is expressing only his private experience; his lines may be for him only a means of talking about himself without giving himself away; yet for his readers what he has written may come to be the expression both of their own secret feelings and of the exultation or despair of a generation" (*OPP*, p. 137).

14. The whole argument of "What Is a Classic?" is interesting in this respect. Eliot's standard of classical value is "universality," which is opposed to the "provincial." The closest English literature comes to a classical age is the eighteenth century, and this too fails because its "restriction of religious sensibility itself produces a kind of provinciality: the provinciality which indicates the disintegration of Christendom, the decay of a common belief and a common culture" (*OPP*, pp. 61–62).

15. But at least a hint about how to make this connection is given in Eliot's "The Classics and the Man of Letters," *To Criticize the Critic* (New York, 1965): "The continuity of literature is essential to its greatness; it is very largely the function of secondary writers to preserve this continuity, and to provide a body of writings which is not necessarily read by posterity, but which plays a great part in forming the link between those writers who continue to be read" (p. 147).

16. Eliot, *After Strange Gods: A Primer of Modern Heresy* (New York, 1933), p. 22.

17. Ibid., p. 35.

18. Eliot, *The Idea of a Christian Society* (New York, 1940), p. 26.

19. Eliot is by this time aware of the ideological motives of canon-formation and indulges in a little critique of his own. He speculates that the revolutionary politics of Wordsworth and Coleridge makes intelligible their "inability to appreciate Pope," and he also notes the "irrelevance of the metaphysical poets to the interests which he and Coleridge had at heart" (see *The Use of Poetry*, pp. 74–76).

20. Eliot expresses his second thoughts about dissociation in several places, but see "Milton II" (*OPP*, p. 173). His attack on Milton's unorthodoxy had the peculiar result of biasing even the defenses provoked by this charge. The most notable of the early defenses, C. S. Lewis' *A Preface to "Paradise Lost"* (London, 1942), seeks to bring Milton back into the orthodox fold, and it is this distorted perception of Milton's career which is still the "canonical reading" of criticism.

21. See Eliot's comment in *The Idea of a Christian Society* about "a state secularized, a community turned into a mob, and a clergy disintegrated" (p. 42). Eliot's feelings about the relation between the cultural elite and the religious orthodoxy are more clearly expressed in *Notes toward a Definition of Culture* (1948): "The artistic sensibility is impoverished by its divorce from the religious sensibility, the religious by its separation from the artistic" (rpt. in *Christianity and Culture* [New York, 1968], p. 99). See also the interesting comments on elites and classes in chapter 2 of this work.

22. See Eliot's comments critical of Arnold in *S.E.*, pp. 385–93.

23. Eliot, *The Idea of a Christian Society*, p. 34. Eliot goes on to associate, as well as to distinguish, his notion from the Coleridgean idea of the "clerisy," but the two groups are so close in function that it seems the idea must have come from Coleridge.

24. See Edward W. Said, *The World, the Text, and the Critic* (Cambridge, Mass., 1983), esp. pp. 290–92. On Eliot's elitism, see Terry Eagleton, *Criticism and Ideology: A Study in Marxist Literary Theory* (London, 1976), pp. 145–51. The identity that Eliot somewhat dissimulates, Harold Bloom addresses openly in "The Dialectics of Poetic Tradition" (*A Map of Misreading* [New York, 1975]):

> Our profession is not genuinely akin any longer to that of the historians or the philosophers. Without willing the change, our theoretical critics have become negative theologians, our practical critics are close to being Agaddic commentators, and all

of our teachers, of whatever generation, teach how to live, what to do, in order to avoid the damnation of death-in-life. I do not believe that I am talking about an ideology, nor am I acknowledging any shade whatsoever of the recent Marxist critiques of our profession. [P. 29]

What Bloom is "acknowledging" is rather more complex than can be clarified by his denial. Bloom's essay obviously and urgently rewrites "Tradition and the Individual Talent," which suggests to me that Eliot's work is still the Ur-text of critical ideology. On the critic as intellectual, I refer to Gramsci's argument in *Selections from the Prison Notebooks:* "Since these various categories of traditional intellectuals experience through an *"esprit de corps"* their uninterrupted historical continuity and their special qualification, they thus put themselves forward as autonomous and independent of the dominant social group" (p. 7).

25. Cleanth Brooks, in Robert Penn Warren's interview, "A Conversation with Cleanth Brooks," in *The Possibilities of Order: Cleanth Brooks and His Work,* ed. Lewis P. Simpson (Baton Rouge, La., 1976), p. 19. I refer the reader to Brooks' "Notes toward a Revised History of English Literature," *Modern Poetry and the Tradition* (Chapel Hill, N.C., 1939), for the particular canonical choices.

26. Brooks, "A Note on the Death of Elizabethan Tragedy," *Modern Poetry and the Tradition,* p. 203. For a somewhat wilder polemic against science, see John Crowe Ransom, *God without Thunder. An Unorthodox Defense of Orthodoxy* (1930; Hamden, Conn., 1965), pp. 117–38.

27. Brooks, *The Well Wrought Urn: Studies in the Structure of Poetry* (New York, 1947), p. 252; all further references to this work, abbreviated *WWU*, will be included in the text.

28. "One was to attempt to see, in terms of this approach, what the masterpieces had in common rather than to see how the poems of different historical periods differed—and in particular to see whether they had anything in common with the metaphysicals and with the moderns" (*WWU*, p. 193).

29. This point was made by Ransom in *The New Criticism* (Norfolk, Conn., 1941), p. 95.

30. It is undeniable, especially in the wake of Frank Lentricchia's argument in *After the New Criticism* (Chicago, 1980), that a defense of criticism is at stake in every new theory or method. What has not been adequately understood is the function of canonical choices in critical revolutions. Lentricchia's presentation of the central figures of contemporary criticism (Northrop Frye, Murray Krieger, E. D. Hirsch, Paul de Man, Harold Bloom) might have focused upon their respective canons, which are certainly not merely the epiphenomena of theory. It is not accidental that Frye, de Man, and Bloom are such vigorous canonizers or that their careers began with such strong revaluations of devalued figures. The lesser influence, on the other hand, of Krieger and Hirsch, while it might be explained by deficiencies in their theoretical formulations, might also be a measure of precisely their lack of canonical interest.

31. See Richard Rorty, "Nineteenth-Century Idealism and Twentieth-Century Textualism," *Monist* 64 (Apr. 1981): 155–74.

32. See Eliot, *After Strange Gods:* "What is still more important is unity of religious background; and reasons of race and religion combine to make any large number of free-thinking Jews undesirable" (p. 20).

33. This subject is discussed in *English Literature: Opening Up the Canon,* ed. Leslie A. Fiedler and Houston A. Baker, Jr., Selected Papers from the English Institute, 1979, n.s. 4 (Baltimore, 1981). There is a welcome feeling in this volume that the canon must be opened, though I would emphasize that this opening does not mean simply a larger canon, that is, one with greater powers of co-optation but multiple, conflicting canons.

The Making of the Modernist Canon

Hugh Kenner

Your whimsical thoughts, if you live long enough, will be back
haunting you. I am now beset by a notion that crossed my mind
twenty years ago. Then it seemed only a mild historical fancy. Now
it resembles a cognitive Black Hole. It is simply this: that *no Englishman alive in 1600 was living in the Age of Shakespeare.* For
there was no Age of Shakespeare in 1600. That age was invented
long afterwards.

Partly, I was thinking of Borges' famous statement that writers
invent their predecessors; partly, I was pondering angry speculations rife in those years, when it was held, if you remember, that the
Beatles, if you remember them, might be unacknowledged Mozarts.
We were all of us being reproved for not celebrating their genius.
Moreover genius, we were being told, never does get properly celebrated. It goes to a premature and quicklimed grave, after which
posterity's accolades need cost posterity exactly nothing.

We are talking about psychic money: that was the currency
bourgeoisiedom denied the Beatles while they were intact. Yes, yes,
mere dollars came fluttering down abundantly upon Ringo and
George and Paul and John. But not for them a reward that was
withheld from Mozart also while he lived: assimilation into the musical canon. It is like the withholding of a full professorship.

I was set to wondering, when did Shakespeare get assimilated
into the canon? Moreover, was there any inherent scandal in his not
having been assimilated while he lived? And to the second question
the ready answer was no. In 1600 there was no canon, literary history not yet having been invented. Nor, save in theater circles, was
Will Shakespeare even so much as a celebrity. Not only no canvasclimber of Drake's, but no learned fellow of the court had any

reason to suppose he would some day be envied for having been Shakespeare's coeval, privileged to stand in the pit at the Globe while Burbage, reciting words about seas of troubles, sawed the air with his hand thus. The canvasclimber, for that matter, could have told Burbage a thing or two first-hand about seas and trouble.

How did it ever become obvious that about 1600 Englishmen were living in the Age of Shakespeare? And is it even obvious now? Roland Barthes would have said it is not; he would have had us believe that such determinations were reversible, were in fact at bottom political, serving as they did to advantage a custodial class whose livelihood was bound up with the preeminence of Shakespeare: a class apt to be relegated to janitorial status should anyone make college deans believe that in 1600 men lived in the Age of—oh, Tom Dekker. It is, of course, professors such as myself who have a fiscal stake in Shakespeare. One Marxist gambit is to make innocents doubt whether there is any other stake.

Meanwhile such fin-de-siècle Englishmen as thought about it—fin, I mean, du seizième siècle—doubtless thought they were living in the age of Queen Elizabeth, not thinking to define their good fortune in literary categories at all. I could as well attribute my presence here to the fact that we live in the age of sterile surgery and penicillin.

By the 18th century vernacular literature had accumulated a long enough history to be thought about historically. By 1783 Dr. Johnson had collected his *Lives of the English Poets,* working from a canon established, interestingly enough, not by himself but by a syndicate of booksellers. It included no poet born earlier than 16xx: none, in short, whose conventions of spelling, syntax and image would be apt to strike an Augustan browser as odd. It was possible to wonder about the present state of literature. If that means, to ask with what names posterity might associate one's own time, then it concedes that our posterity will know us in ways we do not.

So in what age did a literate man about 1810 suppose he was living? Why, in the age of Samuel Rogers, Thomas Campbell, Robert Southey. Those are the names that would have come to mind: names we no longer hear. Our present canonical list is Wordsworth, Coleridge, Byron, Keats, Shelley, to which add Blake:

Hugh Kenner is the Andrew W. Mellon Professor of the Humanities at the Johns Hopkins University. Among his many books are *The Poetry of Ezra Pound* (1951), *The Pound Era* (1971), which won the 1972 Christian Gauss Award, and *A Colder Eye* (1983). In 1984, his books on Joyce, which include *Joyce's Voices* and *Ulysses,* were awarded the first James Joyce Centennial Medal.

and where did it come from? That is unwritten history. How canons are determined is in general unwritten history.

Let me therefore throw what light I can on one canon I have a little knowledge of. The canon of literary modernism: how did that get made? Is it made yet?

As recently as 1931, a year I can just remember, it was not made, was not even adumbrated. That was the year F.R. Leavis published *New Bearings in English Poetry,* and felt obliged, before he disclosed the new bearings, to dispose of pseudo–bearings, the likes of Alfred Noyes and Walter de la Mare. Noyes had lately undertaken a long poem about the great astronomers of history, and Leavis even felt required to deal with that; his dealing was formal in syntax but paraphrasable as a snort. Nor was he overcome by William Butler Yeats, whose intelligence he called "magnificent" but much of whose poetry he described as meditation on the events of the poet's life: an *Irish* life, moreover. Leavis identified one *English* modern poet, G.M. Hopkins; one naturalized English one, the American–born T.S. Eliot (who would later advert to Leavis's "rather lonely battle for literacy"); finally one *echt* American, Ezra Pound. Pound was the author of just one good poem, *Hugh Selwyn Mauberley* (1920); the rest, before and after, was enamel and polish and the doing of inorganic will; such "limited interest" as the *Cantos* had was "technical." Dead 42 years but organic, G.M. Hopkins was O.K. Alive 43 years, T.S. Eliot was more than O.K.; the hope of the time, it was clear, lay with Mr. Eliot.

Whatever else *New Bearings* was, it was an intelligent start at canon–defining, given the state of knowledge in '31. Pointless now to ironize at the expense of Leavis's later career: his disenchantment with Eliot, his growing obsession with Lawrence, his virtual dismissal of Joyce, his grotesque determination that what at bottom had prevented Eliot from being a major poet was American birth. The state of knowledge in 1931, that is the thing to concentrate on. What do you need to know to define a canon?

Wrong question, since there's no generic answer. Better: what did Leavis in 1931 not know? Two things at least of great scope. One was the unprecedented interdependence of prose modernism and verse modernism. Though his magazine *Scrutiny* was later to deal with *Wuthering Heights* and *Hard Times* in a series it called "The Novel as Dramatic Poem," still how *Ulysses* had been the necessary forerunner of *The Waste Land* was something never clear to Leavis, nor how Henry James's habits of diction were refracted throughout a poem Leavis nowhere mentions, Pound's *Homage to Sextus Propertius*. That was a central modernist discovery, that distinctions between "prose" and "verse" vanish before distinctions between firm writing and loose; there is no more dramatic moment in the *Cantos* than the one that affixes to the poem's page scraps of so–

called "prose" that have been extracted and Englished, with neither meter nor ragged right margins, from the contents of Sigismundo Malatesta's post–bag. "Hang it all, Robert Browning," commences *Canto II,* and when Robert Browning had processed old Italian letters he'd felt constrained to put them into blank verse, thus marking the frontier across which they were fetched: from "out there," where prose is, into a genuine *poem.*

But we no longer think language must vest itself in measure when it is brought into a poem. "Give me my robe, put on my crown"—that is a formula it need no longer intone. One test of a sensibility that acknowledges this new bearing is hospitality to Marianne Moore, who can pick her brisk way through unmetered though counted lines that are open to scraps of actual prose, and not the prose of Gibbon or Pater either, but corporation pamphlets about the Icosasphere. Of her, despite T. S. Eliot's firm endorsement, Leavis could make nothing: a defeat of a great critic so humiliating it has vanished from the Index to the reprinted *Scrutiny.* Another test is William Carlos Williams, who comes as close as any real poet does to validating the philistine complaint that modernist verse misrepresents mere prose by "lines." *Scrutiny* was not alone in ignoring Williams in England; he was not even published there until after his ex–compatriot Eliot had died, and even today so unabashed a British pro–modernist as Donald Davie confesses to making little of him.

And of course when we're in Donald Davie's company we may feel sure we're remote from prose/verse naivete. No, it's something else about Williams, his American–ness, the cisatlantic tang of his cadence, that still eludes John Bull.* And now we are ready for the second cardinal fact that was hidden from Leavis in 1931: the fact that the English language had split four ways, leaving English natives in control of but a fraction. No Englishman will contemplate this with any zest, so if you get your literary news from England you'll hear little of it.

Since Chaucer, the domain of English literature had been a country, England. Early in the 20th century its domain commenced to be a language, English. By about 1925 it was clear that three countries, Ireland, America and England, were conducting substantial national literatures in this language. Common words had deceptively different meanings in these three different literatures, and divergences of idiom were guaranteed by the fact that the three literatures drew on radically different traditions and on different intuitions of what literature might be for. It was no longer feasible to

---

*Not every Englishman is in this sense John Bull. Williams has had no better reader anywhere than Charles Tomlinson in Gloucestershire, who's responded to him as Mallarmé did to Poe. It is pleasant that Williams knew that in his lifetime.

retain for the canon only what readers in England were prepared to like, the way they had once liked the songs of the Scotsman, Bobbie Burns, and the Irishman, Tom Moore. (''Bobbie''; ''Tom''; they condescend when they accept.)

And by mid-century it was also clear, if not to everyone, that the decentralization of ''English'' was not the whole story: that there was arguably a new center, locatable in books but on no map. English was the language not only of the Three Provinces but also of several masterpieces best located in a supranational movement called International Modernism.

Such a modernism flourished in conjunction with other modernisms, painted, sculpted, danced. These in turn acknowledged new environments created by new technologies: notably, the invasion of the city by the rhythms of the machine (subways and the crowds they brought, motorcars, pavement drills like the Rock Drill Epstein sculpted.)

Looking back, Virginia Woolf said whimsically that late in 1910 ''human nature changed.'' She meant that by 1910 you could see International Modernism coming, which is true though an observer thenabouts would have expected its literary language to be French. That it proved to be English instead was largely the doing of James Joyce, whose *Ulysses* helps us define the very concept of an International work. To what literature does it belong?

Not to Irish, though its events are set in Dublin. Joyce had explicitly rejected the Irish Literary Revival as provincial, and had not only left Ireland—many Irishmen have done that—but had adduced alien canons of which his systematic parallel with a Greek epic is probably the least radical. Not to English, though most of its words are in English dictionaries and Shakespeare is an adduced presence. No, the parts of *Ulysses* that resemble a novel resemble continental, not Victorian, narratives, and its sense of what business a large work of fiction ought to be about is continuously alien to English expectations. Its fit reader is not someone schooled in a tradition it augments, as the best reader of Dickens will be grounded in Fielding and Smollett; rather, anyone willing to master the book's language, its procedures, its Dublin materials, must do so all on the book's own terms. In Ireland, peevishness about its authenticity is apt to fasten on the claim that most of its devotees are American, and indeed many of them are, though anyone's current list of six *Ulysses* authorities would include one Australian, one German, and one Swiss.

Though the language of International Modernism, like that of air control towers, proved to be English, none of its canonical works came either out of England or out of any mind formed there. International Modernism was the work of Irishmen and Americans. Its masterpieces include *Ulysses, The Waste Land,* the first thirty *Cantos.*

After 1910 it flourished for some forty years. Its last master-piece was *Waiting for Godot,* which an Irishman living in Paris wrote in English after having first detached himself from English by writing the first version in French. One reason Modernism's primary language was English was the emergence in this century of Irish and American self–confidence, affording to no other Indo–European language so rich a variety of social and cultural experience. And International Modernism was not restricted to language; it drew on a variety of 20th century activities which transcend the need for translators: on cubist and non–representational painting, which though mostly done in Paris owed little to any specifically French tradition; on renovations in music, inseparable from the impact (en-abled by the railway) of the Russian ballet on three capitals; on the fact that the first century of world travel has also been the century of world wars; above all on the popularization, through technology, of a science which knows no frontiers and sets down its austere oracles in equations exactly as accessible to a Muscovite as to a New Yorker.

Via technology, science has shaped our century. Three events of 1895 might have foreshadowed the shape had anyone known how to correlate them. The first American gasoline–powered car was designed; an Italian named Marconi sent messages more than a mile with no wires at all; a German named Roentgen discovered that rays his apparatus was emitting passed clean through materials opaque to light.

The automobile was to end the domination of the railroad, the 19th century's triumphant cultural and economic symbol; post–Ford, all men chugged on their own, and a decent car soon meant more than a decent house.

Wireless, transmitting sounds and later pictures, was to termi-nate printed fiction and live drama as the normative media for en-tertainment; the play, the short story, in part the novel, became "art forms," art being the name we give an abandoned genre. (So televi-sion turns old movies into an art called "cinema.")

And X–rays heralded the bending of learned attention on the technology of the invisible, a change with analogies as striking as they are difficult to reckon. When early in our century John Donne's poems began to be revived after more than a century of total neglect, the eye–beams of his lovers in "The Ecstasie" no longer seemed remote from physical reality as they had when everything real was made of brick.

Hard on the discovery of the electron in 1898 came Max Planck's discovery that energy is radiated not in a continuous stream but in discrete packets, called quanta, which are never fractional, always intact, and can be counted like chromosomes. More: when a quantum of energy was emitted, its electron jumped to a new orbit, without occupying even for an instant any of the space between. Mysterious energies, sudden transitions, are as congenial to the 20th-century mind as they would have been unthinkable to our great–grandfathers. It is pointless to ask whether Eliot, who made Planck–like transitions in *The Waste Land,* did so on any scientific analogy (probably not) or had heard at all of the relevant physics (perhaps). The life of the mind in any age coheres thanks to shared assumptions both explicit and tacit, between which lines of causality may not be profitably traceable.

Before the first war the life of the English–speaking mind emanated from London, the last of the great capitals. The skeptical Joseph Conrad, a Pole, walked its streets (and his son became a motor–car salesman). He was England's most distinguished practising novelist in the century's early decades. The principal novelist of an earlier generation was also foreign: Henry James. He lived in Rye and came up to London for the winters. London, he said ecstatically, could always give you exactly what you sought. And England's principal poet was W.B. Yeats, a man who made a symbol of his Irish identity though from 1895 to 1919 he preferred to live at 18 Woburn Buildings, London WC1. That the principal resident talent in those years was foreign in origin and often in allegiance should arrest us: London was attracting world talent the way Rome had in Augustan times when the world had a smaller circumference, and like Rome it was seeing its cultural affairs preempted by the talent it had attracted. (Vergil, Cicero, Horace, Propertius, Ovid: none was native to the Rome that claims them. Ovid had come from wild hills now called the Abruzzi, as alien to Rome as any Idaho.)

And yet another wave came. Ezra Pound, born in Idaho, reached London in 1908 from Pennsylvania via Venice, partly to learn from Yeats, whose skill in fitting the sentence exactly into the stanza was one of the signs of mastery he discerned. His old Pennsylvania classmate Hilda Doolittle ("H.D.") arrived a little later. In 1914 Tom Eliot, of St. Louis and Harvard, became a Londoner too. By contrast the native talent is apt to seem unimportant, or else proves not to be native: even Wyndham Lewis, who went to an English public school (Rugby), had been born near a dock at Amherst, Nova Scotia, on his American father's yacht.

So early modernism (say 1910–1920) was the work of a foreign coterie, the first literary generation to come to maturity in the 20th century, in awareness of Marconi and radium and Picasso, in awareness too of the French poetic avant–garde of the 1880's and '90's. Their work was either written in London or disseminated from there; Eliot brought *Prufrock* in his luggage; Joyce mailed installments of his *Portrait of the Artist as a Young Man* from Trieste as fast as he could have them typed, for serialization in a London feminist paper called *The Egoist*. London was the place to come to: Mecca: the center of the world's sophistication and prosperity, the great inexhaustible settled capital. When Pound and Lewis in 1914 named the whole modern movement "The Great London Vortex," one thing they had in mind was the ingathering power of vortices. *The Waste Land*'s occasion was the failure of that vortex. Eliot wrote in 1921 that London "only shrivels, like a little bookkeeper grown old." The same year Lewis discerned ". . . a sort of No Man's Land atmosphere. The dead never rise up, and men will not return to the Past, whatever else they may do. But as yet there is Nothing, or rather the corpse of the past age, and the sprinkling of children of the new."

A while back we left F.R. Leavis, from whom was hidden, all his life, the truth that England had become, linguistically speaking, a province. Thus American literature was no longer English literature that had happened to get written somewhere else. And the history of England, its climate, its customs, its local pieties, no longer afforded, by sheer impalpable presence, a test for the genuineness of a piece of writing in the language called English. And the capital, a "torture" for Wordsworth, was not England, but a magnet for polyglot talent including Polish and American talent. As late as the 1930's, Faber & Faber's letterhead was designating one of the firm's directors, T.S. Eliot, as "U.S.A. Origin." He was also known as "Tom (Missouri) Eliot." The capital had lured him but not whelmed him.

As the capital ingathered, the provinces stirred. Poems were mailed to *The Egoist* by William Carlos Williams from New Jersey and by Marianne Moore from New York. Williams had known Pound at college; Miss Moore revered the example of James. Though they stayed settled in America all their lives they were never tempted to make easy rhymes for the natives. Their generation, aware of emissaries in London—Pound, Eliot, H.D.—could look toward London for contact with more than mere Englishness. The next American generation, that of Hemingway, Fitzgerald and Faulkner, also drew profit from the transatlantic example. By the time of its apprenticeship there were modern masterworks to study, notably *Ulysses* and *The Waste Land*. However rootedly local, American writing, thanks to some twenty years of looking abroad, has enjoyed ever since an inwardness with the international, the technological century. Today young poets in Germany or Norway expect that it will be Americans who will understand them.

Analgously, in England, Virginia Woolf, hating *Ulysses*, still made haste to exploit its riches. She is not part of International Modernism; she is an English novelist of manners, writing village gossip from a village called Bloomsbury for her English readers (though *cultivated* readers; that distinction had become operative between Dickens's time and hers, and Bloomsbury was a village with a good library.) She and they share shrewd awarenesses difficult to specify; that is always the provincial writer's strength. And she pertains to the English province, as Faulkner and Dr. Williams to the American: craftily knowing, in a local place, about mighty things afar: things of the order of *Ulysses*, even. It is normal for the writers of the Three Provinces to acknowledge International Modernism and take from it what they can; normal, intelligent, and wise. Seamus Heaney and John Montague would not be the authentic Irish poets they are but for International Modernism; Montague is especially instructive in having absorbed it, for his Irish purposes, at second hand from Williams, who had learned from Joyce and Pound and had also innovated, locally, on his own. Montague has learned the way of that. A thing writers can learn from one another is how to learn.

I have been describing the view from 1983. I have also been describing it as seen by myself. Other people have seen it quite differently, and from earlier years it has looked almost unrecognizably other. I can next enlighten you best by being personal and specific. It was in 1947, under Marshall McLuhan's informal tutelage, that I first became aware of my own century. Such a lag was perhaps possible only in Canada. By then an American movement called the New Criticism was enjoying its heyday. Like most critical stirrings on this self–improving continent, it was almost wholly a classroom movement. Stressing as it did Wit, Tension and Irony, it enabled teachers to say classroom things about certain kinds of poems. Donne was a handy poet for its purposes; so was Eliot; so too was the post–1916 Yeats. Thus Eliot and the later Yeats became living poets, and a few Americans such as Richard Eberhart, also a few Englishmen, e.g. William Empson. The Pound of *Mauberley* was (barely) part of the canon, 1920 having been Pound's brief moment of being almost like Eliot, tentative and an ironist. But when Pound was working in his normal way, by lapidary *statement*, New Critics could find nothing whatever to say about him. Since "Being–able–to–say–about" is a pedagogic criterion, he was largely absent from a canon pedagogues were defining. So was Williams, and wholly. What can Wit, Tension, Irony enable you to say about The Red Wheelbarrow? "So much depends . . .", says the poem, and seems to *mean* it; for a New Critic that was too naive for words.

I can still see Marshall chucking aside a mint copy of *Paterson I*, with the words "pretty feeble."

In those years we couldn't see the pertinence of *Ulysses* either. *Ulysses* had been blighted, ever since 1930, by Stuart Gilbert's heavy–handed crib. Nothing as mechanical as that could be organic. Frank Budgen's 1936 book, which might have helped, was too bio-graphical to survive New Critical scrutiny. (The tears Old Critics dropped in Keats's Urn got prompted by his tuberculosis, not his words. So a pox on biographers.) Richard Kain's *Fabulous Voy-ager,* the first book about *Ulysses* in more than a decade, looked like brave pioneering; as, in the circumstances, it was. Not that it took us the distance we needed to go, if we were to see *Ulysses* as pivotal.

Nor to see Pound as the central figure he was. The chain of accidents that brought Marshall McLuhan and me into his presence on 4 June 1948 I'll detail some other time. The *Pisan Cantos* were then newly published. Later I reviewed them for the *Hudson Re-view,* another connection masterminded by Marshall. I'd read them, ecstatic, with Pound's remembered voice in my ear. Soon, thanks to New Directions' well–timed one–volume reprint, I could read to the surge of the same spoken cadences the rest of the poem he'd begun in 1916 or before. Its authority, after what my Toronto mentors used to call poetry, was as if great rocks were rolling. I was 25, and about to become a Yale graduate student under Cleanth Brooks's mentorship. That fall the dismal Bollingen fuss broke—a forgotten minor poet named Robert Hillyer assembling three installments of invective in the equally forgotten *Saturday Review*—and literati in pulpit after pulpit would do no more than affirm the purity of their own political motives. Enthralled by the master, I resolved that if no one else would make the case for Ezra Pound the poet, then I would. Having no reputation whatever, I had nothing to lose. I was naive enough not to guess that I was mortgaging my future; it is sometimes liberating not to know how the world works. So in six weeks in the summer of 1949, on a picnic table in Canada, aided by books from the University of Toronto library, I banged out on a flimsy Smith-Corona the 308 typescript pages of *The Poetry of Ezra Pound* . . . which to my wonderment was instantly accepted by New Directions and by Faber & Faber. By 1951 they got it out. Though most of the reviews were put-downs, Pound before long was a stock on the academic exchange: a safe "subject." What that means is not that I'd "discovered" him, or been magnetically persuasive concerning his virtues. What I'd done, unwittingly, at the threshold of two decades' academic expansion—people peering under every cabbage-leaf for "topics"—was show how this new man with his large and complex oeuvre might plausibly be written about. Whether that was a service to him or to anyone I have never been sure.

In 1956, *annus mirabilis*, I visited Williams, Lewis, and Eliot, with introductions from Pound. He had told me that you have an obligation to visit the great men of your own time. Amid those visits and conversations a book to be called *The Pound Era* first began to shimmer hazily in my mind. Its typescript would not be complete for 13 years during which nothing stood still. Many were making the place of *Ulysses* clearer and clearer; Beckett was defining the trajectory of International Modernism; much attention to Pound was bringing one thing clearly into focus: that what he had always demanded was old-fashioned source–hunting scholarship, the very kind of thing the New Criticism had made disreputable for a generation. Part of a canon is the state and history of the relevant criticism.

For a canon is not a list but a narrative of some intricacy, depending on places and times and opportunities. Any list—a mere curriculum—is shorthand for that. The absence of Wallace Stevens from the canon I use has somehow been made to seem notorious. I account for it by his unassimilability into the only story that I find has adequate explanatory power: a story of capitals, from which he was absent. Like Virginia Woolf of Bloomsbury or Faulkner of Oxford, he seems a voice from a province, quirkily enabled by the International Modernism of which he was never a part, no more than they. His touch is uncertain; fully half his work is rhythmically dead. The life of the live part is generally the life of whimsy. And when, as in "Idea of Order at Key West," he commands a voice of unexpected resonance, then it is a voice unmistakeably American, affirming that it finds around itself a wildering chaos in which minds empowered not culturally but cosmically can discern (or make) precarious order. Whence order may stem, how nearly there is none, is Stevens's obsessive theme. Some splendid poems affirm this. They get lost in the shuffle of *Collected Poems* and *Opus Posthumous,* where, "ideas" being close to every surface, the seminars find gratification. His proponents seem not willing, perhaps not able, to distinguish his live poems from his stillborn: a sign, I think, that he is rather a counter on their board-game than an active force.

The rumor has been put about that Pound despised him. Let me place on record therefore that the night Stevens died, Ezra Pound, having gleaned the news from the blurry TV in a recreation lounge at St Elizabeths, wrote an urgent letter to *Poetry.* In those days I was his contact with *Poetry,* so he addressed it to me. "*Poetry,*" he said, "owes him a memorial issue." He hoped that someone, preferably ol' Doc Wms, would explain in that issue what Stevens had been writing *about*. I passed the word to Henry Rago, who solicited Doc Williams, who complied. Williams did not say what Stevens had been writing about; sick and old himself, he was content to affirm a commonality with Stevens in being mortal.

The question, though, was characteristically Poundian. In the story I have been elaborating for 35 years, everything innovative in our century was a response to something outside of literature. Pound's way of putting that is famous: "It is not man / Made courage, or made order, or made grace." Nor was it Joyce who made Dublin, nor Eliot London. Nor I, for that matter, the canon. I have tried to reconstruct an intricate story, continually guided by my judgment of six people I saw face to face, and listened to intently, never taking notes. They were Pound, Williams, Eliot, Lewis, Beckett, Miss Moore. I'm aware that I never met Stevens: nor, for that matter, Yeats or Joyce.

Heminge and Condell saw Shakespeare face to face. They subsequently enabled the First Folio of 1623, such a homage, observe, as no other dramatist of the time received. That was the beginning of Shakespeare's canonization. For 350 years this year, we have been confirming the judgment of Heminge and Condell. Something a contemporary can speak to is the aliveness of a man, his power to invest the air with forms. My own testimony, for what it has been worth, is that of a privileged contemporary. Yeats was able to proclaim, of Synge and Lady Gregory, "And say my glory was, I had such friends." I cannot pretend to such intimacy. I can hope, like Spence with his anecdotes of Pope, to have left some reasonably faithful portraits, and remember how, despite the smug confidence of Arnold, Spence's evaluation of Pope is no longer thought wrong.

The Modernist canon has been made in part by readers like me; in part in Borges' way by later writers choosing and inventing ancestors; chiefly though, I think, by the canonized themselves, who were apt to be aware of a collective enterprise, and repeatedly acknowledged one another. For our age has been canon–minded. One way to make a canon has been by explicit homages: imitation, translation. Pound made pedagogic lists of dead authors, and translated their texts. To the suggestion that he tended to list what he had translated, he replied that on the contrary he translated what he thought alive enough to list.

Poets translate to get into the language something that was not there before, some new possibility. In our century they have been especially apt to be incited by a sense of communing, in an ancient author, with otherness: with a coherent sense of the world for which we and our words are unprepared. If a translation turns out to resemble the sort of poem we are used to, it is probably unnecessary. Critics and historians (which all of us are informally, even when we may think we are simply reading) are similarly guided: we deplore the unnecessary. Pound discovered that the way for a poet to write the poem he wants to write, life having prompted some chemistry of desire,may be to co-opt an alien precursor whose sense of the world, in wholly foreign words, may guide English words today. Such a poet, the "Seafarer" poet for instance, became part of Pound's canon. Our canon likewise, when our eyes are not on pedagogic expedience, is something we shape by our needs and our sense of what is complexly coherent: what accords with the facts, and folds them into a shapely story, and brings us news from across Pound's godly sea, which is also the sea beside which the girl in Key West sang.

what kind?

The Shaping of a Canon: U.S. Fiction, 1960–1975

Richard Ohmann

Categorical names such as "The English Novel," "The Modern American Novel," and "American Literature" often turn up in catalogs as titles of college courses, and we know from them pretty much what to expect. They also have standing in critical discourse, along with allied terms unlikely to serve as course titles: "good writing," "great literature," "serious fiction," "literature" itself. The awareness has grown in recent years that such concepts pose problems, even though we use them with easy enough comprehension when we talk or write to others who share our cultural matrix.

Lately, critics like Raymond Williams have been reminding us that the categories change over time (just as "literature" used to mean all printed books but has come to mean only some poems, plays, novels, etc.) and that at any given moment categories embody complex social relations and a continuing historical process. That process deeply invests all terms with value: since not everyone's values are the same, the negotiating of such concepts is, among other things, a struggle for dominance—whether between adults and the young, professors and their students, one class and another, or men and women. We don't usually notice the power or the conflict, except when some previously weak or silent group seeks a share of the power: for example, when, in the 1960s, American blacks and their supporters insisted that black literature be

The first and second sections of this paper ("Reading and the Book Market" and "The Next Stage") appeared in different form as "The Social Definition of Literature," in Paul Hernadi, ed., *What is Literature?* (Bloomington, Ind., 1978). I extend my appreciation to Indiana University Press for permission to reprint these two sections.

included in school and college curricula, or when they openly challenged the candidacy of William Styron's *Confessions of Nat Turner* for inclusion in some eventual canon.[1] But the gradual firming up of concepts like, say, postwar American fiction is always a contest for cultural hegemony, even if in our society it is often muted—carried on behind the scenes or in the seemingly neutral marketplace.

Not only do the concepts change, in both intension and extension, but the process of their formation also changes. The English, who had power to do so, admitted *Great Expectations* to the canon by means very different from those used to admit the *Canterbury Tales* by earlier generations of tastemakers. Again, the process may differ from genre to genre even in a particular time and place. For instance, profit and the book market are relatively unimportant in deciding what will be considered modern American poetry, by contrast with their function in defining modern American fiction. As a result, in order to work toward a serviceable theory of canon-formation, it is necessary to look at a variety of these processes and at how they impinge on one another.

Here, I attempt to sketch out one of them, the process by which novels written by Americans from about 1960 to 1975 have been sifted and assessed, so that a modest number of them retain the kind of attention and respect that eventually makes them eligible for canonical status.[2] I am going to argue that the emergence of these novels has been a process saturated with class values and interests, a process inseparable from the broader struggle for position and power in our society, from the institutions that mediate that struggle, as well as from legitimation of and challenges to the social order. I will then try to be more specific about the representation of those values and interests in the fiction itself.

Reading and the Book Market

People read books silently, and often in isolation, but reading is nonetheless a social act. As one study concludes:

> Book reading in adult life is sustained . . . by interpersonal situations which minimize the individual's isolation from others. To persist over the years, the act of book reading must be incorporated . . . into a social context. Reading a book becomes meaningful when, after completion, it is shared with others. . . . Social integration . . . sustains a persistent engagement with books. Social isolation, in contrast, is likely to lead to the abandonment of books.[3]

Richard Ohmann is professor of English at Wesleyan University. He is the author of *English in America* and is presently working on studies in mass culture.

Simone Beserman found, in her study of best-sellers around 1970, that frequent reading of books correlated highly with social interaction—in particular, with the desire to rise in society. Upwardly mobile second- and third-generation Americans were heavy readers of best-sellers.[4]

As you would expect, given the way reading is embedded in and reinforced by social relations, networks of friends and family also contributed in determining which books would be widely read. In her survey, Beserman found that 58 percent of those who read a particular best-seller did so upon recommendation of a friend or relative. Who were these people, so crucial to a book's success? Beserman found that they were of better-than-average education (most had finished college), relatively well-to-do, many of them professionals, in middle life, upwardly mobile, living near New York or oriented, especially through the *New York Times,* to New York cultural life.

These people were responsive to novels where they discovered the values in which they believed or where they found needed moral guidance when shaken in their own beliefs. Saul Bellow's remark, "What Americans want to learn from their writers is how to live," finds support in Philip H. Ennis' study, *Adult Book Reading in the United States.*[5] Ennis determined that three of the main interests people carried into their reading were a "search for personal meaning, for some kind of map to the moral landscape"; a need to "reinforce or to celebrate beliefs already held, or, when shaken by events, to provide support in some personal crisis"; and a wish to keep up "with the book talk of friends and neighbors."[6]

The values and beliefs of a small group of people played a disproportionate role in deciding what novels would be widely read in the United States. (Toward the end of this essay, I will turn to those values in some detail.) To underscore their influence, consider two other facts about the book market. First, if a novel did not become a best-seller within three or four weeks of publication, it was quite unlikely to reach a large readership later on. In the 1960s, only a very few books that were slow starters eventually became best-sellers (in paperback, not hardback). I know of three: *Catch-22, Call It Sleep,* and *I Never Promised You a Rose Garden,* to which we may add the early novels of Vonnegut, which were not published in hard covers, and—if we count its 1970s revival in connection with the film—*One Flew Over the Cuckoo's Nest.* To look at the process the other way around, once a new book did make the *New York Times* best-seller list, many other people bought it (and store managers around the country stocked it) *because* it was a best-seller. The process was cumulative. So the early buyers of hardcover books exercised a crucial role in selecting the books that the rest of the country's readers would buy.

Second, best-sellerdom was much more important than suggested by the figures for hardbound sales through bookstores. *Love Story,* for instance, the leading best-seller (in all forms) of the decade sold only

450,000 hardback copies in bookstores but over 700,000 through book clubs, 2,500,000 through the *Reader's Digest,* 6,500,000 in the *Ladies' Home Journal,* and over 9,000,000 in paperback—not to mention library circulation or the millions of people who saw the film. Books were adopted by clubs, paperback publishers, film producers, and so forth, in large part because they were best-sellers or because those investing in subsidiary rights thought them likely to become best-sellers. As Victor Navasky rather wryly said:

> Publishers got out of the business of *selling* hardcover books ten or fifteen years ago. The idea now is to publish hardcover books so that they can be reviewed or promoted on television in order to sell paperback rights, movie rights, book club rights, comic book rights, serialization rights, international satellite rights, Barbie doll rights, etc.[7]

The phenomenon of the hardbound best-seller had only modest economic and cultural significance in itself but great significance in triggering reproduction and consumption of the story in other forms.

A small group of relatively homogeneous readers, then, had a great deal of influence at this preliminary stage. But of course these people did not make *their* decisions freely among the thousands of novels completed each year. They chose among the smaller number actually published. This fact points to an important role in canon-formation for literary agents and for editors at the major houses, who belong to the same social stratum as the buyers of hardbound books, and who—as profitability in publishing came to hinge more and more on the achievement of best-sellerdom for a few books—increasingly earned their keep by spotting (and pushing) novels that looked like best-sellers. Here we have a nearly closed circle of marketing and consumption, the simultaneous exploitation and creation of taste, familiar to anyone who has examined marketplace culture under monopoly capitalism.

But it is clear, influential readers chose not among all novels published but among the few that came to their attention in an urgent or attractive way. How did that happen? As a gesture toward the kind of answer that question requires, I will consider the extraordinary role of the *New York Times.* The *New York Times Book Review* had about a million and a half readers, several times the audience of any other literary periodical. Among them were most bookstore managers, deciding what to stock, and librarians, deciding what to buy, not to mention the well-to-do, well-educated east-coasters who led in establishing hardback best-sellers. The single most important boost a novel could get was a prominent review in the Sunday *New York Times*—better a favorable one than an unfavorable one, but better an unfavorable one than none at all.

Ads complemented the reviews, or perhaps the word is "inundated": two-thirds of the space in the *Times Book Review* went to ads. According to Richard Kostelanetz, most publishers spent more than half their advertising budgets for space in that journal.[8] They often placed ads in such a way as to reinforce a good *Times* review or offset a bad one with favorable quotations from reviews in other periodicals. And of course reviews and ads were further reinforced by the *Times* best-seller list itself, for the reason already mentioned. Apparently, the publishers' faith in the *Times* was not misplaced. Beserman asked early readers of *Love Story* where they had heard of the book. Most read it on recommendation of another person; Beserman then spoke to *that* person, and so on back to the beginning of the chain of verbal endorsements. At the original source, in more than half the instances, she found the *Times*.[9] (This in spite of the quite unusual impact, for that time, of Segal's appearance on the "Today" show the day of publication—Barbara Walters said the book made her cry all night; Harper was immediately swamped with orders— and of the novel's appearance in the *Ladies' Home Journal* just before book publication.)

The influence of the *Times Book Review* led publicity departments to direct much of their prepublication effort toward persuading the *Book Review*'s editors that a particular novel was important. It is hard to estimate the power of this suasion, but one thing can be measured: the correlation between advertising in the *Book Review* and being reviewed there. A 1968 study concluded, perhaps unsurprisingly, that the largest advertisers got disproportionately large amounts of review space. Among the large advertisers were, for instance:

	Pages of ads	*Pages of reviews*
Random House	74	58
Harper	29	22
Little, Brown	29	21

And the smaller ones:

Dutton	16	4
Lippincott	16	4
Harvard	9	"negligible"

During the same year Random House (including Knopf and Pantheon) had nearly three times as many books mentioned in the feature "New and Recommended" as Doubleday or Harper, both of which published as many books as the Random House group.[10]

To summarize: a small group of book buyers formed a screen through which novels passed on their way to commercial success; a handful of agents and editors picked the novels that would compete for the notice of those buyers; and a tight network of advertisers and reviewers, organized around the *New York Times Book Review*, selected from these a few to be recognized as compelling, important, "talked-about."

The Next Stage

So far I have been speaking of a process that led to a mass readership for a few books each year. But most of these were never regarded as serious literature and did not live long in popularity or memory. Books like *Love Story, The Godfather, Jonathan Livingston Seagull,* and the novels of Susann, Robbins, Wouk, Wallace, and Uris would run a predictable course. They had large hardback sales for a few months, tapering off to a trickle in a year or so. Meanwhile, they were reprinted in paper covers and enjoyed two or three years of popularity (often stoked by a film version). After that they disappeared or remained in print to be bought in smaller numbers by, for instance, newly won fans of Wallace who wanted to go back and read his earlier books. There was a similar pattern for mysteries, science fiction, and other specialized genres.

But a few novels survived and continued (in paper covers) to attract buyers and readers for a longer time, and they still do. Why? To answer that the *best* novels survive is to beg the question. Excellence is a constantly changing, socially chosen value. Who attributed it to only some novels, and how? I hope now to hint at the way such a judgment took shape.

First, one more word about the *New York Times Book Review*. I have argued that it led in developing a broad audience for fiction. It also began, I believe, the process of distinguishing between ephemeral popular novels and those to be taken seriously over a longer period of time. There was a marked difference in impact between, say, Martin Levin's favorable but mildly condescending (and brief) review of *Love Story* and the kind of front-page review by an Alfred Kazin or an Irving Howe that asked readers to regard a new novel as literature, and that so often helped give the stamp of highbrow approval to books by Bellow, Malamud, Updike, Roth, Doctorow, and so forth.[11] Cultural leaders read the *Times Book Review* too: not only professors but (according to Julie Hoover and Charles Kadushin) 75 percent of our elite intellectuals.[12] By reaching these circles, a major *Times* review could help put a novel on the cultural agenda and insure that other journals would have to take it seriously.

Among those others, a few carried special weight in forming cultural judgments. In a survey of leading intellectuals, just eight journals—the *New York Review of Books,* the *New Republic,* the *New York Times Book Review,* the *New Yorker, Commentary, Saturday Review, Partisan Review,* and *Harpers*—received almost half the participants' "votes" in response to various questions about influence and importance.[13] In effect, these periodicals were both a communication network among the influentials (where they reviewed one another's books) and an avenue of access to a wider cultural leadership. The elite, writing in these journals, largely determined which books would be seriously debated and which ones permanently valued, as well as what ideas were kept alive, circulated, discussed.[14] Kadushin and his colleagues concluded, from their studies of our intellectual elite and influential journals, that the "top intellectual journals constitute the American equivalent of an Oxbridge establishment, and have served as one of the main gatekeepers for new talent and new ideas."[15]

A novel had to win at least the divided approval of these arbiters in order to remain in the universe of cultural discourse, once past the notoriety of best-sellerdom. The career of *Love Story* is a good example of failure to do so. After some initial favorable reviews (and enormous publicity on television and other media), the intellectuals began cutting it down to size. In the elite journals, it was either panned or ignored. Styron and the rest of the National Book Award fiction panel threatened to quit if it were not removed from the list of candidates. And who will read it tomorrow, except on an excursion into the archives of mass culture?

In talking about the *New York Times Book Review,* I suggested a close alliance between reviewing and profit, literary and monetary values. The example of the *New York Review of Books* shows that a similar alliance can exist on the higher ramparts of literary culture. This journal, far and away the most influential among intellectuals (in answer to Kadushin's questions, it was mentioned almost twice as often as the *New Republic,* its nearest competitor),[16] was founded by Jason Epstein, a vice-president of Random House, and coedited by his wife, Barbara Epstein. It may be more than coincidental that in 1968 almost one-fourth of the books granted full reviews in the *New York Review* were published by Random House (again, including Knopf and Pantheon)—more than the combined total of books from Viking, Grove, Holt, Harper, Houghton Mifflin, Oxford, Doubleday, Macmillan, and Harvard so honored; or that in the same year one-fourth of the *reviewers* had books in print with Random House and that a third of those were reviewing other Random House books, mainly favorably; or that over a five-year period more than half the regular reviewers (ten or more appearances) were Random House authors.[17] This is not to deny the intellectual strength of the *New York Review*—only to suggest that it sometimes deployed that strength in ways consistent with the financial interest of Random House. One need not subscribe to conspiracy theories in order to see, almost everywhere one looks in the milieu of publishing and reviewing, linkages of fellowship and common interest. Together these networks make up a cultural establishment, inseparable from the market, both influencing and influenced by it.

If a novel was certified in the court of the prestigious journals, it was likely to draw the attention of academic critics in more specialized and academic journals like *Contemporary Literature* and by this route make its way into college curricula, where the very context—course title, academic setting, methodology—gave it de facto recognition as literature. This final step was all but necessary: the college classroom and its counterpart, the academic journal, have become in our society the final arbiters of literary merit, and even of survival. It is hard to think of a novel more than twenty-five years old, aside from specialist fiction and *Gone with the Wind,* that still commands a large readership outside of school and college.

I am suggesting that novels moved toward a canonical position only if they attained both large sales (usually, but not always, concentrated enough to place them among the best-sellers for a while) and the right kind of critical attention. On the one side, this hypothesis conflicts with the one most vigorously advanced by Leslie A. Fiedler—that intellectuals are, in the long run, outvoted by the sorts of readers who keep liking *Gone with the Wind.*[18] On the other side, it collides with the hopes or expectations of critics such as Kostelanetz and Jerome Klinkowitz, who promote an avant-garde fiction called post-modernist, post-contemporary, antinovel, or whatever.[19]

Clearly, I need an independent measure of precanonical status, or my argument closes into a circle. Unfortunately, I don't have a very good one: in part, because it is still too early to settle the issue, but also because I have not yet finished the inquiry I intend.[20] But let me offer two scraps of pertinent information. First, the editors of *Wilson Quarterly* polled forty-four professors of American literature (in 1977 or 1978, apparently), asking them to rank in order the ten "most important" novels published in the United States after World War II.[21] The editors printed a list of the twenty-one novels rated highest in this survey; eleven of them were published in or after 1960. In rank-order, they are *Catch-22, Gravity's Rainbow, Herzog, An American Dream, The Sotweed Factor, Second Skin, Portnoy's Complaint, The Armies of the Night, V, Rabbit Run,* and *One Flew Over the Cuckoo's Nest.* All easily meet the criterion of attention from intellectuals. (Again, it doesn't matter that Norman Podhoretz *hates* Updike's novels, so long as he takes them seriously enough to argue with his peers about them.) As for broad readership, all of the novels except *Second Skin* and perhaps *The Sotweed Factor* have sold over half a million copies—and one may be sure that many of those sales occurred through adoption in college courses.[22]

My second cast of the net is much broader. *Contemporary Literary Criticism* abstracts commentary on recent world literature, mainly by American professors and intellectuals. Its coverage includes critical books, respected academic journals, taste-forming magazines, quarterlies, and little magazines.[23] It claims to excerpt from criticism of "work by well-known creative writers," "writers of considerable public interest," who are alive or who died after 1 January 1960. So it constitutes a sampling of the interests of those who set literary standards, and it monitors the intermediate stage in canon-formation. During the ten years and twenty-two volumes of its publication, up through 1982, it has run four or more entries (maximum, nine; and the average entry includes excerpts from four or five critical sources) for forty-eight American novelists of the period in question:[24]

Auchincloss	Elkin	Piercy
Baldwin	Gaddis	Plath
Barth	Gardner	Porter
Barthelme	Gass	Pynchon
Bellow	Hawkes	Rechy
Berger	Heller	Reed
Bradbury	Higgins	Roth
Brautigan	Jong	Salinger
Burroughs	Kesey	Selby
Capote	R. MacDonald	Sorrentino
Cheever	Mailer	Styron
Condon	Malamud	Theroux
de Vries	McCarthy	Updike
Dickey	McMurtry	Vidal
Didion	Oates	Vonnegut
Doctorow	Percy	Walker

Most of these meet my two criteria. All but a few (Bradbury, Condon, MacDonald, perhaps Auchincloss and Higgins) have received ample consideration by influential critics. Yet most novelists promoted by post-contemporary advocates such as Klinkowitz (Sloan, Coover, Wurlitzer, Katz, Federman, Sukenick, etc.) are missing, while the list includes only a few writers who have had elite approval but small readerships (Elkin, Hawkes, Sorrentino, maybe two or three others). In fact, at least thirty-one of these novelists published one book or more between 1960 and 1975 that was a best-seller in hard or paper covers.[25] On the other hand, the list excludes the overwhelming majority of the writers who regularly produced large best-sellers: Puzo, Susann, Wouk, West, Robbins, Wallace, Michener, Krantz, Forsyth, Chrichton, and so on and on. I conclude that both the *Contemporary Literary Criticism* selection and the *Wilson Quarterly* survey give modest support to my thesis. Canon-formation during this period took place in the interaction between large audiences and gatekeeper intellectuals.

Class and the Canon

To return to the main theme, then: I have drawn a sketch of the course a novel had to run, in order to lodge itself in our culture as precanonical—as "literature," at least for the moment. It was selected, in turn, by an agent, an editor, a publicity department, a review editor (especially the one at the Sunday *New York Times*), the New York metropolitan book buyers whose patronage was necessary to commercial success, critics writing for gatekeeper intellectual journals, academic critics, and college teachers. Obviously, the sequence was not rigid, and some might on occasion be omitted entirely (as I have indicated with respect to *Catch-22* and *One Flew Over the Cuckoo's Nest*). But one would expect the pattern to have become more regular through this period, as publishing was increasingly drawn into the sphere of monopoly capital (with RCA acquiring Random House; ITT, Howard Sams; Time, Inc., Little, Brown; CBS, Holt, Rinehart & Winston; Xerox, Ginn; and so on throughout almost the whole industry). For monopoly capital changed this industry much as it has changed the automobile and the toothpaste industries: by placing much greater emphasis on planned marketing and predictability of profits.[26]

This shift brought publishing into the same arena as many other cultural processes. In fact, the absorption of culture began almost as soon as monopoly capitalism itself, with the emergence of the advertising industry (crucial to planned marketing) in the 1880s and 1890s, and simultaneously with mass-circulation magazines as the main vehicle of national brand advertising.[27] With some variations, cinema, radio, music, sport, newspapers, television, and many lesser forms have followed this path, with books among the last to do so. The change has transformed our culture and the ways we participate in it. It demands rethinking, not only of bourgeois ideas about culture but of central Marxian oppositions like base and superstructure, production and reproduction.[28] Culture cannot, without straining, be understood as a reflex of basic economic activity, when culture is itself a core industry and a major source of capital accumulation. Nor can we bracket culture as reproduction, when it is inseparable from the making and selling of commodities. We have at present a relatively new and rapidly changing cultural process that calls for new and flexible ways of thinking about culture.

My account may, however, have made it sound as if in one respect nothing has changed. Under monopoly capital, even more than when Marx and Engels wrote *The German Ideology*, the "class which has the means of material production at its disposal, has control at the same time over the means of mental production." But does it still follow that, "thereby, generally speaking, the ideas of those who lack the means of mental production are subject to" the ruling class?[29] The theory can explain contemporary reality only with an expanded and enriched understanding of "control" and "subject to." For although our ruling class owns the media and controls them formally, it does not exercise direct control over their content—does not now use them in the instrumental and ideological way that Marx and Engels identified 140 years ago. Mobil "idea ads" are the exception, not the rule.

To return to the instance at hand: neither the major stockholders of ITT and Xerox and RCA nor their boards of directors played a significant role in deciding which novels of the 1960s and early 1970s would gain acceptance as literature, and they certainly established no house rules — printing only those books that would advance their outlook on the world. (If they had done so, how could they have allowed, e.g., the Pantheon division of Random House virtually to enlist in the New Left?) They exercised control over publishing in the usual abstract way: they sought a good return on investment and cared little whether it came from a novel by Bellow or by Krantz, or for that matter from novels or computer chips. And very few of the historical actors who did make critical decisions about fiction were members of the haute bourgeoisie. Was class then irrelevant to the early shaping of a canon of fiction? Alternatively, did the working class make its own culture in this sphere?

My argument points toward a conclusion different from both of these, one that still turns upon class but not just upon the two great traditional classes. Intuitively, one can see that literary agents, editors, publicity people, reviewers, buyers of hardbound novels, taste-making intellectuals, critics, professors, most of the students who took literary courses, and, in fact, the writers of the novels themselves, all had social affinities. They went to the same colleges, married one another, lived in the same neighborhoods, talked about the same movies, had to work for their livings (but worked with their minds more than with their hands), and earned pretty good incomes. I hold that they belonged to a common class, one that itself emerged and grew up only with monopoly capitalism. Following Barbara and John Ehrenreich, I call it the Professional-Managerial class.[30] I characterize it by the affinities just mentioned; by its conflicted relation to the ruling class (intellectuals managed that class' affairs and many of its institutions, and they derived benefits from this position, but they also strove for autonomy and for a somewhat different vision of the future);[31] by its equally mixed relation to the working class (it dominated, supervised, taught, and planned for them, but even in doing so it also served and augmented capital); and by its own marginal position with respect to capital (its members didn't have the wealth to sit back and clip coupons, but they had ready access to credit and most could choose—at least at an early stage in their careers—between working for themselves and selling their labor power to others).[32]

People in the Professional-Managerial class shared one relation to the bourgeoisie and another to the working class: they had many common social experiences and acted out similar styles of life. I hold that they also had—with of course many complexities and much variation—a common understanding of the world and their place in it. In the remainder of this essay, I will look at some of the values, beliefs, and interests that constituted that class perspective, by considering the novels given cultural currency by those class members who produced, marketed, read, interpreted, and taught fiction. My claim is that the needs and values of the Professional-Managerial class permeate the general form of these novels, as well as their categories of understanding and their means of representation.

For my examples I will draw upon such works as *Franny and Zooey*, *One Flew Over the Cuckoo's Nest*, *The Bell Jar*, *Herzog*, *Portnoy's Complaint*, and Updike's *Rabbit* series. But what I say of these books is true of many other novels from the postwar period that have as yet a chance of becoming canonical.[33] To glance ahead for a moment: these novels told stories of people trying to live a decent life in contemporary social settings, people represented as analogous to "us," rather than as "cases" to be examined and understood from a clinical distance, as in an older realistic convention. They are unhappy people, who move toward happiness, at least a bit, by the ends of their stories.

A premise of this fiction—nothing new to American literature but particularly salient in this period—is that individual consciousness, not the social or historical field, is the locus of significant happening. In passing, note that on the level of style this premise authorizes variety, the pursuit of a unique and personal voice.[34] But on the levels of conceptualization and story, the premise of individual autonomy has an opposite effect: it gives these fictions a common problem and drives their material into narratives which, seen from the middle distance, look very similar. I am going to suggest that much precanonical fiction of this period expresses, in Williams' term, a particular structure of feeling,[35] that that structure of feeling was a common one for the class in question, and that novelists explored its contours before it was articulated in books of social commentary like Philip Slater's *Pursuit of Loneliness* (1970) and Charles Reich's *Greening of America* (1970), or in films like *The Graduate*, and certainly, before that structure of feeling informed a broad social movement or entered conversational cliché, in phrases like "a sick society," "the establishment," and "the system." (More avant-garde writers, outside the circuit of best-sellers, had given it earlier expression: the "Beats," Mailer in *Advertisements for Myself*, Barth in *The End of the Road*, etc.)

This structure of feeling gathered and strengthened during the postwar period. It became rather intense by the early 1960s. After 1965 it exploded into the wider cultural and political arena, when black rebellions, the student movement, the antiwar movement, and later the women's movement made it clear, right there in the headlines and on television, that not everyone considered ours an age of only "happy problems."[36]

In retrospect it is easy to understand some of the forces that generated this consciousness. To chart the connection, I will take a broad and speculative look at the historical experience of the class that endowed fiction with value and suggest how that experience shaped that class' concerns and needs, before I turn at greater length to the fiction that its members wrote, published, read, and preserved.

Like everyone in the society, people in the Professional-Managerial class lived through a time when the United States was enjoying the spoils of World War II. It altogether dominated the "free world" for two decades, militarily, politically, and economically. Its power sufficed to give it dominance among its allies and to prevent defections from the capitalist sphere, though the "loss" of China and Cuba gave cause for worried vigilance. Its products and its capital flowed freely through most parts of the world (its very money was the currency of capitalism after the Bretton Woods and Dumbarton Oaks agreements). U.S. values also flowed freely, borne by advertising, television shows, and the *Reader's Digest* more than by propaganda. The confidence one would expect to find in the metropolis of such an empire strengthened the feeling of righteousness that came from having defeated one set of enemies in war and having held at bay another set in peace. Both the war and the cold war fostered a chauvinistic and morally polarized conception of the world. *They* were totalitarian monsters; *we* were an open society of free citizens pursuing a way of life superior to any other, past or present.

Furthermore, that way of life generated a material prosperity that was historically unprecedented and that increased from one year to the next. The pent-up buying power of the war period (never before or since has the broad working class had so much money in the bank) eased the conversion from war production to production for consumers by providing capitalists with an enormous and secure domestic market, and they responded with rapid investment and a flow of old and new products. Affluence, like victory in war, made people confident that they and their society were doing things right.

On top of that, social conflict became muted. Inequality remained as pronounced as it had been before, but no more so, and the working class participated in the steady growth of total product.[37] Though workers could not see any narrowing of the divide between themselves and higher classes, the postwar generation did experience an absolute gain, both from year to year and by comparison with the 1930s; and many *perceived* this gain as a softening of class lines. The sense of economic well-being that results from such an experience of history promoted allegiance to the social order, as did the tightening bonds between unions and management, amounting to a truce in class conflict within the assumptions of the welfare state. Cold war propaganda helped make it possible— especially for those who managed the new arrangements and lived in suburbs—to see our society as a harmonious collaboration.

Developments in business additionally gave support to this image of harmony. There was a rapid growth and sophistication of advertising, which not only sold products but continued to shape people into masses, for the purpose of selling those products and advancing a whole way of life whose cornerstones were the suburban home, the family, and the automobile. Leisure and social life became more private, drained of class feeling and even of the feeling of interdependence.

Politics seemed nearly irrelevant to such a life. Moreover, the boundaries of respectable political debate steadily closed in through the 1950s. On one side, socialism was pushed off the agenda by union leaders almost as vigorously as by Truman, McCarthy, the blacklisters, and the FBI. On the other side, businessmen gradually abandoned the tough old capitalist principles of laissez-faire and espoused a more benign program of co-operation with labor and government. The spectrum of discussable ideas reached only from corporate liberalism to welfare-state liberalism; no wonder some thought they were witnessing the end of ideology.[38]

Consider the experience of the class that creates the canon of fiction in such an environment. Not only were its numbers and its prosperity growing rapidly along with its institutions but every public voice seemed to be saying to intellectuals, professionals, technical elites, and managers: "History is over, though progress continues. There is no more poverty. Everyone is middle class. The State is a friendly power, capable of smoothing out the abrasions of the economic system, solving its problems one by one through legislation that itself is the product of your ideas and values. You have brought a neutral and a humane rationality to the supervision of public life (exemplified beautifully by that parade of Harvard intellectuals to Washington in 1961). Politics is for experts, not ideologues. You are, therefore, the favored people, the peacemakers, the technicians of an intelligent society, justly rewarded with quick promotions, respect, and adequate incomes. So carry forward this valued social mission, which in no way conflicts with individual achievement. Enjoy your prestige and comforts. Fulfill yourselves on the terrain of private life."

But because the economic underpinnings of this consciousness were of course *not* unchanging and free of conflict, because material interdependence was an ever more pervasive fact,[39] whether perceived or not, because society cannot be wished away, because freedom on such terms is an illusion—for all these reasons, the individual pursuit of happiness continued to be a problem. Yet myth, ideology, and experience assured the Professional-Managerial class that no real barriers would prevent personal satisfaction, so it was easy to nourish the suspicion that any perceived lack was one's own fault. If unhappy, one must be personally maladjusted, perhaps even neurotic. I am suggesting that for the people who wrote, read, promoted, and preserved fiction, social contradictions were easily displaced into images of personal illness.

The Illness Story

This fiction of illness locates the experience of personal crisis somewhere in the passage from youth to maturity. This is easy to understand.

Within the configuration of social forces I have described, maturity is equated with independence, in fact with a kind of invulnerability to the intrusion of social tension, an invulnerability to society itself. But even though one may push social conflict and historical process out of sight, one cannot really cease to be social: at a minimum, social *roles* are indivisible from selfhood. To put the contradiction another way: the ideal calls for a self that is complete, integral, unique; but in actual living one must be *some*thing and *some*body, and definitions of "somebody" already exist in a complete array provided by that very social and economic system that one has wished to transcend. Society comes back at the individual as a hostile force, threatening to diminish or annihilate one's "real" self. Furthermore, society has the power to label one as sick, if one is unable to make the transition into a suitable combination of adult roles. So the representation of malaise and neurosis in the favored novels of the period incorporates an ambiguity, sometimes explicit and sometimes latent: I seem to be crazy, but again, possibly it's *society* that's crazy. The balance tips sometimes toward one construction of the ambiguity, sometimes toward the other, but the polarity is always there.

It will be convenient to take *The Bell Jar* (first published obscurely in Britain in 1963 but an American best-seller after its 1971 publication here) as a paradigm. Esther Greenwood's achievements are supposed to make her the "envy" of everyone, but as she puts it, "all the little successes I'd totted up so happily at college fizzled to nothing outside the slick marble and plate-glass fronts along Madison Avenue."[40] In those windows, she cannot see the self she wants to be. An insistent imagery of alien reflections in mirrors, of frightening photographs, of makeup and clothes that conceal the self, of fade-outs and disappearances and false identities makes it clear that Esther is unwilling to equate the person she feels herself to be with the person presented to the world in these various guises. "I knew something was wrong with me that summer," she thinks (p. 2). Patricia Ann Meyer Spacks calls Esther's malaise "negative narcissism"—a helpful diagnosis, though it obscures the way social roles and power relations translate into personal illness.[41]

Esther is on the threshold of maturity. A transition will be forced upon her, but a transition to what? Nothing so simple as winning all the prizes at school. Her summer in New York is a trial run for her in one possible adult role, that of "career girl," and she feels desperately estranged. She puts on a series of acts that humiliate and confuse her and ends by casting her New York wardrobe into the night, "like a loved one's ashes," from the sunroof of her hotel (p. 124). She is holding rites for a possible grown-up identity prepared for her by her past, her gender, and her society.

It is not the only one, of course. The main alternative role that awaits her adult self is that of wife and mother. She can make womanhood itself her identity, as womanhood is constituted by her society and her class. Yet she feels both inadequate to and oppressed by this possibility—marriage would make her "numb as a slave in some private, totalitarian state" (p. 94). Through the course of the story she systematically attempts or witnesses the main activities linked to this role and finds them at best distasteful, at worst ruinous. Courtship: a cold ritual with Constantin, a humiliating deception with Buddy, a brutal assault with Marco. Sex: detached from feeling, whether in Buddy's clinical version or Irwin's suave one. Birth: appropriated by men, their institutions, their technique. Motherhood: Dodo Conway and her "paraphernalia of suburban childhood" leave Esther musing, "Children make me sick" (pp. 130, 131).

Other roles exist, some presented in the very explicit image of the fig tree, with "a wonderful future" (p. 84) at the end of every branch, and Esther starving because to choose one future is to renounce all the others. The identities available to her are destructive, confining, partly because identities are, partly because of the extra divisions that gender adds to the division of labor, partly because Esther is endowed with the class ideal of being unbounded and autonomous. Casting about for solace, she remembers the time when she was "purely happy" (p. 82)—up to age nine. Skiing joyously, she thinks of herself as aiming back through her past at an image of both purity and happiness, "the white sweet baby cradled in its mother's belly" (p. 108). But in present life she can gesture toward purity, toward exemption from adult being, only through madness and a suicide attempt. Her female psychiatrist may guide her back to a hesitant reentry into the social world, but since that world presented her with the impasse that made her mad in the first place, the end of the novel resolves its crisis at best only tentatively.

With a few mutations, Salinger tells the same story in *Franny and Zooey*. Franny Glass' neurosis has patently social origins: the class snobbery and male privilege of Lane Coutell, who represents one future for her; and the appropriation of art and knowledge for competitive self-advancement by the professors and poets and theater people, who represent another. Like Esther, Franny seeks a purity that she cannot envisage in adult life as given by class and gender. Like Esther, she tries to annihilate her social self, not literally but through the spiritual discipline of the Jesus prayer, through the "way of the pilgrim" and its denial of all discriminations between social classes—just as her brother Buddy would have us unlearn the "illusory differences, between boys and girls."[42] And like Esther, Franny returns to sanity and—we are to expect—the untransformed social world, where she will be able to go on toward her adult role of actress, healed through Zooey's agency and through the image of the Fat Lady who is Christ who is all of us: a perfect symbol for the refusal to take society as real.

These novels tell a version of *the* story of the postwar period, a story firmly established earlier in one of the two securely canonical works of the 1950s, *The Catcher in the Rye*.[43] But not much of the acclaimed fiction from 1960 to 1975 is literally about adolescent rites of passage. To make my claim more adequate, I need to posit one transformation of the story: the person hanging onto childhood as the only defense against capitalist and patriarchal social relations is most often a man or woman already implanted in an adult role but only masquerading as a productive and well-adjusted member of society. In other words, the rite of passage marked by illness and movement toward recovery may be, and usually is, an adult crisis, of the sort popularized later by Gail Sheehy in *Passages*.

As an example, consider Alexander Portnoy, who, at 33, is the assistant commissioner of human opportunity for the city of New York; but he feels like a fraud—he cannot love; he cannot act or feel grown-up toward his parents. As he puts it: "A Jewish man with parents alive is a fifteen-year-old boy, and will remain a fifteen-year-old boy till *they die!*"[44] Masturbation is an apt image of his arrested growth, for it joins pleasure to internalized parental disapproval, fixes it on objects (liver, an apple, his sister's underwear) rather than people, and detaches sex from any social function. Why this refusal of adult participation? For one answer, think of the few idealized images Alex retains from childhood of the adult life that might await him: the Turkish bath, for instance, or the men playing baseball. Significantly, these are scenes "without *goyim* and women" (p. 49) and exempt from the pressure toward competitive individual achievement. I suggest that in this, one of the most politically sophisticated fictions of the period, it is rather explicit that "maturity" entails acceptance of distorted social relations: male supremacy, class domination represented as rule by the gentiles ("These people are the *Americans*, Doctor" [p. 145]), and the compensatory drive to best others in school, sport, moral righteousness, public recognition. Even Alex, talking wildly from the analyst's couch, can see beyond the peculiarities of his own parents and Weequahic culture to broad social configurations that make growing up a betrayal of integrity.

We can read this story over and over in the precanonical novels: a man (occasionally a woman) is doing pretty well by external measures; yet somehow the tension between his aspirations and his quotidian social existence grows unbearable. He stops doing what people expect of him and enters a period of disorientation and disreputable experiment. Bellow's paradigmatic hero, Moses Herzog, thinks, "If I am out of my mind, it's all right with me," and his students realize that in their class on Romanticism "they would see and hear odd things."[45] This is the condition of Bellow's heroes, from Eugene Henderson through Charlie Citrine. Updike tells the story too—three times so far in the *Rabbit* novels alone—though his character is no would-be hero of the intellect. Running, space flight, a plane trip to the Caribbean image Harry Angstrom's three excursions into adventurous abnormality, breaking the "stale peace" of marriage, paternity, and work.[46]

Even those precanonical novels that depart from a realistic convention tend to thematize bad social relations as the illness of ordinary people.

A car dealer loses his bearings in Vonnegut's *Breakfast of Champions,* a housewife, in Pynchon's *The Crying of Lot 49,* a businessman, in Heller's *Something Happened.* An established classic of the period, *One Flew Over the Cuckoo's Nest,* takes the problematic to its logical extreme, where normality is submission to totalitarian madness and those who don't fit are shut up in a lunatic asylum. And the same total inversion of socially defined sanity and madness appears, though less thoroughly developed, in the few acclaimed novels that locate their exploration of American social reality in an earlier time: Heller's *Catch-22,* Porter's *Ship of Fools,* McCarthy's *The Group,* Doctorow's *Ragtime,* even Morrison's *Song of Solomon* (published just after the end of my period).

Let me now sketch in a few other lineaments of this story. Against the threat that the project of happy selfhood may shatter into the fragmentations of capitalist production (the division of labor) and reproduction (the family as a separate sphere of consolation and fulfillment), most of these novels offer at least a glimpse of a more integral way of being. Plath gives us those images of childhood happiness and of skiing back to the perfect moment of conception. Roth has Portnoy remember not only the prehistoric world of the Turkish bath but those temporary idylls of oceanic love with his mother. Herzog finds sustenance in images of his childhood family, as does Harry Angstrom—especially the recurring one of himself protecting his sister Mim as they go sledding. Salinger's idealization of childhood needs no commentary. Even McMurphy and Chief Bromden recall times when life was simple and spontaneous. Almost always, these visions of a better way point us toward the past, and most often toward an individual childhood past when the self was engulfed in familial love and society stood at a distance, unperceived.

Such visions of wholeness linger in memory and animate desire, but they collide with the main experiences of adult life. I'll mention three such experiences, beginning with work. Most often, it is a scam: Pynchon, Vonnegut, and Updike, for example, locate it in car lots and salesrooms, where one needs a measure of cynicism to peddle the American dream on wheels. Salinger's Zooey deplores the fake world of television work. Plath gives us the hype of the woman's magazine, Heller, the mutual- and self-deception of the corporate headquarters. Kesey and Pynchon render brief, nightmarish visions of factory and corporation. Occasionally there are images of nonalienating work, but: Rabbit loses his rather satisfying job as a linotypist (this old-fashioned work disappears entirely, with automation); Moses Herzog can't get back to his great book; Esther Greenwood has no idea how to become the poet she imagines; Kilgore Trout is indeed a writer, but he is ignored and savagely lonely; Alexander Portnoy's city bureaucracy defeats the humane purposes his work is supposed to achieve; Chief Bromden knows that a big dam has made salmon fishing all but impossible. Only Salinger, in what strikes me as a sleight of hand, manages to retrieve a sense of wholeness in work, taking it quite out of the system of commodity relations through the spiritual device of the Fat Lady.

The experience of sexuality, no more than of work, can offer a reintegration of the self. When these authors take advantage of the new freedom to represent sexual encounters, what they disclose is remarkable for its botched eroticism. Esther Greenwood sees male genitals as turkey parts; she hemorrhages uncontrollably when she discards her virginity. Dotty Renfrew, of *The Group*, fails to get her diaphragm in, watches with horror as it rolls across the floor of the clinic, and later undergoes a clinical deflowering. For Portnoy, sex emerges from the bathroom only to take shape as exploitative orgies with the "Monkey" and an attempted rape in Israel. Rabbit Angstrom's fantasies barely take him past impotence with his young housemate Jill. And Vonnegut aptly expresses the objectification of sex by providing us with the penis measurements of his male characters and drawings of girls' underpants and a "wide open beaver." Only Kesey offers an uncritical fantasy of the erotic, and his liberated ladies are compliant whores while his proper women are "ball cutters." In virtually none of these novels is there an arena of erotic playfulness uncontaminated by bad social relations, in which one might recover a childlike unity of body and spirit.

Finally, the experience of objects—of the socially produced physical world—runs from the banal to the terrifying. Characters live among and by commodities but experience commodities as antagonistic, destructive to one's individuality, vulgar and homogenized, or full of factitious variety. Characteristic scenes in these novels are Rabbit's drab homes, organized around the TV set; Herzog's farmhouse filled with things that don't work; the cultural hodgepodge of Pynchon's Fangoso Lagoons; the paraphernalia of beauty and fashion in *The Bell Jar*. At a monstrous extreme are Kesey's sterile ward with its hellish machinery and Vonnegut's plastic river. Only Salinger's Zooey is truly at home with commodities, and then only in the sanctified retreat of the Glass apartment, where bought objects have become saturated with love and memory. For most of these writers, the things produced by cooperative human labor are as alienated as the labor itself and the mechanics of *re*production.

Through the story of mental disorientation or derangement, then, these novels transform deep social contradictions into a dynamic of personal crisis, a sense of there being no comfortable place in the world for the private self. These books are narratives of illness.

I want now to touch on the form of the story they tell about it. We might see that story as a version of the comic plot, with society itself as the tyrannical older generation; but these stories do not point toward a new society built around the values of the young or to the marriage feast that solemnizes it. They end, at best, in mere recovery—in the achievement of personal equilibrium vis-à-vis the same untransformed external world. Not all the central figures become whole again, but the movement into illness and toward recovery is the basic story on which the novels play variations.

What are the means of recovery? I think the medical theme asserts itself in the plethora of healers who figure in these stories. Some, of course, are bad therapists, like those who misunderstand or bully Esther Greenwood before the good Dr. Nolan assumes charge of her welfare, or like the timid hacks manipulated by Nurse Ratched in *One Flew Over the Cuckoo's Nest*. Some are shadowy Germanic stereotypes like Dr. Hilarius in *The Crying of Lot 49* and the silent listener Spielvogel in *Portnoy's Complaint*. Almost never does the professional healer effect a cure, and the same holds true for the many self-appointed counselors and prophets who proffer guidance or wisdom. There are the innumerable "reality instructors": those who bedevil Bellow's heroes with well-intentioned or self-serving advice; Rabbit's young educators in new thought, Skeeter and Jill; Kilgore Trout, the unintentional wise man whose book pushes Dwayne Hoover off the deep end; the kooks and true believers who confuse and eventually desert Oedipa Maas.

Yet the central characters of these novels do not heal themselves: if they recover at all, it is with the help of someone who takes on the role of therapist but who does so out of love and personal commitment. Zooey is the archetype here, marshaling all his Glass family wit, backed by his mother's chicken soup, his brothers' anthology of wise sayings, and the saintly presence of the dead Seymour. Contemptuous of psychiatrists, he is able to be one for Franny on her couch because he has the techniques that love and family provide. Likewise, Willie Herzog, just by caring and being there, helps Moses back to sanity—as does Rabbit's sister Mim, by offering him the simple revelation that "people want to be nice." And of course Randle Patrick McMurphy becomes Christ to the men on the ward, choosing his own death, in effect, to restore their health and autonomy.

But if I am right in this analysis, the ministrations of these healers should not produce altogether convincing resolutions. If these novels thematize social contradictions as personal neurosis, one would expect any recovery to be a problem, for individual cures cannot address the causes of the illness. At best, they can produce a kind of adjustment. And indeed, some of the novels acknowledge this impasse. Vonnegut, whose story never really departs from the social, offers no hope for his individual creations, only for the whole human race in a distant future through the somewhat magical agency of more "humane ideas." None of the four possible solutions to Oedipa Maas' puzzle will afford her much personal repose. Roth leaves Alex Portnoy on the couch, ready only to *begin* his therapy under the tutelage of the dubious Spielvogel.

And where the hero does return to health, a strange diminution usually occurs, signaling, I think, a disengagement from the issues that generated the story in the first place. Chief Bromden heads off to see how some men from his tribe have managed to go on spearing salmon on the spillway of the new dam, carrying on the old ways in a pre-industrial pocket that the "Combine" has overlooked. Esther Greenwood steps into a room filled with eyes that will judge her sane; her triumph is simply that she can face them. Franny Glass is able, finally, to sleep. Herzog, also lying on a couch, in an isolated farmhouse in the Berkshires, knows he has recovered because he has "no messages for anyone." Harry Angstrom and his wife Janice, provisionally reunited, curl up together in a motel-room bed and, like Franny, fall asleep. Nothing has changed "out there," but our heroes are now "O.K.?"

In this essay I have barely outlined an intricate social process and a sizable body of fiction. I have ignored vital distinctions: for instance, I have said nothing about the value attributed to these works by different fractions of their readership. Obviously, young people and older people experience class and history differently and have different literary tastes. The same holds even more strongly for men and women. Neither have I spoken of changes in the form and tone of the illness story through fifteen years of rather turbulent history. I have omitted consideration of the balance between explicit and implicit—or even unconscious—criticism in the novels; an analysis that equates Kesey's fiction and Plath's clearly needs refinement. And of course I have neglected even to mention many novels that may come to reside in the canon.

What I hope to have accomplished, nonetheless, is to have given concrete enough form to the following powerful yet vague ideas about culture and value so that they may be criticized and perhaps developed.[47] (1) A canon—a shared understanding of what literature is worth preserving—takes shape through a troubled historical process. (2) It emerges through specific institutions and practices, not in some historically invariant way. (3) These institutions are likely to have a rather well-defined class base. (4) Although the ruling ideas and myths may indeed be, in every age, the ideas and myths of the ruling class, the ruling class in advanced capitalist societies does not advance its ideas directly through its control of the means of mental production. Rather, a subordinate but influential class shapes culture in ways that express its own interests and experience and that sometimes turn on ruling-class values rather critically—yet in a nonrevolutionary period end up confirming root elements of the dominant ideology, such as the premise of individualism. I hope, in short, to have given a usable and attackable account of the hegemonic process and to have added content to the claim that aesthetic value arises from class conflict.

1. See John Henrik Clarke, ed., *William Styron's Nat Turner: Ten Black Writers Respond* (Boston, 1968).

2. I make no large claims for my boundaries. They mark off, crudely, the time when publishing had become part of big business but before subsidiary rights had completely overshadowed hardbound novel publishing. My boundaries also mark the time when people born to one side or the other of 1930 attained cultural dominance and could most strongly advance their reading of the postwar experience. And these years roughly enclose the rise and decline of 1960s movements as well as economic boom and the U.S. intervention in Southeast Asia. Anyhow, things have changed since 1975, both in the great world and in fiction publishing; accordingly I will use the past tense when describing the process of canon-formation, even though many of my generalizations still hold true.

I will speak of "precanonical" novels, meaning those that are active candidates for inclusion, not those that will in fact be canonical at some later time.

3. Jan Hajda, "An American Paradox: People and Books in a Metropolis" (Ph.D. diss., University of Chicago, 1963), p. 218, as cited in Elizabeth Warner McElroy, "Subject Variety in Adult Book Reading" (M.A. diss., University of Chicago, 1967).

4. See Simone Beserman, "Le Best-seller aux Etats-Unis de 1961 à 1970: Etude littéraire et sociologique" (Ph.D. diss., University of Paris [1975]), pp. 280–92.

Surprisingly, neither this audience nor the ways it integrated novel reading into its social existence seem all that different from their counterparts in early eighteenth-century England, as described, for example, in chap. 2 of Ian Watt, *The Rise of the Novel: Studies in Defoe, Richardson, and Fielding* (Berkeley, 1957), or in "The Debate Over Art and Popular Culture: English Eighteenth Century as a Case Study," by Leo Lowenthal (with Marjorie Fiske), in Lowenthal, *Literature, Popular Culture, and Society* (Palo Alto, Calif., 1968).

5. Saul Bellow, in Jason Epstein's interview, "Saul Bellow of Chicago," *New York Times Book Review,* 9 May 1971, p. 16.

6. Philip H. Ennis, *Adult Book Reading in the United States,* National Opinion Research Center (University of Chicago, 1965), p. 25. Other main needs were (1) "escape," which also implies a relationship between reading a book and the rest of one's social life (what one is escaping *from*), and (2) information, which I suspect is a need less often fulfilled by novels now than in the time of Defoe and Richardson. My appreciation is extended to Ennis, who is my colleague, for lots of help when I was first considering these issues.

7. Victor Navasky, "Studies in Animal Behavior," *New York Times Book Review,* 25 Feb. 1973, p. 2.

8. See Richard Kostelanetz, *The End of Intelligent Writing: Literary Politics in America* (New York, 1974), p. 207. Kostelanetz's estimate was confirmed by some of Beserman's interviews. Allan Green, who handled advertising for a number of publishers, including Viking, told her in 1971 that on the average, 50 to 60 percent of the budget went to the *New York Times Book Review* and another 10 to 20 percent to the daily *New York Times.* M. Stuart Harris, head of publicity at Harper, said he ordinarily channeled 90 percent into the *Times* at the outset, though once a book's success was assured, he distributed advertising more broadly (see Beserman, "Le Best-seller," p. 120).

9. See Beserman, "Le Best-seller," p. 168.

10. See Kostelanetz, *The End of Intelligent Writing,* p. 209, based on reports in Harry Smith, "Special Report: The *New York Times Book Review,*" *Newsletter,* 30 July 1969, and "The *New York Times Book Review* (Part II)," *Newsletter,* 8 December 1971.

11. For instance, the Sunday *New York Times* assigned only four of the novels that would become 1965's ten best-sellers to literary intellectuals: Julian Moynihan reviewed Bellow's *Herzog;* George P. Elliott, LeCarre's *The Looking Glass War;* Marcus Cunliffe, Stone's *Those Who Love;* and Peter Buitenhuis, Wouk's *Don't Stop the Carnival.* Only Moynihan wrote a thoroughly respectful and enthusiastic review; it was full of words and phrases like "masterpiece," "new and perennial," "great characters," "beautiful fluidity." Perhaps more important, he drew parallels both to contemporaries like Malamud, Salinger, Mailer, and Philip Roth, and to earlier writers like Joyce and Henry Roth, with the intention of putting Bellow in their company. The review all but says, "this one belongs in the canon." Elliott invoked Greene and Chandler, Cunliffe alluded to Graves and Wilder, but they used these

comparisons in one way or another to demote LeCarre and Stone. Buitenhuis' review was dismissive; his *en passant* allusion was to the Marx Brothers. (I extend thanks to my student assistant, Pierce Tyler, for surveying reviews and digging up such information.)

12. See Julie Hoover and Charles Kadushin, "Influential Intellectual Journals: A Very Private Club," *Change* (Mar. 1972): 41.

13. See Kadushin, Hoover, and Monique Tichy, "How and Where to Find the Intellectual Elite in the United States," *Public Opinion Quarterly* (Spring 1971): 1–18. For the method used to identify an intellectual elite, see Kadushin, "Who Are the Elite Intellectuals?," *Public Interest* (Fall 1972): 109–25.

14. Like the Sunday *New York Times,* many of these journals singled out *Herzog* in the fall of 1964. The *New Yorker* gave it a lead review by Brendan Gill. V. S. Pritchett covered it for the *New York Review of Books,* in the only review of a 1965 best-seller devoted to just one book. The *New Republic* gave a lead review to Irving Howe, and the *Saturday Review,* to Granville Hicks. Only Pritchett was less than enthusiastic.

15. Kadushin, Hoover, and Tichy, "How and Where to Find the Intellectual Elite," p. 17.

16. See ibid., p. 9.

17. See Kostelanetz, *The End of Intelligent Writing,* pp. 107–8, based on Smith, "The *New York Review* Gives Strong Preference," *Newsletter,* 5 March 1969; and p. 110.

18. See, for instance, Leslie A. Fiedler, *The Inadvertent Epic: From "Uncle Tom's Cabin" to "Roots"* (New York, 1979). Though I have not seen it yet, I gather Fiedler's *What Was Literature?: Class Culture and Mass Society* (New York, 1982) argues again for the primacy of people over professors.

19. As Jerome Klinkowitz states in his preface: "For even the well and intelligently read, 'contemporary American fiction' suggests Ken Kesey, Joseph Heller, John Barth, and Thomas Pynchon at best—and at worst Updike, Roth, Bellow, and Malamud." He contends that such a list misses "the direction which fiction will take, and is taking, as the future unfolds before us" (*Literary Disruptions: The Making of a Post-Contemporary American Fiction,* 2d ed. [Urbana, Ill., 1980], p. ix).

20. Since this study *is* work in progress, I will be especially grateful for criticism, leads, and methodological suggestions.

21. Twenty-six of the forty-four responded. The survey accompanies an article by Melvin J. Friedman, "To 'Make It New': The American Novel since 1945," *Wilson Quarterly* (Winter 1978): 136–37. I don't know how the professors were selected or who they were, but I might note that almost every novel on this list was written by a white male with an elite educational background.

22. John Hawkes is the outstanding example of a novelist whose work has consistently impressed critics and professors, without ever appealing to a wider audience. Should any of us be around to witness the outcome, it will be interesting to see if any of his books has a place in the canon forty or fifty years from now.

23. It also excerpts reviews from a very few middlebrow journals like *Time* and *Newsweek.*

24. I omit novelists still alive in 1960, but whose possibly canonical work belongs to an earlier time—Steinbeck, Dos Passos, Hemingway, etc. I *include* those of an older generation (Porter, McCarthy) who did not publish a precanonical novel until the 1960s. I exclude novelists of foreign origin (Asimov, Kosinski, Nabokov) and writers mainly known for their poetry, plays, or criticism, unless (as with Dickey and Plath) they also produced a precanonical novel during this period.

25. I got this count by surveying the hardback and paperback best-seller lists in the *New York Times* from 1969 through 1975 and by checking the annual summaries in Alice Payne Hackett and James Henry Burke, *Eighty Years of Best Sellers, 1895–1975* (New York, 1977) for the rest of the 1960s. When I find time and patience to plow through the *Times* for that decade, my count will probably go up by a few.

26. For an account of this process that attributes it more to industrialism than to capitalism, see John Kenneth Galbraith, *The New Industrial State* (Boston, 1967). I prefer

the analysis in Paul A. Baran and Paul M. Sweezy, *Monopoly Capital: An Essay on the American Economic and Social Order* (New York, 1966). In publishing, the ascendancy of media packaging over simple book publishing has continued apace in recent years. See Thomas Whiteside, *The Blockbuster Complex: Conglomerates, Show Business, and Book Publishing* (Middletown, Conn., 1981). The practices Whiteside describes, along with the growth of national bookstore chains, have further altered the dynamics of publishing, thereby providing another reason for terminating this study somewhere around 1975.

27. See my preliminary study of this process, "Where Did Mass Culture Come From? The Case of Magazines," *Berkshire Review* 16 (1981): 85–101.

28. See, for instance, Raymond Williams, "Base and Superstructure in Marxist Cultural Theory," *New Left Review* 82 (Nov.-Dec. 1973): 3–16.

29. *The Marx-Engels Reader*, ed. Robert C. Tucker (New York, 1972), p. 136.

30. See Barbara and John Ehrenreich, "The Professional-Managerial Class," in Pat Walker, ed., *Between Labor and Capital* (Boston, 1979). The article originally appeared in *Radical America* (May-June 1977).

31. For an interesting account of this contradiction in the lives and work of media intellectuals, see Hans Magnus Enzensberger, "The Industrialization of the Mind," in *The Consciousness Industry: On Literature, Politics, and the Media*, ed. Michael Roloff (New York, 1974).

32. Every term of this characterization is a problem, and the whole subject vexed beyond apparent usefulness. (The debate over the Ehrenreichs' proposal in *Between Labor and Capital* should satisfy anyone on this point, as it applies to Marxists.) There is not even agreement whether the people I refer to constitute a class, a subclass, a stratum, a contradictory location in the class structure, etc. For myself, I don't care which concept the reader prefers, so long as *in this context* we agree on what group we are talking about and agree that it has acted *as* a recognizable group. If the reader feels more at ease with the concept, from mainstream sociology and everyday talk, of the "upper middle class," that's all right too, though such a reader will, if he or she accepts my argument here, have to challenge the whole framework of theory from which that concept derives. Methodologically, I join the Ehrenreichs in holding that the point is not to "define" classes in some ahistorical way and that a notion of class is validated or invalidated by its power in theory, empirical explanation, and political practice. Hence I do not mean to be appropriating a preexisting definition of class in this essay and "applying" it to a particular situation and problem. Rather, I intend my argument and my evidence to help *develop* a more adequate picture of the way class has worked and works in the social process.

33. I am under no illusion that this study itself can stand apart from the canon-formation process; I am participating in that process, as I describe it. There is no help for that. I would insist, though, that my immediate purpose is not to tip the scales in favor of some novels and against others. My tally of precanonical novels includes some that I like very much indeed, some that I can't abide, and—in a fine gesture of impartiality—some that I haven't read. I do, of course, wish to influence the process in a broader way by calling attention to its narrow social base and to the parochial outlook it has produced.

34. Thus the precanonical novels display styles as various as those of Vonnegut, Malamud, and Brautigan; and some novelists, like Updike, get high marks from the gate-keepers specifically for their styles.

35. Williams has used this concept since writing *Culture and Society, 1780–1950* (New York, 1958). Its most exact theoretical formulation is in his *Marxism and Literature* (New York, 1977).

36. It was fascinating, after twenty-five years, to reread the essay from which I remembered this phrase, Herbert Gold's "The Age of Happy Problems" (written 1956; rpt. in a book of the same title, New York, 1962). Gold offers a very precise early sampling of this consciousness.

37. For instance, the poorest 40 percent of families in the country received 16.8 percent of the income in 1947 and 16.9 percent in 1960, while the percentage going to

the richest 5 percent went from 17.2 percent to 16.8 percent. The top 1 percent owned 23.3 percent of the nation's *wealth* in 1945 and 27.4 percent in 1962. These figures come from tables compiled by Frank Ackerman and Andrew Zimbalist, "Capitalism and Inequality in the United States," in Richard C. Edwards, Michael Reich, and Thomas E. Weisskopf, eds., *The Capitalist System: A Radical Analysis of American Society*, 2d ed. (Englewood Cliffs, N.J., 1978), pp. 298 and 301.

38. Godfrey Hodgson calls this outlook "liberal conservatism." See his excellent discussion in chap. 4, *America in Our Time* (New York, 1976). On p. 76 Hodgson enumerates six points of the ideological consensus which are very close to the analysis I give here.

39. That is, people relied on others, through the intermediary of the market, for more and more goods and services. In an ordinary day's "consuming," each of us depends on the past and present labor of hundreds of millions of workers worldwide. But of course this is easy to forget, since that loaf of bread magically appears on the store shelf and the only labor we *see* is that of the checker and the bagger.

40. Sylvia Plath, *The Bell Jar* (New York, 1971), p. 2; all further references to this work will be included parenthetically in the text.

41. Patricia Ann Meyer Spacks, *The Female Imagination* (New York, 1975), p. 145. She takes the concept from Therese Benedek.

42. J. D. Salinger, *Franny and Zooey* (Boston, 1961), p. 67. The two stories, which add up to a sort of novel, appeared earlier in the *New Yorker*. The Glass kids were already culture heroes for the reader of this fiction; people stood in line outside of bookstores on publication day to buy the book.

43. The other securely canonical work of the 1950s, *Invisible Man*, not only exhibits the characteristic inversion of sanity and insanity but comprehends racism itself within the illness story and the adolescent rite of passage.

44. Philip Roth, *Portnoy's Complaint* (New York, 1969), p. 111; all further references to this work will be included parenthetically in the text.

45. Bellow, *Herzog* (New York, 1964), pp. 1, 2.

46. John Updike, *Rabbit Redux* (New York, 1972), p. 16.

47. These ideas derive from Antonio Gramsci, through the later work of Williams and people connected to the Center for Contemporary Cultural Studies at the University of Birmingham and to *Screen* magazine. E.g., Dick Hebdige, whose *Subculture: The Meaning of Style* (London and New York, 1979) is a fine study in this vein. Todd Gitlin has advanced the theory and analysis of hegemony farthest in the U.S. See esp. his *The Whole World Is Watching: Mass Media in the Making and Unmaking of the New Left* (Berkeley, 1980).

Index